FRIONA Main Street

OLD PARMERTON—Historical Seal, 1907

A HISTORY OF

PARMER COUNTY

TEXAS

FIRST EDITION
VOLUME 1

PARMER COUNTY
HISTORICAL SOCIETY

Copyright 1974
By The Parmer County Historical Society

Printed in the United States of America
By Nortex Press, Quanah, Texas

ISBN 0-89015-073-7

Another Quality
Book By

NORTEX PRESS

Quanah, Texas

MARTIN PARMER

The Reading of the Texas Declaration Of Independence

By Fanny V. and Charles B. Normann

This painting was painstakingly prepared after exhaustive research by the artists. They devoted two full years to research, securing the likeness of the Signers when available, talking to members of the families of descendants, and studying the background of each of the Signers.

ACKNOWLEDGEMENTS

The Parmer County Historical Survey Committee wishes to express its appreciation to all of those whose contributions have made this book possible.

To thank each individual would be an impossible task; however there are some whose efforts merit special attention. Among them are Mr. Eugene V. Sofford for his history of Farwell, Mr. Hamlin Y. Overstreet for the Farwell Times of 1908, Mr. Bill Ellis and his entire staff of the Friona Star for two years of complete co-operation and understanding of the problems associated with publication.

The vast majority of the photographs used are the work of Dr. Cliff Ennen, pastor of the Farwell Baptist Church who spent countless hours working with old, faded, snapshots until they were redone into usable prints.

Much statistical information was researched and typed by the ladies associated with the county government. Mrs. Dorothy Quickel, Mrs. Bonnie Warren, Mrs. Benna Felts, and Mrs. Helen Joan Johnson. Wilma Louise Moseley supplied a copy of "Views in around Farwell, 1909," many of the photos used are from this publication.

Miss Juanah Nance is due credit for drawing in the cattle brands and typing the entire chapter.

Mrs. Mary (Jim) Johnston has demonstrated a sincere interest; her work as typist, editorial assistant, and translator-copyist has been invaluable.

Other ladies who have helped with the arduous chore of typing are Miss Jamie Washington, Miss Juanah Nance, Mrs. Virginia Self, Miss Hope Mays and Mrs. Eddie Mays.

The receipts were donated by Mrs. Wana Brewer and edited by Mrs. Lucille Lewis who also drew the maps and "Signpost."

Perhaps the most unique feature of the entire book is the inclusion of work by local artists. The drawings, all original and done especially for this volumn, were contributed by Bobby Wied, Rose Black, Carol Ellis, Ethel Ruth Spring, Paul Wyley, Margaret Charles, Billie Long Homer, Carrie Tatum, Diane Tatum and Debbie Houlette.

Librarians in Virginia, Missouri, Tennessee, and Texas have given freely of their time. Two warrant special mention, Mrs. Billie Fairchild of Friona and Mrs. Claire Kuen of Panhandle Plains Museum of Canyon who have been particularly helpful.

There are many others, to each of them our sincere thanks.

P.C.H.S.C.

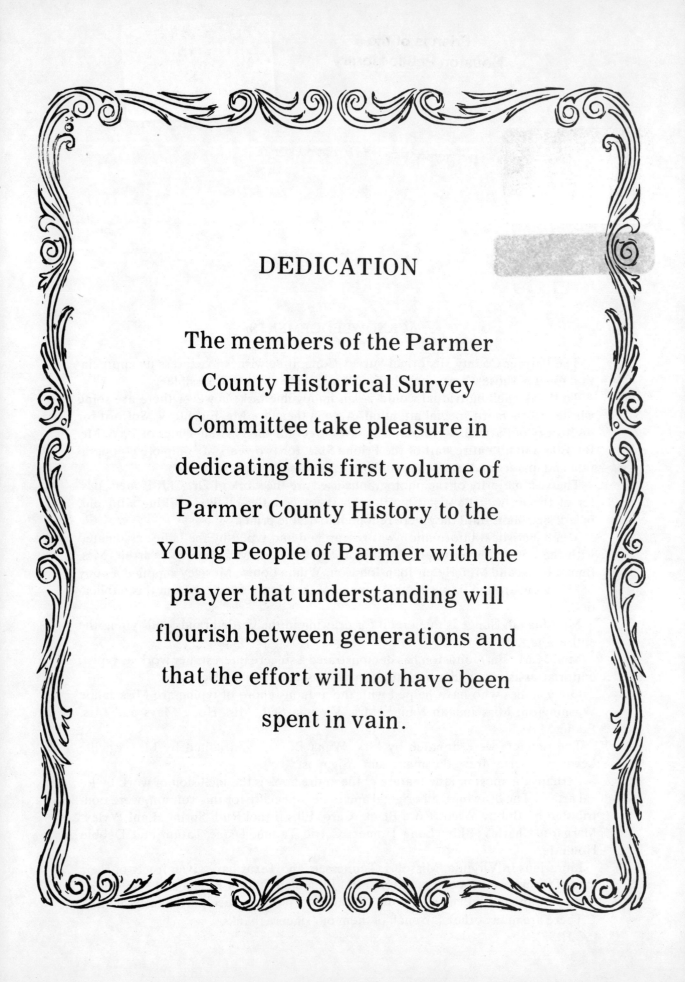

DEDICATION

The members of the Parmer
County Historical Survey
Committee take pleasure in
dedicating this first volume of
Parmer County History to the
Young People of Parmer with the
prayer that understanding will
flourish between generations and
that the effort will not have been
spent in vain.

FOREWORD

Why Write A County History?

At first the answer is a little too obvious: to record the major events of a certain area over a given length of time. Such a mundane approach stifles interest and the resulting manuscript becomes a boring set of statistics filled with names, dates and ancient photographs, all of which are necessary for a true documentation of cold facts, but there is more to counties and histories than warmed over information. Counties and histories are concerned with people, their likes and dislikes, their civic and business endeavours, their politics and their economic ambitions. The County is the bulwark of Americanism; its organization and function stand between the centralization of state government and the incorporated cities within its borders. History is the factual record of people and the events which influenced their lives. The purpose of this book is to present Parmer County, Texas, its origin and its status at the beginning of the year 1930.

PREFACE

To obtain a true understanding of Parmer County, one must start with the land itself. No better place for the complete comprehension can be found than Parmerton Hill, the gentle crest of land partway between Friona and Bovina. Here at the site of the original Court House the scene is one of awe inspiring grandeur. The imagination is confounded, even dwarfed, by viewing thousands of acres of profitable farm land that was once spoken of as the Great American Desert. The panorama is limited only by the defects of human vision and the curvature of the earth. No mountains or forests obstruct the view, rocks and tree stumps, the eroded gullies and the untenable swamp lands are unknown in this Eden. Millions of acres of topsoil ranging from three to eight feet in depth await the plow. Although rainfall which averages only 16 to 20 inches a year creates a hazard for the "dryland" farmer, his brother who practices irrigation is almost assured of success.

Whence came this land?

Was it a freak of nature or the intention of the Creator?

Let us avoid complications with the theologians or the occult and turn to the science of geology for an explanation.

Thirty thousand years ago when the last Ice Age began to melt away billions of tons of water coursed southward from the recently formed Rocky Mountains. Snow and ice dissolve slowly so that the resulting floods were not a sudden deluge. Hundreds, perhaps thousands, of years were occupied by these great rivers that coursed across our land. Rocks and gravel are found near the Gulf coast that had their beginning in the Colorado Rockies. Toward the end of this epoch obstructions that had withstood the rampaging waters divided the flow in two major areas. The Canadian River basin and the Pecos River valley were the main drainage ditches related to our high plains. Running Water Draw remains as a final reminder of the formation of our land.

For millions of years our Llano Estacado, scoured by terrific "northers," had been swept into a vast plain said by some scientists to be the oldest land mass on earth. Across the millions of acres the slowing floods deposited deep layers of silt which in time became our valuable topsoil.

A newcomer's first remark relates to the "flatness" of our country, but it is not flat. The western area is about two thousand feet higher than the eastern. Yet no water pours off the plains into the canyons of the eastern edge. Despite a fall of ten feet per mile, west to east, the rains are absorbed by the land or held in any of a thousand playas, the "buffalo wallows" of western stories.

Parmer County lies about in the center of this geological wonderland. Its formation, its creation, its organization is a drama of people who sought a better life and who had the fortitude to "stay put" regardless of the odds.

It is their story we want to tell.

Left to right, seated, Mrs. Grace Whitefield, Mrs. Mabelle Hartwell, Mrs. Ethel Benger; standing, Glenn Reeve and Otho Whitefield.

Left to right, seated, Hugh Moseley, president; Mrs. Allo Reeve, vice president; Mrs. Ida Jesko, secretary; Mrs. Louisa Wilson; standing, Clyde Goodwine, Miss Lola Goodwine, Mrs. Mary Dixon, and Nelson Lewis. Members not shown are Joe Jesko and Mrs. Orma Flippen.

TABLE OF CONTENTS

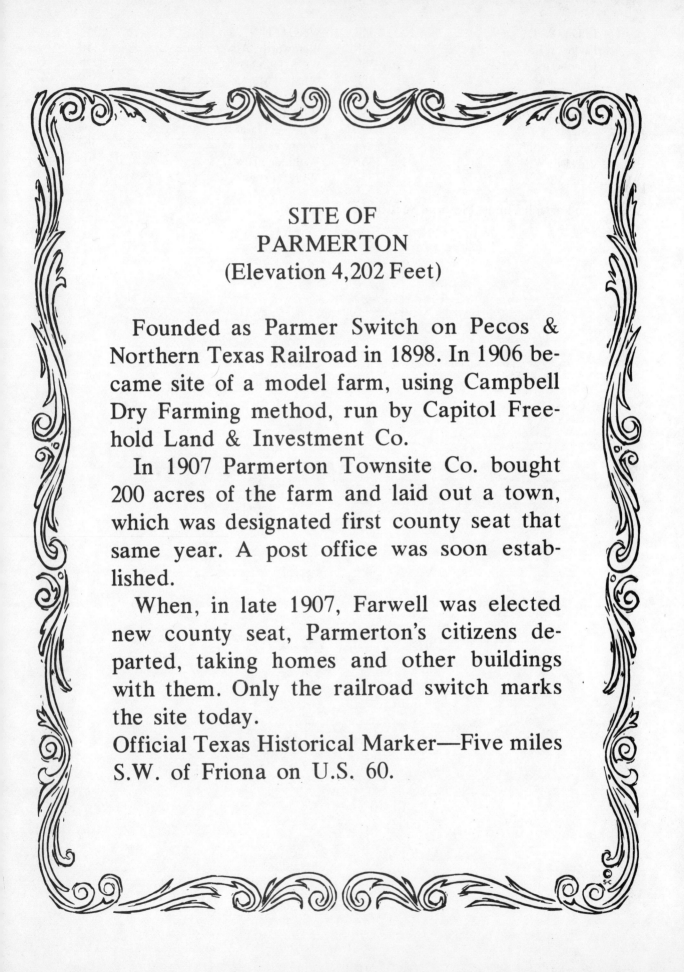

SITE OF
PARMERTON
(Elevation 4,202 Feet)

Founded as Parmer Switch on Pecos & Northern Texas Railroad in 1898. In 1906 became site of a model farm, using Campbell Dry Farming method, run by Capitol Freehold Land & Investment Co.

In 1907 Parmerton Townsite Co. bought 200 acres of the farm and laid out a town, which was designated first county seat that same year. A post office was soon established.

When, in late 1907, Farwell was elected new county seat, Parmerton's citizens departed, taking homes and other buildings with them. Only the railroad switch marks the site today.

Official Texas Historical Marker—Five miles S.W. of Friona on U.S. 60.

Chapter I

In The Beginning

West Texas Historical Association Year-book, Vol. XXIII, Oct., 1947.

EARLY DAYS IN PARMER COUNTY

By Frank H. Hayne

Parmer County was created on August 26, 1876, after the Committee on State Affairs had recommended that a capital reservation tract be established for the purpose of providing a state capital in Austin. The county was named for Martin Parmer who was born and reared in Virginia. He came to Texas in 1825 and located at Mount Prairie in Cherokee County. In 1836 he represented San Augustine in the Constitutional Convention. He died the next year.

On January 10, 1882, the State of Texas awarded a contract to Mattheas Schnell of Rock Island, Illinois, to erect a capitol building in exchange for 3,000,000 acres of land. Schnell later assigned his interest to Taylor, Babcock, and Company, which became commonly known as the Capitol Syndicate. Most of Parmer County became a part of the Syndicate lands, was incorporated in the XIT Ranch, and became a part of the Bovina Division.

In 1898 the Pecos Valley and Northeastern Railroad built diagonally across the county from northeast to southwest. Switches were constructed along the line and given the names of Black, approximately six miles from the northeast corner of the county; Friona, on the Frio Creek eight miles from Black; Parmerton, seven miles from Friona and almost in the center of the county; Bovina, six miles from Parmerton to serve as headquarters of the Bovina Division; Wilsey, six miles from Bovina and seven miles from Texico, which was in New Mexico at the point where the railroad crossed the state line. An effort was later made to develop a townsite at each switch.

An incident which occurred during the building of the railroad across Parmer County is still remembered by some of the old settlers. On December 25, 1898, the rail crew decided to take the engine and caboose and go to Bovina to celebrate the day. The "Christmas Special" was going along at a moderate speed when a herd of antelope came along side and, as is their custom, tried to cross the track in front of the engine. The engineer slowed down, and the crew members who had guns fired from the caboose. Not an antelope fell, but as the engineer started to speed up he noticed a large buck caught on the cowcatcher of the engine. He gave the buck a breeze ride into Bovina where the crew had antelope steak for Christmas dinner.

The Pecos Valley and Northeastern Railroad was acquired by the Santa Fe, and plans were made to build a line from Belen, which was south of Albuquerque, to intercept the Pecos Valley line where it crossed the state line. Judge J.D. Hamlin and John Hutson purchased land on the New Mexico side at this joint and laid out the townsite of Texico. The town started with a boom. It was generally believed that it would be a division point on the Belen cut-off.

The Syndicate people decided to profit by the prospects of Texico's becoming a divisional point and laid off the townsite of Farwell on the Texas side adjacent to Texico. J.D. Hamlin became the Syndicate's agent in charge of the townsite which consisted of 640 acres. Lot sales were brisk. The boom which had started in Texico extended over the line into Farwell. A number of brick business houses were constructed. The mercantile firm of Hopping and Roberson moved from Texico to Farwell. Each town had a post office. Real estate values were soaring, money was easy, and building was going on at a terrific pace.

In the meanwhile, the Santa Fe officials and the Syndicate could not agree on how much land the Syndicate should donate in Farwell for the railroad yards and roundhouse. Suddenly without warning the Santa Fe started construction of a roundhouse at Riley's switch ten miles west of Texico. The Santa Fe had quietly purchased a tract of land there, and laid out their own townsite which became Clovis. This terminated Texico's and Farwell's hopes of ever becoming sizable towns.

Parmer County had been attached to Deaf

Smith County for judicial purposes. It was generally thought that when Parmer County was organized Bovina would become the county seat. Farwell, which was only three and one-half miles from the southwest corner of the county, was not regarded as being favorably situated for the purpose. In 1906 a petition, signed by the necessary 150 voters, was presented to the commissioners court of Deaf Smith County to allow Parmer County to organize. The petition was granted and the court designated Parmerton as the new county seat. The first courthouse was a small box-strip building with a small vault. It was sufficient at the time, however, as there were only three county officials to occupy it. Uncle Bill Townsen was named the first County Judge, Jess McKay, County and District Clerk, and E.T. (Lish) Stevens, Sheriff.

In 1904 the Syndicate Company began an active campaign to sell the XIT lands. The first method of land disposal was to sell large tracts, ranging from 25,000 to 200,000 acres to realtors at prices varying from $2.50 to $6.00 an acre. The realtors in turn, through their sub-agents, sold the land in small tracts. Among other realtors was George G. Wright, of Kansas City, who purchased 100,000 acres in the northeast part of Parmer County. He laid off the townsite of Friona where he built a small hotel and an attractive bungalow for a land office. He also constructed a garage for a fleet of automobiles which he used to carry prospects out to see the lands.

Mr. Wright had agents in the northern states, especially Illinois, Wisconsin, and Missouri. These agents induced prospectors, usually well-to-do farmers, to come out on special excursion trains which were chartered from time to time. The rates were greatly reduced and this caused many to come as a lark as much as for the serious business of land buying. The round-trip fare from Chicago was $25, and from St. Louis, $20. When the excursionists reached Friona, Mr. Wright's salesmen got them in the fleet of Pierce Arrows and showed them the vast expanses of level land covered with a wonderful turf of grass. Wheat growers from Kansas and corn raisers from Illinois saw great agricultural possibilities in the new country, paying ten to twelve dollars an acre

SANTA FE TRACKS and a Syndicate Built Home assure prosperity.

for land which had cost Wright less than half that amount.

Within two years Wright had disposed of his tract, but the transaction resulted in a few actual settlers. Most of the buyers were comfortably situated at their homes in the North and had no intention of pioneering the new country themselves. They had bought their tracts, either quarter sections, half section, or, in some instances, whole sections, purely for speculation.

The result of the large realtor policy, as demonstrated by Wright and others, was not satisfactory to the Syndicate Company which was desirous of effecting actual settlement of the land. The Company created the office of Land Commissioner, a position first held by F.W. Wilsey. Wilsey appointed Judge J.D. Hamlin as resident representative of the owners with headquarters in the newly established town of Farwell. Henceforth land was sold only to actual settlers. Judge Hamlin still (1947) represents the Company, but in recent years he has associated with him his nephew, Hamlin Overstreet, who has taken over the active management of the Company affairs. The most of Parmer County, and considerable portions of adjoining counties, have been settled and developed under the administration of Hamlin and Overstreet.

The county had scarcely been organized when a struggle began over the county seat. The Commissioners Court of Deaf Smith County had put it at Parmerton which was near the geographical center of the county and theoretically was a wise location. It soon developed that no one except the hand full of residents of Parmerton itself wanted to leave it there. Friona, seven miles to the northeast, was ambitious. Bovina, six miles to the southwest, was divided against itself. Farwell, nineteen miles to the southwest, had the most votes. The majority of the Bovina voters decided to support Farwell.

The matter of moving the county seat was the burning issue of the first general election after the organization of the county.

A man's residence was based on the fact that if he had his laundry done in a particular place, that was his legal home. So all the cowboys of the XIT outfit brought their laundry to Farwell to be done once every two or three months, which entitled them to vote in the election.

The day of election came and much activity, both legal and illegal, went on, for not only were county officials to be elected, but the decision of the county seat was the fiery issue. When the smoke had cleared away the tempers began once more to ride an even keel; the results were in favor of moving the county seat to Farwell.

However, there were several contested votes, but all were validated with the exception of one, that of Katerina Rubal Coba, a Mexican. Since that vote had to be validated to clear all votes, and the question at issue, much activity ensued. The newly elected Sheriff, R.C. Hopping, was sent by the newly elected judge, J.D. Hamlin, to El Paso to find this said person. After much vain hunting, the sheriff wired back to the judge the following message, "I have searched the various apartments of El Paso and Katerina Rubal Coba cannot be found." The sheriff had been dubious from the beginning, since there were probably a hundred Mexicans who would answer to the same name. However, B.T. (Press) Abbot finally located the persons in question at Artesia, New Mexico. Coba was brought back and questioned and the vote

was validated beyond question, which gave Farwell the county seat.

UP FROM THE SOD

The following court minutes are presented as an illustration of the legal "bridge" between already organized counties and those seeking to become separate political units. The state legislature of August 21, 1876 established, in a geographical sense, the counties of the Panhandle. Deaf Smith and Parmer were two of the areas named and placed under Oldham for judicial purposes. Deaf Smith was organized in 1890. To facilitate court proceedings Parmer and Castro were removed from Oldham's jurisdiction and placed under the protection of their close neighbor, Deaf Smith.

The inclusion of these notes may come under the "dry bones of history" classification, but they are a part of the story and much work by future writers may be eliminated by their presence in this volume.

Vol. 2 Page 104, Commissioners Court Minutes of Deaf Smith County, Texas, dated Sept. 25, 1906

September 25th, 1906

Be it remembered that on this 25th day of September, 1906, there was begun and holden a special session of the Hon. Commissioners Court of Deaf Smith County, Texas. Hon. W.H. Russell, County Judge, presiding and County Commissioners Geo. L. Muse, T.M. Palmer, Jno. R. Armstrong, with Sheriff J.T. Inmon and County Clerk W.B. Beach in attendance, when the following business was had to-wit:

Be it remembered that on August the 22nd 1906 Came on to be heard the Petition of the Citizens of Parmer Co. Texas, requesting that the Commissioners Court of Deaf Smith County, Texas to which County, said Parmer County is attached for Judicial purposes, requesting said Commissioners Court to order an election and to organize said Parmer County, Texas, as provided in Title 23 Chapter 2 Sayle's Revised Civil Statutes, and it appearing to the Court that said County should be organized. It is therefore ordered, adjudged and decreed by the Court, that said Parmer County shall be and the same is hereby organized and that all the rights and matters and requests asked for in said petition be and the same is hereby granted, and it is further ordered by the Court that Title 23 Chapter 2 of Sayle's Revised Civil Statutes be carried out relative to the organization of unorganized Counties.

The foregoing Judgement was rendered at the August term of this Honorable Court to-wit: August 22nd 1906, and through inadvertance the proper Judgment was not entered on the Minutes of the said Court. It is therefore ordered & adjudged by the Court that said order be entered in said Minutes of this Court Now for then, This Sept. 25th, 1906. W.H. Russell ————————

Vol. 2 Page 90 Commissioners Court Minutes of Deaf Smith County, Texas. Feb. 13th, 1906

For the purpose of maintaining and supporting the public Free Schools in Parmer County, Texas, there shall be assessed, levied and collected for the year 1906, on all property of whatsoever character, both real, personal and mixed situated in or owned in said County on the first day of January A.D. 1906, either by residents or non-residents of said County, the sum of Ten Cents on the One Hundred dollars valuation of said property, except in School District No. 9, composed of parts of Castro and Parmer Counties, and for said District No. 9, there shall be assessed, levied and collected the sum of Twenty Cents on the One Hundred Dollars Valuation as above for said District, and all residents residing in that part of said District No. 9 which is situated in Parmer County;

It is further ordered that there shall be assessed, levied and collected for the year 1906 from each male person between the years of 21 and 60 years residing in Parmer County, all who are, under the laws of the State of Texas, subject to such tax, a poll of 25 cents of each such persons;

It is further ordered that there be and there is hereby ordered assessed, levied and collected a special occupation Tax of a sum equal to one half of the sum levied by the State of Texas on like occupations, for the year 1906 in said Parmer County, Texas.

Court Adjourned until Wednesday, Feb'y 14, 1906 at 9 O'clock A.M.
2004
C.L. Davis--Quarterly report for quarter ending Jan'y. 31st, 1906 examined and **approved.**

Vol. 2 Page 126 Commissioners Court Minutes of Deaf Smith County, Texas. April 9, 1907.

The County of Deaf Smith
The State of Texas.
In Commissioners Court, Deaf Smith
County, Texas. April 9th, 1907.

Be it remembered that at a former term of this Court, there was presented a petition to organize Parmer County, Texas, which said County is attached to Deaf Smith County for Judicial purposes, that thereafter said Parmer County was duly organized, and divided and laid off in election, justices, and Commissioners Precincts, as per order of this Court of record in Vol. 2 pages 111 to 117, inclusive, wherein an election was ordered for the purposed of electing county and precinct officers and to designate a County Seat; now therefore be it ordered that said election be held in the various precincts of Parmer County for the purpose of electing said county and precinct officers and for voting for and designating a county seat for said Parmer County, said election to be held on the 7th day of May A.D. 1907; and it is ordered that the following named persons be and they are hereby appointed judges for said election, to wit:
For Precinct No. 1, W.P. McMinn,
For Precinct No. 2, C.W. Arthur,
For Precinct No. 3, Norman Wilson,
For Precinct No. 4, J.F. Rusk
And it is further ordered that the Clerk of this Court issue notices to said Judges of their said appointment.
W.H. Russell, County Judge.

Vol. 5, Page 128 Commissioners Court Minutes of Deaf Smith County, Texas. May 8, 1907

IN THE MATTER OF ELECTION RETURNS FOR PARMER COUNTY.

Be it remembered that heretofore to-wit: On the 7th day of May, A.D. 1907, there was holden an election in the County of Parmer, State of Texas, which said Parmer County was attached to Deaf Smith County for Judicial purposes, that such election was held in the various voting precincts of said Parmer County, to-wit: Precinct Nos. One, Two, Three and Four, which said Precincts had been heretofore duly laid off and designated by the Commissioners Court of Deaf Smith County as Voting, Justices, and Commissioners; said election was held for the purpose of Designating and establishing a County Seat for Parmer County, and for the election of County and Precinct Officers for said Parmer County, by virtue of an order of election heretofore issued by the County Judge of Deaf Smith County, calling for and ordering said election; and whereas, on the 8th day of May, 1907, due returns of said election were made by the election judges of the various precincts of said County to the County Judge of said Deaf Smith County, to which the said Parmer County was attached for judicial purposes; and thereafter on the said 8th day of May 1907, the said County Judge of Deaf Smith County, made due canvass of said election returns as made and provided by law in such cases, and from such returns makes the following findings, to-wit: That the following named officers were duly elected for the following offices, to-wit:

For County Judge; W.L. Townsen, he having received a majority vote.

For Sheriff and Tax Collector; E.T. Stevens, he having received a majority vote.

For County and District Clerk; J.F. McKay, he having received a majority vote.

For County Treasurer; Norman Wilson, he having recieved a majority vote.

Vol. 5, Page 128 Commissioners Court Minutes of Deaf Smith County, Texas. May 8, 1907.

—continued—

For Tax Assessor: J.B. McMinn, he having received a majority vote.

For Commissioner Precinct No. One: W.P. McMinn, he having received a majority vote.

For Commissioner Precinct No. Two: F.L. Spring, he having received a majority vote.

For Commissioner Precinct No. Three: Tom Hoghland, he having received a majority vote.

For Justice of the Peace Precinct No. Three: C.A. Woodford, he having received a majority vote.

And by virtue of said election and returns thereof it is further found that the town of Parmerton was duly elected and designated the County Seat of Parmer County, Texas, said Town of Parmerton having received a majority vote.

Now, therefore, by reason of said order of the Commissioners Court of Deaf Smith County, Texas, organizing said Parmer County, and by reason of said order of election and election and due return thereof, and canvass of such return, I, W.H. Russell, County Judge of Deaf Smith County, Texas, hereby declare, adjudge and decree, that the above named officers are duly elected to the offices set opposite their respective names; and I further declare order, adjudge and decree that the Town of "Parmerton," aforesaid, is the County Seat of said Parmer County, by reason of said town having received sufficient number of votes to elect it such County Seat.

It is further ordered that a due minutes of all the returns for said election be entered in the minutes of "Record of Election Returns."

It is further ordered that this order by duly recorded in the minutes of the Commissioners Court for Deaf Smith County, Texas.

Witness My hand and seal of office this 8th day of May, 1907.

W.H. Russell, County Judge, Deaf Smith County, Texas.

PARMERTON
By Hugh Moseley

Parmer Switch was the original name of Parmerton which is near the Geographical center of Parmer County and was designated the County Seat at an election held on May 7th, 1907.

Parmer Switch was a passing switch on the Pecos Valley and Northern Texas Railway Company which rail line was built as far West as Bovina in 1898. This rail line was extended in 1900 to Texico-Farwell and finally closed with the Roswell line near Elida, New Mexico.

Parmer County was created by the State Legislature from the Bexar Territory August 21, 1876 and named after Martin Parmer—a signer of the Texas Declaration of Independence.

The Original Townsite of Parmerton contained 200 acres of land out of Section 22 Block "C" Syndicate Subdivision situated in Capital League No. 497. The deed to this 200 acres of land is of Record in Volume 7, Page 130, Parmer County Deed Records.

In 1906, a lush wheat crop had been grown on this Section 22. This was known then as the MODEL FARM and had been established by the Capitol Freehold Land and Investment Company of Chicago.

The Campbell Dry Farming Methods were put into practice on this farm by Mr. Campbell the Farm Manager.

This method, according to C. Frank Hastings, was deep plowing to a depth of a 12 inches and then compacting the sub-soil with packer wheels to hold the available rain water. The Packer Wheels were also referred to as Camel Packers in those days.

The Parmerton Townsite was surveyed by J.S. McClearey and his Plat was filed for Record May 11th, 1907 (four days after county organized) and is of record in Volume 6, page 351 of the Parmer County Deed Records. You may wonder how Parmer County already had six deed records in less than a week.

Parmer County had been previously attached to Deaf Smith County for administration purposes and Judicial purposes and everything that pertained to land in Parmer County was Recorded by that County Clerk in the Deed Records designated Parmer County Deed Records.

Volume 1 Page 1 Commissioners Court Minutes of Parmer County, Texas:

"Whereas, Parmer County has been duly organized as required by law, and at an election held in said Parmer County on May 7, 1907 and the returns thereof duly canvassed by the County Judge, (W.H. Russell) of Deaf Smith County, Texas, on the 8th day of May, 1907, as required by laws, and:

Whereas said County Judge of said Deaf Smith County did on said 8th day of May, 1907, declare and enter an order declaring that the town of Parmerton in said Parmer County, Texas, had at said election been duly elected and chosen as the County Seat of said Parmer County, Texas, and:

Whereas there has been a contest filed by certain citizens of said Parmer County attacking such election and order.

The Officers of the Parmerton Townsite Company, a corporation were as follows:
Wallace Good, President
Norman Wilson, Vice-President
and W.L. Townsen, Secretary.

It is believed by this writer that the Townsite Company owned the 28' x 30' building that was used as the temporary Court House on Saturday, June 8, 1907 when the duly elected County Officials, to-wit:

William L. Townsen, County Judge
W.P. McMinn, Commissioner Precinct No. 1
F.L. Spring, Commissioner Precinct No. 2
E.T. Stevens, Sheriff
and J.F. McKay, County Clerk
met in a Called Session of the Commissioners Court of Parmer County, Texas, and transacted the first Official Business for the County of Parmer.

It was the custom in those days for the Sheriff of the County to make his way to the Court House Steps and announce the Commissioners' Court Meetings in the following words:

"Hear Ye, Hear Ye, The Honorable Commissioner's Court of Parmer County, Texas is about to convine in a called (or Regular) Session. All persons having business to conduct with said Court are advised to take due Notice hereof and govern themselves accordingly."

The Temporary Court House above referred to was used for a few months until a larger building could be built. The Commissioners Court Minutes dated October 19, 1907 reflect that a contract for building a Court House be let to Henry Sloan and C.M. Clark for $1380.00. This building was to be 30' x 40'.

An adobe vault was also authorized to cost no more than $360.

This building was moved to Friona in the summer of 1909 and has served as a Church, a drug store, and later as a used furniture store.

It sat on the lot between Ralph Taylor's Barber Shop and Allen Stewart's Jewelry Store. It partially burned on the night of January 29, 1957 and caused the Death of Robert Houston "Bob" Pierce who lived in the West Room of the building. The Building was torn down and moved and the lot remains vacant unto this day. (1971)

The Railroad Company above mentioned later became known as The Atchison, Topeka, and Santa Fe Railway Company. The Railroad tracts at the town of Parmerton were moved to the South some 44 varas or about 121 feet in 1909. Therefore most of the buildings and the windmill were situated a little farther North than is generally believed. The windmill was 100 yards North of the present North Right-Of-Way Boundary line of U.S. Highway 60. This windmill was used by I.W. Quickel until 1954 for watering his livestock.

The Temporary Court House was quite some distance from the railroad according to Mr. Henry Curtis, who related to this writer in an interview on December 28, 1970, that he rode a train to Parmerton on February 28, 1908 to purchase his Marriage License. Upon arriving there he made his way across the tall grass on foot to the little frame Court House which seemed to him at the time to be about ¼ a mile in distance from the point he was discharged from the train. This interview was had in the Home of Mr. Henry S. Curtis at 801 Second Street, Farwell, Texas, and in the presence of two of his sons, to-wit: Penn Curtis and Duane Curtis.

Mr. Henry S. Curtis and Miss Grace Haynes were married on March 1st, 1908 at The Farwell Inn in Farwell, Texas. Said Marriage License is of Record in Volume 1 Page 8, Parmer County Marriage Records.

The Plat of Parmerton reveals that it was to have 74 City Blocks plus a Public Square in the center of the Plat. Had Parmerton remained the County Seat a Court House would have been built thereon. The Streets of Parmerton were designated to be 60 feet in width except Main Street and Seventh and Eighth Streets which were designated to be 80 feet in Width. These were the streets leading to the Public Square.

The Streets in the Town of Parmerton were named after Famous Texans as follows:

Clement, (Joseph D. Clement) Land Commissioner in 1838.

Austin, (Stephen F. Austin)

Travis, (William Barret Travis)

Crockett, (David Crockett)

Bowie, (Colonel James Bowie)

Houston, (Sam Houston)

Ross, (Governor Lawrence Sullivan Ross)

Cabel, (William Lewis Cable) Mayor of Dallas in 1874

Reagan, (John H. Reagan—Texas Railroad Commission)

Mills, (John T. Mills) (1817-1871) Pioneer jurist.

So far as I have been able to ascertain, the Temporary Court House was situated upon Block 45 of Parmerton Townsite. In the Commissioner's Court Minutes dated August 17th, 1907, Mr. J.F. (Jess) McKay, the County Clerk, was allowed $5.00 for superintending the making of the adobes for the Adobe Vault to be erected on Lot 21 Block 45 in the Town of Parmerton. This Adobe Vault (according to the Plat of Parmerton) was 975 feet North of the Railroad Right-of-Way line, and some 230 feet South of the designated Public Square. I presume the adobe vault was near the Court House on Said Block 45.

The Post Office at Parmerton was established on September 14th, 1907 and was discontinued on August 15, 1909, the mail sent thereafter to Friona. Mr. William Lyles (Uncle Bill) Townsen was the Postmaster during this time.

Although Mr. Townsen lived at Parmerton, the Post Office was at the Courthouse rather than in his home, according to his niece, Mrs. Estelle Dunn Combs.

Although much planning had gone into the Town of Parmerton by its officers, it was destined to failure because the Business Men at Bovina were against the new townsite and also the Capitol Freehold Land Company had its office already established in Farwell and they thought that Farwell would be the logical place for the Court House and County Seat. So, a Petition was presented to the Commissioner's Court of Parmer County,

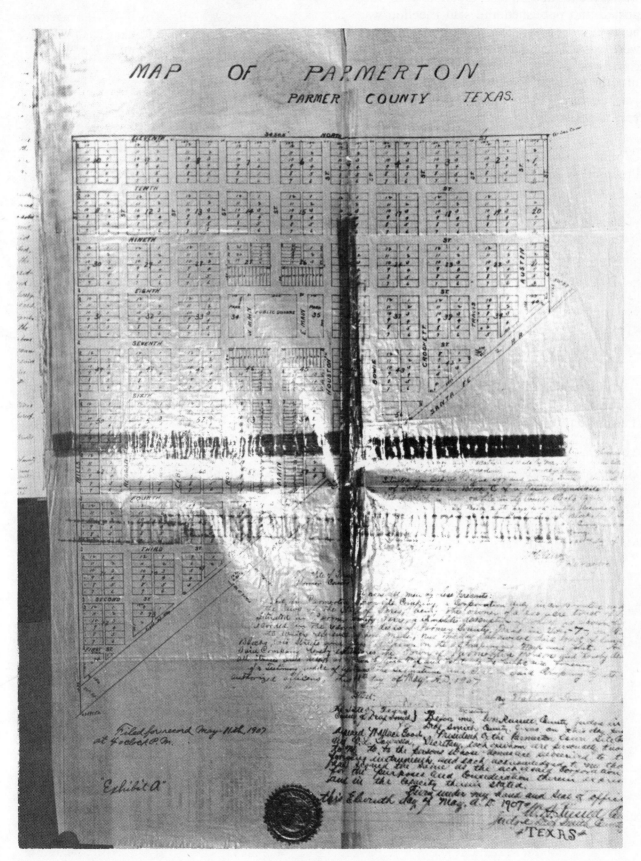

MAP OF PARMERTON

9

calling for a County Seat Election. After which the Notices of said Election were duly posted and published and said Election was held on December 10th, 1907 and 126 votes were cast. The results of the election were canvassed by the Commissioners Court five months later on May 6th, 1908 and Farwell was declared the County Seat having received 99 votes.

Voting Precinct	For Parmerton	For Friona	For Farwell
1	4	0	0
2	1	1	11
3	9	0	0
4	12	0	15
5	0	0	67
6	0	0	6
Totals	26	1	99

After which the Commissioner's Court ordered the County Records removed from Parmerton to the building known as the "Hamlin Brick" in Farwell. It is not clear as to what day the records were actually moved but I believe they were moved on Thursday, May 7th, 1908. The Marriage Records reflect that W.H. Butler and Mrs. Sallie Cress were issued a license on Saturday, May 9th, 1908 dated Farwell, Texas.

PARMERTON MARKER DEDICATION—Henry Curtis, pioneer—left; Henry Tuebal, speaker—center; Hugh Moseley, Master of Ceremonies—right.

The "Hamlin Brick" building situated on Lots 31 and 32 Blk. 18 O.T. Farwell was used as the temporary Court House until said building was razed by fire on the 19th day of May, 1913.

The Comissioner's Court met in a special Called Session to decide what should be done about a temporary Courthouse whereupon it was ordered by said Court that the County Officers should remove their records and furniture to the building located on third street and situated on Lot 29 and the South one half of Lot 30 in Blk. 27 O.T. Farwell.

The First Commissioner's Court Meeting held in the Hamlin Brick was on Monday, May 11th, 1908.

DRILL MOUNTED on a "one-way."

ORIGINAL "Wind shield farmer."

THIS IS THE way we make our bread.

11

Chapter II

Martin Parmer

The "Ring-Tailed Panther from Missouri," so reads the title of a book written in Dallas, Texas, in 1874 by Thomas Parmer about his father Martin Parmer for whom our county was named. Almost a hundred years had elapsed between the birth of the father and the literary venture of the son. Small wonder then that the passage of still another hundred years has left a very dim trail for us to follow. Our efforts have included hundreds of miles to travel, dozens of letters and phone calls to Virginia, Tennessee, and Missouri. Everyone contacted has been sympathetic and cooperative but the trail has been obliterated by the winds of time and hidden by the debris of fallen dreams. Our research is continuing, perhaps a future volume will be able to pick up the thread of fate and weave it into a more satisfying pattern. The best we can do at present is to tell it to you as it was told to us.

We do not wield the ax; we merely pick up the chips!

THE FREDONIANS

The "Fredonians," as the American colonists were then styled, numbered about two hundred men. They took possession of the stone house in Nacogdoches, and commenced fortifying themselves. Having raised the flag of independence, they began to organize their forces and government. Colonel Martin Parmer, one of the most daring and vigilant men in the colony, was appointed to the command of the military; and suitable alcaldes, or, as they preferred to call them, justices of the peace, were chosen for the different settlements. On the 18th they held a court-martial for the trial of Manuel Santos for giving aid and comfort to the enemy, of which he was honorably acquitted.

Martin Parmer was only one of the extraordinary characters that appeared in Texas about that time. His life had been a thrilling romance. He was born in Virginia, in 1775. At twenty years of age he emigrated to Tennessee, where he married Miss Sarah Hardwick. He was engaged for some time in superintending the works of Montgomery Bell, of Dickson County. But his ambition was not satisfied. In 1818, he emigrated to Missouri, and settled fifty miles above the highest

county formed in the then territory—surrounded by the Sioux, Iowa, and Osage Indians. He gave fifty dollars for a bear-dog, and by the chase kept such supplies of meat as drew the Indians around him. One of them, called Two Heart (from the fact that he had killed a white man, and eaten his heart), came to partake of his bounty, when he spread before him a large quantity of meat, and, standing over him with a drawn knife, forced him to eat till it ultimately killed him! Parmer had numerous and fearful fights with the savages, but at last acquired an influence over them, which induced the government at Washington to appoint him an Indian agent. He was elected a colonel of the militia, and then a member of the convention to form a state constitution. It was shortly after taking his seat in this body, that, two of the members getting into a fight, he interfered in behalf of one of the parties, announcing himself as the "Ring-tailed Panther," by which name he was afterward known in the west. After serving two or three terms in the Missouri legislature, Parmer emigrated to Texas, and settled near Mound Prairie. It is said he fired the first gun in the Fredonian war. Among the numerous stories told of him, it is related, upon good authority, that when his bear-dog died, he sent fifty miles for a clergyman to attend the funeral, which he actually did—supposing it to be one of Colonel Parmer's family! His son, from whom the above account is obtained, says he heard the sermon.[1]

PARMER'S POLITICAL LIFE

Information concerning Colonel Parmer's political activities in Missouri was furnished by Mr. Floyd C. Shoemaker, Secretary of the State Historical Society of Missouri, Columbia, in a letter dated November 17, 1939.

He said:

I have your letter of November 13, requesting certain information on Martin Palmer, or Parmer, who lived in Missouri before settling in Texas.

Martin Palmer was not a member of the Missouri Constitutional Convention of 1820, since his name does not appear as a member in the Journal of the Convention in our files. This Constitutional Convention convened at St. Louis on June 12, 1820 and adjourned on July 19, 1820.

Martin Palmer served as a representative from Howard County in the first General Assembly of Missouri. The first session of this Assembly convened at St. Louis on September 18 and adjourned on December 12, 1820. The extra session of the first General Assembly met in St. Charles from June 4 to June 29, 1821, and the second session of the first General Assembly met at St. Charles from November 5, 1821 to January 12, 1822.

Martin Palmer was also elected as a State Senator to the third General Assembly which met in St. Charles from November 15, 1824 to February 21, 1825.

The special session of the third General Assembly met at St. Charles on January 19, 1826. It seems certain that Palmer did not serve in this session of the third General Assembly, since the Senate Journal of this special session of 1826 (p. 9) records the fact that a committee was appointed to inquire into the cause of the absence of certain Senators, among them "Martin Parmer, a Senator from the district composed of the counties of Clay, Ray, Lillard (now Lafayette) and Charlton Counties . . ." This committee later reported that Palmer had "removed . . . out of the State," but that there was no evidence of his resignation in the office of the Secretary of State. (Senate Journal, 3rd G.A., Spec. Sess., 1826, p. 13)

The *History of Clay and Platte Counties, Missouri* says that at the time Palmer was elected to the legislature as a Senator he lived in Clay county "on Fishing River, in the southeastern part of the county."

Louis Houck in his *History of Missouri* (Volume III, page 157) mentions the fact that Martin Palmer "hunted and trapped in the limits of the present Carroll county in 1817. . . ."

Brown states that James Kerr, for whom Kerr County, Texas was named, sat with Colonel Parmer in the Missouri Legislature and that at the close of the session in 1825 they resigned and came to Texas together.[2]

On October 2, 1826 the Mexican government cancelled, unjustly so, many think, the empresario contract it had awarded to Haden Edwards, April 18, 1825, to settle eight hundred families in and around Nacogdoches. Lawlessness prevailed in that area and a small revolution was in the making. It was then that three men who were in later years to sign the Texas Declaration of Independence appeared upon the scene to play important roles in the drama then unfolding, Martin Parmer, John S. Roberts and James Gaines.

The conditions as they existed at that time were described in detail by Henry S. Foote, in 1841 in his *Texas and the Texans,* as related to him by Benjamin W. Edwards, brother of Haden Edwards. The Anglo-Americans had held an election January 1, 1826 at which time Chichester Chaplin, son-in-law of Martin Parmer[3] had been elected by Samuel Norris, according to Foote, ruled with a high hand.

Nacogdoches now became a scene of wild uproar and confusion; acts of lawless and cruel violence marked the history of every day, and indeed of every hour; hands of Regulators as they were called, pervaded the whole country, under the ostensible sanction of the Alcalde, and ready to execute any mandate to which he might give utterance.[4]

The Mexican population, in anticipation, immediately set up claim to all the valuable places occupied by the Americans! The servile alcalde, Norris, granted all the orders they asked; and Gaines, his brother-in-law, was ready with a company of *Regulators* to enforce them. By these means, the Americans were dispossed, driven from their homes, fined and imprisoned. Matters had become intolerable.[5]

Finally the opposition organized and on November 23, 1826 brought Samuel Norris and Jose Antonio Sepulveda to trial before a court composed of Colonel Parmer, President, Captain B.J. Thompson, Major John S. Roberts, J.W. Mayo and William Jones.

—And the Court being sworn in took their seats.

It was determined by the Court that martial Law shall be enforced in the town, and every American be compelled to bear arms, or be put under arrest, and fined according to the pleasure of the Court. This law shall be in force until ordered by the Court.

"ORDER TO THE SERGEANT OF THE GUARD"

You are commanded to bring forthwith every American in the village and compel him to bear arms—if he refuses, put him under arrest.

Martin Palmer (sic)
Col. Commander in Chief

Wm. B. Ligon
Sergeant of the Guard.[6]

On November 25, 1826 "Proclamation was issued, offering a reward of one hundred dollars for the body, dead or alive, of James Gaines charged with high crimes and misdemeanors."[7]

On the 25th both Norris and Sepulveda were found guilty and removed from Austin. The following is from the verdict rendered in the case of Norris:

We, the Court Martial, find Samuel Norris late Alcalda of the District of Nacogdoches, worthy of death, but in consideration of his ignorance, and the influence of infamous advisors over him sentence him to be deprived of the office of Alcalda of said District, and forever incapable of holding any office, trust, honor or profit, in the said District and in case of his resuming or attempting to resume its functions, that his punishment of death shall be inflicted on him.—And that he be forever incapable of holding any office of trust, honor or profit within the said District.

Martin Palmer
Col. Commandant Nacogdoches[8]

On January 1, 1827 Stephen F. Austin issued a circular from which the following was extracted:

A small party of infatuated madmen at Nacogdoches have declared Independence and invited the Indians from Sabine to Rio Grande to join them and wage a war of murder, plunder and desolation on the innocent inhabitants of the frontier—The leader of this party is Martin Parmer, and Jim Collier, Bill English, the Yoakums, and the man of that character are his associates.[9]

This was the beginning of the Fredonian War, which ended March 31, 1827 when the Fredonians crossed the Sabine in exile.

On November 2, 1835, Colonel Parmer was seated at the Consultation at San Felipe as the delegate from the District of Tenehan. On November 11 the Consultation created the Municipality of Tenehaw (Shelby) to embrance the same territory formerly embraced in the District of Tenehaw and Colonel Parmer was thereafter the representative from Tenehaw Municipality.[11]

On November 12 Colonel Parmer placed in nomination Henry Smith for Governor of the Provisional Government of Texas. On November 14, Parmer was elected a member of the General Council of the Provisional Government. He, Stephen W. Blount and Edward O. Legrand were the delegates from San Augustine Municipality to the Constitutional convention at Washington-on-the-Brazos in March, 1836 and there they signed the Declaration of Independence.

On August 16, 1839 Colonel Parmer was appointed Chief Justice of Jasper County, being succeeded January 30, 1840 by Captain Mark B. Lewis. He died March 2, 1850,[12] while preparing to move to Walker County and was buried on the A.C. Parmer survey about twelve miles southeast of Jasper, Jasper County.

When Parmer County was created August 21, 1876 it was named in honor of Martin Parmer, an eccentric Texan of the olden time, and one of the signers of the Declaration of Texas Independence.

The Commission of Control for Texas Centennial Celebrations had the remains of Colonel Parmer exhumed and in 1936 reinterred in the State Cemetery at Austin and a monument erected at his grave.

Colonel Parmer was married four times, each wife dying before he did except his last one. His first wife was Sarah Hardwick. He next married a widow, Mrs. Lornt, his third wife was another widow, Mrs. Margaret Neal. His fourth wife, Zina Kelly, survived him and lived for a number of years in Waller County. Only the names of the children of the first marriage are known to the compiler. They were Charlotte, who married William Liles; William, who married a cousin, Lucinda Caldwell in Arkansas; Martha, who married William Driskill in Arkansas; Emily, who was married to Chichester Chaplin in Texas; Ishom, who was never married; Thomas, who married Rachel Teal; Nancy, who married

Henry Black, and Mary Palmer, who married Henry Black. All the children of Martin Parmer spelled their name "Palmer."

Mr. William P. Zuber who as a boy served in the Texas army in 1836 was married to a granddaughter of Martin Parmer. Mr. Zuber's wife was a daughter of William and Charlotte (Parmer) Liles.

Some of the surviving grandchildren of Martin Parmer in 1940 were Mrs. Low Parker, Trinity, Texas, a daughter of William Parmer, son of Martin Parmer by his first marriage and Mrs. T.M. Brewer, 103 Dresden Street, Houston, a daughter of Martin and Zinna Kelly Parmer.

Other descendants were Mrs. G.J. Creighton, Conroe; Mrs. Phil H. Sticker, 1403 Holman, Houston; and Mrs. J.E. McQuillen, 3401 Avenue K, Galveston.

LIFE IN MISSOURI

From the Liberty Chronicle, Liberty, Clay County, Missouri, we quote part of Mr. Irving Gilmer's article of July 28, 1938.

In 1820 immigration began in earnest and settlements were made along Fishing River, Big Shoal, along the Missouri and throughout the southern part of the county generally by Samuel Tilford and many other pioneers. Although there were numerous bands of Indians in close proximaty to the settlements in Clay and though many of these were semi—hostile no outbreaks or collisions occurred between them and the pioneers until the summer of 1821 up in what is now the northwestern part of the county.

One family especially was accused of acquiring property by questionable means. Their fondness for horses was a particular weakness. On one occasion in the summer of 1821 they visited a camp of Iowa Indians up in the Platt country and took away some horses belonging to the Indians. It was sometime in the month of August in 1821 probably when nine Iowa Indians came down into the Clay County Settlements. To the southeastern part of the county, three miles northeast of where Missouri City now stands lived David McElwee. He had come from Tennessee the previous year, built the house and opened the farm.

At the time of the visit of the Indians, McElwee was back in Tennessee on a visit having taken with him his wife and daughter, Mrs. Margaret Herschel. He left behind to care for the house and farm his sons James and William, and his daughter, Sarah, all unmarried young people. The nine Indians came to Mr. McElwee's one evening and took three horses belonging to the settler and seized another which they were prevented from taking only by the stubborn and plucky interposition of young James McElwee. The Indians seemed greatly elated at the ease at which they had gotten even with the whites in the matter of horse—stealing and at once sent off the three captured animals in charge of two of their number. The other seven Indians went into camp for the night within fifty yards of the McElwee home. The young McElwees were in great terror to be sure, but when their father left he had charged them that if they were ever in any danger from the Indians they had only to let their nearest neighbors know and they would soon be relieved. On this occasion they contrived to let Thomas Officer know of their situation and soon the entire settlement knew that seven Indians had already taken three horses from the McElwee's young folks and were threatening them by their presence with further damage and injury. The next morning early came old Martin Palmer, and with him Patrick Laney, Thomas Officer, James Officer, David Liles, William Liles, James Woolard, Alex Woolard, and with them were Mrs. James Laney, wife of Patrick Laney, and Miss Mary Crawford who had come for companionship for Miss McElwee.

The Indians were a little startled by the appearance of the settlers but stoutly maintained that what they had done was justifiable and altogether proper. Old Martin Parmer was not in a mood to discuss principles. He never let an opportunity pass to have a fight with the Indians. Two years before in a fight of his own bringing on, down on the Wakenda, in Carroll County, he and his party killed three Indians and wounded a number more. His voice was always for war or at least for a fight, when there was the smallest provocation.

The discussion in McElwee's dooryard grew warm and at last Parmer said something to one of the Indians that so incensed him that he presented his gun at Parmer and

16

cocked it, and before he could fire, Parmer shot him dead. A fierce and stubborn little fight then came off in the dooryard. Both whites and Indians ran to cover. Two of the Indians ran into the house where the ladies were, but seeing them coming Miss McElwee ran out of doors and the other two took refuge under a bed. The Indians outside were defeated and scattered, one of them being wounded. Those in the house closed the door tightly and bravely held the fort. But at last the whites climbed to the top of the house and began tearing away part of the roof, when the savages suddenly opened the door and sprang forth hoping to escape by swift running. Some of the settlers were waiting for them and one was shot dead before he had gotten twenty feet from the door. The others escaped.

A variety of sources tell us that Martin Parmer lived and traveled in the Grand River Valley, Clay, Howard, Ray, and Carroll Counties. This area of Missouri lies just northeast of Kansas City.

He is said to have performed the first wedding ceremony in Clay County. The wedding took place beneath a sugar maple tree near the Dillon home and about one quarter mile from Parmer's log blockhouse. The contracting parties were Cornelius Gilliam and Mary Crawford. Miss Crawford was an orphan who had been reared by Mrs. Mary Poteet. Mr. Gilliam, "Neill," was later sheriff of Clay County, state senator, and a gallant officer in the Florida War. (The Florida War was fought between the Seminoles and U.S. troops in an effort to subdue the Florida Indians, 1835-42.)

No authentic information can be given of any permanent settlement made in Clay County, Missouri, prior to the year of 1819. In 1818 and 1819 the territory now included in Ray and Clay, and counties of other territories, were surveyed and opened to entry. Settlers began to move in rapidly, the area around Cooley Lake was particularly attractive. A stage line had been established between Camden and Liberty. This route lay through Goose Gap between Cooley Lake and Fishing River, and the Gap was about a mile from the ridge where Parmer's fortress-like residence stood. The town of Miltonville was later built near Parmer's homestead.

In searching for Parmer's grave an old history gives an account of a party of people who searched near the town of Miltondale, Missouri. They were surprised at being unable to find it even though three trips were made into the area. It was their understanding that he had spent most of his life in the region of Cooley Lake. In reality he lived in Missouri only about ten years.

The search was abandoned when a large rattlesnake was found under a fallen tombstone!

IN PUBLIC LIFE

Governor McNair appreciated the importance and dignity of the office of first governor of Missouri. He made it evident in many ways. When the legislature assembled in St. Charles, the temporary capital, Governor McNair rode over on horseback. It is tradition, according to Walter Williams, that he was the only state officer who wore a cloth coat, cut swallowtail, after the fashionable style of 1821. The governor was further distinguished by a tall hat of beaver. Most of the legislators wore homespun clothes and homemade shoes. Several came in buckskin leggings, fringed hunting shirts and moccasins. A few had wool hats, but the common head covering even of the public men of Missouri was the fur cap of coon or wildcat. The sartorial distinction of Governor McNair made its impression upon the legislators. It is handed down that one member, Palmer, from the Grand River Valley, insisted on occupying for a single night the same bed with Governor McNair, so that, as he said, he could go back and tell his constituents on Fishing River that he had "slept with the governor of Missouri."

This legislator, Palmer, or Parmer, for tradition preserves both ways of designating him, was not overawed by his public position. He took an a active part in the proceedings. Governor McNair did not limit his relations with the general assembly to the delivery of messages. On one occasion Duff Green and Andrew McGirk became so heated in argument during a session that McGirk threw a pewter inkstand at Green. A fist fight was started. Governor McNair came forward and tried to restore order. He took hold of Green and was trying to pull him away. Palmer, who called himself, the "Ringtail Panther," pushed the governor to one side and shouted:

"Stand back, governor, you are no more in a fight than any other man. I know that much law. I am at home in this business. Give it to him, Duff!" [1]

MARTIN PARMER—IRONWORKER

In our search for information concerning Martin Parmer's early life we were consistently confronted with the name of Montgomery Bell. During the summer of 1973 we spent a night at a state park in Dickson county Tennessee named in honor of this pioneer industrialist. Only one of his old iron furnaces remains. A crude circle of stonework, tumbled into ruin, and vine covered, it tells a story of American progress into what was in the early eighteen hundreds a true wilderness.

How or when Martin Parmer met Montgomery Bell or how long he remained in his employ we do not know. We are told only that at age twenty he came to Tennessee and for some time was a superintendent for the works of Montgomery Bell. In as much as Parmer's association with Bell was undoubtedly an important period in his early life, a brief summary of Bell's operation is included in this record.

Montgomery Bell was born in Chester County, Pennsylvania in 1769. From an older brother he learned the craft of manufacturing felt hats. His skill must have been considerable for in 1789 he moved to Lexington, Kentucky to establish his own business and to care for a recently widowed sister and her children. His journey led through the beautiful Cumberland mountain country and he was impressed by the vast number of rushing streams whose potential for generating mechanical power was wasted. The mountain ranges were covered by thousands of acres of hardwood forests. Outcroppings of limestone and iron ore were visible in cliff-sides and along the banks of creeks and rivers. Bell was intrigued by the preponderance of these natural resources and after a few years as a successful hatter he invested in property in Dickson County, Tennessee about two hundred miles southwest of Lexington, Kentucky.

His new venture consisted of purchasing an iron furnace from a Mr. Robertson who had met with only small success in it's operation. There were a great many of these furnaces in central Tennessee during the early eighteen hundreds. They were built of rough native stone in the form of a round chimney-like tower. Charcoal was obtained by burning the native hardwood in crude kilns. Iron ore was dug from the surrounding mountainsides. Limestone was present in great quantities. The furnace was filled with a mixture of these three ingredients and a fire kindled at the bottom to ignite the charcoal. By means of huge volumes of air forced up through the mass of materials the charcoal generated extremely high temperatures. As the iron melted from the crude ore the limestone disintegrated into gases which improved the quality and workability of the finished product. Near the base of the furnace a group of molds caught the molten metal forming it into ingots called "pigs" because of their stubby, round shape.

Bell's need for water-powered machinery caused him to change the course of a small, swift river, the Harpeth. He used slave labor to cut a tunnel 96 yards long, 6 feet high, and 15 feet wide, through solid rock. The water thus diverted created a "mill race" of astounding force that drove the machinery necessary for the foundry's operation.

In one year Bell had increased production in the original furnace and built several additional ones. In 1808 he advertized for 5000 cords of wood to be delivered to his locations. At one period he had one hundred-fifty thousand dollars invested in land and equipment. He owned 10,000 acres of land spread over five counties. During the War of 1812 his foundry, probably under the supervision of Martin Parmer, cast the cannon balls used in Andrew Jackson's defense of New Orleans, Louisiana. Bell amassed a fortune of seventy-five thousand dollars and gave twenty thousand dollars to establish a school for poor children.

Bell's business suffered badly in the depression of 1819 and despite a recovery in the late 20's he died alone and in very humble circumstances in 1855.

Martin Parmer's departure from the Bell organization may have been prompted by slackening of business he may have felt a yen to see the "other side of the mountain." Whatever his reason, we find him living in Missouri in 1816.

MARTIN PARMER—
A CHRONOLOGICAL SKETCH

1778—Born in Virginia on June 4th, 1778
1798 Moved to Tennessee
1816 Moved to Missouri
1817 Lived in Carroll county, Missouri
1820—22 Representative in Missouri State Government
1824 November 15-February 25, 1825 State Senator in Missouri Legislature
1826 Moved to Texas with James Kerr, a fellow Legislator
1826 Fought in Fredonian War on the side of Texas colonists.
1827 Fled into the United States—across Sabine River into Louisiana
1831 Returned to Texas
1831 Again expelled into Louisiana
1835 Returned to Texas—Constitution Delegate
1835 Elected to general council from Tenaho
1836 Signs Texas Declaration of Independance at Washington-on-the-Brazos
1839—40 Chief Justice—Jasper County, Texas
1850 Died March 2nd; buried in Jasper County
1836 Reburied in State Cemetary, Austin

CHAPTER II FOOTNOTES

Parmer's Political Life

1. Yoakum's **History of Texas**, Vol. I p. 247.

2. John Henry Brown, **History of Texas**, I, 136.

3. Chichester Chaplin had married Emily Parmer, daughter of Martin Parmer. Foote was mistaken in stating that Chaplin was a son-in-law of Haden Edwards (Henry S. Foote, **Texas and Texans**, I, 229). Yoakum, probably following Foote, made the same misstatement. (Henderson Yoakum, **History of Texas**, I, 239)

4. Henry S. Foote, **Texas and the Texans**, I, 233.

5. Henderson Yoakum, **History of Texas**, I, 244.

6. The **Austin Papers**, Dr. Eugene C. Barker, vol. 2, part 2, 1515-1522.

7. **Ibid.**

8. **Ibid.**

9. **Ibid.**, 1558.

10. H.P.N. Gammel, **Laws of Texas**, I, 531.

12. Judge Fulmore said that Colonel Parmer died in 1837 (L.T. Fulmore, **The History and Geography of Texas As Told in County Names**, 90). Reverend Thrall states that he died soon after the Revolution. (Homer S. Thrall, **A Pictorial History of Texas**, 597). (Mr. Dixon says that Colonel died in 1857. **Men Who Made Texas Free**, 153).
The following is self-explanatory:

Navasota, Texas
March 4, 1936

Mr. L.W. Kemp,
Houston, Texas.

Dear Mr. Kemp:
Replying to your letter of Feb., 29th. I was quite elated to find that you too are in favor of having Martin Parmer's remains taken to the State cemetary at Austin. And that you will recommend an appropriation for this purpose.

I talked with several of his descendants, at Old Washington who were there for the centennial celebration. They all agreed that he be taken to Austin. Do you want me to get a written statement from them to that effect? Also is there a questionnaire to be filled out as to proof of the grave being that of the designated person? There is a sandstone marker over the grave but the inscription has worn off. I interviewed, with Mr. Glenn and Mr. Smith, several very old men who stated that they had known of the location of the Parmer grave since they were boys and had hunted in its vicinity. Will it be necessary to get affidavits from them since the inscription is indistinguishable? As to the date of his death; the family Bible of his daughter Matilda Palmer (Morris) now owned by her daughter Mrs. A.E. Nation, carries the following entry—"Colonel Martin, Palmer Died March 2nd. A.D. 1850." This entry was made by Matilda's husband. Of course you have his birth date of June 4, 1778.

You may be interested in knowing that I have traced the Revolutionary War record of Martin's father and the connection has lately received the approval of the Daughters of the American Revolution.

Thanking you for your prompt reply to my letter and awaiting further instructions from you, I am,
Sincerely yours,
Sterrett McAlpine Terry
(Mrs. J.W.)

Life In Missouri

1. On February 28, 1835 Colonel Parmer received title to one league of land in Zavala's Colony situated in what is now Orange County (v. 22, p. 199, Spanish Archives). In Headright Certificate No. 39 for one labor of land issued to him February 1, 1838 by the Board of Land Commissioners for San Augustine County it is not stated when he came to Texas. He was living in Jasper County, October 22, 1849 when he sold the certificate to James McMahan (File 116, Jasper 1st Class, General Land Office.)

19

The Fredonians

1. Missouri Historical Review, Vol. XVII, no. 1, Oct. 1922, p. 16, p. 3, and p. 17, p. 2 & 3.

In Public Life

1. Montgomery Bell State Park is eight miles north of Highway 40 about thirty miles west of Nashville, Tennessee.

Martin Parmer—Iron Worker

1. "Virginia Wills and Administrations—Years 1632-1800," by Clayton Torrence, lists Pledge Parmer, Amherst County, 1795; John Parmer, King George County, 1799. Any relationship between Martin Parmer and these men is unknown at this time; however they are the earliest of this name to be found in Virginia.

Chapter III

The XIT Ranch

THE VIEW FROM PARMERTON HILL

The traveler who makes bold to undertake the journey into the XIT story will find himself also following the trail of Parmer County history. Of the ten panhandle counties touched by the finger of fate Parmer was the one most completely covered in the creation of the world's largest fenced cattle ranch. The path he treds will not always be well defined and smooth. There are areas of vagueness, dusted over by the sands of time. Very early in the journey he will be confronted with a decision; should he follow the Factual route or turn aside upon the Romantic byway?

The one marked Factual is the widest and most popular but it leads through Logic and becomes mere computer fodder, very soon bogged down in columns of figures and bone dry statistics. The results are passed out on plastic cards devoid of sentiment or humor.

The Romantic trail, with all it's meanderings, is the one most frequented by the casual voyager who does not ignore facts but who desires a little sugar—coating on the pill of knowledge.

For those who demand the pinpoint accuracy of names and dates the Panhandle Plains Museum Library at Canyon, Texas has tons of records given them by the Capital Reservation Lands Co. of Chicago, Illinois. They have been subjected to casual perusal and technical research. These records represent one of the most valuable gifts ever made by a business organization to an institution dedicated to the preservation of American history. These records will be alive and well when the profound mumblings of politicians are gathering the dust of centuries in marble mausoleums.

Perhaps the most valid approach lies somewhere between the seriously academic and the fancifully romantic. Parmer County lies way south of the geographical center of the XIT spread. Parmerton "hill" is part of an undulating upland that runs from north to south through the heart of the county. Our trail crosses the swelling prairie at a point where men will someday build a group of buildings beside a newly laid pair of rails and

ORIGINAL RANCH HOUSE at Buffalo Springs

ORIGINAL BUNK HOUSE at Buffalo Springs

declare Parmer to be a part of the rapidly expanding western civilization. At this stage of our fanciful journey we are atop the highest wave in a sea of grass. Far, far, to the north a misty bank of clouds hang over the miles broad valley of the Canadian. We squint our eyes beneath the broad brim of our hat but even so we cannot overcome the limit of human vision nor the curvature of the planet earth and so we are unable to follow the green waves until they break upon the imaginary shores of Oklahoma. Somewhere in that dim distance is a place called Buffalo Springs. Here the first XIT cattle were pastured after a contest of trail driving that was in itself a true saga of the old West.

Buffalo Springs was very early given over to marketable steers. From the gently rolling country near the springs and down across the whole of Dallum county such pastures as Farwell Park, Matlock, and Carrizo were stocked with the offspring of lanky longhorn cows and beef type bulls brought in from the midwestern states.

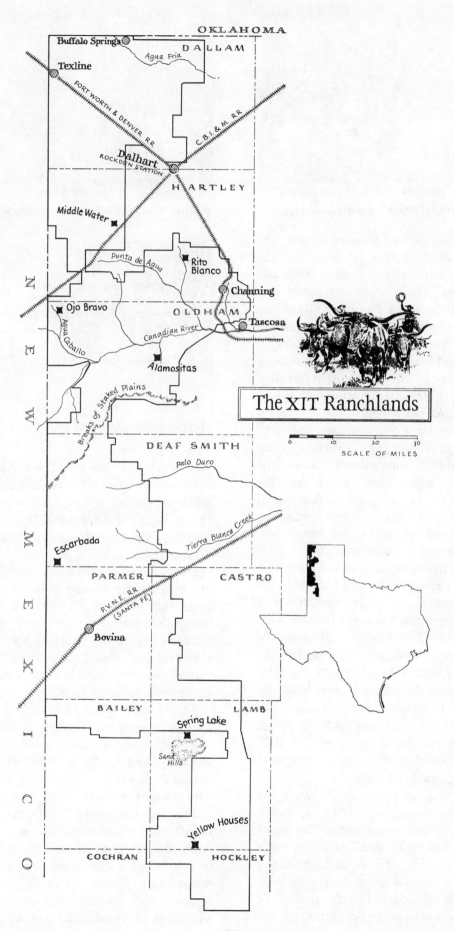

OKLAHOMA

DALLAM

Buffalo Springs

Agua Fria

Texline

FORT WORTH & DENVER R.R.

C. B. I. & M. R. R.

Dalhart
ROCKDEN STATION

HARTLEY

Middle Water

Punta de Agua

Rito
Blanco

Channing

Ojo Bravo

OLDHAM

Canadian River

Tascosa

Agua Caballo

Alamositas

Breaks of Staked Plains

The XIT Ranchlands

DEAF SMITH

Palo Duro

0   10   20   30
SCALE OF MILES

Tierra Blanca Creek

Escarbada

PARMER

CASTRO

P. V. N. E. R.R.
(SANTA FE)

Bovina

BAILEY

LAMB

Spring Lake

Sand
Hills

Yellow Houses

COCHRAN

HOCKLEY

N E W   M E X I C O

ORIGINAL HORSE BARN at Buffalo Springs.

WOODEN WINDMILL and Pen on Escarbado pasture.

BOVINA HEADQUARTERS OF XIT—Division 8.

In the western part of Hartley County the Middlewater division was set aside for the care of cattle culled from incoming herds and other divisions. These were not cattle suffering from disease nor handicap. Realizing that the bull is half the herd the management of the XIT had spent thousands of dollars on good grade and purebred males to improve the native breed. The cattle that strolled across the Manilla pasture were off color, ungainly, or just plain ugly!

Down in Oldham County the big valley of the Canadian splits the areas governed by the Ojo Bravo and the Alomocitos divisions. The Rito Blanco pasture and much of the Alomocitas area was devoted to the use of polled black Angus bulls. Ojo Bravo was the northernmost stronghold of the Herefords, the breed that won popular acceptance with the majority of cattlemen. Black Angus also proved to be extremely popular largely due to the favoritism shown by George Findley, a Scot, who was general manager for the XIT.

South of the Canadian the divisions of Escarbado, Springlake, and Yellow Houses were almost exclusively Hereford domain, although a few of the pastures were ruled by Durham sires. In 1910 the black Angus were the only pure bred stock left upon the range and when the last cattle were sold in 1912 they were declared to be, "for all practical purposes," a pure bred herd.

From our vantage point atop Parmerton hill we feel the magnitism of the far north range. There is something about the sheer magnitude of the scene that befuddles one's reason. A motor trip of several hours along the dirt roads that criss cross the region only adds to the magic of unbelief; instead of simplifying or explaining the extent of the

XIT it has the reverse effect. Although one may visit the sites of every headquarters and make a valiant effort to comprehend the ranch in it's entirety the final result is as baffling as a schoolboy trying to describe the Grand Canyon.

Despite our enchantment with the northern range we realize that there are other areas that we must fit into the magnificent image. We pull our gaze away from the far distance and to the southwest we see a dust cloud arising from Bovina eight miles away where sweating men are driving half wild cattle into railroad cars.

To the south the XIT lands roll over all of Parmer county and spill into Bailey. South and east they invade Castro, then Lamb, Hockley, and Cochran counties. These are the lands of ancient riverbeds and wide lakes whose waters may be either "salt" or "sweet."

The southernmost division bears the beautifully romantic name of Casas Amarillos, Yellow Houses. Here great herds of south Texas cattle were turned onto the range. Life giving water lay not too far beneath the surface and outlandishly tall windmills pumped it into tanks.

XIT COWBOYS in 1909 North of Bovina.

XIT LOADING CREW at Bovina.

GARCIA

SPRING LAKE DIVISION MONUMENT—Lamb County.

GARCIA LAKE WATERING PLACE between Mustang Lake at Bovina and Escarbado pastures. Following big rains the mile wide lake bottom would be covered with water.

Resignedly we turn away from the task of expressing true appreciation. Dwarfed by the geographical prospect we refuse to be tempted into a discussion of the day to day business transactions attendant upon a gigantic operation.

Writers of western fact or fiction should stand for a few hours on Parmerton hill. They would soon realize that there was more trail dust than gunsmoke, more hard work than playacting and sometimes more sweat than rain!

CHANNING HEADQUARTERS of XIT Ranch. Other buildings associated with the operation have been destroyed by fires and storms or so vastly remodeled as to be unrecognizable.

Little more than half a century old, Channing sits in the dusty, northwest corner of the Panhandle, center of what was once the largest spread in the world under fence—the XIT Ranch of Texas.

The XIT general headquarters in Channing, above, was built around the turn of the century and has changed little since then; but the way of life it served is gone. Few Texana students forget the story of the ranch's inception, however, for it was responsible for the largest state house in the nation—the Texas Capitol.

In 1882, the Sixteenth Texas Legislature set aside three million acres of its public lands in the Panhandle as payment to whomever would contract to build a "suitable" state capitol. The contract went to Mattheas Schnell of Illinois, who shortly assigned his interests to a group that came to be known as the Capitol Syndicate.

While ground breaking for the capitol got underway, the area was inspected; and by 1885, Abner Blocker, a trail driver, had devised the brand which would give the ranch its name. During the next year, more than 110,000 cattle were bought and the first ranch house was built. At its peak, the XIT was running 150,000 cattle on its ranges.

In 1887, the ranch was split into seven divisions (later eight), each of which operated as a separate ranch with its own headquarters and equipment. The division foreman reported monthly to the manager at general headquarters, then at the Rito Blanco division.

In 1890, the general headquarters was moved to Channing to make use of the railroad which had been run through in 1888. From this headquarters all business affairs—paying wages and accounts and buying supplies—were conducted. Until the growth of Amarillo, Bovina, and more railroad lines, Channing continued to serve daily freight runs for supplies from each of the ranch divisions.

Slow to show profit, the syndicate in 1901 decided to sell land wholesale to meet obligations. By 1912, the XIT was out of the cattle business. Today, less than 2 percent of the original acreage remains intact.

But the memory of those days lives on. Every August in Dalhart, 30 miles north of

Channing, the remaining XIT cowboys gather for the three-day XIT rodeo and reunion.

FROM A TO IZZARD Amarillo News
Credit To Wes Izzard
Prairie 'Droodlers'
Had Fun With XIT

Here's the solution of the XIT puzzle.

The story goes that when the XIT was founded along the west edge of the Panhandle it was generally believed nobody could ever change the brand into something else.

BUT SOME SMART COWPOKE—who was fancy with a running iron—finally figured out that a Texas star with a cross in the center could be fashioned from the XIT.

News of the accomplishment passed from cow camp to cow camp. And it became a pastime with scores of waddies to try and duplicate the feat. Playing with the puzzle became something of an early prairie version of "Droodling."

There was a slight hitch in the solution of the puzzle. All of the lines wouldn't conform as long as the XIT was blocked out perfectly on a steer's hide.

But if the top of the "T" was slapped on at a little angle, it was easy to make a Texas star out of the brand. The new brand was called the Star-Cross.

Dozens of readers sent in sketches showing how the brand was doctored. The diagram in this column explains it.

In addition to those we've already mentioned as having sent us letters and drawings, these good people came to our rescue:

Dale Worley of Canadian, Roscoe Mikel of Amarillo, Glad Snodgrass of Floydada,

Ralph Rittenhouse of Borger, Ralph Davis of Clayton, Jim Housley of Amarillo, Edgar Exum of Amarillo, Roy Grimes of Stratford, Mrs. Gene McGlasson, Jr., of Canyon, L.E. Fitzgerald, Bartlesville, Okla., Hix Wilbanks of Spearman, Ray J. Bones of Boise City, and Goose Ramey of Dimmitt.

AB BLOCKER

It has long been recognized that dedication is not restricted to any one profession. I recall a one-armed nego who prided himself on his ability to dig a straighter, smoother, better graded ditch, than any other man. Fifty years later and two thousand miles removed I learned of another working man who felt the same way concerning his chosen life's work.

Ab Blocker, the designer of the XIT brand, was born on a Texas farm in 1856. Very early in life he discovered that cotton farming was not for him. The lure of wide skies and broad prairies imbued him with the burning ambition to move more cattle faster and in better condition than any other man.

He delivered the first herd to the XIT's Buffalo Springs pasture. His boot heel raked the ground to form the most famous of all cattle brands.

"That brand will hold'em," was his only comment when asked to design a brand that would confuse rustlers.

Of the twelve million cattle that walked north out of Texas, his brother John at one time had eighty thousand on the trail, many of them under the watchful care of Ab.

His pride in a job well done prompted him to say "I have looked down the backs of more cows and drunk more water out of more cow tracks than any other man who ever pounded a herd toward the North Star."

He remained active and an expert horseman until he died at the age of 87.

A COW CAMP TRAGEDY

The day to day life of an average cowboy was not the glamour filled epic described by Hollywood movies and "Western" writers who have never been this side of the Mississippi River. Long periods of "batching" in line camps, trying to outguess the Panhandle

A KNIGHT of the plains.

weather, being mid-wife and guardian to a bunch of half wild cattle was not an occupation for those of weak spines and timid dispositions.

There were times of fun and pranks. Practical jokes, always embarrassing and often painful to the victim, were the order of the day. Despite the harshness of the environment, sentiment was not wholly lacking and many lifelong friendships developed. Oftentimes only a first name or a nickname identified a man to his fellows, but there existed a mutual respect between these men who were destined to become legendary characters.

Back in the 1920's a cowboy was found dead at a cowcamp where he lived alone. An undertaker was notified and the body was embalmed. Two men started from Bovina to Farwell with a coffin in a pickup truck. The highway south of the railroad tracks was being graded and time after time they became stuck in the loose dirt, arriving late at Farwell they learned that an autopsy had been called for. They held it just before sundown in the basement of a mercantile store. All the cowboy friends of the deceased were gathered around when the doctor came and began his work. As the doctor progressed with his job fewer and fewer cowboys remained until at last only the men from the morturary and the doctor were left. When the autopsy was completed it was suggested that the body be buried that same night. The dead boy's friends refused and the funeral was postponed until the next day which was Sunday. Interment was made at Mt. Olivet, south of Farwell. The dead boy's name is not known.

The autopsy revealed that the cowboy had been poisoned by strychnine. + He had apparently used it in place of baking powder or soda when he prepared his biscuits for supper.

Strychnine was not stored in chuckwagons but small amounts were sometimes kept at line camps for prairie dog extermination.

Copied from FORT WORTH STAR-TELE-GRAM
Page 4, Section one, Sunday, January 13, 1963

FAMOUS XIT RANCH MEMORY NOW

Cowboys who pounded leather on the famous XIT ranch more than 50 years ago have a right to shed a sentimental tear because the last vestige of the 3,000,000-acre spread in the Texas Panhandle has been moved.

Sale of the last 39 acres of the former cattle empire was announced in Fort Worth last week by Hamlin Y. Overstreet of Farwell, last of the representatives of the ranch holdings.

Overstreet said he has passed a deed to the 39 acres to Hurshel R. Harding of Farwell. The land, within the city limits of Farwell, now is industrial property, lying between two main lines of the Santa Fe Railway, one of which runs to Chicago and the other to Houston and Galveston.

The Representative made his announcement while visiting in the Fort Worth National Bank with two friends, Joe A. Clarke, executive vice-president, and Brandon Stone, vice-president.

The land transaction in Farwell, Overstreet reminded, marks the completion of a bright chapter in Texas history. The original spread of 3,000,000 acres was given by the State of Texas in 1882 in exchange for the construction of the $3,000,000 state Capitol in Austin.

The XIT was the largest fenced ranch in the continental United States, and perhaps the largest in the world.

Overstreet explained that in 1951 the Capitol Freehold Land Trust, owner of the ranch, was closed when the remaining 25,000 acres was divided among 10 shareholders. A part of the acreage went to Hames H. Douglas, Jr. of Chicago, including the 39-acre tract which was sold to Harding.

The Story of the XIT goes back to 1875 when the state officials found they were getting cramped in the old capitol in Austin, and a constitutional convention set aside the 3,000,000 acres of state land with which to get a new capitol.

However, nothing was done about the proposed new capitol until Nov. 9, 1881, when fire destroyed the old building. Gov. Oren M. Roberts called a special session of the Legislature, and it stuck a bargain with Charles B. and James V. Farwell, Chicago brothers, under which they agreed to build the new capitol and accept the 3,000,000 Panhandle acres in payment.

The red granite Capitol stands in Austin today as the largest state capitol building in the United States.

The Farwells borrowed money in England to develop the ranch. The debt was liquidated in 1909.

The original ranch covered all or portions of 10 counties, Dallam, Hartley, Oldham, Deaf Smith, Parmer, Castro, Bailey, Lamb, Cochran and Hockley.

The 10-county spread perhaps helped perpetuate the story that the XIT name meant "ten in Texas."

In 1885 the first cattle started moving into the XIT pastures from South Texas. Thousands of cattle drummed along the dusty trail to their new home on the XIT.

Came the time for branding and the ranch needed a brand. Ab Blocker, who drove one of the first herds into the 3,000,000-acre pasture, had the responsibility of choosing a brand.

Blocker dug his boot heel into the sand and inscribed the letters, XIT—a brand that would be difficult for the cattle rustler to change.

Overstreet is a nephew of the late Judge James D. Hamlin, who was resident

April 11, 1918 Stock Law passed 291-151 "horses, mules, jacks, jennetts, and cattle may not run at large in Parmer Co."
Commissioners Court Notes

29

THE CAPITOL AT AUSTIN—The Texas pink granite exterior, the terrazzo floor depicting the history of Texas under six flags, and the enduring reminders of Texas men and events preserved in stone, pictures, and documents make the State Capitol and its grounds one of the most beautiful in the United States. Construction was started in 1882 on the massive structure, which was paid for by three million acres of land from the Texas public domain. This Central Texas landmark is the nation's largest Statehouse, ranking next in size to the United States Capitol that it resembles.

representative of XIT until his retirement. Judge Hamlin died 12 years ago.

The Farwells began fencing the ranch in 1882. Sale of parcels of the ranch began in 1901, creating smaller ranches and townsites that were to grow into sizeable cities in the Panhandle. The last of the cattle was sold in 1912.

All that remains of the far-flung cattle operations are the mineral rights on the land, reserved by the Capitol Mineral Rights Company.

Time for obsequies will come this summer when the fast-fading remnant of XIT cowboys gather for their reunion. They will shed a tear for XIT, death of which marks the passing of an era in history.

July 9, 1928 Jack Rabbit scalps—5c each.
Commissioners Court Notes

TRUE WEST
May-June, 1965

SUMMERING ON THE XIT

By Bill Derrick
as told to Harvey LaFon

In the Spring of 1904, I was on a trip from my home in Vici, Oklahoma, to visit cousins in New Mexico. I was on the Santa Fe train and had my saddle with me in an old coffee-sack in the baggage coach. You could check your saddle then the same as your trunk or valise. I understand that custom has since been discontinued. I usually worked for the Pursells or Teagues at Canadian, Texas, in the wintertime, and worked at other ranches in the summer.

When the train stopped at Bovina, Texas, C.R. Smith, the foreman of the X.I.T. came aboard looking for hands to make up the roundup crew. They always hired extra hands in the summer months, but kept only the regular cowboys in the winter. I hired out on the train and, after getting my saddle loaded in the spring wagon, Mr. Smith and I started for the Escarbada headquarters, a sub-division of the X.I.T. about thirty-miles north of Bovina. A short distance from the outskirts of town, Mr. Smith informed me we were now on X.I.T. territory. I asked about the way the ranch lay and he told me the south line ran by the north side of Bovina, then went to the New Mexico line, then east to a point about eighteen miles southwest of Hereford and near the town of Friona, then north about six miles to what was known as the Tierra Blanca Camp. It was so called because of the outcropping of white caliche knolls or small hills. From there the line ran north twenty or twenty-five miles to the south bank of the Canadian River and Tombstone Camp. Some cowboy was buried there—just one tombstone. Again the boundary turned west to the New Mexico line—then south to a point about straight west of Bovina.

Smith asked how I would like to help Bill McCaty break some horses for the round-up wagon and how I was with broncos. I told him I didn't set myself up as a bronc rider but managed to ride the ones I got on, and would be glad to help McCaty. After spending the night at Escarbada, McCaty and I gathered the horses from the horse pasture and drove them to the old N.D. line camp on the New Mexico line. That camp consisted of a round corral, several small pens, a large square corral made of logs and, of course, the horse pasture.

After breakfast the next morning, McCaty and I started to rope and handle a small bunch of the horses. We had extra ropes and tied several to log and rock drags. That got them used to the rope and prevented them from getting rope-burned or getting too far from camp. The drags would give if pulled on pretty hard. After McCaty and I saddled the ones we had in the round corral a few times, I would snub them for him and he would ride the buck out of them. Some of the horses were old-timers at the game and had already been broke once, but started in bucking again—those kind never did break out entirely and Bill would sure use the quirt on

them. Not so, the young ones—he handled them just as easy as he could. He said the old ones knew better than to buck, but the colts didn't.

McCaty was a real hand with horses and one of the best riders I ever saw. I wound up riding about as many as he did, just for the heck of it. I was nineteen years old at that time, over six feet tall, weighed about 190 pounds and was just about as much man as the next one—at least, I thought so.

Some of the colts never bucked a jump, but most of them did. I remember one little blue-grey horse that Bill took a shine to. One day he was working him in the big log corral. All at once he flew to the north side and jumped and fell right on top of the log fence, then went on over. I saw Bill quit him on the fence and then jump down on the other side. He hollered for me to come on and help him. When I got there, the pony was down and Bill had his head pulled up with the bridle reins and was standing on the saddle horn with one foot holding him down. Bill said, "That's one pony I aim to own."

After we had some of them going pretty good, we would ride and locate the roundup wagon and stay a day or so. One day Bill was riding this same pony at the roundup and had him starting to cut pretty good. The pony had a cinch sore and Bill had the saddle loosely cinched. Anyway, he picked him up a little too quick with the spurs and got throwed, saddle and all. Bill just laughed. Walked up to him and patted him on the neck and said, "You little son of a gun, I wouldn't take a hundred for you."

After about a month we had the horses going pretty good. Learned to neck, rein, and to stand when being mounted. We delivered them to the horse wrangler and joined the roundup crew. One day C.R. said, "Bill, come and go to Escarbada with me and stay all night." The next morning we started for the wagon with some extra provisions. C.R. had two water buckets filled with butter and eggs. He mounted and I handed him the eggs.

I was riding a horse known as Old Wobbly, so named because he sunfished. When I got on him with the bucket of butter, I guess he didn't like it and proceeded to come unwound. He would sun first one side, then the other. At the time, C.R. was yelling, "Don't spill the butter, Bill! Don't spill the butter!"

I managed to stay aboard and still had the bucket of butter, after I had his head pulled up. A cowboy's life in the summer on the X.I.T. would be considered pretty rough for people nowadays. The chuck-wagon was their home, the ground their bedroom, and the sky the ceiling. But most were used to that and didn't complain.

I don't recollect how many cows the X.I.T. had at that time, but the roundup crew worked from about the middle of May till late in the summer. They started that time from the southeast side and worked north. The circle men were throwing in good-sized bunches all the time to the rope and branding crew, who threw the cows with the branded calves back to the territory already worked.

Along in June, they took the wagon outfit to Bovina, where they unloaded some replacement cows. I don't remember how many—maybe a thousand or more. Those cattle had to be dipped, and were driven north of the headquarters eight or ten miles, where they had some pens and a dipping vat. The vat had a large corral on each end and each narrowed down to the vat so the cattle could be driven in. Some of those old wild cows would jump in with a big splash.

I worked one end and Ray Anderson worked the other. We had them all run through by noon and Ray and I were a mess. Our clothes were soaked with cow and dip. About that time two men and two women drove up. I don't know who they were, but they looked at us and laughed. After we had changed our clothes back of the post corral at the windmill, we washed them out and hung them on the braces of the windmill tower, and as we went to the wagon I picked up a large flat cow-chip. Ray did also.

After we filled our tin plates at the chuck box, we set them beside us on the ground and set our coffee cups and a big sourdough biscuit on them. Everytime we took a bite of biscuit we would park it right back on the cow-chip. Those people would look at us in astonishment, but Ray and I didn't let on like we noticed. We had a good laugh afterwards.

The cowboys had to take, in turn, a two-hour guard every night on the horse herd, with the horse wrangler taking the first turn. The one they had that year was still not much

more than a boy. One evening about supper-time, one of those fast moving thunderstorms came up, with the lightning something fierce.

He had finished his supper and gone to relieve the man on guard when the lightning struck and killed three saddle horses, and the rest took off in every direction. He came up and said to the foreman, "Well, Mr. Smith, I guess I'm going to have to give them to you. I can't stay with them any longer."

The boss didn't pay much attention to him and waited for things to settle down some. He was raised in that country, a cowhand and a foreman all his life, and it took a lot to perturb him. Several of the hands had already taken off after the fleeing remuda and soon had them in the rope corral.

C.R. was roping some of the night horses, when lightning struck again off to the south and knocked up a cloud of dust. It hit close to where it had killed the horses. C.R. looked over at the wrangler, who was leading the horses out as he roped them, and said, "Kid, I'm a hell of a notion to give 'em back to you!"

After the roundup was over that summer, I was sent to the Tierra Blanca Camp on the east line to take George Baldwin's place, as he wanted to go home for a spell. Some of his folks had died. That was mainly a fence riding job. I would go north one day and stay all night at Tombstone Camp and ride back the next. Then to the corner south and then west. I'd meet the other fence riders at Friona and return to Tierra Blanca Camp the next day. They had telephones in all the camps even in those days. The lines came out from Hereford and went around the ranch on the barbed wire fence; all were connected to headquarters. It was a wonderful thing for an outfit of that size, and saved many a long ride.

There were a lot of wild mustangs on the ranch, which were not much good for anything but to paw the snow off the short grass in winter for the cattle. Sometimes they would spook, run into the fence and break the phone line. The line riders were always quick to make repairs, as the phone was really appreciated.

A little telephone operator at Hereford had been calling Baldwin up of an evening and playing music for him. The first time she called after he had gone, I didn't tell her I wasn't Baldwin, but she knew right away. After I told her who I was, I asked her to call the same as ever, and I would really enjoy the music.

I rode to Hereford once in a while and we would take in a show. I always remembered her for breaking the monotony for me, as that job was pretty lonely.

After the cowboy, George Baldwin, got back that fall, I went to the Escarbada for a few days. C.R. Smith paid me off but helped me get a job at a ranch southeast of Bovina called the Yellow Houses. They had artesian wells and did a lot of irrigating but that's another story. The last I heard of Bill McCaty, he and Earl Sode had a dude ranch each of Tucson, Arizona. Incidently, Earl Sode was a champion bronc rider at that time. I don't suppose they are with us anymore, as they were older than I.

Chicago Sunday Tribune: June 18, 1944
Part 2—Page 8
RITES TUESDAY FOR J.V. FARWELL IN LAKE FOREST
Pioneer Merchant Dies at Age of 85.

Services for John Villiers Farwell, 85, pioneer Chicago merchant and civic leader, will be held at 4:15 p.m. Tuesday in First Presbyterian church, Lake Forest. Mr. Farwell died of a heart attack early yesterday in his home, 121 S. Stone Gate, Lake Forest.

Mr. Farwell was president of John V. Farwell Company, wholesale dry goods firm, which was founded in 1865 by his father, John Villiers Farwell Sr., one of the merchants who helped to build Chicago.

"Business Sold in 1925"

In 1925 the business was sold to Carson Pirie Scott & Co., but the original Farwell company is still in existence as owner of the former Carson Pirie Scott & Co. warehouse at Monroe St. and the river, now leased to the government.

Mr. Farwell was born Oct. 16, 1858, in the old Farwell home at 19 S. LaSalle St. He was graduated from Lake Forest academy in 1874 and from Yale university in 1879. He was director of the Chicago World's Fair in 1893 and had been a member of the executive committee of the Chicago Plan commission since its organization. He was also chairman of the board of the Y.M.C.A., and president of the First State Pawner's society, 42 S. Clark St.

"Helped Raise Funds for Y"

In 1862, his father donated the Farwell home on La Salle St., to be used as headquarters for the then newly organized Y.M.C.A. In 1883, the son along with Cyrus H. McCormick, helped raise funds for the Y.M.C.A. building which now stands on the site of the old Farwell home.

Mr. Farwell is survived by a daughter, Mrs. Katherine Farwell Carpenter of New Haven, Conn.; four stepsons, Perry Dunlap Smith, Hermon Dunlap Smith, Lawrence Smith, and Elliott Smith; a stepdaughter, Mrs. W.D. Harvey; a brother Arthur L. Farwell, and a sister, Mrs. Henry N. Tuttle of New Haven. Mr. Farwell married Miss Ellen Sheldon Drummond in 1884. She died in 1912, and in 1919, he married Mrs. Harriet Flower Smith who died in 1938.

Chapter IV

Bovina

BOVINA

Bovina is located on the Llano Estacado or Staked Plains between two forks of Running Water Draw and has an elevation of 4070 feet above sea level. Bovina was originally the Hay Hook line camp, division number eight of the famous XIT Ranch. One of the earliest structures built in Parmer County was the headquarters building of this Ranch and stood about 400 yards north of the present city of Bovina.

A switch on the Pecos and Northern Texas Railroad in 1898 was called "Bull Town" by train crews because a herd of bulls was in the habit of getting on the railroad track near a cottonseed warehouse and the trains would have to stop while the crew drove the animals from the track. When the name was officially bestowed it was given the Latin word for "bull" or Bovina in order to dignify the name. Bovina was one of the largest cattle shipping points in the United States at the turn of the century. Herds of cattle were driven here from distant ranches in the plains country. The Bovina Post Office was established January 31, 1899 with William M. Guy being appointed the first postmaster.

Prepared by the Personnel:
WORKS PROJECTS ADMINISTRATION
O.P. No. 665-66-3-299

As its name implies, the oldest town in Parmer County, Bovina was a cow town and at one time attained the distinction of being the largest shipping point of cattle in the world. It got its name from the latin "bos," meaning ox or cow.

Today it clings close to the Santa Fe Railroad, a small modest village, slightly noticed by the way many tourists who go hurrying through it on their way to places of more note. It is not incorporated.

Thirty-five years ago, Bovina was started on its career with about a dozen souls, a general store, livery barn and barber shop and section house where borders were accommodated with meals. Rooms were not a necessity then, for beds were carried as a

WAGON TRAIN AT BOVINA, 1906.

HEADQUARTERS—South and West Land Co.—Bovina—1906.

far distant ranches for groceries and the town lay for the most part silent and inactive until a drove was sighted coming in for shipment to market. Then everything came alive, cowboys rode here and there, cattle bawled and rushed for the tanks of water, the old stock pens—still standing—were pushed to capacity to hold the huge droves, sometimes from many different ranches.

This condition existed until settlers began coming in about 1905, settlers from the developed east with slight idea of farming in a semi-arid country. Bovina received them all, looked curiously at them, wondering what they came for with farm horses, farm tools and the farmer's instincts. To them this was a cattle country and nothing else. Grass, short and succulent grew, but no plow had broken the soil and to the ranch owner or cowboy, it was a sacriledge to take from the cattle the native grass and give them only a promise of grain to be grown.

EARLY DAY BOVINA.

EARLY DAY SCENE at Bovina—A group in front of the W.L. Townsen boarding house.

NEW HOME NEAR BOVINA

TOWNSEN HOTEL IN BOVINA.

Immigrant cars were unloaded and hopeful, but doubtful families moved out of Bovina across the unbroken prairie to their sections, half or quarter to build their homes.

The tale of loneliness, hope deferred, hot winds and lack of rain on these distant farms soon broke the spirit of most of these pioneers who had lived too long in comfort and plenty. This one went "back" and then another one followed, all passing through Bovina and Bovina looked on and smiled, thinking that soon all would get enough and leave them in peaceable possession, but they reckoned without their host, for among these immigrants were a few with the pioneer spirit who saw a future in farming this land that needed only moisture to make it productive and set about finding ways to conserve the moisture and those stayed.

Most of these families were young people with small children and at first schools were not needed, but as the needs for schools came, parts of the families moved to Bovina where the one teacher school existed and children began to be educated in their new home.

Bovina, always hospitable, received them, treated them well and went on growing and

introducing new forms of business. A bank opened, another boarding house, residences were built and then a new school building was demanded for the expanding scholastics.

Other families came to take the place of those who had left and gradually the country around Bovina became settled, not thickly, but a few years had dotted the prairie with fences, homes, windmills and every year added a new family or two to Bovina.

This is the outline, the bare facts about Bovina, the little town on the Santa Fe rail-

DRUMMERS (travelling salesmen) traveling through Bovina. The children are local.

36

RAILROAD WATER TANK at Bovina in 1913.

road, but the story of the kindness, the generosity, the goodness of the old timers of Bovina can never be told for it lives in the hearts of those who partook of it. The wind may carry it to distant parts and wherever lives anyone who at one time dwelt in Bovina lives love for Bovina.

A few of those old timers still live there, but most of the dwellers are new comers who have moved into a growing town to go into business there.

Bovina will never be a city, it may never be known beyond the confines of a small territory, but its spirit will live as long as any descendent of any pioneer who knew it, lives.

BIBLIOGRAPHY
Mrs. Minnie Olivia Aldridge . . Farwell, Texas

OLD TIMER REMEMBERS
BOVINA 57 YEARS AGO

Hastings came to the little settlement of a couple of stores, a railroad and acres of cattle pens that was Bovina, in 1902. This was four years after the railroad pushed through and made the settlement a shipping point for XIT Ranch.

After XIT made this their shipping yard, other ranches started bringing cattle here to meet the rails and go to Kansas. Hastings refused to say Bovina was the largest shipping point in the world, pointing out that he couldn't be sure such a claim is correct since he didn't tour all the world and look for a larger one. But it was huge.

CATTLE TOWN
From early spring to late fall, cattle were loaded at the "Bull Capitol" day and night. The railroad had been built from Amarillo to Roswell and Albuquerque in 1898. It made Bovina a permanent settlement but never provided a large population. Often cattle came in faster than cars could be brought here to take them away so the herds had to be held out of town and grazed sometimes for as long as three weeks.

While the herd was waiting for cars, cowhands had come to Bovina and they didn't even wear pistols and they weren't the trouble-seeking type character television westerns make them seem to be, Hastings recalls.

LAW ENFORCEMENT

Maybe some towns in the cattle country were wilder than Bovina, but none in Parmer County was. "There has never been a saloon in the county," Hastings states, "and it was against the law to wear pistols. That law was enforced, too, but people were as much or more law-abiding then than they are now." Hastings admits there was some cattle rustlin' "but so what, some one stole my milk cow one night long after this place became civilized."

When the County of Parmer was established, Hastings became deputy sheriff but he had been acting as unofficial lawman before that. Hobos often came through town and broke into one of the stores so Hastings would get his horse and ride down the railroad track until he overtook the culprit.

This bit of public service caused him to have a narrow escape once. Hastings and Ray Davies, another Bovina oldtimer who still lives here, found a store had been burglarized. They started down the railroad track thinking another hobo was what they were searching for. They had no guns.

A vacant house was located where Parmerton elevator now stands and when Hastings and Davies came to it, they began a search of the premises. First they looked in the sheds and outbuildings around the house. Hastings noticed some muddy footprints leading into the house so went inside to investigate. He opened a closet door and found

OLD JAIL CELL used in Bovina.

BOVINA HIGH SCHOOL group 1911-1912.

BOVINA BASKETBALL TEAM, 1914—Back row: Hallie Hoghland, Miss Sprawls, Mr. Fritch, and the Schlenker girls. Seated: Matilda Tidenberg, Gertrude Lambert, Pearl Dean, and Irene Tidenberg.

himself looking into the faces of three or four "rough fellers."

Hastings called to Davies to bring his gun and come help him take the varmits back to town. When the men, two of which were desperate ex-convicts, discovered they had been tricked and neither Davies nor Hastings had a gun, they wished they had used the three shotguns they had with them in the closet but by that time, the two Bovinans had seized the weapons and were using them to persuade the outlaws to go quietly.

"We didn't know we were taking such a risk," Hastings admits. "We never needed guns to bring hobos back to town and never imagined we would encounter such rough men."

Hastings' policy as deputy was "let 'em fight." He says fist fights were fairly common and attempting to stop them wouldn't have been as easy for him in Bovina as it is for Mr. Dillon in Dodge City.

BOVINA SCHOOL

The Bovina School Board was founded about the same time as the townsite was platted. Joe E. Burham was hired as the first teacher in 1910. This old school house was an old residence near the city waterworks. It consisted of two small rooms with a double door between them. It had a pot-bellied coal stove which was supposed to heat the entire building. Frank Gonzolez Velasco got a dollar a month to take care of this stove. There were 20 children in the first three grades. Eulalia Sprawls, a young lady almost 18, was hired as second teacher. The school continued to grow so that by the fall of 1913 Lem Fertch was principal, Pearl Dean and Eulalia Sprawls taught the primary grades. The two latter boarded at the XIT headquarters in Bovina during the early days. Benton Graham was principal in 1914. He was succeeded by Leora Tidenberg, Madge Lively. Roy Hecox was railroad depot agent. He married Eulalia Sprawls. He was one of the first men to be drafted from the county when the

BOVINA SCHOOL, 1920-21—Back row, left to right, E.V. Day, Superintendent and teachers Sam Martin, Gertrude Lambert, and Irene Tidenberg. Some of the students are identified as follows: Back Row: 5. George Richards, 6. L.D. Parker, 7. Ray Bullock, 8. Nannie Mary Ezell, 9. Ella Tidenberg, 10. Roy Bullock, 11. Leona Glover, 12. Ida Woelvel, 13. Mary Wakefield, 14. Odessa Potts, 15. Frank Spring, 16. Lillian Ezell. Second Row: 1. Bonnie Potts, 2. Unknown, 3. Stanley Wakefield, 4. Joe Wilson, 5. Gladys Stagner, 6. Opal Venable, 7. Alice Hild, 8. Mary Spring, 9. Helen Lambert, 10. Mack Richards, 11. Lester Norton, 12. Mary McDonald, 13. Ruby Bullock, 14. Lowell Stagner, 15. Sammie Dee Collett, 16. —— Richards, 17. Margaret Ezell. Third Row: 1. Unknown, 2. Unknown, 3. Unknown, 4. Floy Wakefield, 5. Ruby Denny, 6. Cleva Lee Denny, 7. Unknown, 8. Unknown, 9. James McDonald, 10. Norma Lee Wilson, 11. —— Caldwell, 12. Unknown, 13. Oscar Lee Parker, 14. Melvin Wakefield, 15. Grace Caldwell. Fourth Row: 1. J.D. Denny, 2. Unknown, 3. Joe Williams, 4. Pete Richardson, 5. Unknown, 6. Unknown, 7. Unknown, 8. William McDonald, 9. Elmer Englant, 10. Unknown, 11. Unknown, 12. Henry Tidenberg, 13. Earl Richards, 14. Herman Woelfel, 15. Otto Woelfel.

OLD TIDENBURG PLACE north of Bovina adobe—
top to bottom.

D.O. STALLINGS, Frankie Barnes, Luther Barnes,
Grandpa Stallings, Mrs. D.O. Stallings, Fray Stallings,
Mrs. Frank Hastings, Mrs. Luther Barnes.

United States entered World War I. His wife took his place at the depot when he left and after her Aubrey Sprawls, her brother, took the job. Mrs. Hecox registered at West Texas for a refresher course and returned to resume the teaching in Bovina. "Moth" McDonald, as she was called, was a cook hired by the railroad who cooked for the workers as they spread rails, her tent always pitched at the "end of track" where the workers also set their camp. She was always a good friend to young folk like Eulalia and often brought a meal or two and sometimes a cake or pie to cheer them up. Mr. Williams had the livery stable, Norma Wilson opened a lumber yard, Porter Johnson was the blacksmith. The Bovina Mercantile Store was run by four businessmen—Tom Houghland, Luther Boyne Barnes, Frank Hastings and A.J. Oliver, this latter serving in the capacity of bookkeeper. The new school was opened May 1, 1911. It was a two story brick building. Bovina was bound to grow because Parmer County became noted for its production of milo. In fact no other county in the entire United States or anywhere else in the world produces as much milo each year as Parmer County. The farmers take their business to Bovina as well as Friona. Both places are also known for the tremendous part they played in the rise of the feedlot industry.

When the XIT determined to parcel the ranch to prospective buyers it was decided to sell at a minimum of 50,000 acres rather than a few acres to each person that came along. It was only after noticing how successful some buyers were with townsites that it began developing for colonization. When the Bovina division was made, John R. Arm-

MRS. DeLANO, Marie Kaiser, Oscar Robert, George Rankins, Mrs. Lillie Chesher—at Bovina Mercantile.

strong was sent as foreman and manager. Born in Vernon County, Missouri, May 22, 1869, his parents, Mr. and Mrs. James D. Armstrong, moved to Kimble County, Texas, September 13, 1880. When he was 20, he and a friend named James Frazier, drove a herd of horses to Ballinger where they sold them, took a train for Tascosa and went to work for Foreman Judge Eubank. He married Florence Nichols, June 17, 1900, Rev. Burnett, Baptist preacher conducting a revival, riding 30 miles from Hereford to perform the ceremony. John R. Jr. was born February 6, 1907. He stayed on as foreman until a large part of the land was disposed of, then took charge of all the land south of the Canadian, as general foreman. He was a kind-hearted man, but despite this he met an untimely death on the streets of Bovina, November 17, 1908. He was buried in Farwell. His wife made her home there and later married a Mr. Golladay.

BOVINA'S LONGHORN overshadowed by things to come.

One of the landmarks in Bovina is the gas station founded in 1925 by J.H. Leake. When he moved to Mineral Wells his sons Clifford and Everson bought him out. Bovina and the surrounding farms were mostly settled by young couples trying to make a start in life. Hence the need for a school system did not seem important in the early years. As time went on and families increased the one teacher school developed into the wonderful school system that makes Bovina a progressive modern town. Bovina started as general store, livery barn, barber shop, section house where 35 boarders were accommodated, meals served three times daily. Later there was a blacksmith shop, a dry goods store. The Methodists, Baptists, Church of Christ, Pentacostal Holiness, Mission Bautista Mexicana all built modern structures. The Gaines Hardware Store also served the town for many decades. The high school put out a paper called The Pentalphia. Markobrad built Bovina's second blacksmith shop, and the town had Darsey's Drug and Bovina Drug. One of the annual events, started in 1963 is Bull Town Days. In 1969 the unveiling of the statue of a bull and of the historical marker made the event even more impressive. Now a town of some 2,000 people it continues to take the lead as a shipping and grain center. Bovina incorporated as a city shortly after World War II.

THE FRIONA STAR
Friday, July 2, 1948

In Tribute to Bill Mersfelders, Pioneer Resident, HISTORY OF PARMER

COUNTY CLOSELY RELATED WITH
EARLY DAY MERCHANT
by George McLean.

Bill Mersfelders, one of the earliest and most prominent citizens of Parmer County, passed from the scenes of this life and was buried at Clovis, Saturday, June 26, and I being a lifelong and intimate friend of his, was honored by being chosen as one of his pallbearers. I, therefore, feel it incumbent upon me to write a few words relative to his useful and colorful life, that the memory of his usefulness to Parmer County may be remembered a little longer.

When I first knew Bill the Santa Fe railroad, near the close of the last century, had built to a point where Bovina now is located. This was several years before any station had been located at Friona, and Bovina soon became known as the largest live cattle shipping point in the world.

At that time the large ranchers ordered their cars one year in advance in order to have them ready when the fall shipping season arrived. As the Farwell Brothers owned three million acres around Bovina, it was an ideal place to hold cattle for shipment.

Bill Mersfelder had arrived here at about that time and wished to install a general store and eating place. The Farwells had not, at that time, sold any of their land, and there was no land there on which to locate his store, so Bill located his business in a large dugout on railroad land, southeast from where the depot at Bovina now stands. This was the first private business established within the limits of Parmer County, and it sure flourished financially, as cowboys who had been out on the range for several months had lots of money to spend.

Bill also had a contract with the Santa Fe Railroad to load all cattle on the cars and he kept a loading crew of from 10-20 men all the time. Cattle loading went on both day and night. At that time the railroad eating house was at Bovina, and was operated by Mrs. Nichols. The cattle buyer and train crews ate at the railroad house. The cowboys and the train crew were a noisey bunch.

At that time, there were no local officers and no law or preachers in the county, so

THE STATE OF TEXAS,
County of *Deaf Smith*

To any Regularly Licensed or Ordained Minister of the Gospel, Jewish Rabbi, Judge of the District or County Court, or any Justice of the Peace, in and for said County—GREETING:

You are Hereby Authorized to Solemnize the Rites of Matrimony Between

Mr. George F. McLean and *Miss Ollie Whitaker*

and make due return to the Clerk of the County Court of said County, within sixty days thereafter, certifying your action under this License.

Witness my official signature and seal of office, at office in *Hereford*
the *29* day of *Novr.* 1905

T. B. Beach, Clerk,
of County Court, *Deaf Smith* County.

By _____ Deputy.

I, *W. B. Mersfelder*, hereby certify that on the *30* day of *Nov* 1905
I united in Marriage *George F. McLean* and *Miss Ollie Whitaker*
the parties above named. Witness my hand, this *30* day of *Nov* 1905

W. B. Mersfelder a J.P. & Ex-Off. Notary Public.

Returned and filed for record the *4* day of *Dec* 1905 and recorded the *13* day of *Dec* 1905

W. B. Beach County Clerk.
By *J. H. King* Deputy.

when it came necessary for a wedding ceremony to be performed, a group of the citizens took Bill, who was then under 21 years of age, over to Hereford and had him appointed as Justice of the Peace for Parmer County. My wife and I were the first couple to be married in the county.

Bill took in money from his store faster than he knew how to spend it, and as there was no organization for the county, he decided to organize it. This was done, although there were not enough real people in the county to form a legal organization.

To overcome this handicap, the cow ponies were named and voted to fill out the legal requirement. When the ponies had been voted it was found that they were still a vote short, so my old dog was registered and voted. When the organization was completed, Bill bought a tract of land about midway between Bovina where Friona was afterward built, and called it Parmerton, and established the county seat of Parmer County there. A courthouse was built and a town started. The county seat, however, was later

moved to its present location at Farwell. The Parmerton court house was moved to Friona, where it is now occupied as a store building.

Owners of all this vast tract of land—the Farwells of Chicago—were very religious people and when they came to Bovina and found no church or Sunday School, they mentioned the fact to Bill Mersfelders. Bill was always ready to tackle anything so Joe McHenry, an Indian preacher of Methodist faith, my sister and myself got the cow punchers together and a Methodist Sunday School was organized at Sam Arnette's cow camp just outside of Bovina.

The Farwells donated some money for the Sunday School and the cow punchers donated quite a sum. Our treasurer was a waitress at the railroad eating house, and she decided to pitch "crackalue" with the cowboys on the station platform and win enough money to build a church house. The cowboys were experts at "crackalue," however, and she soon lost all the Sunday School money and thus the first church in Parmer County came to an inglorious end.

Bill was in every venture of any note in Parmer County in those early days, but now he was gone on a longer and permanent venture, where his many friends trust his spirit will rest in peace and glory throughout all the Aeons of Eternity.

Volume I, Deaf Smith County Court Records, page 626, item 988.

Bill Mersfielder made bond on November 24, 1902 to become justice of the peace and exofficio notary public for the unorganized county of Parmer. J.R. Armstrong, Ira Aten-surities.+

His jurisdiction was Precinct III of Deaf Smith County.

+Ira Aten was manager of Escarbado Div. of XIT Ranch, J.R. Armstrong succeeded him in this position.

THE FRIONA STAR
Friday, August 13, 1948

READER ASKS MORE YARNS OF OLD WEST

The Star office is in receipt of a letter from a lady at Clovis, New Mexico, relative to a story by George McLean that was carried in the Star a few weeks ago, relative to bringing the law into Parmer County. The writer complains of the brevity of George's account of the matter, but wants more frontier stories. The letter follows:

Clovis, N.M. July 28, 1948
Friona Star,

Gentlemen:
Your story of Bill Mersfelder was wonderful. My first husband, Clark Kane, was in the bunch of cow punchers that took Bill to Hereford and got law in Parmer County. Mr. McLean did not make his story as realistic as my husband told me. He said there were eight cowpunchers, all three sheets in the wind,—McLean among them. As they came back to Bovina, Bill, at the corner of the stock yards, gave a yell, saying: "The law has come to Bovina!" They threw the lines to the

wind and stradling those wild ponies took off, everybody yelling, straight for the store. One tried to go on one side and another on the other. One pony went right through the window into the store, broke out most of the show cases and tore up things in general, and thus the law came to Bovina.

Clark Kane died and I married again and our daughter sent me the clipping. I sure enjoyed this story, as Mr. Kane has told me a lot about the cattle shipping time at Bovina. It now seems like a dream, but I have been to some wild old times, when things were wide open. No law. But my husband helped to bring the law to Parmer County. Have McLean write more of the old times. I was there, but I can't write but do love to read of it as it happened.

Yours truly, Lorietta Morzingo

THE STATE LINE TRIBUNE
Monday, March 1st, 1954
SPECIAL Public Schools Week Edition

"Bovina School Started In Railroad Section House"

Piecing together the history of Bovina Schools has been no simple matter. All official files that might have been used to throw some light on events of past years were burned in the fire last fall (17 September, 1953) which consumed the main Bovina school building.

Superintendent W.H. Willoughby has been head of the administration of Bovina Schools for a comparatively short while (since July 1st, 1949) but he cooperated in assisting "The Tribune" to interview several long-time residents of the Bovina Community who could recall important names and dates.

Following is a compilation of facts garnered from conversation with several pioneer Bovina residents. We are sure the public will be kind enough to remember everything set forth here is strictly from the memories of Bovina residents, and that no official records are available to substantiate this story.

As best as pioneers can recall, the first school in Bovina was held in the "section house" of the (Panhandle and Santa Fe) railroad, under a private tutor. The first school that could be genuinely regarded as a "public" school opened in 1905. It was held in the Catholic Church for two or three years.

Old timers say that about 1907 school was held in one of the downtown business buildings, up on the second floor. Miss Alice Mersfield was the first public school teacher in that building.

Then, a big event of the school's history came up. The first brick school building was constructed in the year of 1911. It was made up of eight classrooms, and was a part of the building that burned in the fall of 1953. It was remodeled previous to that fire, however.

The school continued its steady growth, and in 1927 an addition was made to the original brick building. The addition provided seven more classrooms and a study hall. It could truly be called a complete "system" at that time.

Chapter V

Farwell

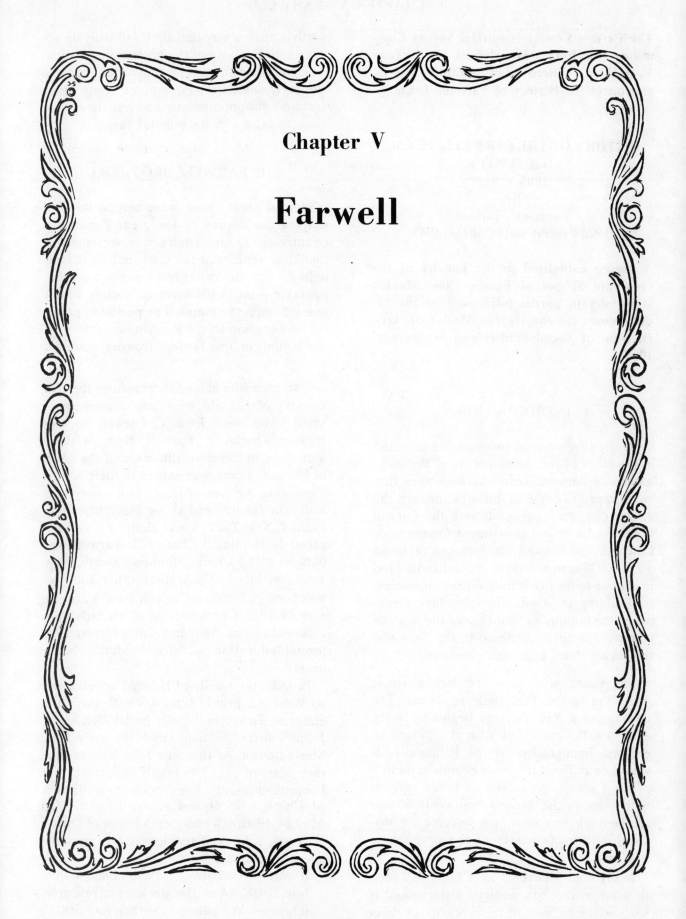

The Parmer County Historical Survey Committee gratefully acknowledges Mr. Eugene V. Sofford's generosity in permitting the inclusion of his History of Farwell, Texas.

HISTORY OF THE FARWELL, TEXAS COMMUNITY,
1905—1952
by
Eugene V. Sofford
B.A., Central State College, 1947

A thesis is submitted to the Faculty of the Graduate School of Eastern New Mexico University in partial fulfillment of the requirements for the Degree Master of Arts, Division of Social Studies and Psychology, 1955.

INTRODUCTION

Nearly fifty years of progress are included in the story of the development of the community of Farwell, Texas. Settlers were first encouraged to come to this area through the efforts of those connected with the Capitol Freehold Land and Investment Company of Chicago. The Farwell brothers had received a 3,000,000 acre rectangle of Panhandle land in exchange for funds to build the state capitol building in Austin. In turn, they established the famous XIT ranch, and the story of its development is a tribute to the Farwells, their associates, and their cowboys.

The ranch was once the largest single operation in the Panhandle of Texas. The liquidation of XIT holdings, beginning in the early 1900's, coincided with the period of greatest immigration to the Panhandle. It would be difficult to give a complete picture of the Farwell community of today without telling about this great ranch venture, and the men whose names have become synonymous with many phases of the progress of this area.

Many colorful events have been recorded thus far in the community's history, and it shall be the purpose of this work to set them forth in such a way that they will truly be appreciated by those of the present generation. The gown has undergone many changes since the early days. It has overcome many disasters and disappointments and has risen each time to face a more hopeful future.

THE FARWELL BROTHERS

Men of great vision were responsible for shaping the destiny of the great Panhandle country of Texas. Theirs was seemingly a thankless venture at the start, but their long fight for law and order has become an indispensable asset to the civilized society which now occupies the plains. The period of greatest immigration to the Panhandle came with the taming of this lawless frontier country.

Two men who helped to transform the cow country of the old west into a country of small farms were John V. Farwell and his brother Charles B. Farwell. Both of these men lived in Chicago, Illinois, and the town of Farwell, Texas, was named in their honor. They were the sons of Henry and Nancy Farwell. The family lived at Big Flats, Chemung County, New York, where Henry Farwell engaged in farming. [1] Charles B. Farwell was born at Mead Creek, Steuben County, New York, on July 1, 1823. His brother John V. was born in Steuben County, New York, on July 29, 1825. Charles received his early education at Elmira Academy. John received his formal education at Mount Morris Seminary. [2]

In 1838, the family of Henry Farwell started West in a prairie schooner with their five children, Henry Jackson, Charles Benjamin, John Villiers, [3] Simeon, and the only girl, Maria Louise. At this time John V. was thirteen years of age. The family emigrated to a homestead about a hundred miles southwest of Chicago, in Ogle County, Illinois. [4] On May 24, 1900, at a banquet in honor of Queen Victoria, John V. Farwell was the principal speaker and said:

It was my privilege to see Chicago in July, 1938, from the deck of a prairie schooner. We entered the then incipient city of say 3,000 people, via the Michigan Avenue—Lake Shore Drive, then a succession of sand ridges, down to old Fort Dearborn, just in front of Rush Street Bridge of today, which then had a ferry on the river for foot passengers only.[5]

There was a small cabin on the land where the Farwells settled, but it had to be made habitable. In 1840, the Farwells built the first brick house that arose from the prairies of Illinois.[6] During their first years in Illinois, the Farwells encountered rather difficult times. They raised wheat and sold it for forty-five cents per bushel, or at $18.00 for a wagon load.[7] Forty bushels of wheat were required to equal one wagon load, and it cost $24.00 to produce the wheat and get it to market.[8]

Charles B. Farwell moved to Chicago in 1844 and found employment in various mercantile concerns. He became interested in politics and served as clerk of Cook County from 1853 to 1861. In 1870, as a Republican, he was elected to Congress over John Wentworth in a closely contested campaign. In 1887, he was elected to the United States Senate to fill the vacancy left by the death of John A. Logan. Farwell was married on October 11, 1852, to Mary Eveline Smith of South Williamstown, Massachusetts. Only four of their nine children reached maturity.[9]

John V. Farwell started out for Chicago in 1845. He worked his way into town on a load of wheat, with $3.25 in his pocket from his father and a Bible from his mother.[10] He first took employment in the office of his uncle, the county clerk. For his services he received the handsome sum of twelve dollars a month.[11] He next went to the firm of Hamlin and Day at a salary of $250.00 a year and remained until December 16, 1949. In the spring of that same year he had married Abigail Gates Taylor.[12]

Charles and John had built a house on Randolph Street. John brought his bride there to live. John V. transferred his services to Wadsworth and Phelps, a wholesale dry-goods house. This was in 1849 and at a yearly salary of $600.00.[13] On the fourth day of April, 1851, their first child, a daughter, was born. John's wife died on May 9, 1851 with a request that their daughter, Abby, should be trained up in the fear of God that she might be brought to join her again in heaven.[14]

Farwell joined the firm of Cooley, Wadsworth And Company, and three years later in 1854, he married Emeret Cooley, a sister of his partner. The firm name was changed in 1862 to Cooley, Farwell, And Company, the partners being Francis B. Cooley, J.V. Farwell, and Marshall Field.[15] Cooley retired in 1864 and Levi Z. Leiter became a partner, the firm being known as Farwell, Field And Company. Field and Leiter left the firm in 1865 to take over the retail store of Potter Palmer. The firm they left became John V. Farwell And Company.[16] In the same year, John V. Farwell took his two brothers, W.D. and Charles B., into the company, of which he remained president until his death in 1908.[17]

In 1851 the firm had sales of $100,000.00, and by 1868 sales were ten millions. The store was burned in 1870 and no sooner was it rebuilt than it was again destroyed by the Great Fire of 1871. A site was then selected on Market Street for a new store, and Farwell rebuilt on a yet larger scale, with unwavering faith in the future growth of the city of Chicago.[18]

Charles B. and John V. Farwell were both in their sixties when they launched out on possibly the greatest venture of their lives. They became interested in the building of the capitol building of Texas in exchange for 3,-000,000 acres of land in the Panhandle district of Texas. Quite a number of the nobility of England became interested in this project as well as wealthy Englishmen well-known as philanthropists. John V. was acquainted with Lord Tweeddale, who joined in this large venture with the Farwell brothers.[19]

A law had been passed on February 20, 1879 in the Texas Legislature appropriating 3,050,000 acres for the purpose of building a State Capitol. Included in this land were parts of the following counties: Dallam, Hartley, Oldham, Deaf Smith, Parmer, Castro, Lamb, Bailey, Cochran, and Hockley. Fifty thousand acres of the land were to be reserved to meet the costs of surveying.[20]

Mattheas Schnell, of Rock Island, Illinois, was given the contract for the Capitol Building. Schnell assigned a three-fourths interest in the contract to the company composed of Abner Taylor, A.C. Babcock, John V. Farwell, and Charles B. Farwell, of Chicago. On May 9, 1892, he assigned the remaining one-fourth interest to the John V. Farwell Company.[21] The Capitol Building was completed in April, 1888 at a total cost of $3,224,593.45 to the Farwell Company, for which full title was given to the 3,000,000 acres of land. A careful survey of these lands was made by A.C. Babcock in which his inspection tour took his surveying party over 950 miles and ended on April 27, 1882.[22]

The XIT was established by the Capitol Company as a temporary institution to secure the use of the land until the time of the farmer should come.[23] In order to raise funds for fencing all this land and to stock it with cattle, John V. Farwell went to Europe to secure the necessary capital. As the Farwell Company maintained offices in Paris, Manchester, and Belfast, Farwell was well-known in those cities.[24] In order to borrow English money, Farwell found it necessary to form an English Company. In 1855 the Capitol Freehold Land And Investment Company, Limited was organized. Its authorized capital was equivalent to about $15,000,000.00 in American money. Directors of the company were: the Marquis of Tweeddale, Lord Thurlow, Edward M. Denny, Sr. William Ewart, and Henry Seton-Karr. In America, John V. Farwell, Charles B. Farwell, Walter Potter, and Abner Taylor completed the board.[25] In a newspaper article J. Evetts Haley wrote:

> After a fumbling start, the ranch served as a privately operated experiment station in the improvement of Hereford, Shorthorn, and Aberdeen-Angus breeds. Much profit accrued to the Panhandle through the reputation for good cattle which the XIT helped to establish.[26]

The herd maintained on the ranch averaged from 125,000 to 150,000 head of cattle.[27] According to Mrs. Florence Golladay, who lived on the Bovina section of the ranch from 1900 to 1908, the ranch was divided into seven sections, with section having a name. The ranch started in Dallam County, Texas, and extended to Lubbock, Texas. It was approximately one hundred miles wide and two hundred miles long. The Capitol Company began to sell portions of their lands in the early 1900's.[28]

In the fall of 1898, J.J. Hagerman was building the Pecos Valley branch of the Santa Fe Railway.[29] This line crossed the ranch in a southwesterly direction from Amarillo. The railroad had been completed to Bovina, Texas, in 1898 and was extended on to the present town of Farwell, and thence to Roswell in 1900.[30] The XIT saga is rich in the exploits of bad men, cattle rustlers, prairie fires, blizzards, and other items standard in the story of the cowboy's battle with a country hard to tame.[31] In the winter of 1884, the XIT lost nearly a million acres of grass by fire. One of the worst fires to break out was in 1894 and crossed into the Syndicate range south of Farwell, Texas. The fire broke out in New Mexico, and a strong west wind blew it eastward into Texas.[32]

John V. Farwell was convinced that there were great possibilities for successful farming in the ranch region.[33] The XIT began to liquidate its holdings in the early 1900's. This led to one of the greatest periods of immigration to the Texas Panhandle.[34] The first sales of land of any consequence were made in 1901. George W. Littlefield bought 235,858.5 acres in July, 1901. In the same year, the Rhea brothers bought nearly 50,000 acres north of Bovina for $2.00 an acre. Heavy sales of land continued until 1904 when the company directed its interests toward colonization. George H. Heafford, Hardy W. Campbell, and Charles E. Wantland were granted an option for large bodies of land in Parmer and Dallam Counties. These men formed the Farm Land Development Company and began to sell to small buyers.[35]

F.W. Wilsey was appointed land commissioner by the Syndicate Company and began his work in 1905. In 1905, James D. Hamlin, of Amarillo, was engaged as resident representative of the company, and made his headquarters at the newly established town of Farwell on the Texas-New Mexico line.[36] When land sales were first pushed, land could be financed with 10 per cent cash payments, and the rest in nine annual notes at 6 per cent interest. Later, a larger margin of one-fifth in cash was required, and the remainder in eight years at the same interest.[37] Through the years, the Farwell office sold 200,000 acres of land, practically settling and developing Parmer County. Thus in its final phase, the Syndicate turned into a genuine colonizer of the grasslands of Texas.

In his later years, John V. Farwell was greatly interested in religious activities. Though a member of the Methodist Church, he frequently spoke for different churches. He was also interested in Dwight L. Moody's work and contributed large sums of money to the Moody Bible Institute.[38] He also gave the land for the first Y.M.C.A. building in Chicago. Fifty dollars of his first year's salary of ninety-six dollars was given to help build the first Methodist building to be erected in Chicago.[39]

John V. and his brother Charles B. lived in Chicago until they died. Charles died in his eighty-first year on September 23, 1903. John V. died in his eighty-fourth year on August 20, 1908.[40] These men are famous for their great interest in the many phases of the growth of the Panhandle-Plains country. It is quite evident that the colonization of this vast plains area was greatly stepped up as a result of their persistent efforts. Many others who helped to tame the wild range "have since loped over the divide to what, we trust, may be greener pastures."[41]

EARLY DAYS IN FARWELL

Farwell is a twin city with Texico, New Mexico, and is located on the New Mexico line in Southwestern Parmer County, Texas. The town site was surveyed in early September, 1905, by W.D. Howren of Amarillo, Texas. Before his surveying party could proceed with its work, it was necessary to burn off the grass which was about four feet high over the entire area. Mr. Howren states that there were a number of blue quail and some antelope in the area at that time. The surveying crew camped east of the town site at a mill known as "Little Joe." Texico was a thriving village at that time, with three stores, one church, and five saloons. The population of Texico in 1905 was about three hundred. Immediately after completing his surveying of the town of Farwell, Mr. Howren proceeded to survey the remaining lands in Parmer County.[1]

Nearly 586 acres of land were included in a grant by the Capitol Freehold Land Investment Company, of London, England, and were set aside to be known as the town of Farwell. This grant was made and signed by Sir William Ewart, of Belfast, Ireland, and the honorable Sir Herbert Maxwell, London, England, trustees for the company. It was specified that the land was to be subdivided into blocks, streets, and alleys. The Pecos and Northern Texas Railroad Company tracks were made the dividing line between the state lines of Texas and New Mexico.[2]

The R.H. Kemp Lumber Company has the distinction of being the oldest business in Farwell. It was established on the Texas side of the line in 1904. This was before there was any town on this side of the line, but the company was serving Texico and the area with lumber. Milton Brown came here as manager of the yard on August 15, 1904 and remained here until 1910. He recalls a terrible blizzard in November of 1906 when it snowed for four days with scarcely a let up. His company was having a difficult time supplying coal to all those who needed it at the time. Kemp Lumber was the only company that had a source of supply at that time. Mr. Smith, who was running a bakery at Texico, called the yard for a ton of coal, and was assured that he would get it. Mr. Brown had one of his employees to take the coal to Mr. Smith, but he refused to accept it on the grounds it was not a full ton of coal. The coal was brought back to the lumber yards and sold to another party. Mr. Smith called the lumber yard and wanted his coal. He was told that it had been sold and that this was the last ton of coal to be had. It was necessary for the bakery to be closed for several days as a result of this failure to accept the coal when it was first delivered.

Two of the first houses that were built here, and that still remain, are the Sam Randol and the Ted Sheets residences. They were built in 1906 and are still in a good state of repair. Both have been remodeled several times during the years.[4] R.C. Hopping built a home here in 1906. His home was furnished modestly. It had a Majestic stove and burned coal. His wife, Lelia, had a vegetable garden. At this time Hoppins was in a grocery business at Texico with Harry and Clyde Robertson.[5]

A post office was established at Farwell on December 26, 1906. It was discontinued on November 30, 1907, and re-established on January 3, 1908. Mrs. Minnie B. Francis was

BRICK BUSINESS BLOCK at Farwell, Texas.

appointed as post mistress and served in that capacity until 1923.[6] In order to encourage the establishment of business on the Texas side of the line, the Capitol Company persuaded several business men in Texico to come over here and set up business. Coker and Triplett, dealers in general merchandise, came over in 1907. The Maddux Hardware Company came at this same time. However, these businesses remained here only a short time.[7]

On May 8, 1907 Parmer County was duly organized. There was a called meeting of the Commissioner's Court at Parmerton, the temporary court house. W.L. Townsen was county judge and presided over the meeting. Also present were W.L. McMinn and F.L. Spring, commissioners; J.F. McKay, county clerk, and E.T. Stevens, sheriff. The court determined that meetings be held at Parmerton until the county seat was determined and settled according to law.[8]

Parmerton remained the county seat for only a short time. A wooden structure was constructed to serve as a courthouse, but soon there was pressure from the citizens of Farwell to move the county seat to its present location. Parmerton was located in the geographical center of the county, and in order to make such a move, an election had to be held. According to state law, when the move was more than fifteen miles or five mile from the geographical center of the county, twothirds of the qualified voters of the county had to vote in favor of such a move.[9] According to legend, Farwell won the election by voting some New Mexico neighbors and at least one burro who had more spirit than the voters. This is the story told by Bob Kyker, for years the town's barber, historian, and

leading wit. He also recalled that the XIT moved the whole muddy Pecos River off its land and into New Mexico with only four Santa Fe tank cars. Kyker came to Texico in 1905. Soon thereafter, he began barbering in Farwell and continued to ply his trade for the next forty-five years.[10]

An election was held on December 10, 1907 for the purpose of determining whether the county seat should be moved to Farwell. Farwell received two-thirds of the votes cast, and was declared to be the county seat of Parmer County, Texas, by order of W.L. Townsen, county judge. The original court house in Farwell was a two-story wooden building located where the present water tower is situated. Fire destroyed this building at an early date. Rooms in the "Farwell Real Estate Exchange" were rented as a temporary court house.[13]

Another election was ordered to be held on November 16, 1907, for the purpose of determining whether the city was to be incorporated as a city or town to be known as Farwell. W.H. Abbey was appointed as the presiding officer at the election and was authorized to select two judges and two clerks to assist in holding the election.[14] The results of this election favored incorporation of the town. Forty-four votes were cast in favor of incorporation with no dissenting votes being cast. W.L. Townsen declared the town incorporated to be known as "Farwell" in accordance with Chapter I, Title XVIII of the revised Statutes of the State of Texas.[15]

It then became necessary to elect city officials for the town of Farwell. An election was held on December 31, 1907. George Landers was the newly elected mayor. Charles Dycus was elected as marshall, Clyde Roberson, Vick Anderson, Tom Johnson, John DeOliveria, and Saunders Gregg were elected as aldermen for the town of Farwell.[16]

The location of Farwell seemed quite strategic for growth. The railroad was bringing many settlers to this part of the country. The Capitol Land Company had hopes of influencing the Santa Fe Railroad to locate its shops here. A half-section of land was offered to the railroad to locate its shops at TexicoFarwell, but railroad officials were holding out for more land. When they saw that it was

ONE-STORY BRICK Business Building, cost $2,500, renting for $300 per annum. This building is included in our sale.

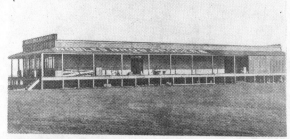

WHOLESALE GROCERY HOUSE at Farwell, Texas.

WAREHOUSE WITH Trackage Facilities, Farwell, Texas.

not forthcoming, they decided to locate the shop ten miles from Farwell at a place known as "Riley's Switch."[17] Thus it was that the city of Clovis, New Mexico had its beginning. This was in 1907, and the townsite for Clovis was laid out by the railroad people. Prior to that, all that was there was a switching track from Texico. The only railroad then reaching into New Mexico was the Pecos Valley Railway Company from Pecos to Roswell; Pecos Valley and Northern Roswell on to Texico; and the Pecos Valley, Northern Texas into Amarillo. In 1902 the Santa Fe Railroad leased the Pecos Valley lines, and the lines became the Santa Fe Railroad.[18]

In 1905 the Santa Fe Railroad began building the famed "Belen Cut-Off." With the decision to found Clovis, construction began there, and the two sets of track met and become one, twelve miles east of Vaughn. Old timers recall that the tracks of the Santa Fe once went south out of Texico to Cameo. One Sunday the railroad brought in about three hundred men to take up this twenty-three miles of trackage. They completed this job in one day to prevent an injunction being obtained the following day to stop the removal of the tracks. The tracks were taken up as a result of the railroad's decision to locate its terminal in Clovis instead of in Texico-Farwell.[20]

The Santa Fe Railroad built its depot at Texico in 1908. A freight depot was built at Farwell at the same time. The freight depot was placed on the Texas side in order to take advantage of the cheaper freight rates in Texas. Many shippers still take advantage of the lower rates by having their freight billed to Farwell. They then transport the freight by trucks to various points in New Mexico. Farwell soon became a great shipping center in the early days. This was particularly advantageous to the freight agent, who received a certain percentage of the fees at that time. As early as 1908, three wholesale grocery houses had located at Farwell. They were situated in the north part of town where they would have trackage facilities to load and unload their goods. These wholesale houses were the Nobles Brothers Grocers, the Radford Brothers Grocers, and Waples-Platter Grocers. A Mr. Garten was in charge of the depot in those days. W.W. Vinyard came as station agent in 1914. He has remained in that position up to the present time.[21]

The area around Farwell has been predominately a farming country. The first farms were in operation in 1906. Even in the early days farmers worried about drouths and crop failures. As long as West Texas was favored with rains, it blossomed like a flower garden. The products of the West were shipped to the East every fall. Good businesses were established. To the western man the world seemed a good place to live. Then for three years only scattered showers came. Since there were no crops there was no

BANK BUILDING at Farwell, Texas.

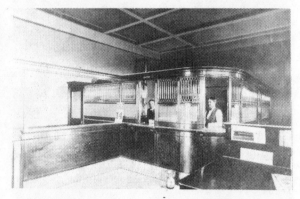

INTERIOR OF Bank Building at Farwell, Texas.

money. Hopping and Robertson Grocery was selling merchandise on credit. They could not collect the money that their customers owed. The business had to be closed in the fall of 1909. Hopping sold his home in Farwell and cleared his indebtedness. Then he bought an eighty acre tract of land on credit from J.D. Hamlin, who was the land representative in Farwell. Hopping built a dug out house and went to work breaking out the land. He used a grubbing hoe and a shovel. Water was hauled from Jim Oden's mill. When his crops were ready to sell, lightning struck in the haystacks. In a little while, the whole summer's work was burned to the ground. Hopping and his wife Lelia were certainly discouraged. But friends came to the rescue, and Wallace Good offered Hopping the managership of the Sixty-Nine Ranch. The offer was accepted, and Hopping moved his family to a four-room house known as the "Four Mile Camp."[22]

On December 21, 1908, The First National Bank of Farwell was chartered. D.A. Linthicum was the first president of the bank.[23] This bank building is one of the few buildings in Farwell to have survived the various fires that have swept through the business district of the little town. In order to stimulate the growth of Farwell, the Capitol Land Company built and paid for a magnificent three-story hotel. This building was erected in 1908 and was located on Third Street where the water tower is situated today. A Mr. Stuart was contractor for the building. Clark Smith was the first manager of the hotel.[24] The Farwell Inn, as it was called, was built to accommodate prospective customers of the Capitol Land Company. Excursion trains were sponsored every few weeks to bring prospective land buyers from the East. In turn, the hotel became a mecca for the traveling salesmen who traversed the then scarcely-populated plains. The inn is described as having elaborate suites of rooms. A beautiful ballroom was finished in ultra-fashionable decor.[25] Another hotel was once located on First Street. It was a two-story frame building and was located one block south of the Kemp Lumber Yard. Parties arriving in Farwell as far back as 1908 claim it was in use at the time of their arrival. It was known as the Farwell Hotel and served also as a boarding house. Meals were served for twenty-five cents, and rooms could be rented for fifty cents per night.[26] The Parmer Hotel, also a frame building, was located on Second Street. It stood adjacent to the property owned by D.M. Whitley. In later years, it was moved to Clovis. The Farwell Hotel was torn down in later years to make room for a new building.[27]

A number of medical doctors practiced in Farwell in the early days. Dr. Oliver was about the first to come. He came in 1906, and was followed in 1907 by a Dr. Taylor. Dr. J.Q. Burton came in 1908.[28] In 1910, Dr. Burton was appointed as the first county physician of Parmer County. For his services as county physician, he received ten dollars a month.[29] For a short time there were two drug stores in the town. T.C. Linthicum established a drug store here in 1908. S.C. Faville had a drug store here at about the same time, but remained in business for only about one year. Then for many years the town was without a drug store. The Red Cross Pharmacy at Texico served the twin cities for a number of years.[30] Nearly all of the business establishments at this time were located on Third Street which is now known as the Court

BRICK BUSINESS BLOCK at Farwell, Texas. This block adjoins the Hamlin Block.

VIEW SHOWING relative position of Hamlin Block and one-story Brick Business Building, both of which are included in our sale.

House Street. J.D. Hamlin constructed a group of business buildings which covered one entire block. This block was referred to in those days as the "Hamlin Block" or as the "Hamlin Bricks." These buildings were located in the block where Claude Rose now has his residence. In fact, residences have taken the place of many of the early business buildings of the town. B.E. Nobles had a retail grocery store in the "Hamlin Block." Mr. Linthicum's drug store was located there too. The barber shop occupied one of the Hamlin buildings. The Porter Hardware was another business which occupied the block.

At this time the XIT Ranch was still in the cattle business. There were over twenty thousand head of cattle on its ranges. Cattle rustling was still a common occurrence. Being situated on the state line made Farwell a strategic point since the rustlers would do their best to get the cattle over the line into New Mexico. There they felt that they would be safe, and that the Texas Rangers would have no jurisdiction over them. Legend says that the XIT once built a long board fence down the state line to keep out trespassers. W.E. Farwell, who helped to lay out the town of Farwell, says that it was a barbed-wire fence, but a remarkably stout one.[32] While the XIT still maintained its herds, six Texas Rangers were kept busy patrolling the state line. Though all the herds were not sold until 1912, the fence along the state line was removed in 1908. D.M. Whitley was hired by the county officials to complete this job. [33]

Probably the "biggest" business in town in the early days was Jess McKay's livery stable. This was before the days of the automobile,

and McKay had a thriving business for several years. A blacksmith shop was also here in the infancy of the town, and was run by a Mr. James.[34]

According to the records, the town's first jail was built in 1908. The cost of this structure was $212.50.[35] One can well imagine what a sturdy structure it must have been. At this time the county was paying sixty dollars a month for the use of rooms in the "Farwell Real Estate Exchange" and for a grand jury room in the upper story of the "Hamlin Bricks."[36] These buildings were rented again, and this time the commissioners agreed to pay seventy-five dollars per month for the county offices.[37]

Bob Kyker recalled a period from 1909 through 1911 when it stayed so dry that even the tumbleweeds never grew above three inches high. He said that the people would have moved out of this country if they could have. They couldn't leave because they were so poor. None had enough to buy a railroad ticket, and all the horses were so nearly starved they couldn't pull wagons, so the people just stayed.[38]

In the year 1910, R.C. "Coke" Hopping was asked to make the race for sheriff of Parmer County. He was successful in this race, and this meant that he could move his family back to their dug out home, just two miles east of Farwell.[39] Commenting on conditions of the towns in this region, Hopping said:

Texico, Bovina, and Farwell were wicked, wild, and gory, and enticed rowdies, murderers, and gamblers. The rustlers were still mavericking the calves and yearlings. In order to tame the Llano Estacado the sheriff's office would need

HAMLIN BLOCK, Farwell, Texas cost $15,000, renting for $2,000 per annum. This entire block is included in our sale.

a rugged man and one full of courage.[40]

Cattle thieving was to be one of Coke's most perplexing problems. He was also appointed cattle inspector in 1910. He was empowered to make arrests on short notice if necessary. Fent Stallings was hired as deputy to assist him. Coke served as sheriff of Parmer County until 1918. Law breakers of the worst type soon left Farwell and Parmer County shortly after Coke went into office. Perhaps they left because the entire county was now well organized, and because Farwell and Texico became law-abiding towns.[41] At the expiration of his fourth term as sheriff, Coke refused to make the race again. He sold out his holdings in Farwell and moved to Littlefield.[42]

All indications point to the fact that the town was booming in 1910. The population had risen to 800, and the town could now boast of having its own newspaper. B.F. Fears was now publishing "The State Line Tribune."[43] In addition to serving as the resident representative of the Capitol Land Company, J.D. Hamlin had formed a company of his own in the interest of selling properties in and around Farwell. The concern was called the Farwell Development Company. There were offices in Chicago, Illinois and in Farwell, Texas. James D. Hamlin was president, and James M. Hamlin was vice-president. Leonard A. Hardie was secretary and treasurer, and C.C. Marshall was manager. The purpose of the company was to induce prospective buyers to come from the East and buy property in Farwell. A thirty-two page booklet was published which described in glowing terms the advantages of settling in Farwell. This booklet, published in about 1910, contained a number of interesting views of various business buildings and homes that were here at that time.[44]

The entire "Hamlin Block" was offered for sale in this booklet, and it was stated that these buildings were erected at a cost of $15,000.00. The following businesses were located in these buildings: the Nobles Grocery, the Cash Drug Store, the Barber Shop, and in the upper story were the offices of W.L. Sims and S.G. Bratton, attorneys. J.D. Hamlin also maintained offices on the second floor over the drug store.[45]

HOTEL, Farwell, Texas, cost $40,000.

TWO-ROOM RESIDENCE, cost $600, renting for $90 per annum. This residence is included in our sale.

RESIDENCE WITH Six Rooms and Hall, cost $3,000, renting for $300 per annum and is included in our sale.

An excellent view of the Farwell Inn was included in the booklet. The hotel was a three-story brick structure and was built at a cost of $40,000.00. The rooms were elaborately furnished, and a beautiful ballroom added glamour to the building. A water tower was located beside the hotel and was used to supply water for the inn. The Farwell Post Office, a one-story brick building, was located in back of the Hamline Real Estate Exchange.[46] The Coker and Triplett General Merchandise Store was still here at the time, and it was interesting to note the horses and buggies in front of the store.[47] An ice plant was also here, and the Malone brothers had a lease on the ice and the electric power plant. The Texas Company's plant was located next to the ice plant, and J.L. Walling was manager of the company.[48] An interesting view was given of the wholesale district at that time.[49] Some of the homes that were pictured in the booklet included those of J.M. Hamlin, J.G. Weatherley, J.M. Kindred, and James A. Oden. It seems that James Oden had the nicest home in town at that time.[50] The few pioneer settlers who remain in Farwell are agreed that the town had a larger business district then than it has at the present time. The town seemed to have an opportunity for real growth, and the time seemed ripe for happiness and prosperity in the little town.

Early in 1910, the county commissioners approved the establishment of a road beginning at the east line of Parmer County and extending to the eastern limits of the city of Farwell.[51] This was a wonderful step forward for the community, for there were no open highways in evidence in those days. Since there were no cars as yet, there was no great need for too many highways. Of course these early roads were not paved and became quite muddy in case it did happen to rain. However, it seemed that most everyone depended on train service when they needed to go any distance.

W.M. Shitley, who served as city constable from 1910 to 1920, relates that trouble began to develop in the city government in 1910. The finances of the little town had reached a sad state, and the problem was further intensified when a Mr. Oliver absconded with about $500.00 of the city's money.[52] A petition was presented to R.W. McDonnell, county judge, to order an election to be held on November 5, 1910, for the purpose of determining whether the voters were in favor of abolishing the corporation of the city of Farwell. The election was held in Hamlin Hall, and the citizens of the town voted at this time to allow the corporation of Farwell to lapse.[53]

BIRD'S EYE VIEW, Farwell, Texas.

COUNTRY RESIDENCE of J.M. Hamlin, near Farwell, Texas.

COUNTRY RESIDENCE of J.M. Kindred, near Farwell, Texas.

COUNTRY RESIDENCE of J.G. Weatherly, near Farwell, Texas.

James A. Odem residence at Farwell.

It was found that the outstanding debts of the defunct city of Farwell amounted to $1,000.00. A.M. Billingsley and W.P. Gordon were appointed to audit the city books.[54] Payment of back city taxes was ordered so that the debts of the town could be paid. The county attorney was empowered to enter suit to compel the payment of these taxes.[55] The incorporation of the town was legally abolished on November 16, 1910.[56] Fent Stallings was appointed as receiver for the abolished city of Farwell, and he promised to discharge all the duties incumbent upon him as receiver of the defunct village of Farwell, according to the best of his skill and ability, and according to the constitution and laws of the United States and of the state of Texas.[57] Thus the city government of Farwell came to a rather inglorious end. The city was not to be incorporated again until 1950. The First National Bank of Farwell was also abolished in 1910, but a short time later, a new bank was established. It was chartered under the name of The Texas State Bank of Farwell. Some of the same men who had organized the town's first bank were the organizers of the new bank. The same building on Third Street served as headquarters for the banking institution. The amount of capital stock in the bank was divided into one hundred shares of $100.00 each. Oscar Cliett, J.R. Stegall, B.E. Nobles, and T.C. Linthicum, each bought five shares of stock. The remaining eighty shares were bought by D.A. Linthicum. The five men named above served as the board of directors for the new bank.[58] J.R. Stegall operated the bank for a short while. Then George Eads was in charge for a time. In 1912, the bank was bought by H.E. Guy, who continued to operate the bank under the name of The Texas State Bank of Farwell.[59]

There were only two windmills in Farwell in the early days.[60] Many families were using cisterns. Still others were hauling water from their neighbor's farms. Coal stoves were in use, and the electric system at that time was not very reliable. Water was plentiful, but people had not yet learned about drilling wells. Very few people were financially able to buy the equipment for the wells. A public water tank was approved in 1910, and the county commissioners authorized the paying of ten dollars per month as rent for the tank.

WAREHOUSE AND COAL YARDS with Trackage Facilities, Farwell, Texas.

There were no public waterworks at this time.[61]

In a special election of 1911, returns showed that the voters of the community favored the prohibition and sale of intoxicating liquors within the state of Texas. A total of 136 citizens voted in this election. Ninety-nine votes were cast in favor of prohibition, and thirty-seven votes were cast to do away with prohibition.[62] Then the citizens of Parmer County participated in an important election on September 9, 1916, on the question of whether there should be prohibition in the county. Of the 159 votes that were polled, 141 were cast in favor of prohibition. The county has been "dry" ever since that time.[63]

The first automobile in town was owned by Jim Oden. Oden bought the car in 1912. It was a Model T Ford, one of those with a high top. Bob Kyker owned the second car in town.[64] Pretty favorable rains came to this area from 1912 until about 1929, and the farmers were able to realize fairly good crops. People worked hard and managed to get by. Money was not so plentiful, but people had plenty to eat. People were not too busy to visit with each other then, and they were always ready to help a neighbor in distress. Good times were enjoyed by all at singings and picnics, and at the socials which were held at the country schools.[65]

Disaster struck the little city in the form of a devastating fire on May 19, 1913. The fire swept through the buildings in the "Hamlin Block" and destroyed them all.[66] The flames broke out in the building occupied by the Smith and Dodson Dry Goods Store. It was believed that the fire was the work of an arsonist, but this was never proved. The flames spread rapidly to the other businesses in the block. The fire-fighting equipment of those days was rather limited. It consisted merely of a two-wheeled cart which was kept in the fire house at Texico.[67] Farwell has never had a fire station of its own, and the one station at Texico has served both towns. Farwell has always had the waterworks for both towns, and cooperation has existed in the use of the water and of the fire station. However, by the time the meager fire equipment arrived on this occasion, the buildings were all ablaze. Fire fighters failed to save any of the buildings in the block. Various citizens did manage to remove the county records and some of the court room furniture to safety. Court was held temporarily in the store building formerly occupied by the Pecos Hardware and Furniture Company. [68] This building was located one block south of the buildings that burned. The businesses taken out of circulation by the fire were not rebuilt. A little later, a barracks-type building was moved in about where Claude Rose lives today. This building then served for several years as the court house. [69]

A bond election was held on August 9, 1913 to determine whether the people favored building a new court house. There were ninety-nine votes in favor of issuing $50,-000.00 in bonds for the new building. Eighty-one votes were cast against the issuance of these bonds. The bond issue carried, and officials made plans for the erection of a three-story court house building. [70] However, work did not actually begin on this building until 1916. Plans which were submitted by C. Risser, architect, were approved. [71] W.M. Rice, of Amarillo, Texas, was selected as the contractor for the building. The cost of the building without its furnishings was $43,-243.65. [72] W.M. Rice was also given the contract to build a new county jail. County officials specified that it was not to exceed $3,000.00 in cost, and that it was to be built in back of the court house building on Third Street. [73]

ARCHITECTS: July 1, 1916

C. Risser and Company of Amarillo, Texas, was selected as Architect for the Court House to be erected for Parmer County,

Texas, subject to the selection of plans and a mutually agreeable contract.

SEE: Parmer County Commissioners' Court Minutes, Volume 1, Pages 499, 500 and 501.

ARCHITECT'S PLANS AND SPECIFICATIONS:

Court House Building Plans:

Court House Building Plans, Date, Volume and Page.

Plans modified, Aug. 21, 1916, Vol. 1, Page 505.

Plans accepted, Sept. 18, 1916, Vol. 1, page 507.

Architect's Fee, Sept. 19, 1916, Vol. 1, Page 509.

Architect's Fee, Oct. 12, 1916, Vol. 1, Page 513.

Architect's Fee, Oct. 30, 1916, Vol. 1, Page 515.

ARCHITECTS: October 12, 1916

It is ordered by the Court, that Order Number 16 of this Court passed on September 19, 1916, be and the same is hereby rescinded. It is further ordered by the Court that a total price of $1320.00 be allowed the Architects, C. Risser and Company, to be paid one-half to Wm. Townes, surviving member of the Co-Partnership of C. Risser and Company, and one-half to the administrator or administratrix of the estate of C. Risser, deceased, when legally proven.

SEE: Parmer County Commissioners' Court Minutes, Volume 1, Page 513.

CONTRACTOR: 19 September 1916

W.M. Rice of Amarillo, Texas, was employed as general superintendant of construction in the erection of the Court House Building at the County Site in Farwell, Texas. Fee agreed upon was 8½ percent of the aggregate cost of Labor and Material to be paid as follows: $500 on October 1st, 1916 and each month thereafter during which work on building is progressing until the aggregate sum of $2500 shall have been paid to contractor and the residue of his fee computed as set forth in contract shall be paid to him when the building is completed and turned over to the said Board of County Commissioners.

THE COURT HOUSE

SEE: Parmer County Commissioners' Court Minutes, Volume 1, pages 507-509.

CONSTRUCTION CONTRACT: 11 November 1916

W.M. Rice Construction of Amarillo, Texas, was awarded a Contract for the completion of the Court House now in course of erection for Parmer County, at Farwell, Texas. The Honorable James D. Hamlin, County Judge of said Parmer County, formally executed and signed the Contract in behalf of and binding upon said Parmer County and the Commissioners Court thereof.

SEE: Parmer County Commissioners' Court Minutes, Volume 1, pages 517-522.

SURETY OR PERFORMANCE BOND: 11 November 1916

W.M. Rice Construction Company, as Principal and J.M. Neely and J.D. Thompson, as Sureties. Amount of Bond: $15,000.00.

SEE: Parmer County Commissioners' Court Minutes, Volume 1, Page 521-522.

COST OF COURT HOUSE BUILDING: 13 August 1913

The Building was to cost no more than $50,000 which amount was voted in Court House Bonds on 9 August 1913.

SEE: Parmer County Commissioners' Court Minutes, Volume 1, pages 381-386.

COST OF COURT HOUSE CONSTRUCTION:

The amount of $43,243.65 is mentioned in the Minutes of the Commissioners Court, dated 11 November 1916, as the computed cost of the Court House Building.

SEE: Parmer County Commissioners' Court Minutes, Volume 1, Page 519.

According to B.N. Graham, who was county clerk from 1916 to 1926, county officials moved into the new building in 1917. It was the pride and joy of the entire county, and especially to the people of Farwell. The new building was modern in every respect and was a welcome addition to the county officials, who now had spacious offices in which to work. Serving as first judge in the court house was James D. Hamlin, F.W. Reeve, Frank L. Reed, F.L. Spring, and F.W. Mc-Elroy, were commissioners. B.N. Graham was the county clerk. Coke Hopping was sheriff, and J.C. Temple was justice of the peace.

Graham recalls that J.C. Temple performed the first "mail order" marriage vows he had ever seen. He relates that early one morning before eight o'clock, an old fellow who lived north of Farwell drove up to the side of the court house in his covered wagon. The old fellow came in and inquired when the train from Amarillo was to arrive, informing the court house personnel that he was expecting his bride-to-be to be on the train. When the train pulled in, the bride was on board. The couple returned to the court house, bought their license and inquired about the justice of the peace. The ceremony was performed by Mr. Temple, but the unusual part of the ceremony was the way the participants were situated. There was a bench approximately ten feet long which extended along one side of the room, and as the vows were being read, the bride sat at one end of the bench, and the groom sat at the other end. Mr. Graham served as witness and stated it was an exceedingly solemen wedding.

Beginning in January, 1917, a newspaper called the "Texico-Farwell News," was published at Texico. R.M. Hudson and sons were the publishers. This paper was published for three years and ceased publication after the first issue of 1920. Commenting on the growth of Texico-Farwell, editor Hudson said:

> More automobiles are seen on the streets of Texico-Farwell on any afternoon than may be seen in the same time in any other town between Amarillo and Albuquerque. This is only an indication of where real life and business have a home.

The Criterion Theater was built in 1917. Such pictures of "The Pearl of the Army—With Comedies," "Dante's Inferno," and "Charlie Chaplin," were being shown in those days. Archie Green, Manager, advertised a superb program of Photo Plays. Tickets were

POWER PLANT, Farwell, Texas.

twenty-five cents and thirty-five cents.[76] D.M. Whitley says that the theater was located on Second Street, one block from the present post office. The building was moved out in 1921, and the electrical wiring in the building was used to wire Mr. Whitley's home.[77]

Farwell seemed to be booming as several new businesses made their appearance in town. J.L. Herrington had begun construction of a frame building to be used as a hotel. There were to be twelve rooms on the first floor and twenty on the second floor.[78] B.E. Nobles announced the opening of a dry goods store, and stated that he would carry a full line of millinery in ladies' ready to wear clothing. Mr. Wiggins was dressmaker and milliner.[79] Barry Hardware opened a store in Farwell. The store retailed hardware, implements, harness, furniture, and well supplies. Mr. Smith, of Clovis, was in charge of the store.[80] The business was located in a building owned by Mrs. Florence Golladay. It was situated directly across the street from the present post office.The store remained here about five years and then was closed.[81]

Farwell was becoming quite modern. Thirty street lights were installed by the Stateline Utilities Company. This company was furnishing electric power to the town. It also had a contract to furnish water to the town. The reservoir tank at the Farwell Inn was serving as the city water tower. H.N. DeBerry was manager of the utilities company.[82] The charter of the Stateline Utilities Company was amended, and the name changed to that of Southwest Utilities Company. The capital was increased to $100,-000.00. Farwell soon could boast of having

VIEW OF ICE FACTORY and Texas Oil Company's Plant, Farwell, Texas.

EARLY INDUSTRIAL PLANT

current twenty-four hours a day. The utility company had connected Texico-Farwell with the Clovis plant. The ice plant was rebuilt and had facilities for supplying surrounding towns with ice.[84]

C.A. Wulfman completed a six room bungalow on Third Street, and V.V. Knowles had built a home on Avenue B and Sixth Street. W.M. Taylor and T. Eustace Allen, Ford agents in Farwell, completed their garage on Avenue A and Third Street. They reported having sold thirty Ford cars in 1917.[85] According to a census just completed by the Texico-Farwell Commercial Club, Texico had a population of 614, and Farwell's population stood at 508. Editor Hudson reported that eight months before each town had only 400 inhabitants.[86]

Improvements were being made at the Santa Fe Depot. Unsightly trackage was removed from around the passenger depot. The south side plot was prepared for parking. Double tracks were laid on the road side bed, and brick paving was laid from the west side of the depot to the state line. A new and roomy freight depot was built. Agent W.W. Vinyard remained at the passenger depot, and his assistant, J.W. Daniels, transacted the business at the freight depot on the Texas side. It was rumored that excavation would begin on the Texas side for an eight stall roundhouse to accommodate the cut-off, or Galveston branch.[87]

G. Clark Smith had assumed the management of the Farwell Inn. The hotel was completely destroyed by a fire in the fall of 1920. Faulty wiring was blamed for the fire. If there had been anything with which to fight the fire, the city might still have a hotel. The

water-works system, located right next to the hotel, was completely frozen, and no water was available to fight the flames. A small fire had started near the roof on the south side of the building. It was a slow-moving fire, and residents were able to carry out the furniture, fixtures, and even some doors and windows. Outside the building, there was a howling north wind.[88] In 1915, Bob Kyker had set up his barber shop in the hotel. The pioneer barber managed to haul his barber chair from the building.[89]

In 1917, a promoter turned up and announced plans to start a new industry. Residents of Texico-Farwell were introduced to a scheme to turn out tires and "Cannon Ball Motors." C.A. Roberson, the promoter, had a half page advertisement in the Texico-Farwell News. He announced the establishment of the Western Tire Manufacturing Company. He called upon the citizens to buy shares in the business that was soon to be the biggest in all the West.[90] Mr. Roberson reported that rubber tires would be made by April 1, 1917. A building had been erected on the north side of the railroad to house the tire plant. This was on the property now occupied by the Henderson Grain Company. Steel and brick were on the ground to build an office building for the company. The three-story office building of the Cannon Ball Motor Company was built at a cost of $50,000.00. The Texico Hotel stands today as evidence of this promotion scheme.[91]

Everyone had hopes of seeing Farwell become a large city. Real estate offices were selling a number of lots to prospective home builders. Keating-Robertson Realty Company advertised:

BLOCK OF RESIDENCES in Farwell, Texas.

BARN, SHEDS, and Lots, Farwell, Texas cost $800 and included in our sale.

Farwell will soon be one of the most beautiful residential towns of all the plains country.The present industry, now under construction—The Western Tire Mfg. Co.—is sufficiently large to insure the city's growth well up to the 10,-000 population mark.[92]

The first unit of the Western Tire Manufacturing Company had 26,600 square feet of floor space. In connection with the plant was a reservoir with a capacity of over one million gallons. The company was capitalized at one million dollars. In one week, the stock sales ran to $150,000.00. After many delays, Roberson announced that machinery for the tire plant was in transit, and that work would begin July 1, 1917.[93] The year 1918 rolled around, and still no tires had been made. Mr. Roberson promised that the plant would make tires within forty days. Mr. Van Ness, an engineer brought from Akron, Ohio, said that Farwell was an ideal place for the manufacture of rubber tires and other rubber goods.[94]

C.A. Roberson also announced the bringing of the Mountain States Motor Company to Texico-Farwell. This company was to manufacture the "Cannon Ball Motor Car."[95] A charter for the company was applied for and granted. The company was capitalized at ten million dollars. Roberson addressed more than 500 citizens at the Criterion Theater. He told them that the Cannon Ball Motor Company would be manufacturers, assemblers, and distributers of automobiles, farm tractors, and trucks.[96]

Incorporators of this company were: C.A. Roberson, W.L. Mansfield, J.D. Hamlin, D.A. Randall, and J.C. Milne. By October 5,

1917, one half million shares had been bought by more than 450 people.[97] Big plans were made for this company. It was announced that the annual capacity of the motor company would be 200,000 autos, trucks, and tractors. The plant was to cover fifty acres of land, and 35,000 workers were to be required to operate the plant.[98] W.A. King was employed as the engineer and plant manager. No cars were ever manufactured here, but some were shipped into Farwell from Illinois. Roberson sent the following telegram from Chicago:

First shipment of Cannon Ball cars goes forward to you by express. These are the Four—38 cars as per specifications our Mr. King was authorized to build sometime ago. The Six-Sixty "Star of the Highway" is now under construction.[99]

W.A. King announced that the manufacturing plant would be ready to start in another sixty days. Each time the dead line arrived, the time would be set up again for beginning the manufacturing of the tires and cars. The stockholders were becoming uneasy. C.A. Roberson continued to assure them that they had nothing about which to worry. A dozen tires were finally manufactured, but no "Cannon Ball Motors" were in evidence. The stockholders finally discovered that the promoters had vanished with the stock money.[100] Formal charges against these men were not pressed until 1921. The case was held in Federal Court in Santa Fe, New Mexico. Roberson had been a resident of Texico, and he had conducted a good part of his business from the administration building of the Cannon Ball Motor Company in Texico. Charges had also been brought against M.M. Craig, B.S. Triplett, and F.W. McElroy. These charges were dropped as no grounds for action against these men could be found. C.A. Roberson was charged with fraudulent use of the mails in selling Cannon Ball stock.[101] Roberson was found guilty in five of sixteen counts before the court. James D. Hamlin, Fent Stallings, and R.O. James, of Farwell, Texas, and D.A. Randall and J.C. Milne of Pueblo, Colorado, other officials of the company who were jointly indicted with Roberson, were acquitted of the charge.[102]

The charges under which Roberson and the other officials of the Cannon Ball Motor Company were tried were those of obtaining money under false pretenses in connection with the promotion of the Cannon Ball Company, and the misrepresentation of the worth of the stock. The case occupied eighteen days of a tedious, legal battle. Roberson at one time during the trial stated that if any one was guilty of the charges outlined in the indictment, he himself was to blame for he had conceived the idea of the Cannon Ball Company, and had asked his friends to join him.[103]

W.A. Gillenwater, attorney for Roberson, filed a motion for a new hearing. Roberson was being held in the State Penitentiary. The motion for a new trial was denied. Judge Colin Neblett, J.S. District Judge, passed sentence on Roberson on February 5, 1921. Roberson was sentenced to ten years in Leavenworth prison and payment of costs amounting to $7,800.00.[104] It is no wonder that the citizens of Texico-Farwell are still wary of any one desirous of selling stocks or of starting a new industry.

Another disaster occurred on October 18, 1918. One of the buildings formerly used as the court house went up in flames. The building was then being used for offices by Dr. McCuan and the Hines Abstract Company. The fire started in Dr. McCuan's office. The adjoining building, occupied by the Chauchon Tailor Shop, also burned.[105]

Farwell had an elevator in 1919. C.R. Holman and Son—Elevàtor, was the name of this business concern. They later sold to a Clovis mill.[106]

James McDowell was now publisher of the Texico-Farwell News. Room and board could be obtained at the Modern Cafe. Board was $7.00 per week, and a room could be had for $1.50 more per week.[107] B.F. Fears was still editor and publisher of The State Line Tribune. Reese and Lokey, attorneys, had offices in the Court House.[108] The Capitol Land Company was advertising for settlers who "would develop this splendid country which is unsurpassed in climate, soil, and water."[109]

The three wholesale distributing houses located at Farwell made plans to move to Clovis. Nobles Brothers, Waples-Platter Company, and the Radford Grocery Company, all of which had big distributing houses in Farwell, made their move in 1920.[110] Early day Farwell was plagued by fires, deceived by promoters, and suffered the loss of its outstanding business houses.

The material in this chapter will include the years from 1921 through 1929. Fire had played a great part in determining that the main business section of the town should be moved to Avenue A or along Highway 70. It was there that The Plains Buying And Selling Association established a store in Farwell in 1921. The business was located in the building now used for a warehouse by the Furniture Mart. The building was then owned by Bart Osborne and A.B. Crane. Albert Thomas was manager of the company from 1921 to 1924. J.E. Randol then managed the association for several years. Then in 1927, Randol established the Randol Mercantile Company. This business was sold to Bart Osborne in 1932, and the business became the Osborne Mercantile Company. Randol then opened a wholesale candy and school supplies business, which covered seven counties in West Texas. This business was in operation until 1946, when Randol moved to Muleshoe, Texas.[1]

Other businesses were soon established on the new Main Street, and in 1921 a new bank building and a hardware store were built. Bill Bryant first put in a hardware store, and when the building burned, he rebuilt and established a grocery store and butcher shop. The Texas State Bank burned at the same time and was rebuilt in 1922. H.E. Guy was president of the bank at this time. However, the bank was soon closed because of several difficulties that arose.[2]

While the citizens of Farwell had experienced a number of problems, they were greatly shocked at the new trouble that came to light. This difficulty came to a climax when Mr. Guy, president of the bank, shot a Mr. P.E. Parker in front of the bank on March 5, 1922. The man was shot as the result of a quarrel that occurred between the two men earlier in the day. The trouble grew out of an alleged error that was made by a clerk in the bank who failed to give Mr. Parker credit for $15.00. A check for this amount was turned down when drawn on the bank by Parker.

It was alleged that Guy, who was also in charge of the bank at Texico, started from the bank in Farwell to the latter bank with $500.00 in currency. When carrying such an amount of money, it was the usual custom to be armed. Witnesses said Parker was outside the bank in Farwell and renewed the argument with Guy. Parker was said to have made some passes at Guy, and the banker drew his revolver and fired at Parker. The bullet entered Parker's abdomen, and he died the next morning. Following Parker's death, a formal charge of murder was filed against H.E. Guy. Guy contended that the shooting was in self-defense. Parker was forty-five years of age and was survived by his wife and two sons.[3]

The murder trial was under way in April of 1922. Judge Sam G. Braton, Carl A. Hatch, and John P. Slaton, represented the defendant, while County Attorney Lokey, represented the state. Judge Tatum was hearing the case.[4] The jury returned a verdict of not guilty, and W.A. Massie, the foreman of the jury, read this verdict on April 30, 1922.[5] Guy then reopened the bank at Farwell, but it soon became insolvent and was ordered to be closed. The assets of the bank were taken in charge by the Comptroller of Currency.[6]

After several years, the Guaranty State Bank was established in Farwell on January 17, 1925. Henry Wilkinson was president of the bank, and B.F. Ashbrook was vice-president. Gordon Phillips was cashier, and Thornton Braden was bookkeeper. The directors of the bank were: J.A. Pitman, R.H. Young, J.H. Head, Wilkinson, and Ashbrook. The capital stock of the bank was $20,000.00. Then in 1927, the Guaranty State Bank was reorganized as the Security State Bank. The bank received its charter on November 13, 1927. Deposits at that time were only $83,000.00. J.H. Head was president of the bank, and G.D. Anderson was vice-president. Directors of the bank were: J.A. Pitman, D.F. Ashbrook, G.W. Brumley, J.H. Head, and G.D. Anderson. The bank has been in its present location since 1927. J.H. Head, president of the bank, died in 1947, and G.D. Anderson, vice-president of the bank, was elected to the presidency. Directors of the bank were: G.D. Anderson, R.W. Anderson, G.W. Brumley, Belva Anderson, and J.A. Pitman. The capital stock of the bank was raised to $100,000.00. Deposits were now nearly two and one-half million dollars. In 1930, the deposits had been $153,000.00; and in 1940, they were $413,000.00; and by 1952, they had reached $2,870,000.00.[7]

Another new business, The Texas Grocery, was established by W.W. Hall in May, 1922. Hall operated this store in a little building on the lots now used by the Phillips 66 filling station. This building now serves as a garage for Mrs. Jess Newton. Hall relates that he bought meat from Coltharp's Meat Market and made hamburgers, which he sold at ten cents each. He also built the first tourist cabins in this section of the country. They were built in 1922 and were located one block south of his little store. Tourist accommodations were almost unknown at that time. Six cabins were made out of cotton sack ducking, and Hall says that they were more like tents. The sides could be rolled up, and there was a kerosene drop light in each cabin. One dollar per night was the charge for one of these cabins. Hall furnished the kerosene, which was located in a barrel in the middle of the lot. The only modern provision at that time was a water hydrant, also in the middle of the lot, and which served all six cabins. However, many people commented that these were the best accommodations to be found between St. Louis and the West coast. Hall operated his store and tourist cabins until 1928. During this time, Jess Newton ran a little cafe across the street from Hall's grocery. It was located on the property now occupied by the Piggly Wiggly Store.[8]

During the 1920's, the Post Office in Farwell was located in back of the Texas State

Bank building. On July 16, 1923, Gustav A. Wulfman was appointed as post master of Farwell. Wulfman served in that position until the year 1933. It might be well to mention that during the early 1930's, the post office was located in a frame building where the Piggly Wiggly Store is now situated. It was moved to its present location in 1936. Mrs. Noma Lokey was appointed as post mistress in 1933 and served in that position to the present time.[9]

Still, other businesses were in operation here in the early 1920's. O.C. Sikes opened a Ford Agency here in 1924 at the corner of Second Street and Avenue A. This was in the same building now occupied by Sikes.[10] The town had been without a drug store since 1913, but in 1925, a Mr. Ament and George Sasser opened the Fox Drug Store. This was in the same building now used by the Rose Drug and Gift Store.[11] E.E. Jakson was running a tailor shop in those years. The Farmers Grain Company was operating here and was advertising lump and nut coal for sale. The O.K. Wagon Yard was featuring "Chick Chow" to make chickens grow.[12] Loyd and Sikes opened a Chevrolet agency here in 1926 and were in a building at Third Street and Avenue A. By 1930, O.C. Sikes had given up the Chevrolet agency to Charles Lunsford. Lunsford moved the agency to Friona and soon closed the business there. Sikes then opened another Ford agency and has remained in that business until the present time.[13] It is interesting to note that the town's newspaper, **The State Line Tribune,** was being published by Stanley Seigler.[14] The paper was bought by W.H. Graham in 1926, and he has continued its publication to the present time.[15]

Several competent physicians have practiced here during the years. In 1923, Dr. D.W. Clark was the resident physician in Farwell and had been appointed as the County Health Officer.[16] Two other doctors who were practicing here in the 1920's, were Dr. McCuan and Dr. Presley. They were partners and had their offices in a building on Second Street.[17] Dr. V. Scott Johnson came to Farwell about 1930 and remained until 1946. The town has been without a medical doctor since that time.[18]

PLOUGHING SCENE near Farwell, Texas—

Farwell could boast of having a cotton gin in 1925. It was operated by J.S. Edwards, who moved his equipment in from East Texas. The equipment was old and was scarcely suited to gin the type of cotton that was grown in this section. The gin soon closed and afterwards burned. A Mr. Holman was operating the Farwell Elevator, and R.A. Hawkins was running the Doggett Grain Company. This company later became the Henderson Grain Company.[19]

During the early 1920's, the Capitol Reservation Lands Company began to direct its interests toward selling land to prospective farm buyers. Hamlin Overstreet became associated with the company in 1925, and his uncle, J.D. Hamlin, put him to work to help sell land to settlers. Modern farm homes were built on many of the tracts of land and sold with the land at cost.[20]

Farming in those days was accompanied with hazards of dust and drought, of violent windstorms, and of hail. Production was often uncertain and harvest even more so. The Capitol Company gained the reputation during these years of never foreclosing on a settler who was really trying to make his land pay, but "carried" many hard-pressed creditors for years. Those who were more fortunate were able to pay off their land in one year. The company often loaned money for improvements, and even kept up a nursery near Farwell for the wives of settlers who wished to plant shrubs and trees.[21]

In about 1924, a pamphlet was issued called "Capitol Reservation Lands." It was hoped that this pamphlet would help to spur the sales of land in Parmer County. At this time, 500,000 acres of land were being offered for sale as farm homes. The trustees of

VIEW SHOWING PART of Wholesale District, Farwell, Texas.

CORN SHELLING PLANT, Farwell, Texas.

the company were listed as Francis C. Farwell, Charles F. Harding, and George Findlay. The main offices of the company were still located in Chicago, and branch offices were at Farwell, Texas, and at Dalhart, Texas.[22]

Tracts of land were being offered from 160 acres up, at reasonable prices and on liberal terms of payment. These tracts were offered to actual settlers, who were seeking a new location where virgin land was ready for the plow, where soil fertility and an abundance of pure water, united to spell opportunity for human betterment. Pictures were given of various farms in Parmer County. The pamphlet described Farwell as being about 418 miles Northwest of Ft. Worth, Texas; ninety miles West of Lubbock; ninety-six miles Southwest of Amarillo, and on the junction of the two main lines of the Santa Fe Railway System.[23]

The soil was described as being rich and productive, with no trace of alkali. It was further stated that the lands offered in the sale were in an altitude of 3,000 to 4,000 feet, and afforded an invigorating atmosphere conducive to health and energy. The lands were said to be underlaid with an inexhaustible sheet of soft water, ninety-nine per cent pure, at a depth of from fifty to 225 feet. Rainfall in the country was said to have averaged 22.80 inches annually. This report was based on U.S. Government statistics over the last twenty-three years.[24]

It was said that the efficient farmer here had never had a complete crop failure. Broom corn, Kaffir corn, milo maize, oats, millet, sorghum, Sudan grass, and almost every variety of vegetable, were advertised as yielding abundantly in this country. Wheat

was listed as one of the staple crops, with yields of forty to fifty bushels not being uncommon. The average yield over a period of years was listed as being from fifteen to twenty bushels to the acre. From one-fourth to one bale of cotton per acre was said to grow here. Indian corn was described as a ready money crop, producing from twenty to fifty bushels per acre.[25]

Kaffir corn and milo maize were the pioneer grain crops of this part of Texas, and were yielding from forty to sixty bushels of grain to the acre. Sorghum cane constituted the leading forage and hay crop yielding from three to five tons to the acre. Though originally a treeless prairie country, all varieties of quick growing ornamental trees and shrubs were being planted by the settlers. Many of the homes were surrounded by beautiful groves as well as all kinds of flowers and vines. Black walnut trees were being planted and were proving to be suited well to the region. Paper shell pecan trees were also being planted in great numbers.[26]

Potatoes, cabbages, turnips, tomatoes, peas, beans, beets, okra, and all varieties of melons and squashes were being grown here in great profusion. Orchards and small fruit patches were being planted. Several pictures of young orchards were given in the pamphlet.[27]

The country was characterized by the number and quality of Hereford, Durham, and Angus cattle which thrived on the native grasses of the area. Pure water and an abundance of grain were said to have made this country ideal for hog raising. Cholera and other diseases were advertised as being almost unknown here. Raising hogs was said to be a "mortgage lifter."[28]

Well-sustained churches of most denominations were to be found in all communities through Parmer County. The population was composed of a high-grade, law-abiding class of real American citizens. Good schools were afforded, and the larger schools provided daily transportation for the children from the farms to the school and back home again. The roads were pictured as being smooth and easily traveled. Prospective buyers were urged to call on or write James D. Hamlin, resident representative, at Farwell, Texas. [29]

On December 31, 1950, Hamlin Overstreet liquidated the interests of the Capitol Reservation Lands Company in Farwell. He had reduced their holdings by sale to settlers to a bare 20,000 acres—the last of the 3,000,000 acre tract that the first Farwells and their associates had gotten in exchange for building the Capitol at Austin. The remaining land was divided among ten stock holders in the company. [30]

About the biggest business in town was conducted at the elevators during the fall of the year, when threshing of hand-cut maize, went on for weeks at a time. The maize was cut in the fields and hauled into town by the wagon loads by the farmers of the community. This has all changed now with the introduction of mechanized equipment and irrigation in the county. [31]

As the year 1926 drew to a close, the inhabitants of Farwell were getting ready for a big Christmas. Crops had been good, cattle prices were high, and the farmers and ranchers were in a holiday mood. They were unaware that tragedy had struck at their community once again. During the early hours of the day before Christmas, Sheriff J.H. Martin knocked at the door of County Attorney, J.D. Thomas. When Thomas came to the door, Martin explained that there was some trouble about a farmer by the name of George J. Hassell. Hassell, who was a big burly man about forty years old, had moved to Farwell, from Oklahoma, about a year before and had rented a farm belonging to Judge J.D. Hamlin. The family kept to themselves and little was known about them. There were eight children ranging from Alton who was twenty-one, to Sammie, the baby, who was two. Later it developed that these were not Hassell's children but his step-children. Likewise,

they were his nieces and nephews for he had married his brother's widow.

Hassell had recently held a farm sale and had rented the farm to the Lindop family. Sheriff Martin explained that the Lindop family had just come to his office for help. Hassell was boarding with the Lindop family for the time being. He explained that his family had gone to Oklahoma. Hassell had been questioned previously about the disappearance of his family, and had told a straight-forward story, and had been released on his own cognizance. Sheriff Martin told J.D. Thomas that the Lindop family had just come from the farm home and were badly upset. They said that Hassell had returned to the farm after being questioned, in a kind of daze. He hardly spoke to any one and ate very little. He soon retired to his room, and after a bit, the Lindops went to bed. They could not sleep, and Mr. Lindop kept his gun near at hand. Early the next morning, Hassell called to Lindop who went to the door of his room and asked what he wanted. Hassell asked him to get a doctor, telling him he was terribly sick. As Lindop was leaving with his family, Hassell called out again and told him to get Sheriff Martin, too. [32]

Lindop then dashed into Hassell's room and found him holding his arm. Blood was streaming to the floor, and Hassell's eyes were protruding from their sockets as if they would burst. Lindop quickly got his family into the car and drove into town for the sheriff. When Sheriff Martin reached the farm, Hassell was weak from the loss of blood, but was not in serious condition. The sheriff drove him to the Baptist Hospital in Clovis, New Mexico. [33]

On being questioned about his attempted suicide, Hassell made a very revealing confession. He admitted that he had killed thirteen people. A woman and three children had been murdered in California. His wife and eight children were killed on the farm three miles northeast of Farwell, Texas. With a feeling of security, the murderer had gone about his business as usual. He had answered all inquiries about the whereabouts of his family. A public sale had been held at the farm on the very spot where Hassell had buried the bodies of the victims. Hassell was tripped up by leaving packed suitcases of baby clothes in a closet of the farm home. Some of the ladies attending the sale wandered through the house and glimpsed some baby clothing. Immediately their suspicions were aroused. Hassell stuck to the story that his family had gone to Oklahoma.[34]

A searching party was organized on December 24, 1926, and excavation was made of a dug out, which had been freshly covered. The dug out soon yielded the bodies of nine victims. The dead were: Mrs. Hassell, about forty-three; Alton, twenty-one; Virgil, sixteen; Maudie, fourteen; Russell, twelve; David, seven; Johnie, six; Nannie, four; and Sammie, who was two. The face of Mrs. Hassell was horribly dented from the blows of a hammer, and the older boy had most of his head blown away. Russell's body showed signs of having been chopped with an ax. The bloody ax was found buried, but the hammer was not located. A razor was found in the house and showed signs of blood and flesh clinging to it.[35]

A special grand jury was called to hasten the trial of Hassell. The crimes had been committed on December 8, 1926. Hassell's wounds were not of a serious nature, and he was placed in the Farwell jail by Sheriff Martin. The slayer was soon quietly spirited out of the Farwell jail and taken to Plainview, Texas for safekeeping. His removal was prompted by reports that mob violence was anticipated. A wire had been sent to Blair, Oklahoma to ascertain if the Hassell family had arrived there, and when a negative answer came back, crews of men had begun plying shovels to the freshly covered dug out close to the Hassell home. At a depth of four feet, layers of blankets were encountered by the diggers. Under these blankets, wrapped in blood-stained sheets, were found the nine murder victims. With the exception of the three smaller children, who had been choked with stockings that had been tied around their necks, the other members of the family had been dealt deadly blows over the head. Bullet wounds were found in the older boys. The bodies were removed from their dug out crypt and taken to Farwell to await burial instructions. Mrs. Hassell and her eight children were laid to rest in the Farwell cemetery on December 25, 1926.[36]

Hassell continued his confession by saying, "I would have given anything in the world if I had not made the first lick, but I had started it, and I finished it."[37] He then choked the three smallest children to death. The daughter's room was entered and Hassell struck her twice with the hammer and finished by choking her. Virgil and Russell were sleeping in the back room. He started choking Russell and hit him with the ax. Virgil came in and started wrestling with him. Hassell ran into another room, grabbed a shot gun, and shot Virgil through the heart. The oldest boy, Alton, was away at the time working, but returned in several days. Alton was told that the rest of the family had gone to visit relatives at Shallowwater, Texas. That night Hassell says that he drank some more whiskey and got up at four in the morning and shot Alton while the boy was asleep.[38]

The grand jury convened at Farwell on January 10, 1927. Reese Tatum was the presiding judge. Serving as jurors in the case were: H.D. Ellison, J.J. DeOliveria, W.E. Williams, J.F. Foster, J.O. Ford, Jack Carr, Ben T. Galloway, R.L. Hightower, N.E. Wines, E.M. Sherrieb, W.S. McDaniel, and W.C. Crowell. McDaniel served as foreman of the jury.[39]

Hassell was found guilty of murder and was sentenced to death in the electric chair by Judge Reese Tatum on January 12, 1927. The case was appealed, but on June 15, 1927, the Court of Criminal Appeals affirmed the sentence. While awaiting execution in the penitentiary at Huntsville, Hassell asked a guard to bring him a pencil and a slip of paper. He then drew a rough sketch of a street in Whittier, California, and marked an X near the north end. The guard was told that if the Whittier police were notified and would go to the house marked out on the paper, that they would find the bodies of a woman and her three children. They were to pry up the boards on the back porch, and the bodies would be found buried under the porch. Officials notified the Whittier Police, and the four bodies were uncovered as Hassell had said they would.[40]

When confronted with the evience of these bodies, Hassell made a full confession of his crimes to J.D. Thomas, County Attorney.

Hassell then recited the most detailed statement of a life of crime that had been published. He stated that his first "impulse to commit a crime" was when his step-mother killed his father. That was in 1905 when Hassell was seventeen years of age. He had left home in 1901 when his mother died. Hassell soon got into trouble in Abilene, Texas and was convicted of embezzlement. For this he was sentenced to two years in the Texas State Penitentiary. After serving his time, he joined the army under an assumed name and deserted after a few months. Hassell then married, but after two years he and his wife separated. They had a child who was a year old at that time. Hassell enlisted in the Navy and was sent to San Francisco where he deserted and started back to Texas. He took up with a woman at San Angelo, Texas, and they went back to California. This woman had three children, and she and the children were later murdered by Hassell. Hassell then enlisted in the Army again at Fresno and was sent to Fort McDowell. It was learned that he had deserted previously, and he was given two years in the Federal Penitentiary. After serving part of his time at Mare Island, he finished his term at Fort Leavenworth. Upon his release the naval authorities claimed him, and he was taken to Marine Barracks at Norfolk, Virginia, where he served a year. It was particularly noticeable in his confession that Hassell had been drinking heavily before every one of his major crimes.

Hassell confessed that he and his wife had quarreled over his relations with his step-daughter. He said that he had a pint of whiskey at the barn, which he went out and drank. On his return to the house, another quarrel followed. Hassell related that he then took a hammer and hit Mrs. Hassell with it twice. He took a stocking and tied it around her neck and finished by choking her to death. This occurred during the night while Mrs. Hassell was in bed. The baby was sleeping in the same bed with its mother, and was awakened during the struggle with Mrs. Hassell. Hassell proceeded to choke the baby to death in the same way.

George Hassell was the only man in the history of Death Row at Huntsville to gain weight. He ate heartily and showed no signs of remorse for the brutal crimes that he had committed. Thus Hassell's killings by his own confession, numbered thirteen. Hassell offered no comment when informed of the results of the search in California. He was led to the electric chair on the night of February 12, 1928, and as the burning current shot through his body, he paid the penalty for his terrible deeds. No one came forward to claim his body, and the chapter was closed on one of the most brutal crimes on record.[41]

Meanwhile, business went on as usual in Farwell. Various civic improvements began to come to the town. The town was soon to have natural gas piped into its homes. The West Texas Gas Company was the first to make an application to lay a gas line in the streets and alleys of Farwell, but no agreement was entered into since the company did not specify a definite time limit in laying the pipe or at what price the pipe would be laid. This application was made in 1927.[42] It was not until 1930 that an ordinance was passed granting a franchise to the Southern Union Gas Company, of Dallas, Texas, to lay pipe lines and to maintain a gas plant for the distribution of natural gas in Farwell. The company was not to be required to extend its lines more than 150 feet to any consumer, at $1.50 for the first 1,000 cubic feet.[43] Construction was begun on the gas line in April, 1930, and was ready for service by July, 1930.[44]

Another change came when The Texas-New Mexico Utilities Company was granted a franchise in 1929 to take over the operation of Farwell's light plant. The company was also granted the right of way through the streets and alleys of the town to maintain its poles, guy wires, braces, and transformers.[45]

Growth has continued to the present time, and people have continued to move to the city and build fine new homes here. This growth may be traced to the expansion of irrigation practices in this area. Many farmers have made use of the precious water here and have built their homes in Farwell. While it is true that the little city has been blasted by dust, drouth, and depression, improvements in the way of farming seem to have given the town hopes for a much brighter future.

The development of the Farwell school system has been quite rapid through the years. The first school was conducted in the old rock Congregational Church building in 1907. Early in 1908, some portable buildings were constructed on the present school property, and school was held in these buildings until 1910.[1] The following statement was made by W.L. Townsen, County Judge of Parmer County, Texas:

I, W.L. Townsen, county judge of said county do hereby certify that on the 4th day of May, 1908, I made an entry upon the records of the commissioner's court of said county declaring the Farwell Independent School District duly incorporated for free school purposes.[2]

The above document began the educational development of the Farwell schools. The first school board members were elected on May 11, 1908, and twenty-nine votes were cast in the election. J.M. Hamlin was elected as president of the board, and Alex Shipley was elected as secretary. Ed Shopbell was elected to serve as treasurer that first year. Joe Francis, J.M. Kindred, R.C. Hopping, and John Simmons were the other members of the board. Hamlin, Kindred, and Shipley were to serve for one year.[3]

The first teachers in Farwell were Miss Minnie Harbison, T. Guy Rogers, and Lewis Mersfelder. They were re-elected for the fall and spring terms of 1908 and 1909. The salary of Mr. Rogers was set at $100.00 per month, and the other two teachers received $80.00 per month for their services.[4]

An election was to be held at Hamlin Hall on June 27, 1908 to determine if the board of trustees should have the power to annually levy and collect a tax upon all taxable property in the Farwell school district for the support and maintenance of public free schools.[5]

Another election was called to vote $12,-000.00 worth of bonds to purchase a school site and erect a school building.[6] R.W. McConnell was County Superintendent at this time, and the county commissioners ordered that he be allowed $25.00 for transportation for each school year.[7] McConnell reported that there were 152 pupils in the city

PUBLIC HIGH SCHOOL Building at Farwell, Texas, cost $20,000.

of Farwell in 1909.[8]

Joe Francis and Ed Shopbell resigned from the school board, and C.G. Bratton and B.E. Nobles were elected to fill their vacancies. The board ordered that an inexpensive ladder be made for the purpose of extinguishing any fire that might originate on the roof, and that a cheap belfry and flag pole should be made.[9]

The Farwell High School Building was erected in 1910 at a cost of $20,000.00. According to the corner stone on the building, J.M. Hamlin was still president of the school board, and J.B. Younger was now secretary. B.E. Nobles, Alex Shipley, J.M. Kindred, D.A. Linthicum, and C.L. George were the other members of the board. O.G. Roovermoore was the architect, and J.H. Heckman and M.W. Easum were the contractors. The building, a two-story red brick structure, had a full basement, and a windmill was located just to the east of the school.[11]

No records were available on the school from 1910 to 1915, but E.A. White was superintendent in 1915 at a salary of $1,000.00 for the nine month term. Miss Mable Kinney, Miss Eva Hendricks, and Miss Hazel Wilson were teaching in the school. Each of these teachers was receiving $60.00 per month. The board members at this time were: J.L. Walling, Bob Kyker, J.A. Oden, J.J. DeOliveria, R.C. Hopping, A.R. Carter, and T.J. Allen. Walling was president of the board, and Kyker was secretary.[12] Mr. Vaughn was janitor at the school and received $40.00 per month for his services.[13]

The board then agreed to re-elect Superintendent White for a two year period and raised his salary to $1,200.00 per year. The teachers in the system were to receive a $5.00 monthly raise beginning on September 1, 1916.[14] L.E. Thompson of Canyon, Texas was hired as the manual training teacher for the school term beginning September 4, 1916, at a salary of $85.00 per month.[15] The board decided that all pupils attending school from another district should be charged tuition. Those who were in the first three grades of school were to be charged $1.00 per month; those in the fourth through the sixth grades, $1.50 per month; in the seventh and eighth grades, $2.00 per month; and those in the ninth and tenth grades were to be charged $2.50 per month. At this time Farwell had only a ten grade school system.[16]

In the school board election of 1917, F.B. Hiner and W.W. Taylor were added to the board.[17] A.R. Carter resigned, and F.W. McElroy was appointed to fill his vacancy.[18] Constant changes were made through the years as one teacher resigned and another was elected to the position. Domestic Science was added to the curriculum in 1917, and Miss Mary Harris was the teacher.[19] Mrs. Lucy Gathings was elected as a primary teacher.[20] Miss Lurlene Boone was elected at the resignation of Miss Hendricks, and Flora Best Hopping replaced Miss Wilson.[21]

More new teachers were added to the faculty in 1918. Miss Fannie Boyle was hired as a primary teacher at $75.00 per month, Miss Ada Wilkerson was grade teacher at $70.00 per month, and Miss Rosemary Cox was hired for the grades at $70.00 per month. Miss Anita Piece was the new Domestic Science teacher and was also a regular class room teacher. C.H. Wirth was hired as manual training instructor at $1,200.00 per year. A major step was taken that year as the board decided to add the eleventh grade to the system for the 1918-19 term and thereafter.[22]

Serving on the school board in 1918 were: J.M. McCuan, J.J. DeOliveria, F.W. McElroy, B.N. Graham, J.A. Hiner, J.J. Oden, and W.W. Taylor. Then in 1919, another group took over, including McElroy, DeOliveria, C.B. Daniel, A.L. King, R.A. Hawkins, W.S. McDaniel, and B.F. Fears. Chester M. Pressley was later named to fill the vacancy left by Fears.[23] C.H. Wirth, E.A. White, Mrs. Fannie Boyle, Mrs. L.E. Canon,

Miss Josephine Nichols, Miss Rosemary Cox, Mrs. B.J. Lipscomb, and Miss Madge Nixon were then teachers.[24]

It was moved by the school board that no pupil from the Texico school could enter the Farwell school unless it was satisfactory with the Farwell school board.[25] A joint session was held with the Texico board to discuss the advisability of suspending school because of the flu epidemic. Both boards agreed to suspend school after hearing a thorough discussion of the matter by Dr. G.A. Foote.[26] School was suspended for six weeks due to the epidemic, and classes were held on Saturdays to make up for lost time.[27] The schools were closed again on December 19, 1918 because so much sickness still prevailed. They were not reopened until January 20, 1919.[28]

Board members expressed themselves as being opposed to any of the teachers of the school dancing during the school term, and requested that Superintendent White call their attention to that effect.[29]

Miss Madge Nixon, Miss Fannie Boyle, and Miss Rosemary Cox were retained for the 1919-20 school term at $75.00 per month. Miss Maud Smith was hired as Domestic Science teacher at $80.00 per month. Other new teachers were: Miss Ruth Thomas, Miss Ruby Forbes, Miss Ada Belle Thacker, Miss Ruby Lawler, and Miss Juanita Avant. Each of these teachers received $80.00 per month for their services.[30]

The women in the community became part of the school board in 1920. Ladies who served were: Mrs. J.H. Aldridge, Mrs. Carrie Thomas, Mrs. S.H. Withers, and Mrs. J.D. Hamlin. Men who worked with them were: C.B. Daniel, F.W. McElroy, A.L. King, and J.J. DeOliveria.[31] W.H. Younger was elected as superintendent of the school at a salary of $200.00 per month for a nine month period. Miss Smith, Miss Mills, Miss Sanders, Miss Redfern, and Miss Cullum were unanimously elected as teachers. Mr. Sherrer was principal, and Miss H. Parks was a primary teacher.[32]

In 1922, W.W. Hall, Alford Berggren, C.M. Pressley, and D.W. Clark were elected as school trustees. Miss Blanche Ford, Miss George, Miss Proter, and Miss Avant were teachers. W.M. Gourley was hired as the system's first agriculture teacher. He was to teach half time at Farwell and half time at Bovina.[33] C.B. Daniel resigned as a board member, and Charles Davis was nominated to fill his vacancy. T.E. Lovelace, S.T. Lawrence, and A.L. King were elected as trustees for two years.[34] W.H. Younger resigned as superintendent, and J.W. Reid was elected in his place. Henry Love was hired as coach and teacher for the fifth and sixth grades. Miss Othelia Graham was hired as teacher of English and Spanish.[35]

In 1924, S.T. Lawrence resigned as school trustee and was replaced by W.S. McDaniel. Miss Lois Berry was engaged as Home Economics teacher at $200.00 per month. Judge Hamlin was authorized to borrow $3,000.00 from the Capitol Land Company for payment of teachers' salaries. This sum was to be paid back with eight per cent interest with the first local taxes of 1925.[36]

Four new grade teachers were hired. They were: Miss Stamps, Mrs. Hromas, Miss Hall, and Miss Wilson. Miss Bessie Walker became head of the English department at a salary of $1,125.00 a year. All teachers were re-elected to their respective positions for the 1926-27 school term. Herman Sawyer was elected as superintendent of the Farwell school at a salary of $2,250.00 per year.[37]

New board members were: R.A. Hawkins, J.J. DeOliveria, J.P. Tate, and Eddie Smith. Miss Sheffield was hired to teach the third and fourth grades, and Mrs. O.C. Siles was to teach the seventh grade and Spanish.[38]

Teachers for the 1928-29 school term were: B.H. Hopkins, Mrs. Sikes, Miss Mary Stone, Miss Retha Sanders, Miss Turner, Miss Clark, Miss Bess Wallace, Miss Greta Brister, and Miss Hale. Sawyer was re-elected as superintendent at $2,400.00 per year.[39] F.J. Doose was given the contract to furnish gasoline for the school trucks. Truck drivers were J.M. Carpenter and Bob Moore.[40]

In 1929, Superintendent Sawyer resigned to move to Canadian, Texas, and Mr. Guy Tabor was elected to fill his vacancy. L.J. Young became the new agriculture teacher, and his wife taught English and Spanish. Miss Bertha Lee Parks was hired as Science teacher, and Royal Terrill became coach and principal. R.V. Ham was employed as janitor and bus driver at $100.00 per month.[41]

THE STORY OF THE CHURCHES

About seven years after the turn of the century, a rock church building was constructed on First Street in Farwell, two blocks south of the present Security State Bank. This was on the property now owned by Mr. and Mrs. Loyde Brewer. Mrs. J.O. Ford says that the rock for the building was brought and transported from Tolar, New Mexico. According to Hamlin Overstreet, the first school in Farwell was conducted in this church building.[1]

A deed was made on July 3, 1907 to the Congregational Church of Farwell in consideration of $706.00. The property consisted of lots No. 15 and No. 16 in Block 16 in the town of Farwell. As long as the Evangelical Congregational Chuch maintained worship in the building, the property was to remain theirs. It was further stipulated in the deed that if the church ceased to be the Congregational Church or if services were suspended in the house for one year, that the property was to be sold and disposed of at public auction. C.C. Marshall was listed as president of the church board.[2]

The church was quite an ornate structure for its time, and a minister's home was maintained on the property just to the east of the church building. Several members of the church were pictured in front of the building in the early days of the church. Since there are now no living members of the church, no one was able to identify any of the pictures.[3] The church flourished for several years, and Mr. Calhoun was minister for the group. By 1913, the membership was greatly reduced, and Mr. Calhoun left to accept another ministry. Services were discontinued in the church very soon thereafter, and the building then stood vacant for a number of years.

Then in 1935, Mr. J.O. Ford bought the building and used the rock to construct a double garage and storage room on his farm. The old rock church only survived three decades, but pioneers will remember it as helping to shape a large phase of Farwell's history in religion and education.[4]

Another church had its beginning in Farwell in 1907. A deed was made to the Christian Church on May 1, 1907, and F.M. Glenn, H.W. Shurlock, and J.M. Simmons were the

CONGREGATIONAL CHURCH and Parsonage, Farwell, Texas.

CHRISTIAN CHURCH, Farwell, Texas.

trustees of the church. The church property was located on Second Street and consisted of lots No. 14, No. 15, and No. 16 in Block 30 in the town of Farwell.[5] A meeting of the congregation was held for the purpose of securing a loan from the church board of the American Christian Missionary Society for completing their church building. Thomas H. Jones was church clerk, and it was voted to borrow $750.00 to complete the building.[6]

Some of the early members of the church were: Mr. and Mrs. M.M. Craig, Mr. and Mrs. S.C. Hunter, Mr. and Mrs. J.M. Kindred, Mr. and Mrs. Benny Franklin, Mr. and Mrs. J.P. Mason, Mr. and Mrs. Jim Wallings, Mr. and Mrs. B.E. Nobles, and Mrs. Minnie Francis. The B.O. Faville's came in 1910 and placed their membership with the group. Some of the early day preachers were Wright C. Moore, G.W. Davis, and a Brother Field. S.G. Battenfield arrived in 1918 as minister for the church, and remained until the group disbanded several years later.[7] A picture of the church building indicated that the structure had stained glass windows, and that there was a steeple on the building.[8]

The membership of the church was once well over 100 in number. A revival closed at the church in 1918 with thirteen being added by baptism. The meeting was held by the local minister, S.G. Battenfield. O.N. Robison was then president of the church board, and announced that Bible School opened at the church each Sunday at 10:15 a.m. It was also announced that the Sunday School attendance was running above 100, and that additions were being expected at every service.[9]

Then in 1924, as many members had either died or moved away from the community, the church trustees were faced with a great decision. Attendance had dropped to such a degree that a preacher could no longer be supported, and so it was with great reluctance that the trustees decided to discontinue their services and to sell the church building. The building was bought by the Methodists at Oklahoma Lane, and they moved the meeting house out to their community. The Christian Church still retains title to its lots in Farwell, and B.O. Faville serves as the only living trustee of the church. The last trustees of the church were Jim Walling, Mrs. Pearl Grady, and Faville. Sumner Davidson was the last treasurer of the church.[10] So it was that the Christian Church only served the spiritual needs of Farwell for a few years, but memories of the church's influence are still cherished by many in the community.

The Baptists and the Methodists never had a building in Farwell up to and including 1952, but always maintained their houses of worship in Texico. The Baptists had met for a short time in Farwell as early as 1818, but they had met in private homes. The group disbanded in 1919 and united with the church at Texico.[11] Both Baptists and Methodists have had strong congregations from a very early day.

The history of the churches in largely the history of families. Several families had moved into the Farwell community and decided to make an effort to establish the Church of Christ here. In 1921, they engaged the services of W.M. Speck to hold the first gospel meeting for them. The meeting was conducted under a tent just south of where Lovelace Grain Company now stands.

73

Among those present at that meeting were: J.S. Williams, Jim and Charles Lunsford, and Willis and George Magness. These men and their families made up the original membership of the Church in Farwell. They had made an earlier attempt to establish a congregation in the Oklahoma Lane community, but had failed.[12]

Members met in their homes for awhile, and then they obtained the use of the Court House for several years. Revival meetings in those days were well attended and quite successful as well. In the meeting held by W.M. Speck, there were thirty-two who responded for baptism. U.R. Beeson held the next meeting and baptized thirty-four. John W. Hedge came for the next meeting and baptized quite a number. Among the people to come into the church during this time were the C.M. Crows, the Ebb Randols, and the Bob Kykers. The first elders of the congregation were T.P. Burk, C.J. Moore, and J.S. Williams. Bob Moore was serving as treasurer, and contributions many times were not over $5.00 per Sunday.[13]

As the congregation grew numerically as well as spiritually, members began to see the need for a meeting house of their own. Title was obtained from the Capitol Freehold Land Company to lots No. 21 and No. 22 in Block No. 13 in the town of Farwell. The deed was made out on May 5, 1925, to the Elders of the Church of Christ and to their successors in office. A restrictive clause in the deed provided that if the property should cease to be used by the church, that it would then revert to the Capitol Freehold Land Company.[14]

Members of the church were canvassed for contributions toward erecting a church building. The most any individual gave was $100.00, and it took several years for some of the members to pay out their pledges. A stucco building was erected on the present church property at Avenue C and Fifth Street in Farwell. The building had a seating capacity of about 175, and there were two small classrooms and a baptistry included in the building. W.T. Millen painted the baptistry scene, which clearly depicts the beautiful mountain area around Hot Springs, New Mexico. The building was equipped with folding chairs at first, and the complete cost of the building was $2,200.00. Only $300.00 of this amount had been paid out for labor. The members did nearly all the labor on the building themselves. A note was signed at the lumber yard for the material, and it was paid for as the members paid their pledges.[15]

Prior to 1925, candidates for baptism had been taken to the Christian Church and were baptized in their baptistry. The first individual to be baptized in the new baptistry at the Church of Christ was W.W. Hall. The preacher holding the meeting at that time was E.A. Bedicheck. This was in 1925, and he also returned in 1926 for another meeting with the church. Hall recalls that people used to come from miles around to attend these meetings. Banners would be stretched across Main Street advertising these revivals, and great interest prevailed in hearing the visiting evangelists. It seems that times have greatly changed since then, and that people have allowed other interests to influence them.[16]

CHAPTER V. FOOTNOTES

The Farwell Brothers

1. Reminiscences of John V. Farwell, by His Elder Daughter, Vol. I, p. 15. Chicago: Ralph Fletcher Seymour, 1928.
2. Dictionary of American Biography, Vol. VI, pp. 294-5. New York: Charles Scribner's Sons, 1931.
3. Reminiscences of John V. Farwell, op. cit., p. 17.
4. Dictionary of American Biography, op. cit., p. 295.
5. Reminiscences of John V. Farwell, op. cit., p. 18.
6. Ibid., p. 20.
7. Ibid., p. 32.
8. Ibid., pp. 33-35.
9. Dictionary of American Biography, op. cit., p. 295.
10. Reminiscences of John V. Farwell, op. cit., p. 48.
11. Ibid., p. 48.
12. Ibid., p. 57.
13. Dictionary of American Biography, op. cit., p. 295.
14. Reminiscences of John V. Farwell, op. cit., p. 84.
15. Reminiscences of John V. Farwell, Vol. II, p. 21.
16. Ibid., p. 122.
17. Dictionary of American Biography, op. cit., p. 296.
18. Reminiscences of John V. Farwell, op. cit., p. 123.
19. Ibid., p. 199.
20. J. Evetts Haley, The XIT Ranch of Texas, pp. 50-1. Norman, Oklahoma: University of Oklahoma Press, 1953.
21. Ibid., p. 52.
22. Ibid., p. 53.
23. Ibid., p. 58.
24. Ibid., p. 60.
25. Ibid., pp. 72-3.
26. Amarillo Daily News, Nov. 8, 1953.

27. Haley, **op. cit.**, p. 83.
28. Statement by Mrs. Florence Golladay, Farwell resident, personal interview, March 5, 1954.
29. Haley, **op. cit.**, p. 148.
30. Statement by Mrs. Florence Golladay, personal interview, March 5, 1954.
31. **Amarillo Daily News**, Nov. 8, 1953.
32. Haley, **op. cit.**, pp. 173-5.
33. **Ibid.**, p. 208.
34. **Amarillo Daily News**, Nov. 8, 1953.
35. Haley, **op. cit.**, pp. 218-19
36. **Ibid.**, p. 221.
37. **Ibid.**, p. 223.
38. **Reminiscences of John V. Farwell**, Vol. II, pp. 37-8.
39. **Dictionary of American Biography, op. cit.**, p. 296.
40. **Ibid.**, pp. 294-5.
41. Haley, **op. cit.**, p. vii.

Early Days In Farwell

1. Letter by W.D. Howren, State Land Surveyor, Amarillo, Texas, to the author, November 30, 1953.
2. **Deed Record, Parmer County, Texas**, Bk. II, pp. 499-500, Dec. 28, 1905.
3. Statement by Milton Brown, personal interview, May 24, 1954. Mr. Brown is now residing in Clovis and owns the Clovis Lumber Company.
4. Statement by Tom Randol, personal interview, March 2, 1954. Mr. Randol came to this area in 1903 and has lived here all that time.
5. R.C. Hopping, **A Sheriff-Ranger In Chuckwagon Days**, p. 162, New York: Pageant Press, 1952.
6. Letter by Victor Gondos, Jr., National Archives and Records Service, Washington, D.C., to the author, Feb. 24, 1954.
7. Statement by Hamlin Overstreet, personal interview, April 9, 1954. Mr. Overstreet came to Farwell in 1906.
8. **Commissioners Court Minutes**, Vol. I, p. 1, June 8, 1907.
9. Statement by Wilfred Quickel, personal interview, March 3, 1954. Mr. Quickel is the City Clerk of Farwell.
10. **The State Line Tribune**, Farwell, Texas, May 14, 1953. All files of the Tribune were destroyed from 1910 through 1939. The files from 1940 up to the present time are complete and intact in the Tribune offices.
11. **Commissioners Court Minutes**, Vol. I, p. 49, May 6, 1908.
12. **The State Line Tribune**, Sept. 10, 1953.
13. **Commissioners Court Minutes**, Vol. I, p. 52, May 11, 1908.
14. **Ibid.**, pp. 26-27, Nov. 9, 1907.
15. **Ibid.**, pp. 30-31, Nov. 23, 1907.
16. **Ibid.**, p. 36, Jan. 4, 1908.
17. Statement by Tom Randol, personal interview, March 2, 1954.
18. **Clovis News Journal**, Feb. 11, 1954.
19. Letter by W.D. Howren, to the author, Nov. 30, 1953.
20. **The State Line Tribune**, June 12, 1941.

21. Statement by W.W. Vinyard, personal interview, May 24, 1954.
22. R.C. Hopping, **op. cit.**, pp. 165-169.
23. **Deed Record, Parmer County Texas**, Bk. XXIX, p. 189, Dec. 21, 1908.

24. Statement by Hamlin Overstreet, personal interview, April 9, 1954. Mr. Overstreet has resided in Farwell since 1906.
25. **The State Line Tribune**, Sept. 10, 1953.
26. **Ibid.**, June 9, 1949.
27. Statement by D.M. Whitley, personal interview, April 15, 1954. Mr. Whitley has been a Farwell resident since 1906.
28. Statement by Mrs. Golladay, personal interview, March 5, 1954.
29. Commissioners Court Minutes, Vol. I, p. 116, May 9, 1910.
30. Statement by D.M. Whitley, personal interview, April 15, 1954.
31. Statement by Hamlin Overstreet, personal interview, April 9, 1954.
32. **The State Line Tribune**, May 14, 1953.
33. Statement by D.M. Whitley, personal interview, April 15, 1954.
34. Statement by Tom Randol, Personal interview, March 2, 1954.
35. **Commissioners Court Minutes**, Vol. I, p. 54, May 11, 1908.
36. **Ibid.**, p. 72, Nov. 27, 1908.
37. **Ibid.**, p. 98, April 13, 1909.
38. **The State Line Tribune**, Feb. 15, 1951.
39. R.C. Hopping, **op. cit.**, p. 169.
40. **Ibid.**, pp. 171-172.
41. **Ibid.**, p. 190.
42. **Ibid.**, pp. 245-246.
43. Walter Prescott Webb, editor, **The Handbook of Texas**, Vol. I, p. 587.
44. **Views In and About Farwell, Texas**, Chicago: Manz Engraving Co., n.d. This booklet was borrowed from Mrs. Golladay of Farwell.
45. **Ibid.**, p. 2.

46. **Ibid.**, pp. 3-4.
47. **Ibid.**, p. 9.
48. **Ibid.**, pp. 18-19.
49. **Ibid.**, p. 23.
50. **Ibid.**, pp. 24-32.
51. **Commissioners Court Minutes**, Vol. I, p. 193, Feb. 19, 1910.
52. Statement by D.M. Whitley, personal interview, April 15, 1954.
53. **Commissioners Court Minutes**, Vol. I, p. 237, Nov. 10, 1910.
54. **Ibid.**, p. 249, Nov. 15, 1910.
55. **Ibid.**, p. 250, Nov. 17, 1910.
56. **Ibid.**, pp. 204-208, April 28, 1911.
57. **Ibid.**, pp. 209-210, April 29, 1911.
58. **Deed Records, Parmer County, Texas**, Bk. XV, pp. 598-599, Oct. 29, 1910.
59. Statement by Tom Randol, personal interview, March 2, 1954.
60. **The State Line Tribune**, Jan. 3, 1952.
61. **Commissioners Court Minutes**, Vol. I, p. 251, Nov. 17, 1910.
62. **Ibid.**, p. 298, July 24, 1911.
63. **Ibid.**, p. 510, Sept. 9, 1916.
64. **The State Line Tribune**, Feb. 15, 1951.
65. Statement by Tom Randol, personal interview, March 2, 1954.
66. **Commissioners Court Minutes**, Vol. I, p. 367, May 19, 1913.
67. **The State Line Tribune**, April 2, 1942.
68. **Commissioners Court Minutes**, Vol. I, p. 367, May 21, 1913.

69. Statement by Mrs. Golladay, personal interview, March 5, 1954.
70. **Commissioners Court Minutes**, Vol. I, p. 367, May 21, 1913.
71. **Ibid.**, p. 505, Aug. 15, 1916.
72. **Ibid.**, p. 519, Nov. 6, 1916.
73. **Ibid.**, p. 537, March 14, 1917.
74. **The State Line Tribune**, Jan. 3, 1952.
75. **Texico-Farwell News**, Jan. 12, 1917. The copies of this newspaper are filed in the Curry County Court House at Clovis, New Mexico.
76. **Loc. cit.**
77. Statement by D.M. Whitley, personal interview, April 15, 1954.
78. **Texico-Farwell News**, March 2, 1917.
79. **Ibid.**, April 13, 1917.
80. **Ibid.**, Feb. 16, 1917.
81. **Ibid.**, March 2, 1917.
82. Statement by Mrs. Golladay, personal interview, March 5, 1954.
83. **Texico-Farwell News**, Aug. 3, 1917.
84. **Ibid.**, Jan. 11, 1918.
85. **Ibid.**, July 19, 1918.
86. **Ibid.**, March 23, 1917.
87. **Ibid.**, Feb. 9, 1917.
88. **Ibid.**, Oct. 27, 1917.
89. **The State Line Tribune**, Sept. 10, 1953.
90. **Ibid.**, Feb. 15, 1951.
91. **Texico-Farwell News**, Jan. 12, 1917.
92. **The State Line Tribune**, Sept. 10, 1953.
93. **Texico-Farwell News**, Feb. 2, 1917.
94. **Ibid.**, June 22, 1917.
95. **Ibid.**, Jan. 25, 1918.
96. **Ibid.**, Feb. 9, 1917.
97. **Ibid.**, Aug. 31, 1917.
98. **Ibid.**, Oct. 5, 1917.
99. **Ibid.**, Oct. 26, 1917.
100. **Ibid.**, March 29, 1918.
101. **The State Line Tribune**, Sept. 10, 1953.
102. **The Clovis Journal**, Jan. 20, 1921.
103. **Ibid.**, Jan. 27, 1921.
104. **Loc. cit.**
105. **Ibid.**, Feb. 10, 1921.
106. **Texico-Farwell News**, Oct. 18, 1918.
107. **Ibid.**, Jan. 10, 1919.
108. **Ibid.**, April 26, 1919.
109. **The State Line Tribune**, May 23, 1919. This copy was borrowed from Fred Geries of Farwell.
110. **The Clovis Journal**, March 25, 1920.

1921-1929

1. Statement by J.E. Randol, personal interview, May 10, 1954. Mr. Randol now lives at Muleshoe, Texas.
2. Statement by G.W. Magness, personal interview, May 25, 1954.
3. **The Clovis Journal**, March 9, 1922.
4. **Ibid.**, April 27, 1922.
5. **District Court Minutes**, Vol. II, pp. 170-5, April 30, 1922.
6. **Ibid.**, pp. 217-23, May 8, 1923.
7. Statement by R.W. Anderson, Vice-president, Security State Bank, personal interview, May 28, 1954.
8. Statement by W.W. Hall, personal interview, May 26, 1954.
9. Letter by Victor Gondos, Jr., National Archives and Records Service, Washington, D.C., to the author, Feb. 24, 1954.
10. Statement by O.C. Sikes, personal interview, May 29, 1954.
11. Statement by Claude Rose, personal interview, May 28, 1954.
12. **The State Line Tribune**, Feb. 29, 1924. This paper was borrowed from Fred Geries of Farwell.
13. Statement by O.C. Sikes, personal interview, May 29, 1954.
14. **The State Line Tribune**, Feb. 29, 1924.
15. **Ibid.**, Dec. 30, 1926. This paper was borrowed from Fred Geries of Farwell.
16. **Commissioners Court Minutes**, Vol. 88, p. 169, Feb. 13, 1923.
17. **The State Line Tribune**, Dec. 30, 1926.
18. Statement by W.W. Hall, personal interview, May 26, 1954.
19. Statement by Fred Geries, personal interview, May 25, 1954. Mr. Geries came to Farwell in 1917.
20. Statement by Hamlin Overstreet, personal interview, April 9, 1954.
21. J. Evetts Haley, **The XIT Ranch of Texas**, p. 224. Norman, Oklahoma: University of Oklahoma Press, 1953.
22. **Capitol Reservation Lands**, Chicago: n.d.
23. **Ibid.**, p. 2.
24. **Ibid.**, p. 3.
25. **Ibid.**, pp. 4-5.
26. **Ibid.**, pp. 6-9.
27. **Ibid.**, pp. 10-11.
28. **Ibid.**, pp. 12-13.
29. **Ibid.**, pp. 14-15.
30. Statement by Hamlin Overstreet, personal interview, April 9, 1954.
31. **The State Line Tribune**, Sept. 10, 1954.
32. R.J. Vernon, "Thirteen People Dead," **Famous Detective Cases**, Vol. I, No. VI, Aug., 1935, pp. 48-9.
33. Clyde Morley, "Mantrap Woman," **Line-Up Detective Crime**, Vol. V, No. III, Oc.-Nov., 1951, pp. 22-5.
34. **The State Line Tribune**, Dec. 30, 1926. This paper was borrowed from Fred Geries of Farwell.
35. **The Clovis Journal**, Dec. 30, 1926.
36. **Loc. cit.**
37. **The State Line Tribune**, Dec. 30, 1926.
38. **Loc. cit.**
39. **District Court Minutes**, Vol. II, pp. 373-4, Jan. 4, 1927.
40. Clyde Morley, **op. cit.**, p. 59.
41. R.J. Vernon, **op. cit.**, p. 85.
42. **Commissioners Court Minutes**, Vol. II, p. 333, Nov. 9, 1927.
43. **Ibid.**, p. 475, Jan. 10, 1930.
44. **Ibid.**, p. 477, July, 1930.

Growth Education

1. Statement by Hamlin Overstreet, personal interview, April 9, 1954.
2. **Minutes of Farwell Independent School District**, Vol. I, p. 1, May 4, 1908.
3. **Ibid.**, pp. 2-3, May 11, 1908.
4. **Ibid.**, p. 4, May 18, 1908.
5. **Ibid.**, p. 5, June 11, 1908.
6. **Ibid.**, p. 7, Aug. 7, 1908.
7. **Commissioners Court Minutes**, Vol. I, p. 75, Dec. 22, 1908.

8. **Ibid.,** p. 131, Aug. 17, 1909.
9. **Minutes of the Farwell Independent School District,** Vol. I, pp. 8-9, Nov. 14, 1909.
10. **Views In And About Farwell, Texas,** p. 11, Chicago: Manz Engraving Co., n.d.
11. **Loc. cit.**
12. **Minutes of Farwell Independent School District,** Vol. I, pp. 20-21, Aug. 13, 1915.
13. **Ibid.,** p. 26, April 13, 1916.
14. **Ibid.,** p. 28, May 6, 1916.
15. **Ibid.,** p. 29, May 18, 1916.
16. **Ibid.,** p. 35, Sept. 17, 1916.
17. **Ibid.,** p. 38, April 16, 1917.
18. **Ibid.,** p. 40, May 16, 1917.
19. **Ibid.,** p. 45, Sept. 3, 1917.
20. **Ibid.,** p. 41, June 9, 1917.
21. **Ibid.,** p. 44, Aug. 3, 1917.
22. **Ibid.,** pp. 54-5, May 28, 1918.
23. **The State Line Tribune,** Feb. 26, 1953.
24. **Texico-Farwell News,** Aug. 23, 1918.
25. **Minutes of Farwell Independent School District,** Vol. I, p. 67, Sept. 10, 1918.
26. **Ibid.,** p. 69, Oct. 7, 1918.
27. **Ibid.,** p. 71, Nov. 16, 1918.
28. **Ibid.,** p. 73, Jan. 15, 1919.
29. **Ibid.,** p. 77, Feb. 22, 1919.
30. **Ibid.,** p. 87, Aug. 16, 1919.
31. **The State Line Tribune,** Feb. 26, 1953.
32. **Minutes of the Farwell Independent School District,** Vol. I, pp. 97-98, May 3, 1920.
33. **Ibid.,** pp. 117-18, May 16, 1922.
34. **Ibid.,** p. 127, April 26, 1923.
35. **Ibid.,** p. 128, May 3, 1923.
36. **Ibid.,** pp. 135-6, July 12, 1924.
37. **Ibid.,** pp. 140-1, April 26, 1926.
38. **Ibid.,** pp. 145-47, May 12, 1927.
39. **Ibid.,** pp. 148-49, April 18, 1928.
40. **Ibid.,** p. 151, Aug. 8, 1928.
41. **Ibid.,** pp. 160-65, May 4, 1929.

Churches

1. **The State Line Tribune,** Aug. 23, 1951.
2. **Deed Records, Parmer County, Texas,** Bk. IV, p. 208, July 3, 1907.
3. **Views In And About Farwell, Texas,** p. 20. Chicago: Manz Engraving Co., n.d.
4. **The State Line Tribune,** Aug. 23, 1951.
5. **Deed Record, Parmer County, Texas,** Bk. XVII, p. 103, May 1, 1907.
6. **Ibid.,** Bk. VI, pp. 560-64, May 14, 1907.
7. Statement by B.O. Faville, personal interview, June 1, 1954. Mr. Faville has operated the Red Cross Pharmacy in Texico since 1910.
8. **Views In And About Farwell, Texas, op. cit.,** p. 21.
9. **Texico-Farwell News,** July 5, 1918.
10. Statement by B.O. Faville, personal interview, June 1, 1954.
11. **Texico-Farwell News,** April 26, 1919.
12. **The State Line Tribune,** Dec. 20, 1951.
13. Statement by G.W. Magness, personal interview, May 25, 1954.
14. **Deed Record, Parmer County, Texas,** Bk. XXXIV, p. 113, May 5, 1925.
15. Statement by J.E. Randol, personal interview, May 10, 1954.
16. Statement by W.W. Hall, personal interview, May 26, 1954.

BIBLIOGRAPHY

BOOKS, ENCYCLOPEDIA, AND PAMPHLETS

Capitol Reservation Lands. Chicago: n.d. Pp. 16.

Church Bulletin, Farwell, Texas, 1953. Pp. 4.

Dictionary Of American Biography, Vol. Vi, Pp. 294-6.

Haley, J. Evetts, **The XIT Ranch of Texas.** Norman, Okla.: University of Oklahoma Press, 1953. Pp. 245.

Hopping, R.C., **A Sheriff-Ranger In Chuckwagon Days.** New York: Pagent Press, 1952. Pp. 216.

Reminiscences Of John V. Farwell, by His Elder Daughter, Vol. I. Chicago: Ralph Fletcher Seymour, 1928. Pp. 198.

Reminiscences Of John V. Farwell, by His Elder Daughter, Vol. II. Chicago: Ralph Fletcher Seymour, 1928. Pp. 235.

Texas Almanac, Dallas, Pp. 32.

Views In And About Farwell, Texas. Chicago: Manz Engraving Co., n.d. Pp. 32.

Webb, Walter, Editor, **The Handbook of Texas,** Vol. I, Pp. 587.

LETTERS AND PERSONAL INTERVIEWS

Anderson, R.W. to the author, May 28, 1954.

Brown, Milton to the author, May 24, 1954.

Crow, C.M. to the author, May 20, 1954.

Faville, B.O. to the author, June 1, 1954.

Geries, Fred to the author, May 25, 1954.

Golladay, Mrs. Florence to the author, March 5, 1954.

Gondos, Victor to the author, Feb. 24, 1954 (Letter).

Graham, B.N. to the author, May 25, 1954.

Hall, W.W. to the author, May 26, 1954.

Howren, W.D. to the author, Nov. 30, 1953 (Letter).

Magness, G.W. to the author, May 25, 1954.

Magness, J. Willis to the author, May 20, 1954.

Overstreet, Hamlin to the author, April 9, 1954.

Quickel, Wilfred to the author, March 3, 1954.

Randol, J.E. to the author, May 10, 1954.

Randol, T. Sam to the author, May 19, 1954.

Randol, Tom to the author, March 2, 1954.

Rose, Claude to the author, May 28, 1954.

Sikes, O.C. to the author, May 29, 1954.

Thomas, Mrs. J.D. to the author, May 31, 1954.

Vinyard, W.W. to the author, May 24, 1954.

Whitley, D.M. to the author, April 15, 1954.

MAGAZINE ARTICLES

Morley, Clyde, "Mantrap Woman," **Line-Up Detective Crime**, Vol. V, No. III, Oct.-Nov., 1951, pp. 22-5, p. 59.

Vernon, R.J., "Thirteen People Dead," **Famous Detective Cases**, Vol. I, No. VI, Aug., 1935, pp. 48-9, p. 85.

NEWSPAPERS

Amarillo Daily News, Nov. 8, 1953.

Clovis News Journal, Feb. 11, 1954.

Texico-Farwell News, (1917-19).

The Clovis Journal, March 25, 1920; Jan. 20, 1921; Jan. 27, 1921; Feb. 10, 1921; March 9, 1922; April 27, 1922; Dec. 30, 1926.

The State Line Tribune, May 23, 1919; Feb. 29, 1924; Dec. 30, 1926; Jan. 13, 1927; Jan. 18, 1934; July 7, 1938; (1940-54).

UNPUBLISHED MATERIALS

Commissioners Court Minutes, Vols. I, II, and III.

Deed Record, Parmer County, Texas, Bk. II, pp. 449-500; Bk. IV, p. 208; Bk. VI, pp. 560-64; Bk. XV, pp. 598-99; Bk. XVII, p. 103; Bk. XXIX, p. 189; Bk. XXXIV, p. 113; Bk. XLII, pp. 155-66; Bk. LXII, pp. 505-24, pp. 582-3.

District Court Minutes, Vol. I, pp. 204-08; Vol. II, pp. 170-75, pp. 373-4.

Minutes of Farwell Independent School District, Vols. I, II, and III.

Official Minutes Of The City Of Farwell, Vol. I, pp. 1-6.

Chapter VI

Friona

Prepared by the Personnel:
WORK PROJECTS ADMINISTRATION
O.P. No. 665-66-3-299

FRIONA, TEXAS

About 1906, the George G. Wright Land Company of Kansas City, Missouri, contracted with the Capitol Freehold Land and Investment Company of Chicago to sell several thousands of acres of land owned by the company in the Panhandle of Texas. The lands were mostly in Parmer and Deaf Smith Counties.

As a preparation to instituting this gigantic sale of land, a local office or headquarters was necessary as a base to bring prospective land buyers to and from while making the sales or showing the land. Accordingly, what might be termed the northwest half of Section 6 in Township 1 South, Range Four East, or that part of this section lying on the north side of the Santa Fe railroad track, was chosen as the site for a proposed town to be used as a base of the sales operation.

This tract of land was then surveyed and laid off into town lots and blocks with streets and alleys, and named Friona, from the Frio Draw, which lies immediately to the south of the townsite. Thus we find the city of Friona coming into existence as a land boom town and within the next year and one half, it had an almost mushroom growth with buildings to house the various lines of business interprises such as are necessary to the welfare of the people in a thrifty and growing town and community.

Having thus founded a base for operation locally, the land company, inaugurated a vast advertising campaign of the lands and established agents and sub-agents in many localities in the central states of Ohio, Indiana, Illinois, Iowa, Missouri, Nebraska and Kansas. It was the duty of these agents to interest prospective land buyers and home seekers in the lands of the Friona territory. The agencies converged and united at Kansas City on the first and third Wednesdays of each month and formed large "Land Excursion Trains" which reached Friona (the following day) on the first and third Thursdays of each month.

GEORGE G. WRIGHT HEADQUARTERS—Friona, Texas.

Each train brought from 250 to 500 prospective land buyers, many of whom bought tracts of land containing 160 acres up to 640 acres, which were to be converted from grass land to farm land. Upon many of these tracts the new owners soon built homes and settled thereon.

Thus we find this vast and fertile domain, which had for years been the home of immense droves of cattle, grazing over pastures of almost unlimited extent, and inhabited only by a few cattle owners and their cowboys, now cut-up into small farms and inhabited by many men and their families, who came here to make their homes. They came to apply themselves to an entirely different form of agriculture than that of the single production of cattle, which was that of plowing up the sod land and producing food and grain crops.

Following the first influx of farmer-settlers there were a few years of unusual drought, which coupled with the lack of knowledge on the part of the settlers as to the manner of cultivating crops in this semi-arid climate, caused almost complete and total farm failures. Many of them became discouraged and returned to their former homes or to other localities far from the Friona Country. Those who remained found that the growing of cattle and sheep was a safer and more profitable business than that of trying to grow feed and grain crops. They therefore again divided the lands into pastures of much smaller dimensions and practically every farmer provided himself with a nucleus of a herd of cattle or sheep (or both) and conditions

FRIONA'S FIRST DEPOT

SANTA FE RAILWAY STATION—FRIONA, TEXAS

began to assume a more prosperous and satisfactory appearance.

More moisture and a better knowledge of the proper methods of farming in this area, caused the production of more bountiful crops and this made stock farming more profitable. During the Winter of 1910 or 1911 the country was covered with a deep snow, which remained for many days, and most farmers (not being prepared for such conditions) soon had their store of feed consumed and most of them lost large numbers of sheep and cattle from cold and hunger. It is said that the cattle, in their extremity actually ate the bark from the cedar fence posts in an attempt to satisfy their hunger. Following this, better crops were grown and pastures were richer and the few remaining settlers became permanent residents, very few leaving or coming after the first exodus during the years of 1908 and 1909.

During 1914 occasional new settlers began to arrive, and this continued until the fall and winter of 1917 when a considerable number of cattlemen began leasing pastures not many miles out of Friona and moved their families into Friona. It looked for a year or so, that the country was again rapidly filling-up with new people. This condition however; was suddenly halted and again many people moved away. During the winter of 1918-19 one of the deepest snows ever known in this locality, covered the ground for a period of seven weeks and was accompanied during much of this time by zero weather. This caught most of the people unprepared as to feed and shelter for their livestock, which at that time was practically all cattle as cattle were more profitable than sheep. Although

all kinds of feed obtainable was shipped in with all the dispatch the railroad company could command, hundreds of head of cattle perished from cold and hunger. In one four acre lot or corral at Parmerton, six miles southwest of Friona, there were at one time enough dead cattle that, it is said, one could walk entirely over it without stepping upon the ground by stepping from one carcass to another. Skinning began and the hides were hauled into town by the wagon load, weighed by the ton and shipped out by the car-load. This catastrophe reduced many of the apparently prosperous cattle raisers to bankruptcy and the population of Friona again decreased.

Better conditions for farming and cattle raising followed and the country again began to look prosperous and the population remained normal until in the early "twenties" when the Syndicate people again started another land sale program, with their sales people working largely in Oklahoma and Central and East Texas, bringing their prospects in by automobile and returning them to their homes by the same means, and quartering them in the new Syndicate Hotel that had been built on the Ozark Trail about 12 miles to the southeast of Friona. The hotel was situated at the southeast corner of Section 11, Township 5 South, Range 4 East. (last sentence added by Hugh Moseley)

It was just at this time that power farming was becoming popular and within a short time dozens of farm tractors were busy both day and night turning the sod of the large pastures to the south of Friona, which had heretofore been scarcely touched by the plow. Thousands of acres of formerly rich pasture land was converted into rich farming land and wheat, cotton, corn and grain sorghums were produced in abundance for several years. Many acres of farmland, lying north of Friona, were sold during this time by private agencies and the same influx of settlers was made there, until the city of Friona became the center of a vast area of farm land.

During the first six years after Friona was started there was but one church established. It was organized as a community church and was under the protection of the Congregational Church Organization, but in 1914 two other churches, the Baptist and Methodist, were organized, as the surrounding territory was filled-up there was a demand for more churches until the city now has five church buildings.

Friona's first school was a frame building, erected in 1908, but which soon became inadequate for the needs of the district and a five room brick school building was completed in 1912. It was then a three teacher, third class high school. In 1916 the departments of domestic science and manual training were added and two more teachers were employed and the school was raised to the rank of a second class high school. It was so continued until 1921, when the number of teachers was raised to six. In September of 1921, shortly after the term had begun, the five room brick building burned to the ground. A very cheap five room frame building was hastily constructed and school was continued in this during the remainder of that term and the term of 1922-23. During this time a consolidated school district had been formed of the original Friona district and three smaller districts. The consolidation of the district was completed in February 1923 and the fourth school building was completed in January of 1924. During the year of 1924 the district was converted into an independent school district, and efforts were at once begun to secure State Affiliation which was accomplished in 1924-25 and it then became a first class high school with complete State affiliation. Although the new school building was pronounced by many to be far larger than the school district would ever need, within two years it became necessary to build additional room. In the year of 1931 it became neces-

sary to issue more bonds for the building of another school building of even greater dimensions in order to house the school. The number of teachers had been raised to 19.

A scoop shovel was the only grain elevator in Friona, up until the spring of 1916, but on January 27, 1916 a contract was let by George T. Courtright and W.H. Warren for the erection of Friona's first grain elevator. At this writing, there are five elevators and during the harvest of 1931, two hundred thousand bushels of wheat were shipped from these grain elevators. Four million bushels of wheat were produced that year in Parmer County and over half of that amount was sold or marketed through the Friona grain elevators.

During 1926 or 1927 Friona secured its first public utility. Representatives of Texas Utility Company met with the Friona Chamber of Commerce and arrangements were made whereby that company would build a line into the town or establish a generating plant to furnish lights and power.

A cotton gin was built in 1926 or 1927. It burned in 1931 and was replaced by the present building and equipment and 1934 over two thousand bales of cotton were ginned.

The City of Friona was incorporated on March 21st, 1928. Mr. John White was elected mayor and Mr. J.A. Blackwell and Mr. Jesse M. Osborn were elected commissioners. The Order signed by Parmer County Judge, Ernest F. Lokey, confirming the Incorporation of the City of Friona, was inadvertently omitted from the Commissioners' Court Minutes of the above date. This was noticed some time later and was called to the attention of the Parmer County Judge and Commissioners' Court and the matter came on to be considered in a regular meeting of the said Court and order and decree was duly passed on the 4th day of January 1930 and is recorded in Volume Two at page 473 of the Commissioners' Court Minutes of Parmer County, Texas.

The population of the City of Friona gradually increased and it became apparent that a more extensive and efficient water system should be installed in order to supply the citizens with water for public and domestic use, so during the term of the first city officials an election was called by an almost unanimous

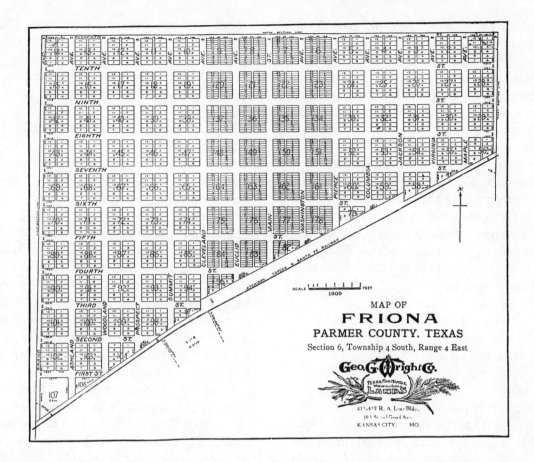

MAP OF
FRIONA
PARMER COUNTY. TEXAS

Section 6, Township 4 South, Range 4 East

Geo. G. Wright Co.

TEXAS PAN HANDLE
WHEAT and CORN
LANDS

411-412 R. A. Long Bldg.,
10th St. and Grand Ave.
KANSAS CITY.   MO.

vote that the contract for a complete water system to be municipally owned and that city warrants should be issued to pay for the same. Later a franchise was granted to The West Texas Gas Company to install and operate a system of gaslines for the purpose of supplying gas for fuel and lights.

The present board of Friona City officials is as follows: Floyd W. Reeve, mayor; Frank L. Spring and Opal C. Jones, commissioners; John White, city Tax Assessor-Collector and city Secretary and Treasurer; Logan Sympson, city water superintendent and city fire marshal; L.D. Cummings, Corporation Judge; Chas. M. Jones, City Marshal and A.D. Smith, was serving as City Attorney

BIBLIOGRAPHY

John White, Friona, Texas
Approved and signed by:
John White

The above is not dated, but is believed by this compiler, Hugh Moseley, that the interview was had in the latter part of 1933 or the early part of 1934. This was copied from the Parmer County file in the archives of the Panhandle-Plains Historical Museum in Canyon, Texas, on May 26, 1970.

Hugh Moseley

FRIONA, PARMER COUNTY, TEXAS

Friona is a beautiful little town, located on the main line of the Sante Fe Railroad, twenty-four miles southwest of Hereford, Deaf Smith County, and thirty miles northeast of Texico. A second railroad is surveyed and partly under construction from Texline southward through Friona. It commands a very large trade territory and is destined to be a distributing point for a vast part of the prosperous Panhandle country.

Friona will probably be the county seat of Parmer County. It is situated on gently rolling prairie, free from draws or ravines: is supplied with an abundance of purest water; has at this time a fine hotel, livery stable, two general stores, mail, telegraph and express facilities. A building is already erected in which a bank is to be established in the near future.

The climate is absolutely unsurpassed for healthfulness.

All indications point to the rapid growth of this, one of the newest of the Panhandle towns, and opportunities for business men, tradesmen, and mechanics are numerous.

The tributary lands, once the cattle ranges, have been divided up and sold to settlers who are now moving in and converting them to farms. Now is your time to locate for business, or for a home. Lots are offered at reasonable prices, for cash or on good terms. The first buyers have the pick and will reap the harvest. Come to Kansas City over any line of railroad. From Kansas City we go over the Santa Fe in our own train direct to FRIONA: leaving the first and third Wednesdays of each month.

Write, for further information, to
GEO. G. WRIGHT CO.
411-12 R.A. Long Bldg.
10th St. and Grand Ave.
Kansas City, Mo.

COME-ON FOR LAND BUYERS—This reproduction of a publicity piece for the old George Wright Land Company was the back side of a map of Friona, printed in 1906. Notice the glowing terms used by the author to describe the property. Such printed pieces were common 50 years ago as developers sought to settle up the then sparsely-populated Texas Plains.

HISTORICAL SKETCH
FRIONA'S ORIGIN IS TRACED BY WRITER

Friona Star, Sept. 3, 1970
By Mrs. N.R. Cox
(Mary Catherine Crawford)

The town of Friona came into existence about 1906—less than seventy years ago. Development was begun by the George G. Wright Land Company of Kansas City, Missouri. The Wright Land Company secured an option to sell land owned by the Capitol Land Syndicates. This Chicago based syndicate owned and managed the famous XIT, (Ten-Counties-in-Texas) Ranch. At one time the XIT Ranch was said to be the largest ranch in the United States, or perhaps in the entire world.

Parmer County land was included in the more than 300,000 acres of West Texas Land which was sold by the state of Texas to build the state capitol building in Austin. The XIT Ranch was put up for sale in 1901, when its British investors found that profits from cattle-raising were coming in too slowly.

The Wright Land Company began land-selling operations around Friona on a large scale in the fall of 1907. The completion of a railroad connecting Amarillo and Clovis made it possible to bring large numbers of prospective settlers to see the country. For a period of two years (1907-1909), bi-monthly excursion trains were run from Kansas City to Friona.

Trainloads of a hundred to a hundred and fifty people were brought from Missouri, Kansas, Illinois, Indiana, Ohio, and other states. Excursionists were met at the station by a convoy of 18 to 20 "taxis," and carried on sight-seeing tours of the prairie country. They were taken in relays to points 18 to 20 miles northwest or southwest of town to hotels for an overnight stay.

Some land-buyers were taken to spend the night at Star Ranch about 18 miles southeast of Friona. There where the community of Lazbuddie is now located. Other excursionists were driven to a hotel at "Old" Findlay, a town now non-existent, which was located about 18 miles northwest of Friona. The Findlay hotel was a long, two-story structure with more than twenty rooms.

According to a map and prospectus put out by the land company, the town of Friona had a "fine hotel, livery stable, two general stores, mail, telegraph, and express facilities. A building is already erected in which a bank is to be established in the near future."

A.N. (Uncle Andy) Westworth, one of the first settlers, recalled that when he arrived in Friona, on the first excursion train in the fall of 1907, a box car served as a station. The present railroad station was built in 1908.

John White, long-time editor of the Friona Star, made his first trip to Friona on the excursion train in October, 1908. He later said he remembered nothing of the town—possibly because there was so little of it. The excursionists were whisked out of town in a calvacade of approximately twenty company cars to "Old" Findlay. There they were made comfortable for the night. The next morning they were taken to see the country.

Mr. White recalled with amusement the rush there was among the different company cars to get back to the land office to sign up for the farm land. The race was to sign up for a choice quarter section before another person beat him to it. Mr. White said he came out ahead in this race by signing up for his quarter section before leaving Findlay. He wished to get land adjoining that owned by a friend in Illinois, who had told him it was good land.

After much of the farm land around Friona was sold, the Wright Land Company next centered its efforts on developing the town. It became a trade center and shipping point for farms and ranches for many miles around. "Old" Findlay was located in Deaf Smith County, to be exact; but much of the farmland in Parmer County was sold there.

Land, which was sold at $22.50 per acre, had been paid for by the company at the rate of about a dollar and a half per acre. The Capitol Land Syndicate from whom the Wright Land Company secured an option to sell land in Parmer and Deaf Smith Counties had its headquarters at Farwell, Texas.

The Wright Land Company withdrew its colorful sales promotions around 1910. Excursionists paid the regular round-trip railroad fare here; but Pullman accomodations were furnished free by the land company. On one occasion a hundred cots were furnished overnight "guests" at Star Ranch by the company.

A brochure on the town of Friona, around 1907, or 1908, pictures some of the business places and "typical" homes of Friona citizens. These included photos of the home of George W. Clark, the residence of D.W. McMillan, one of the land agents and the home of John Saxine, land office representative. This home was situated near the railroad; and it was quite a show place with many beautiful flowers and trees. At one time town lots sold at $65.00 a piece; and many considered that too high a price.

By 1909, the town boasted two grocery stores—one run by R. Overfelt, a boarding house operated by a Mrs. Karr, "Doc" Seamond's livery stable, a bank, post office, and a lumberyard. A pharmacy was owned by Dr. E.E. Rohrabaugh, the town's first doctor. There was a Union Church, a two-room school, a newspaper office with a Mr. Harris as editor, and Flanders' photograph gallery.

FIRST TEAM? . . . What well may be the first baseball team ever assembled in Friona is shown in this 1908 photograph. Identity of the players is not known.

Mrs. Karr's, the first boarding house in Friona, was situated in a two-story yellow frame house one block west of Main Street. The Friona Hotel, which described as "21 rooms and modern" in a land booklet, was operated by a Mr. Clark. It occupied the approximate location of the present Friona Hotel on the west side of Main Street.

The building used by the town's first pharmacy served originally as the first courthouse for Parmer County. It was at Parmerton. Developers of Friona once planned for the county seat to be located here. They had set aside land in the center of town for a courthouse square. After a county-wide election in 1908, the county seat was moved to Farwell. There it has remained since, although a later election was held in an unsuccessful attempt to move the county seat to Friona.

NOTE—George G. Wright of Jackson County, Missouri, on May 10, 1910 deeded to the County Commissioners of Parmer County and their successor in office the following: ALL BLOCK 50 Original Town of Friona for the use of the Public forever for Court House Purposes only. (See Parmer County Deed Record Vol. 8 p. 150.)

THE FRIONA STAR, Friday, June 23, 1950.

Beautiful trees . . . the greenest of grass . . . that is the spacious park on North Main street in Friona after 44 years of efforts by Friona citizens to maintain a park within its limits!

And its a rich and unique history behind this local park project. The Main Street Park, which incidentally is a county park rather than city owned, was designated as park land by George C. Wright and presented to Parmer County. This was part of Wright's plan when in 1906 he laid out the city of Friona, having purchased the 368.2 acre townsite in October of that year from the Capitol Freehold Land and Investment Company of London, England for the amount of $5,523.00. In November of 1906 the city was officially named, and the park, blocks, streets and alleys were marked off.

Locust trees were planted and watered from storage tanks located behind Mr. R.H. Kinsley's hardware store which now is the Plains Hardware and Furniture location. These trees became big shade trees but were in a few years killed by borers. Then Mr. Kinsley drilled a well near the center of the park in 1926 and the present elm trees were planted. The well was drilled at cost and paid for by the local women's clubs.

THE FRIONA STAR, Thursday, April 16, 1953.
Jodok Tells of Early Excursion Trains, Land Prospecting in Early Days Here.

It was in the latter part of one of the latter years of the present century when a train of some five or six Pullman coaches pulled onto the siding at a small place that was marked on the railroad map or time table, as Friona. This arrival was about four o'clock in the afternoon. To be a little more exact as to date it was on or about the 10th day of October in the year 1908.

The train was one of those then popular semi-monthly "Home Seekers" excursion trains of the Geo. G. Wright Land Company of Kansas City, and Friona was its destination. The train made two trips each month and was run for the exclusive transportation of prospective customers of the land company.

It appears that, perhaps three or four years earlier in the century, the George G. Wright Land Company had entered an agreement with an English syndicate to sell about a million acres of land for the syndicate, that was located in the great Panhandle of Texas, said land having been ceded to the syndicate by the state as partial payment for the building of the State House at Austin. And it seems that the syndicate evidently chose the right man for the job, for it was not long 'til George G. had his agents, solicitors and his boosters well scattered through the Central states of Ohio, Indiana, Illinois, Iowa, Missouri. And these agents were no tenderfeet nor slouches at the job.

Thus it was that on the regular railroad excursion dates of each month, from 150 to 300 home-seekers and prospective land buyers were congregated at Kansas City from these various states by the well organized army of solicitors, and loaded the George Wright special and headed for Friona. The train mentioned in the opening paragraph of this story was one of those trains and carried a reported 281 prospective homeseekers. Practically all these homeseekers were men. Perhaps a dozen of them had their wives with them. There were no children. They wined and dined and slept on the train.

THE FRIONA STAR, Thursday, August 27, 1953.
First Well Developed In 1908, Survey Tells.

CASTOR BEANS AND SUDAN· ARE TWO MORE OF THE FLOURISHING PARMER COUNTY CROPS THAT WITH THE AID OF IRRIGATION AND SOIL FERTILITY PROGRAMS ARE NETTING ENVIABLE GOOD YIELDS LOCALLY, IN CONTRAST TO THE DEARTH OF CROPS IN THE UN-IRRIGATED SOUTHWEST THIS YEAR.

WITH PARMER COUNTY IRRIGATION MUCH IN THE NEWS THIS MONTH, EMPHASIZED BY THE DIVERSIFIED AND BUMPER CROPS IN THE COUNTY, THE FOLLOWING HISTORY OF LOCAL IRRIGATION HAS BEEN PREPARED BY JOE OSBORN.

JOE HAS SPENT CONSIDERABLE TIME THIS SUMMER GLEANING THE FACTS ON EARLY-DAY IRRIGATION IN THE VICINITY, AND HE IS USING THIS RESEARCH IN CONNECTION WITH HIS SCHOOL WORK AT THE UNIVERSITY OF TEXAS.

THE STAR IS GLAD TO PRESENT THIS BIT OF LOCAL STORY: By Joe Osborn

The official records of the State Board of Water Engineers show that the first irrigation well in the High Plains was at Plainview in 1911; however, Parmer County had been irrigating for several years by then.

In 1906, George Hitts, a commission merchant in Indiana, became interested in the High Plains, attracted, no doubt, by the extensive promotional campaigns of the land companies in charge of disposal of the XIT Ranch. In that year, 1906, he purchased a farm at the present town of Springlake. In 1907, he traded this property for 1400 acres located in the eastern part of Parmer County, joining the present site of the Black community. This is located in and around section 20 of the Harah Survey.

According to his son-in-law, R.P. Conway, George Hitts was a very far-sighted person, "visionary" fellow who predicted that "this country would someday be a garden 'spot.'" In 1908 the first irrigation well in this immediate region was drilled on this place.

It was a 4" well drilled to 200'. Mr. Conway says that they hit water at 141 feet and that the water level remained there as long as the well was used until 1924. The pump was set at 160 ft. This early well was powered by a 10 h.p. Witte Engine from Kansas City. Conway related that he remembers this fact clearly because the motor "gave us some trouble!"

With this 4" well a large variety of garden crops were raised, however Hitts wasn't satisfied with its output and in 1910 he drilled a 12" well about 200 yds. south of it. This well was powered by a 40 h.p. Bessemer one-cylinder motor. It burned oil and operated similar to diesel motors now. To start it the "hot-head" had to be heated by a blowtorch about 30 min. and then the motor was "turned over" by compressed air as it was too heavy to turn by hand. Homer Brumley of Hereford estimates that the motor weighed ten tons. Mr. Brumley said he saw the engine being moved in 1928 when it was sold from the place to McDonald, a pioneer irrigator at Hereford. He said the flywheels on each side were mounted under the front and it was "drug" or trailed using the flywheels for back wheels to McDonald's place north of Hereford. John Aldridge of Farwell remembers the motor and pump as a "massive piece of equipment" in 1918, when he was by the place.

Both the 4" and the 12" wells were pumped

by a double-action pump of similar or exact construction to windmill pumps then and now. The 4" well seems to have been abandoned when the larger one was drilled. The 12" well was operated with the double-action pump until 1915 when a centrifugal pump was installed. The output of the well with the double-action pump, Conway said, was 250 g.p.m. and after the centrifugal pump, was installed the output was stepped up to 450 g.p.m.

After obtaining a water supply, Hitts laid concrete tile three inches in diameter with a 2 inch hole under three acres north of the well. This sub-irrigated tract was planted to various garden crops, an apple orchard, gooseberries, blackberries, strawberries, sweet potatoes, etc. Conway says that they raised them with a great deal of success however the market was limited. He said most of the produce was marketed in local towns. He mentioned that at that time alfalfa hay was worth only $7.50 a ton.

Hitts was especially interested in proving the ability of the country to raise garden crops and since his water supply was limited he does not seem to have watered much else. He is credited with being the first man in the United States to cure sweet potatoes successfully, Conway said, in connection with his business in Indiana and because of his interest in this crop planted twenty acres of them.

Hitts seemed to have been on the right track but just 30 years too early. He operated the farm from Indiana, coming down to see it often to supervise farming operations. The place had 1400 acres in it originally so the irrigation operations were only a part of its work. In 1923 Hitts became discouraged with his Texas farming attempt and turned complete control of the place over to his son-in-law, R.P. Conway, who abandoned the well in 1924 and sold the place to A.C. Hayes in 1928 and moved to Hereford where he still lives. The place is now in four different farms and Clyde Hayes owns the land around the well sites.

The holes and casing of these early irrigation attempts are still on the Hayes place and are occasionally checked by the Board of Water Engineers. In addition to the two holes mentioned there is a huge 24" hole and casing 100 yards east of the site of the 12" well.

This was drilled sometime between 1915 and 1923 and with it Hitts hoped to water 800 acres which it was the high point of. After drilling reached an unknown depth, the hole started caving in badly and it was abandoned. Hayes mentioned that he has thought of putting a smaller casing inside one of these large wells sometime and utilizing it for a well of his own.

Hayes occasionally plows up the 40 year old tile in the sub-irrigated patch. The apple trees are all dead now but a few pear trees are still living. A Bois d'arc, hedge that survives is dying slowly. The old casings, dead trees and one old irrigation valve are the mute reminders of the ambitious attempts of a man who foresaw the potentialities of a country that are just now being realized. Geo. Hitts died in Indiana in 1926 thinking that this country might not be worth irrigating after all.

In 1923 Hitts became discouraged with his Texas farming attempt—especially with the irrigation which he spent an estimated $250,000 on and with very little success. His son-in-law attributes this failure to the poor machinery and lack of a good market for their products. He says that the old timers had been calling them foolish "damn yankees" for attempting to irrigate for years and finally in 1923-24 they decided that maybe the cynics were right.

The holes and casing of these early irrigation attempts are occasionally checked by the Board of Water Engineers. The records of the state board show annual checks on the water level in the 4" well from 1938. From this date until 1948 the water level remained at 138 ft. In 1949 the level sank to 140 ft. and in 1950 check showed a depth of 142 ft. The last check, 1952, found the water level down to 148½ ft. The nearest well now in operation to the point of this checking is an 8" well located about 400 yards north of it.

THE FRIONA STAR, Thursday, April 23, 1953
"Uncle John" White Tells of Early Hotels; Alludes to Wampus Cat Tale.

That was many years ago and the day of the closed car had not yet come to pass, and the snow continued to fall, and the hands of the chauffeurs, riding in the open cars were becoming numb from the effect of the falling snow melting on them, as, it being in the early part of October, people generally had not begun carrying gloves with them in readiness for a change in the temperature from balmy autumn to the depth of winter, and the condition was something similar to holding one's hands in a tub of ice water.

At least one of these chauffeurs complained that his hands were becoming so numb that he would have to stop and place his hands under the hood of the engine to warm them. It chanced, however, that one of his passengers had in his overcoat pockets a pair of those old fashiond "jersey" gloves. They were knitted cotton just like the material of those old fashioned sweaters which ladies used to wear. The passenger drew them from his pockets and handed them to the chauffeur and they felt so good to his cold, wet hands, that he made the remainder of the trip in comfort. The shades of night were beginning to lower when this car, which was among the first to arrive, reached its destination.

The destination was a two-story frame hotel building which had been built and was owned and operated by the people of the land company, and where these people entertained as their guests the train load of home-seekers and prospective land buyers. It was some eighteen miles out on the prairie north west of Friona. The building was perhaps 60 to 74 feet long and about 25 or maybe 30 feet wide. The ground floor contained the lobby, the dining room and the kitchen, while the upper room was used as one vast bedroom and its floor was covered with one-person cots placed in rows across the short way of the building, with narrow aisles between the rows, leaving a space between the cots sufficient for the occupants to move between them while preparing for their night's repose.

The cars continued to arrive from Friona in singles, pairs or groups until all excursionists had arrived, which was some two hours or more after night fall. The building was comfortably warmed throughout and bright fires glowing in the coal-burning stove; and the guests were agreeably surprised to find the same force of cooks and waiters there to serve them that so ably served them on the train during their trip to Friona, and the first

88

call to supper was issued at about the usual supper time. It was then jet black outside and the snow still falling, though the wind was abating. It was about nine o'clock when the last of the guests had arrived and all had been fed. Some of the guests going outside to see about the weather, found that the wind had entirely subsided and the stars were shining brightly, and after all had been warmed and fed, they began ascending the stairs to the large bedroom on the second floor. That room was soon a babel, (sometimes almost a roar) of voices as the guests were being assigned to their individual cots.

This tumult of voices continued for, perhaps an hour, but was beginning to die down as the guests retired to their respective cots for the night but just at that time two belated drivers arrived with their cargo of guests and after eating their supper, came up to the sleeping room.

Of course, some one wanted to know what had made them so late, and they at once began telling about what a large "wampus" they had encountered on their way out, and it looked for awhile that they would not be able to get by it. It was sure a big one—the biggest they had ever seen, and it refused to give the road and threatened to attack them. It sure was a big 'un and if it had "sot" onto them, they might all have been killed. Then the other fellows in the room began to tell what big "wampuses" they had seen and how dangerous they were; but our boys maintained that this one was the biggest one that ever was, for they had seen lots of "wampuses." There weren't any more as big as that 'un. And so the talk went on until some "sucker" probably from Illinois bit. And he took the whole thing, hook, sinker, cork and all and made off with it. There was then a few seconds of deathly silence in the room, for they all wanted to know. He just asked what sort of a creature is one of them "wampuses." Then one of the boys told him, and such a shout and noise as went up. There were yells and screams and guffahs and cackles and gurgles, almost enough to blow the roof off, and it lasted for several minutes. Then when all was silent again the "biter" broke the silence by saying: Well. I just wanted to know and it seemed like no one else was going to

ask what it was and now I know, and that started another roar.

Early Friona's Bear and Wolves

During the nineteen twenties a young man became engineer on the Santa Fe railroad and made regular runs out of Amarillo to Clovis, New Mexico, then back to Amarillo. The east end of his run was Waynoka, Oklahoma.

He often told of experiences on these runs. During the early days of Friona, when Prospectors and Land Hungry men were brought to Parmer County, one interesting story was of a pet bear. One day, the train had stopped at the depot in Friona. The train conductor was standing by the train door when he was nudged from behind. Thinking it was a fellow worker wanting his attention, he turned around to see a grown bear. He was so startled that he climbed the ladder to the top of the train.

Another story is of prairie wolves. On a fall night run a new fireman kept seeing objects jump across the track in the flashing train light and asked this engineer—Noah A. Lane—what the objects were. Mr. Lane, loving a joke, said that they were prairie wolves crossing the track. Upon arriving in Amarillo the young fireman resigned his job and went back to New York City, his original home. He said he couldn't live in a country so full of wild wolves. (The wolves were only huge tumble weeds that had broken from their stems by strong winds and being blown about.)

Mr. Ed White Sr. remembers the Bruner Bear. The Bruners ranched northwest of Friona and would bring the Pet Bear into town riding in the back seat of their car—says Mr. White. The Bear owners moved to Amarillo and became neighbors of Mr. Pane's. But one day the grocery-boy became frightened by him and scattered his groceries on the ground. The bear had to be disposed of as City folks and bears don't mix. Several Friona people have had their picture taken with the Bear. The Bruner boys would go swimming in the farm pond but Brother Bear, fearing for their safety, would pull them out!

THE HEREFORD BRAND
Tuesday, June 19, 1923
TWO BROTHERS DROWNED IN Friona LAKE: SEARCHERS FIND BODIES TUESDAY
Russel and Mark Reeve were repairing Telephone Line When Boat Capsized and Brothers Go Together

HIGH WAVES HAMPER RECOVERY

Volunteers From Friona, Hereford, Farwell and Elsewhere Put in Hours Dragging, Diving and other efforts without avail until Early Tuesday afternoon.

The body of Russel Reeve was brought to the surface about 1:00 Tuesday afternoon with the aid of grab hooks fastened on the end of a windmill sucker-rod. It was found near the telephone pole where the nephew who was with them had said the accident happened. The body was brought at once to Friona. A short time afterwards the report reached here that the second body had also been brought to the surface from the same pool. No more details were available before going to press.

Friona, June 17----Perhaps the saddest affair in the history of this community occurred here about four o'clock Sunday when two brothers, Russel and Mark Reeve, aged respectively 27 years and 23 years, were drowned in a lake about eleven miles north of this place.

The young men were out in a small boat trying to repair a telephone line when in some manner the boat rocked and Mark fell overboard. He was unable to swim and became slightly strangled but Russel sprang to his assistance and brought him to the boat and told him to hold on and they would get to shore, but in his alarm he tried to get into the boat and thus upset it. Once more Russell rescued him but again he let go of the boat. Again the brother undertook his rescue and the two went down together and came up no more. William Guyer, their nephew, a boy of about 16 years of age, was with them in the boat and made several attempts to rescue them by diving but failed to reach them. Seeing his own strength was failing and that the boat was drifting away from him, he swam to it and floated safely to the shore which was about 200 yards away. The water where the brothers went down was about twelve feet deep. A call for help reached town and within an hour nearly every man and boy and several of the ladies and girls of the town were on their way to the lake. This fact alone would prove the very high esteem in which these young men were held by the entire community.

Russel Reeve came to this country from Indiana about the year 1916 and Mark, with his mother and three sisters came a few years later and all located on their farm about nine miles west of town where they have since resided. They were two of America's noblest young men and their untimely death is a severe loss to the entire community.

Large parties of Hereford men hurried to Friona at the first report of the drowning of the two men to lend what aid they could. Sunday night Dr. Hicks was called to attend to Mrs. Reeve.

The unfortunate accident stirred the community and deep interest has been manifest and much sympathy expressed. Returning searchers reported that the big lake, swollen by recent heavy rains, carried choppy waves that made boat work unsafe and hard. A raft was anchored over the spot where the boys went down and two Mexicans dived and dragged all of Sunday night and part of Monday without result. Every conceivable plan was tried up to noon Tuesday without result.

Survivors:

mother: Mrs. Adeline Reeve

brother: Floyd White Reeve

sisters: Rachel, Margaret, and Frances of the home

Mrs. F.T. Schlenker; Mrs. John Guyer; Mrs. Bert Ashton

Mrs. Oscar Schlenker; Mrs. Ray George

FRIONA STAR, Friday, May 28, 1948
PIONEER FRIONA NEWSPAPER MAN OBSERVES 80th BIRTHDAY

J.W. White, pioneer resident of Parmer County and founder of The Friona Star, last Sunday observed his eightieth birthday. The occasion was observed much in the same fashion which "Uncle John" has lived—quietly, among his relatives, and his friends and fellow townsmen.

Mr. White moved to Texas as a young

UNCLE JOHN WHITE

man, locating in Parmer County. Since that time, he has engaged in farming, insurance business, city clerk, and probably greatest of all have been his endeavors in the newspaper field.

"Uncle John," as Mr. White has come to be called by hundreds of friends and neighbors in the Friona territory, actually founded the Friona Star. In 1925, answering an ever-growing need for a community publication, Mr. White made a deal to have The Star printed in Clovis. A few weeks later, he sold the publication to Seth B. Holman of Hereford, and remained with the paper as editor and manager.

When Mr. Holman sold the Hereford and Friona papers to Lindsey Nunn and Dave Warren in 1929, Mr. White remained as editor for several months and was later replaced by Mr. Barfine, who operated The Star for a period of 11 months. When Dave Warren took over the interest of Mr. Nunn, he returned operation of The Star To Mr. White.

With exception of the 11-month period, Mr. White has been continuously manager and editor of The Star since it was founded.

Many times, it seemed that the newspaper could no longer exist—and several times its continuation has been due solely to the sacrifice, persistence and determination of John White. For several months he set the paper by hand and printed it on a small job press in order to retain mailing permits and to offer the best available service to the community.

"UNCLE JOHN" WHITE
Late Editor Describes Early-Day Friona

Friona Star
Sept. 3, 1970

(Editor's note: The following piece was written by long-time editor of the Friona Star, J.W. ("Uncle John") White, on the 35th anniversary of his arriving in Friona. It is reprinted here because of its historical significance.)

This is Tuesday, August 16th, 1949. Thirty-five years ago, August 16, 1914, on Sunday forenoon, in company with my wife and children and the handful of personal belongings, I arrived at Friona to make my home. I have lived here ever since, and expect to fulfill my days in Friona, I have never regreted that move.

At that time Friona had an estimated population of 150 people. There was but one church building. The Union Congregational. The Baptist had recently organized, the Methodist organized within the next few weeks, with nine members, but neither church had a building. There was a 2 story brick school building, employing three teachers, known as a 3rd class high school. The only kind of grain elevators here at that time was scoop shovels. There were several vacant houses, but as the weeks passed by, these houses were bought by farmers and cattlemen and moved to the country.

There were no paved streets and wagon roads led out from the business part of town in all directions heading straight toward the place the drivers wished to go, without regard to street lines. No one knew there were such things.

A few acres here and there over the prairies had been broken out and were in cultivation, making little green spots on the prairie, something like, I suppose, oasis are on the deserts. As I remember it, there was but one automobile owned in Friona. There are more now. In fact, anyone that does not own an automobile now is not considered to be much "Pumpkins." I still do not own one and more than likely I never shall. Would not be allowed to drive if I had one.

At that time, the airplane was only beginning to be considered as a real fact, but not

LOOKING SOUTH ON MAIN STREET, FRIONA—ABOUT 1910.

more than two persons would ever be able to ride together in one. They just would not be able to carry more. At that time a man simply could not make a living at farming in this country. The soil and climate were fit only to grow grass. True the few fields of fine row crops growing here at that time bore evidence to the contrary, but—

I soon learned that I was the only man who had little enough sense to move to Friona.

Since the George G. Wright Land Boom had ceased, everybody that was able had been moving out, just as the houses moved out of town for a while after I arrived. When I would meet a man and stop for a little chat, of course his first question was, "What is your name?" And when I had told him, his ejaculation was, "Oh, you are the new man." And by this I soon came to understand that no one had moved here for a long time, and which I learned later to be a fact. I did not mind this, and was, later quite proud of it, as it won for me the only distinction I have ever enjoyed—that of being the "ONLY DURNED FOOL IN THE PANHANDLE."

And even that was a short-lived distinction, for it seemed that it was only a few months until people began moving to Friona, and not many weeks passed that some new family did not arrive.

The cattle men were very kind to me, however, and they told me if I succeeded in raising any "feed"—as row crops were called then—that they would buy it, as they sometimes used a little "feed" but mostly depended on grass for their cattle, and that sooner or later I would be able to get hold of a "little bunch of cattle," then I would be all right.

We moved immediately from the car to a little farm, which I had rented during a previous visit two weeks before, but we had not been quite as "durned fools" as our neighbors had suspected. We had two fine horses, three fair milk cows, and our two or three dozen hens. We did not put in much of our time driving into town, but when we came we brought some eggs, some cream and sometimes some butter, which the people here seemed very glad to get, thus we were never hungry because we had nothing to eat. We fared well. We never had to sleep out of doors and we had enough clothing, though it was not fine nor costly, but about the same as our neighbors had, and they sure were GOOD neighbors.

People told us our big eastern horses could not stand this climate and should not rush them. We had no occasion to rush them, for the simple reason, that they walked as fast as our neighbors' horses trotted. Neither would

92

EARLY DAY FRIONA . . . This is a view of Friona, taken close to the time written about by "Uncle John" White in the accompanying article. It is taken from the vacinity of the old Bill McGlothlin place, looking east toward the business district of town.

OLD LOCATION . . . The location used by Friona State Bank for some 40 years, at Fifth and Main, is shown shortly after it was completed, sometime in 1910. The building was used in recent years as the Masonic Hall, and now is owned by the Calvary Baptist Church for its mission.

they eat this sorghum grain, so I bought some corn from some one who had shipped a car load in and when I fed them, I would put corn in their boxes and a bundle of maize in the manger, and do you know, those horses were as big fools as my family and I had been. They pounced in on those bundles of maize and devoured them before they paid any attention to the corn. We had also brought three pretty nice hogs with us, and had it not been for them, I do not know how I would have gotten rid of the corn, for even our hens did not care for it when they could get those nice little maize grains for food.

We also brought with us, what we considered a mighty good plow in Illinois. I had a small strip of sod land to plow, so I hitched my big horses to the iron plow and started in on the job and was getting along just fine so I thought. While I was at it one of my neighbor's drove by and yelled out to me to take that old two-horse plow back to Illinois with me. I replied, "Who said I am going back to Illinois?" Two other men in wagons, driving in from New Mexico with loads of grain, and when they saw us turning the sod, the one on front turned in his seat and called out to his neighbor, "Turnin' it with TWO, By Gog!"

One of my neighbors that I gained when I came here told me there were two kinds of home seekers that came in on the "Wright" excursions. Some were "kickers" and some were "stickers," and there were more kickers than there were stickers and that accounted for the sparse population at that time. But in the thirty-five years great changes have been wrought, and many of those good neighbors have gone hence. The city has grown from its

150 souls to an estimated 1,600 or 1,800 people. The territory has become populated, and all have learned that this country will produce many things other than whitefaced cows and calves, in fact there are not so many things in the line of agricultural products that cannot be produced here.

Bank Opened In 1908
FRIONA STAR,
Sept. 3, 1970

Friona State Bank traces its beginning to June 1, 1908, when George C. Wright, owner of the George G. Wright Land Company, opened the first bank in Friona.

The bank, which opened as First State Bank, was first located in a wooden frame building at the corner of Sixth and Main Streets, at the same location where Friona Federal Credit Union is located today.

D.W. McMillan managed the bank for Wright, who served as bank president, although he did not live in Friona.

The land developer sold the bank to A.W. Henschel, who was working for the George G. Wright Land Company as early as 1908. Henschel had been in the Goodwine home in Indiana before they moved to Texas.

Henschel went to work for the bank in Friona around 1910 or 1911. He bought it from Wright in 1919, and became its second president.

Construction on the red brick building at Fifth and Main had begun in 1909, and it was occupied during 1910. This building became the bank's second home, and housed the operation for the next 40 years of its history.

ORIGINAL BUILDING . . . The above building, which was located at Sixth and Main Streets, where Friona Credit Union is located today, was the first location of Friona State Bank, which opened its doors as First State Bank on June 1, 1908. The above shot, taken a few years later when John Gischler had a general mer- chandise store at the location, shows the Gischler family. Left to right are Mr. and Mrs. John Gischler, Luella (Mrs. Carl Maurer), Constance (Mrs. Lawrence Walker), Viola (Mrs. George Treider), Ruben and Elwin Gischler.

Henschel was killed in an automobile wreck on September 22, 1926, the day after the bank suffered its first armed robbery. On January 31, 1927, Margaret M. Henschel, his widow, became the bank's third president.

Bank Presidents

Name	Tenure
·+George G. Wright	1908-1919
A.W. Henschel	1919-1926
Mrs. A.W. Henschel	1927-1930
+Bruce McLean	1930-1944
+S.H. Osborn	1944-1959
Frank A. Spring	1959-present
+Inactive president	

Friona Bank Robbed
FRIONA STAR,
Sept. 3, 1970

Bank robbery is a crime which has been dramatized all the way from the old western movies to the more up-to-date "cops and rob- bers" flicks.

And, in reality, most banks of any age have experienced at least an attempt at the illicit removal of their cash.

Friona State Bank has experienced three robberies in its history, but the last one was over 34 years ago. The amount of money taken in the robberies ranged from only $95 to $3,713. Robbers were apprehended in two of the hold-ups, and convicted of their crimes.

The bank was first robbed early in the morning of Monday, September 21, 1926. G.D. Anderson, cashier; and Jesse M. Os- born, assistant cashier, were the only ones in the bank when three armed men entered the building (at Fifth and Main) at about 9:20 a.m.

One robber took charge of the door and

the other two covered the bank officials. Anderson and Osborn each reponded to the admonition to "Put 'em up" but Henschel failed to act until a third admonition with a gun placed in front of him, convinced him that the intruders were serious.

During this time, three customers arrived in the bank—A.B. Cole, a farmer living at the edge of town; Roy C. Cox, a garage operator, and Mrs. R.O. Sampley.

The robbers tied up Osborn and Anderson with their hands behind their backs, and ordered Henschel to open the safe, or they'd "blow his head off." Henschel told them to "blow away," for he could not open the safe, as the time lock was on.

The robber then ordered Henschel into the vault and closed the door. The men took what money was in sight, which amounted to about $95 being only what had been taken in after closing time Saturday evening and earlier that Monday morning.

After the robbers left, the bank officials pushed upon the vault door, which had not been securely fastened, and spread the alarm. Within a few minutes, high-powered cars filled with armed men went out in all directions, in pursuit of the bandits. However, they were unable to sight them, or to even be certain they were on their trail, according to an account in the Friona Star.

On Wednesday of the following week, Henschel, Anderson and Roy Cox went to Amarillo in an effort to identify two men whom Amarillo officials thought might have been implemented in the robbery.

Upon their return from Amarillo, the car driven by Mr. Henschel overturned near Summerfield and he was killed.

Nine months later, on Friday, June 3, 1927, the bank was robbed again. This time the robbery happened during the noon hour. Mrs. Carl (Luella) Maurer recalls that two men were inside the bank, and one was outside. The Maurers lived across the street south of the bank.

Mrs. Maurer said she noticed a fellow out front, sitting on the bicycles of her children. She inquired what he wanted, and he said he was "just looking around."

The two men who entered the bank found Jesse M. Osborn, assistant cashier, alone in the building. They forced Osborn to open the safe, removed $3,713.30 in cash and escaped.

One of the bandits wore a mask, and it was he who forced Osborn to the rear of the bank at the point of a gun. Two customers, Floyd T. Schlenker, and a second man who was unidentified, entered the bank during the robbery, and they, with Osborn, were locked in the vault where they were found about thirty minutes later by G.D. Anderson, when he returned from lunch.

Following the robbery, Carl Maurer and others gave chase in their cars. They followed the bandits northwest of town, following the tracks in the dirt, to the breaks west of Vega, at a place known as "Mohair Canyon."

They were unable to locate the men, but did find money sacks and wrappers, where the bandits evidentally divided the money. It was later learned that one of the bandits had a gun pointed at Maurer, and would have shot him had he come any closer to his hiding place behind a rock.

Red Cummings was arrested within three weeks in El Paso. He was tried and convicted of taking part in the robbery, and sentenced to 14 years in the penitentiary.

Jim Bryant was also arrested, tried, and received 14 years in jail.

Many years later, E.G. Gonser of Friona was on a hunting trip to New Mexico and was directed to a stable in Santa Fe when he needed to leave his horses overnight.

The man running the stable, and leather goods store, upon finding out Gonser was from Friona, is said to have told him "I robbed the bank in Friona once." He said he learned leather work while in prison, and had gone into business in Santa Fe.

Friona State Bank was robbed the third time on Monday, June 29, 1936, at about 3:30 in the afternoon. Two armed men entered the bank. Those present were Mr. and Mrs. Charlie McLean, Orma White (Flippin) bookkeeper, and Hugh P. Lee, a customer.

Orma was in the back, doing her posting work, and did not know what was going on at first.

Mr. and Mrs. McLean, Lee and Orma were forced to the back and asked to lie down. Having corralled the employees into the bank, the intruder announced, "This is a hold-up." He then proceded to rifle the cash drawer of its contents, and asked McLean to go into the vault and get all the money it contained.

McLean did as he was told, but not knowing where all the money had been placed that morning, missed some of it. There was in the vault what the bank called its "dummy" bag, filled with packages of worthless papers, and this bag was handed over to the stick-up man.

The men then left, having with them $964 in actual money.

Less than a week later, Fort Worth police arrested two escaped convicts after a high-speed chase and an accident in which one of the men was hurt. When captured, the two had with them over $600 in cash and practically all the travelers checks which had been taken from Friona State Bank.

One of the men, Herbert Alvin Stanley, had been serving a 99-year sentence in Huntsville for a 1930 murder in Fort Worth. The other man was T.C. Britton. He also had a criminal record.

The two men were tried and sentenced to prison terms in Alcatraz by a Federal court in Amarillo.

By co-incidence, Frank A. Spring, the current bank president, had quit his job at the bank four days prior to the robbery, for another job. F.B.I. men investigating the robbery asked Spring about the "circumstances of his leaving."

Spring said he was a "relieved man" when the bank robbers were caught.

THE FRIONA STAR, Sunday, September 2, 1973

NOW FRIONA PUBLIC LIBRARY
"Old Hotel Glories In Its Past, Serves The Future

Part of the heritage of the Panhandle and South Plains of Texas includes "prospecting." Not prospecting for gold or silver or precious gems, but something more tangible and productive ... land ... rich, fertile farmland.

According to a Works Projects Administration (WPA) report filed in early 1940 or 1941, the Syndicate Hotel, located 12 miles southeast of Friona is "the most pretentious building for many miles around, looks much

FIRST CARETAKER . . . Mrs. W.C. Wilkerson is pictured at the left with other unidentified persons in a picture made in front of the Syndicate Hotel. She was the first caretaker of the hotel when it opened in 1926. Mrs. Wilkerson is the sister of Mrs. E.G. Adams of Friona, who served as caretaker after her sister left the hotel.
(E.G. Adams Photo)

out of place, surrounded on all sides by flat farm country."

"It reflects the past glories of the time when money was more plentiful and people were eager to begin a new life in a new land. Although it is now drab and worn looking, it is still a handsome building."

The Syndicate Hotel was constructed in 1925 and opened for business in 1926 by the Capitol Freehold Land and Investment Company, Limited. They built the hotel to accommodate land buyers who were brought into this country when the ranches were being sold to farmers.

Former caretakers of the now defunct hotel said most of the prospective land buyers were brought from East Texas and Oklahoma, as well as Arkansas. Many of the prospects were oil people who had been in on the early oil finds in the East Texas-Oklahoma areas.

When constructed, the hotel was a nine-room, two story stucco structure and was erected at a cost of $18,000, according to the report. And when it was first opened, it was operated by Mr. and Mrs. W.C. Wilkerson, who had moved to Parmer County from Oklahoma. Mrs. Wilkerson, who visits her sister, Mrs. E.G. Adams in Friona, and her husband had a number of helpers as at times they had more than 135 "prospectors" as guests to feed.

The first floor of the building housed the

AN IMPOSING STRUCTURE . . . At one time, the old Syndicate Hotel, above, was perhaps the most imposing structure around in Parmer County, as it set majestically aloof east of Hub. The old hotel housed hundreds of prospective land buyers in the years gone by. When it was officially closed as a hotel, it was purchased by the Friona American Legion and now houses the Friona Public Library and the American Legion meeting rooms just south of the city park in Friona.

(E.G. Adams Photo)

lobby, dining room, office, bath, kitchen and living quarters for the caretakers. Upstairs were two large bedrooms, a hall and a bath.

Installed was a Delco light plant, and a windmill furnished water which was piped into the hotel, with large coal stoves being used for heating and cooking purposes.

During the busy years as a hotel, the Syndicate Hotel group "sometimes couldn't sleep them all," recalled Mrs. Adams, who also worked as caretaker at the hotel in the later days it was in operation. "The drivers would bring in the prospective buyers five at a time and it could be that several car loads would come in at one time.

"Once in awhile, some of the men had to stay in town. We had 17 beds, but that wouldn't take care of all the men.

"Lots of wives, but very few children came along on the buying trips. The oil people sure bought a lot of land. I remember that a man by the name of Gammon bought quite a bit of land, and was one of the first to be brought in by the Capitol Land Syndicate," she added. "He is still alive and lives in the home of Mr. and Mrs. Jim Griffith on fifth Street now."

When the prospective buyers were brought to Parmer County, they stayed for two nights at the Syndicate Hotel and were fed five meals. "No, there was really no big problem in cooking for 100 or more men," recalled Mrs. Wilkerson. "We had plenty of help and it was nothing unusual to cook at least a quarter of beef for a meal. We also had lots of canned vegetables and fruits. We raised our own back during that time. A lot of the meat was canned also, and we served fresh vegetables when they were in season.

"Seventy-five men were brought in at once when the hotel first opened," she added, "and the men came in too early. My sister had to go to her house and get more silver, she added her own since there wasn't enough yet at the hotel. And the Delco light plant hadn't

been installed yet, so my sister (Mrs. Wilkerson) used coal oil lights all over the place."

In later years, after the hotel closed as a part of the land acquisition parcel offered in Parmer County, Mrs. Adams continued to live on the premises as caretaker before moving into Friona. After it closed formally as a hotel, many snowbound people and duck hunters still utilized the facility.

As late as the WPA report in 1940 or 1941, it was reported "At the present time only a part of the hotel is being used. Vinton Bolte and wife, whose maiden name was Mary Pesch, and family are living there and acting as caretakers for the property. The place has not been operated as a hotel since 1931, but there is quite a bit of unsold land surrounding it, and if there should be another land boom, the hotel would again be opened for business."

The predicted land boom was interrupted by World War II and following the war it became obvious to many that the land boom would probably never happen, so the facility was listed for sale.

It was first purchased by the Muleshoe American Legion, who pondered the situation and found they had no solution to attempting to cross the draw (Running Water Draw) with the huge structure, so a decision was made to sell it again.

The second purchasers were the members of the Friona American Legion, who are the present owners of the building. They moved the building to its present location just south of the Friona City Park.

In the interim years since it was moved to Friona, the building housed a number of varied businesses before it was converted to the use of the Friona Public Library. After extensive remodeling in the building, although many of the original features and fixtures are still part of the structure, the large arched windows in front are gone, although faint marks can be seen where the imposing windows were removed and made smaller.

The American Legion utilizes the upstairs portion of the building, which formerly housed the prospective land buyers and the former bedrooms have been converted to meeting rooms. All the downstairs is used by the library, and where hungry land buyers were fed in the dining room, now children browse through the children's section of books and in the former caretaker's bedroom, you can find the best in fiction.

The lobby remains that . . . a lobby for the library and what was the kitchen is a work and reference room.

A place to dream of tomorrow and to build the future still holds true, but now, it is through books and study . . . the old hotel still holds the promise of a better tomorrow as people of all ages live through the works of another age and time.

A hotel no more, but still a vital part in the future for the Friona area. Still part of the heritage that is Parmer County and Friona.

To Editor Bill Ellis and to all of the subscribers who have cooperated with him in establishing a library of "old issues," we are indebted for the following articles. We hope you will find them of interest in that they reflect the growth of Friona and Parmer County.

FRIONA STAR, September 9, 1927.
2,000 ACRE WHEAT FIELDS WILL BE SEEN HERE DURING THIS SEASON
Wheat acreage in this vicinity expected to far surpass all previous plantings; Bit outfits run drills night and day in order to get ground seeded while there is ample moisture in store.

Wheat sowing in the Friona territory is in full swing just now, many farmers working night and day. A few farmers are finishing this week. Ford Welsh and Marvin Whaley each are sowing about two thousand acres. Mr. Welsh has been running three outfits with a night shift of workers and has averaged about 200 acres a day. Other men with large acreages are Turner Parr Company, J.C. Wilkison, Osborn Bros. and Fallwell Brothers. They expect to finish within the next few days. The smaller crops by Carl Maurer, L.L. Lillard, F.W. Reeve and others and those of a quarter-section, 160 acres, and smaller are well under way.

Practically all this earlier planted wheat is on summer fallowed land or well prepared land. If the weather continues favorable during September and October quite a large acreage of wheat will be planted after the row crops are harvested.

The wheat being sown far surpasses the acreage of last year here, and a like condition is manifest all over the Panhandle. It is becoming a difficult matter to supply the demand for wheat drills. According to the Amarillo Daily News, 800 drills have been sold by the International Harvester Company alone this fall, and of course that is not taking into consideration any of the old drills that are in use or any sold by any of the other companies.

THE FRIONA STAR, Friday, October 21, 1927
TEXAS UTILITIES COMPANY TO INSTALL ELECTRIC LIGHTS IN FRIONA
Local Business Men Meet To Arrange Final Details of Cost.

Company Officials agree to put in street lights until town is incorporated, after which regular contract may be signed. Funds necessary raised by subscription list circulated by J.J. Horton.

At a meeting of the business men of the town with F.H. Oberthier, manager of the Texas Utilities Company of Hereford, and Mr. Scott, general manager of the same company, at Mr. M.A. Crum's real estate office last Friday night, arrangements were made whereby the town will be lighted by electricity in the near future.

The terms of the contract provide that the town will buy at least ten street lights at a flat rate of $2.25 each per month for a period of not less than eighteen months, and that the work of installing these will begin within three months, and that the current will be turned on within six months from date of contract.

As the town is not incorporated, these lights will be paid for by voluntary subscriptions for the time above mentioned, and it is expected that the town will have money in the treasury from revenues raised from taxes by the time this contract shall have expired. The use of current in public and business buildings and in private homes will, of course, be a matter to be decided by those in charge of such buildings, but it is expected that the greater number of .private houses and practically all the business houses will subscribe for lights and power where needed.

FRIONA STAR, Friday, June 17, 1927
FAMILIES OF EARLY SETTLERS MEET

A most enjoyable meeting of members of the families of the earier settlers of Friona and vicinity occurred at the home of Mrs. Minnie Goodwine at the south side of town Sunday.

Each of the families taking part in the occasion took baskets of food and a regular picnic dinner was enjoyed together. It is estimated that over one hundred persons were present, consisting in a large part of the Goodwine, Schlenker, Reeve, Guyer, and Clennin families, and was given in honor of members of these families who are visiting here from a distance. They were Mr. and Mrs. F.E. Clennin, recently of California, Mrs. Adaline Reeve and daughter, Miss Rachel; Mr. and Mrs. L.E. Goodwine and son, David Leland; Mr. and Mrs. Willard Schlenker; Harold Schlenker, all of Long Beach, California; Miss Florence and Beth Schlenker and Mrs. W.W. Burns, of Des Moines, Iowa.

Among those present from the neighboring town were Mr. and Mrs. R.G. Clennin and children, Mr. and Mrs. L.E. Gordon and children, of Tulia, and Mr. and Mrs. Homer Fox, of Hereford.

In addition to these quite a number of the intimate friends of the families from Friona and vicinity were also present. It is needless to say that the day was most happily spent by all present.

THE FRIONA STAR, Friday, March 25, 1927
RAZING AN OLD LANDMARK

The old frame building on the east side of Main Street, formerly occupied by the T.J. Crawford store, is now being razed and the material removed from the ground.

This is one of the oldest buildings in the town, having been built about 1907 or 1908. It was a two story building and the upper story was for a time used as a hall for public functions of various kinds.

It is rumored that when this building is removed it will be replaced by a modern structure in the no distant future, similar to the one recently completed by Mr. Crawford which now houses his store.

If this rumor becomes fact it will be another valuable addition to the business portion of the town.

THE FRIONA STAR, Friday, March 25, 1927
STREET GRADING NOW GOING ON IN OUR TOWN

The work of grading the two blocks on Main Street was begun Tuesday afternoon. The block between Sixth and Seventh Streets was first prepared for the grader and has been graded.

After grading, the street will be surfaced with gravel of a kind known as caliche, which forms a hard smooth surface and which we hope will give us a permanent hard-surfaced thoroughfare.

THE FRIONA STAR, Friday, February 11, 1927
SYNDICATE OIL TEST

The oil test on Capitol Syndicate land, being put down by the Humble oil company 15 miles east of Farwell, was down 900 feet last Sunday. The bit is in red clay and it is expected another strata of water will be drilled through before long. Since losing the tools in the well some time ago no further difficulties have been encountered and the bit is going down at a rapid rate.

THE FRIONA STAR, Friday, December 2, 1927
"Material For Friona Lights Ordered and Rolling"--Judge Kelso
Utilities Company Prepares To Install Electric Lights

Power plant here expected to be ready for operation by Christmas time.

Workmen busy all week remodeling buildings on property to be occupied by plant. Friona enthused by prospect.

The arrival here Saturday evening of a huge truck and trailer bearing a huge 80-horse power oil engine which was unloaded on the property recently purchased by the Texas Utilities Company, was the first evidence that Friona is soon to be blessed with a series of street lights.

The large combined engine and generator was unloaded Sunday morning and workmen have been busy all week overhauling it and getting the plant ready for complete installation as soon as the ground for its location can be made ready for it.

Other workmen for the company have been busy repairing and remodeling the buildings on this property which faces on Main Street and lies just one lot south of Seventh Street. Some of the smaller buildings will be removed entirely from the premises.

It is reported that the installation of the power plant will be accomplished by Christmas and if the poles and lines and other equipment, which have been ordered and are expected to arrive at any time, shall be installed by that time, we are told that there is no reason why Friona shall not have electric light and power by Christmas day.

Our people are enthusiastic over the prospects of the coming of lights and are high in their appreciation of the efforts being put forth by the Texas Utilities Company to give us the service so much earlier than the date given in the contract. Of course we realize that there are many hindrances which may occur, and for which this company can in no way be responsible, but the fact that the company is making every possible effort to give us service at the earliest possible date surely meets with our approval.

INCORPORATION IN 1928

Early in 1928, a petition was presented to Parmer County Judge E.F. Lokey "to determine if tract could be incorporated into a town with a commission form of government, to bear the name of Friona, to elect a mayor and two commissioners to hold office until the first Tuesday of April following if the town is incorporated and to show that the town has 200 inhabitants."

Names appearing on the petition will be recognized by many present citizens. They were Mr. and Mrs. J.A. Blackwell, O.F. Lange, Raymond Jones, J.L. Landrum, Howard G. Morris, J.A. Guyer, W.H. Warren, M.A. Crum, J.J. Horton, John Gischler, Reubin T. Guschler, B.T. Galloway, Mr. and Mrs. H.P. Eberling, W.Y. Preston, Mr. and Mrs. J.R. Roden, F.L. Spring, L.R. Dilger, Jack Anderson, A.B. Short, V.E. Hart, V.E. Weir, C.S. Burns, Carl C. Maurer, E.S. White, T.A. Glossup and H.A. Bennett.

The petition was considered Feb. 10, 1928. It carried 65 to 34. Election was held in the office of The Friona Star with M.A. Crum as presiding judge. John White was named mayor and J.A. Blackwell and Jesse Osborn as commissioners.

FRIONA STAR, Friday, March 23, 1928.
FRIONA NOW INCORPORATED CITY BY VOTE 65 FOR AND 34 AGAINST

Incorporation Has 65 Votes Wins By Majority of 31 Votes

Friona enters stage of cityhood at Incorporation Election Monday. A satisfactory voting strength was shown. Proposition wins almost two to one. White, Mayor, Blackwell, Osborn Commissioners.

At an election held here Monday for the purpose of determining whether or not Friona should become an organized municipality or remain a mere hamlet, 101 votes were cast.

There is perhaps 125 legally qualified voters within the described limits of the corporation. Of this probably 125 voters, 101 came to the polls and expressed their preference in the matter; sixty-five voting in favor of the proposition and thirty-four in opposition, giving a majority of thirty-one in favor of incorporating.

Since no nominations had been made for either of the offices and none had entered the race voluntarily for either office, the voters were left the privilege of making their own ticket, and many and varied were the candidates voted for. There were nine persons who received votes for mayor and perhaps twice that many for commissioners. A rather novel feature was that each person voted for mayor also received a few votes for commissioner. Of the votes cast for mayor John White received 34, being a plurality of ten votes. This being the same number that was cast against the proposition, it might appear that those who voted for the new mayor, also voted against the proposition.

Of the votes cast for commissioners Jerry A. Blackwell, of the Blackwell Hdw. & Furn. and Jesse M. Osborn, cashier of the Friona State Bank, received the highest number of votes, there being 22 for Mr. Blackwell and 20 for Mr. Osborn, and they were declared elected as commissioners.

A complete history of the laws that govern the city of Friona would be too lengthy and the following notes contain only the early ordinances that were passed when Friona was in infancy.

The first ordinance to be entered on the books involved the problem of sanitation. Adopted May 1, 1928, not even two months after incorporation, the law was for the regulation and cleanliness of outside toilets, with the specific reference that the buildings must be fly-proof.

In 1928, traffic problems existed just as they do today, and the second law on the books was to establish a speed limit (20 miles per hour) and to regulate the driving of tractors on Main Street, also to establish curb parking.

When the officials passed a law to regulate and suppress hog raising or keeping within the city limits, they were specific on what the property owner could do. The ordinance states "no hogs in blocks 62, 63, 76, 77, 82 and 83—no one to keep more than one hog to the city lot in any other block, all lots of pens must contain not less than 600 square feet of space for each hog confined therein."

All of the above laws were passed in the very beginning of Friona city government. Then in June of 1928, one of the most important grants for the comfort of the citizens was made. It was the initial agreement with Texas Utilities Co. to construct, maintain and operate an electric lighting and power plant, furnishing electric lights and power to the public.

The fifth law pertaining to Frionans declared it unlawful for a person to be intoxicated on the streets of the city or in any public place. A twin ordinance to the one above forbade fighting within the city limits.

It was declared unlawful to allow any kind of domestic animal to run at large within the city limits, such as horses, mules, burros, cattle, hogs, sheep, etc.

More or less taken for granted now was the rule that all poles used for support of wires for public utilities should be placed along the alleys or streets other than Main Street.

Progress continued and the next franchise to better living conditions was the grant of West Texas Co. to establish natural gas for lights, heat and power. Following on the heels of this franchise was an ordinance letting the contract for the construction of the waterworks.

From that time, the number of laws appearing on the books to govern Friona, have increased as rapidly as the situations arise to demand the regulations.

But none show the growth and the demands quite so much as the first early laws that are recorded here.

THE FRIONA STAR, Friday, October 25, 1929
OUT OF 80 VOTES CAST IN WATER WORKS ELECTION, 76 FAVORED PROPOSITION; TO START SOON

The question as to whether or not Friona shall have a municipally owned water system seems to have been definitely decided by the election here Monday.

The election was called for the purpose of deciding whether the proposition that the city should install a municipally owned water system at a contract cost of $38,130.80 be accepted or rejected. There was a total number of eighty votes cast, seventy-six for the proposition and four opposed.

As was stated in last week's Star, the advertisement for bids for the construction of such a system brought a return of five bids for the contract, and at the letting held in the city the bids were opened and it was found that the Sherman Machine and Iron Works of Oklahoma City had placed the lowest bid, which was $38,630.80, and was awarded the contract subject to the vote of the people cast in last Monday's election.

PROPOSED REMOVAL OF COUNTY SEAT

A page ad in the Star of November 23, 1928, pushed reasons why boosters thought voters ought to move the county seat from Farwell to Friona.

The ad, headed, "Friona—a logical location for the county seat of Parmer County," contained a large picture of a proposed courthouse, which backers said could be built in Friona for $35,000.

(Farwell claimed, in an ad in the same paper, a new courthouse would cost $150,-000.)

Some interesting copy from the big ad:

FRIONA—Is within two miles of the legal center of Parmer County.

FRIONA—Is but three miles east of the exact or geographical center of Parmer County.

FRIONA—Already has the largest scholastic population in Parmer County and the largest voting population.

FRIONA—Now has a larger population and more vacant land to be occupied than any other locality in the county and is, therefore, destined to become the center of population for the county and is, therefore, the logical location for the county seat.

FRIONA—Has the best gin within a hundred mile radius.

On the other hand, the ad charged:

FARWELL—Is on the extreme edge of the county and only five miles from the southwest corner.

FARWELL—Can never become the population center of Parmer County.

FRIONA STAR, Friday, August 9, 1929
FARMERS, TIRED OF CHICKEN THIEVERY, ORGANIZE TO PUT STOP TO SUCH PRACTICE HERE

At a meeting in the county court house August 3 a number of farmers and poultrymen of Parmer County voted to organize a Parmer County Anti-Theft Association. A true county representation not being present due to the rains threatening in the Bovina and Friona territory, the members present decided to get the organization started by adopting the constitution and by-laws, paying their dues and electing a temporary chairman and setting the date for another meeting at which time the entire county may be represented.

The next meeting will be held in the Bovina school building on Thursday night, August 15. The meeting will be of much importance to the association and all who possibly can should be present. All officers for the association will be elected at this meeting and the constitution and by-laws will be read and open for amendments, new markers will be added and a number of chickens will be marked to show each member how to mark his property.

It is very important that each community of Parmer county be represented at this meeting, as one of the executive officers of the association will be elected from each community represented.

The business of the Parmer county association is to fight the thief and here is the way it does it.

It pays a reward for the conviction of any thief who steals from a member of the association.

It gives each member a method of positively identifying his chickens, turkeys and other livestock anywhere he may find them.

It will send out notices to all the produce houses within a reasonable distance of Parmer county, giving them the name and association number of each member.

It provides a means whereby the farmers and poultrymen of the county can wage an organized fight against the thief.

Many other counties have used this same method to rid their counties of thieves and Parmer county can do the same thing. Come to the meeting Thursday night at Bovina and bring your friends with you.

FRIONA STAR, Friday, August 23, 1929
WILL LIKELY REACH A MILLION BUSHELS

A few weeks ago the Star carried a story as to the amount of wheat grown in the Friona territory and shipped from the Friona depot, stating that a possible million bushels might be shipped.

Later estimates seem to justify this supposition, in view of the fact that it is found that many large crops and parts of crops have not yet been removed from the farms where they were grown.

It is estimated that about 500 carloads have been shipped from Friona already, each carrying an estimated load of 1550 bushels, or a total of 778,000 bushels, lacking only 225,000 of the possible million bushels.

Investigation or inquiry disclosed the fact that on two farms alone in this locality there are very close to 80,000 bushels and perhaps more than that. Two other farms have about 8000 each, while many other farmers have varying amounts still in store on their farms. Marvin Whaley, one of Friona's most extensive wheat men has not sold any of his crop,

103

which is estimated conservatively to be at least 40,000 bushels. L.F. Lillard and F.W. Reeve are two others who still have large amounts in storage in their own bins.

Thus, judging from the large part of the lacking 225,000 already located it seems more than possible that the 1,000,000 bushels before predicted will have been shipped from the Friona territory and from Friona elevators, before the entire crop has been placed on the market.

FRIONA STAR, Friday, October 4, 1929
ONE 'PHONE SYSTEM TO BE USED HERE

The probability of Friona having two rival telephone systems was averted when Roy Baily last week sold the new system he had about completed to the State Telephone Company, with local offices at Lubbock.

Mr. Bailey had only recently moved his family here with the intention of making Friona his home, but after disposing of his business interests here removed his family last Saturday to Roswell, New Mexico, where he will enter the feed business. By his genial disposition, honorable bearings, energy and industry, Mr. Bailey had made friends of all Friona people who has been fortunate enough to make his acquaintance, all of whom regret his departure.

FRIONA STAR, Friday, October 11, 1929
CHAMBER OF COMMERCE TAKES UP MANY PROBLEMS OF CONCERN TO ALL CITIZENS OF FRIONA

The regular meeting of the Chamber of Commerce which was held last Monday night at the school auditorium was quite interesting and enthusiastic, although a comparatively few of the members were present.

Among the subjects that received consideration were more and better roads into town, better streets in town, early evening and Sunday closing of the stores and other business places, loyal support of the local cotton gin and inviting the County Track Meet to Friona.

Especially did the deplorable condition of Main street come in for its share of consideration and criticism and the mayor replied that he and the city commissioners would be only too glad to do any amount of good work on this and other streets if the people will only place the means at their disposal to pay the cost.

The regular meeting night was changed from the first Monday to the first Thursday night of each month.

THE FRIONA STAR, Thursday, June 14, 1951.
Inquiring Reporter Dubs Jack Anderson Qualified Historian of Parmer County
By Phyllis Dishman—Star Staff Writer

Don't let the sign on Jack Anderson's Barber Shop fool you. It's more than a barber shop; it's a meeting place, a museum, and a panorama of Friona's past.

And don't let Jack fool you. He is more than a barber. He's a former cowhand, a coach, a historian; in short, a character.

Just stop by his barbershop and be convinced. Especially if you need a shave or hair cut. Jack says he is the best barber on the east side of Main Street. He used to be the best barber in town—in fact, at one time he was the best barber in Parmer County—being the only one.

As long as anybody needs a hair cut, Jack's place is open, from sun-up to twelve o'clock if necessary. He has been barbering F.L. Spring for 40 years, and says Mr. Spring has survived the ordeal successfully.

Jack started into the business 43 years ago down in Bovina by the simple expedient of opening up a barber shop. Before that he had been riding herd out on the range, and got his experience cutting the cowboys' hair as they perched on wagon tongues, instead of going to barber college.

Finally he decided there were too many cowboys out on the range (at least one too many) and not enough barbers in town, so he came in off the prairie, opened up a shop and began collecting the pictures which today line the walls of his shop and provide both conversation for customers and facts to settle any arguments.

In 1926 he moved to Friona, opened up his shop in its present location and settled down to keeping a pictorial record of events past and present.

For instance, you'll find a picture of an old time chuck wagon, a bundle of bed rolls, and some self conscious looking cowboys who look with scorn upon the camera man. This chuckwagon was from the old Block outfit and the picture was made decades ago. Slightly yellow from age, now, it is still an authentic relic of the Good Old Days.

Then there are a couple of pictures of the team of oxen which T.N. Jasper kept at Friona years ago. Mainly they were just a curiousity, but they served also as beasts of burden for Jasper's trade wagon, hauling lumber and other supplies.

A picture of Texico, New Mexico, made in 1907, decorates the west wall and portrays life in the Gaslight Era, with its wooden sidewalks and its horse and buggy atmosphere.

Jack's interest in riding and in horses did not end with his career out of doors. He kept horses for years, and pictures of them dominate his collection.

You'll find shots of quarter horses owned by Marvin Whaley, a beautiful palomino, a picture of Man of War, and one of the last mare and colt that Jack owned.

Among the most interesting pictures which he displays are three showing the ravages of nature in the unpredictable Panhandle, including an ice storm, a spring flood, and one of the threatening clouds of a duststorm that swept the prairies about ten years ago. These pictures were all made in 1940-1941 by Lee Spring, who is now a senior student at the University of Texas Medical School.

FRIONA STAR, Thursday, January 15, 1953. STATE BOUNDARY AGAIN QUESTIONED, REVIVING MEMORIES OF OLD TIMERS IN THIS LOCALITY.
By F.W. Reeve

Editor's Note: Articles in the Amarillo paper over the weekend telling of a state official maintaining that the Texas-New Mexico boundary was some sixteen miles off—too far west—has created considerable talk and a lot of reminiscing in the counties along this boundary.

Now, personally, we are hopping mad at the gentleman and his claims—we think he is very inaccurate and his contentions, if carried out, would be unjust. We have always understood that the boundary was only about 2.7 miles too far west in this area, and that's

as far as we'll budge. The peculiar location of the towns to our west on the state line actually place their interests more closely with new Mexico and Clovis anyway, many contend, and we wouldn't buck the crowd and raise any fuss there, but we sure wouldn't want 16 miles of Parmer county farm land to be given back to the Indians!

At any rate, our friend, F.W. Reeve, brought us the article printed below that we think quite clever and most interesting— bringing back lots of memories to the old-timers and serving as informative lore to the newcomers.

The story in the Saturday and Sunday edition of the Amarillo Daily News, regarding the dispute over the location of the New Mexico-Texas state line started quite a reminiscing. There are still several people living who remember many of the circumstances and several of the legends concerning the correcting survey that was conducted at federal expense in the early part of the county's history.

When the county was organized the state line was plainly in a mess. A glance of the ordinary plainsman's naked eye could plainly establish the accusation of general confusion and irregularities.

Mis-location of the state line was taken for granted. It came to be concluded that the then marked line was established for the convenience of moneyed cattle interests. The exact line made little difference to anyone. West Texas and New Mexico land and oil at that time had no measureable value.

A few years after the turn of the century, several farmers who had invested their life savings in this panhandle land began to be quite distressed as to the validity of their land titles. The big land companies became disturbed. It was hard to sell land that might be in Texas, New Mexico or no-man's land.

As a result of the commotion a federal correcting survey was finally ordered. The senior Senator from Illinois was delegated as a special committee to see the order was diligently and properly carried out. This senator was a good man. He was interested in the biggest land holding company in the country. Therefore the correcting survey was rushed through in record time and no doubt with intended thoroughness.

105

One of the legends concerning that survey had its setting north of here in the Canadian River brakes. At present an apparent mile or two jog in the state line gives some credence to the authenticity of the legend.

The legend is to the effect that about the time the surveying crew reached the Canadian brakes from the north, a Kentucky Methodist circuit rider joined the crew as a scout and guide. Also as a companion for the senator. In the minds of Washington and Chicago dignitaries this country was still infested with roving and ravaging Indian tribes. Inspired Judgement was deemed advisable—hence, the eloquent speaking guide. Sure enough, a morning or two after the preacher had joined the crew, they discovered an Indian standing on a knoll to the south with an army rifle in one hand and a big feather in his hat or cap. (The cowboys could never quite agree as to the Indian's Headgear.) The warning Chief's mission was to wave the surveying crew around his supposedly winter camp.

When the U.S. Crew had got established some two or three miles to the west and started peacefully on their south course the good elder felt called on to give thanks for their miraculous evasion of blood shed. He in no sense censured the poor heathen for standing stout for what he considered justice.

There were several cowboys with the crew. Their duty was to haul water, gather fire chips, make and break camp and do the cooking. These cowboys had lots of fun, especially over the Indian Chief Episode. They insisted the Indian favored in appearance their company preacher and friend. They speculated as to what a little more Methodist grace might accomplish if applied to the Chief.

But it was definitely not in keeping with cowboy tradition to ask questions or accuse anybody. The fun and wit was still going strong when the crew made camp on Frio Draw. This time they camped some quarter of a mile from a sheep ranchman's windmill. This rancher also had the only grocery store and post office in Easter, New Mexico, a good place to visit. In their loafing hours this rancher gathered lots of their fun and implied meaning. He also dated back to where it was not good manners to ask pointed questions.

By the time the group broke camp on Frio Draw, the preacher had helped the senator to realize how important it was that the new location should not meet with the disapproval of the awful "hell-dive" at Texico.

It was true that Texico had a preponderance of open liquor stores and open gambling houses.

As for building up a scare complex the cowboys simply winked and grinned. But the element of discretion must have had some influence with the surveying crew and their Eastern advisories. If they ever worked that part of the line it was probably at night or during a blinding storm. The good elder frequently gave thanks that they got through to the sand hills without blood shed.

A few years ago our own Judge A.D. Smith worked up a rather complete briefing on the legal phases of the state-line issue. His findings were based entirely on federal and state records—no legends. Some of the top legal minds pronounced the judge's efforts as scholarly and complete and of probable value when the time is ripe.

FIRST RESIDENCE IN FRIONA, TEXAS

The First Residence in Friona, Texas was built for Geo. G. Wright on Lots 1 & 2, Block 75, Corner of 6th & Euclid streets.

This residence was sold to Ann. E. Hanson of Tuscola, Illinois, who also purchased Se. 5 and East half of Sec. 32 situated 5 miles north of Friona.

Mrs. Hanson leased the above residence to Olson Bros. who operated a grocery & general mdse. store on main street—east side—between 6th and 7th streets, in Block 62. This house still standing as of Sept. 23, 1962.

The Geo. G. Wright referred to in paragraph 1 was a real estate operation selling for Capitol Freehold Land and Investment Co. of Chicago, owners of the XIT Ranch.

Friona Townsite was all of Sec. 6. Wright's operation began in the year 1906 and the main operation closed early in 1910. All of his auto drivers were discharged Dec. 1909.

EARLY CITIZENS OF FRIONA, TEXAS

A.N. Wentworth
John F. Lillard
G. Stuckey
Alan Stuckey
R.H. Kuenzli
Mrs. Flanders
Wm. Crawley
S.A. Harris
Rev. Hensel
John Evans
Steaman Stevick
J.W. Varr
R.V. McWilliams
Frances Kohl
O.M. Jacobs
J.B. Overfelt
D.W. McMillen
Dr. C.S. Fergus
Dr. Rohrabaugh
Chas. Dorton
Wm. McCandlish
H.C. McCoy
John Gischler
Louie Kohl
Lawrence Lillard
Heney H. Morris
Geo. W. Clark
W.J. Foster
G.M. Chester
D.W. Hanson
G.M. Orbaugh
Jeff Ogg
George Marsh
Beaver Towles
Samuel Marsh
Mr. & Mrs. Mary
Reece
A. W. Henschel
R.H. Ames

W.G. Harris
Florence Hill Hanson
Henry Hanson
John Hanson
Sherman
Carlyle
Bilderback
J.C. Cady
Harley Cady
Charley Cady
R.O. Messenger
T.J. Crawford
Chas. Saxine
John Saxine
Byron Foley
Julius Eskert
Robert Vell
Ralph Brown
Jesse Letton, Jr.
G.S. Jefferson
Jesse Letton, Sr.
Lee Griner
Booker Diamond
Bert Shattuck
Henry Idecker
Janie Tiefel
Henry Tiefel
J.C. Wynn
Amos Lyon
Horton
Chris Ziehr
J.W. Yelverton
Thos. Yelverton
W.J. Yelverton
Chyde Seamond
Wesley Evans
"Red"
Ves. Marrion
S.A. Harris (Editor)

EARLY BUSINESS OWNERS, FRIONA, TEXAS

Olson Bros. Mdse.
J.F. Lillard & Sons Mdse. (later) Livery
J.B. Overfelt Mdse.-Lumber
D.W. & J.H. Hanson, Gen. Mdse.
G. Stuckey & Sons Well Drilling
A.N. Wentworth, Drilling & Blacksmith
McMillen & Fergus—Real Estate, Ranching, Lumber & Banking

FIRST BRICK SCHOOL BUILDING in Friona, Texas.

THE FRIONA STAR, Thursday, March 5, 1953.

Historical Background of Friona Schools Told by Floyd Reeve at Masonic Meet

In keeping with the "Public School Week" theme, F.W. Reeve talked before the Friona Masonic Lodge Tuesday evening choosing as his subject, "An Early Settler Looks at Our Schools." Mr. Reeve told of the school progress here from the first rural schools to the present.

His very interesting bit of local history follows, presented in two installments:

By F.W. Reeve

Interest in school ran deep in the heart of Friona pioneers. Not all of these early settlers possessed superior formal education. They had little high-brow disposition among them; but they all had a deep urge to see this expanse of clean nature turned into a superior land of American homes.

From the first they pinned their hopes on good schools.

In the fall of 1909 a young immigrant family moved to Friona. The family consisted of husband, wife and month-old baby girl. They unloaded their immigrant car about where the stock pens are now located. There they hitched four horses to their wagons loaded with their stuff and supplies and headed to their new home, although their house was not yet built. They thought they knew where they were going because the man had been here for a few weeks the year before and built sheds and fences. From the railroad they

MISS GRACE BREWER'S 6th grade—1926.

drove up the hill to a watering tub. The tub was located about 200 feet east of the present Main Street crossing. An old boy by the name of "Daddy" Foster lived nearby in his scale shed. He was a coal dealer and of course loaded the newcomer with coal. They had not yet learned the merits of cow chips. This Dad Foster was, figuratively speaking, the chamber of commerce, the law, but in truth a good friend to all tenderfeet. He described in detail to these new people the route to their destination. Each prairie dog town, lake, old campground or distant dugout was described minutely. He even warned against the deceitfulness of the mirages. He knew those details would shorten the distance.

The trail led near the spot where the post office is now located. It then angled off just north of the present Jasper home and at that point the new parents caught sight of the school house. It was off to the right of the trail on the site of the present grade school. It was a new looking 20 by 40 frame building. Some dozen or twenty children came running out to the trail to see a new family coming in.

The young man did not remember seeing the schoolhouse the year before when he was here. Did his baby cause him to look more earnestly for the school?

Early in the game Friona sentiment seemed to catch fire with a desire for good and even better schools. They, earlier than most places, caught the idea of enlarging their district. The Friona district succeeded in getting the out-lying districts' school funds transferred to her budget. In turn she was wisely generous in paying the parents for transporting their children to school. Of course there was some imposing and confusion over the transportation problem. There was no legal pattern for people to follow, but it finally worked out to the advantage and approval of all school minded people.

Harold Schlenker deserves credit for driving the first regular school bus route. The Rhea District fixed up a Model A touring car with a "tarp" over the top. Harold regularly and without fail brought his brothers, sisters and children enroute to Friona schools. Schlenkers lived 20 miles out. All the distance was trail road. Friona paid the boy

MISS VERSA ODOM'S Class in 1926—Friona.

while he went to school.

The whole country was learning. They found out they could legally and economically have their children transported with tax money.

In 1923 the Friona School district voted to consolidate with the adjacent district. And the following year it became an independent school district. John White, T.J. Crawford and J.A. Guyer were three of the first trustees of the big new district.

In 1921 lightning set fire to and totally destroyed the school building. A temporary frame structure was quickly built by mob citizenry, that is, every body brought their hammer and saws and went to work. Nobody questioned but that the material would get paid for, and it was. The Rockwall Lumber Company was the pioneer and only lumber company at that time. It did its part heroically.

This hastily built building, again supplemented by the use of the Congregational Church, furnished school facilities until the new $52,000 building was completed in 1924. A $35,000 addition was built in 1928.

FRIONA SCHOOL TEACHERS

1908-1909
Roxie (Witherspoon) Fertch

1909-1910
Floy (Knowed
Floy (Knowd) Crawford
Tennie Davis

1910-1911
Nell Killum
Edith (Maurer) Lillard
Elsie (Goodwine) Clennin (Deceased)

1911-1912
Lynn Fertch
Elsie (Goodwine) Clennin
Oliva (Durice) Brownlee

1912-1913
Lynn Fertch
Lucy V. Goodwine, New York, N.W.
88 Morning Side Drive
John Priddy

1913-1914
W.H. Saffold
Glenna (Colson) Carter, Corpus Christi, Texas, 1533 5th St.

1914-1915
W.H. Saffold, Seonard, Texas
Glenna (Colson) Carter
Frank Jackobs

1915-1916
W.H. Saffold
W.H. Yonger Jr. (Deceased)
Glenna (Colson) Carter
Esther (Schlenker) Burns, Des Moines, Iowa

1916-1917
W.H. Yonger, Jr.

1917-1918
Hap McFee (Deceased)
Ina (Jordan) Hale, Amarillo, Texas
Esther Schlenker Burns
Catherin (Stevins) Lyons, Clearwater, Minn.
Edd Treavie

1918-1919
Hap McFee
Ina (Jordan) Hale
Esther (Schlenker) Burnes
Catherin (Stevins) Lyons
Gunnie Parker
Mary Ducas (Cullum) Clennin, Rye, Colorado

1919-1920
Amelia (Fickie) Warren

1920-1921
John Richburg
Floyd Golden
Elsie (Pool) Golden

1921-1922
Floyd Golden
Elsie Golden
Mac Nobel
Murrel Sanders

Friday, September 16, 1927
"About 330 students enrolled, with over 100 in high school. Crowded conditions are in evidence and it became necessary to wire for another teacher to help with the high school work.

(Miss Esther Schultz—new teacher)

Friday, October 28, 1927
"Prof. Conway is advocating the organization of a Parent-Teacher Association ..."

Friday, Dec. 9, 1927
"At this time I wish to call attention of the parents of children to your child's report card. Any child making lower than C grade is either below normal or is failing to put forth his best efforts .... It is my opinion that school is of practically no value to a child who constantly makes below a C grade. And to say the least of it, the child making such grades is of no value to the school."
J.A. Conway, Supt.

Friday, January 27, 1928
Addition—expansion and equipment to cost $35,000.

February 24, 1928
2 teacher additions
William McClure
Carl C. Maurer—7th grade—moved to Congregational church building.

Friday, May 4, 1928
Graduation—next Wednesday and Thursday
11 high school
52 from 7th grade

The Friona Star, Friday, May 3, 1929
18 seniors graduate—May 9

Friday, August 17, 1928
News of building a frame structure 44 x 30 feet to be divided into 2 class rooms. (northwest corner)
F.W. Reeve purchased 10 trucks (school buses) for transportation.

Friday, September 14, 1928
Enrollment and classification:
Primary 35 Miss Eloyse Pitman
Second 27 Miss Ruby Haines
Third 30 Miss Esther Jennings
Fourth 23 Louise Watson
5th & 6th & 7th Miss Inez Osborn, Miss Harrison, Mr. Armstrong, Mr. Boston
5th—30 6th—38 7th—48 (231)
Freshman 51
Sophomores 32

Juniors 20
Seniors 14
Grand total (348)
High School Teachers: J.A. Conway, F.H. Rose, Billy McClure, Marie Phillips, Miss Debbie Askew, Miss Ruth Holmes

August 23, 1929
  J.A. Conway-Supt.
High School:
  George A. Heath
  Mrs. Alice V. Conway
  J.H. Mims
  Marie Gardner
  Elizabeth Cherry
  Beth Pitts
5th 6th 7th:
  M.A. Armstrong
  Inez Osborne
  Esther Jennings
  Louise Watson
  Vivian Boston-4th
  Esther Reeve-3rd
  Mrs. Marie Whitle-2nd
  Eloyse Pitman-Primary

Football of 1927-28

Vega 0—Friona 7
Happy 0—Friona 12
Canyon 20—Friona 12
Vega 16—Friona 12
Sudan 0—Friona 13
Portales 12—Friona 6

Team: Roy Hall, Hadley Reeve, J.D. Curry, Reeve Guyer, Bill Hamlin, Elvin Johnson, Earl Beasley, Eugene (Pete) Richardson, W.H. (Shorty) Jones, Granville McFarland, Harris Evans, Arthur Baker, Edward Spring, Otho Whitefield (captain).

FRIONA STAR, Friday, May 24, 1951.
Five Graduated in 1916.

Graduation, 1951, in the new auditorium was quite different to that held by the first graduating class in 1916, members of that group recall.

Fred White, one of the five members of that first class, tells of the 1916 exercises being held in a 24 x 30 ft. auditorium, part of the three-room school which burned in 1918 or 1919.

Members of the 1916 class were Fred White, Clyde Goodwine, Elvin Gisher, Ethel Sutton, and Dempsey Winn. White has stayed in Friona, operating an electrical business here, while Clyde Goodwine has remained here as a farmer. When last heard from, Gisher was engaged in insurance business in California; Ethel Sutton was married and living near San Francisco; and Winn was a Certified Public Accountant in Amarillo.

William (Sport) Younger was superintendent of the school at that time; he was the son of Rev. W.H. Younger, then Baptist pastor at Canyon.

The local faculty consisted of three teachers.

White was valedictorian in 1916, and Ethel Sutton was salutatorian. Immediately after the graduation exercises a reception was held in the Friona Hotel, located on the site of the present hotel, though it was a different building.

FRIONA—CHURCHES

Although records for verification on the history of the local churches are few, old-timers agree that building began on the first Friona church around 1908. Begun as a non-denominational meeting house for worship services, the building in its early stages was known as the Friona Union Church. With labor and funds being donated, some 100 residents of an area probably extending to near Lazbuddie and out to the Rhea community, launched their church-building project, only to come to the end of the rope—financially—before the building was completed.

Reports are that the various members of the congregation then turned to their own "church" mission boards, in an attempt to secure sufficient money to complete their work—with the understanding that the new church would be named after the "Mother Church" which supplied the finances. In the end, the Congregational Church agreed to underwrite the venture, and the members titled their edifice the Congregational Community Church.

Mr. and Mrs. Hurlburt, both ministers, served the local pastorate, as well as making every-other-Sunday visits to other little churches in the area.

Some time in the "early 20's," most long-time residents agree, the church was destroyed by fire and it was some years later before it could be rebuilt, with members donating labor to dig the basement, and both funds and labor for the foundation, upon which Bob Hicks laid the adobe brick he had made himself. Again the Congregational Church board was approached, and again funds were received to complete the church.

Covered with stucco now on the outside, and redone on the interior some years ago, that same building still serves members of the Friona Congregational Church, who are proud to point out that the church was "paid out" some years back with a mortgage burning ceremony being held.

Some of the charter members of the church are still represented in services by members of their families, although none of them still reside in the area, and the majority are dead. Included in the charter group were the Bill Goodwines, Fred Clennins, Wilbur Forbes, Harry Hughes, George Maurers, George Livings, and John Geischlers.

In the meantime, the population of Friona and surrounding area was increasing, and two other denominations formed their own groups for worship services. First were the Baptists, and then a short time later—only a few weeks, to be exact—the Friona Methodist Church was organized.

Weather-beaten ledgers at the Methodist Church show that a "class" was organized on November 3, 1914, with W.M. Pearce as minister. Some 14 charter members were listed, none of which are now known to be living.

History of Friona Methodist Church

The Friona Methodist Church was organized in May, 1914. The group had worshipped with the community church prior to the organization in 1914. The nine charter members were Mr. and Mrs. J.T. Berry, Misses Lois and Irene Berry, Mr. and Mrs. A.J. James, Mrs. Fearne Taylor, W.H. Saffold and Mrs. Gertrude Sherrieb. (Mrs. Sherrieb was Clyde Sherrieb's mother.)

The first building for the local Methodist Church is still in use as the fellowship hall

BAPTIST-METHODIST CHOIR CONCERT,

AT THE SCHOOL HOUSE.

SATURDAY DEC. 11, '15.

PROGRAM

Anthem—"Savion, Blessed Savior" - Choir

Piano Solo "Pass me not by Oh, Gentle Savior,
Miss Nellie Meade

Vocal Solo "In The Valley of the Moon"
Miss Cecil Sutton

Reading "The Governor' Last Levee" Mrs. Carter

Flute Solo, "Sur de Carnival De Venise"
Mrs. Chauchon

Double Quartet, "The Angels' Song" .
Misses Schlenker, Powell, Meade, Schlenker,
Messrs Younger, Messenger, Gischler, Farmer

Recitation Musical, "The Village Blacksmith," .
Miss Luella Gischler

Ladies Trio, "A Meadow Song."
Mesdames Chauchon, Crawford, Carter

Piano Duet, "Soldiers' March from Faust"
Mesdames Carter and Crawford

Ladies Quartet, "Rockin' in De Win' "
Mesdames Carter, Crawford,
Misses Schlenker, Meade

Vocal Duet, "Sweet Genevieve"
Misses Cecil and Ethel Sutton

Reading, "Eugineer Connor's Son" Miss Schlenker

Flute Solo, "Grand Fantasie de Concert Sur
Abeon de Weber" Mrs. Chauchon

Double Trio, "Old Time Favorites"
Mesdame Carter, Ballard' Crawford,
Misses Meade, Schlenker, Mrs. Saffold

Chorus, "Who Knows What The Bells Say," Choir

Pantomine, "The Holy City" Miss Lola James

ADMISSION 15 AND 25 CENTS

and is known as the Methodist Annex. Rev. W.M. Pearce was pastor of the church at that time.

The foundation for the basement was run in 1930, but the depression postponed further building until '39 when the basement building was completed with Rev. L.L. Hill as pastor.

Rev. O.B. Annis, who was here from 1931 to 1933, two of the depression years, still chuckles about his use of the excavated basement site. To pay the church benevolences, he raised pigs in the incompleted basement.

The building committee appointed in

October of 1939 for construction of the basement included A.S. Curry, J.W. Parr, O.G. Turner, B.T. Galloway, W.C. Osborn and E.V. Rushing.

The present sanctuary was completed November 14, 1948 with Rev. C.C. Hardaway as pastor. B.T. Galloway was chairman of the building committee at that time.

The present church plant, which is valued at $142,000, has become inadequate for the growing church's needs. As a result, on May 13, 1956, the present building committee was appointed to negotiate the building of the first units of a $135,000 building program. Construction is scheduled to begin in November.

From nine members to a membership of 435, the church has seen many changes. Dedication of the sanctuary was held March 13, 1955.

A list of former pastors and the years they were at the Friona church is as follows:

William M. Pearce, 1914-1916; Z.R. Fee, 1916-1917; B.Y. Dickinson, 1917-1921; Preston Florance, 1921-1923; I.E. Walker, 1923-1926; L.B. Gillam, 1926-1928; Carter E. Porter, 1928-1929; D. Van Pett, 1929-1931; O.B. Annis, 1931-1933; Herschel Thurston, 1933-1935; G. Reginald Hardy, 1935-1936; L.L. Hill, 1936-1938; J.L. Price, 1938-1942; E.A. Irvine, 1942-1944; David Binkley, 1946; Dewitt Seago, 1946'1948; C.C. Hardaway, 1948-1949; J.E. Tidwell, 1949-1952; U.S. Sherrill, 1952-1955.

Rev. Hugh Blaylock is pastor of the church at the present time, having come to the church in 1955.

The first Methodist Church, now known as the "annex" and used for fellowship meetings, was constructed of adobe brick. Later, launching a building project, the members got themselves a basement completed, and then, for more years than many of them care to remember, were stymied by lack of funds to complete the top half of the building, and observed their Sundays "downstairs."

The buff brick structure with which current Frionans are familiar was completed in 1948, after which the old basement was completely turned into Sunday School classrooms. Dedication of the new building was held on March 13, 1955, when all debts against the structure were wiped out.

TEMPORARY BAPTIST CHURCH, originally Parmerton Court House.

The First Baptist Church of Friona was organized January 20, 1914, with 14 members. Charter members of the church were Mr. and Mrs. Silas Thomas, Mr. and Mrs. D.H. Mead, Mr. and Mrs. B.C. Taylor, Mrs. T.D. Ballard, Mrs. Lillie Bocock, Mrs. Minnie Maxwell, Miss Willie Owens, Mrs. William McCandish, Mr. and Mrs. J.N. Messenger and W.H. Safford.

The first meeting place of the little group was the school house. In February of 1914, J.T. Burnett was called to the church as pastor.

In May, 1914, the church purchased a building on Main Street in which to worship. This building was sold in 1924 and was occupied by Weir's Second Hand Store. The structure was destroyed by fire last year.

After the sale of the building, the group held worship services in the school house and the Methodist Church until Thanksgiving Day of 1926. A basement had been built just north of the present church auditorium and a basket lunch was served in the new basement on that Thanksgiving Day. The church membership then totaled 76.

In 1929, an auditorium was built above the basement. In 1934, a pastor's home was built and in 1943 a building fund was started for a new and larger auditorium.

CONGREGATIONAL CHURCH, FRIONA, TEXAS

When the spirit of progress led ambitious people from the crowded sections of the north and mid-west United States to begin building homes in the newly founded town of Friona, Texas it did not dim their ideals to

UNION CONGREGATIONAL CHURCH—Friona, Texas

ORIGINAL CONGREGATIONAL CHURCH—with rainbow.

the fact that a place of worship was a part of their ambition; and, in less than one year after the community was given a name— quoting from record, June 14, 1908, "Pursuant to a call the people of Friona assembled to consider the organization of a church." The group being of various denominations agreed that a union organization was practical. Plans were made to begin the construction of a building. Later developments revealed that local contribution was inadequate for completion of the building and it was obvious that some individual or missionary society would have to assume responsibility in order to continue with the work. This opportunity was extended to all denominations represented and none responded except the Congregational—there was one member of the Congregational Church—Mrs. J.W. Karr—at that time in Friona.

The Congregational people agreed to render aid on the condition that the organization remain a Union Congregational Church. The money furnished was to be conferred as a grant, or loan, without interest, providing that the church raise a voluntary offering annually for the Congregational Church Building Society. The term "Union" was explained later to mean Congregational.

In a testimony signed by three Friona citizens Aug. 7th, 1908, The Union Congregational Church of Friona, Texas became a corporation, formed in the support of public worship; directors, J.W. Karr, R.V. McWilliams and D.W. McMillen; John F. Lillard, Notary Public. The department of State,

Texas, fixed its seal to the charter August 28, 1908, with W.R. Davis, Secretary of State; H.M. Little, Chief Clerk.

December 8, 1908 a meeting was called by the Missionary pastor, Rev. John G. Lange of Amarillo. A quorum of the church was present; past activities of the organization were reviewed and the future discussed. As a result the group pledged itself to one bond of fellowship. Names of the charter members are: Mrs. R.V. McWilliams, R.V. McWilliams, Gurteude Karr, J.W. Karr, Mrs. D.W. McMillen, D.W. McMillen, Mrs. C.S. Furgus, C.S. Furgus, Wm. McClandish, C.B. Olsen, Carrie M. Olsen, Mrs. Seth Roush.

The following articles of Faith were adopted:

I. We believe in one God, the Father Almighty, Maker of heaven and earth and of all things visible and invisable.

II. We believe in Jesus Christ the Only Begotten Son of God to be our Saviour and Lord, who was crucified for our sins, and rose for our justification.

III. We believe in the Holy Spirit, our Teacher, our Comforter and our guide.

IV. We believe in the Divine inspiration of the Bible, both the old and the new testament Scriptures as our rule of faith and practice.

The laymen carried the work of the church with the occasional support of the District Superintendent, Rev. C.S. Murphy and the visiting ministers of the Panhandle Congregational Church, Amarillo, Farwell, Spring Lake. The Council Manual was adopted May 9, 1909. At this date a vote carried to proceed with the dedication of the church building; May 23rd, 1909 was set for the event and invitations were sent to Amarillo, Farwell and Spring Lake churches to be present and assist with the dedication.

RESIDENCE OF Rev. W.A. Hensel, Friona, Texas.

UNION CONGREGATIONAL May Pole Dancers.

On May 23rd, 1909. Superintendent C.S. Murphy, acting moderator, the Congregational Church of Friona, Texas was recognized with appropriate services; the articles of faith were found to be in accord with Congregational Churches; a house of worship was almost complete; the membership numbered twenty-one; and in general prospects for a future for the church were good.

Rev. J.L. Parker came as supply pastor during July 1909. August 1, 1909, W.A. Hensel accepted pastorate of the church and remained as leader until January 8, 1912.

A program of real church activities began with the year 1910. New officers were elected; three deacons, Mr. William Goodwine, Mr. Jefferson and W.S. Hensel; three trustees, Mr. John Orbaugh, J.W. Karr and D.W. McMillen; church clerk, Mrs. R.H. Kinsley. Mrs. Kinsley has been annually elected to date—January 1938—making a record of twenty-eight years of devoted, efficient service in the office of church clerk.

Misses Elsie and Lucy Goodwine were baptised into the church, March 27, 1910. Sunday April 17, 1910, D.W. McMillen was sent as a delegate to Spring Lake. On Nov. 29th-30th, 1910, the Friona church entertained the Panhandle Association of Congregational Churches.

A Home Missionary Society was organized March 2, 1910, through the ministry of Mrs. Firman of Chicago, President of the National Federation of Women's Congregational State and Home Missionary Society. The initial enrollment was twenty. Mrs. T.D. Ballard was elected first president, Mrs. C.M. Orbaugh, Vice-President, and Mrs. William Goodwine,

Secretary. The first regular meeting, March 18, and a first Missionary program was given May 1st.

The ladies of the church had an Aid in progress for financial benefit and later the two societies merged into the Ladies Aid. Good service has been their motto, and to date they are alert: Quarterly Teas, Annual Chicken Dinners and Bazaars, and occasional planned entertainment enhance the interest as well as increase the bank deposit slips of the four monthly meetings of the Aid.

The Christian Endeavor begun January 2, 1910 with a membership of nineteen, was very successful for a number of years. The Panhandle District Convention met with the Friona C.E. in June 1923. Since 1932 there has been little interest manifested in a Senior Endeavor. The Junior organization functioned for a year or two. Both are inactive at the present.

The honor of having a Cradle Roll in the church and Sunday School is attributed to three ladies, Mrs. Hensel, Mrs. Kell, and Mrs. R.H. Kinsley. These ladies contributed the one dollar necessary to purchase supplies and canvassed the homes for the babies' names. Nine names were on the first roll hung in the church. Present enrollment is six.

In the early days before the automobile was common, the home department functioned along with the cradle roll in that it reached the mothers and others who were not able to attend services regularly. This department has been dropped.

By February 11, 1911, the membership read forty five; and at the date the fiscal year was changed from August 1st to April 1st.

The church was given a Bible by Brother E.K. Warren and Rev. Wm. H. Hurlbut presented the gift January 15th, 1912. The resignation of Rev. W.A. Hensel was accepted Jan. 15th, 1912, and the church voted to call Rev. Wm. H. Hurlbut as pastor.

Changes took place as time advanced. Loved pastors felt the urgent call to other fields and left rich, lasting memories with the Congregational people at Friona. One change which showed the flint of the membership occurred Aug. 7th, 1921 in the early hours of the morning, about 2:00 a.m. during an electrical, rain storm. Lightning set the building afire and it was completely destroyed with all furniture and fixtures, several tons of coal, two pianos, a baby organ. Insurance was One Thousand Dollars, and grant about $775. A canvas the next day resulted in a subscription over the one thousand dollar figure for a new building.

Services were held in the public school building until that, too, was destroyed by fire. Then the homes opened doors for worship. Work soon began on a new structure for the Congregationals and dedicatorial services were held June 17, 1923 on the completion of an adobe house.

Some visiting ministers here during the Panhandle Association, June 8, 9, 10-1922, were Dr. Easterbrook, Colo.; Dr. Ricker, Dallas; Dr. Dana of New York and Mr. Powell of Dallas, Tex.

Mr. and Mrs. Dickey conducted a three-week revival beginning July 25th, 1925. They gave and received worthily, two who were loved by the entire community.

District superintendents coming to Friona Congregational Church, Rev. C.S. Murphy, Dr. A.E. Ricker and Lucian Marsh.

The membership has come to this church from many faiths: United Brethren, Friends, Congregational, Presbyterian, Episcopal, Evangelical, Roman Catholic, Christian Church, Methodist, Baptist, Assembly of God, Church of God, German Lutheran and on confession of faith. The present membership is ninety five, thirty eight men and fifty seven women. The Sunday School enrollment is eighty two. The Ladies Aid has thirty nine on its roll.

The pastors serving this church for a long or short period are: Rev. J.L. Parker, July 1909; Rev. Wm. Allen Hensel, 1909-1912; Rev. Wm. H. Hurlbut, Jan. 1912-Feb. 1916; C.M. Stevens Feb. 1916-Oct. 1917; Dr. A.K. Wray supplied 1917; Rev. C.W. Duncan, Dec. 1, 1917-Jan. 1, 1918; Rev. L.J. Grantham, 1918; Rev. Fred William, Nov. 1918— May, 1920; Rev. Richard Jones, Dec. 1, 1920—July 1, 1921; Rev. Chester Shiflet, July to September, 1921, supplied; Rev. Martin for one week in 1921; Rev. F.A. Fons, supplied; Rev. John Peyton, June 1, 1922—May 1924; Rev. W. Stark, 1926-1927; Rev. W.T. Wilson, supplied; Rev. A.M. Shelton, supplied 1925; Rev. Truman Douglas supplied, 1924; Rev. Chester Mardis, 1924; Rev. Homer Shankweiler, student, 1927; Rev. John L. Beattie, Oct. 1, 1927-Oct. 1, 1931; Elmer Richardson; Homer Milford, July-September, 1932, held a Bible School; Rev. Samuel (Father) Pearson, April 14, 1933—April, 1934; Rev. Kenneth Park, January 4, 1935— July 1937; Rev. C. Carl Dollar, February 16, 1938.

Mr. and Mrs. Logan Sympson, January, 1938 Mrs. Kinsley supplying data from church record.

Do You Remember

Homer Fox Recalls Churchgoers of 1913; Tells Incidents in History of Friona Congregational Church and Members

HOMER FOX

A short time ago Tess and I drove around over Friona just to see the many new houses that had been built the last few years. It wasn't long until we found ourselves looking for the old houses that we knew and they were hard to find. How the place has grown.

We finally made it around to the corner where the little Congregational Church stands; it is not the same old church as the other one burned, but it is on the same lot. I lived just around the corner in the same block at Mother Reece's boarding house so I didn't have to back-pedal much to remember a lot of things about this little church. I remember the congenial, good natured, hard working pastor, Rev. Hurlbut; he had a fair sized job on his hands, because he had a pretty large flock to look after in the early days, and they were well scattered; and a lot of time he was their lawyer, doctor, general adviser and preacher. You see this little Congregational Church was the only church in Friona and everyone that attended church (and most of them did) had to go to this one.

I was like most kids brought up in those days, and maybe they still are that way, I don't know. I was, and am a Democrat, cause Dad was; I was and am a Presbyterian because my mother was. I never heard of a Congregational denomination, so the thing that eked into my dull head and left the print there for good, was Congregational church. Sure that means everybody's church, one church, one community; it sounded pretty good to me.

Well, I remember the first Sunday I attended the little church and the Rev. Hulbert clinched this impression that I already had formed in my mind, he was near the door when I entered and he extended his hand and said, "Come in Son, you are welcome to God's Church and one God's House." One community, one where a bunch of the finest people on earth came to mix and worship.

I thought about the rigs that were hitched around the church—buggies, wagons, spring wagon, horses and mules, can't remember a single car at that time. They came from far and near, maybe some would only get in a few times a year. The Houlettes, George Taylors, Boatmans, Spahns, B.Z. Taylors, F.W. Reeve; most of these lived pretty far out as I remember; also the Kaisers, Trieders, Reeds, Jeskos, James Singletons, and many more. Some would come on Saturday and spend the night with friends, some would leave home early and go back the same day, bring their own lunch or eat at the hotel, but spend the day with their friends visiting, hungry for news and compansionship. I wonder what the people of That community would have done without that little Congregational Church?

Most every Sunday this little church was pretty well filled up and the close-in ones were pretty faithful. The Coles, Rorbaughs, Ballards, Dugans, Suttons, Stevicks, Henschels, Kinsleys, Wynns, Hansons, Wentworth, Geo. Clarks, Sherribs, Meades,

Gischlers, Clennins, Goodwines, Drakes, Yelvertons, Maurer, Lillards, Weirs, Tiefels, Crawfords, and of course a lot more thatn I can't think of right now.

You could sit back and look that crowd over and find as good talent as you could find any place, and how they loved to do things for one another, and how they enjoyed these Sundays together. I remember one bright sunny morning in September 1913 just as Rev. Hulbert was dismissing his congregational, Mother Reece stuck her head in the door and yelled, "Clennin's house is on fire," and almost due south as the crow flies, we could see the house smoking. A man at the hotel told me to take his horse and buggy and go ahead. I rushed to the store to get out the fire extinguishers, everyone had them in the stores, especially in those days, no waterworks, anyway when I got to the store, some fellows had already broken the glass out of the door and had the extinguishers. One old boy yelled and said "we couldn't wait, we had to have these d--- fire extinguishers." I hopped in the buggy and me and the old grey mare took off. As we came up out of the draw, the Tiefel brothers had their old two spot side winder "Mason" headed for the fire. I pulled old grey in next to the rail, took the corner on two wheels and passed that car. I didn't hold that lead long but it always made the Teifel boys faces red to mention it in company. We all got out there, we had enough willing help to put out the town but no water. The windmill tank was dry and the house burned to the ground and I mean slowly. We had plenty of time to save most of everything in the house, but as usual a lot of it was broken up through too much haste. The people just stayed on, they forgot about dinner, they wanted so bad to do something for a neighbor in distress, you could see it in every face, and they did. A pat on the back, a word of encouragement from a kind heart, in words and deeds they helped the Clennins a lot. It was a hard blow to the Clennins, no insurance on the house, but they rebuilt that fall. But if it hadn't been for that little Church they probably would never known half of the friends and well wishers they had.

I have seen a lot of Churches of every size and kind in all these years, but like a fairy story to a little kid, this little Congregational

FRIONA WOMEN AT CLUB MEETING.

church on the corner will always be the Community Church—"God's House."

Club Starts 47th Year

The Wednesday afternoon meeting of the Friona Woman's Club marked the beginning of the 47th year for the organization. The first meeting was held on the front porch of the Friona Drug Store early in September of 1909. They met in the Friona Club House which was a dream of the members who organized the club.

Mrs. Pearl Bartlett was the only person present who was present at the first meeting. She has been an active member of the club since it was organized. Mrs. Edith Lillard has been a member of the club for more than 40 years. Others who have been active in the club for more than 35 years are Ethel Reeve and Malinda Schlenker.

The covered dish luncheon was followed by an interesting meeting centered around the theme "Texas." Those present answered roll call with, "My first impression of Texas." Mrs. R.N. Gore's subject of discussion was titled, "The Meeting Place of Texas."

Mrs. Edith Lillard accompanied the group as they sang "Texas, My Texas." Hostesses were Mesdames R.N. Gore, John Davis and L.F. Lillard. Mrs. Bert Shackelford was voted in as a new member, and Mrs. Grace Brodt of New York was a visitor.

From the first meeting of the club until the most recent one, the membership has grown from about 20 to 40. There are also three associate members, one charter member, and one honorary member. The charter member is Mrs. Pearl Bartlett and the honorary member is Mrs. Margaret Henchel Reeve of Alameda, California.

Mrs. Reeve donated the land on which the present club house is built. The club house was erected in 1939 through the joint efforts of the Friona Woman's Club and the Modern Study Club.

These two clubs and the Progressive Study Club are Friona's only federated clubs. All three clubs meet regularly in the club house and it is also used by other civic and private groups on special occasions.

In 1939 the Friona Woman's Club sponsored the Junior Study Club, which later became known as the Modern Study Club. The

FRIONA WOMAN'S CLUB and Mrs. Euler's old Summerfield School.

Progressive Study Club was organized in 1951. All three are members of the Seventh District of the Texas Federation of Women's Clubs.

The club motto is, "The best we can do for one another is to exchange our thoughts freely"—Froud.

This motto was chosen by the members when the club was organized and has never been changed. The time of meeting is still the same, too. It is 2:30 p.m. on the second and fourth Wednesdays of each month.

The city park, which so many enjoy in 1956, was a gift from the Friona Woman's Club. When it was first established, it was set with locust trees. After a few years, the borers killed most of the locusts. Then it was set with Chinese elm trees by members of the club.

Many improvements in the community have been made by the efforts of members of this club. Most of them have been active in church and civic groups while their families were growing up. This club has always been willing to cooperate with the schools, chamber of commerce officials and any other group in any undertaking for the good of the community.

Study Club Is 25

The Tuesday evening meeting of the Modern Study Club was a birthday party and silver tea. The cake, which formed the center of the table decorations, was topped with a silver "25" and birthday decorations were used throughout the entertaining rooms.

Mrs. Charles McLean of Houston sent the club a floral arrangement for the piano and the planter was a gift from her to the club. Mrs. McLean was formerly a member of the club.

The highlight of the evening was "Our Silver Anniversary in Retrospect," which was given by Illene Osborn. Mrs. Osborn is the only charter member of the club who is now active in it. Those present answered roll call with a club memory. Nelda May provided music.

Hostesses for the evening were Louisa Wilson, Decimae Beene, Mildred May, Valoris Osborn, Anita Taylor, and Fern Awtrey. Guests, besides Nelda May, were Mrs. John Lamb, and the following former members: Doris Boggess, Lorraine Welch, Martha Clements, and Clydie Black, all of Friona, and Fleta Terry and Carmaleet Terry of Bovina.

FRIONA HOTEL—21 rooms and modern.

KEEP COOL! Roden Spring and Shaffer in the Old Drug Store

W.M. ANDERSON, Contractor

IN FRIONA'S NEW DEPOT

LOOKING SOUTH on Main Street, Friona—About 1910.

LOOKING NORTH ON Main Street in the late 20's—
two story building is present hotel—moved in from
Rhea after original building burned in 1924. This building was Rhea Brothers land headquarters.

SOUTH ON MAIN STREET

UP NORTH ON MAIN STREET

LOOKING SOUTH down Main Street—Friona

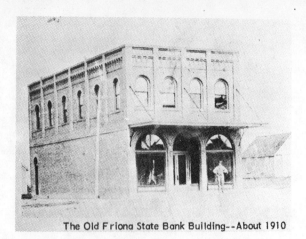

The Old Friona State Bank Building--About 1910

FIRST BRICK BUILDING in Friona (Bank)

CO. OP. STATION in 1929—Marathon Gas, U.S. Tires, Quaker State Oil, and a real Extra—Ladies Rest Room! Left to right: Unknown, A.A. Crown, mgr. Unknown, Wright Williams.

FRIONA CONSUMERS CO-OP—1929

SANTA FE GRAIN ELEVATOR (Men unknown).

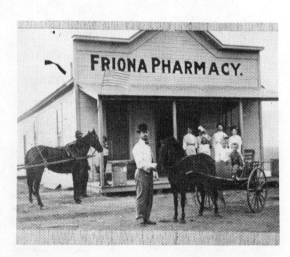

FRIONA PHARMACY owned by Dr. Rohrbaugh.

FRIONA PHARMACY Dr. Rohrbaugh, Physician.

A GARAGE BUILDING in Friona, Texas

THE OLD AND THE NEW.

RESIDENCE IN Friona, Texas

RESIDENCE OF Geo. W. Clark, Friona, Texas.

Gethering for celebration, large building in background was first school building in Friona.

GATHERING FOR celebration, large building in background was first school building in Friona.

123

RESIDENCE OF D.W. McMillan—Friona, Texas.

TWENTY BURRO TEAM—FRIONA.

HAPPY FARMERS

"HOWDY, MAM" Nelda Goodwine and Bruner Bear.

A BEVY OF FRIONA'S FINEST—Left to right—Elsie Goodwine Clennin, R.G. Clennin, T.J. Crawford, and Mrs. Crawford, Lucy Goodwine, Edith Mayer, Ralph Brown, Lawrence Lillard.

F.H.S. STUDENTS—1928, left to right: Watson Whaley, Rosa Hall, Otho Whitefield, Red McFarland, Wade Wright, Chick Schlenker, Dalton Allen, Hadley Reeve, Unknown, J.D. Curry, Earl Beasley, Tracy Campbell.

FRIONA'S SECOND TERM of school was 1909-10, students past the primary grades were—Lucy Goodwine, Clarence Ogg, unknown, Floy Node, Emile Clennin, unknown, Tessie Clennin, Clyde Kime, Miss Grinner, Elta Hinsel, Sterling Stowel, and Clyde Goodwine (wiping dust from his eye!)

FRIONA BALL TEAM—1911

FRIONA BALL TEAM—1908.

F.H.S. FOOTBALL TEAM—1928.

FIRST BRICK SCHOOL IN FRIONA.

AURTHUR HILTON and Friona School Buses.

FRIONA SCHOOL BUSES

ONE OF THE FIRST IN TEXAS.

THE IRON HORSE

TRAIN WRECK, FRIONA—1908.

EARLY TRACTORS REPLACED HORSES.

BREAKING SOD WITH STEAM RIG.

CASE COMBINE was motorized but horses pulled it through the field.

HARVESTING WHEAT—left to right: George Messenger, Clyde Goodwine, Leland (Jim) Goodwine, Fred White, Logen Simpson, and John White.

STEAM ENGINE and thrasher still in use. Owned by M.H. Sylvester.

LEFT: Grace Hort—Right: Orma Flippen

PIONEER IRRIGATION WELL.

FIRST SANTA FE ELEVATOR.

GRAIN ELEVATOR

J.N. JASPER and his oxen—Friona.

FIELD OF Irish Potatoes near Friona.

OIL WELL SOUTH of Friona drilled by Williams.

COYOTE HUNTERS—FRIONA.

FRIONA'S OLD JAIL CELL

FRIO DRAW AFTER A RAIN

WHEN THE DRAW COMES UP.

CECIL SUTTON in Front of Friona Jail in 1912. This jail was built of 2'' x 4'' lumber spoked together in crib style. It had one window with round iron bars across the window.

PILES OF GRAIN Marooned by high water.

FRIENDS! ROMANS! COUNTRYMEN!

WHERE DO WE GO FROM HERE?

FIRST CAR WRECK

CLARIDGE FALLWELL, clear the road!

CHARLIE BANIUM—dare devil!

CLARIDGE FALLWELL— SPORTSMAN!

LAND OF MILK AND HONEY

GEORGE G. WRIGHT'S autos and drivers for land seekers. Mr. Saxene lived in home behind the autos and he was in charge of the autos.

131

PROSPECTIVE SETTLERS.

RED CUMMINGS

JIM BRYANT

BELLES OF THE BALLET—F.H.S.—1928. Left to right are: Otho Whitefield, Harry Hamilton, Pete Richardson, Bill Hamlin, J.D. Curry, Unknown, Granville McFarland, Reeve Guyer, Rosa Hall, Unknown.

GEORGE WILLIAMS, oil well driller.

GROUP OF PEOPLE from Iowa in 1906.

HOPE MAYS is shown giving a reading entitled "Creed" by Hal Borland, during the marker dedication Wednesday, a part of Friona's July 4th celebration.

FRIONA MARKER DEDICATION, 1973, left to right are Hugh Moseley, David Mosley, and Frank Spring.

Chapter VII

Communities

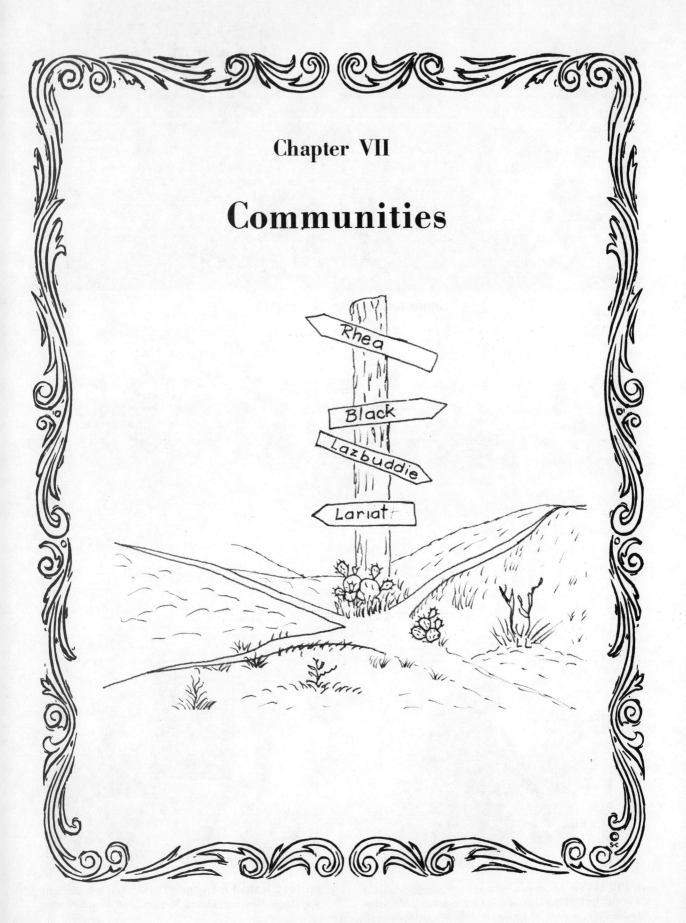

BLACK, TEXAS

Named in honor of E.B. Black, who came to Hereford, Texas, in 1901 and bought several hundred acres of Parmer County land from his brother-in-law, J.E. English. These lands became known as the English and Black Subdivision of Parmer County. The Townsite of Black was carved out of this subdivision. The Black Post Office was established April 26, 1912 and it was discontinued November 30, 1914, mail sent thereafter to Summerfield. Re-established March 6, 1915.

Discontinued May 31, 1920, mail sent thereafter to Summerfield. Re-established February 16, 1926.

Postmasters and Dates
of Appointment:

Joseph C. Baker	April 26, 1912
Joseph J. Erdman	March 6, 1915
Albert S. Bell	April 5, 1916
Thomas E. Baker	March 16, 1917
Bettie M. McCrate	February 16, 1926
Woodrow McCrate	April 9, 1936
Geneva L. Deaton	December 8, 1936
William C. Neill	November 1, 1939
Leslie L. Deaton	April 1, 1945

BLACK FAMILY HISTORY

The earliest ancestor of E.B. Black about whom we know was William Black who was living in Lunenburg County, Virginia in 1757 and who died in Halifax County, Virginia in 1789. His son, Thomas Black, was born about 1745 and lived in Pennsylvania County, Virginia where he was a captain in the Revolutionary Army. He married Susannah Richardson. Among other children they had Nathaniel S. Black born April 23, 1789 in Halifax County, Virginia who married Elizabeth Ann Wilkes May 1, 1809, in Halifax County, Virginia.

With some of his brothers and a sister he migrated to Harris County, Georgia and later to Alabama. His son, Caswell Bond Black was born July 5, 1841 while the family was still in Virginia. He became a captain in the Civil War serving in the 34th Alabama infantry. His second wife was Frances A. Johnston. Both are buried in Society Hill, Russell

County, Alabama; Caswell having died May 10, 1874 and Frances July 30, 1868. It was their youngest child, Epinetus Bushrod Black, born October 13, 1866 who came to Texas, first to East Texas, then to Cleburne as he was orphaned at an early age. He migrated to Deaf Smith County in 1901 and bought land in Parmer County.

By W.A. Black

Neither my father nor our family ever lived in Parmer County. He and my mother's uncle, J.N. English of Cleburne, Texas bought 2222 acres of land on the north side of the railroad from the Capitol Syndicate in 1901 (November) and I think this was the first year they put the land on the market. In 1902 my father established E.B. Black Co., Furniture and Undertaking in Hereford moving from Cleburne, Texas where he had worked in a dry goods store. He moved from there thinking that in establishing his own business in a new area he would benefit financially. This proved to be true although there were many times during drouths, depressions and World War I when financial survival seemed doubtful. Although my father lived at all times in Hereford, his trade territory was quite large as he had the only furniture store and the only undertaking establishment to take care of Parmer County for many decades.

Regarding the Black Community: I do not know when first the railroad switch and later the station was put in and named Black (the station was later moved). It is possible the station was named "Black" because my father was the only individual landowner there at the time, but more probably because he knew quite well the Santa Fe officials in the Amarillo division. Before the roads were paved, the road came to Black from Hereford on the north side of the railroad then crossed over to the south side and continued to Friona. At one time a townsite was laid out on the south side of the railroad. I do not know if any lots were ever sold but the town did not develop. The land my father bought was leased to the Bullock Brothers in 1907 and during the lease, about 1000 acres were

SANTA FE WINDMILL tower at Black.

BLACK MERCANTILE in 1930—Glen McCrate, owner.

broken out for farming. I recall quite well the remains of the steam fired tractor used in this operation in the 1920s. During the 1920s, wheat was about the only money crop.

As I was growing up, I recall quite well the numerous prairie fires we had and the severe winters. One winter the ground was frozen so long and the snow was so deep that it was necessary to rig up a sled to take a body to the cemetery for burial. In 1918 my father took back the land and soon thereafter established a herd of pure-bred Herefords. He had a dispersal sale of this herd in the late 1920s—I think it was 1928. After the original purchase my father bought land to the west and to the east of the 2222 acres. After my mother's death in 1941, my father divided the land between the four children. I am the only one who still owns my portion although my sister, Mrs. Jesse Stanford, deeded her portion to her two children, Mary Barnard (Mrs. Dick Barnard) and Bill Stanford in Plainview. Mr. and Mrs. Barnard still operate E.B. Black Co. in Hereford although the untertaking establishment is now the Gilliland-Watson Funeral Home.

Black School District No. 1

Black School District was designated as District No. 1 soon after formal organization of Parmer County. According to the official survey, as recorded it was in "the Northeast corner of Parmer Co., then on a line west with the North line of said county to point in the west line of Capitol League No. 447, thence south with the west line of said League 477 to the southwest corner of Capitol League 486, thence east parallel with the north line of League 486 to the east line of said Parmer County then north with east line of said county to the place of beginning."

The Black Community had its beginning when the Santa Fe Railroad came through the area in 1898, and the first buildings were in connection with the railroad and its business, such as loading docks, coal chute, pumping facilities for water, etc.

The surrounding land for many miles was owned by the XIT Ranch. In 1901, E.B. Black and Captain English bought land on the north side of the railroad. In 1906 Mr. Black broke and cultivated this grass land for farms and homes were built as the land resold. Black derives its name from this E.B. Black.

In 1908, the Wright Land Co. came in to sell land for the XIT Ranch. About every two weeks, excursion trains brought interested people, along with land promoters and soon this land was sold to settlers from all over the United States. Hotels had been built to house these people while looking over the area. One in this area was given to the county for a schoolhouse in 1910. The Commissioner's Court appointed election officials to hold an election for school trustees for District 1, February 14, 1910. They were T.S. Bullock, C.F. Kelner, George F. Cornish. The first teacher was Miss Laura Edwards.

In 1908 George Hitz of Indiana had bought land, moving to the area in 1911, and the Walco Drilling Co. drilled the first irrigation well about 1913, a 12" one, southwest of where Black now is. This later became the Conway Place and is now the farm owned by Clyde Hays.

Due to the land boom and increased population, school enrollment increased until

SCHOOL GROUP at Black, Texas in 1925. Teachers were: Eloyse Pittman, Major Vurton. Children not identified.

more room was needed, so in 1918 the schoolhouse was moved from near the railroad to the southeast corner of a section about a mile or less southwest of the present location on a farm which was the A.O. Drake farm later, but at that time a bare pasture area. It was re-built into a two or three room house with a coal room added.

The first teachers here were Annie Lee Riley Appling, (now of Claude, Texas), Mary Lou Roberson, also Linnie Mae Donald Roberson. This was from 1918-1922. School Trustees at that time were Ray Conway, Jess Stanford and Elbert Overton. The parents of Mary Lou Roberson lived at Summerfield until 1914, then moved to Hereford. She now lives in Lubbock.

The W.T. Riley family and nephew, Elbert Overton, ran a ranch three miles southeast of Black beginning in 1916. Annie Lee Riley Appling taught her first school at Black in the new building and location in 1918-1919.

Though some records are unavailable for a number of years; other early day teachers were Eloyse Pittman and Roberta Campbell. Also others with salaries are:

1920—Luella Gischler Mauer and Mary Hicks.

A 1923 School Census slip was found, listing school children at that time . . . Jess Stanford was "Census trustee." Bennetts-3, Browders-3, Paul Coneway, Hazel Galloway, D.W. Hanson, Hinds-6, Johnson-3, McKinley-3, Overton-1, Schiehagens and Mary E. Stanford. Other teachers and monthly salaries:

1924-1925 Edith Hunter & Mary V. Davis $110 each

1925-1926 Edith Hunter $120, Emmett McAdoo $115

1926-1927 Eloyse Pittman $125, Major Bruton $125, Milford Alexander $125

1927-1928 Bonnie Curry $100, Eloyse Pittman $125, David W. Ray $100 for 6 months.

In 1924, the school house was moved to its present location, with a two room school and a teacherage built.

The following is copied from Volume 1, Number 1, dated November 1927 of the Black School newspaper:

THE LONG LOOK
NOVEMBER 1927
STAFF—Woodrow McCrate, Business Manager; Lex Alexander, Associate Editor;

137

BLACK SCHOOL

Beulah Mae McCrate, W.R. Scheihagen, Jr.; Margaret Guinn; Elvis Bell; Elizabeth McMurry; Lozeda Deaton; Sidney McKinney; Bonnie Curry; Audaline Mann; Eloyse Pitman; Lanelle Scheihagen; David W. Ray; and Clifford Mann, Art Editor.

PUBLISHED BY BLACK PUBLIC SCHOOL, BLACK, TEXAS, PARMER COUNTY.

OUR FACULTY

Pictures of Miss Bonnie Curry, David W. Ray and Eloyse Pitman appear at top of page 1.

"Cast all your fears on God that anchor holds"

"Rich gifts wax poor when givers prove unkind;'

"Things seen are mightier than things heard"

"Sweet it is to have done the thing one ought"

"To lose the good and secure the evil, you need only to neglect to choose the good."

Bonnie Curry

Once upon a time the King was leaning out the window as his soldiers filed past. The court fool came up behind him, and seeing the broad expanse of the part of one's anatomy which is naturally most prominent when one is leaning out a window, he gave it a great smack.

The king turned on him in rage and ordered him off to be whipped but one of the men begged the king to spare the fool because he was only a fool. At last the king said, "Well, if he can give me an excuse that is worse than the act, I will forgive him." So they called the fool and asked him what excuse he had. He said, "I thought it was the Queen."

"No nation can rise higher than its womanhood." Boys are as good as girls make them be .... What the world needs, is not more men but more man under each hat."

David W. Ray

"Life is the gift of nature; but beautiful living is the gift of Wisdom."

Things don't turn up in this world until somebody turns them up. Tact is something that when you ain't got it ev-body knows you ain't, and when you has got it nobody notices.

Our patiences will achieve more than our faces.

The secret of getting on is getting started.

When you get to the end of your rope tie a knot in it and hold on.

Eloyse Pitman.

A RURAL HIGH SCHOOL FOR BLACK
By Eloyse Pitman

The greatest need of Black today is a Rural High School. We have boys and girls in our community who are anxious for the opportunity of a high school education and it isn't within their reach. They realize that in this age of higher education they will be handicapped thru life if they must depend on only their work of grammar school. Many of these students want to go to college and specialize in the work of their choice, but how can they until they finish their high school work.

Transferring the students to other high schools does not solve the problem. Those who are unable to pay the added expense are left behind. Anyway a person of that age is to young to be sent away from home. Even tho he has had the best of training he is at a plastic stage, the most critical period in his life. He is climbing "Fool Hill" and the chances for getting him up the hill in good repair depend mainly on the influence of the home.

Why should our people have to go away to find the right school. Why not have one here? If for no other reason for the development of the country. To attract the kind of people we want to move in and the kind we want for our neighbors will not come if they find that we do not have a high school, for their aim in life

YOUNG PEOPLE on steps at Santa Fe Depot—Black, Texas. Left to right: Cliff Johnson, Margaret Guinn, Beulah Mae McCrate, Virginia Perkins, Lozeda Deaton, Mildred McMurry. Two others unidentified.

is to give their children, "A better bringing up than they themselves have had." And what about the people who are already here? If they don't care to send their children off they will be left no alternative than to move out and find homes where there are also advantages.

As a concluding thought let us visualize an auditorium large enough for all of us to have a comfortable seat when we meet at the school. A well equipped stage for our program and entertainments. Students and parents wouldn't you be happy to see this come true?

Those who fight against the public school are waging a losing fight.

Lets all Boost and Talk for a HIGH SCHOOL. If we will; this subject over which we sleep we shall some day cease to dream.

"The billows are heaving behind,
     The breakers are foaming before.
We need all the strength we can find.
     Each ounce you can put on the oar.
Are you doing the best that you can
To keep the old galley afloat.
     Are you power or freight?
     Are you pulling your weight—
Are you pulling your weight in the boat?

It isn't the task of the few—
     The pick of the brave and the strong.
It's he and it's I and it's you
     Must drive the good vessel alone.

Will you save, will you work, will you fight?
Are you ready to take off your coat?
Are you serving the State?
Are you pulling your weight—
Are you pulling your weight in the boat?"
                                        Guietman.
                                        E.V. Pitman

BOOST FOR A RURAL HIGH SCHOOL
By: Bonnie Curry

Can a community progress without an educated citizenry? No it can not. All people are more or less interested in an education or at least a high school education.

How many of you want to send your children to a town school? There are but very few in spite of all the many advantages the city school offers. The parents can usually see the danger of sending a young child away from home. If a child insists upon going with the wrong crowd even in a small community what will he do in town? A child can not make a grade and be out two or three nights a week.

Who can realize a high aim in life with only a grammar school education? No one. Who can become a governor without an education. No one. Can anyone become a president without an education? Certainly not. We may say our aim is not in that direction. Even tho it is not. Where are the leaders coming from? For a democracy to live, it must have educated leaders.

The public school is one of the greatest institutions in the world. The public school is for all the children of all the people. It is for the convict's son as well as the minister's daughter. It is the melting pot for democracy, equal rights to all, special favors to none.

He who fights against the school shall return to ignominous dust unhonored, unwept and unsung. His trouble is under his hat. No one shall ever call him blessed or honor his name.

Look ahead, not back; up, not down. If what is old were good enough, we'd never need the new.

                                        B. Curry

HONOR ROLL

Students on the honor roll must make an average of "Eighty" on attendance, deportment and grades.

Audaline Mann, Geneva Deaton, Glen Roberson, Nethla Crawford, Mazie Miller, Owda Bell, Floyd Starns, Richard Lawhorn, Jim Guinn, Adam Ernest Scheihagen, Maurika Crawford, Gladys Hicks, Gwendolyn McKinney, La Elizabeth McMurry, Lex Alexander, W.R. Scheihagen, Jr., Leo Lawhorn, Beulah Mae McCrate, Elmer Maples, Woodrow McCrate, Allen Guinn, Virginia Perkins, Lozeda Deaton.

HIGH HONOR ROLL

Students on the high honor roll must make an average of "Ninety" on attendance, deportment, and grades.

Sidney McKinney, Clifford Mann, Audaline Mann, Oleta McKinney, Elvis Bell, Geneva Deaton, Pauline Mann, Margaret Guinn, Ethmer Smith, George Brown.

WHY WE NEED A
RURAL HIGH SCHOOL
By: Clifford Mann.

First, Because no community can progress where the inhabitants are not EDUCATED.

Second, A good school draws people to the community.

Third, It is very inconvenient for children to go to town to school. Country children should be educated in the country.

Fourth, A good school is attractive in appearance.

Fifth, The auditorium could be used as a community hall and for religious services.

Lastly, No person can obtain a college education without finishing high school.

THE LONG LOOK.
By: Sidney McKinney.

People come up out of the valley and get the long look. When Columbus crossed the ocean he had the long look. Washington took a long look when he started out to whip the English with his small army.

You too can get the long look, if you will look far enough. Don't quit school while you are young but take the long look and go on to college and make something out of yourself.

Every Community Should
Furnish Its Own Entertainment.

If we had a high school here it would be far better and easier for the parents to see plays and entertainment here than going to town.

Ethmer Smith.

More Ready to Give
and More Ready to Go.

If we had a Rural High School, people would be more willing to give their money for school benefits and more boys and girls would be ready to go out into the World's Work.

George Brown.

If we had a High School here, it might cause children whose parents did not have the money to send them off to school, to finish here and then someone might be interested enough in them to send them on to college.

W.R. Scheihagen, Jr.

The quotations on this page are from the students in Black Public School. Printed exactly as they appeared in their themes. Others to be printed later. They all dream of a day when they will go to college. Helping them find and getting them ready for the task born by their side is the work of the Public School.

Office Dog.

VICTORY FOR THE BEARS—October 21st, 1927, marked the beginning of the Black Bears Soccer Ball history. They won the opening game of the season. Defeating the Summer Field Coyotes to the tune of 9 to 2.

The Bears were the first to park the ball over the goal line. Early in the first half the Coyotes rushed the ball into the Bears backfield but missing their aim they fought on the defensive thru out the rest of the game.

In the second half, the Coyotes returned with new snap and vigor and succeeded in booting two goals, but the Bears soon broke up the packs trick and the lone Coyotes limped off the field in defeat.

The Line Up. SMITH, Ethmer, Captain, BROWN, George, MANN, Clifford; THOMPSON, Lessley; BELL, Elvis; GUINN, Allen; McKINNEY, Sidney; McCRATE,

Woodrow; PRICE, Ralph; ALEXANDER, Lex; BROWN, Paul; LAWHORN, Leo.

Soccer Football is the most interesting game I ever played. It is regular football robbed of its brutal tackling, basket ball robbed of its technicalities and old soccer ball robbed of its limitations. The rules are made up from the three games mentioned and in playing the game one can pass the ball, dribble it or kick it. It is a very swift game and would be better named as: "Speed Ball."

GIRLS BASKET BALL GAME

Black Basket Ball team lost the first game of the season to Summer Field. The girls played a good game. The line up was: Lozeda Deaton, Allamae Thompson, Oleta McKinney, Beulah Mae McCrate, Virginia Perkins, Elizabeth McMurry, Audaline Mann, Geneva Deaton, Maesie Miller, and Owda Bell.

Ringling Bros. and Barnum Bailey Shows Combined, marked a red letter day on the Black School calendar. The students and teachers went to Clovis and saw the largest circus in the world.

Remember The Sham Trial Oct. 14? The surprise program of the literary society was a "Price, McMurry" success. After the argument and while some of us were recovering from the fall an orchestra from Clovis rendered an enjoyable program of instrumental music and songs.

Always remember the Hallow-ween Party, but never mention it.

Page six shows pictures of six men and they may be the School Board Members.
Below this is the following statement:

"WHY NOT THIS INSTEAD"

Then follows a free hand drawing of a beautiful little flat top masonry type school building with the flag pole out in front upon which is the Stars and Stripes.

Below the drawing is this quotation:
"So Built We The Wall—For The People Had A Mind To Work;"

Nehemiah—

CADILLAC

The town of Cadillac, Parmer County, Texas, is composed of 14 city blocks, each 300 by 300 feet. Streets were designated as First, Second, and Third. Avenues crossing streets at right angles were to be called Silver, Carpenter, McMillan, Vorpe, Davis, Foster, Ford, and Jackson.

At the request of George G. Wright, a resident of St. Paul in Ramsey County, Minnesota, B.C. McCleary surveyed the townsite and recorded his plot in the Deaf Smith County courthouse on February 9, 1907. Volumn 6, page 22, gives the location as section 104 in Thomas Kelly's subdivision. This proposed town was near the point where Parmer, Lamb, and Castro counties meet.

A rumor of the day suggested that a railroad from Tucumcari, New Mexico, to an undetermined point in the lower panhandle would pass through the proposed town. Both projects failed to materialize.

Lakeview School

The Lakeview School District was brought into existence in 1928 when it was decided to divide the Black School District. It extended from the dividing line approximately 10 miles south to the Lazbuddie District and joined Castro County on the east and ran about eight miles west to the Friona Independent School District.

The two-roomed building was located 11 miles southeast of Friona and built facing the east toward a lake which was dry except during the rainy season. It was a farming and ranching community. The board members consisted of three enthusiastic farmers who were eager to have a good community for the people, Mr. E.B. Whitefield, Mr. J.M.W. Alexander, and Mr. C.A. Guinn.

LAKEVIEW STUDENTS

Mrs. Cora Carter had been elected to be principal at Black but when she was given her choice of staying there or taking a position at Lakeview she chose the new school. Miss Floyd Bridges was the primary teacher.

A letter from Mrs. Carter (now Mrs. Floyd) stated that they started school in September 1928 with a nice new building and desks. They knew something had to be done about the purchase of maps, library books, and other teaching supplies. An auction sale was planned, and the merchants in Friona very generously donated items to be put up for sale. Mr. J.A. Conway, school superintendent at Friona, gave his services as entertainer and very efficient auctioneer. Contributions from men and ladies hair cuts from a barber shop to a fancy pair of garters from a variety store really helped bring in the money.

Mr. Ira Miller of the Lakeview community promised the teachers an extra check for $25.00 if the auction sale brought $50.00. They got that much and a lot more, so they invested in a good used piano. Later they started a project for stage scenery and more library books. "It was a very pleasant year," said Mrs. Floyd.

For the next school term, 1929-39, Mr. and Mrs. Van Boston were elected as teachers and they remained with the school seven

LAKEVIEW STUDENTS

LAKEVIEW SCHOOL

years and lived in the new three-roomed teacherage.

LAKEVIEW STUDENTS, 1928-1929—Students attending Lakeview the first year it had school. Our apologies if anyone is left off this

LAKEVIEW SCHOOL before removal to Friona.

RED TOWER, now Home Ec. cottage

ORIGINAL LAZBUDDIE STORE

list that should have been on it. Bell, Onida; Crow, Clifford; Hazel, Elmore; Guinn, Jim; Hand, L.R.; Haws, Bob, Jim, Lola; Highfill, Jack, Wilda; Hinda, Dean, Leslie; Jones, Euel, J.D.; Maggard, Helen, Robert; Mahler, Aveline, Clifford, Loren; Mandershied, Elaine, Wayne; Maples, Dan, Ethel, Leonard; McKinney, Garland, Gwendolyn; Miller, Claude, Grace, Massie; O'Brien, Julia, Tom; Redinger, Elmeda; Russell, Edwin, Gilbert.

LARIAT

Named by W.H. Simpson of the purchasing department of Santa Fe. It was named for the cowboys' rope or lariat. The post office was established December 9, 1925.

LAZBUDDIE

Lazbuddie was named for D. Luther (Laz) Green from Vernon, Texas, and Andrew (Buddie) Sherley from Anna, Texas. These men bought several sections of land in Parmer County in 1924. When they decided that they would need to set up a commissary, Wayne Sherley suggested that they should call it the Lazbuddie Commissary. It became the Lazbuddie Store and Post Office. This Post Office was established on May 4th, 1926.

THE STATE LINE TRIBUNE
Monday, March 1st, 1954
SPECIAL PUBLIC SCHOOLS
WEEK EDITION

"Lazbuddie School Did
Lots of Moving Around"
By
Barbara Hinkson
(Now Mrs. Glenn Lust)

The history of Lazbuddie and how it got started, and how it has progressed during the past 47 years is quite a tale: as, I imagine, is the history of most schools.

The Lazbuddie School was started back in 1907 with one teacher, whose name is not available, and seven pupils. The pupils who started to school that first year were:

Daisy, Grace and Charley Paul Lyle and Robert Oak, and Mary and Fred Kaiser. Greta and Grace Paul are still living in the community. There was only a four month term that year due to the fact that the teacher left. (Moved away.)

The first trustees for the school were: Joe Paul, Peter Kaiser, Frank Reed, and R.E. Oaks.

We all feel pretty proud to have one of those first four trustees, Joe Paul, still living in the community with us. Mr. Paul served on the (school) board for a number of years.

The school was not known as Lazbuddie back then, but was called the "Star Ranch

"OLD ADOBE" part of the school system.

School." It was named after the Star Ranch, which at that time made up much of this section of the country.

The next year, in 1908, the school got going. The school was located two miles east of the corner south of the school, around Pyrtz'es. For the next four years, from 1908 to 1912, F.A. Cook taught the school. For two of the four years he lived in a tent and on the side he was a county surveyor.

In 1913, Lurlene Boone was the teacher; in 1914, Ralph Stapleton; in 1915, Elsie Goodwine and in 1916, Lucy Goodwine taught the school.

About this time the school took traveling fever and moved to one mile north and one mile west of the present location. It stayed at that location two years, from 1917 to 1919, during which time Lyda Saine was schoolmarm.

The School again desired to move, this time it went a little east of the old Star Ranch headquarters, which is about one mile north and one mile east of where (Lazbuddie School) it is now.

The School was making steady progress and in 1919 it became a two teacher school. The first two teachers to teach (under the two teacher system) were Miss Erma Worth and John Essex. During the 1920-21 term John Essex was back and Ann Mason was the other teacher. The next year in 1922 Erma White and John Younger taught.

The school had another attack of (traveling) fever in 1922 and moved to the "old dobie" which was located one mile south and one-half mile east of the (Lazbuddie) Corner Store.

During the next six years the school stayed at "Adobie." The teachers during that time were Miss Dollie Clark and Grace Paul in 1922-23, Mina Payne and Grace Paul 1923-24, and Viola Trieder and Grace Paul 1924-25.

In 1925 the school again decided to roam and this time finally settled where the present Lazbuddie School is (today). This same year the school consolidated with Red Tower (School District of Castro County) and became a three teacher school. This was when the school took on the name of Lazbuddie. The name came from two men, Lazarus Green and Buddy Sherley. They combined the two nicknames and came up with Lazbuddie.

The old school building must have been very tough and strong because the same building was moved all (of the above described) four times. The reason for all these moves was to try to keep the school in the center of the few families whose children made up the school (pupils). This old building is still with us as it was made into a teacherage; and at present, after considerable over-hauling, is the superintendent's home.

During the 1925-26 term Miss Grace Paul and the two Blankenship girls taught the school. This year must have been a killer because the school jumped from 22 pupils to over 70. Well, the little ones were thick on the stage. Some sat on bricks, nail kegs, etc., and the rest were scattered wherever they could find a place to drop. They had moved the Red Tower (School) building in but it wasn't near enough to take care of over 48 new students. Naturally there weren't half enough books to go around and things looked pretty bad. By the way, the old Red Tower building is the present (at this writing) home economics cottage.

Then to make bad things worse, the school didn't have but one trustee for about a three-month period during the year. All the old trustees had moved away and no one else had lived in the community long enough to qualify to become one.

Gee! What a hectic year!

In 1926, J.B. Lewis came to the school and he actually became the first superintendent of the school. He began to get things done and in 1926-27 a new brick building, (the present grade school) was erected.

SUPERINTENDENT'S HOME

STAR RANCH HEADQUARTERS—1906

OLD STAR RANCH BARN

Three of the trustees at the time the brick building was built were Otto Treider, Bob Bledsoe, and John Steinbock.

Up until then the school had only seven grades. In 1927 they acquired nine grades, and a little later became an eleven grade school.

Mr. J.B. Lewis stayed two years and in 1928 Mr. Haskins became superintendent. He served in this capacity for six years and it was during his administration that Lazbuddie became an accredited high school. The school became a lot better after it became accredited and somewhere around 1929 or 1930 the home economics and vocational agriculture departments were established.

Prepared by the Personnel:
WORK PROJECTS ADMINISTRATION
O.P. No. 665-66-3-299

W.P.A. Report of 1934-35
THE STAR RANCH

The Star Ranch headquarters is located in Parmer County, two miles northeast of Lazbuddie, Texas, and about twenty-seven miles east of Farwell.

The Capitol Freeholder Company deeded sixteen leagues of land to Thomas Kelly of Kansas City, Kansas, on December 15, 1902 and on the same date deeded 10,240 acres to Andy Laird. On October 24, 1904, Andy Laird deeded his acreage to Thomas Kelly. On September 8, 1906, Thomas Kelly filed a dedication and platt after surveying two tracts, divided it into 108 separate sections and improved it. He built the ranch headquarters and called it the Star Ranch.

In 1907 W.W. Ryan, trustee for Thomas Kelly, started selling out 2,560 acres in small tracts. All but four sections of this land was sold by March 22, 1907. On March 22, 1907, these four sections were sold to William Reed. On January 26, 1924, Mary J. Reed sold to W.O. Reed and on October 3, 1924, W.O. Reed sold to the A. Sherley estate, the present owners.

It is reported that the herds that were fed out on this ranch by Thomas Kelly, were sent to Kansas on foot. The cattle were first fed at the ranch, then sent to Kansas. They were fed on Kansas grass and were fed one carload of shelled corn every day. They were sent from Kansas on to Liverpool. The owner is reported to have made a nice profit in spite of the expensive feeding.

The old ranch house is still standing, reminiscent of prosperous ranching days. Although at the present time the house is in a very run-down condition, one can easily see that at one time it was a very fine home. The house is a two story frame structure and is built in the shape of a "T." On the ground floor there are two large bedrooms and a large hall. A stairway runs to the second floor. To the rear there are several rooms of

STAR RANCH SCHOOL

FISHING AT SODA LAKE

average size. On the second floor there are two large rooms to the front and one large room running to the back that looks as if it might have at one time been used as a dance hall. The ceilings are all beaded and the faded wallpaper still can be recognized as being the best. The house faces east, away from the highway. There is a porch on the east and south sides. At present it is practically fallen down. It has been propped up with anything that could be found at hand. A large dinner bell can still be seen on the top of the house.

The barns and corrals still stand but like the house are in a very dilapidated condition. There is also a large windmill and storage tank.

A large part of the land surrounding this old ranch house is in cultivation.

BIBLIOGRAPHY
Bill Sherley . . . . Lazbuddie, Texas
Press Abbott . . . . Bovina, Texas

Star Ranch, which had been purchased from the syndicate in 1902 by Thomas Kelly, a member of the Livestock Commission of Kansas City, was one of the largest and best known ranches in the country. Land comprising 55,136 acres was purchased from the Capitol Reservation Land Company. Ten thousand acres were purchased by A.L. Laird, first foreman of the ranch, making a total of 65,136 acres, or slightly over 160 sections of land, constituting Block "H," Kelly Subdivision.

It is told that in measuring this land A.L. Laird, first "boss" of the ranch, attached a speedometer to his buggy wheel and with a compass in his lap, took the measurements. Cattle were brought in by Kelly, and Star Ranch became an active cattle ranch with 30 windmills, various outbuildings, bunkhouses for cowboys, and corrals for horses.

One building, a dugout, and about eight windmills were already there, having been put there by the syndicate; the dugout known as Red Tower Camp, was there about 43 years ago, according to an old settler. Directions or locations around the ranch used to be given according to names of windmills, according to Mrs. F.L. Reed, of Friona, whose husband purchased a part of Star Ranch in 1908. A few of the windmills were: Red Tower, Keefer, Four-mile, Carter Corner, and Cottonwood—important, for they meant water for thirsty stock and humans in a dry country.

Star Ranch functioned on this large scale only from 1902 until 1908 when the last of the Kelly cattle were shipped to Kansas for summer feeding on their way to market at Liverpool, England. Ben Curtis came as second manager of the ranch in 1903, and he was manager until the ranch was sold in 1908.

Almost at once this land was placed on the market for retail to homesteaders, as Kelly believed the land was fit for farming and would eventually make an agricultural country. Conditions since have proved the wisdom of his vision. By 1906 much of the land had been sold in tracts ranging from 80 to 640 acres. In some instances three or four sections were sold to one purchaser. Kelly gave liberal terms and 25 years time, thus encouraging the small farmer to own a home.

The land was also listed for sale with the George G. Wright Land Company, which ran

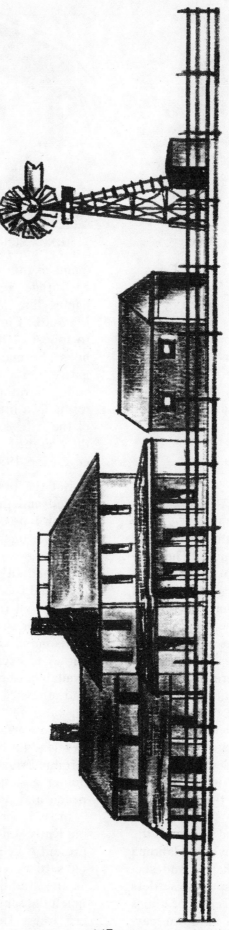

THE STAR RANCH headquarters as it was
April 1st, 1906.
Located in Parmer County, two miles
Northeast of Lazbuddie.

FOURTH OF JULY at Star Ranch.

KNOX SCHOOL BUILDING and Carpenters.

excursion trains from Kansas City to Friona and brought the people out to Star Ranch in a special fleet of automobiles owned by the company. Some of the settlers buying farm-ranch tracts who are still represented here are: Joe Paul, who built in 1907; John Treider, Stephen Jesko, and Pete Kaiser, who built in 1908. R.L. Bledsoe is also an early comer to the Star Ranch, or Lazbuddie community.

A HISTORY OF THE
OKLAHOMA LANE AND
ITS CHRISTMAS TREE
By Harold Carpenter

In the years prior to 1916, this community was part of the great XIT Ranch. "The Syndicate" as it was known had not sold any land in this area. Ranch affairs were administered through the Bovina Division. Windmills, some of them hand dug by the range hands, dotted the prairie. Line shacks and half dug-outs served as seasonal homes for the cow-boys. Barbed wire fences were few and far between. A lone traveller might chance upon an iron surveyor's stake. The little towns of Bovina, Farwell and Texico were the nearest permanent settlements. Herds of cattle dot-ted the plains. Antelope and deer were infre-quent visitors, wandering in from the "brakes" of New Mexico and the caprock to the south.

The year of 1915 found land agents of the "Syndicate" circulating all over Oklahoma and West Texas. Quarters, halves and sec-tions of land were sold to prospective settlers for as little as $100.00 down. Teams of mules and horses were even taken as down pay-ments as the "Syndicate" made a big push to encourage agriculture in this area. Soon names like Magness, Dosher, Hammonds, McGuire, Christian, Fowler, Perkins, began to appear on land deeds in the county court-house. Permanent homes began to take form, native grass began to disappear and the young farming settlement began to take form. Two little schools, Knox, located west of the A.L. Tandy farm, and Sunnyside, on the present Earl Routon farm were complet-ed during 1917.

But the first crop had already been har-vested and the first Christmas observed.

John Bates, Ben Bates, E.W. McGuire and John Scribner had all moved their families and possessions to this community in 1916. They had all settled close together for com-pany and moral support, putting down a do-mestic well from which each family hauled water for livestock and household use. Christmas Eve found these four families to-gether to exchange what few presents were available. Christmas day was beautiful, warm and sunny. The four men spent the day work-ing on a new home for one of the families. The Fowlers, also observing Christmas in a new land far from their native Oklahoma, en-tertained relatives, enjoyed a baked chicken dinner and spent the afternoon setting out peach and plum trees.

In 1917, the Christmas Tree was held in the old Knox School, located direcily west of the present A.L. Tandy farm. This is the year that old settlers recall that a peach tree was used as the traditional tree and the effect was much the same as we have today in our mod-ern trees. Decorations for this tree were home made. Strings of cranberries and pop-corn livened up the appearance. The sacks of treats that Santa handed out that night were made of bright colored mosquito netting and were filled with treats that were "store bought" with the proceeds of the first box supper that had been held a few weeks pre-viously. The sacks were hand made by the women of the community. For this program someone made a talk. The little school house was filled.

A program of some sort was planned for the Christmas of 1918, but the flu epidemic and heavy snows cancelled their plans. World War I was coming to a close and now families were filtering into the community. Chester Fowler and Mable Ayres Ellison were to present a program. They were to be a doctor and a nurse. Vashti recalls this was the year that her brother, Chess, got his first long pants.

1919—The weather was favorable and Old Timers report that the community had a "Tree." By this time the families of Foster, Christian, Magness, Hammond, Rhodes, and Perkins who came in 1918, had moved into the community and attended the get-to-gether.

In 1920, the Christmas Tree was held in the old Sunnyside School, located on the corner of the persent Earl Routon farm. Another peach tree wrapped in green crepe paper was used. About 12 or 14 families were present. Among these families were the George Mag-nesses, the Fowlers, the McGuires, the Fos-ters, the Doshers and the Hammonds.

1921 was a year of progress. A real cedar tree was brought in from the breaks by Tom Foster, John Christian, Carl Fowler and the newly married Clyde Perkins. The celebra-tion was held on the present location of the Oklahoma Lane Methodist Church, as the two little schools of Knox and Sunnyside had been consolidated. The school had only two teachers and P.A. Lee was the superinten-dent. This year of 1921 was also important as the year that the date of the first Friday night in December was officially set as the date for the annual box supper to raise funds for the purchase of Santa's sacks. This date re-mained the same down through the years despite basketball games, deaths in the com-munity, snow or shine until the Oklahoma

OKLAHOMA SCHOOL BUILDING before the Lane was added. School District Number 10.

Lane School house became the present Methodist Church years later. This was the year that Carrie Foster and Lucille Magness took the pruned limbs from the 1921 tree and made large gaudy hats of them. They painted their cheeks a violent red and went about school switching the other children and otherwise making a nuisance of themselves. They were severely reprimanded by teacher P.A. Lee. He remarked, "If I were to tell you what kind of girls you remind me of it would make you mad."

Some family names you will recognize who came and stayed were: McGuire, Fowler, Hammonds, Foster, Tandy, Christian, Mag-ness, Roberts, Perkins, Balls, Robertson, Ayres, Rhodes, Meeks, and Miller (of course we are not certain of the year each family came).

In 1922, another big snow storm racked the high plains. No trip to the breaks. Same old peach tree covered with crepe paper. Okla-homa Lane was still only a two-teacher school. The superintendent was Mr. N.C. Smith, who later became rural mail carrier and remained such for many years, and Miss Ann Foster was the other teacher. But the little school was fast becoming overcrowded. The late R.G. Hammonds donated the school a box car, to be used as temporary class-rooms and Superintendent Smith took the overflow students and taught them there.

1923—A great year for the community. A giant new building of tile with coal furnace and basement classrooms was built. Another big snow storm that year, but the tree had al-ready been brought in. Christmas shopping trips that year were made with wagons and teams. The celebration went on as scheduled despite bad weather.

GEORGE ROBERTS and family, February 6, 1919. Back row: left to right—Joe, Oda, Ruth. Second row: Thelma, John, Earl. Seated: Mr. and Mrs. George Roberts with Lonnie standing between them.

MRS. ROBERTS with her turkeys (Okla. Lane)

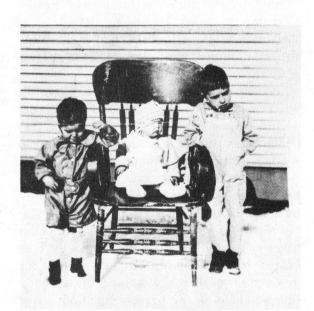

MABEL AYERS, Maurene Tandy holding Jurhee Wood.

RAY GLEN AND JURHEE WOOD

CHURCH GROUP at Oklahoma Lane Community.

PICNIC GROUP at Oklahoma Lane—not dated.

150

MRS. ROBERTS and Mrs. Alexander (Okla. Lane)

SUNDAY AFTERNOON, Oklahoma Lane

GROUP PICTURE, Oklahoma Lane Community—not dated.

D.W. CARPENTER of Oklahoma Lane planting milo.

SHERMAN WOOD AND FRIEND

GLEN WOOD CHILDREN.

STANDING, left to right: Gertrude Fowler, Susie Wood, Maude Wood, Bertha ——, and Lillie Rury. Seated left to right: Guy Mounce, Carl Fowler, Sherman Wood, Frank ——, and Clyde Rhodes. Picture bears no date.

CLAUDE ALEXANDER, Carl Fowler and Mr. Wood.

GLEN WOOD AND VELVA AYERS.

F.W. AYERS thresher at work in early 1920's.

HAROLD CARPENTER posing with his dogs.

OKLAHOMA LANE—Group Picture—not dated—people unidentified.

In 1924 a traveling Christmas tree salesman came through Farwell with a giant Christmas tree. His plans were to cut up the big tree and sell it as several smaller trees. Carl Fowler, brother of Chester and Vashti Fowler, happened to see him before he cut it up and made a bid for it. The man was happy to sell it and Carl triumphantly brought home the biggest tree ever. Carl Fowler's sister, Vashti, has served on more tree-decorating committees than anyone else in the community.

In 1925, another snow storm prevented a trip to the breaks for a cedar tree. The tree committee resorted to the ever faithful old peach tree wrapped in crepe paper, and the people came to the celebration in wagons. Mrs. Ed. McGuire recalls that the H.G. Hammonds family came by their farm in a wagon. They piled on a load of blankets and heated bricks to keep their feet warm and proceeded on to the school house.

The year 1926 brought a surge of new settlers. For several years, families moved in by the score and broke out the native grass. The depression of the thirties saw many families become discouraged and move on. A church and Union Sunday School had been in operation in the old school house for several years.

It was a hard land but a rewarding one. Many of the first settlers have lived to see a community of modern churches, irrigation wells, farm to market roads, electricity, telephones, and other modern conveniences.

But the Oklahoma Lane Christmas Tree has remained the same. Always to be held on Christmas Eve night, always old Santa with a gift for everyone and always the Spirit of the old time Christmas.

O'NEAL SCHOOL

The O'Neal School was located near the home of a family by that name who lived north of Bovina four miles. The Tidenberg children who came to Bovina in 1909 attended this school the first year they were here transferring to Bovina later. The school closed when the O'Neal family moved about 1912.

RHEA

The Rhea community is located in the northwest part of the Rhea subdivision in Parmer County which was a block of land

EASTER SUNDAY with the Schlenker family (picture not dated) at Fuqua Ranch. Louisa Schlenker on front row with X on dress.

bought from the XIT by John and Joe Rhea for a cattle ranch and was sold for farming land in the early 1900's. F.L. Spring and Charles Schlenker were the first farmers in the area moving there in 1906. Later several other families moved into the community including J.W. Barnett, Charlie Stewart, J.W. Scaceny, H.B. Hunters, Carl Copeland, A.J. Grim and J.R. Champion, all of whom stayed only a few years then moved away.

A one-room school house was built in 1908 with fourteen pupils attending. The first year Miss Cora Hutchinson taught for a couple of months then a Mr. Miller finished the term. In 1909 Miss Malinda Reeve from Indiana taught the school and continued several years until she married Floyd Schlenker. The Rhea school continued until 1949 when the district was divided, part going to Friona and part to Bovina.

The school building was used for Sunday school and when it was possible to find a preacher service was held there. Also we had a "Literary Society" that met twice a month at which time anyone who had a special talent was welcome.

Elections were held here too, in fact it was the meeting place for any special event.

FRIONA STAR, Friday, September 27, 1951

RHEA

It was that the Reinkinds, the Gallmeiers, the Droeges, Schroeders, Schlingers and Schultz came, saw, bought and eventually conquered.

It was between 1906 and 1910 that most of

HOTEL FINDLAY Decoration Day in 1910.

ON THE WAY HOME from Findley, May 30, 1910.

LEAVING "Old Findley"

them drifted out here, joining the Walz family from Arcadia, Indiana, Will Schumns from Ohio, and the Porths from Kansas.

Here they met to fight together the hazard of building a house, drilling a well, growing a crop, raising a family, creating a life. In comparative isolation, they were all new to the land, miles from supplies, from doctors, from everything but a church and a friend.

Today the community encompasses about 40 families on its 100 square miles of land, many of them represent three generations in a family that is still farming the same land. Many of the families have intermarried, and both of these factors help account for the strong community spirit prevailing there.

But, like most stories of pioneers, the first years were discouraging. Those people had to meet and control the problems of drouth, bugs, prairie fire. The beautiful grain crops which the land agents showed off so proudly began to look suspiciously like experimental farms; it was the same old story of a Paradise forced to meet reality face to face. Some of the families, discouraged and broke, went home to the Middle West but there were those who stayed.

And what was life like? Well, truly it was the era of the independent, staunch, anti-socialist thinker. There were no subsidies, no guarantees, and quite frequently no profit.

Farming was a heart breaking experience. Those men of the soil born to the settled farmland of the Middle West were used to establish ways of farming. As Mrs. Charles Schleinker pointed out, "Nobody that came down here knew what would work."

Here they discovered their standby tools would not do. Grains grew too tall, moisture was too light. They deserted their breaking plows and rollers for listers. They had only draft animals to help them farm a half section or a section of land instead of 40 or 80 acres. It took time; but they learned.

Some investigated the possibilities of ranching. They could buy cattle below the breaks, purchase yearling calves for $12.50 and sell at a remarkable profit—but there were deadly quirks in the cattle market.

Water was a big problem. Even backyard gardens on whose success even subsistence sometimes depended, had to be irrigated. They experimented with tiles laid three feet deep, like pipes, through which the water seeped and nourished the plants.

For doctors and dentists it meant either a trip to Hereford or Clovis or using homemade medicines. Every housewife kept a supply of the old standbys: horehound roots, sassafras bark, hard rock candy, whiskey, mustard for plasters, turpentine and lard.

There were no roads in the area, transportation was by horse-drawn buggy. You could drive from Friona to Rhea and stop for only three gates.

154

PICNIC AT Fuqua Ranch in 1911.

SUNDAY SCHOOL group taken at Rhea School, 1909.

The farmers who settled found the influence of the bigger ranches creeping into their lives. The XIT spread didn't break up until 1912, the Rhea ranch still ran thousands of cattle, and the Escabada ranch still has its headquarters just over the Deaf Smith County Line. Fenced-in farmland wasn't always popular. Unfenced land wasn't always practical.

Originally the community was knitted together by the post office. It was in the Gallmeir home, and the profit was made strictly out of the sale of postage stamps. Eventually the patrons found that there wasn't enough profit in the business to warrant all the time it took, so the Post Office was dissolved.

It's interesting to note that at the time of its establishment the people from Indiana had hoped to name the post office Fort Wayne, after their old home town, but finally, government authorities settled on Rhea.

When the Rhea postal office was eliminated, the citizens began to get their mail out of Bovina. Charles Schlenker delivered the mail on Monday and Friday. Mrs. Schlenker always left a light in the window for him, so he could find his way home easily after those deliveries, and the neighbors for miles around would know mail was on its way.

Of course social life was a community affair, and it centered around the church and the school.

Community parties included sing songs, box socials, pie suppers, special holiday parties, Christmas programs, a community tree and sometimes even amateur dramatics. The women had sewing bees and later meetings of the Home Demonstration Club to spark their social activities. Bridal showers were always given and the entire community attended and weddings were gay occasions.

These activities, perhaps more than any other feature, laid a solid foundation for community fellowship and understanding. Even today community affairs are eagerly anticipated. Although the school has now been disbanded and the children ride a bus into Friona, the gatherings are still gala and everybody comes.

Perhaps the secret of the integration at Rhea lies in the influence which the church has had upon all their lives. Each Sunday for weekly services and each special festival day the church is opened, not only to members, but to all the citizens of that community, regardless of their denomination.

Mrs. Herman Schuler who was formerly a Gallmier, recalls the first time she attended church in Parmer County. It was the first Sunday after the family arrived here, on February 3, 1910, and although they were still unpacked and unsettled, the family dressed and attended church. There was no church building there and no pastor, but services were held with the same reverence and devotion, although it convened in the parlor of the residence, a square table was used for a pulpit and the speaker was Pastor Lohman, who drove 30 miles from Hereford in a surrey to deliver the message. The S. and W. Land Company donated 40 acres and $1,000 to the project. The men gave their labor, hauling material from Friona. Then the Lutheran pastor from Fort Wayne, O.E. Schmidt, came down to Texas to serve his flock.

History of Lutheran Congregation
Friona, Parmer Co., Texas

The small beginning of Immanuel Congregation, 18 miles northwest of Friona, Texas, was made in March, 1908 when Mr. Herman

155

THE RHEA CHURCH

THE CONRAD DROEGE HOME—Standing (left to right) are William Schumm, George Sachs, Herman Reinking, Mr. and Mrs. Conrad Droege, Ida Reinking, and Mr. and Mrs. Schulz.

F. Reinking from Decatur, Adams County, Indiana, negotiated a contract with the Wright Brothers for ten sections of land to be sold exclusively to Lutherans. The Wright Brothers from Kansas City, Missouri, had purchased a large tract of grazing land from the Farwell Syndicate, owners of the XIT Ranch, who desired to settle this land with thrifty out-of-state farmers. One of their real estate agents was Mr. J.J. Vorpe from Van Wert, Ohio. The Wright Brothers used high-pressure methods of salesmanship to pro-mote a boom for settlement project. Special Coaches and even special trains were run weekly from Chicago and Kansas City to Friona to accommodate the fortune-seeking farmers from the Central States. Hundreds of people came to Friona in those days.

Friona, at this time, was only a village with a few stores, a lumber yard, a bank, and a small hotel. Most of the people slept in the pullman train in which they had come for the two or three days' stay inspection tour. In those days the automobile was yet a novelty to the adventurous farmers who had come to these wide-open spaces to see for themselves what this great country was like. The Wright Brothers had a dozen or even more automo-biles at the disposal of the prospective land-buyers. They had the people shown to the best spots of land to insure the sale of their land. It was during the boom years of this Panhandle of Texas that Mr. Herman Rein-king came to Friona in search of good farm-ing country.

In his youth, Mr. Reinking had seen Iowa and Nebraska develop into rich and fruitful states. Now he was 60 years of age, and after seeing the Panhandle of Texas, he felt sure that this was for him a second chance to help settle a new country at a low cost of land. With a spade in hand he got out of the car that hauled him around in the country and examined the depth of the fertile soil. After serious consideration and study he put the following proposition to the Wright Brothers Land Company:

A. They should set aside ten sections of land to be sold exclusively to German-Lutheran people in one plot.

B. They should donate and set aside forty acres of the half-section of land which Mr. Reinking had chosen for himself. These forty acres were to be deeded to the German-Lutheran Congregation, Missouri Synod, as soon as feasable after it had been organized.

C. And they were to donate $1,000.00 for the erection of a Chapel on the forty-acre church ground. Without quibbling the Wright Brothers agreed to the propositions and promised to give a bell for the Chapel after it was built. But this last promise was not kept.

The same day Mr. Reinking contracted for 280 acres and made the above proposition legal and returned to his home in Indiana, filled with joy over his accomplishments and full of hope for a prosperous future for the new colony in the Panhandle of Texas, then called Ft. Wayne.

HERMAN F. REINKING

Upon arriving at his home-town, Mr. Reinking gave a report of his trip to the Decatur Democrat. This newspaper gave him a nicely written article, which was read by many. Soon many of his friends in the Bleeke settlement, Preble, Freidheim, Flatrock, and Fuelling Congregations became interested in the Texas Panhandle and made excursions to this new country. In the space of a few months the ten sections of land which had been reserved originally were sold to German-Lutheran people. This prompted the Wright Land Co. to reserve additional sections of land.

It now became necessary for the people who had purchased the land to get together to formulate plans for a concentrated effort to get people to move down to Texas. Several meetings were held in Decatur. By this time not only Mr. Reinking was the spokesman for the new colony, but men like Charles Gallmeier, Ferdinand Bultemeier, Carl Bultemeier, Carl Schroeder, Conrad Droege, Jacob Schueler, Carl Oetting, Henry Heckman, Fred Heckman, Charles Lavall, and many others were heard. Some were willing to start up anew in this colony, others offered financial assistance to those who would need loans but no one seemed willing to be the first settler, because, no water or shelter was near this new colony. Finally funds were raised by free-will offering to have a 4 inch well drilled and a colony house built on the forty acre church property, for the housing of the first settlers in the colony. After these two obstacles were taken care of, Mr. Reinking decided to go with his son, Herman, age

THIS PICTURE REMINDS us of the pioneer days. It shows the colony house built perhaps in 1908 or 1909, and the church built in 1910. At first the colony house was to the left of the church near the colony well and accommodated the first early settlers. Later on it was moved to the right of the church and served the Christian Day School. Still later on with a few additions it served as the parsonage until the new parsonage was built in 1954.

19, in the spring of 1909, and to have his daughter, Ida, who was in Pasadena, California, to come and keep house for him and his son, since Mrs. Reinking would not leave her home in Indiana.

In the month of March, 1909, Mr. Reinking engaged a box-car and loaded three horses, one cow, one brood sow, two dozen chickens, farm implements and feed and he and his son rode the freight train for six days to Friona. This was the longest, most uncomfortable trip that the writer of this memoir ever made. It was truly unromantic. Arriving in Friona on a bright, sunny day at this time it was unknown to Hoosiers that in the Panhandle the sun shines every day and that clouds seldom appear on the blue sky, the unloading was uneventful except for smiles and curiosities of the older citizens of Friona. After a good night's rest in the hotel, we loaded our wagon with our necessary household goods, food, poultry and livestock and arrived at the colony house at sun-down.

There was no corral, so the livestock was tied to the wagon for the night, and my father and I set up to keep house and to retire. Our three horses were strange and were rather restless. They were tame, heavy draft horses, however, something frightened them, and about midnight all broke loose, and dashed into the darkness. Early, before daylight the next morning, my father instructed me to go northwest following a certain star, until I should come to the old ranch house in the draw, here I should seek help from Mr. Schulz who lived there, and Mr. George Sachs, both of whom my father had met on his first trip. He would go in the direction to the northwest where lived a family by the name of Houlette and whether we found the horses or not we would return to the colony house by night. What an experience that was with coyotes howling in the night and rattlesnakes slithering in the grass by day. Fortunately my father had found the horses near the well about six miles north of the colony house and was eagerly awaiting my arrival. We were thankful to have our horses back.

The next day we purchased hobblers at a small store in Hollene, New Mexico, and a field was fenced off, to keep our livestock from straying away. Next, we tried to make a garden. The ground was so hard and dry, we couldn't plow nor spade it, and it just wouldn't rain. After the hay and grain which we had brought along from Indiana was all fed, it became necessary to buy corn and hay in Friona or Bovina every week. And it just would not rain! In order not to be idle, we hauled loose stone from the draw north of the colony, and since my father was a good mason, he proceeded to build a stone house. This now, greatly remodeled and enlarged house, is the beautiful home of the Herman Schueler family today. While we were building our house, the Conrad Droege house was being built and later the dugout of Charlie Lavall. Next was the Charles Gallmeier house, then the Carl Schroeder house, several months later the Charles Bultemeier house (for the Earnest Schroeder family). These three families moved here the 3rd of February, 1910, all suffering hardships and privation for it just WOULD NOT RAIN. No one even thought of irrigation wells!

Because I knew Pastor Arthur Lohman, a Missouri-Synod Lutheran minister, who was stationed at Canyon, I contacted him and he came to conduct services for us in the colony house. After the service he took the picture showing Mr. William Schumm, Mr. George Sachs, Herman Reinking Jr., Mr. and Mrs. Conrad Droege, Ida Reinking, and Mr. and Mrs. August Schulz at the colony house. Pastor Lohman served us the best he could from Canyon, and we would change off getting him and returning him to the Friona

Depot. Now had come the time to organize this congregation and to adopt a constitution. The name chosen was Immanuel German Lutheran Congregation U.A.C. Next came the building of the Chapel for which $1,000.00 was lying in wait at the Friona Bank. It was placed there by the Wright Brothers Land Co. as Mr. Reinking had contracted with them. The people who by this time were members of Immanual Congregation: Mr. and Mrs. Carl Gallmeier and their children, Mr. and Mrs. Conrad Droege, Mr. and Mrs. Carl Schroeder and children, George Sachs, William Schuman, Ida and Herman Reinking, Charlie Lavall, Mr. and Mrs. Earnest Schroeder. Mr. and Mrs. Schulz did not become members, nor did the Fahsholz family join. Neither did Mr. Herman F. Reinking join because he was preparing to return to his home in Indiana for valid reasons.

After the dedication of the Chapel the congregation assembled regularly every Sunday. Pastor Lohman served them as often as he could, and on the Sundays when he was not present reading worship services were conducted by me. I was given this honor because I had been in Concordia College for three years. Ida was a great help to me during the week reading and rereading the assigned sermon from Dr. Walther's Sermon book and selecting the hymns and prayers. Pastor Lohman was highly pleased with our congregational life and encouraged us to continue in the good work.

In one of these long rides to Friona after services, Rev. Lohman talked to me very seriously to consider going to Springfield to study for the Holy Ministry. This council quickened me to the care. It was then that to me came a divine call summoning me into the full-time service of His church. My mind was soon made up and on the last Sunday in January—1911, I bid farewell to the beloved people in the colony to leave for the seminary at Springfield, Illinois. We had sold our livestock and implements to the Walz family and my sister Ida continued the school a while longer and then decided to live in Hereford. As I remember it, this is the story of how Immanuel Congregation came into being. May God in His great love continue to bless this His church and may He ever keep

her in pure doctrine and supply her faithful ministers for the future.

By Rev. Herman J. Reinking

RHEA SCHOOL

The Rhea school was established about 1908 or 1909. The first directors were J.R. Champion, J.W. Barnett and Chas. Schlenker. There were four families living in the community who had children of school age. The men got together and built a one-room school house which was located about one half mile north of the Barnett home on the Frio draw, approximately in the center of the Rhea Bros. subdivision and was called the Rhea school. The school room was furnished with a pot bellied stove and a long home-made table with benches around it on which the children sat with the teacher sitting at the head of the table.

There were thirteen pupils the first year: Madeline, Calvin, Homer, Jay and Dorothy Barnett, Willard, Esther, Mabelle, Florence, Bula and Harold Schlenker. Lula Champion and Don Adams. Miss Cora Hutchinson was the first teacher. The second year a Mr. Miller taught and the third year Malinda Reeve taught, she later married Floyd Schlenker.

The J.W. Barnetts and the Champions moved away and the school house was moved to a new location which was three quarters of a mile south of Chas. Schlenker and one half mile east of the H.B. Hunters, following the center of population.

By 1923 more families had moved into the community and it was necessary to build a larger two-room building. Floyd Schlenker, Clarence Dixon and Henry Helms at this time were trustees. Land was given by a non-resident across the road from the Floyd Schlenker home where the new building was built, the lumber was hauled from Bovina in a wagon pulled by burros. The old school building was moved nearby and was used for a teacherage. There were about thirty pupils at this time. The J.B. Fowlers were the first teachers.

Later the number grew to approximately eight and another two-room building was built.

RHEA SCHOOL BUS, Harold Schenker, driver.

SUMMERFIELD SCHOOL, now Euler's barn.

In 1949 the Rhea school district was divided, part going to the Friona school district and part to the Bovina district.

Some of the teachers who taught at Rhea were: Miss Cora Hutchinson, Mr. Miller, Malinda Reeve Schlenker, Abbie Reeve, Jack Storm, Miss Winn, Mr. and Mrs. J.D. Fowler, Marie Gardner, Vivian Boston, Mr. Nolan, Mr. Overstreet, Corrine Tipton, Gladys Sides, David Sides, Nelda Goodwine, Mr. and Mrs. Wallace, Greta Paul, and Dolly Clark.

SUMMERFIELD SCHOOL
NEWSPAPER ARTICLE, Nov. 17, 1968

Searching for information to compile a history of the Summerfield School, Mrs. Johnson, who herself is a former teacher, has found that the first school was in the half-dugout home of a Mrs. Millet, who taught the Wilson and Loflin children and her own children about the turn of the century.

The first school was built in 1901 or 1902, according to recollections of Mrs. J.L. Roy Rogers, 306 N. Lawton, whose family, that of the late W.L. Sain, moved to Summerfield from Johnson County in November of 1902. The building was new then, she says.

She entered school when the term began the following January 1, and Miss Lenna Greer, later Mrs. Persy Estes, taught several terms and was the only teacher.

A second teacher was added to the faculty for the 1911-12 term, when Miss Edith Maurer now Mrs. Lillard of Friona, was the principal and Miss Mattie Highsmith, now Mrs. Ford of Clovis, N.M. the assistant. Miss Hortense Russell, now Mrs. Woodard of Amarillo, followed Miss Highsmith.

Ray Johnson, who came with his parents to the community in 1908, remembers that Will Harris was the teacher in 1910. Mrs. Rogers says Johnson attended high school in Hereford and rode back and forth on the train, which had a convenient schedule that brought him to Hereford early in the morning and took him home after school was dismissed.

Mrs. Rogers also recalls an odd fact caused by the location of Summerfield at a point where Deaf Smith, Castro and Parmer Counties come together. The three counties took turns paying the teacher her salary in the early days.

As the school building was in Castro County and Miss Greer boarded with a family whose residence was in Parmer County, when it was her turn to draw her pay from Deaf Smith County she was in a unique position, being paid by one county while she lived in another and worked in a third.

The wooden school building was used for church services as well as classes, Mrs. Rogers says, and her family drove in by buggy from their farm six miles to the south, to attend church twice a month and a Methodist minister another Sunday.

The congregation which came in from scattered farms, many for long distances, usually heard the preaching, then had "dinner on the ground" before an afternoon Union Sunday School. The Presbyterian minister from Hereford sometimes preached after Sunday School.

Names of Laura Edwards and Mr. Edelman are also mentioned among early teachers in the school. A brick building replaced the old wooden school about 1920, when Miss Bessie Foster, now Mrs. O.G. Hill Sr. of Hereford

Billie Longhomer

RHEA SCHOOL, 1910—Back Row, Don Adams, Lula Champion, Madaline Barnett, Malinda Reeve, Esther Schlenker. Second Row, Jay Barnett, Edna Hunter, Maybelle Schlenker (Hartwell), Calvin Barnett. Front Row, Homer Barnett, Harold Schlenker, Bula Schlenker, Florence Schlenker, Dorothy Barnett.

was principal.

Mrs. Johnson, then Miss Billee Smith, came to Summerfield as a teacher for the 1921 term, when the brick building was new

and Miss Dell Slaton was the other teacher.

After it was no longer used for school, the brick building served as a community center until it was destroyed by fire.

Chapter VIII

Trails Across Parmer

Paul Wyly

TRAILS ACROSS PARMER

According to the census of 1880, Parmer County had a population of zero. This is not too surprising when we remember that a scant four years prior to this census Parmer County was "created" by politicians drawing three straight lines on a map of the Panhandle. The eastern boundry of New Mexico completed the square and placed Parmer astride the path of westward expansion. The census figures, of course, referred to permanent residents; realizing this we cannot help but wonder who did the counting! Although Parmer was without visible signs of habitation it had for many years been the scene of an extensive transient population.

Running Water Draw, or "creek" as the old maps call it, had been used as a major highway since long before the Romans paved the Appian Way. Prehistoric men and animals ranged along this ancient path centuries before the American Indians demonstrated its value to the Spanish explorers. Cattlemen found it to be a boon to their moving huge herds across the area. Rancher Stinson's cows grazed its grassy banks in the early 1800's. Long before the region was mapped it was spoken of as the "Comanche Trail to Santa Fe." It may have been its popularity with the Comanches that led the first European travelers north to a more barren but safer route. Despite the known perils we find one lusty soldier brave enough to follow it in the completion of his assigned duties.

Mexican authorities and businessmen were anxious to establish a direct trade route between Santa Fe and San Antonio. To this end Corporal Jose Mares was dispatched from Santa Fe on July 31, 1787. He traveled in a southeasterly direction but we have no proof that he crossed Parmer County on his way to San Antonio which he reached on October 8 of the same year. Upon his return early in 1788 he used Comanche guides and most historians agree that he crossed a part of what later became Parmer County, Texas. It is very likely that he used the Comanche trail since he logged only 710 miles between the two cities.

Parmer County's next well-known visitors

AN OLD TRAIL STILL IN USE.

POOR PROSPECTS

were members of the ill-fated Texas-Santa Fe expedition. Texas' second president, Mirabeau B. Lamar, was interested in extending the boundaries and influence of the new republic into the western wilderness. Although termed a voyage of merchants the caravan erred in taking a large military escort and a few cannons.

They departed Texas on June 2nd, 1841 and eventually reached Santa Fe under the most dire circumstances. Failing commercially as well as politically, their only real accomplishment was proving Running Water Draw to be a feasible route.

Today's road maps show the most direct route to be some 696 miles in length and recommend a driving time of 13 hours; a far cry indeed from the weary weeks required by Senor Mares and those who followed his trail.

In more recent times a winding route across the southwest was established in an effort to increase "tourism"—a coined word of recent vintage. The trail was marked by tall concrete obelisks, set on wide bases and

PRAIRIE FIRE—Menace to travelers and settlers.

OZARK MARKER—Nazareth, Texas. Nelda G. Bragg and Glee G. White.

bearing the names of towns along the way. It has been suggested that one reason for the twists and turns in the trail was the unwillingness of some towns to purchase a marker. One early resident of Friona was heard to say, "We don't need a tombstone! Friona isn't dead—yet."

Where the Ozark trail started and where it ended is largely a matter of speculation. It was promoted in the early 1920's and markers have been spotted in Arkansas, Oklahoma, Texas, and New Mexico. Bovina and Farwell in Parmer County were noted as well as El Paso in far west Texas.

These monuments to tourism have almost completely disappeared due to their having been erected squarely in the middle of the host towns' main highway intersection. Some were blasted to bits, some thrown in the dump, others buried, a few remain on back roads or in city parks and on courthouse lawns.

The moccasined foot of the Indian, the flint-hard hoof of the longhorn, the narrow high pressure tire of the Model T Ford are no longer with us, but we still follow their lead when we travel the trails across Parmer.

RUNNING WATER DRAW

Running Water Draw contrary to its name, very seldom had any running water, only after big rains that fill the brakes above it. The only exception is near the town of Running Water.

This draw had no head but comes from the brakes in Eastern New Mexico near Melrose. There it crosses the divide and runs into the Pecos River.

Crossing the Texas line it runs in an east-to-southeast direction just south of Bovina, Flagg and Running Water. South of Plainview in Hale County, it runs into Blanco Canyon, or Salt Creek. Running across Crosby and Dickens Counties it disappears in the brakes of the lower Cap Rock section.

It is one of the creeks of this section that does not give traces of the Spanish influence by its name, however, the country around that was drained by this draw, and called Los Llanos del Agua Corriente, by the old guides of the early days.

Here in early days buffalo ranged, Indians roamed and had their camping grounds. As early as 1878 the white man had begun to range cattle down this far to the south.

Today part of the rich grass lands along its banks still furnishes grazing for the descendents of these early herds of Texas longhorns, but have been changed by time and new blood until they are not easily recognized as the progeny of those hardy, long-legged vari-colored breeds. Most of this land, however, has given over to the farmer who produces much feed, cotton and potatoes where once the grama and curly mesquite waved in the Texas breezes.

FRIO DRAW

Frio Draw heads in Eastern New Mexico, crosses Texas line west of Bovina and running in an east and northeasternly direction joins Tierra Blanco or Tule Creek south of Hereford on through the south part of Randall County and into the Palo Duro Canyon, thus into Red River.

The nature of this small creek is very similar to all those that drain the Staked Plains of Texas. It stays dry most all the year; only runs following the big rains in the spring.

Here on this creek in the late seventies a ranch was started, being the first ranch to be laid out south of the then ranch headquarters of Leigh Dyer on the Tierra Blanco. The new ranch was in charge of L.G. Coleman. The ranges adjacent to water were, of course, taken first, and this part of the country saw ranching expeditions long before the lands to the south and west were taken up.

Along the Tule Creek, Indian traders and buffalo hunters made their way in the early days, and many years before them the Spanish invaders passed through, as evidenced by the Spanish names that still distinguish these waterways. According to A.P. Stone of Muleshoe, Texas, he heard a legend at Big Spring in the early 80's concerning these creeks or rivers as they were then known. According to this legend these little creeks used to be rivers but had been filled in with sand, in the early days when the Indians roamed the plains, and never again was known to run. Long years have passed since that time and now farms and small ranches operate up and down this little draw.

Chapter IX
Brands

BRANDS

By Tom Grady

Brands, estray cattle and horses has been a way of life for me starting as a boy and then as a rancher during which time I spent a number of years as an Inspector for the Cattle Sanitary Board of New Mexico.

My family came to Texico in 1902, I went to both the Texico and Farwell schools, graduating from Farwell High School. In many ways my family was connected with the settlement and development of this area.

Not so long ago a reputable newspaper, in a cattle state, printed a two column headline saying, "First Cattle Brands were used on the XIT ranch in Texas," which is so stupid as to be inexcusable: the XIT is but yesterday's child, even though it does not exist today. A radio commentator recently stated, "That branding originated on the ranch of a Spanish pioneer in Texas, he also stated that branding was exclusively an American process; necessary at the outset, but so crude and cruel as to be practically obsolete now." So much malarky, it is neither Spanish, Texas, New Mexican, American, crude, cruel, nor obsolete.

The Oriental Institute of the University of Chicago, probably is the best authority in this field, by virtue of long research, but it is not the only one, that can prove that branding was done at least two thousand years before Christ. Tombs in Egypt not only show ancient brands, but picture the actual work of branding, except that the costume of the cowboys is quite different, the scene might just as well be in New Mexico, Texas, or Montana. Mostly the sign or name of some ancient God seems to have been chosen for the brand. Sometimes there was a temple brand. One pictured an ox with the brand on its rump showing that it belonged to herd number 43. We also find that early Egyptians, Romans, Greeks and others fire branded criminals and slaves.

During this same period, branding of livestock was a common practice. There is Biblical evidence that Jacob, the great herdsman, branded his stock. Chinese characters have been branded on animals so long that prob-

ably not even Confucius could have said when the practice started.

In America, offenders in the Plymouth Colony had scarlet letters sewed on their clothes. If these letters were unlawfully removed, the offenders were burned in the face with a hot iron. In 1673 Connecticut adopted branding instead of the death penalty. Branding was used on animals in England about the eighth century. Hernando Cortez doubtless brought the first branding irons to America. He needn't have bothered, because there were no other cattle or horses on this continent to mingle with his for quite awhile. His brand was the three crosses. In 1540 Coronado came northward on the greatest treasure hunt in American history, entered what is now Arizona, and roamed the southwest for two years.

He had branded cattle with him. That was over four hundred years ago. It wasn't long as time goes however before other Spaniards over here owned competitive herds and of course the enterprising Yankee came onto the scene soon afterwards and, with his coming, practical necessity called for brands. So brands were used. The branding of cattle and horses, like other events in the history of our country has changed through the years. In the days of the open range it was necessary to use a clear, legible brand, which usually was a large one, for each owner's stock could scatter over a large area and become mixed with those of other owners.

There were no fences to keep them apart, so the advantages of a large, clear brand were many to the estray men as they went about their daily work. In the event the brand was not clear, someone was invariably catching the animal, picking the brand with a pocket knife to see just what the brand was and to whom the animal belonged. These early day brands in many cases took up the larger part of an entire side of an animal. There were those who put their brand on both sides, so regardless of which side they were looking, they could see their brand, should the animal belong to them.

In the present time due to well fenced pastures, the likelihood over most of the range country of the stock mixing with neighbors has come to a minimum, so that the large brands are no longer a necessity. Then too, the leather industry through the years has strenuously objected to the large brand damaging so much of the hide which in turn caused the feeders to also object.

The branding irons of the early days were in most cases made from a steel rod about two and one half feet along, bent on one end to form a hook, these were called running irons. I have seen a wagon box rod used. However, this is not to say that bars and stamp irons were not used. Stamp irons have a tendency to blotch a brand, and this is especially true if the iron has become too hot. For an iron to be at its best for branding it should be ash color, if it is blue, then it is too cold, leaving you with a brand that will not peel. If it is red then it is too hot and likely to blotch. There is a late method out called freeze branding, using dry ice and alcohol.

They say the hair turns white, and it has been reported that using this method that the brand fades out after a period of time. New Mexico law states that a brand must be made with a hot iron. At one time many range riders carried on their saddle, an iron ring, to be used wherever they found an animal needing branding. They would heat the ring over a small fire, then using a pair of saddle pliers to hold the ring, would do their branding.

Another device used was a saddle iron, this was a short rod, bent on one end and the other end threaded, along with this was a small pipe of the same length of the rod above also threaded on one end, connecting the two together, this formed a branding iron, broken down this was carried in a scabbard. The above two devices are still used in the rough country.

Brands are read left to right, that is on the left side from the head to the hip, on the right side from the hip to the head. And from top to bottom. A bar is a bar and not a minus sign, a cross a cross and not a plus sign. Using the letter T for example. A letter lying partially on its face or back is called a tumbling T. If the letter is all the way over it is called lazy, when there is a tail coming off the bottom then it is a drag T. When the angles are rounded as with a M, N, or W it is read a running M, etc. I would call the brand of the Winrock Center in Albuquerque a running

W, broken R. When there is a quarter circle under the letter, then it is called rocking T. Then you have stripes, hackmores, garters, butt bars and etc. Character brands are usually ones that do not fall into a category as to come under a classification, so the owner gives it his own interpretation.

There has been a great deal of talk about burning, altering or running a brand, which means changing the rightful owner's brand into another by burning over the old brand into one which the thieves would sell the animal by, than ever happened. For it was a common practice for cowboys sitting around the wagon or bunk house to let his imagination soar into how many ways he could work a brand over. However, in the past the cowman has had his share of this trouble.

During my years as an inspector, after everyone thought that brand running was a thing of the past, I had three cases of this nature. A conclusive proof that a brand has been altered is to kill and skin the animal in question and examine the brand from the flesh side. The new part of the brand will be soft, whereas the original or older part is hard.

Then too, after the hide has dried, the original part will show plainer than the last brand put on. There is a method used by thieves in branding stolen stock by taking a wet sack, laying it upon the animal, and applying the hot iron. Such action would give the appearance that the brand had been there for a period of time. This method I am not familiar with for I was never on that side of the fence. However, I was approached by a thief saying he would brand the calves in this manner if I would pass the stolen calves, I could get a cut after the sale. My reply was "No Soap." Probably the most famous case of brand burning in this area was that of the XIT brand being changed into a STAR CROSS. The story goes that the thief was apprehended, but they could not prove that the brand could be run. The defendent was told that if he would show the court how he had changed this brand and de´ t from future operations of this kind, the charge would be dropped.

In talking about brands and their history, a few words should be said about marks, as they were an essential part of identification along with an owner's brand, especially in the range country. When I say marks, I am referring to all marks, as all marks were not made in the ears. The dewlap was one mark, made by cutting the loose skin on the lower part of the neck about three inches which would hang down just in front of the forelegs. Then there was the waddle which was made by cutting a part of the skin downward either on the side of the jaw or the forehead. I have also seen this mark on the body of the animal.

In New Mexico such marks are listed in the brand book as Verrugas, translated this means wart. We seldom see any such marks in use today. I suppose that the most famous ear mark to come down through history was Chisum's JINGLE BOB. It was made by starting to cut an underslope from the outer edge of the ear, toward the head, but not completing the cut leaving a part of the ear attached to hang loose which would bob up and down, hence the Jingle-Bob.

At the time the cattle industry engaged in trail-driving herds to the markets and pasture to the north there was a practice of using a road or trail brand, usually a single letter or figure. You will find a number of such brands recorded in the old brand books. There were advantages to this practice, the brand was fresh and plain, the trail herd may have been bought, which had several brands in the herd. Then too, one owner might have several herds on the road at one time, so he knew at once which of his herd his stray belonged to.

Texas records brands by counties, that is to say by counties in which the owner runs his cattle. At times this has led to confusion and in many instances a lot of work in establishing the ownership of stolen or estray animals, this is the result of the same brand being issued in adjoining or nearby counties. At one time there was an inspector at Amarillo that advocated dividing West Texas into districts with the district number being part of the owner's brand.

Just the other day there was a meeting of concerned cattlemen held in Hereford, Texas, trying to find a solution to duplication of brands in the Panhandle of Texas. This meeting was the result of the mixing and die up of cattle in the severe storm this past January. (1971)

Through the kindness of Earl De Oliveira,

who loaned me his father's brand book of the Panhandle Stockman Association from which I gathered a number of names of ranchers and operators of this area. Mr. De Oliveira was the Cattle Inspector at Farwell for a number of years. The Panhandle Association later merged with the Texas and Southwestern Association. There was one date in this book listed in pencil, 1911.

Among the names were:

Van Natta—Amarillo, range Bailey, a big steer outfit.

Landergin Bros.—Parmer and Bailey Counties—One time on the VVN.

J.A. Oden—range—Parmer and Bailey Counties. The Oden home was at third and Avenue F in Farwell.

C.S. Hart, Portales, range—Parmer County.

J.R. Stegall—range—Parmer, Bailey and Roosevelt Counties.

Janes Bros.—Bovina—The brand drag Y—range Lamb and Bailey counties. Their ranch was just east of the present town of Muleshoe.

Jim Leftwich, Farwell—range—Parmer County. The home place some four miles NE of Farwell.

S.F. Tipton, Farwell—range—Parmer and Bailey Counties. Unknown to me.

F.W. Jersig, Bovina, who ran the 69 brand.

E.K. Warren & Son, Bovina, Home address, Four Oaks, Michigan. Range—The Muleshoe and YL ranches in Parmer, Bailey and Lamb Counties. Warrens used the U-brand on their cattle. The Warren fortune was said to have been made in the manufacture of imitation of whale bone used in women's corsets. Quills from turkey feathers were processed as a substitute for whale bone.

S.G. Bratton, Farwell, who later became a United States Senator from New Mexico, and then appointed a judge on the Federal Court of Appeals.

The Terrazas along with a number of other Mexicans were listed in this book. The Terrazas had a number of brands listed and were reputed to own an unbelievable number of cattle.

The many phases of the livestock industry have made drastic changes since the turn of the century and I am sure there will be changes in the years to come. Therefore with more people than ever before engaged in the industry; a record number of cattle in our country; with meat consumption per capita the highest in history; I am sure there will be a demand for cattle to produce this beef, and with this demand there will always be a need for BRANDS.

PARMER COUNTY BRANDS

Name	Location	Brand	Placement	Date
A.N. Wentworth	Friona, Tex.	ANW	Right jaw	10-15-1907
A.A. Chapman	Farwell, Tex.	"A"	Left thigh	10-2-1908
A.N. Wentworth	Friona, Tex.	AW	Right hip	11-4-1908
Mrs. Florence Armstrong	Farwell, Tex.	V	Right hip	4-15-1911
Allington & Mulkin	Friona, Tex.	A	Left hip	10-25-1911
Addison Ballard	Friona, Tex.	AB	Left hip	12-29-1911
B.P. Abbott	Bovina, Tex.	VK	Left hip	10-21-1912
Addison Ballard	Friona, Tex.	A	Left hip	5-13-1913
A.J. Oliver	Bovina, Tex.	⌒	Left hip	10-23-1913
A.J. Oliver	Bovina, Tex.	⌂	Left hip	10-23-1913
M.C. Sanders	Bovina, Tex.	◁	Left hip	11-3-1913
G.A. Wulfman	Farwell, Tex.	AX	Left hip	5-13-1914
A.W. Henschel	Friona, Tex.	AH	Left hip	12-7-1914
David R. Scyoc	Friona, Tex.	A	Left hip	4-15-1915
W.H. Alderson	Muleshoe, Tex.	ALD	Left side	4-28-1915
L.G. Anderson	Bovina, Tex.	A	Right hip	6-16-1915

Name	Location	Brand	Position	Date
A.W. Wood	Bovina, Tex.	A	Left hip	6-29-1915
A.O. Drake	Black, Tex.	A+	Left side	10-20-1915
T.J. Hooser	Farwell, Tex.	ATH	A—Left jaw	6-15-1916
			TH—Left side	6-15-1916
Joe Butcher	Bovina, Tex.	AV	Left hip & thigh	9-14-1916
Ralph Paul	Friona, Tex.	A	Right hip	3-3-1917
A.C. Young	Friona, Tex.	AC	Left hip	11-26-1917
Abbott & Martin	Friona, Tex.	D	Left shoulder	11-26-1917
Chester A. Lyon	Farwell, Tex.	A	Right hip	2-16-1918
R. & P. Looney	Bovina, Tex.	A	Right side	4-10-1918
A.C. Yocham	Summerfield, Tex.	AY	Right hip	
R.A. Hawkins	Farwell, Tex.	AV	Right side	9-9-1918
Edgar Chase	Bovina, Tex.	A	Left jaw	4-16-1919
W.A. Dosher	Farwell, Tex.	AD	Left shoulder	7-16-1919
W.A. Wilson	Black, Tex.	AL	Left side	10-21-1919
W.H. Fugua	Amarillo, Tex.	A-	Right side	4-21-1919
Jeff Watson	Friona, Tex.	Æ	Left hip	12-11-1922
W.Y. Preston	Friona, Tex.	AP	Left side	9-18-1923
S.A. West	Hurley, Tex.	CD	Left shoulder	1-31-1925
A.L. Chesler	Portales, N.M.	G	Right side	4-27-1911

George Daugherty	Friona, Tex.	66	Right hip	3-8-1915
F.W. Jersig	Bovina, Tex.	69	Left side or hip	4-28-1915
Smith & Donald	Hereford, Tex.	U	Right hip	5-3-1916
F.W. Jersig	Bovina, Tex.	⌐69	Left side	5-8-1917
J.D. Ford	Farwell, Tex.	67	Left hip	7-25-1922
M.U. Towy	Friona, Tex.	6	Left hip	2-25-1927
John Armstrong	Farwell, Tex.	6	Right shoulder	9-19-1929
S.M. Wilson	Bovina, Tex.	ꝋS	Left shoulder	12-15-1908
J.E. Slater	Farwell, Tex.	MS	Left side	1-3-1910
Seamonds & Son	Friona, Tex.	A\	Right hip	4-24-1914
Stacy Queen	Bovina, Tex.	f	Left thigh	2-1-1915
Harry W. Sheriff	Friona, Tex.	∽	Left side or hip	11-25-1915
O. Stevick	Friona, Tex.	S̲	Left side	5-25-1916
E.M. Sheriff	Friona, Tex.	[S]	Left hip	10-25-1916
D.W. Hanson	Friona, Tex.	Ⓢ	Left hip	4-23-1917
D.W. Hanson	Friona, Tex .	S	Left jaw	8-29-1917
D.W. Hanson	Friona, Tex.	∽	Left shoulder	4-21-1920
William Schwede	Farwell, Tex.	S̲+	Left hip	10-8-1921
J.H. Stagner	Bovina, Tex.	+S	Left hip	1-3-1922

R.H. Kinsley	Friona, Tex.	S̴	Left hip	11-20-1920
W.M. Sherley	Lazbuddie, Tex.	S-	Right hip	11-8-1926
John Barnett	Bovina, Tex.	7b	Left hip	5-16-1908
Ike Brown	Farwell, Tex.	I K	Left hip	11-30-1909
J.L. Parker	Farwell, Tex.	BM	Left hip	6-28-1910
Erick Boysen	Friona, Tex.	EB	Left hip	5-25-1911
H.J. Ballard	Friona, Tex.	JL	Left side	10-21-1911
Bovina Merchantile Co.	Bovina, Tex.	H	Left shoulder	1-15-1912
Jerry Blackwell	Texico, N.M.	JB	Left hip	1-29-1912
J.K. Billingsly	Bovina, Tex.	B	Left shoulder	7-31-1913
E.P. Billingsly	Bovina, Tex.	B	Left hip	7-31-1913
Bell Stock Co.	Black, Tex.	B	Right jaw	11-18-1913
A. Beckham	Bovina, Tex.	BK	Right hip	12-10-1913
D.M. Ballard	Friona, Tex.	9	Left hip	7-17-1914
Beggen Bros.	Bovina, Tex.	G	Right hip	10-13-1914
Mrs. C.F. Fowler	Farwell, Tex.	BBF	Left side	10-16-1916
W.J.Bond	Farwell, Tex.	B	Left shoulder	8-7-1917
B.T. Hendrickson	Farwell, Tex.	BH	Right hip	8-17-1918
Miss Billy Castella	Bovina, Tex.	BC	Right hip	2-3-1919

L.F. Buttemeier	Rhea, Tex.	⌂B	Left hip	9-13-1920
D.R. Bennett	Black, Tex.	⌂B→	Right side	1-26-1921
W.A. Bryant	Farwell, Tex.	B	Left side	10-17-1921
G.W. Bussey	Friona, Tex.	⅋	Left hip	3-21-1929
F.C. Clennin	Friona, Tex.	FCC	Right ear	4-24-1911
Joe Colon	Bovina, Tex.	Z	Left jaw	4-26-1911
D.M. Ballard	Friona, Tex.	⊤	Left hip	10-16-1911
C. Warther	Parmerton, Tex.	CW	Left side	10-23-1907
J.C. Copeland	Bovina, Tex.	X	Left hip	6-2-1911
J.C. Copeland	Bovina, Tex .	77	Left hip	6-2-1911
Chas Cady	Friona, Tex.	C−	Left hip	8-12-1912
Carter	Farwell, Tex.	C̲	Left hip	5-12-1913
Geo. W. Clark	Friona, Tex.	Ĉ	Right hip	6-11-1913
C.F.L. & I.C.		C	Left thigh	4-20-1914
J.E. Cary	Friona, Tex.	+	Left hip	7-17-1914
Chas. Widmire	Friona, Tex.	C	Left shoulder	8-20-1915
Christian Treider	Friona, Tex.	C	Left hip	11-25-1915
Carl Dotson	Friona, Tex.	C̄	Left shoulder & right hip	5-1-1916
Clyde Roberson	Summerfield, Tex.	CE	Left shoulder	3-23-1917

Chas. Buttemeier	Rhea, Tex.	C̲	Right hip	11-18-1917
Clarence Alexander	Farwell, Tex.	CA	Left hip	12-6-1917
Coneway Brothers	Black, Tex.	U	Right shoulder	3-22-1918
C.E. Christian	Farwell, Tex.	C	Right side	2-22-1919
C.M. Benton	Friona, Tex.	CL	Left side	7-21-1919
C.D. Owens	Bovina, Tex.	CD	Left hip	12-5-1919
C.M. Crow	Farwell, Tex.	C	Right hip	5-8-1920
C.S. Phillips	Friona, Tex.	©	Left thigh	3-29-1921
C.J. Smith	Rhea, Tex.	C S	Left hip	5-24-1921
C.J. Mobley	Farwell, Tex.	C J	Left hip	10-31-1921
T.B. Morse	Farwell, Tex.	CM	Left hip	7-21-1923
Beaulah Dudley	Bovina, Tex.	C	Left side	8-8-1927
Craig Walling	Farwell, Tex.	IC	Left side	4-8-1929
Elmer Crume	Texico, N.M.	C/	Left shoulder	12-21-1929
Booker Diamond	Friona, Tex.	B-◇	Left side	8-20-1907
D.W. Dunn	Farwell, Tex.	⊢D	Left hip	7-7-1911
J. Davies	Bovina, Tex.	JD	Left hip	7-10-1911
E.E. Rohrabaugh	Friona, Tex.	dR	Right hip	11-6-1911
Gose Dee	Bovina, Tex.	DEE	Left hip	1-4-1913

Name	Location	Brand	Location on animal	Date
Merton Dickson	Farwell, Tex.		Left side, hip, or shoulder	1-20-1913
C.E. Dotson	Farwell, Tex.		Left shoulder	5-6-1913
Gose Dee	Bovina, Tex.		Left side	5-16-1913
D.M. Davis	Friona, Tex.		Right shoulder	11-18-1913
O.B. Danields	Farwell, Tex.		Right hip	12-10-1913
S.H. Withers	Farwell, Tex.		Right jaw	12-10-1913
C.H. Dale	Big Square, Tex.		Left loin	3-27-1915
Davis & Truman	Friona, Tex.		Right hip	7-13-1915
M. Schubert	Farwell, Tex.		Right hip	3-11-1916
J.M. Teague	Friona, Tex.		Right hip	8-31-1918
Virgil Davis	Farwell, Tex.		Left hip	7-30-1921
A.D. White	Friona, Tex.		Left hip	7-18-1928
W.S. Looney	Bovina, Tex.		Left hip	5-28-1909
J.E. Hermes	Bovina, Tex.		Left shoulder	6-21-1913
E. Richardson	Friona, Tex.		Left ribs	10-20-1913
Geo. T. Courtwright	Friona, Tex.		Left hip	11-13-1913
E.M. Sheriff	Friona, Tex.		Left side	2-7-1914
P.P. Lee	Friona, Tex.		Left side or hip	3-9-1915
E.A. Taylor	Friona, Tex.		Left thigh	12-30-1915

E.E. Taylor	Friona, Tex.	Ê	Right side	4-18-1916
E.W. McGuire	Farwell, Tex.	EC	Left side	6-15-1916
Elmer Paul	Muleshoe, Tex.	E	Left side	12-18-1916
Elbert Overton	Black, Tex.	EO	Left hip	3-1-1917
E.H. Englant	Bovina, Tex.	EH	Left hip	7-24-1917
R.B. Ezell	Bovina, Tex.	EZL	Right side	12-20-1917
J.P. & E.M. English	Friona, Tex.	E	Left hip & side	1-26-1918
Coneway Bros.	Black, Tex.	Ē	Right hip	8-14-1918
E.H. Meeks	Farwell, Tex.	∃ᴴ	Left side	8-4-1920
Mrs. A.R. Schlenker	Bovina, Tex.	Ψ	Left hip	9-20-1921
Elmer Euler	Friona, Tex.	E	Left shoulder	2-14-1922
Edgar Chase	Bovina, Tex.	EC	Left hip	4-29-1922
Evans Bros.	Friona, Tex.	Ŧ	Left hip	3-18-1929
Elbert Thomas	Friona, Tex.	E	Left hip	4-3-1929
F.L. Spring	Bovina, Tex.	Ŧ	Left thigh	8-6-1910
C.F. Brownlee	Friona, Tex.	Ᵽ	Right hip	8-6-1910
F.S. Langer	Bovina, Tex.	ⅎ	Either side	1-11-1911
Bovina Live Stock Co.	Bovina, Tex.	F	Right hip	11-10-1911
F.W. McElroy	Farwell, Tex.	ꟻ	Left hip	9-9-1912

177

Henry Franck	Star Ranch	Ħ	Left hip	3-8-1913
C.M. Faville	Farwell, Tex.	Ⓕ	Left hip	7-7-1914
F.S. Gray	Friona, Tex.	⊓	Left hip	4-28-1915
Francis Kohl	Friona, Tex.	FK	Right hip	6-10-1916
J.W. Maxwell & Son	Farwell, Tex.	FJ	Right hip	6-1-1917
A.L. Tandy	Farwell, Tex.	FT	Left side	6-21-1918
Mamie Fowler	Farwell, Tex.	⟨F⟩	Left side	7-1-1922
M.D. Fincher	Black, Tex.	⟨F⟩	Left hip	5-6-1924
J.H. Kohl	Friona, Tex.	JK	Right hip	12-11-1908
Mrs. J.R. Champion	Bovina, Tex.	JR	Right hip	2-1-1909
J.H. Leftwich	Farwell, Tex.	JL	Left hip	3-1-1909
W.J. Hahn	Farwell, Tex.	JH	Right shoulder	8-19-1909
Leftwich, Kindred, & Leftwich	Farwell, Tex.	LKL	Left hip	2-5-1910
D.W. Dunn	Farwell, Tex.	JD	Left hip	7-7-1911
J. Davis	Bovina, Tex.	JD	Left hip	7-10-1911
J.L. Walling	Farwell, Tex.	JXL	Left hip	8-25-1911
D.S. Johnson	Bovina, Tex.	J	Right hip	9-2-1911
Jerry Blackwell	Texico Route	JB	Left hip	1-29-1912
Mrs. Belle Melugin	Texico Route	J	Left side	2-2-1912

178

J.M. Spohn	Friona, Tex.	JS	Right hip	5-16-1912
J.F. Lillard	Friona, Tex.	I	Right hip	9-17-1912
Jim Dudley	Farwell, Tex.	J	Left side	9-21-1912
Joe Paul	Bovina, Tex.	P	Left hip	12-20-1912
Stephen Jesko	Friona, Tex.	J	Left jaw	1-13-1913
Otto Treider	Friona, Tex.	Jo	Left hip Left shoulder	1-31-1914
J.W. Ford	Friona, Tex.	J	Right hip	3-14-1914
E.L. Donelson	Farwell, Tex.	JX	Left hip	5-8-1914
W.H. Jarrell	Texico Route	J	Right hip	12-20-1921
Jim Martin	Bovina, Tex.	H	Right shoulder	9-20-1915
J.W. Johnson	Farwell, Tex.	J	Left side	5-29-1916
J.N. Johnson	Farwell, Tex.	JJ	Left side	6-2-1916
J.L. Osborne	Farwell, Tex.	JL	Left side	7-28-1916
John Ellis	Black, Tex.	JE	Left hip	3-1-1917
W.J. Smith	Farwell, Tex.	J2	Left shoulder	3-23-1917
J.G. Rose & Wife	Summerfield, Tex.	JJ	Left hip	4-6-1917
F.W. Jersig	Bovina, Tex.	R	Left hip	5-8-1917
J.M. McCuan	Farwell, Tex.	J	Right hip	5-31-1917
J.M. Casey	Farwell, Tex	M	Right shoulder	6-20-1917

179

J.E. Staley	Farwell, Tex.	E	Left thigh	11-12-1917
J.E. Johnston	Texico, N.M.	E	Right hip	12-5-1917
J.S. Potts	Bovina, Tex.	K	Right hip	7-5-1918
Gordon R. McCuan	Farwell, Tex.	J	Right shoulder	4-12-1919
N.A. Laughlin	Summerfield, Tex.	J-L	Left side	4-22-1919
J.A. Hiner	Summerfield, Tex.	AH	Left side	2-3-1919
James Williams	Friona, Tex.	J	Left hip	6-13-1919
J.E. Taylor	Friona, Tex.	E	Left hip	10-28-1919
J.B. Abbott	Bovina, Tex.	JB	Right hip	11-6-1920
Joe Blake	Farwell, Tex.	B	Right side	11-21-1921
Charles Jefferson	Friona, Tex.	J-	Left side	5-20-1920
Dale McCuan	Farwell, Tex.	J	Right side	4-9-1921
J.F. McKiney	Summerfield, Tex.	JF	Left side	9-10-1921
Mrs. Texie Walling	Farwell, Tex.	J L	Left shoulder Left hip	10-4-1921
A.J. Jarrell	Bovina, Tex.	(J	Right hip	11-7-1922
Glenn Hightower	Farwell, Tex.	T	Left thigh	8-14-1944
F.E. Turner	Bovina, Tex.	J	Left hip	11-17-1924
W.T. Hughes	Bovina, Tex.	J7	Left thigh	5-24-1926
Mrs. Belle Melugin	Texico Route	J	Left hip	8-28-1926

J.H. Drager	Bovina, Tex.	J3	Right shoulder	10-5-1926
Mrs. J.W. Crawford & J.J. Crawford	Black, Tex.	J◇	Left hip	2-19-1927
J.B. Finley	Farwell, Tex.	ꭻF	Left side	9-22-1927
C.F. Kellner	Boom, Tex.	K	Left shoulder	10-10-1907
K. Killam	Bovina, Tex.	KK	Left shoulder	8-31-1910
Guy Kempson	Bovina, Tex.	K̄	Right shoulder	10-19-1910
Peter Kaiser	Bovina, Tex.	K1	Right side	10-17-1911
Jim Stokes	Bovina, Tex.	K2	Right shoulder	7-10-1912
W.W. Chivington	Summerfield, Tex.	⋀	Left shoulder	4-21-1913
M. Killam	Bovina, Tex.	K̄	Right side	7-8-1913
B.W. Kieran	Bovina, Tex.	−K	Right shoulder	5-25-1917
Oneal Bros.	Texico Route	⋁	Left side	1-1-1918
G.H. Miller	Bovina, Tex.	K̲	Left side	5-26-1919
B.K. Greeson	Summerfield, Tex.	KX	Left hip	1-10-1927
Frank L. Spring	Bovina, Tex.	ꭻF̲	Left thigh	10-17-1907
W.W. Meyer	Farwell, Tex.	A̸	Either side	5-23-1908
John F. Lillard	Friona, Tex.	ꞀL	Left jaw	11-4-1908
M.E. Lassen	Friona, Tex.	L	Left hip	5-12-1909
Frank L. Spring	Bovina, Tex.	F̄	Left thigh	5-31-1909

Name	Location	Brand	Location on animal	Date
C.W. Gurnee	Bovina, Tex.	L	Right hip	10-30-1909
R.C. Oden	Farwell, Tex.	L⊣	Left thigh	4-27-1910
C.E. Dodson	Farwell, Tex.	⊥	Right thigh / Right shoulder	9-28-1910
Fred Langer	Bovina, Tex.	⅂	Either side	1-11-1911
John F. Lillard	Friona, Tex.	LL	Left hip	2-6-1911
Mrs. L.V. Linthicum	Farwell, Tex.	◇M	Either hip	11-10-1911
Fred Langer	Bovina, Tex.	G̅	Right hip	1-20-1912
S.F. Tipton	Farwell, Tex.	Lₒ	Right thigh	2-22-1912
R.P. Lee	Friona, Tex.	L̲E̲	Either side	6-19-1912
Lawerence F. Lillard	Friona, Tex.	M̅	Right hip or side	12-12-1912
J.H. Leftwich	Farwell, Tex.	⊥K	Left side	5-31-1913
John Lucas	Bovina, Tex.	L6	Right hip	11-12-1913
David H. Lawrence	Friona, Tex.	⌒L	Left hip	4-10-1915
D.C. Vassey	Bovina, Tex.	L̲	Left hip	2-11-1921
W. Kamradt	Rhea, Tex.	L̅	Left hip	4-24-1914
C.L. McLellan	Farwell, Tex.	M	Right hip	5-20-1915
Ed A. Porth	Rhea, Tex.	⌒L̲	Left hip	10-2-1915
L.E. Gordon	Friona, Tex.	E	Left hip	11-2-1915
Laura Trieder	Friona, Tex.	T	Left hip	11-27-1915

L.J. Hopping	Farwell, Tex.	L	Left hip	10-3-1916
Lee Osborne	Farwell, Tex.	t	Left side	11-1-1916
Lawrence Johnson	Summerfield, Tex.	LJ	Left side	1-29-1917
J.L. Osborne	Farwell, Tex.	L	Left shoulder	3-2-1917
Mrs. L. Carter	Friona, Tex.	t	Left shoulder	4-10-1917
C.L. Gilmore	Farwell, Tex.	LG	Right hip	8-29-1917
L.F. Fluss	Farwell, Tex.	4	Left hip	5-11-1918
A.S. Curry	Friona, Tex.	LD	Left side	7-31-1918
L.F. Beckner	Friona, Tex.	LX	Left hip	1-16-1920
August Bultemeier	Rhea, Tex.	b	Right hip	7-21-1921
Lillian Hughes	Friona, Tex.	H	Left hip	7-17-1922
Elma Lawhon	Summerfield, Tex.	JΓ	Left side	10-18-1922
Luther Hastings	Bovina, Tex.	LH	Left hip	2-21-1925
J.J. Herndon	Texico Route	LH	Left side	5-4-1927
Frank McSpadden	Bovina, Tex.	M	Left thigh or Left hip	5-31-1910
R.E. Maddux	Farwell, Tex.	tSS	Left jaw, left shoulder, left hip	1-19-1911
Tom Maxwell	Friona, Tex.	M	Left hip	4-24-1911
W.E. Moorman	Texico Route	7L	Left hip	4-5-1913
D.H. Meade	Friona, Tex.	H	Left side	4-7-1913

W.A. & W.H. Massey	Friona	⋔	Left hip	3-31-1914
F.W. McElroy	Farwell, Tex.	MC	Right hip	12-4-1913
M B. Tryer	Summerfield, Tex.	MB	Right hip	5-22-1916
Paul Elmer	Muleshoe Route	M	Left side	12-16-1916
J.J. Miller & Co.	Farwell, Tex.	M.A.C.	Left hip	3-27-1917
M. Alexander	Farwell, Tex.	MA	Left side	6-22-1917
R.A. Mitzelfelt	Farwell, Tex.	M3	Right hip	7-16-1917
M.W. Wells	Bovina, Tex.	ME	Right hip	11-15-1917
W.D. Monroe	Farwell, Tex.	M	Right hip	12-10-1917
L.J. Morris	Farwell, Tex.	M3	Right hip	4-10-1918
Carl Maurer	Friona, Tex.	TX	Left hip	4-23-1918
P.L. Maride	Friona, Tex.	∿	Left shoulder	9-25-1918
J.J. Miller	Farwell, Tex.	⟨	Left side	1-13-1920
Earl Miller	Bellview, N.M.	M	Right side	5-13-1922
T.J. Crawford	Friona, Tex.	MK	Left hip	1-13-1923
Mrs. Ward Thompson	Bovina, Tex.	MK	Right hip	7-21-1923
Mervin Wilterding	Muleshoe Route	M—	Right hip	8-31-1925
McSpadden Bros.	Friona, Tex.	× △	Left jaw Left shoulder	3-6-1913
Wm. Candlish	Friona, Tex.	⅄	Left hip	4-25-1913

Mrs. E. Nichols	Farwell, Tex.		Left shoulder	4-14-1911
Horace Nichols	Farwell, Tex.		Left side	5-29-1911
Fowler Nichols	Farwell, Tex.		Left shoulder	(no date)
D.M. Ballard	Friona, Tex.		Left hip	4-1-1912
W.F. Newton	Texico Route		Left side	1-22-1917
N.L. Marney	Farwell, Tex.		Left hip	10-2-1920
W.F. Perry	Friona, Tex.		Right hip	11-7-1921
William Halzerland	Muleshoe, Tex.		Left thigh	10-23-1923
N.B. Morton	Friona, Tex.		Left thigh	1-5-1928
R.E. Oakes	Bovina, Tex.		Right hip	5-10-1910
J.M. Hamlin	Farwell, Tex.		Left hip	11-12-1910
R.S. Overstreet	Farwell, Tex.		Left hip	11-12-1910
Bovina Livestock Co.	Bovina, Tex.		Right side	3-1-1912
O.L. Smith	Bovina, Tex.		Right thigh	5-27-1913
J. Frank Owen	Friona, Tex.		Right hip	10-19-1914
Orvil Stevick	Friona, Tex.		Left hind quarter	7-8-1916
D.M. Ballard	Friona, Tex.		Right hip	10-16-1916
Wayne Riley	Black, Tex.		Left hip	3-1-1917
O.D. Godard	Farwell, Tex.		Left hip	6-9-1917

Name	Location	Brand	Position	Date
H.W. Wright	Friona, Tex.	Ⴇ̄	Right hip	8-28-1917
J.L. Osborne	Farwell, Tex.	⅗	Left hip	8-31-1918
Jim Perkins	Farwell, Tex.	ᵒᵒ	Left side	9-27-1918
O.A. Owens	Bovina, Tex.	OA	Left shoulder	12-5-1919
J.R. Walker	Friona, Tex.	O	Left shoulder	1-3-1920
M.B. Buchanan	Friona, Tex.	⌒	Left shoulder	7-2-1923
O.D. Knight	Friona, Tex.	O-	Left hip	8-16-1927
Riley Pierce	Friona, Tex.	X	Left hip	7-6-1914
August F. Porth	Rhea, Tex.	₽	Right hip	2-16-1915
Ed A. Porth	Rhea, Tex.	P̳	Right hip	2-16-1915
Martin Porth	Rhea, Tex.	P̳	Right hip	2-16-1915
R.L. Payne	Muleshoe Route	P	Right hip	2-15-1917
C.R. & A.J. Pierce	Farwell, Tex.	(P)	Left hip	5-31-1917
J.B. Roberson	Boom, Tex.	T	Left shoulder	12-10-1907
Miles Ross	Bovina, Tex.	Я	Right hip	8-25-1911
Frank L. Reed	Bovina, Tex.	W	Right hip	2-6-1912
K.K. Runnels	Texico Route	R̄	Right hip	4-24-1912
J.W. Ford	Friona, Tex.	R	Left hip	10-2-1912
George Hitz	Black, Tex.	Rₓ	Right hip	7-7-1913

M. Renner	Rhea, Tex.	R	Right hip	1-2-1918
T.D. Roberson	Farwell, Tex.	R	Right side	3-21-1918
A.A. Russell	Farwell, Tex.	AR	Left side	10-6-1924
Ralph L. Gallagher	Bovina, Tex.	R	Right shoulder	3-17-1927
A.F. Randall	Bovina, Tex.	R-	Left thigh	8-26-1929
J.C. Stallings	Farwell, Tex.	JS	Right hip	10-4-1909
Charles Schlenker	Rhea, Tex.	♀	Left side	10-19-1909
Charles Smiley	Parmer County	?	Left hip	11-4-1908
S.M. Wilson	Bovina, Tex.	S	Left shoulder	12-5-1908
Ed Hunt	Texico, Tex.	ST	Left side	7-19-1909
J.E. Slater	Farwell, Tex.	MS	Left side	1-3-1910
Ira A. Stoughten	Friona, Tex.	IS	Right hip	12-16-1910
Seamands & Son	Friona, Tex.	Ŝ	Right hip	4-24-1914
Stacy Queen	Bovina, Tex.	f	Left thigh	2-1-1915
Harry W. Sherrieb	Friona, Tex.	ᔑ	Left hip	11-25-1915
O. Stevick	Friona, Tex.	S̲	Left side	5-25-1916
E.M. Sherrieb	Friona, Tex.	[S]	Left hip	10-25-1916
Spradley & Thurmond	Friona, Tex.	S̲	Left hip	12-29-1916
D.W. Hanson	Friona, Tex.	Ⓢ	Left hip	4-23-1917

William Schwede	Farwell, Tex.	S̲ᵗ	Left hip	10-8-1921
J.H. Stagner	Bovina, Tex.	+S	Left hip	1-3-1922
R.H. Kinsley	Friona, Tex.	S	Left hip	11-20-1922
W.M. Sherley	Lazbuddy, Tex.	S–	Right hip	11-8-1926
Mrs. M.V. Townsen	Parmerton, Tex.	OTO	Right side	11-22-1907
John Treider	Friona, Tex.	J	Left side	11-27-1909
F.C. Thieman	Bovina, Tex.	T̄	Right shoulder	10-29-1910
Jacob Tiefel	Friona, Tex.	H̄	Left thigh	7-26-1911
E.F. Englant	Texico Route	T	Left side	1-16-1912
T.H. Hughes	Friona, Tex.	H	Left hip	4-17-1912
H.L. Tiefel	Friona, Tex.	H̲	Left side	9-20-1912
G.W. Taylor	Friona, Tex.	T	Right side	10-14-1912
W.E. Schlenker	Bovina, Tex.	TL	Left side	5-1-1912
A.L. Chesher & Son	Farwell, Tex.	8	Either side	6-13-1914
J.A. Oden	Farwell, Tex.	F	Left hip	7-29-1914
James Oden	Farwell, Tex.	人	Left hip	7-29-1914
Thomas Short	Farwell, Tex.	J	Left side	7-29-1914
B.T. Lucas	Friona, Tex.	T̄	Left shoulder	11-26-1914
Mulherin & Hargraves	Friona, Tex.	T⊥	Left hip	1-9-1915

J.A. Tidenberg	Bovina, Tex.	T (overline)	Left side	1-29-1915
W.L. Copeland	Farwell, Tex.	I	Left hip	11-22-1921
George Treider	Friona, Tex.	⊥	Left hip	11-25-1915
Laura Treider	Friona, Tex.	⊤	Left hip	11-27-1915
Mrs. L.B. Englant	Bovina, Tex.	Ŧ	Left side	2-26-1917
W.T. Riley	Black, Tex.	∇	Left side	3-1-1917
H.A. Thomas	Farwell, Tex.	⋀	Left shoulder	4-26-1917
Mrs. G. Carter	Friona, Tex.	T	Left shoulder	7-9-1917
T.E. Parker	Farwell, Tex.	T-P	Left side	9-12-1917
Tom Hastings	Bovina, Tex.	T-H	Left side	9-29-1917
S. Mulherin	Friona, Tex.	I	Left hip	2-4-1918
Otto Treider	Friona, Tex.	┕	Left hip	5-1-1918
G.W. Turner	Friona, Tex.	T	Right hip	7-12-1918
W.L. Johnson	Summerfield, Tex.	I	Left hip	7-12-1918
T.N. Jasper	Friona, Tex.	T	Left side	7-12-1918
T.H. Hughes	Friona, Tex.	Ħ	Left hind quarter	3-11-1919
T.O. Cunning	Bovina, Tex.	TC	Left hip	4-21-1919
C.W. Dixon	Texico Route A	TY	Left hip	1-18-1921
E.E. Talkington	Friona, Tex.	T	Right jaw	4-7-1921

189

Name	Location	Brand	Location on animal	Date
Danna Gardner	Bovina, Tex.	I	Left thigh	5-14-1923
H.L. Tidenburg	Bovina, Tex.	∠	Left side	1-22-1925
W.H. Tedford	Friona, Tex.	TZ	Right hip	11-3-1927
J.A. Richards	Bovina, Tex.	T̄	Left hip	8-5-1929
Cash Richards	Bovina, Tex.	T̄-	Left hip	8-5-1929
C.H. Vaughan	Farwell, Tex.	V	Left hip	4-11-1910
E.K. Warren & Son	Hurley, Tex.	U-	Either hip	4-1-1911
R.V. Moorehead	Hurley, Tex.	৬	Left side	8-29-1911
Joseph Paul	Bovina, Tex.	ʊ	Left hip	10-23-1911
Chas. K. Warren	Hurley, Tex.	U-	Left side	7-15-1912
W.G. Paute	Hurley, Tex.	U	Left hip	10-24-1912
L. Smith	Friona, Tex.	⌒	Left hip	12-30-1915
Adaline Reeve	Friona, Tex.	U̲	Left hip	7-11-1918
Roy Hawkins	Bovina, Tex.	U	Right hip	2-13-1919
Floyd Reeve	Friona, Tex.	V̲	Left hip	10-27-1911
B.P. Abbott	Bovina, Tex.	VK	Left hip	10-21-1912
F.L. Reed	Friona, Tex.	V	Right hip	4-27-1914
Mrs. J.A. Oden	Farwell, Tex.	VT	Left shoulder	7-29-1914
V.E. Weir	Friona, Tex.	VE	Right hip	12-3-1917

V.F. Hodge	Friona, Tex.	⩔F	Right hip	5-2-1918
J.E. Ball	Bovina, Tex.	V−	Left hip	7-8-1918
W.H. Fuqua	Amarillo, Tex.	V⩤	Left hip	4-21-1920
E.E. Warren	Friona, Tex.	−V−	Right hip	9-9-1920
J.W. Woltman	Farwell, Tex.	V∧	Left side	12-10-1921
George G. Wright	Friona, Tex.	⌢V	On any part of animal	1-4-1923
John Armstrong	Farwell, Tex.	V̲	Right hip	9-19-1929
E.K. Warren & Sons	Three Oaks, Mich.	O−	Leg or hip	9-23-1908
William Reed	Star Ranch	W∾	Right hip	10-26-1908
Jim Rogers	Star Ranch	W±	Left side	7-15-1909
J.L. Walling	Farwell, Tex.	JXL	Left side	8-25-1911
C.T. Word	Canyon, Tex.	T-T	Right shoulder	1-15-1912
W.E. Goodwine	Friona, Tex.	WE	Right side	1-20-1912
D.M. Davis	Friona, Tex.	W	Right side	6-11-1913
C.P. Wirth	Farwell, Tex.	⌢W	Right side	8-9-1913
Carl Porth	Rhea, Tex.	⋀W	Left hip	9-11-1913
Jay Williams	Bovina, Tex.	JW	Left hip	11-27-1914
J.P. Hammett	Bovina, Tex.	⌂	Left hip	2-4-1918
W. Watkins	Farwell, Tex.	W−	Right hip	7-23-1915

M.S. Weir	Friona, Tex.	W̄	Right hip	3-31-1916
W.D. Sipe	Farwell, Tex.	WA	Left hip	6-24-1916
G.W. Brigg	Farwell, Tex.	-W	Right hip	9-2-1916
J.N. Watson	Farwell, Tex.	W	Left hip	9-30-1916
J.H. Doak	Farwell, Tex.	W-D	Left hip	10-30-1916
W.W. Wells	Bovina, Tex.	3W	Right hip	11-17-1917
A.W. Alexander	Summerfield, Tex.	A∧A	Left side	1-24-1919
J.G. Wood	Farwell, Tex.	W̲	Left hip	7-21-1919
W.H. Simmons	Friona, Tex.	WH	Left side	7-3-1920
Mrs. Texie Walling	Farwell, Tex.	J L	Left shoulder Left hip	10-4-1921
W.E. Goodwine	Friona, Tex.	W̲	Right hip	11-20-1922
W.T. Talbot	Friona, Tex.	WT	Right hip	6-23-1923
W.H. Foster	Friona, Tex.	WHF	Right side	2-21-1925
W.M. Wilterding	Muleshoe, Tex.	W	Right hip	8-31-1925
Erma White	Farwell, Tex.	W̲	Right hip	7-18-1928
Mrs. Texie Walling	Farwell, Tex.	W	Left side	4-8-1929
F.C. Herbart & Co.	Texico, N.M.	XT	Left thigh	6-1-1909
J.F. Hill	Farwell, Tex.	+	Left hip	5-30-1912
Riley Pierce	Friona, Tex.	X̲	Left hip	7-6-1914

Name	Location	Brand	Position	Date
W.S. McDaniel	Farwell, Tex.	XV	Left hip	5-15-1915
G.C. Taylor	Friona, Tex.	ΔX	Left side	9-27-1915
J.K. Billingsley	Bovina, Tex.	X	Left side	3-28-1916
B.W. Kieran	Bovina, Tex.	X	Right shoulder	5-25-1917
D.M. Ballard	Friona, Tex.	X-	Left side	7-9-1917
L.H. Hoffman	Rhea, Tex.	⋀	Left hip	9-13-1920
R.G. Hammonds	Farwell, Tex.	-X	Left hip	4-19-1924
W.H. Hughes	Friona, Tex.	X	Left shoulder	4-24-1925
Will Wilson	Friona, Tex.	X	Right hip	12-28-1926
W.G. Harris	Summerfield, Tex.	⊥	Left side	2-2-1915
A.O. Drake	Black, Tex.	⅄	Left hip	10-9-1915
B.F. Taylor	Farwell, Tex.	H	Right side	11-28-1916
Joe P. Hammett	Bovina, Tex.	Y	Left hip	8-27-1917
Mrs. Pearle Grady	Texico, N.M.	Z	Left hip	5-13-1912
H.P. Spohn	Friona, Tex.	Z	Left hip	1-6-1914
O.A. Gamble	Friona, Tex.	4	Left hip	5-2-1918
H. Geries	Farwell, Tex.	N	Right hip	3-24-1919
Derris S. Jones	Farwell, Tex.	Z	Left hip	5-1-1919
R.H. Kinsley	Friona, Tex.	Z	Left hip	5-1-1919

Edward Kohl	Friona, Tex.	O	Left hip	8-4-1909
Jim Walker	Friona, Tex.	O	Left jaw	11-1-1916
John Hudson	Bovina, Tex.	O	Left thigh	10-18-1917
Burton Brown	Friona, Tex.	O̅	Right hip	11-8-1917
John Armstrong	Farwell, Tex.	O	Right shoulder	9-19-1929
B.C. Roberson	Summerfield, Tex.	II	Left hip	4-23-1913
S.F. Dave	Rhea, Tex.	14	Left hip	6-24-1914
A.B. Horn	Farwell, Tex.	II	Left shoulder	6-30-1917
Robbins & Gamble	Friona, Tex.	II̲	Right hip	5-2-1918
Bernard Roberson	Summerfield, Tex.	II̲	Left thigh	10-18-1922
John Armstrong	Farwell, Tex.	I	Right shoulder	9-19-1929
L.F. Anderson	Bovina, Tex.	2̄	Left shoulder	12-1-1913
Henry Elfers	Bovina, Tex.	4	Right shoulder	8-13-1915
Joseph Jesko	Friona, Tex.	2	Left hip	8-16-1917
W.P. Kays	Texico, N.M.	22	Right shoulder	6-24-1920
H.J. Helms	Bovina, Tex.	22	Left hip	5-5-1925
John Armstrong	Farwell, Tex.	2	Right shoulder	9-19-1929
John Armstrong	Farwell, Tex.	3	Right shoulder	9-19-1929
George P. Garrison	Hereford, Tex.	3̄	Right hip	5-5-1914

E.T. Stevens	Farwell, Tex.	4	Left hip	10-12-1908
McQueen Bros.	Bovina, Tex.	4	Right shoulder	2-16-1909
C.F. Schroeder & Co.	Rhea, Tex.	4 4	Right side	8-29-1911
Tiefel Bros. & Winn	Friona, Tex.	4	Right side	6-19-1912
Ernst Schroeder	Friona, Tex.	4 4	Right side	10-15-1912
A.M. Brownlee	Friona, Tex.	4	Right hip	11-1-1915
Grace Paul	Friona, Tex.	4	Left shoulder	3-3-1917
R.E. Brownlee	Friona, Tex.	4⌐	Right side	4-21-1917
J.A. Guyer	Friona, Tex.	4X	Left side	10-28-1922
G.E. McLellan	Friona, Tex.	4/	Left hip	3-18-1926
John Armstrong	Farwell, Tex.	4	Right shoulder	9-19-1929
J.E. Schluter & M. Schubert	Farwell, Tex.	5	Left side	3-13-1914
Bob Gray	Bovina, Tex.	56	Right hip	6-9-1917
M.O. Venable	Bovina, Tex.	5L	Right side	4-16-1923
Opal Venable	Bovina, Tex.	5	Right hip	5-26-1925
John Armstrong	Farwell, Tex.	5	Right shoulder	9-19-1929
George Daugherty	Friona, Tex.	66	Right hip	3-8-1915
F.W. Jersig	Bovina, Tex.	69	Left side	5-8-1915
F.W. Jersig	Bovina, Tex.	⌐69	Left side	5-8-1917

J.O. Ford	Farwell, Tex.	67	Left hip	7-25-1922
M.Y. Towry	Friona, Tex.	6	Left hip	2-25-1927
John Armstrong	Farwell, Tex.	6	Right shoulder	9-19-1929
Mrs. M.E. Ricks	Bovina, Tex.	73	Left hip	1-6-1909
E.R. Ricks	Bovina, Tex.	⊢	Either hip	1-6-1909
E.T. Stevens	Farwell, Tex.	7+	Left side	1-28-1909
J.H. Aldridge	Bovina, Tex.	7H	Left hip	11-11-1910
M. Killam	Bovina, Tex.	7K	Left hip	5-27-1913
A.L. Chesher	Farwell, Tex.	∧	Left side	5-13-1914
S.J. Justice	Farwell, Tex.	17	Right thigh	10-10-1914
A. Alonquist	Bovina, Tex.	A	Left side	10-27-1914
Mrs. A.M. Brownlee	Friona, Tex.	7L	Right side	11-10-1914
J.H. Alderidge	Bovina, Tex.	7K	Left shoulder	11-19-1914
L.B. Moorman	Texico Route	7L	Right hip	1-9-1915
Allien S. Jersig	Bovina, Tex.	Ŧ	Left side	4-28-1915
Jo Shelby Jersig	Bovina, Tex.	ŦS	Left hip	4-28-1915
P.L. Gaede	Muleshoe, Tex.	7H	Right hip	7-12-1916
B.J. Nelson	Farwell, Tex.	7N	Left hip	3-12-1917
B.T. Bell	Black, Tex.	Ƶ	Left hip	7-13-1917

W.A. Gillham	Farwell, Tex.	77	Left hip	8-18-1917
G.L. Brown	Friona, Tex.	77	Left thigh	11-8-1917
J.O. Cantrell	Friona, Tex.	7	Right hip	2-14-1918
J.C. Temple	Friona, Tex.	71	Left hip	8-12-1918
Robert H. Schueler	Rhea, Tex.	4	Left hip	8-21-1918
John Kloepper	Farwell, Tex.	711	Left side	8-28-1918
Waite Miller	Hurley, Tex.	7-	Either side	8-28-1918
A.J. Smith	Muleshoe, Tex.	UP	Left hip	10-10-1918
Jack Dunn	Farwell, Tex.	7	Left side	11-15-1921
Jack Dunn	Farwell, Tex.	7r	Left shoulder	11-29-1921
Albert Wiley Smith	Friona, Tex.	UP	Left hip	12-29-1922
Mrs. Emma L. Smith	Friona, Tex.	UP	Right hip	12-29-1922
Loyal F. Lust	Dimmitt, Tex.	X	Left side	3-19-1927
Sam Aldridge	Farwell, Tex.	7H	Left hip	9-2-1927
J.A. Parker	Bovina, Tex.	7	Left hip	3-12-1929
John Armstrong	Farwell, Tex.	7	Right shoulder	9-19-1929
C.M. Cooke	Farwell, Tex.	8	Right side	7-23-1923
John Armstrong	Farwell, Tex.	8	Right shoulder	9-19-1929
J.A. Oden	Farwell, Tex.	9	Left thigh	7-29-1914

D.W. Hanson	Friona, Tex.	96	Left side	4-5-1919
John Armstrong	Farwell, Tex.	9	Right shoulder	9-19-1929
W.W. Meyer	Farwell, Tex.	⅄	Either side	5-23-1908
J.B. McMinn	Summerfield, Tex.	T	Left hip	7-1-1908
Grady Stegall	Farwell, Tex.	+	Left side	1-16-1909
Stephen Jesko	Bovina, Tex.	∥	Left side	5-21-1909
T.B. O'Neal	Bovina, Tex.	Ⓚ	Right hip	8-26-1909
Chas. Schlenker	Rhea, Tex.	⏝	Left side	10-19-1909
W.H. Hitson	Farwell, Tex.	I	Left thigh	11-6-1909
Tom Grady	Texico, N.M.	↳	Left hip	12-31-1910
Mrs. E. Nichols	Farwell, Tex.	Ā	Left shoulder	4-14-1911
Floyd Schlenker	Bovina, Tex.	Â	Left side	10-21-1911
J.E. Cary	Bovina, Tex.	+	Left hip	11-18-1911
O.G. Ray	Friona, Tex.	Ⓔ	Left hip	2-25-1912
Chas. Gallmeier	Rhea, Tex.	◇̄	Left hip	5-8-1912
Mrs. Pearle Grady	Texico, N.M.	Az	Left hip	5-13-1912
A.J. James	Friona, Tex.	◇	Right shoulder	5-27-1912
J.F. Hill	Farwell, Tex.	+	Left hip	5-30-1912
Rady Wilson	Farwell, Tex.	+	Left hip	5-30-1912

Name	Location	Brand	Position	Date
A.C. Schlenker	Bovina, Tex.		Left hip	5-12-1913
R.A. Gregory	Friona, Tex.		Left hip	10-14-1912
G.C. Taylor	Friona, Tex.		Left shoulder	11-2-1912
F.E. Clennin	Friona, Tex.		Right hip	10-20-1913
B.F. Taylor	Friona, Tex.		Left side	12-11-1913
Delmer D. Taylor	Friona, Tex.		Right hip	4-29-1930
A.L. Chesher Jr.	Farwell, Tex.		Either side	6-13-1914
D.M. Ballard	Friona, Tex.		Left hip	7-17-1914
J.E. Cary	Friona, Tex.		Left hip	7-17-1914
Miss Daisy Paul	Friona, Tex.		Left shoulder	7-18-1914
Charlie Wilson	Farwell, Tex.		Right side	8-20-1914
C.W. Harrison	Farwell, Tex.		Left shoulder	9-22-1914
J.W. Dugan	Friona, Tex.		Right hip	9-25-1914
Chas. Fahsholtz	Texico, N.M.		Left side	9-30-1914
E.G. Taylor	Friona, Tex.		Left hip	10-7-1914
C. Delano	Bovina, Tex.		Left hip	10-14-1914
Albert Bell	Black, Tex.		Left hip	10-17-1914
H.P. Oliver	Farwell, Tex.		Left hip	10-26-1914
Matt Jesko	Star Ranch		Left hip	11-9-1914

L.E. Eastland & Son	Bovina, Tex.		Left shoulder	11-9-1914
E.M. Ross	Bovina, Tex.		Right hip	11-20-1914
R.M. Glaze	Hurley, Tex.		Left hip	1-19-1915
David H. Lawrence	Friona, Tex.		Left hip	4-10-1915
George Sacks	Rhea, Tex.		Left hip	4-9-1915
D.B. Williams	Bovina, Tex.		Left hip	8-20-1915
Arthur Davies	Bovina, Tex.		Left hip	10-5-1916
J.W. White	Friona, Tex.		Right hip	9-15-1915
Seamonds & Son	Friona, Tex.		Right hip	10-18-1915
W.E. Bledsoe	Muleshoe, Tex.		Left shoulder	5-30-1916
J.L. Green	Bovina, Tex.		Left side	6-16-1916
Katherine Hamlin	Farwell, Tex.		Left side	8-2-1916
A.J. Bistor	Bovina, Tex.		Left thigh	9-19-1916
T.E. Baker	Black, Tex.		Left hip	3-13-1917
Mrs. J.G. Rose	Summerfield, Tex.		Left shoulder	4-6-1917
D.M. Ballard	Friona, Tex.		Left side	4-23-1917
Mr. & Mrs. J.G. Rose	Summerfield, Tex.		Left shoulder	5-1-1917
R.S. Barnes Jr.	Friona, Tex.		Right hip	5-31-1917
W. Reede Curtis	Friona, Tex.		Right side	6-16-1917

Name	Location	Brand	Location on Animal	Date
S.T. Lawerence	Friona, Tex.		Left shoulder	6-27-1917
C.D. Caldwell	Bovina, Tex.		Left side	7-9-1917
D.R. Doolittle	Friona, Tex.		Right hip	7-23-1917
W.A. Doolittle	Friona, Tex.		Right hip	7-23-1917
Frank Hastings	Bovina, Tex.		Left side	8-29-1917
C.R. Holman	Farwell, Tex.		Left thigh	9-13-1917
Floyd Schlenker	Friona, Tex.		Left side	9-24-1917
Charles Hawkins	Bovina, Tex.		Right side	11-3-1917
W.H. Warren	Friona, Tex.		Right hip	11-12-1917
Will Hall	Friona, Tex.		Left side	12-20-1917
H.D. Ford	Friona, Tex.		Left hip	1-11-1918
O.S. Gallatin	Friona, Tex.		Left hip	1-26-1918
J.H. Stagner	Bovina, Tex.		Left shoulder	3-23-1918
C.F. Vance	Summerfield, Tex.		Right hip	4-26-1918
T.F. Tipton	Farwell, Tex.		Right jaw	2-11-1919
Ross Glaze	Hurley, Tex.		Left hip	3-3-1919
J.A. Hiner	Farwell, Tex.		Left side	2-3-1919
R.L. McMurtry	Farwell, Tex.		Around right hip bone	6-19-1919
Floyd Schlenker	Friona, Tex.		Left side	8-8-1919

Name	Location	Brand	Position	Date
R.L. Galloway	Friona, Tex.		Just back of shoulders	11-1-1919
R.L. Galloway	Friona, Tex.		Left shoulder	2-17-1920
Clyde C. Seamonds	Friona, Tex.		Left hip	3-10-1920
Fred Thomas	Friona, Tex.		Left hip	3-8-1920
Edd K. Massie	Friona, Tex.		Left hip	4-19-1920
Charles Tidenburg	Bovina, Tex.		Left hip	8-28-1920
W.D. Knight	Friona, Tex.		On nose	11-29-1920
J.C. Denny	Bovina, Tex.		Left hip	1-14-1921
O.B. Roberson	Summerfield, Tex.		Left hip	1-27-1921
W.H. Massie	Friona, Tex.		Left hip	6-11-1921
W.A. Bell	Texico Route		Left thigh	6-17-1921
Frank Woodard	Friona, Tex.		Left thigh	9-21-1921
J.M. Sphon	Friona, Tex.		Right shoulder	10-20-1921
Ed Ross	Bovina, Tex.		Right hip	10-25-1921
Charles Hinkson	Muleshoe, Tex.		Left shoulder	11-5-1921
Merton Dickson	Farwell, Tex.		Left shoulder	2-21-1922
C.J. Smith	Texico Route		Left jaw	4-4-1922
J.O. Ford	Farwell, Tex.		Left hip	7-24-1922
Lowell Stagner	Bovina, Tex.		Left shoulder	9-16-1922

Name	Location	Brand	Location on animal	Date
W.R. Hayworth	Farwell, Tex.	✝	Right side	12-12-1922
J.J. Boulmare	Friona, Tex.	⚓	Left side	8-11-1924
W.D. Knight	Friona, Tex.	⚓	Left hip	10-27-1924
I.D. Merrill	Friona, Tex.	○	Left hind leg	2-25-1927
Wayne Bennett	Lariat, Tex.	⚓	Left side	7-1-1929

Chapter X

Old Letterheads

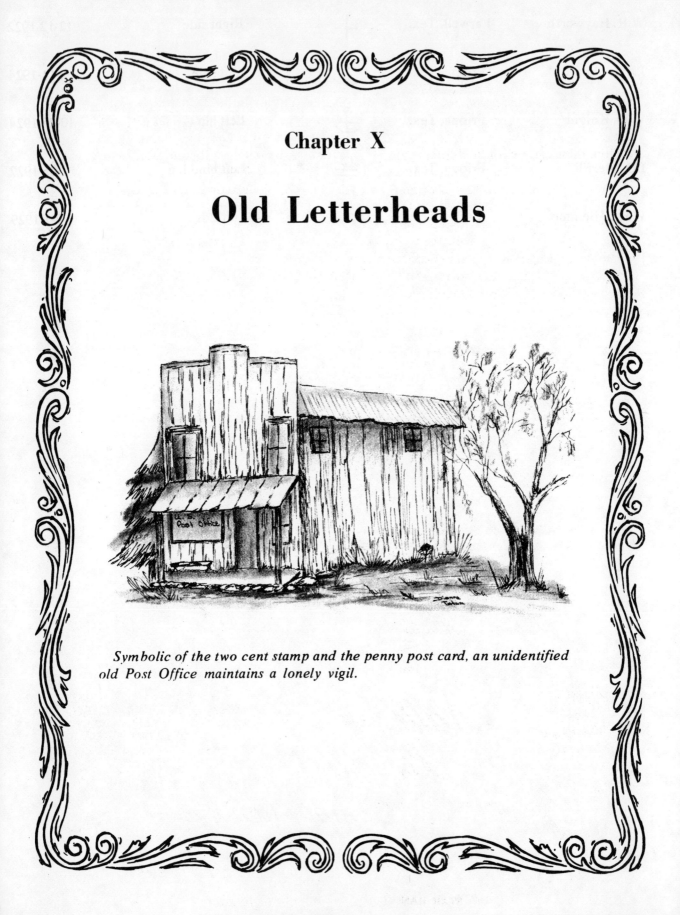

Symbolic of the two cent stamp and the penny post card, an unidentified old Post Office maintains a lonely vigil.

Unlike the Oklahoma land rush that broke upon the unclaimed Indian Territories as an all-consuming tidal wave, the settling of the Parmer County prairies resembled the more orderly advances of incoming ocean swells that each in turn covered more and more land. Swift horseless carriages rode the waves of immigration, their cargoes of land-hungry farmers enchanted by miles of deep topsoil to be had at bargain prices. The business of buying farms, establishing homes, and purchasing farming tools was of primary importance to both newcomer and salesman. The correspondence necessary to file and record deeds, mortgages, liens, contracts, titles, and taxes created a mountain of paper work. The newly formed office of county clerk found itself the target of bankers, lawyers, manufacturers, serious-minded farmers and non-resident fortune seekers.

The flamboyant letterheads and very descriptive language indicate that problems existed, even in the good old days.

TELEPHONE CENTRAL 348.

F. W. WILSEY, LAND COMMISSIONER.

The Capitol Freehold Land & Investment Co. Ltd.

617-619 FIRST NATIONAL BANK BUILDING

Lands subject to sale and prices to change without notice

Chicago, August 12, 1908.

IN ORDER TO BORROW money in England, John V. Farwell found that he must form an English company. The Capitol Freehold Land and Investment Company, Limited, was organized in 1885 with a capital of three million pounds sterling ($15,000,000).

Chicago, St. Louis, Kansas City, St. Joseph, Omaha, Fort Worth.
Thos. Kelly, President & Manager. Frank C. Mills, Vice President. E. B. Overstreet, Vice President.
R. H. Lee, Vice President. Jesse Sherwood, Vice President. Chas. Kelly, Secretary & Treasurer.

National Live Stock Commission Co.

Annual Sales Exceed Fifty Million Dollars

Union Stock Yards, Chicago, Sept. 25, 1908.

Long Distance Phone 941 Yards.

THE STAR RANCH and Cadillac Township people.

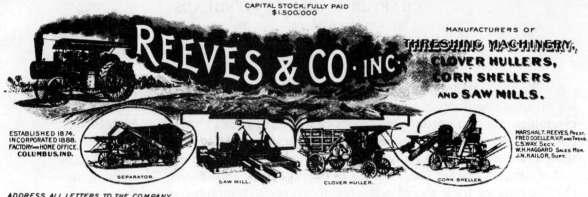

REEVES & CO· INC·

MANUFACTURERS OF
THRESHING MACHINERY,
CLOVER HULLERS,
CORN SHELLERS
AND SAW MILLS.

ESTABLISHED 1874.
INCORPORATED 1888.
FACTORY AND HOME OFFICE.
COLUMBUS, IND.

SEPARATOR.
SAW MILL.
CLOVER HULLER.
CORN SHELLER.

MARSHAL T. REEVES, PRES'T.
FRED DOELLE R.V.P. AND TREAS.
C.S.WAY. SEC'Y.
W.H.HAGGARD SALES MGR.
J.N.KAILOR, SUPT.

ADDRESS ALL LETTERS TO THE COMPANY.

Oklahoma City, O.T. July 6, 1908

THIS LETTERHEAD places Oklahoma City in "O.T." (Oklahoma Territory). Stationery evidently printed before Oklahoma achieved statehood in 1907 but used in 1908.

J.M. JEMISON
WHOLESALE & RETAIL
Grocer and Butcher
100-102 E. MAIN ST.
DENISON, TEXAS
PHONES 273

GENERAL SUPPLY CONTRACTOR
FOR RAILROADS, SCHOOLS, HOTELS
AND GOVERNMENT WORKS

Midland, Texas Jan 27th 1913

O. B. HOLT, VICE-PRES.
P. SCHARBAUER, VICE-PRES.

W. H. COWDEN, PRESIDENT.

E. R. BRYAN, CASHIER.
M. C. ULMER, ASST. CASH.

No. 4368

The First National Bank
OF MIDLAND, TEXAS.

CAPITAL $100,000.00   SURPLUS $100,000.00

MIDLAND, TEXAS, 4/3 1913

CLARKE & COURTS, GALVESTON

ALEX SHIPLEY, PRESIDENT.
FRED W. JAMES, V. PRES.

J. C. NELSON, CASHIER.
J. R. HULL, ASST. CASHIER.

NO. 8767.

THE CLOVIS NATIONAL BANK

CAPITAL STOCK $25,000.

CLOVIS, NEW MEXICO, December 6, 1912.

OFFICE OF
DISTRICT AND COUNTY CLERK
PARMER COUNTY

FARWELL, TEXAS
June,
Ninth,
1912.

THE FIRST STATE BANK & TRUST CO.

CAPITAL $100,000.00
ORGANIZED 1907.
RE-ORGANIZED 1909.

S.B. EDWARDS, President
H.B. WEBB, Vice Prest.
A.P. MURCHISON, Cashier.

HEREFORD, TEXAS.   December 13th, 1912.

JNO. E. HILL, Pres.   B.N. BROWN, Vice-Pres.   P.E. BRISCOE, Sec. & Treas.

STEPHENS LITHO & ENG CO ST LOUIS

Independent Paper Cutter Co.

"ABSOLUTELY INDEPENDENT"
MANUFACTURERS OF
STICKFAST AND TAKE-UP TWINE HOLDERS,
ROLL PAPER CUTTERS, ETC.
UNDER ORIGINAL PATENTS.
"FOR THE JOBBING TRADE"
505 NO. SECOND ST.

St. Louis,   May 22, 1915.

WASHINGTON   JEFFERSON   BIG STICK   NO. 17 JUMBO

H.A. NOBLES, Vice-President   M.C. NOBLES, President   A.G. STANLEY, Sec'y & Treas

NOBLES BROTHERS GROCER CO.
CAPITAL $400000.00
WHOLESALE GROCERS

MAIN HOUSE
AMARILLO,
TEXAS.

BRANCHES AT
PLAINVIEW
TEXAS
DALHART
TEXAS
FARWELL
TEXAS
LUBBOCK
TEXAS
MEMPHIS
TEXAS

JUSTICE BRAND

FARWELL, TEXAS
8-24-18

Board of County Commisioners
Parmer County

SOLD TO

Terms   net

MEMBER OF
U.S. FOOD
ADMINISTRATION

THE COUNTY OF DALLAS

QUENTIN D. CORLEY
COUNTY JUDGE

Dallas, Texas, 12/12/13

F. W. REEVE, COMMISSIONER PRECINCT No 1, FRIONA, TEXAS
F. L. SPRING, COMMISSIONER PRECINCT No. 2, BOVINA, TEXAS

R. A. HAWKINS, COMMISSIONER PRECINCT No. 3, FARWELL, TEXAS
HENRY BLEDSOE, COMMISSIONER PRECINCT No. 4, MULESHOE, TEXAS

JAMES D. HAMLIN, COUNTY JUDGE

COMMISSIONERS' COURT
PARMER COUNTY, TEXAS

Francis C. Farwell, Charles F. Harding and George Findlay,
Trustees
Capitol Reservation Lands

TEXAS CAPITOL BUILDING.

102 SOUTH MARKET STREET
Chicago, Ill.

TELEPHONE MAIN 4874

Sept. 29, 1921.

PARMER COUNTY

FARWELL, TEXAS

Sept, 29, 1927

208

D. L. WHITNEY, Manager.

Ind. Telephone 1083.

F. N. BURLEIGH,
F. B. FAUST, } Salesmen.

"Square Deal" Realty Company,

Notary Public.   Correspondence Solicited.

Topeka City Property — Kansas Farms — Texas Lands.

433 KANSAS AVENUE.

Topeka, Kansas,_____190

PAID UP CAPITAL $400,000.00

FOXWORTH-GALBRAITH COMPANY

OF ALAMOGORDO, N.M.

LUMBER

DALHART, TEXAS.   MCH. 26, 1908.

HOUSE PHONE
207

Hebron Produce Co.

OFFICE PHONE
174

J. P. RAFTER, Proprietor

Eggs,   --   Poultry,   --   Butter,   --   Cream

Hebron, Nebr., _May 5_ _____190 8

DONLEY COUNTY

OFFICERS:

GEO. F. MORGAN, CO. JUDGE
C. A. BURTON, CO. AND
DIST. CLERK.
J. T. PATMAN, SHERIFF AND
TAX COLLECTOR.
G. W. BAKER, TAX ASSESSOR
J. M. CLOWER, TREASURER
J. C. KILLOUGH CO. ATT'Y
E. R. CLARK, SURVEYOR

COMMISSIONERS:

W. G. SMITH,   PRECINCT NO. 1.
J. D. JEFFRIES,   PRECINCT NO. 2.
E. E. McGEE,   PRECINCT NO. 3.
B F. NAYLOR, PRECINCT NO. 4.

CLARENDON, TEXAS,___9-22-___190 8

THE STATE OF TEXAS

RALPH STEINER, M.D.
President

Texas
State Board of Health
Department of Vital Statistics
R.P. BABCOCK, STATE REGISTRAR
Austin, Texas

January 10, 1913.

PHONES:
BELL 389 MAIN
HOME 2879 MAIN

Coldren Land Company

OFFICES
NEW YORK LIFE BLDG.
KANSAS CITY, MO.

100,000 ACRES IN THE
PAN HANDLE OF TEXAS.
LOW PRICES, LOW RATE OF
INTEREST. LONG TIME.

WE ARE OWNERS, NOT AGENTS.
TERMS: TEN YEARS TIME ON DEFERRED PAYMENTS. 6% INTEREST

ASSOCIATED LAND CO.

Successors to

Geo. G. Wright Co.

TEXAS PAN HANDLE
WHEAT AND CORN
LANDS

LONG DISTANCE
TELEPHONE
MAIN 4120

411-412 R. A. LONG BUILDING
TENTH STREET AND GRAND AVENUE

INCORPORATED. PAID UP CAPITAL $100,000.
620-622-624 GUMBEL BLDG. EIGHTH & WALNUT STS.

Kansas City, Mo. July 11, 1 02.

WE ARE OWNERS, NOT AGENTS
TERMS; TEN YEARS' TIME ON DEFERRED PAYMENTS. 6% INTEREST

Associated Land Co.

TEXAS PAN HANDLE
WHEAT AND CORN
LANDS

410-411-412 R. A. LONG BUILDING
TENTH STREET AND GRAND AVENUE

LONG DISTANCE TELEPHONE
BELL 4120 MAIN

SUCCESSORS TO GEO G. WRIGHT CO.

KANSAS CITY, MO., June 19, 1908.

CHARLES K. WARREN, Manager,
Three Oaks, Michigan.

B. P. ABBOTT, Foreman,
BOVINA, TEXAS.
On Pecos Valley Div. Santa Fe R. R.

E. K. Warren & Sons

OWNERS Y RANCH

RANCH in
CASTRO, LAMB, BAILEY,
and PARMER COUNTIES, TEXAS.

<u>CATTLE FOR SALE</u>   3 Oaks, Mich. July 2, 1908

County Clerk,

    Farwell, Texas.

Dear Sir:-

    We are enclosing you herewith Warranty Deeds and Release of
Trust Deeds for the following described land in Parmer County: East 1/2
of Section 17, Block Z and N.E. 1/4 Section 1 in Block X. Also N.E.
1/4 of Section 48 in Block Y, situated in Parmer and Baily County.

    Kindly record these and send us bill for same and we will remit
promptly.

        Yours very truly,

            E.K.Warren & Sons.

            Chas K Warren

Sten.#2.

Mrs. Jeannette Hartwell

Bovina Texas

Dr.
Frederick E. French

TO **Francis C. Farwell, Charles F. Harding** and ~~George Findlay~~
CAPITOL RESERVATION LANDS, CR.   *Trustees*
Room 1136—208 South La Salle Street

<u>2nd Notice</u>   Chicago, Ill., Nov 20th 1928

1928				
May 1	To rent of 5168.05 acres pasturage under Lease No. 1643 from the 1st day of November 1928 to April 30th 1929		904 41	
	add 10% from November 1st		19 79	924 20

Rec'd Paymt.
1/22 29
Capitol Reservation Lands
By James D Hamlin

211

MANUFACTURERS OF
THRESHING MACHINERY.
CLOVER HULLERS.
CORN SHELLERS
AND SAW MILLS.

ESTABLISHED 1874
INCORPORATED 1888
FACTORY AND HOME OFFICE.
COLUMBUS, IND.

ADDRESS ALL LETTERS TO THE COMPANY

Dallas, Texas. April 7, 1908.

Mr. J. F. McKay,

    County Clerk,

        Parmerton, Texas.--Parmer Co.

Dear Sir:-

    Enclosed we return you copy of Chattel Mortgage, which you sent us and which we desire that you file and return to us the original with your certificate thereon, showing a certified copy is filed in your office. Had you read carefully our instructions of March 3rd and also our letter of March 20th, you would not have sent us the certified copy but would have sent us the original as we instructed and requested.

    Kindly give this matter your immediate attention and let us hear from you by return mail and oblige.

        Yours truly,

AFM:FL.

MANUFACTURERS OF
THRESHING MACHINERY.
CLOVER HULLERS.
CORN SHELLERS
AND SAW MILLS.

ESTABLISHED 1874
INCORPORATED 1888
FACTORY AND HOME OFFICE.
COLUMBUS, IND.

ADDRESS ALL LETTERS TO THE COMPANY

Dallas, Texas. April 11, 1908.

Mr. J. M. McKay,

    County Clerk,

        Parmerton, Texas.

Dear Sir:-

    We are just in receipt of the enclosed original mortgage. What in the mischief do you mean by returning this mortgage to us in this condition? You should have filled out the certificate on same and have sent it in to us in proper form. We are only asking of you what is regular and legal and for which we have paid our money.

    We now ask that you fill the certificate out on this mortgage and return it to us by early mail to Dallas, Texas. We are satisfied this matter has been overlooked by you personally and we send it to you by registered mail in order to know that you get it and we shall expect an immediate return with the certificate thereon properly filled out and signed by you.

        Yours respectfully,

AFM:FL.

Encl.

CHICAGO March 30th 1908.

J. F. McKay Esq.,
County Clerk.
Dear Sir:-

A few weeks ago I purchased Lots 1 & 2 of Sec. 18 Township 16 So, Range 1 East, Capitol Syndicate Sub. in Parmer County and it is my desire to improve it by allowing some one to have use of the soil for building a fence and making some such improvement. If you should know of anyone desiring the use of my land in return for some such improvement being made I shall thank you to learn of it and take it up with you.

I do not aim to take any undue privileges in making this request yet if you should know kindly advise me and oblige,

Very truly yours,
Wm D Petzel.

CHICAGO Mar 4th 908.

J. F. McKay Esq.,
Dear Sir:-

Some time ago I mailed you several deeds and abstract and later a money order to cover the cost of same and taxes but yet I have failed to receive either of the above. It occurred to me that perhaps you had overlooked my address. Kindly have me when ready and oblige,

Very truly,
Wm D Petzel

213

ASSOCIATED LAND CO.

Successors to

Geo. G. Wright Co.

TEXAS PAN HANDLE
WHEAT AND CORN
LANDS

INCORPORATED, PAID UP CAPITAL $100,000.
411-412 R.A. LONG BLDG. GRAND AVE AND TENTH ST

LONG DISTANCE
TELEPHONE
MAIN 4120

Kansas City, Mo.   2/25/08.

Mr. J. T. McKay, County Clerk,

Farmerton, Parmer County, Texas.

Dear Sir:-

We have yours of the 14th calling attention to the
fact that it would be necessary for us to either send stamps
with our instruments, or else pay your bill for such stamps
that may be used in returning said instruments to us.

This is one of the surprises that we do not often
meet. It is indeed too bad that the matter of postage on
our business should be cutting into your revenues to such an
extend us to warrant an action of this kind. This is the
first instance of our many years of experience that we have
been called upon to pay postage for return of instruments
sent for recording.

We do not want to work a hardship in this matter,
and would suggest that you kindly turn over all instruments
that you have recorded for us to Mr. Allen T. Sims, with
whom we will arrange for the return of the documents to us.

In connection with this matter I wish to say that
it is the smallest piece of business that has ever been called
to our attention, especially in view of the fact of what our
company is doing for your county at the present time. Parmer
County was almost an unheard of proposition until we commenced
operating there, and is through our efforts that settlers are
coming into the county.

We would pleased to have the names of the County
Commissioners who passed on this proposition, as we believe
it would do them good to have their names mentioned in connection with such a transaction in some good lively paper.

Kindly follow our suggestion above mentioned, and
turn all of our instruments hereafter to Mr. Sims for return
to us.

Yours truly,

ASSOCIATED LAND CO.

W-R

SOLE AGENCY

CORBITT & BILES

"THE YAZOO VALLEY LAND PEOPLE"

MEMPHIS TENN.

TAKE THE I.C.R.R. SOUTH

ELMER C. BOLLINGER

MISSISSIPPI & LOUISIANA LANDS

FOR SALE

YAZOO VALLEY LANDS
A SPECIALTY

Seymour, Indiana.   June 2nd, 1908.

County Clerk, Parmer Co. Texas,

Dear Sir:-

I bought some lots at Friona, Texas and have just found
out where to have them recorded. I will enclose the deed for same
together with draft for $3.60 which if it is too much you can return
stamps for the difference. Hoping you will attend to this at once and
return the deed to me, I will probably be down in July with some buyers
and will try and call on you.

Thanking you in advance for your prompt action in
this matter,

I am very respt yours,

214

L. G. BYERLEY COMPANY

Texas Panhandle Corn and Wheat Lands

5 TO 10 YEARS TIME, 6 PER CENT.

419 R. A. LONG BUILDING
TENTH AND GRAND AVENUE
LONG DISTANCE PHONE
BELL MAIN 709

KANSAS CITY, MO., March 3, 1908.

Recorder of Deeds,

    Parmerton, Texas.

Dear Sir:

    I want to get a list of all the non-resident land
owners in your county. What would you charge to make me
up a typewritten list, giving owners name and address,
and the number of acres of land he owns in your county?

    Let me hear from you in regard to this matter by
return mail.

        Yours very truly,

        L. G. Byerley Co.

P. S. We are enclosing you stamped envelope for your
reply.

Chapter XI

Home Sweet Home

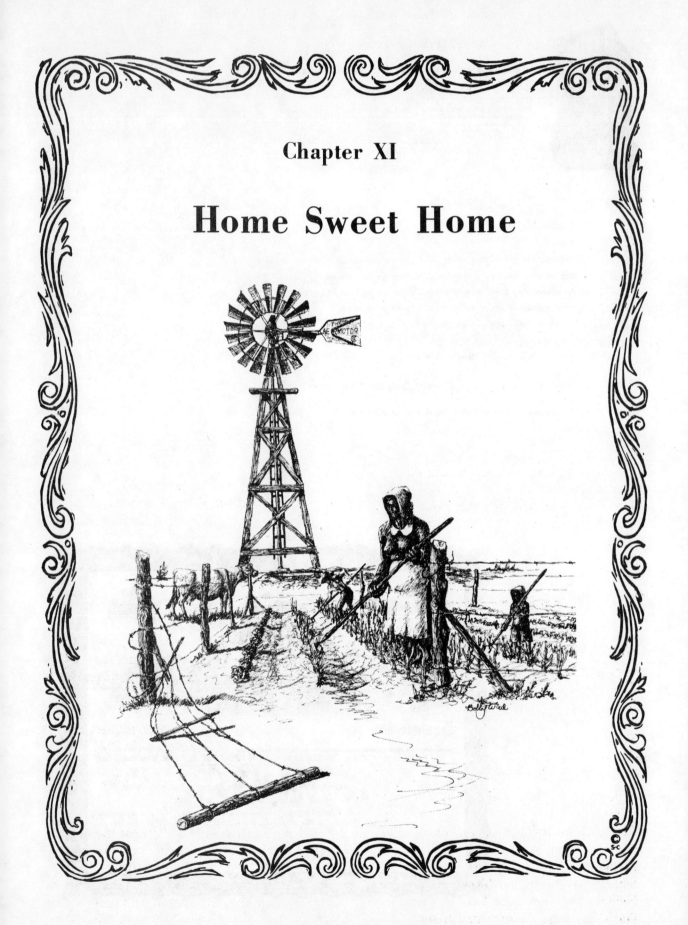

CHAPTER XI—HOME SWEET HOME

"Backward, turn backward, O Time in Your Flight,
Make me a child again Just for tonight!"
(Elizabeth Akers Allen—
"Rock Me to Sleep"-1860)

One of the nicest things about growing old is reaching the point where Time, Memory, and Nostalgia are all blended into a mosaic pattern of diffused light and whose sharp edges have been rubbed smooth by the passing years.

Not all hardship was born of poverty, nor did well filled pockets promise idleness. Practices that now appear to have been the epitome of inconvenience were, in the old days, considered a way of life. Early settlers no doubt gave us the saying that "necessity is the mother of invention."

Can you remember?:—
Plucking ducks for down pillows.
Drying beans and corn for winter use.
Salting and smoking pork.
Hanging beef on the windmill.
Pressure cookers and water bath canning.
Changing straw in a mattress.
Tomatoes wrapped in paper to ripen.
Cabbages, turnips, and carrots buried to avoid freezing.
A noisey rooster that didn't know when Sunday came.

Jacking up one rear wheel of a model T so it would crank.
Hauling water, coal and wood.
When Christmas meant more than gifts.
Corn cob dolls and stick horses.
Cleaning coal oil lamp chimneys.
Icy trips down the path—especially after dark.
Trying to keep the bread starter from freezing.
Box suppers and pie auctions.
When Sunday School and Church were the highlights of the week.
Churning butter and scrub boards.
Sad irons that grew heavier and heavier.
Fixing blowouts on 30 x 3½ clincher rims.
Sand, snow, and rain blowing in.
Heated rocks and feed bags to warm feet.
Gathering eggs before they froze.

Stone crocks of milk in a trough of cold water.
Flypaper and feather dusters.

"The good old days" may be as beauty is said to be—"in the eye of the beholder."

When a girl was married, her neighbors gave her a house warming. They started a Recipe Book. This was the contribution of one guest.

A Recipe For A Good Day
Take a little dash of cold water,
A little leaven of prayer
A little bit of sunshine gold,
Dissolved in the morning air.
Add to your meals some merriment
A thought for kith and kin,
And then as a prime ingredient,
A-plenty of work thrown in.
Flavor it all with the essence of love
And a little dash of play.
Let a nice old Book and a glance above,
Complete a well-spent day.

How to Gain Weight
and Influence Husbands
Recipe for curing meat—makes enough for 280 pounds of meat.
4 lbs. brown sugar
10 lbs. salt
1 lb. red pepper
2 lbs. black pepper
4 oz. Salt Petre
Dissolve salt petre in a little water. Make mixture moist. Rub over meat. Turn every day or so, adding more of the mixture as it is absorbed.

A PENCILED SCRAWL, BARELY LEGIBLE, REFLECTS A FARMER'S SAD PLIGHT
Translated by Lucille Lewis

Nature of the suit as follows—to wit:— about the 30th day of Oct. 1912 at the hour of about 8:30 A.M. defendents received and undertook to ship for plaintiff, from Roswell, New Mexico to Texico, New Mexico, about 188 head of hogs and started with them at last said hour and did not get to Texico until about 10 o'clock A.M. the 31st day of October 1912, negligently delaying them about 6 hours beyond time necessary and ran against the car containing said hogs violently and suddenly stopped and started and negligently jerked and jolted them and shipped them negligently in a car saturated with creosote and poisoned said hogs and as a result of said negligence about 12 of them were dead on arrival at said Texico and others dying which continued until more than 60 of them died if said hogs had been shipped with promptness and dispatch and handled with ordinary care they would have been of the market value of said Texico when they would have arrived there of about $1200.00 but shipped as they were and handled as they were only of the market value of about $200.00 to the damage of the plaintiff in the amount of $1000.00 for which plaintiff sues together with interests and costs.

HOG KILLING TIME

By Mr. E.C. Temple

The first norther had struck, so it was time to kill hogs. The day before, the men made the wooden vat for the scalding, put up the scaffold for hanging the butchered hogs, and made trestles to lay them on for the cutting and quartering. At rooster crowing time, dark as pitch, Ida crawled out of bed in the shivering cold, lit the coal oil lamp on the bed stand, struck a match to the kindling laid in the heating stove, and woke the family. Breakfast had to be over before the helpers came to start the day's work. The cook stove in the house had to be used to heat boilers, tubs, and kettles of water for the scalding vat. Other water could be heated on the stove in the wash shack in the back yard, also in the iron black wash pots near the hog pen.

The workers, or killers, came early, guns under their denim coated arms, ready to shoot to kill. The first 300 pounder was dead. Men grabbed the feet and drug him, or else tied ropes around him to tug and lift him to the huge vat of steaming water, where strong hands and backs turned him over and over until the bristles came off easily upon being rubbed by the palm of the hand. The same strength got him hoisted to the scaffold

HOG KILLING TIME, Ben Buchanan, Melt Crow.

where razor sharp butcher knives were used to scrape him clean of bristles, from top to bottom. Every nook and cranny of him was cleaned until the pinkish white skin glowed clearly and almost was irridescent as pearl. This was only the beginning of Mr. Porky. The scaffold had a heavy crossbeam at the top, in the middle of which a heavy iron hook was suspended by a heavier chain. The hog's hind feet were fastened together with an equally strong chain. One of the links had to be inserted onto the iron hook, making a pulley, by which he was hoisted up, head down. Then the artistry of the main butcher was put to use.

The huge animal was sliced from head to tail, called gutting. The entrails, heart, liver and all insides were lowered into a huge wash tub, as they were separated carefully from the hog's linings. A large hog's insides filled an enormous vat or tub to the brim, with the steaming mass.

It was the women's job to separate from the tub the chitterlings, to cook or use for part of the lard rendering—also cut the heart and liver from the big intestines from which all fatty globules were removed for lard.

After the hog had drained and cooled sufficiently he was again hoisted to the trestle. Again the huge knives or cleaners were used. Off came his head—not to be thrown away. Even ears were saved, scalded in lye water to remove the outer skin and bristle and cooked along with the other parts of the usable head, from which was made spiced head souse. After the hams and shoulders had been cut from him, the feet and knuckles were disjointed to be made into pickled pig's feet—an art of preparation in itself. Then the bacon squares separated, the pure fat or sides cut into strips of skin also. Then cut into small cubes by the quick swish of sharp butcher knives. After the hog had been dissected into his components of hams, shoulders, bacon rashers, fats for lard, the remainder of lean strips were cut for sausage, which was ground by the old fashioned hand method. It was seasoned with sage, salt and pepper and red pepper. Later years we were able to buy prepared seasonings, but now it was our own taste—a pinch or spoon of this or that until it tasted right. After the sausage lay overnight a small amount was cooked for breakfast to judge the taste—too flat called for more seasoning. Too much seasoning called for more strips to be ground and added to the mixture.

Then came lard making day, which was more strenuous than the first day. The huge wash pots were used again. Fires built under them. Another testing, the fires had to be just right, as to blaze and embers, not too hot or low. The cut of fatty part of the hog was poured in the pots. Huge wooden ladles, long, long handles were used to enable the stirrer to stay back from the fire and not scorch face, hands, or catch a blowing calico dress on fire. The stew had to cook slowly. Slowly at first until the first grease had been rendered enough to make liquid for the whole pot full. Then the constant turning of the fatty gobs was a chore. In the cold north wind to the back and the scorch of the fire in front. A good lard maker knew when it was "done," the liquid turned a certain clear color, and the skin had curled and crinkled into brown crunch curls. A big milk strainer or such was used (when the grease had cooled sufficiently) to strain the lard into huge lard cans. A bucker or long handled dipper was also used to convey the lard to the strainer and can. The skins were dumped into other containers, kept ready for soap making. If white lard was wanted, a pinch of soda was dumped into the pot as it boiled.

MRS. D.W. CARPENTER making lye soap—Okla. Lane

Lye Soap

Take 5 pounds of cracklings or fat scrape meat 1 can of lye and 1 gallon of cold water.

Put the water into the wash vat and pour in the lye. It will boil like fury!

Put in the meat scrapes or cracklings and cook until all the meat has dissolved. Take fire away and stir until cool.

Cold Lye Soap

1 gallon water
1 can lye
5 pounds meat drippings or tallow

Pour the water into wash pot and add the lye then the meat drippings or tallow. This mixture will boil on its own. When boiling stops, pour mixture into clean containers to harden.

SOURDOUGH STARTER

1 c. whole milk
1 T. sugar
1½ t. salt
one-third c. white cornmeal

Scald milk. Remove from fire and stir in the sugar, salt, and cornmeal. Mix thoroughly and place mixture in large fruit jar or pitcher. Cover the container and place it in a pan of water which is hot to the hand (120 degrees F.)

Allow to stand in a warm place for 7 or 8

hours or overnight. Make a soft dough by adding the following to the fermented mixture:

1 c. warm water
2 c. flour
1 T. sugar

Beat thoroughly. Place the sponge in the hot water bath and allow it to rise until it is very light and full of bubbles. The resulting mixture is called starter. You will need to keep the starter refrigerated, but must not freeze it.

To set the starter, pour it into a mixing bowl and add lukewarm water or potato water. Then stir in flour to make a thick sponge. Cover and set in a warm place overnight.

The next morning you will need to spoon the starter for the next batch into a jar with a tight fitting lid and put it back in the refrigerator.

After taking the starter out of the sponge, stir in about ¼ c. melted margarine, salad oil or bacon drippings and 2 T. of sugar for each 2 c. of sponge, then add flour to make a stiff dough.

Grease the top of the dough and sides of the bowl, cover and allow to rise until light— approx. double in bulk. Turn the dough out onto a well floured board and knead about 10 minutes. Then shape into loaves and let rise a second time.

When the loaves are about double in bulk, place into hot oven 425-450 degrees for about 12 min. Then reduce temperature to 350 degrees and bake until golden brown.

SEVENTY-YEAR OLD CULTURE

To feed Culture:
1 c. flour
1 c. milk
¼ c. sugar
1 c. culture
(1). Feed once a week.
(2). Do not use for 24 hrs.
(3). Always leave 1 cup culture.
(4). Store in crock, glass or plastic jar— keep covered.

CULTURE BISCUITS

1 c. flour
1 t. baking powder
¼ t. salt
¼ t. soda
one-third c. cooking oil
1 c. culture

Mix together and knead on floured board 10 times. Pat to ¾" thickness. Cut into shapes. Bake 15-18 minutes at 425 degrees.

PANNED POTATOES

Put a lump of butter, enough to fry, in a baking pan; pare and slice Irish potatoes as for frying, put in pan, sprinkle with salt and pepper, and cover with rich milk. Cook in oven until potatoes are tender and milk is all absorbed. These are excellent.

SPANISH RICE

Three small onions and a cup of rice. Fry onions and rice in 1 tablespoon of butter or lard, season with salt and pepper to taste. Add boiling water 3 or 4 times, or until rice is tender. Just before serving, add 4 tablespoonsful of tomato catsup or chili sauce.

WAY TO BAKE BEANS

Soak a quart of beans overnight. Boil soft in the morning. Rinse well and add 1 pound of salt pork, 1 small cup of sugar or molasses and ½ teaspoonful of soda. Bake in covered dish or bean pot for 12 hours. Cover with water when ready for the oven.

BAKED BEANS

Soak the beans over night and cook three hours (the longer the better). Have ready some stale bread dried and baked brown. Roll it fine. To a quart of the beans add the fine bread crumbs, 1 tablespoonful of sugar, 2 cups of sweet cream and a lump of butter the size of an egg, salt and pepper to taste. Bake in moderate oven. This is nice for a school lunch when cold and will keep a long time.

FOR SWEET POTATOES

Wash, pare and quarter your potatoes; put them in a kettle with a pint of water, a pinch of salt, a cup of sugar and a tablespoonful of butter. Let the water cook dry and watch to prevent burning. The sugar and butter will brown nicely on the potatoes, which makes them good.

GLAZED SWEET POTATOES

Boil medium-sized potatoes 45 minutes; then drain, pare, cut in halves lengthwise and sprinkle with salt. Heat 4 tablespoonsful of butter, and add 1 tablespoonful each of water and brown sugar. Place the potatoes in a buttered shallow bake pan. Use the mixture to baste them and brown in a hot oven.

TO MAKE KRAUT

Put double handful of salt in barrel, cut heart out of cabbage and throw in barrel; take a nice, clean spade and chop up what is in the barrel. To every 10 common-sized heads sprinkle on a double handful of salt until barrel is full. Put on board, weight down and set in cool place. This is a good receipt.

GREEN PEAS AND NEW POTATOES

This is an odd dish, but the noted housewives of New England declare its deliciousness. It is made by boiling green peas and new potatoes together. Boil the peas for 20 minutes; then add the potatoes, which should be small. Put in 1 teaspoonful of salt, and boil 20 minutes longer. Pour off the water, add 1 teaspoonful of butter, 1 cupful of cream or rich milk; heat through and serve.

HOMINY WITHOUT LYE

Shell a gallon of large-grained white corn, put in an iron dinner-pot, cover with water in which 3 tablespoonsful of baking soda have been dissolved. Let this soak overnight. In the morning put on a hot fire and let boil 2½ to 3 hours, or until the husks or skins are all loose and will slip easily from the grains. The soda turns the corn yellow. Now drain off all soda water and throw away; put the corn in a small tub or large dishpan and wash several times in fresh water, or until the husks are all washed out. I usually use a broom to wash husks off with and find it much easier on my hands. Next put back on the stove and boil a few times in 3 or 4 fresh waters. Your hominy will be white and tender and you will have about 2½ gallons. Drain all water from it; mix in a little salt and put away in a stone jar. And some of these cold mornings, after frying your sausage for breakfast, put in a cupful of this hominy and fry in the sausage fryings, and you will have a delicious dish with which the good man will be well pleased.

SALADS

CORN SALAD

One gallon chopped cabbage, 1 gallon corn, 1 quart sugar, 6 tablespoonsful ground mustard, 1 tablespoonful cayenne pepper, ½ teacupful salt, enough good vinegar to make it good and juicy. Boil ½ hour. Seal up in glass jars.

LIMA BEAN SALAD

To a pint of lima beans add 1 shreaded onion and 3 hard boiled eggs cut not too fine. Cover with salad dressing, toss together lightly and serve in spoonfuls on lettuce leaves.

VEGETABLE SALAD

Wash and drain some nice lettuce, onions, and radishes. Chop all very small and sprinkle with salt, pepper and a little vinegar. Have boiling hot some nice meat fryings and pour over the salad. Stir all well together and cover until ready for use.

WHITE HOUSE SALAD

Take a small head of cabbage and chop very fine; then add 1 cup good vinegar, 1 tablespoon of sugar, salt and pepper to taste. Add 1 well-beaten egg; then take 2 to 3 stalks of celery and cut as fine as possible with a silver knife. Mix all thoroughly together and serve at once.

TOMATO AND CUCUMBER SALAD

Select medium-sized tomatoes which have just turned pink. Slice off the stem end; take out the center. Chop the centers moderately fine, mix with chopped cucumber, salt and pepper to taste, and pack into the tomato shells. Set on the ice to chill, and serve with mayonnaise dressing.

TULIP SALAD

Cook until tender, medium-sized beets. When cold, cut a slice off each end, take out insides, being careful not to break them. Place each one on a lettuce leaf and fill with finely chopped boiled eggs, potato, lettuce and thin salad dressing. Place slices of boiled egg on top. It is very pretty and delicious.

Dressing for lettuce: 2 eggs, 3 tablespoonsful of sugar, butter size of a marble, ½ cup vinegar, ½ cup sweet cream, salt and pepper to taste; heat, then pour over lettuce. Good for slaw too.

BEAN SALAD

Cook the beans until they are thick. For two quarts of beans I boil 10 eggs very hard; then cold slice them, then place a layer of beans, then eggs; sprinkle lightly with salt and pepper; then beans and eggs again until my dish is full. Then pour vinegar until they are sour. I usually taste, for some do not like as much vinegar as others; and for a change, I often add a raw onion sliced very thin.

SALAD DRESSING

Eight eggs (yolks only) beaten light, 1 cup sugar, 1 tablespoon salt, 1 tablespoon mustard, 1 tablespoon black pepper, a little cayenne, ½ cup cream. Mix all. Put 1½ cups vinegar in a granite kettle, and bring to a boil; add 1 cup of butter and let boil again. Pour this onto the above mixture and stir well. When cold seal in bottles or glass cans, keep in a cool place. This will keep for weeks.

CREAM SALAD DRESSING

Take 2 or 4 eggs, or the yolks left from baking; to this add 1 pint of vinegar, 1 cup of cream, either sweet or sour; ½ cup of sugar, 1 tablespoon of mustard, some of pepper and salt, and a little flour. Beat the eggs well and add the vinegar; stir the sugar and mustard and flour and salt together; this prevents the mustard from floating on the vinegar. Put all together, adding the cream just after the dressing is cooked. As this dressing will keep several weeks if put in a glass jar and set in the cellar or a cool place, it is very handy to have, and as I use it I keep adding cream to make it a creamy consistency. As dressing stiffens when standing, just stir it up a little with more cream and, if needed, a little vinegar.

PIES

DRIED APPLE PIE

First cook the apples until they will mash up; then mash well with the potato masher, sweeten and season with nutmeg and bake with two crusts.

BUTTERMILK PIE

Two cups of buttermilk, 1 cup of sugar, 2 tablespoonsful of flour, ½ spoonful soda, 1 egg and stir together. This makes two pies.

SQUASH PIE

One cupful of squash mashed fine (cooked), 1 cup of brown sugar, 1 egg well beaten, two-thirds cupful of sweet milk, ¼ teaspoonful each of ginger and lemon, with a little grating of nutmeg. Bake with one crust.

RHUBARB PIE

Make the pastry same as for any other pie, and line a deep pie tin. Then wash the rhubarb and cut into small pieces without removing the pink skin. Draw out part of the acidity by pouring boiling water over the fruit; let stand 5 minutes, then mix a large tablespoonful of apple sauce with the rhubarb, using 1 cup sugar to 2 cups of the rhubarb and dot the pie over with a large tablespoonful of butter. Bake with lower crust only.

BETTER HALF'S VERDICT

My wife makes the best pumpkin pie I ever ate, and the best part of it is the chocolate coating on the top. White of 2 eggs beaten to a stiff froth; add pulverized sugar and grated chocolate with ½ teaspoonful extra vanilla. Spread on top of the pie and let harden for a moment in the oven.

PUMPKIN PIE

Use 1 egg, 2 small cups of sugar, 1 tablespoonful of cornstarch, 4 heaping tablespoonsful of pumpkin, 1 tablespoonful of ginger and milk to fill. This is for 2 pies. Beat sugar, egg and starch and add the pumpkin hot; last of all add the milk.

WITHOUT APPLES

When you are hungry for a green apple pie and apples are not to be had for love nor money, try the following and see if you can tell the difference. Crush finely one large Boston cracker, pour upon it 1 teaspoonful of cold water, add 1 teacupful of fine white sugar, juice and pulp of 1 lemon, a little nutmeg. Bake between 2 crusts.

BLACKBERRY DUMPLINGS

Place a quart of berries, sweetened, on the stove and bring to a boil. Make a biscuit dough and drop small pieces in the boiling berries. Cover and let boil from 15 to 20 minutes. Serve with cream.

WATERMELON ICE CREAM

Fill freezer can ¾ full of whipped cream, flavored and sweetened to taste then add ¾ quart of diced watermelon rolled in sugar. Freeze and serve with diced melon on top.

THIS IS LUSCIOUS

Into a deep and rich undercrust that has been delicately baked, put ripe strawberries sufficient to fill, then sprinkle with a generous supply of sugar. Then whip some rich, yellow cream until it is stiff and spread a couple of inches thick on the pie and serve during the day it is made.

ICE CREAM CAKE

Take ½ cup of sweet milk, 1 cup of sugar, ½ cup of butter, 2 cups of flour, 1½ teaspoonful of baking powder, whites of 3 eggs well beaten and 1 teaspoonful of vanilla. Make three layers and bake in a hot oven. Frosting: Yolks of 3 eggs, 1 cup of sugar, ½ teaspoonful of vanilla, beaten 15 minutes when it will be like cream. Put this on each layer and on top of the cake then set in a hot oven for a few minutes until the frosting is a little set. When the cake is cold the frosting will be firm.

FRUIT SNAPS

Take 1½ cups of sugar, 1 cup butter, ½ cup molasses, 3 eggs, 1 teaspoonful soda, 1 cup raisins, 1 teaspoonful each of cloves, cinnamon, and allspice. Mix soft as can be rolled. They improve with age.

MOLASSES COOKIES

Take a cup of butter and lard melted, 1 cup of molasses, 5 tablespoonsful of cold water, 1 teaspoonful of soda, salt, ginger, and cinnamon, use just flour enough to handle. Bake in quick oven. These are very nice.

GINGER COOKIES

One cup of molasses, two-thirds cup of sugar, 1 cup of lard, 1 cup of water, 1½ teaspoonsful of ginger, 1 teaspoonful soda, 1 teaspoonful of allspice. Keep in a covered jar after once cooled, and they will keep well three weeks.

COOLING DRINKS FOR SUMMER

Fill a jar full of dandelion blossoms, cover with water and let stand for 24 hours. Drain the liquor from the blossoms, add one-third more water than liquor and ½ pound of granulated sugar to a quart of the liquor. Bottle and leave uncorked for a week, strain and bottle again, then cork tight.

GINGER ALE

To 10 gallons of water put 12 pounds of sugar, 6 ounces of bruised ginger (unbleached is the best). Boil it 1 hour, put into a barrel, with 1 ounce of hops and 3 or 4 spoonsful of yeast. Let it stand 3 days; then close the barrel, putting in 1 ounce of isinglass. In a week it is fit for use. Draw out in a jug and use as beer.

DANDELION WINE NO. 2

The blossoms gathered at first of dandelion season are good to make wine of, but at last are poisonous. Take 1 gallon blossoms, put in a crock, add 1 gallon boiling water, let stand three days. Then add the rinds of 3 lemons, 3 oranges, and boil on the stove 15 minutes then strain off the liquor. When luke warm add the juice of the lemons and oranges and 4 pounds of white sugar, 2 tablespoonsful of yeast (or a yeast cake). Let stand in a warm place to work for a week then strain and bottle.

LEMONADE FIZZ

The juice of 1 lemon, 1 tumblerful of cold water, sugar to taste, ½ teaspoonful of soda. Squeeze the juice from the lemon, strain, add it to the water with sufficient sugar to sweeten the whole nicely. When well mixed, put in the soda, stir well, and drink while the mixture is effervescing.

NOODLES

Beat 1 egg with a fork until foamy.
Add 3 tablespoons milk.

2 teaspoons K.C. Baking Powder

And enough flour to make a stiff dough.

Divide into three parts.

Roll each part very thin with a rolling pin or large bottle.

Place on clean dish towel over the back of a chair to dry.

After about 30 minutes, remove to bread board and roll as for cinnamon rolls.

Slice very thinly. Toss lightly to separate into nice long strips.

Drop slowly into boiling beef stock or chicken broth.

Cook until tender.

"DO-NUTS"

Cream together:

1 c. sugar

Butter the size of an egg

3 eggs

3 t. salt

Nutmeg, cinnamon, vanilla

1 c. sweet milk.

About 5 c. flour and 1 t. baking powder for each cup of flour. Roll about a half inch thick and drop into hot fat, turning as soon as they reach the top of the fat again. When nicely brown, drain on a clean towel.

SOUR CREAM COOKIES

½ c. lard

1½ c. sugar

2 eggs

3½ c.   flour

½ t. salt

½ t. soda

2 t. baking powder

1 c. sour cream

1 t. vanilla

Mix together and roll out on bread board. Cut out and bake in a hot oven until lightly brown.

AUNT RUTH'S HERMIT CAKES

1 c. sour cream

1 t. soda

1½ c. sugar

3 eggs

2 T. mollasses (sic)

3 T. melted lard

3 c. flour

1 t. each cinnamon, cloves, and vanilla

1 c. raisins

Mix together and drop from teaspoon on greased pan. Cook in medium hot oven until light brown.

HOME DEMONSTRATION LAKEVIEW CLUB—Mrs. T.A. O'Brian, Mrs. M.B. Buchanan, Mrs. Jewel Robason, Mrs. Edith Mercer, Mrs. Mandershied, Mrs. Melt Crow, Mrs. E.B. Whitefield, Mrs. L.R. Hand, Mrs. C.A. Guinn (seated), Mrs. Julia O'Brian Fairchild, Mrs. E.H. Cummings, Mrs. Fred Baker (all seated).

MRS. BESSIE BOATMAN canning utensils—circa 1924.

HAND CRANK MACHINE, National's Expert "B"—courtesy Gib Boatman.

FLUTER AND IRONS—Courtesy Gib Boatman.

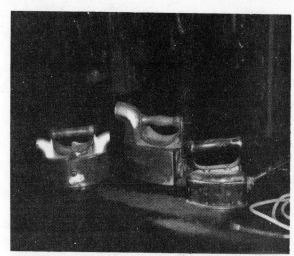

CHARCOAL BURNING and gas fired irons—courtesy Gib Boatman.

HOME IS WHERE the Heart is.

SUE AND SHIRLEY SMITH preserve a relic.

Debbie Houlette - 74

Debbie Houlette 74

Chapter XII

Family Histories

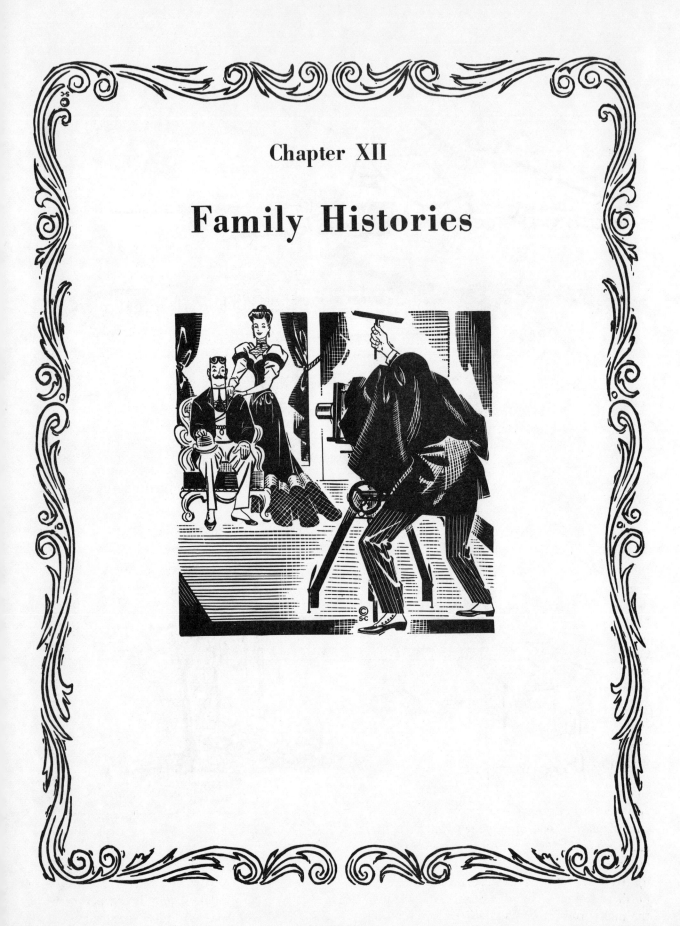

HISTORY OF THE
ALEXANDER FAMILY
as told by Lex Alexander

The Alexander Family moved to Friona in January, 1926, from Dallas, Texas. The Alexander family consisted of Mr. J.M.W. Alexander, and wife, Irven, four sons, Audley, Carl, Milford and Lex; and one daughter, Norene. The two younger sons, Milford and Lex moved with the family, leaving the three older children in Dallas. Lex, the youngest of the children, was 13 years old at the time.

My father, along with some of the neighbors in Dallas, visited the State Fair of Texas in October of 1925. They saw a "booster" train which was on exhibit at the Fair from the Panhandle Country. There were several salesmen on hand when they toured this exhibition of the various agricultural products, selling them on the idea of buying some land and moving to the Panhandle of West Texas. Apparently they were good salesmen, because my father and his two companions made arrangements that day to be shown this property in West Texas. During their stay there they were guests at the Syndicate Hotel. Also while there they each bought property—my father buying 140 acres seven miles east of Friona and 5½ miles south of Black.

The latter part of November or the first part of December, my father and Milford, who at that time was about 19 years old, came out to the recently acquired land and built a two-room house and a barn with a grainery, had a well drilled and a windmill erected. The family moved from Dallas in January of 1926—thus the beginning of the early settlement of the Alexander Family in the Panhandle Country.

The next week after having just settled in our new house, it came one of the biggest snowstorms in the history of the Panhandle. In March of the same year, a prairie fire came within thirty feet of our house, however our family fought the fire all afternoon and up into the night. We were unsuccessful in putting the fire out and it burned throughout the night, but luckily we had escaped losing our possessions. However, needless to say, some members of the family were not too enthused over this "new life," especially my mother.

I started to school at Black, Texas to a two-teacher school, riding a horse to and from classes. In the fall of 1926 when school started again, my father had converted an old model A Ford truck into a school bus, taking all the children in the surrounding community (who were all new-comers) to school. In 1928 the older boys and girls who had finished the seventh grade at Black were transferred to Friona High School. During this year the Lakeview School District was organized by my father and other men of the community. This was a grade school.

My father farmed his land, as well as the adjoining 220 acres, which was owned at that time by friends from Dallas.

Dad was elected to serve as one of the County Commissioners of Parmer County from 1929 to 1939. During his tenure in office, many roads were constructed in his district, thereby giving access to the main highways.

Audley, the eldest of the children, moved to Amarillo in 1928 or 1929. During the depression years, he moved to Friona and lived with the family until securing permanent employment at a Chevrolet house in Muleshoe, Texas.

Carl, the second oldest, at that time was a traveling salesman representing a Coal Company out of Oklahoma City, where he maintained his residence.

Norene, the only girl in the family, lived most of her life in Wilmer, Texas, having married a Wilmer boy before the family moved to the West.

After my father retired as County Commissioner, he decided to run for county judge and was defeated. My parents and Milford decided to move to the Ozarks in the fall of 1940. They purchased a farm in Seligman, Missouri and lived there until the death of the parents. My father died at the age of 81 and my mother at 83. They are buried in

MR. AND MRS. ALEXANDER, Olive Baston—center.

Cassville, Missouri, which is about twelve miles from their farm home. Milford, having moved with our parents to the Ozarks, still maintains his residence in Springfield, Missouri.

AN INTERVIEW
with
GABE D. ANDERSON
on
16 June 1970

Mr. Gabe D. Anderson moved to Friona, Parmer County, Texas, on April 16th, 1925 and was employed as a bookkeeper at the Friona State Bank by Mr. A.W. Henschel, President of the Bank at that time. Mr. Jesse M. Osborn also worked at the bank in the capacity of Cashier. One day in September 1926 two men came into the bank and pulled a gun on Gabe Anderson and demanded the money. Mr. Anderson said the hand gun looked as large as a small cannon and he gave them the money which amounted to about ninety dollars. The armed robbers then forced Anderson, Henschel, Osborn, and a bank customer by the name of Roy Cox, into the bank vault. The robbers told the foursome to remain in the vault for ten minutes before coming out. Gabe Anderson says he remembers that he felt safe while in the vault because he was sure that a bullet from the hand gun could not penetrate the vault nor the vault door made of steel.

The following Monday morning, Mr. Henschel and Mr. Anderson got into the Henschel automobile and drove to Amarillo to see if they could identify a suspect lodged in the Potter County Jail as being one of the bank robbers, but to no avail.

Upon the return trip from Amarillo, Mr. Henschel and Mr. Anderson were accompanied by a man who worked for the Pinkerton Detective Agency, who wanted to come to the Friona Bank to see if he could lift finger prints left there by the bank robbers. Near Summerfield, Texas, Mr. Henschel was in the process of passing another automobile driven by a Mr. Spencer Hough, when the back wheels of the Henschel automobile began slipping on the edge of the south barrow ditch causing Mr. Henschel to lose control of the automobile and causing it to swerve toward the north barrow ditch.

Anderson, riding in the back seat, felt the car slipping its back wheels and fearing danger, threw himself upon the floor boards of the automobile just a split second before the car hit the enbankment of the north barrow ditch. Upon impact, Anderson was thrown through the roof of the automobile in the same horizontal position and as the car began to turn over on its side, he was thrown down the borrow ditch and as he skidded along the ditch his face was scratched by the weeds and the hard surface of the ground. Mr. Anderson says he is thankful to this day that the roof of the automobile was constructed of net wire and cloth.

After he slid to a stop in the ditch, he got upon his feet and started back toward the car, picking up from the ground his hat and placing it again upon his head, before returning to help free the others from the wrecked car. An ambulance was summoned to take Mr. Henschel and the man from the Pinkerton Agency to the hospital in Hereford. Anderson hitched a ride to Black where he used a telephone to inform Mrs. Margaret M. Henschel of the accident and to tell her that her husband had been taken to the hospital in Hereford, after which Anderson spent that night in the home of John Key who lived near

Black. When the ambulance arrived in Hereford, Mr. Henschel was admitted to the hospital, but the Pinkerton Agent would not allow himself to be entered into the hospital for fear of his life should the bank robbers find out that he was there. The agent instead rented a cell in the County Jail and hired a nurse to tend him until he was able to travel. Two or three days later, Gabe Anderson went to Hereford to visit the agent and while visiting with him at the jail, the Pinkerton Agent remarked to Gabe that he had seen many car wrecks but that Gabe was the only man he had ever seen thrown through the top of an automobile and still keep his hat on.

Mr. A.W. Henschel died in the Hereford Hospital on the 23rd day of Sept. 1926, as a result of his injuries suffered in this car wreck. Gabe Anderson says he believes Mr. Henschel's head was crushed between the left car door and the ground as the car turned over. Mr. Henschel was laid to rest in a cemetery in the state of Minnesota. Mr. Henschel died intestate and left no children as per the Affidavit of Heirship recorded in the Deed Records of Parmer County, Texas, in Volume 42 at page 451. Said affidavit was signed by Mrs. Geo. Maurer, Mr. F.L. Spring and Mrs. Margaret M. Henschel, the widow. This affidavit also states that A.W. and Margaret M. Henschel were married on July 15, 1906. It was dated the 2nd day of April A.D. 1930 and acknowledged by Jesse M. Osborn, a Notary Public in and for Parmer County, Texas.

Check District Court Indictments for dates of the bank robbery.

The State of Texas vs. Jim Bryant

The Bank Robbers were Jim Bryant and Red Cummings and Gabe Anderson has their pictures in his Bank Deposit Box at the Bank which he showed to me, Hugh Moseley, on the 24 day of June June 1970.

Jim Bryant was the one who pulled a gun on Jess Osborn.

The Friona Bank was robbed on a second time in the year of 1927 of $3000.00. This bank robbery occured during the noon hour while Gabe Anderson was out to lunch, and upon his return he discovered Jesse M. Osborn and Floyd Schlenker locked in the vault wanting out.

The men were also wanting out because of the darkness in the locked vault. In the excitment Jess Osborn had forgotten that an electric light had been installed in the vault with a pull chain for turning it on and off. Gabe Anderson says that Jesse M. Osborn kept repeating "Get us out of here, it is dark in here." The vault was in those days rarely locked because the cash was kept in a smaller vault near the front of the bank, therefore, it took Gabe Anderson a few minutes to locate the combination to the lock on the vault. There were by this time several towns people and customers in the bank discussing what had happened and this added to the confusion and caused further delay in Gabe Anderson's being able to find the combination that had been written on paper and kept in a secret place.

AFFIDAVIT OF HEIRSHIP

In Re: A.W. Henschel

Recorded Volume 42 page 451 of the Parmer County Deed Records

A.W. Henschel died on or about 23rd September 1926 in Hereford, Texas. He was a resident of Friona, Parmer County, Texas, and lived in the second story of the Friona Bank Building.

He died intestate and left no children.

A.W. and Margaret M. Henschel were married on 15 July, 1906.

This affidavit is dated 2nd April 1930.

(s) Mrs. Geo. Maurer

(s) F.L. Spring

(s) Margaret M. Henschel

Notarized on 2nd April, 1930 by Jesse M. Osborn, a Notary Public in and for Parmer County, Texas.

Also see QUIT CLAIM DEED

Margaret M. Henschel to the Friona Methodist Episcopal Church, dated 20 March 1947 and recorded in the Parmer County Deed Records at Page 118 of Volume 118.

CLARENCE ASHCRAFT

Clarence Ashcraft, or Slim, as he is better known, first came to the Panhandle country in 1914. He got a job cowboying and for several years took part in cattle drives, horse

MR. CLARENCE "SLIM" ASHCRAFT

herding and general ranch work. Somewhere along the way his talent for cooking was discovered and for a spell he had the dubious honor of being the first to arise and the last to retire. Rumor has it that there was never a complaint about his cooking. If this be true it may reflect on Slim's culinary skill or because the first man to gripe would find himself in the cook shack or behind the chuckwagon when the next meal was due.

All in all Slim's life on the range was eventful to say the least. His stories of a cowboy's everyday existence, while contrary to the Hollywood concept, are extremely entertaining.

At this writing he has been employed as a custodian for the Friona Schools for more than twenty years. In 1971 he and a fellow employee, Dan Hodgson, were honored by having the School Yearbook dedicated to them.

F.W. AYRES FAMILY

Frank Wesley Ayres and his wife, Bertha, and three children Mable, Alvin, and Velva; also Frank's mother and father, Joe and Ellen Ayres, and sister; Clarence Givens and wife Josie and three children Lester, Mattie and Sylva, left Frederick, Oklahoma in Tilman County and came to the Panhandle in December of 1916 and settled 10 miles east

of Farwell, Texas. There was one other family between us and town; the Fowlers (C.F.) settled there in 1915. We had to fence our land and break it out as it was all grassland then.

We soon built a small one-room school house and the first teacher was Kitty Cole from Texico, N.M. They named the school house Sunnyside School.

Five years later they had to build a big new brick school house as the 12 mile strip along the old dirt road was settled up with "Oakies." This road was called Okla Lane. Also named by this name was the new school house.

Written by Mable Ellison for the Ayres

THE FAMILY OF JOHN BENGER

For several years John Benger, of Beaver County, Okla., had heard of Parmer County, Texas. He thought some day he would enjoy living there as it seemed to be the "land of milk and honey."

In the fall of 1927 a land agent, Mr. P.B. Griffith, brought John and Mary Benger to Parmer County and sold them some land 7 miles south of Friona. On their first trip to Friona they stayed in the Syndicate Hotel. Then on a return trip to Friona, John began working hard building a house on his land.

Late in the summer of '28 Mr. John had a sale in Oklahoma. He sold everything but his most valuable possessions. He then loaded his wife, Mary, and their 5 children in a Ford truck and started on the two-day journey to Parmer County, Texas. These five children included Dorthea, Lucille, Johnie, Noel and Ira.

John and Mary were very happy when they finally arrived at their new home. Their homestead consisted of one large room and a "bath." Later Mr. John added a lean-to for a kitchen and bedroom, and the large room was divided into two bedrooms and a living room.

The source of water was quite a distance from the house. It was a windmill. The Bengers carried their water to the house in a cream can.

The Benger children missed their Oklahoma friends at first. But soon school started and they met many boys and girls. Several friendships were made with those they rode with on the bus each day. The children attended classes in the "old red brick schoolhouse" in Friona. Dorthea graduated as salutatorian in the class of '30 from Friona High School.

After the Bengers lived in Texas awhile the family purchased a new Pontiac car. They took frequent trips to Clovis where the family thoroughly enjoyed shopping in Woolworth's.

In taking a trip from their house, which road to take was no problem for the Bengers. There were no roads, so Mr. Benger just started off across the pastures angling toward his destination.

The family garden was a rather large one down by the well. Vegetables for the family's use were grown, and Mrs. Benger preserved the food in cans using a pressure cooker and a can sealer.

Mary Benger enjoyed raising chickens. At times, she would have several hundred. She raised baby chicks and had both fryers and laying hens. Egg money was used for the children's school clothes and the family's food.

Mr. Benger butchered his own hogs and cured the meat himself.

Mrs. Benger made all the bread that the family ate.

Recreation for the family included many different games. Mr. Benger and a neighbor, Mr. Watson, spent many hours playing dominoes. The children played ball, horseshoes and croquet. The boys also built a raft and floated it on the lake that was just a short distance from the windmill.

The family attended church at Hub. This was an interdenominational congregation.

Many Sundays were spent with a large number of guests for dinner and afternoon visiting. Some Sundays the family would attend the "singings" that were held in various locations in the area.

The main cultivated crops grown on the Benger farm were kaffir, corn and wheat. When Mr. Benger and the boys worked in the field, Mrs. Benger and the girls prepared a large noon meal and took it to the field where the whole family ate together.

R.F. BLANKENSHIP

Our parents, Mr. and Mrs. Robert Franklin Blankenship were married in a small town near Little Rock, Arkansas in 1899. They came to Indian Territory at Salisaw, Okla. in 1901 and in 1907 moved to Checotah, Okla. where they bought a pretty little home. During the year 1924 we moved to Friona, Texas.

Our father loved horses and cattle and he raised some pretty ones there in his young days.

There were 7 children in our family: William Arvis (deceased), Ora Lee, 2 children, lives in Tulsa, Okla., James Monroe, 1 son, lives in Oklahoma City, Okla., Golda Mae, 4 children, lives in Carthage, Mo., Rose Elizabeth, 1 son, lives in Hereford, Texas, Jetta Louise, 4 girls, lives in New Port, Oregon, Carl Edward, 4 children, lives in Gardena, California.

Ora Lee graduated from Northeastern College at Tahleguah, Oklahoma and taught school after graduation. Later she went to a career in nursing.

Carl Edward had a career in the U.S. Navy serving in both World War II and the Korean War.

Our father passed away in Dec. 1948, and our mother passed away in Dec. 1966.

Note: This family settled in the Hub community 6 miles south of Friona. They returned to Arkansas in 1936. Information in letter to C.L. Vestal.

A.H. BOATMAN

A.H. Boatman came to Parmer County in 1927 from Anadarko, Oklahoma. He bought land south of the Hub community and returned to Oklahoma to arrange transportation for his family.

In 1928 he chartered a railroad boxcar and loaded wagons, tools, and livestock for the Texas trek. A.H., his wife the former Bessie Squanders and two sons Clifford and Gilbert arrived at the Syndicate Hotel in Jan. of 1928. The hotel manager, Mrs. Wilkerson, allowed the family to occupy one of the small upstairs bedrooms.

The couple's daughters, Esther, who was employed as a beautician, and Lillian, a student, remained in Oklahoma until the end of the current school term.

Bessie Boatman soon became known for her skill in producing and conserving home grown fruits and vegetables. Their farm also provided animal food products which she cured or canned. A willingness to share her knowledge with other homemakers resulted in visits and demonstrations throughout the community. She and her neighbors formed the Homeland Community Club whose membership expanded so rapidly that soon another club at Hub was founded. The pioneer ladies at Rhea also organized a club for bettering living conditions. The combined efforts of these clubs brought about the hiring of Miss Roselle McKenny as the county's first Home Demonstration Agent.

Mrs. Boatman's contributions to a better life continue to this day. She has made more than five hundred garments for the young ladies at Girls Town, Whiteface, Texas.

JAMES G. AND NELDA BRAGG

James G. Bragg graduated from high school in Brown County. He heard of harvest work in the plains country, so he came to Sunnyside in Castro County in 1925 to work in the harvest. The next two years he worked in the harvest in Parmer County, working there for E.B. Whitefield, Ira Miller and others. He liked the country so well that he kept coming back seeking employment.

JAMES AND NELDA Goodwine Bragg's Wedding

With his experience as a tractor driver, James Bragg soon became known as an operator of heavy machinery and went to work for Parmer County as a road maintenance operator of their heavy machinery. He worked in the Lazbuddie precinct and then worked under J.M.W. Alexander, road commissioner of Precinct no. 1, for a great number of years.

He married Nelda Goodwine in June of 1934. They have three children, Clyde Ray, Janel and Betty.

LOYDE A. BREWER

Loyde A. Brewer was born in Vici, Oklahoma. His parents were William Newton Brewer and Jenny Benger Brewer. There were 5 children in this family: Velda, Glenn, Loyde, Clarence, and Opal.

When Loyde was 5 years old his father died. The mother kept the children together and remained at Vici till her health failed. At this time she moved to her parents home, Mr. and Mrs. A.N. Benger near Fargo, Oklahoma. The two girls stayed with their mother, and the boys lived with other relatives.

After his mother died in July 1928, Loyde came to Friona to live with an uncle, Mr. A.C. Benger, and family. This new family consisted of Uncle Art, Aunt Bertha and cousins, Clara and Nadean. They had moved from Beaver County Oklahoma to 8 miles southwest of Friona in the spring of 1928.

Loyde entered the seventh grade of the Friona school that fall. Being a very studious person, he enjoyed a good school year and came out with top honors when the class graduated into high school in May 1929.

Again death struck Loyde's family when his Aunt Bertha became ill with cancer and died in August of 1929.

School started in the middle of September and Loyde and Clara were freshman and Nadean was in the sixth grade. With all the family responsibility and fall harvest about ready, Uncle Art was a very busy man. He managed by doing much of the work himself and with the assistance of neighbors, he added 2 muchly needed rooms to their little two room house.

Loyde remained with his uncle until he graduated from high school.

TEENAGED LOYDE BREWER

F.P. BROOKFIELD

In a wagon filled with various household goods, pulled by 2 mules, followed by 4 horses driven by oldest son, Wilbur, F.P. Brookfield left Floyd County, Texas, for his destination to Friona, Parmer County, Texas in February, 1925. At the same time the 1925 Overland touring car brought Kate Brookfield with Edith, Floyd, and Price and the dog and cat.

The family lived in an adobe house on a half section of land six miles west of Friona. All of the Brookfield children attended Friona schools, except Mary who finished high school at Floydada and joined the family in Friona in May, 1925.

Permission to Print: Mary (Brookfield) Richards

M.B. (BEV) AND OPAL BUCHANAN

The W.Y. Buchanan family, Richardson, Texas seeking new country, when economic conditions plunged drastically downward during 1901, moved to Hale County with their children as they were hearing much about the new west and what a wonderful future the plains country had. They settled near Plainview.

M.B. (Bev) was one of these children, the youngest boy and 17 years old.

They worked on a ranch southeast of Plainview and also worked for themselves. One of the well established men of the town offered them the use of his mules and horses

BEV BUCHANAN looking at cattle.

to break the native sod so they could do some farming.

After working there for several years they kept looking further west for grass for their expanding livestock project. They moved south of Dimmitt in 1921 and still looking for more grass land turned their attention to Parmer County. In 1923 they moved to a two story house about two miles east of the present place of Hub. This was on the Ozark trail. The next year Bev and his Dad purchased a place further east in the Sullivan Subdivision about 14 miles southeast of Friona. Bev made this his permanent home, batching here for a number of years. He married Opal Whitefield, Feb. 14, 1927. Their son, Bill, was born Oct. 28, 1928.

But it was in 1923 while still living at the two story house east of Hub with his family that he and his sister, Edith, and Ed Massey, Friona, attended the first picture show to be shown in Friona. It was on a Saturday night at the old red school house.

Bev, a breeder of fine angus cattle, continued to expand his farming and ranching interest down through the years. The continued influx of people settling up the country caused him to cut down on the ranching as the grass was being plowed under for farming, and turn more to farming. All the early farming was done with mules and what horses he had were for working cattle. He had perhaps the first mule drawn combine in the country. Using it for a number of years or until about 1929 when the tractor began to do the work that the mules had been doing.

One of the big problems of the early days was prairie fires. Miles and miles of dry grass spelled trouble and any time one saw smoke rising into the air they hunted the highest

THE COWBOYS—Nix Harp, Bev Buchanan, Diddy Wright, Vernon Wright, Jeome Buchanan.

place they could get to see about where the fire was. And the highest place was generally the windmill. And if it looked as if a fire was spreading they gathered what tools they needed to help fight it and away they went. And then it was by horse back, buggy or wagons. Cars came later.

As always with the prairie country weather played an important part. Fair years, good ones and bitter ones. After a number of years in the twenties with good crops and fair prices everything seemed to change at once. The big depression set in, prices tumbled to almost nothing and then it ceased to rain. Months and months of dry weather and increasing winds soon were blowing the dry top soil about and great clouds of dust was being carried hundreds of miles to the east and south. The top soil was drifting high around buildings and along fence rows and around any object that was there to stop it. There were months and months of blinding dust, no crops and very little grazing from the scant rainfall that did come. Livestock stayed thin all year. Times were hard with very little money but many were raising most of their own food, watered from the windmills that furnished water for the home and livestock. If we produced a little wheat, part was taken to the flour mill at Hereford to be made into flour for home use, or corn was made into meal. A beef or hogs were killed in cool weather and cured for home consumption. In the early years a beef could be hung from the windmill and would keep there all winter. That beef surely was good eating. After nursing his cow herd through one hard winter he got caught in a late winter storm, the 21st of May, with a driving rain and the temperature of 30 degrees that chilled twenty odd head of cattle to death in a short time.

But by making a little each year and with the help of modern machinery and the increase of rainfall, beginning in 1941, when we recorded 45 inches of rain events changed rapidly again and for the better. Bev continued to expand his acreage, but this time with the help of irrigation it was developed for farming. The angus herd was reduced and more time devoted to farming.

Bev, a long time Mason, served on the Selective Service Board from the start and until after the war had ended. Other community activities kept him busy.

Opal was active in Eastern Star and the Womans Federated Club of Friona, and was active in the Lakeview Home Demonstration Club when it was organized and until it ceased to exist.

Their son, Bill, went through grade school at Lakeview and graduated from Friona High School in 1944, entered the armed service in 1945 and served four years. After his discharge he returned home to farm with his father. He was married in March of 1950 to Elsie Jo Boren, who was teaching in the Friona schools at that time. She was from Blue Ridge, Texas. They have three children, W.Y. (Bill), Michel Jerome (Mike), and Felisa Ann (Lisa). Bill and his wife were quite active in the community life, but tragedy struck early when Bill was killed in an accident at the farm in 1964.

Bev always had a buyer for his good angus calves, good years or poor ones. He shipped most of his calves from the loading pens at all stations as all livestock were shipped by rail then. As there were no trucks for hauling he always drove his calves to the pens at Black. To make things easier he generally drove the cows with them then seperated them at the loading pens and then took the cows back home. He had the record of having shipped the heaviest load of grass fed calves from this part of the country.

Bev was best known around here as one of the old time cattlemen. He was an excellent trainer of cow horses. Always ready to stop his work and help a friend in need. He stayed quite active until ill health forced him to curtail his activities in the late sixties. He passed away in 1969.

J.S. BUTCHER

Mr. and Mrs. J.S. Butcher and two daughters, Mable and Hazel, moved to Farwell, Texas in Aug. 1907 from Woodward, Oklahoma, which was then Indian Territory. The Butchers were originally from Illinois, moving to Oklahoma in 1900.

When they moved to Farwell there were no highways, the grass was knee high, and herds of cattle were driven across the open prairie as there were no fences. There were sand storms the next spring after they arrived.

J.S. Butcher and J.C. Temple owned a grocery store in Farwell from 1907 until 1909. Mable Butcher is now Mrs. Huber and lives in Texico. Hazel is Mrs. Scott Weir and lives in Friona.

WILBUR CHARLES

In 1926 Wilbur Charles and his wife, Nettie, their four children and his father and mother moved from near Woodward, Oklahoma to a place southeast of Bovina. The house had been built by the Syndicate Land Company, from whom they had purchased the land. They were six miles from town and had to take their children to town to school. They went by a neighbor's place on the way to town and took their children. In the afternoon the neighbor would bring the children back to their place where Mr. Charles would pick them up.

A field west of them had been plowed up and the high winds blew the dirt into their house so bad they had to carry it out in scoop shovels. In 1931 he bought a quarter section north of Bovina and in 1938 bought a half

MR. AND MRS. WILBUR CHARLES, Elizabeth and children.

section north of that for $10.00 an acre. Mr. Charles relates that on one day he had 1200 acres of wheat blown out by the high wind. They had plenty to eat and wear from their cream and eggs.

The Methodist preacher a Rev. Biggs and his wife, were moving from Bovina to Hedley and spent the last night with the Charles family. They put them on their best bed. Soon after the retired Mr. Charles heard a noise and knew that a slat had fallen from the bed—then another and another. He went to see about the visitors and found them sitting on the bed with all the slats on the floor. They removed the springs and feather bed and got a rope and tied the rails together so it would hold the bed up. He recalls the flood in 1931 when it rained eleven inches, and several people were drowned in the Running Water Draw east of Bovina.

A near tragedy was avoided at his farm one day when a neighbor girl, Bonnie Jean Ballew, was riding one of his horses. The horse started running toward a shed with a low roof. They could not stop the horse and Mr. Charles knew that the horse would go in the shed. He called to her to lay down on the horse, which she did. He said that was one time in his life that he was really scared.

Mr. Wilbur Charles and Miss Nettie Morton were married in Oklahoma July 5, 1918. Their five children are still living. They are Mrs. Ellen Marie (Vernon) Estes of

MR. AND MRS. CHARLES, Mr. Charles' parents and friend.

Bovina; Mary Elizabeth of San Jose, California; Jimmie, of Deming, N. Mex. who had a Drive-In eating place and Mark, with the Frontier Lines of Albuquerque. They have 16 grandchildren and 12 great-grandchildren.

W.F. (BILL) COGDILL

W.G. (Bill) Cogdill bought unimproved grassland 10 miles southeast of Friona, in Parmer County October, 1925. On March 13, 1926 he moved his wife, Sarah, and two daughters, Helen and Willie Ellen (Billie) to a rented farm 1½ miles west of Hub by means of a Buick Touring car. The two girls shared the back seat with a dog and a setting hen (nest and all.)

To Bill, this promised to be a excellent opportunity for a man to become a land owner. Bill and Sarah were glad to give up the role of tenant farmer in Central Oklahoma and the ever present threat of tornadoes. Armed with ambition, determination, and the down payment of $1 per acre on 340 acres, Bill and Sarah began a new life as citizens of Parmer County. Their first home was a four room frame house; nothing out of the ordinary there, but what was out of ordinary was water! The wonderful windmill!—no more drawing water from a cistern. A big snow the last of March 1926 was the family's initiation to the ways of West Texas.

The family moved to what was once the headquarters for the Hayhook Ranch in 1927. Bill had his grassland in cultivation now and raised corn, milo, wheat, and cattle which were the main sources of income.

In 1929, the family moved to the James ranch, and from there to the Hutton place in 1932. During this time, through the depression, "dust bowl" and financial reverses, Bill lost his land. He managed to salvage enough money to buy 240 acres 5 miles southeast of Friona known as the Beasley place. After retirement, Bill and Sarah moved to Friona.

Many comical incidents occurred and many hardships were endured which would only be interesting to the ones who lived them.

Sarah died October, 1967 and is buried in the Friona Cemetery; Bill still makes his home in Friona. Helen married Leonard Haws in 1934 and now resides near Carthage,

Missouri. Billie married Carl Fairchild in 1937 and resides in Friona.

The dog lived to a good old age, and about two-thirds of eggs in the setting hen's nest hatched.

T.J. CRAWFORD FAMILY HISTORY
By Mary Katherine Cox

Mr. T.J. Crawford, pioneer settler and merchant, came to Friona, Texas in the fall of 1907. He operated the T.J. Crawford General Merchandise Store at the corner of Sixth and Main Streets in Friona, for about thirty-four years. This period was from 1914, until his retirement January 1, 1948.

When Mr. Crawford came to Friona, he was employed as bookkeeper and manager of Rockwell Brothers Lumber Company. At this time, the town of Friona, was about a year old. Mr. Crawford was born in Columbia, Tennessee, November 14, 1877. He moved to Waxahachie, Texas, with his parents, the late Mr. and Mrs. Andrew Crawford, in 1891.

On June 12, 1911, Mr. Crawford and a young school teacher, Miss Ella Floy Knode, were married. They were married in Roswell, New Mexico, at the home of the bride's mother, Mrs. S.K. Smith. Mrs. Crawford came to West Texas to teach in the public school at Friona. She taught the school term of 1909-10, which was the second year the school was organized. At this time, it was a one-room school of about twenty pupils. Mrs. Crawford was the second superintendent of the Friona public school system. She taught first grade at Farwell, Texas, in 1910-11.

Mrs. Crawford was born September 19, 1889, at Omaha, Nebraska. She was the daughter of Smith Knode and Susan Katherine Priest Knode. Mrs. Crawford lived in Kansas City and Hiawatha, Kansas. She came to Texas, at the age of 7 years, living at Cleburne, Texas, during her girlhood years.

In 1914, Mr. Crawford purchased a general merchandise store owned by D.W. Hanson and father. The hardware part of the store was bought by R.H. Kinsley. The store was a two-story frame structure with wooden stairs on the outside and back of the building.

On Hallowe'en, pranksters often attempted to tear down the stairs. Mr. Crawford was wont to stand guard on such occasions to prevent this from happening. In those days, strange sights such as cows upon roof-tops and overturned outhouses were not unusual on the morning after Hallowe'en.

In 1926, the old store building was torn down. It was replaced by a more modern, one-story brick building. The Friona Post Office occupied one section of the building for approximately two decades. Later, the Ethridge-Spring Agency was housed here.

The promotion of a good public school system was a major concern of Mr. Crawford. He served several terms as a trustee of the Friona Independent School District in the 1920's and 1930's. He held offices of president and of treasurer of the school board at different times. Mr. Crawford was secretary of the board when a two-story, brick elementary and high school was built in 1927. He also served several terms on the City Commission of Friona, during the same period.

The first home of Mr. and Mrs. Crawford was the old A.N. Wentworth house. In about a year, they set up housekeeping in the home at Sixth and Cleveland, which remained the family home for more than fifty years.

Mrs. Floy Crawford was active in the school and cultural life of the town. She was an accomplished musician; and she taught piano in the early years. She was a pianist, and sometimes chorister of the Union Congregational Church. Mrs. Crawford was a charter member of the Senior Friona Woman's Club, organized in 1909. She was president of the club when it became federated with the State Federation of Women's Clubs in 1922. She was elected president of the Parmer County Federation of Women's Clubs in 1930; and she held this office for two years.

Through the efforts of Mrs. Crawford and other civic-minded citizens, a county agriculture agent and a county home demonstration agent were secured for Parmer County in the early 1920's. Mrs. Crawford helped to organize the Friona Parent-Teachers Association in December, 1927. She was president of this organization in 1931-32, and in 1933, when she passed away on November 3, 1933. The PTA raised funds to provide a hot lunch program, a school band, and other worth-while projects for the Friona schools.

Children of the Crawford's are: Mary Katherine (Mrs. N.R. Cox) of Midland, Texas; Helen Elizabeth (Mrs. George W. Atkins) of Rockwall, Texas; Dorothy (Mrs. A.C. Watson) of Tucumcari, New Mexico; and Margaret Jean Crawford of Lubbock, Texas. Mr. and Mrs. Crawford have ten grandchildren and thirteen great-grandchildren in 1974.

Mr. Crawford sustained a leg injury in a gun accident in his home in September, 1965. He died in a nursing home in Tucumcari, New Mexico, December 23, 1968, soon after observing his 91st birthday.

J.W. CRIM

My father came to Lubbock the summer of 1913 from Kaufman County, Texas. It was a big event in all of our lives. We had made the big trip West. My brother and I were in our teens. The next ten years were to see another change. Bromo, my brother, was the first to get married and needed a place to go. In 1921 we heard about some ranches at Lamesa, Texas that were being sold for farms. We went to see them but did not like that part of the country. We heard from Sam T. Lawrence who had moved to Parmer County. He said that 100,000 acres, that joined the old Star Ranch on the west, had belonged to the X.I.T. but a syndicate had been formed and the land put on the market. Mr. Lawrence encouraged us to have a look. In the summer of 1921 my Dad, Bromo and I came to Farwell. We were shown some land all the way to the drift fence east of Farwell. We took several days to look it all over good, but did not make a deal. In February 1922 we came back and closed the deal for a section of land of which only 40 acres were broken out. We were impressed and the land was level and did not need any clearing or grubbing. My brother, Bromo, moved immediately and began breaking out some more of the land. He started in the fall of 1922, worked all winter and in the spring had 400 acres broken out. He worked with three sulky plows and three mules each. He worked some Mexican help from Lubbock. It was a good year. It had rained and there was plenty of stockwater. Bromo made a good crop, planted maize, some cotton and corn.

In 1924 I married Mabel McQuary, from Lubbock, and we moved on up to a 3-room mansion that I had built. I had $400 worth of new furniture and in the summer I had moved my plows, tools and mules and milk cows.

Moving the plow tools and livestock took some doing. I had four mules to the wagon and lead four. On the wagon I had farming tools, one lister, one cultivator and one drag harrow, also enough feed to make the trip. It took two long hard days to Muleshoe. I made camp where the water tower now stands. My Mother made me a sack full of sugar tea cakes. (I fail to remember what else I had to eat, just the tea cakes.) Everything was bedded down and all was well, when out of the night came a herd of cattle that belonged to the Mashed O Ranch and began to eat all the feed I had brought with me. I hooked up my team and, everything in place, started on out to the place. It was about 14 miles. I went north about 4 miles through the gap at the cattleguard into the Blackwater Ranch. I took a trail to the left on to the farm. There was one house from our house to Muleshoe, the Harding Place.

In 1924 I fenced the inside of the drift fence to make a lane about 2 miles long up to the house. This drift fence was between the X.I.T. and Star ranches. We then fenced around the section that we bought, not so much to keep other stock out as to keep ours in. I always kept up a night horse to get up my work horses the next morning. Once something in the night spooked the horses so that they broke out. My neighbor, Matt Jesko, Bromo and I tracked them all the way to Earth, Texas before we caught up with them. At least 25 miles and two days were lost for each of us. There were 14 head in this escape.

My brother was not much pioneer and his wife was less. He left Parmer County and engaged in the grocery business in 1928. My Dad took over the other half of the farm and put a hand there to do the work. We were beginning some real good years; 1927-28-29 were tops. In 1931 we had 32 inches of rain. I had 20 head of cattle, 18 mules, and I bought the quarter-section of land that joined my place on the road south. I sold sudan that year for 35 cents and maize for 40 cents.

Things were sure in good shape that year.

Two miles north and three east of our house the school house was located. It was 24x28 ship-lap house, and it served as a church on Sunday, also.

As I remember, there were only three families: The Jesko families, the H.G. Hennington family and the Ross Glaze family. Farther east was the Paul family. One of the Paul girls was the teacher. Two of the students were Vernice and Helen Upton, children of my uncle, Jim Upton, who farmed the west half of the place. This was 1926. They stayed until 1928, moving to Bailey-boro, Texas.

The girls came along in the odd years: Mablena in 1925, Lois in 1927, Evelyn in 1929; the boys in the even years: "Buck" in 1932, Max in 1934, Weldon in 1936.

THE DEAN FAMILY
IN PARMER COUNTY

From Wolfe City, 60 miles northeast of Dallas, my mother, Mrs. Nancy Jane Dean, my brother O.L., my little sister Mabel and myself reached Farwell, by train, at 5 o'clock P.M. on August 5th, 1908.

Another brother W.E. had come to Farwell earlier in the year, and was auditing the books of Parmer County. W.E. met us at the train and took us to the hotel where he was staying— a hotel managed by a Miss Mary Bruff from Kentucky.

For some time Uncle John McGuire, (mother's brother) had been living on a government claim in New Mexico and had been writing glowing accounts about the joys of living on a homestead—the fresh air, the wonderful crops, and above all, the homesteads, almost free, for filing! He had asked us to come and see! He was sure we would want to file on homesteads. Mother was persuaded!

So we rented our house at Wolfe City, sold our furniture, gave away our books (much to my displeasure) and came west.

The next morning we sent Mabel to Taiban, New Mexico, where a family (our friends) had charge of a hotel. She was to stay there while we drove out to Grady, New Mexico to look at some land there that had, as yet, no filings. Mother and I filed on two claims. But this land was in litigation with a railroad company who later won the case and we lost the filings.

We drove back to Farwell, spent another night there, and the next day, went by train to Taiban, where Uncle John's son was waiting for us; picked up Mabel and drove to our Uncle John's homestead for a visit—which stretched out to a month.

My Uncle's family went back to Hall County, Texas to help out in the harvest.

W.E. went to Lander, Wyoming, to look after some property that another Uncle my deceased father's brother, Robert Dean, had left to me. When he came back we all went to Farwell and stayed another year. We liked Farwell!

In April, 1909, after we had bought relinquishments we moved out on our claims, lived there for 14 months, proved up and moved back to Farwell and lived there 'til 1912.

I, Pearl, entered Canyon College in the summer of 1910—preparatory to teaching—to review my high school work. I had the same math teacher who been my math teacher at Wolfe City. He was Dean of Men at the college.

My entrance number was 150.

I was elected as primary teacher at Farwell. Also I had First and Second Year Latin Classes (after 2:30 recess). I was reelected in 1911. Mabel was a senior and graduated from high school in May 1912. Our superintendent left us at Christmas for a better job in San Antonio so my roommate, Miss Clara Berry became superintendent and she and I took over all of his work. I already had First and Second Year Latin Classes after 2:30 so I had solid geometry at recess—2:30-2:45. After that came the Plane Geometry, Algebra, First Year Latin, Second Year Latin—each a 45 minute class. We finished Second Year Latin at 4:00. I was so tired at the close of school I didn't apply again.

The trustees at Bovina asked me to teach in their school in 1913-14 so I did. I came to Bovina the 2nd Saturday of September, on the next day—Sunday, the first Methodist church building in Bovina was dedicated by their presiding Elder W.O. Kyker—September 1913.

There was dinner on a table made from lumber borrowed from the Cicero Smith Lumber Yard in Bovina. But such a dinner! Enough for two Bovinas, and such good food! Everybody in Bovina was there. It was a very small town at that time, but they were like one big family.

So my new roommate, Miss Eulalia Sprawls and I joined the family.

I had 12 pupils: Frank Spring, of the Friona Bank, his cousin, Sam Aldridge, Ruth Johnson (Mrs. Bergren's niece), and J.V. Beauchamp—all beginners—all 5 years old. Second grade—Rondal Berggren, Lillian Oliver, Oscar Rogers, Helen Lambert and Ella Tidenberg. After 2:30 P.M. I had other classes.

From High School—First Year Latin and two boys in Second Year Latin. Trustees were: Mr. Spring, Mr. Aldridge and Mr. Oliver. Later Mr. Pierce McDonald.

The young people of Bovina invited us to all their parties and we loved their parties and all of them.

Mabel had graduated in May, 1912, and we had moved to Canyon, where she entered college as a junior, with the provision that if she could not do the work she would be a sophomore. She did the work well, and in 1914 graduated from College.

The College building burned in 1914 but the Seniors graduated. Classes were held in any church building, any other vacant building anywhere classes could be held.

After Mabel graduated from College, we moved to Anson, where she taught in 1915— 5th grade and first year Latin. I rested!

In July 1916 I was appointed as Postmaster in Bovina, so I had spent a few weeks working with O.L.—assistant Postmaster in Anson. I was Postmaster in Bovina until March, 1918. My husband, H.T. Hastings who I had married December 9, 1917 didn't want me to work. So Miss Eula McDonald, former Postmaster, returned to Bovina.

Mabel was married to Henry Reynolds in 1915 and they moved to Haskell where he taught.

When Mother saw I was going to live on the plains, she moved to Bovina to be with me but she liked the people here and was with me for a week after I was married.

Mabel and Henry taught in Bovina one

year, while I was Postmaster. They bought a farm exactly 5 miles north of our farm which is ½ mile west of Bovina. So Henry became a farmer.

A few years later Mabel was appointed County Treasurer—an office which had been filled by Mr. Roy B. Ezell, and by his widow, Mrs. Della Ezell who also died in office. They were the parents of Marvin E. Ezell, present Postmaster in Bovina. Mabel was in office at Farwell until 1973, when she became the victim of a very bad accident—a fall from the steps of the Parmer County court house. She now lives in San Antonio, Texas.

My Experiences in Parmer County, Texas
Ola Delano

From Apache, Oklahoma, to Bovina, Texas, was a lonely trek. Our two buckboard covered wagons rumbled and squeaked along for days over dust-filled ruts of early wagon trains and of trail-drive chuckwagons. A dead-level western horizon was our destination; yet occasionally we crossed ravines, washes, and dry creek or shallow river beds. All, we learned, could be treacherous. Ravines were often wider than they appeared, for gully-washers had tunnelled beneath the ravine banks and left narrow earthen shelves that gave way beneath the weight of our wagon and team, at one time breaking a wagon wheel. Since there was quicksand in both, our teams and wagons seemed to bog just as often in the dry creek as in the running river.

Cotton crops and cotton prices in Apache had been disastrously bad in the fall; at least, this was the circumstance that the Delanoes experienced. Elmer Delano, after accepting penury settlement from Mr. Simpson, for a year's cotton, pulled up stakes and headed for the West Texas area set aside for homesteading. In the first large wagon with jet sideboards and pulled by a team of large sturdy farm horses were Mr. and Mrs. Elmer Delano with five of their nearly grown family—Harry, Reuben, Jean, Ellen, and Blanche. Chancey, our infant and I followed in the smaller wagon pulled by a pair of Indian ponies. We were traveling very light, carrying our feather mattresses and other bedding, necessary clothing for the trip in

trunks, and food and water. Charley, the oldest of the Delano boys, went to Bovina by train in charge of household goods and farm implements and animals. Chancey and I had one dozen Rhode Island red hens and a fine Rhode Island red rooster on the train with Charley, and I had given him minute and urgent instructions to take them through safely and in good health. This he did.

Few people were on our lonely road West. Occasionally vultures circled overhead; and once, for miles, a dusty coyote with tongue hanging trotted along near our wagons. He knew he was quite safe from our guns, for we needed our ammunition for game. And the boys did shoot a rabbit now and then. Two weeks and a day after leaving Apache, we drove into Bovina, the cattle shipping center of the Plains.

Within a few days, Elmer and Chancey had staked their claims on the southern half of a section about three miles of town. Charley and Harry staked their claim a mile south of us on a section nearer town. The boys then helped their father build a dugout for a temporary home of the family.

Chancey got a job at the XIT ranch where we lived for a little over a year. It was while there that our little daughter passed away. Her death defeated us and all our plans, and my only desire was to return to Oklahoma and my people. Mrs. Armstrong, whose husband was the foreman of the XIT headquarters in Bovina, had been quite warmhearted toward me, and she insisted that she needed my company and friendship. Certainly I needed hers, but little did she know—!

Cattle rustling was rampant and these rustlers were insolent in their brand blotting and arrogantly brash with all law and order. Mr. Armstrong had, at last, rounded up the names and evidence against a den of theiving coyotes. As Mr. Armstrong was crossing the street the day before the trial, three men on their horses, riding toward him, charged at breakneck speed down the street. Each man sent a bullet through his body. Face down he fell into the knee-deep powdery dust and the riders pounded over his body. About one-hundred cowboys from various ranches were on the streets of Bovina that day, but Mr. Armstrong lay for four hours before anyone had the guts to step out to claim his body.

Late that afternoon, two Bovina citizens, returning from a business trip to Farwell, heard of the killing. They put the body, covered with blood-caked mud and flies, in an open wagon and drove to the XIT to break the news to Mrs. Armstrong. One of the men came in and began relating the tragic news to me.

Poor Mrs. Armstrong, holding her nursing baby in her arms, had unknown to me quietly stepped behind me. She heard all. Suddenly she dropped her infant and started running. When we were at last able to catch her, she froze into an emotional immobility and stared off into space. For days she was like this; her eyes were blank and her face unexpressive. It was a long time before even her little baby had any meaning for her.

Mrs. Armstrong and I withdrew to her bedroom, but I was aware that Mr. Armstrong's body was being prepared for burial in the living room. He was undressed and his bloody garments were dropped into a galvanized tub. They called me to take the tub to the basement. The butchers cut open his body to find the bullets. (Their activity suffocates me even in remembrance.)

As far as I know, the law never did get those clothes in the basement. They haunted me as long as I was on the XIT. I had one further experience concerning the clothing. Mrs. Armstrong had gone to live with her folks in Farwell. I was alone at the headquarters and I kept hearing strange noises from the basement. I knew a ghost was there. Finally, when I could stand the suspense no longer, I opened the basement door. Our old billygoat snorted a bleat as he hurtled by me. He was long gone and grazing before I could breathe again. Accidently locked in the basement by one of the boys who had gone for fire fighting equipment, he had spent two days enjoying himself eating harness, brooms, and other various and sundry items.

When Mrs. Armstrong could not handle the ranch, Chancey and I were placed in charge until a new foreman was found. I was given Mrs. Armstrong's pretty team of dappled grays. Oh! They were magnificent as they stepped out as a matched team, frisky as colts, flinging superb intelligent heads, prancing on exquisitely slender strong limbs. They seemed to sense my pride and love for them and they returned this affection by yielding faithfully to my every wish or expectancy of them. But from the beginning there was a certain amount of envy displayed by the ranch employees over my complete possession and control of the dappled grays. Of course, this was understandable; besides being a well-trained buggy-team, they were intelligent and well-trained riding horses and very easy riding.

When there was a prairie fire, all hands, including women if necessary, were called upon to fight the flames. This also included all stock that was needed. They needed my grays! Without a word to me, a s-- of b---- harnessed my team to a long corregated iron sheet and was ready to take off with them. Like a weasel caught asleep, I could not stop them. All right, but if they had to go, I'd go too. No one would hold their reins but me. It was a frightening experience. My poor darlings screamed with fright and pain as we charged over the endless prairie with the corrugated sheet booming and rumbling over the cracking and roaring flames. Their bodies—bellies and legs—were burned damnably. For sometime after the fire, they limped about the corral, their heads hanging low, their spirits seemingly broken. I took every moment I could from ranch duties to doctor them, and they did get well. The cowboys showed their sympathy in many ways, one being that they asked me to doctor their own favorite mounts of severe burns.

There were several ways used to fight the prairie fire. Two other ways that I know of are these. The cowboys would work in teams—in threes to a dozen. A couple of the men would tie fresh cow hides to two posts; then each would grab a post, stretching the hides between them, and run through the flames or around the edge of the moving flames. This would smother the fire for a few minutes or until other team members would come behind them and sweep out the blaze with wet gunny sacks or wet brooms. Another method was to kill an animal, usually a yearling, cut off the head and split the carcass in half; two men, each grabbing the foot of a hind leg would drag this across the torrid prairies. The men suffered bad burns, suffocation, exhaution; and as you see, they too, were ill after the heinous destruction.

To the men of the west, a burned-out range with its burned animals stretched in a run in death was the range's most pitiable hardship. Men gave their lives to stop this hell that out-deviled the devil's planned hell. There were five of these devastating fires while I lived in Bovina.

Chancey and I stayed on the XIT until Mr. Simpson asked us to return and take over the cotton farm. That spring Chancey put in the cotton crop, and we picked it and had it ginned. Chancey's pay for the summer's work was a good span of work mules. This we thought was good pay. Chancey, however, wanted to be near his father's family, so we returned to Bovina.

There were three of us again. Vivian was born. Living had meaning for me again, and the West, I thought, would be good.

Chancey opened a barber shop. This seemed at the time a good plan. On the weekends, especially after pay day on the ranches, he was busy from dawn until late at night. Chancey and I could feel ourselves getting ahead financially. But money did not come in fast enough and Chancey began to speculate; I seldom saw any of his hard-earned cash. Because I felt the need of cash and complained, Chancey got me a job as a waitress in a cafe which was poorly run by a woman and her half-grown son. Chancey later bought a part interest in the cafe so that I could have something to say about how it was run. This was not satisfactory either; however, I did learn that a cafe, properly handled, could be a money making project. We made a proposal to the owners that we buy them out-right or that they buy back the shares that we had put into the business. They sold us the business.

When we returned to Bovina from Apache, Chancey had a small dugout dwelling built for our home. About three feet of the dwelling was below ground surface, and about two feet was a lumber rectangle frame above ground. We had only one room. There were glass windows on all four sides. The upper walls were of adobe. The roof was of corrugated iron. Each ripple in the iron brought in the daylight. These ripples let in other things too, for I soon became accustomed to lizards, spiders, vinegaroons, and scorpions finding their way into my house. I

didn't like it, but I could brave them. One evening, exhausted from my cafe work, the heat of the day, and other trying problems, I threw myself across my restful feather bed for that sweet repose and needed sleep. I was lying with my face buried in the crook of my left arm with my right arm sort of thrown across my sweet Vivian. A crisp soft slithering sound alerted every nerve in my body. I threw myself from the bed with the baby in my arms. A rattler was oozing his oily, reptilian body into the room between the beam and the corrugated roofing. Its neck coiled downward, and the black forked tongue fluttered in and out of the beady-eyed ugly face. I rushed from the dugout, fixed my screaming baby safely in the wagon, grabbed an ax; then, oh, did I go after that roof! I started where I thought the snake was and I swung the ax into that roof a dozen times or more. Each time leaving a gaping hole. Then I went to where he might have been. I had turned the roof into a sieve when Mr. Delano, my father-in-law, came along.

"What are you doing up there, Kid," he called in anxious surprise.

Well, he soon found out. Too exhausted to cry; even too spent to be frightened, I told him of the snake. We cautiously crept into the now darkened cellar. There was the snake all right! Right in the middle of my beautiful white bed. His tail with fifteen rattlers and about three feet in length, was still alive and writhing. It had worked itself near the foot of the bed. The head and another two or three feet lay near the center. I had cut him right in two.

I simply could not go back into that dugout or any other dugout to live. We moved into our tiny restaurant.

We were doing very well in the restaurant business. Our problems were that our place was too small for the number who were now eating with us, and supplies were hard to get. I had, however, three big hot meals each day—meals that were appetizing and of sufficient quantity to go the rounds. Though Chancey pled, I would not have charge accounts. If we had to pay cash for our supplies; then anyone who ate with us had to pay when they ate. We did have some exceptions. There were hungry people dragging through going back East who could not have bought a biscuit at a cent a dozen. These people I was always able to give some kind of a meal or two until they moved on.

Eventually, I saved enough money to build a larger place—a larger restaurant, several rooms for a home, and several extra rooms as a sort of a rooming house. We had beds for ten or twelve men. I would never rent a room to one individual; I stuck to the need for four men in a room, with two men on each bed. I usually made them pay before I'd put them up for the night. In the restaurant, though the place seemed full from early morning until late at night, I did not allow lounger-hangouts or dawdlers.

Chancey enlarged my obligations somewhat by telling the cowboys that I would do their washing for them. And I did their washing and ironing. I had a big black pot that I kept boiling all the time with someone's clothing. I made my own soap with hog-lard and lye. Sometimes I made my own lye with wood ashes. The washing and ironing brought in a tidy sum each month. However, I was now using some of the women of the community who wanted to make a little money. I remember that I kept one woman busy ironing and another busy mending and sewing on buttons.

So many of the impoverished down-and-outers traveling east were on the downgrade morally as well as economically. Some were so terribly mean, and I saw several very tragic situations. Broken down wagons brought in starved families, starved teams, and a starved dog or dogs slinking in their shadows. I listened several days to the rows of a family camped with their wagon-home (did I say home?) not too far from the restaurant. The man and woman battered one another about while they shouted vile abuse and vile cursings. Then he started out on his brow-beaten cowed "kids." From pain-filled yawls and pleas for mercy, I knew the kids were being cuffed, kicked, and pinched. Finally I saw the man twisting the arm of a scrawny little ten-year-old. The rascally s-- of a b---- was lashing at the twisting child with a razor strap. Like a fire-eating hell-cat, I hot-footed over to their place. I snatched the strap from him and verbally went after the man. My arm ached to beat him to a pulp. I have nothing but contempt for anyone who mistreats a child; boiling in oil is good for this scum of the earth.When I was through with this louse, he was groveling and cringing. Oh, he was very sorry for what he had done. He begged me to shake hands with him as he pledged a promise never to strike any member of his family again.

O, shame on me that I believed him! I took his hand. It crawled, and I, too late, jerked my hand back. He strolled away, almost swaggering. When he reached his wagon, however, he immediately hitched up his hog-backs and high-tailed it out of Bovina. My hand, however, continued to feel his crawling handshake; so I washed it and scrubbed it with lye soap. Frankly, it still felt a little dirty.

The rainy seasons turned the streets of Bovina into quagmires. An ancient sway-backed plug and a little bone-yard mare were beaten by a friend as they tugged at a heavy load in a muddy street. The big horse heaved and struggled to keep the load moving. The little mare was trying too, but they couldn't get footing in that slick swamp. The driver continued to use the bull whip even though the shoulders of the old horse were raw from the sawing of a wornout harness collar. The little mare fell. The scoundrel jumped from the wagon and tried by sawing at the bridles to drag her to her feet. When he couldn't, he beat her over the head with the handle of his whip. Again I was insane with anger. (I remember now that I was wearing a beautifully embroidered white linen suit.) In rage, as I stood knee deep in mud, I snapped the wet leather whip from the man and began to lash at him in fury. I remember Chancey's voice barely coming through to me. "Give me the whip, Kid! Give me the whip!"

In his peeve, he had knocked out the right eye of the mare. The men standing by unharnessed the horses and took them off the street. Shortly afterwards, the little mare died. It took a six horse team and about eight men to get that heavy load out of the street so that traffic could continue.

While finishing out one of the railroads that came to Bovina, the Mexican workers were camped about a mile from town. There was some kind of rebellion that had aroused the Mexicans into a frothy, horn-tossin' mood. I do recall that it was especially hard for the workers to get food and other supplies. It was cold and there was sickness in their camp. Anyway, the men of Bovina felt the need for protective help. They had **all** left town to go get the law to help them. They didn't seem to have had any fear for the women folk for we had been left behind. Well, I don't remember that I had been afraid either until all the women folk began to gather at the restaurant. Night came and our men folk had not returned. Just before dusk, about four of the Mexican men came to the restaurant. We were all frightened by now, but I told the other women to go back into the residence part of the cafe and I would talk to the men. They seemed terribly agitated and perplexed. They couldn't speak English, nor I Spanish. One man took me gently by the arm and tried to pull me with him. I tried to act unafraid and smiled, but I pulled away from him. He tried again, "Where," he said as he patted my arm, "hombre?"

I pretended I didn't understand at all, but I knew "hombre" was **man.** When he persisted in asking the same question, I finally answered, "Hombre—poolhall."

He looked at me quizzically for a moment, shrugged his shoulder and left me, going to join a group of noisy drinking Mexicans.

I locked the restaurant and joined the other women. We locked ourselves in various rooms. We had worked ourselves into quite a scare. About midnight someone scratched on my window. I was afraid to answer so I waited for another lead. Someone placed his face against the glass and called, "Senors!"

No, it wasn't Clancey. I stared in terror. The figure struck a match and held it in front of his face, and again put his face against the pane and called, "Senora!"

This was the same man that I had talked to earlier. I am sure that he stood at my window the remainder of the night softly calling, "Senora!"

The next morning, I returned to the front of the restaurant. The Mexican was there waiting. Now he had an interpreter. The Mexican's wife was in labor pains. Would I please come. I sent for a mid-wife that lived out on the Hereford road. I had delivered my babies with a doctor's care, but I knew the loneliness of the woman, and her need; so I went to her at once. The baby was still-born, but the mid-wife was able to save the poor little woman's life. I was so contrite and touched by the unhappy people, I wanted so much to do something to help them. I did take those most concerned with the mother and her family to the restaurant where the Bovina women and I fed them. One of Vivian's prettiest little lace infant dresses was put on the baby. We made the coffin and we buried the little one that day. The Mexican people were so very appreciative and henceforth they were always counted among my best friends.

What did we do for fun? I really don't remember! We often dressed in our best and went to meet the passenger trains when they came in. The cowboys were often there in their Sunday best and on flashiest saddles. Sometimes they would put on a mild bronco show. We women folk liked to visit with the people going through. We especially wanted to talk to women of the "outside world."

In 1925, Chancey sold our business and we moved to Arkansas with my father-in-law's family.

THE CLARENCE DIXON FAMILY

We moved from Castro to Parmer County in 1920. We had both been raised near Dimmitt. After we were married in 1915 we bought a section of land eight miles south of Dimmitt for $6.00 per acre. Then we had a chance to sell this land after improving it and breaking the land for crop for $20.00 per acre. The land 918 A we purchased in Parmer County in the Rhea Community cost us $20.00. Our land joined the New Mexico line. The house had burned down so for a few weeks we had to live in an old granary until we could buy a house and get it moved onto our land.

Just east of us was the German colony, at that time they had their own church and school.

Our two older children, Rosella and Buckie, were four and two years old when we came to Parmer County.

As time came near for them and other children in the community to start to school we realized we needed a larger school building, so in 1923 a nice two-room building was built just across the road from the Floyd

C.W. DIXON'S first home in Parmer County.

FRANCES AND TREVA DRAKE

Schlenker home. The lumber was hauled out from Bovina by burros.

During these years we helped organize a Sunday School and Literary Society.

In 1929 when our children were old enough to go to high school we built a home in Friona and moved to town in the winter. It was at this time we joined the First Baptist Church. We have seen this church come from a membership of about 50 to a membership of over 600 and from a small basement to a beautiful brick building with an ample auditorium and class rooms.

Two years after our youngest son Jim was born we bought some land six miles east of our first home and built a brick home. We had survived the dust bowl days. On this land we had ample space to raise sheep, cattle, wheat and row crops.

There were lot of coyotes in the country, so Clarence always kept a bunch of greyhounds. Coyote hunting was the chief attraction around our place.

We built a home in Friona in 1952 and retired from all the heavy work. In October of 1972 Clarence had an operation. A blood clot hit his heart and God called him home.

Mary, his wife and three children, Rosella Landrum, James Wright (or Jim) still live in Parmer County. Clarence Eugene (or Bucky) lives near Clear Water, Kansas. We have eleven grandchildren and six great grandchildren. God has been good to us in every way.

Written by Mrs. Clarence Dixon

A.O. DRAKE FAMILY

Three years after the city of Friona was organized, Mr. and Mrs. A.O. Drake and their two small children, Frances and Treva, arrived to make their home in the Black Community. Mr. Drake, who bought his first Texas land 40 miles northwest of Friona, came to the Panhandle from Iowa. He lived here until his death in 1960.

Bessie Miller and A.O. Drake were married September 30, 1903 in the home of her parents, the late Mr. and Mrs. H.T. Miller of Mt. Ayr, Iowa. Mrs. Drake remembers that the material from which her wedding dress was made was sent to her by one of her brothers from Manila. He was a soldier in the Phillipines during the Spanish American War.

The couple grew up on adjoining farms and attended school together. She was the youngest of eleven children and he was second in a family of five. She says, "The thing I remember most about my grade school days was the hatred I felt for Art. We walked down the same road to a crossroads and I was always glad when we got to the corner where the Drake kids turned off."

Soon after Art's and Bessie's wedding, which was one of the social events of the year in the community they moved onto a farm owned by his parents. They farmed and raised cows, hogs and chickens.

In 1908 the young couple decided to leave their family and friends and move to the Panhandle of Texas. Art had made a trip down here and was attracted to the area, by the price of land. After he purchased the land northwest of town, he rented a farm five miles out and after having a farm sale in Iowa, loaded his livestock in an immigrant car and moved onto it.

Early in 1909 Mrs. Drake and their two

small daughters, Frances and Treva, made the trip by train.

"When the train stopped, I thought we had reached the jumping off place," said Mrs. Drake. "Art didn't know we were coming, so the girls and I walked up to the hardware store . . . right there where Elroy's is now . . . and asked if anyone knew him. Someone said I could probably find him across the street eating lunch, so we just walked in and sat down beside him," she continued.

At the time there were no fences and most of the land belonged to Capitol Freehold Land Syndicate. There was free grazing everywhere, so Mr. Drake went to Roswell, bought 1000 ewes and hired a sheepherder. He constructed a portable house and the sheepherder and his wife lived in it and followed the sheep anywhere the grass was good.

The Drakes farmed one section of land. Mrs. Drake recalls that she heated water outdoors, washed clothes on a rub board, ironed with flat irons heated on a coal stove, did her cooking, sewed for the family, dried and preserved fruit, cared for chickens, churned and did many other chores expected of a farm homemaker in those days.

While the family lived at Black, four other children were born to them. They were Owen, Arthur, Pearl and Earl. Owen was killed in France while he was serving in World War II in 1944. Pearl died in 1929.

The family attended the community activities and church services at the school house in that community and the children attended school there. Church services were conducted every other Sunday and Mr. and Mrs. Drake both joined the Methodist Church in 1911.

When Frances, the oldest child, completed grade school, the couple decided it would be wise to move close to town so all the children could go to high school. In 1919 they bought one quarter section just east of Friona and moved onto it. The house Mrs. Drake lived in was built in 1921.

At the present time the Drake Addition and Welch Acres are part of the original Drake farm, with well kept lawns and paved streets are now located on land which was once the Drake farm.

One of the most trying experiences Mrs. Drake remembers is having her home struck by lightning. She related the incident in these words:

"We lived in a four room house . . . two rooms upstairs and two downstairs. I had been worried for a long time that the wind would blow it over. After being accustomed to large spacious Iowa farm homes, ours seemed like a cracker box.

I nagged Art until he drove stakes in the ground and fastened guy wires to the corners so I would feel safe.

Then one afternoon he started to town and asked me to ride along. At first I thought the girls and I would make the trip with him then decided we should stay at home. Before he had been gone very long, a storm cloud came from the west and I went out to see about my chickens.

When I got back to the house, Frances and Treva were inside and the house was filled with smoke. I didn't see any flames downstairs, so went upstairs to see what was wrong. Lightning had struck chimney and clothes hanging on a line nearby had caught fire.

Some of the clothing was flaming, so I raised a window and threw it down to the ground. I had always been told that articles burning from lightning were hard to put out, but hadn't really believed it until then. I had to go out and push the flames down under the water to put them out.

Another incident she remembered vividly was having her chickens killed by coyotes. At the time the chickens were confined in three cornered pens and a coyote came up in the daytime and killed all except one.

Portions copied from **The Friona Star,** Thursday, September 15, 1966.

ROY EASTEP

Roy Eastep came to Parmer County in 1928 from Lancaster, in Dallas County. He kept hearing much about this country from various ones and after going to Oklahoma to help an Uncle that then decided he did not need help came on west with a car load of men who were coming to look this country over. He became a believer after seeing this

ROY EASTEP AND CATTLE.

EASTEP'S BACHELOR QUARTERS.

ATTACHED CARPORTS, aren't new!

then purchased a place about 13 miles southeast of Friona.

With the help of a brother, Walter, they built a shack with an attached garage and livestock shed. As they had no windmill nor the wherewith to have one put up they hauled water from a neighbor for a number of years. The early farming was done with teams, mules and horses, before they could afford a tractor.

Living became hard when prices fell and then the big drought but Roy stuck it out until times got better. Adding another quarter of land to his holdings that joined him on the north. Then with the help of modern machinery and irrigation crops improved as did the prices. He batched until his retirement in 1963. Now spends his time between the place here and with his sister in Lancaster.

A FEW MEMORIES

THE HARRIS EVANS FAMILY
By Harris Evans

I was born in the town of Margaret, Texas, in 1909. My parents were J.L. and Nettie Evans. My father died when I was fifteen months old.

Mother moved to Floydada, Texas in 1911 where we lived for a short while. On my fifth birthday, Mother married W.F. Perry, and very soon afterwards we moved again; this time to Curry Co., N.M.

As I remember, we moved in early December in 1914. We traveled in two covered wagons. Rutted wagon trails were the only roads at that time. The weather was cold and we had intermittent snow most of the way. My brother, Ralph, and I had the job of gathering fuel for the bachelor stove which cooked our food and doubled as a source of heat. We would take a No. 2 washtub between us and run out on the prairie and gather cow chips. This was the only source of natural fuel on the high plains in those days. It burned so rapidly that it kept us busy much of the time.

Our home north of Bellview, N.M. was a half dug out. It consisted of one large room which could be partitioned by drawing heavy curtains across it. It was heated by a wood burning stove. The wood was hauled from the breaks a few miles away. We farmed while we lived in New Mexico.

I started to school at the age of six in a little one room school called Crocket. We had to walk about three miles. I remember the first snow of the year. It came in the afternoon while we were at school. Most of the children walked home barefooted through about three inches of snow. It had been a very dry and lean year, and their parents hadn't gotten around to buying winter clothing.

In 1917 we moved back to Texas, this time to Friona, which was to be our permanent home. My stepfather bought a blacksmith shop from John Sutton. During the busy season the last thing we heard at night and the first we heard in the morning was the bell-like ringing of his anvil as he pounded out plowshares or shaped horse shoes. I remember in the winter of 1918-1919 the shop was never closed for two weeks. The farmers and ranchers built sleds day and night to try to get feed to the starving cattle.

1920 was a very dry year, and many people made grocery money picking up bones and selling them. There were still quite a few buffalo bones on the prairie but mostly cattle bones from the cattle that died in the winter of '18-'19.

I got my first job and started a bank account. The bank was owned by Al Henshel. He gave me a job sweeping the floor and carrying in coal and carrying out ashes, for which he paid me the magnificent sum of ten cents. He insisted that I put the money in the bank.

It was not long before I began to get good jobs like helping Grandma Houlette wash. She paid 25 cents. Or hoeing the garden for Mrs. Wentworth at 25 cents for once over. Oh, yes, the winter I was ten years old I hit a real bonanza. I started killing and skinning cats. Their skins brought from 55 cents to $2.00 apiece. Grandma Houlette had about twenty black cats that she just couldn't stand to dispose of. When she found out I was getting money for them, she gave them to me. It was like striking a gold mine.

After about three years Dad sold the blacksmith shop, and we moved to a farm three miles north of Friona. The farm belonged to Uncle Andy Wentworth. From then on farming and stock raising was our way of life. Sometimes it would rain enough to make a pretty good crop. But most of the time we lived by selling chickens and turkeys, milking cows and raising hogs and cattle.

Winford F. Perry was born into the family while we lived in N.M. Two girls, Lora and Clara Mae, were born while we lived in Friona. We lived in the old house which was torn down in the 1960's to make way for the building now occupied by the telephone company.

I worked for cattlemen and farmers or anyone who would hire me to get money to go to school on. I drove a school bus for four years for F.W. Reeve in the winter. I always had credit at the T.J. Crawford General Store, and if I needed it Al Henshel was always standing by. These men deserve a large place in the history of this Panhandle country. They are the type of men who made this area what it is.

We lived in South Dakota for eight years during the 1950's where we farmed and ranched. Have lived in Friona since 1959.

In 1939 I married Myrtice Wyly, who had moved with her family to the Friona area in 1927. We raised three sons and a daughter. Wilson, the oldest, lives in Dallas where he is in business. Larry, or Jim as he is now called, is in Indianapolis, Ind. where he worked for Allstate Insurance Co. Brian has a while to go on his military service. Crista married Richard Archer, and they live in Borger where he is a draftsman with an engineering company. We have four grandchildren.

We have watched this area develop from bare prairie land to what it is today. It would take a large book to hold our memories of the times and many wonderful people we have been priviledged to know. If we had our lives to live over, I don't know of any changes we would make or any other place we would want to spend it.

ELMER EULER FAMILY

We came to Friona in the fall of 1920, coming from Hydro, Oklahoma in a Model T Ford. It took two and a half days to get here with the small high-pressure tires. They were all new, but we had several flats on the way, over the dirt highway. A flat then was most unhandy. You carried your own patches. After the tube was patched, you pumped your tire up with a hand pump. Our top was down in the wind and the heat, as the top was supposed to hinder speed, if speed could be used in connection with Model T.

We had our three children under school age—Lee, Raymond and Louise.

After spending our nights at McLean and Dawn, we arrived in Friona about noon. We ate dinner at the Friona Hotel.

The business part of town consisted of Crawford's General Store—groceries, meat market and dry goods. Just across the street south was a Fountain and Short Order, owned by Glenn and Scott Weir. Across the street east was the Post Office. Also, there was Rube Kinsley's Hardware & Implement; Oscar Lange's Lumber Yard; Music's Grocery and Red Jones' Barber Shop.

We had a house waiting for us in Friona. It belonged to the Andy Wentworth's. They were in California for the winter. The house was one of the nicest in town at that time. (It was lately the McGlothlin home.) There was a barn and lot there; so, when our immigrant car got here, there was a place for our six mules and one saddle horse, wagons and implements.

Mr. Wentworth owned the city waterworks, so Elmer had charge of that while they were gone. It consisted of one windmill and one large wooden tank. Some people had their own wells.

Our closest neighbors and friends in town were the Worth Weir's and the J.C. Young's. Mrs. Young was the former Lola James.

There was one doctor here when we came—Dr. Pillans. He said no one ever got sick here, so he left.

Elmer soon built a barn and corral on our place; also a chicken house which blew over one night, breaking up our setting hens and their eggs.

In the meantime we had bought the Summerfield schoolhouse and had it moved to our place. We lined it with white building paper and moved in. We lived in it seven years, then moved into our new house we had built on the place.

In the spring of 1921, Elmer began breaking the sod with two sod plows hooked together. Before that we had fenced the whole place, as this country was open range. There were no roads, just trails. Our closest friends and only neighbors out in the country were the Goodwine's.

Our children rode horseback to school for several years, until all three were riding, with dinner buckets and books.

In those early years, we had no refrigerator (a few had ice boxes), no pressure cooker—only coal oil lamps and coal oil cook stoves. To keep warm in winter, we wore long underwear and slept between wool blankets. We didn't look on these as hardships. It was only a way of life we had always been used to. We did have better things to eat then. Good home-made bread (with everlasting yeast), butter, cottage cheese and fried-down sausage. A quarter of beef hanging high in the shade in cool weather—seemed better, too.

We attended Sunday School and church in

FRIONA WOMAN'S CLUB, 1924.

a little white church on main street where Methodists and Baptists worshipped together. Each had one fourth-time preacher, I believe. Mr. John Messenger and Mr. Harve Mead were our two deacons. I used to think of Mr. Mead as Moses, because he was everything from janitor to Santa Claus.

The Congregational Church was where it is today, but not the same building. The first one was burned down by lightning.

The Friona Woman's Club was very active when we came. I think Mrs. Goodwine was president. I am enclosing a picture of the club women attending a meeting at our house in 1924.

I have mentioned three of our children; so, in order to include all of our family, I will pass on up to 1929 when our fourth child was born. We named her Gertrude Ann.

Our place was two miles southeast of Friona and we lived there till 1964 when we moved to town.

E.L. "HAP" FAIRCHILD

After graduating in May, 1929 at Gore Consolidated school near Wakiti, Oklahoma, Hap Fairchild and friend followed the harvest from Oklahoma to Canada, coming back in the late summer. Hap looked for work and in December, 1929, a Mr. Ray Walker had bought land near Friona, Texas. So looking for something to eat, he took a job with this guy and got to Parmer Co. Dec. 27, 1929. He was paid $2.50 a day and room and board and did manage to save some money—even paid back the backer the $10 he made the trip on. They came in a 1928 Chevrolet truck, finding the hills hard to pull near Miami.

They lived in a 12 x 14 shack which was to be used later as a chicken house. They hauled water ½ mile.

We didn't have time for too many activities and entertainment as we picked maize and corn by hand from day-light to dark. Sold the grain in the head, corn on the ear and hauled it to Friona.

Beans and potatoes were their favorite stand-by in the way of food. They cooked beans at night when they came in from the field so they could have them the next day. One day a couple of guys came by while they were in the field working and ate all the beans!

Most of the entertainment was pitch playing.

O.D. FLEMING

O.D. Fleming, with his wife, Elizabeth, and five children, namely Velma Lee, Lawrence, Raymond, Natham and Dortha, left Vernon, Texas on March 1, 1921 on their way to Chama, New Mexico. There he planned to homestead. They traveled by covered wagon and reached Hereford, Texas, about the middle of June of that year. After spending one night in the wagon yard there, they came on to Bootleg and camped at the old Garcia Lake where O.D. worked on the old Harrison Highway in building culverts with a team of horses and fresno for two months.

When his work there was finished, he went back into Hereford to get his paycheck. While in the barber shop getting a haircut, Frank Reed asked him if he would like to have a job on the old Star Ranch down close to where Lazbuddie now is. So instead of going on to Chama to homestead, as planned, he decided to take a job on the ranch.

The Flemings lived five years in the upstairs of this sixteen room ranchhouse, and the Frank Reeds lived downstairs.

Raymond was five years old when they moved to Parmer County and attended this first year of school in the Old Dipping Vat School about a mile from the ranchhouse, so called, as that was where all the cattle were dipped. The only children in this school were the Fleming and the Reeds with Miss Grace Paul as the teacher. She lived about two miles from school in another ranchhouse,

which is still standing. They either walked to school or rode in a wagon. Once Bud Reed, the driver, got the team running so fast they turned the wagon over and scattered kids all over the prairie. They got up bawling and followed the team back home instead of going on to school.

With the exception of a few times when they came into Friona to buy coal, their only means of heating and cooking was by the use of cow chips. One of their Saturday jobs was always going down to the windmills where the cattle watered to get the chips.

In the spring of 1927 O.D. bought a ranch in Trinidad, Colo., where they moved until he sold it in 1929 and they moved back to Friona and lived on the Reed place three miles north of town. The children went to school in Friona one year, then they moved to the Treider place near Lazbuddie where they stayed till moving to Melrose, New Mexico in January, 1934.

Mrs. O.D. Fleming passed away in 1940, and O.D. died in 1966.

Velma Lee and Dortha live in Tampa, Fla., and Lawrence and Nathan live in Colo. Three other children born after the Flemings moved to Parmer County were Fred, who lives in Lubbock, Texas; Doris; and O.D. Jr., who live in Colo.

Raymond Fleming met and married Marie Beall in 1936 at Melrose, New Mexico. They moved to Friona with their two children in 1953 where he has been in the construction business most of the time since. Their son, Ray Dean, graduated from Friona High School in 1956, spent three years in the Naval Air Force, married a Lockney, Texas girl, Janis Widner, in 1959, and are presently in the department store business in Friona. They have four children.

Their daughter, LaVon, graduated from Friona High School in 1959, married a Friona boy, Don Reeve, son of Mr. and Mrs. Glenn Reeve, that same year. Don graduated from West Texas State College in 1963, taught school in Friona two years, and they moved to Dimmitt in 1973 where they now have the Chevrolet dealership. They have three children.

Raymond served as Mayor of Friona from 1958 to 1964 and again from 1970 until the present time.

PRICE BRUCE—second teacher at Twin Mills School, 1910-1911. J.W. Ford, holding her arm.

J.W. FORD

J. Wilbur Ford and his wife, Mary, moved to Parmer County about six miles west of Friona on September 3, 1908. Mrs. Ford came with her family, the J.M. Spohn family, earlier in the year to Deaf Smith County, from Kansas. Mr. Ford also came from the same place in Kansas. They were married at Hereford, Texas. Being unsuccessful in getting water at their first location, they later moved to Parmer County.

They hired some men who had homesteaded in New Mexico and had their own plows and teams to break out the prairie for their first crop. Their first two crops were destroyed by cattle on the XIT Ranch. Like many other early settlers, they suffered from dry weather and dust storms. After the dust storms they would have to remove the dust by the shovel full. Mrs. Ford remembers that, after a severe dust storm one day, her husband suggested that they have boiled eggs for supper as there would be no dust in them.

Returning from church one Sunday night, they found a "loco" cow standing in front of their chicken house door. Mr. Ford got a whip to chase the cow away so he could close the door. In the mixup, the cow somehow took the offensive and chased him around the house. He called for his wife to open the door so he could get in the next time around. When he got in, he was going so fast he went through the kitchen and hit the wall on the opposite side.

Mrs. Ford was the lucky winner of a Chevrolet car in a drawing held by the Chamber of Commerce on July 3, 1937.

There were two children, Leslie, now living in Illinois, and Florence, who is Mrs. Milton Gore of Mineola. Mrs. Ford is also living near her daughter in Mineola.

BEN T. GALLOWAY

Ben T. Galloway first came to Friona in the summer of 1917. Mrs. Galloway and daughter, Edith, came later on in the fall of the same year. They came from Coleman, Texas in a "Model T" car and made it as far as Post, where they stopped for the night and came on the next day. Their household goods came by train. Mr. Galloway at first engaged in ranching, but the winter of 1917 and 1918 was a hard year on cattle and the ranching business was unprofitable that year. He became an employee of the Kinsley Hardware and in 1929 put in a hardware store of his own, taking on the agency for the Baldwin combine and later the Case tractor. He built a new building on the west side of town on Highway 60 and moved his business to that location, disposing of the hardware but retaining the agency. The business was later taken over by his son-in-law, Bill Hannold.

JOHN GISCHLER (1867-1932)

Who knows all the reasons a particular man became a pioneer while his neighbors refused to venture from the safety and security of their homes? Often the excuse of a family served as a deterrent to an adventurous spirit, but not so with John Gischler.

As a very young man he had left the lakes and hills of Canada for the prairie and sky of North Dakota, settling with his bride in Harvey. When his beautiful and beloved wife died of tuberculosis in 1908, he sold his well-established grain business, left his five children with relatives in Canada and headed for Texas. Within a year he had purchased the only store in Friona (Mann and Seamond's General Store), brought his children to live in what they called "the yellow house with the green roof" (the Teifel house), and was busy in the affairs of the newly founded community.

In 1911 Mr. Gischler moved his store from the original building (located where Plains Hardware stands now) to the building at the southwest corner of the main street intersec-

JOHN GISCHLER, Mrs. John Gischler, Luella, Constance, Viola, Reuben, Elwin.

tion (first bank in Friona, later Roden's Drug Store). Just prior to that he married Ella Graybill of Troutsville, Virginia. She had moved to Friona with her sister and brother-in-law, the D.H. Meades.

As an accommodation to area farmers, Mr. Gischler added a produce service to his general store in order to provide a market for the eggs and cream they needed to sell. The older Gischler children helped their father by candling the eggs and testing the cream for butterfat and helping wait on customers on Saturdays and paydays for the railroad section hands. As a youngster, Carl Maurer would haul eggs into town with his burro, Babe, and an old wagon with no axle—a 2½ hour trip from their farm. Luella (who later became Mrs. Carl Maurer) recalls that her father always bought the eggs, even knowing many of them were ruined by the long, hot, bouncing trip.

Once Mr. Gischler accepted a team of mules on a $400 grocery debt. Shortly afterwards, he used the team to take a group of Boy Scouts, including his oldest son Elwin, to Palo Duro Canyon for a two-week outing.

Also at the insistence of wheat farmers who learned of his background in Harvey, he agreed to open the first grain handling station in the area. Wagon trains of wheat pulled by as many as 22 burros were brought to be shipped from the station, with all of the wheat having to be shoveled by hand into the railroad cars. The caravan of burros and wagons always drew a large crowd of by-standers when they arrived in Friona.

The Gischler family were early members of the Congregational Church.

In order that his children might graduate from a fully accredited 11 year school, Mr. Gischler moved to Hereford from 1916 to 1918. Upon their return to Friona in 1918, Mr. Gischler again resumed ownership of the General Store and built Gischler Grain Elevator and a new family home south of the depot where Friona Grain Co-op now stands. His son Reuben assisted him in the grain business.

Mr. Gischler died in 1932 and Mrs. Gischler died in 1944. Of the five children, Viola, Mrs. George Treider, and Luella, Mrs. Carl Maurer, are still Friona residents. Elwin and his wife, Marcelle, live in Oregon; Reuben and his wife, the former Pearl Clements, live in Eugene, Oregon. Constance, Mrs. Laurence Walker, resides in California.

John Gischler's pioneering spirit and his German industriousness joined with the particular talents of those other early settlers to give a unique quality to Friona. Unlike many frontier towns which started so promisingly only to disappear from the landscape or barely survive, Friona has continued to thrive, despite drouth, depression and dust. Today it is not only prospering but green—a tribute to all the pioneers who saw the future in Friona.

ROSS MORRISON GLAZE FAMILY HISTORY

The cowboys who moved from place to place with the herds of cattle helped to organize the counties of the Panhandle and South Plains. Our father, Mr. Ross M. Glaze, told us that his name was on the organizational list of five counties in this region.

The cowboys who were employed on the ranches near Parmer County became some of the early settlers of the county. One such early settler was Ross Morrison Glaze who had been employed by Colonel Slaughter on the Diamond A, The Drag Y and later the Mashed O Ranch. He drove herd to the Dakotas for the cattle to graze in the summer and then return to the Panhandle for the winter season.

In 1912, Ross M. Glaze purchased a quarter of section of land in the south central part of Parmer County from a Mr. Zachman who lived in Kansas City. In 1913 he brought his bride, Miss Ida Hanna, to live on the farm. The house was a large two-story house built of pre-cut lumber which was shipped from Kansas City to Bovina, Texas, by rail and freighted by wagon to the homesite. The house was built with a basement in which was a furnace to burn wood or coal. It also had a fireplace for heat. Needless to say there was no wood to burn and coal was rather expensive so the furnace was left idle. The post office nearest to the residence was Hurley, Texas, after the railroad was built from Clovis to Slaton. Before that, mail was brought by route from Bovina some two or three times a week.

Mr. Glaze leased some land near his farm on which he raised cattle. Part of the land was used also to raise feed for the cattle. As all good ranchers try to take care of their livestock as best they can, when the snows of winter covered the prairie and fences, the dogies were brought to shelter in the basement of the house. Once a fire burned coming from the north in the Blackwater pasture to within about a quarter of a mile of the house before it was brought under control and stopped. Brooms and wet gunny sacks were the weapons used to fight the fire. When the cattle were ready for market, they were driven to Bovina to board the cattle train for the markets in Kansas City.

Hurley was the center of activity. There was a general store, school, post office, church and a square that was reserved for a courthouse when such should be needed. However, when Bailey County was organized, the County Seat went to Muleshoe. A Methodist circuit rider came to preach at the church in Hurley. Many times he made his stop with the Glaze family. Of course he drove his horse and buggy on his rounds. (Note: An historical marker just north of present Muleshoe marks the site of Old Hurley.)

When the early cars came into popularity, Mr. Glaze bought a 1918 Buick which was a great improvement over the wagons or horse and buggy. Then followed a Model T and other cars and the years progressed. In the 1920's Mr. Glaze acquired more land in the form of three quarter sections which were west of his original purchase.

To this union were born four children: Ida Lou (Mrs. Finis Whitten), Mary Hester (Mrs. Hester Branham), Ross Morrison, Jr., and James Benton Glaze.

Both Mr. and Mrs. Glaze resided in the original house until their deaths in 1958.
Submitted by: Ida Lou Whitten and Mary Hester Branham

HISTORY OF GOODWINE FAMILY

William Edward Goodwine was born May 16, 1869. He died March 19, 1923. He was the third child of four children born to Charles P. Goodwine and Margaret Rarey Goodwine. Minnie Goyer Goodwine was born October 16, 1872. She died October 26, 1943. Minnie was the tenth child and the youngest daughter of a family of eleven children of Vespassion Goyer and Lucy Remington Goyer.

William and Minnie Goodwine were both children of early Howard County, Indiana pioneer families that came to Indiana from Ohio, Pennsylvania, New York, and originally from Germany.

They grew up in Howard County, Indiana and attended the same school, the Loop School, which was a one room school with one teacher. They received a common school education. They were active in the organizations of the community. They took part in the literary groups, singing groups and did church work. They were married December 23, 1891, at the Vespassion Goyer home.

William Goodwine was helping his father, who ran a dairy. They established their home in a small house in the back yard at his father's house. They continued with operation of the dairy for about nine years until about 1900 when the dairy was sold. They moved with their three children to a small town named Center, Indiana, where they farmed, raised grain and hogs and also a small flock of sheep. In about 1906 they became interested in finding a new location some where in the Southwest. It is not known what prompted this decision. It may have been the low prices for farm crops or what was considered high prices for farm land that prevaled at that time.

Mr. Goodwine made two trips to the

VOLUNTEER WHEAT—Rose Hill Farm

ROSE HILL FARM—The Goodwine Home

Southwest in 1906 and 1907 to look at land. On one of these trips he went to Oklahoma. The other trip was to the coastal region of Texas. He went south as far as the Matagorda Bay and Palacios. He told of a boat trip they made down the river to Matagorda and of the Spanish moss that hung down from the trees, practically dragging on top of the boat. He apparently found no land that appealed to him on either of the trips.

In July, 1908, he came with the George G. Wright Land Company on one of their excursion trains to Friona, Texas. The George G. Wright Land Company had laid out the town of Friona in the fall of 1906, from land that belonged to the Capitol Freehold Land Company. This company had received this land from the State of Texas in exchange for construction of the State Capitol building in Austin, Texas. In addition to buying the town section of Friona, they entered into a contract to sell, as agents, other land located north and west of Friona. By the summer of 1908 they were selling a tract of land in the southwest corner of Deaf Smith County, known as the Findley tract. The land company had laid out a small tract into town lots and erected a hotel and small office building. It was to this location that the company took their land prospectors by auto after their disembarking from the excursion trains at Friona. Findley was probably 25 miles from Friona, if you followed section lines, but to travel at an angle across from Friona it would be approximately eighteen miles. To most of the land seekers who were familiar to the speed of a horse and buggy, the distance seemed less than 18 miles. The land and country appealed to Mr. Goodwine and his

brother-in-law, Ulysses Goyer, who had accompanied him on the trip.

The level land with no stumps or rocks to plow around looked very good. They did not buy at this time, but returned to Indiana and brought their wives back with them in August of 1908. The women now had a change to pass their judgement on the proposed purchase. On this trip both families purchased land. Mr. Goodwine bought one half a section three miles west of Dinley and on the south side of a section line, the southwest corner of the tract, being about one and a half miles northeast of Escabarda Headquarters. Mr. Goyer bought land two miles north of Findley. After making arrangements for someone to drill wells on both properties, they returned to Indiana on the excursion train and started making preparations for moving their families to the new location the following spring.

Mr. Goyer owned a steam threshing rig that he had operated in Indiana. He thought with the steam engine and large gang plows, he could make good money in the Panhandle breaking sod for others, and was anxious to get started. He bought two gangs of five twelve-inch bottom moulboard plows and shipped his threshing outfit, plows and some teams and farm machinery plus his household goods to Friona. He left by train just after Christmas and arrived in the early part of January of 1909. He bought the office building the land company had erected at Findley. The building was about 20 x 20 feet and was divided into four rooms. They moved directly from the cars on the railroad track at Friona and began making their home at Findley.

The Goodwine family was not able to finish their business before March 1, 1909. Mr. Goodwine loaded household equipment and

256

THE GOODWINE CHILDREN who came to Texas. Back row—Lucky, Clyde, Elsie. Front row— Glee, Nelda, Lola, Leland.

such tools as he thought he might need to farm in Texas. He loaded four milk cows, five horses, some chickens and a dog. The farm machinery consisted of a double disc breaking plow, one 14-inch moulboard sulkey plow, one 14-inch plow, two wagons, one carriage, one two-row knife planter, one wooden frame harrow, one hay rake, and various hand tools. The animals were loaded in one end of the railroad box car and the farm machinery in the other end. The horses were in one end of another car and the household goods in the opposite end. Feed and water for the various animals had to be loaded into both cars.

Mr. Goodwine had hired a single man that wanted to come west to look at the country. His name was Asa Knight. They left from Kokomo, Indiana with Mr. Knight in charge of one car and Mr. Goodwine in charge of the other. An emigrant car, with livestock in it, was allowed one person to accompany the car to care for the stock. This arrangement saved the cost of one fare.

The cars arrived in Friona on the ninth day of March, 1909. As soon as they arrived, Mr. Goodwine wired his wife to come with the rest of the family of seven children by passenger train. They arrived in Friona about 11:00 A.M., Friday, March 12. Between the time Mr. Goodwine arrived and the family arrived an eight inch snow had fallen. Little did they realize how few times in the next sixty years they would see that much snow fall without wind.

Mr. Goodwine and Asa Knight met the family at the depot. He had rented a house that still stands in block 85 of the original town of Friona. This house was a little over one block in distance from the depot. They walked to the house. The father and mother carried the two younger children and Asa Knight carried a third. The older children helped with the luggage. The large part of the household furniture was already unloaded and in the house. The stove was up and burning. The first order of business was to prepare lunch as most of the children were at the stage in life that they were always hungry. After lunch, the afternoon was taken up with setting up beds and arranging furniture. By night everyone had a place to sleep.

It would be of interest to some, that during the time Mr. Goodwine and Mr. Knight were unloading the cars, there were ten other emigrant cars being unloaded at the same time. It is not known if these ten cars represented ten different families or if some others in the group had shipped more than one car, as the Goodwines had. Two of the families in the group were the Messengers and his brother-in-law, Mr. Moffitt. Mr. Messenger was the grandfather of Steve Messenger, now an accountant in Friona. These families settled north in Deaf Smith County. The Messenger place, now on Highway 214 was on the east side of the road, just after you cross Tierra Blanca draw. The Moffitt place is across on the west side of the road, now owned by Ralph Smith.

An incident happened as these families were moving out to their place from the cars that had brought them from Iowa. They had a dog that they brought with them to Texas. The dog was running and following along with the wagon. It surprised a jack rabbit, and not having had experiences with that kind of rabbit, did not realize that he could not catch it. In chasing the rabbit he went over a rise of land and out of sight of the wagon. Those driving the wagon thought that the dog would join them again when he became tired of the chase. They gave it no further thought and when the people reached the farm the dog had not found them. It was too late for a search. Some four weeks later, a letter from the old neighbors in Iowa reported that the dog had showed up at their former home.

Another incident happened to Mrs. Goodwine on the second night she was in Friona. It was Saturday night and Mr. Goodwine had gone to town to see if he could pick up any news of the new community. The children were all in bed and Mrs. Goodwine thought she was the only person in the house that was awake. She heard the cry of a small baby. The thought crossed her mind that surely no one would abandon a baby on her door step in a new country with her having seven children of her own. She went to the doors in front and back of the house but found no one. She could still hear the baby crying. She remembered an opening on the outside of the house leading to the basement. She went to the door and opened it. She could tell that was where the sound was coming from. She called, asking if anyone were down in the basement. A woman answered that she and the baby were there in bed and explained that she was Mrs. Otto Treider. She and the baby were there because they had arrived in town late. They had lived in the house before the Goodwines and were in the process of moving to Star Ranch. She was invited to come up to the fire but she preferred to stay where she was as the baby had gone to sleep and the bed was warm. The snow had delayed their move. The baby was Juel Treider, who still lives in the Lazbuddie community.

On the 15th of March, the first Monday after arriving in Friona, Lucy, Clyde and Leland Goodwine entered school in Friona. Elsie Goodwine, the older sister, had finished high school the previous spring in Indiana and the three younger children were not of school age. The school building was a one room frame building located in the center of the block where the grade school cafeteria now stands. The teacher was Miss Roxie Witherspoon. She was from Hereford, Texas. The pupils consisted of twelve or fifteen boys and girls scattered through all the grades. The school had only opened the fall before for a nine months term.

With the family settled in their temporary home, Mr. Goodwine went about making plans for improving the Findley land. The first requirement was to get a water well. The arrangement he had made for drilling a well the previous fall, when he bought the land, had not produced a well. The driller had drilled until they struck red bed and had abandoned the hole. He had been instructed to move to another corner of the half section and drill another well. This hole was dry as the first one had been. The driller of these holes explained that in his experience, there was no water found after they had drilled to red bed. Mr. Goodwine realized that he would have to have water to be able to make a home and farm the land. He decided to try again on another corner. This time he secured a new drilling company. The G. Stuckey and Sons had just moved to the territory from Upper Sanduskey, Ohio. G. Stuckey was the father of the late Pearl Kinsley. The son in the company was her brother. Allen Stuckey and Ruben Kinsley, Pearl's husband, were the partners. At the end of the week, Allen and Ruben came in from work and reported they were at 303 feet down and about 155 feet of this was in the red bed. The next morning a man who was working for the land company came down to the house and told Mr. Goodwine that he noticed red clay on the drillers shoes the night before when the drillers had come from work and advised him to stop spending his money. He told him of the number of holes that had been drilled in that area that had proven to be dry. Before the drillers resumed work the next Monday Mr. Goodwine instructed them to abandon the hole.

The next move was to contact Mr. George G. Wright when the next excursion train arrived, to try and get a refund of the money he had paid on the place. He was basing his claim on a verbal guarantee, made by some of the company's agents, that water could be found anywhere at 150 feet or less.

Mr. Wright was not receptive to the idea of refunding the money but did suggest that he would consider trading other land for that piece of land at Findley. The land that he showed him was in the Willis Sub-division, southeast of Friona. Mr. Goodwine told him that he had made a few trips to the Findley property with a team and wagon, and had come to realize the importance of the distance from town. Therefore, if he was going to trade the land, it would have to be close enough to Friona that he could see the train go by. Mr. Wright then said he had a quarter section adjoining the town section, and showed Mr. Goodwine the northwest quarter of section seven. They made a trade; Mr. Goodwine giving one half section of Findley land for the northwest quarter of section seven, just south adjoining the Friona township. Mr. Wright did give him a two mile piece of pasture fence that was to be moved because it was not on a section line. He also agreed to pay all expenses over $200.00 that the water well might cost. The price of the Findley land had been $18.00 per acre and the trade made the Friona land cost $36.00 per acre.

The well was dug on this newly acquired land and Mr. Goodwine's brother-in-law, Ulysses Goyer, broke the sod. They started making arrangements to have a house and barn built. After the crops were planted, the rest of the summer was spent in building fences. When not busy at that, he helped the carpenter with the building of the home and the farm buildings. The crops made roughage for the horses and cows. There was some grain crop.

Not everyone who came to Friona to settle made it through the first difficult months. It is unknown if Mr. Goyer tried to drill another well, or not, when he didn't get water. But he did trade his Findley land for other nearer to Friona and moved the house on it. The land company discovered they had already sold that piece of land to another person and so he had to move again to a location about eight miles northwest of Friona. The land company did pay for the moving of the house the second time. Ulyses Goyer once said that the only money he made while in Texas was in the moving of the house. He also found that his plan to make money breaking sod had come into some difficulty. There was only a short time after the infrequent rains that the sod could be broken or that crops could be planted. After one year he became discouraged and moved his family back to Indiana. Other families followed the same pattern.

The Goodwine family moved into the house on the farm in August of 1909. The barn and other farm buildings were finished later. A silo was erected in 1913. Also, a cow barn was built adjoining the silo.

The first year the crops were short but did furnish roughage for the horses and cows for the next year. There was also seed to plant another crop. The next three crops followed the same pattern and several new varieties were tried as an experiment. The Santa Fe Railroad had an agricultural agent stationed at Amarillo, Texas, Mr. H.M. Bainer. He assisted and advised the farmers in the territory in finding new crops that might be adapted to better methods of cultivation. Mr. Bainer, as agent for the railroad, often furnished seed for these new crops. The only requirement was that farmers plant the seeds and if they did well enough to show promise, the farmer had to return the same amount of seed that he had furnished. Among the crops that Mr. Goodwine tried were black emmor, flax, fetarita, and giant white maize. Another crop that was grown at that time was German millet. This was sowed broadcast for a hay crop and when moisture was favorable, made a seed crop. It was threshed and the straw bailed for hay.

Mr. Goodwine was one of the earlier farmers to try wheat, but it was several years before he made a crop with an outstanding yield. In 1913 he raised a crop of wheat, but it rained before they were able to cut it. The wheat shattered, resulting in a volunteer crop that was harvested the next year. However, the next year the rains came again and the wheat shattered its seeds, resulting in yet another volunteer crop. This crop was the third crop that was harvested from only one planting.

After several short crops, the farmers realized that they would need some livestock to be able to make a living at farming in this area. The Syndicate had moved all their cattle from this part of the land in 1909 and completed liquidation of all their cattle from other divisions in 1911. This left vast areas of land that had not been sold, some had been purchased by buyers in the east for speculation rather than homesteading, available for grazing of livestock by the new settlers. Pastures the size the syndicate used were not practical for the new stock farmers and the cost of fencing on land they did not own was not practical. So a number of persons purchased flocks of sheep, as a herder could be used for them instead of a fence.

Mr. Goodwine first bought a small herd of

cows, about 35 head, at a price of $35.00 per head in the year 1910. Then in 1912 he and Mr. F.E. Clennin, who had settled just south of the Goodwine farm, bought about 1100 head of sheep at a price of $4.50 a head. They were delivered to them that fall in September. In November they noticed some of the ewes rubbing on posts and losing patches of wool. There was no veterinarian in the area that they could contact for information, but there was a Mr. Ralph Lee, west of town, who was in the sheep business. He had experience with sheep in Kansas. He examined the sheep and said they were infected with scabies, caused by a small mite that irritated the skin of the animal, causing a scab to form. The treatment was to dip the sheep in a medicated liquid. The treatment was to be repeated in 12 to 15 days and the flock moved to a clean pasture to prevent reinfection.

They located a portable vat near Hereford that could be rented, but by the time it could be installed and corrals made, it was the middle of December before the dipping was completed. The sheep had lost a lot of wool by this time and had become weak from the infection. A number of the sheep died each day. After they were moved to a new pasture there were two severe blizzards that winter that lasted 24 or 30 hours. The wind and snow was so bad around the sheds that it buried nearly the entire flock. They dug the sheep out of the snow and by spring had about 500 left of the original 1100 sheep. They also had to go through the dipping procedure again, as some scabbies were still found. That summer Clyde Goodwine and Mr. Clennin's son took alternate weeks herding the sheep. When they sold the sheep Mr. Clennin and Mr. Goodwine bought cattle, which proved to be a better investment for them.

The year of 1913 was the first good crop year for the Goodwines. In 1914 the prices began to get better, and cattle became the best investment for cash to meet the needs of the early settlers. Mr.Goodwine added two more quarter sections of land to the farm. One quarter was planted to crops. The other was still in grass and additional grass land was leased. The farm became more of a joint farming-livestock operation.

The increasing price of livestock and farm commodities caused the country to become more prosperous. By the 1920's most people had abandoned their horse drawn buggies and carriages and purchased cars for their transportation. This was one sign of prosperity. The severe winter and spring of 1918 and its record snow storms, caused large numbers of death loss in cattle. The fact that most of the feed for cattle had to be shipped in to the area for the weakened livestock caused many of the cattle operators to go broke. Travel was so difficult that being able to locate and have feed shipped to the railrod depot in no way guaranteed that it would be able to be taken to the cattle on the range. Mr. Goodwine did not suffer too much death loss, but before he could recover from the hard winter the cattle prices began to drop, due to the end of World War I, and he was set back financially.

The moisture from the big snows caused Mr. Goodwine and many other farmers to return to wheat in addition to their cattle. Mr. Goodwine died in 1923 and did not see the expansion of the wheat farming. Clyde Goodwine, the eldest son, took over the farming with the advise and consultation of his mother, Mrs. Minnie Goodwine.

A few good wheat years caused more expansion in wheat farming. With the increase, horse drawn headers and threshing machines became obsolete. Tractors and combines came into use. A new wave of settlers came to the area due to this expanding wheat crop. These settlers came from east Texas and Oklahoma and were more adjusted to dry land farming. An exceptionally good wheat crop was harvested in 1926 and the expansion continued. This trend continued until the beginning of the depression in the 1930's.

In 1931 there was another large wheat crop produced with a yield per acre as good as the crop in 1926, and with much larger acreage. But due to low prices much of that wheat did not pay to be harvested. As a result, many of the new farmers, as well as some of the older settlers had to give up their land and left the country. Some of the settlers were able to stay on their land, either by refinancing or else had other resources.

This brings our family up to the 1930's. The stories of the depression and drought are too vivid on the memories of everyone, and can best be left for future historians to record.

THE SEVEN GOODWINE SISTERS. Back—Elsie, Lucy; Middle—Glee, Lola, Nelda; Front—Floy, Margaret.

The Goodwine's had nine children: Elsie, Lucy, Clyde, Leland, Glee, Lola, and Nelda came with their parents to Friona from Kokomo, Indiana. Floy and Margaret were born in Texas. Mr. Goodwine was heard to remark that he had the house of seven gabbles, two of which were "Texas Longhorns."

The entire family worked together making a home in Texas. The boys worked on the farmland doing the farm chores and the girls helping with the housework. The family entered into the activities of the community, schools, church and clubs. Mother Goodwine was active in the P.T.A. and was choir leader in the church for a number of years. She was a charter member of the Friona Women's Club. Father Goodwine served on the school board, church boards and was county commissioner for several years.

Six of the Goodwine children were techers. The older girls were awarded teaching certificates after passing county examinations or having completed high school and some college work between teaching sessions.

Elsie Pearl Goodwine Clennin, the older daughter, taught her first term of school in the James School in the fall of 1909. She taught one term in the Star Ranch School, and two terms in Friona, all in Parmer County.

The salary for teachers was $40.00 per month. She married Richard G. Clennin of Friona in 1913. They had two daughters, Pearl Lucile Clennin McNitt and Iona Marie Clennin Whitlow. Elsie died in the flu epidemic of 1918.

Lucy V. Goodwine entered school in Friona in the spring of 1909 and attended school the next year. Like her sister Elsie, she took the county teachers examination, and began teaching when 16 years of age. She taught in the Jesko school, Star Ranch, and Friona School in Parmer County. Lucy received her Bachelor of Arts Degree from West Texas State College. She was a history major but took manual training as an elective course and was qualified to teach manual training. She taught manual training in Hereford and Wichita Falls high schools. She received her Masters Degree from Columbia University in New York City and was working toward her Ph.D. She died of cancer in 1959 in New York City.

Clyde V. Goodwine was a member of the first graduation class of Friona High School. There were five members in the class of 1916. In 1918, Clyde entered West Texas College and joined the S.A.T.C. unit, in which one could get a college credit and military training at the end of World War I. He continued in school and prepared to teach. He taught one year in New Mexico and one term in Friona. He also did substitute teaching several times in the Friona school. He has served on various cooperative boards, draft board, juries, and is active in farm improvement programs. He now owns and lives on the original Goodwine home place.

Leland Earl Goodwine attended school in Friona until his senior year. Father Goodwine was ill so he dropped out of school and ran the farm as Clyde was in school in Canyon in the military program. He is married to Margaret Lois Reeve Goodwine, a Friona girl. They have two children, David Goodwine and Lois Marie Goodwine Mullis. Leland worked for Richfield Oil Company until retirement. They own a home and live in Belleflower, California.

Valley Glee Goodwine White graduated from Friona school, worked in a small hospital in Hereford, Texas, and later went to Alamagordo, New Mexico, where she worked as an aide in a hospital there for about a year. She returned home to care for her ailing father and then married O. Fred White on April 22, 1925. Fred White operated an automotive electrical shop in Friona. They live in Friona and have one son, John Fred White. He is married to Sue Cranfill White of Friona and have a bookkeeping and tax service in Friona.

Lola Florence Goodwine graduated from Friona High School. She went to West Texas College one year and one year at the College of Industrial Arts. She worked as Parmer County welfare agent for two years. She was an employee of Friona State Bank until retirement. She still lives in Friona in the Goodwine home.

Nelda Ardis Goodwine Bragg graduated from Friona High School, went one year to Swarthmore College in Pennsylvania, where her uncle was vice-president and taught astronomy. Later she attended Texas State College for Women. Before receiving her degree she taught in the Rhea School and Friona School in Parmer County. Also she taught in several other schools in the area. Nelda was married to James G. Bragg on June 6, 1934. They have three children, Clyde Ray Bragg, Janel Bragg Roper and Betty Bragg Wells. James and Nelda Bragg are retired and live on a small farm near Canton, Texas.

Floy Berniece Goodwine Enochs graduated from high school in Friona, attended West Texas State College for Women. She taught two years in a one teacher school near Bovina in Parmer County, the State Line school; also for two years in Bailey County, Texas. She then taught in the Deer Park, Texas school for 20 years where she served as an elementary school principal until her retirement. She completed work for a Master's Degree at Texas Technological College in 1943. Floy married Homer Cleo Enochs in

THE GOODWINE CHILDREN. Back row—Lucy, Clyde, Leland, Glee, Lola, Nelda; Front row—Margaret, Floy, James Bragg (Nelda's husband) holding daughters Betty and Jenel. Boy on left is Clyde Ray Bragg, boy on right is John Fred White, Glee's son.

1948. Homer was a widower and had two children by his former marriage and Floy had taught these children when they were in first grade. They were Mary Lynn Enochs Short and David Homer Enochs. Homer and Floy have one son, Leland Robin Enochs. Floy and Homer are retired and live in Dear Park, Texas.

Minnie Margaret Goodwine Price graduated from high school in Friona, Texas, went to Texas State College for Women and then taught for one year in Deaf Smith, County. She went back to Texas State College for Women for her B.A. Degree. She taught several years in Vernon, Texas, where she met and married Clyde Joseph Price. They have two sons, Christopher J. Price and Jimmy Ray Price. She received her Master's Degree from the University of Arizona at Tuscon, Arizona. C.J. Price died in 1966 of a heart attack. Margaret is still actively teaching and lives in Yuma, Arizona.

The experiences of the Goodwine family are similar to the good and bad times of many pioneers in a new country. But with everything that happened there are many happy, humorous and rewarding experiences. After having experienced the extreme weather that this area can produce, drought and floods, blizzards and sandstorms, these people have learned to know their neighbors and the country and to call it home.

August 17, 1907 Bank of Bovina wins at bid of 5½ percent.

Commissioners Court Notes

THE JAMES TAYLOR GREEN FAMILY

The James Taylor Green family resided in Marlow, Oklahoma, Stephens County that is, after Indian territory became Oklahoma State. Taylor sold land and farmed. In early 1920 he came out west to see and came home with great tales of country which sounded like the "Promised Land" but Mattie (his wife) was not at all interested in moving. However, in 1926 she came with him on one of the many trips which took two days each way in a Model T. She came home all excited so in 1927 Taylor found a place one-half mile east of Lubbock and they bought it but could not get possession until the fall of 1928. They moved to Silverton as Taylor was on the road all the time. He worked for the Syndicate Land Co. and sold any number of farms in Parmer County. They did move on January 1, 1929 and lived at that farm many years.

PEARL B. GRIFFITH

My parents, P.B. and Ethel Griffith, moved from Ellis County, Okla. to Parmer County in October, 1926. The land here was on a boom again and my dad bargained for a section of land southeast of Friona, then went to working for the Syndicate Land Co. hauling prospective buyers in here for land. The children were Jim, Tom, Paul, Nola Gertrude and Lauretta. The girls all entered school at Friona, my oldest brother Frank and wife Goldie lived south of Follette, Texas. They moved here one year later and lived on a

BACK ROW—Tom and Jim; Middle row—Olive Rector, Nola Adams, Paul and Frank; Front row—Laurett Brookfield, Ethel and Pearl Griffith, and Gertrude Elliott.

farm southeast of Friona, till they moved to Friona where they now live. The Foister Rector family lived at the Griffiths' old homestead from 1927 until 1935, then we moved to Friona.

The first crop the folks made here was a good maize crop and about the time it was ready to harvest a high wind came out of the west and blowed it flat on the ground, good wheat crops were raised but the price was 25c a bushel, but in all the let downs the folks never lived as hard here as they did in pioneering in Ellis County, Okla. they lived here until 1942, then moved to Pleasant View, Colo. to another farm. All the children were married then but Jim and Paul.

Tom married Emily Bender in 1929. They live at Bovina, Texas, own a farm two miles south of Bovina, just had one daughter, she is married to Billy J. Charles. They live in Bovina.

Nola married Raymond Adams. The Adams Drilling Co. have contributed much to the development of irrigation in this era, with their equipment and knowledge of making a good well. They live in Friona.

Gertrude married Dick Elliott. They moved to a farm five miles north of Cortex, Colo. in 1932, where they have made their home, raised five of their six children, all children are married but one. Dick died in the spring of 1972. Lauretta married Floyd Brookfield. They live in Friona, have two children. Ronny lives in Tuscon, Ariz. and

ETHEL AND PEARL B. GRIFFITH

263

THE FARM HOME of P.B. Griffith family, southeast of Friona, 1926 to 1942.

FRANK O. and Goldie Griffith home, southeast of Friona.

C.H. GUINN, father of C.A.—1927.

C.A. GUINN IN 1918.

GUINNS, Jim, Margaret, C.A., John, and Allen Guinn, 1928.

Joan Gail Browning lives in Dallas, Tex. They too have contributed much to the development of irrigation to the Co. by their well drilling business.

Jim married Zay Dee Rule and they have a rest home in Friona caring for the elderly folks.

My parents lived on the Colorado farm until winters were so bad and so much snow they couldn't get out all winter, so they moved to Cortez and lived there four years, came back to Friona on a visit. Dad took sick and they never went back to Colorado. They bought a home in Friona where they spent the rest of their lives. Dad passed away in December, 1952, and mother in December, 1968. Both are buried in the Friona Cemetery. Paul lives at the home by himself.

Submitted by Mrs. Foister Rector.

C.A. GUINN

In the spring of 1928 the Black School District was divided and Lakeview School was designated. Mr. E.B. Whitefield and Mr. J.M.W. Alexander and Mr. Ira Hand were nominated trustees; upon the death of Mr. Hand, C.A. Guinn was appointed to fill his unexpired term so actually there were four men on Lakeview's first trusteeship.

Mrs. Carter and Miss Bridges were the first school teachers of Lakeview and then Mr. and Mrs. Van Boston taught until the late 30's.

When the Guinn family moved here, a person could "cut across country" all the way into Friona without opening or closing a gate.

A Mr. Thompson (Sideline) and a Mr. Thomas (Will) contracted and built the Lakeview school building which incidently is still in use on the grade school grounds here at Friona. The author (Jim) and his brother John C. (Pete), Jim's daughter Cynthia and Margaret C. all used this same school building.

The C.A. Guinn family settled in the Lakeview Community (which was then part of the Black Community (February, 1926. This family consisted of Myrtle and Clarence Guinn and sons Allen and Jim and daughter Margaret. The next year John C. was born. Jim and John C. both attended Lakeview school and graduated from same.

Mr. C.A. Guinn is deceased and Mrs. Guinn resides in Muleshoe, Texas.

D.E. HABBINGA

Dick Habbinga and Selma Kleim were married Dec. 17, 1921 in Abernathy, Texas. They decided to land near Friona so Dick and Selma and his father and mother made their first trip to Friona in a "Model T" sedan. They purchased 320 acres of land 12 miles southeast of Friona in the Lakeview Community.

In 1923 Dick and his brother, Henry, came to the place to build a house. They stayed with the Alton Tedford's, who lived nearby, until they finished building a chicken house. When they had finished the chicken house, they furnished it for a place to stay until they could get the house built. When the house was finished, they moved their household furnishings from Abernathy with teams and wagons. It was in the winter and so cold the men had to walk to keep warm. They spent

DICK HABBINGA'S FIRST HOME

DICK HABBINGA and his father.

THRESHING ON THE Dick Habbinga farm.

two nights on the road. After they had moved, they started on other improvements, such as fences, barns, orchards, etc.

They first farmed with teams of horses, then they bought a Fordson tractor with one-row equipment, and later on purchased two-row equipment. They milked cows, so had plenty of milk and butter. They raised their own feed for their hogs, chickens and horses. They used coal for fuel for cooking and heat.

For entertainment they would celebrate birthdays. The neighbors would meet at the home of the one who had a birthday and spent the evening playing pitch. Each family would take cake and sandwiches for refreshments. The Habbinga's were the first ones in the community to have a battery radio and on Saturday nights the neighbors would gather at their place to listen to the radio, play pitch and eat popcorn.

HISTORY OF BERT AND CLEO HADLEY

My wife, two year-old daughter and I came to Parmer County, Texas in February of 1925. We moved from Arlie, Texas, a small community in Childress County.

I came out to the plains in 1924 and looked for land to buy. I decided to buy 10½ miles south of Friona, 80 acres for $30.00 an acre. It was sod and had no fences or improvements on it. That same year I built a two-room (12 foot by 24 foot) house on the land. Then in February of 1925 we moved to our farm. We shipped our four head of horses, a milk cow, a hog, a few chickens, plow tools (which were few) and household goods here in a box car.

The first year was a busy year for us getting settled, digging a water well, building fence,

A.H. HADLEY and daughter Lottie.

A.H. HADLEY in cotton "trailer."

making a chicken house from adobe bricks, breaking the sod out so we could farm the land and our second daughter was born in August. We had to use a walking one bottom breaking plow to break the sod. This was so slow that we only got part of the land in cultivation the first year.

In 1930 we built a five-room house (two bedrooms, a kitchen, living room and a bathroom). The same house is still on the farm and has been remodeled and built onto in the 40's.

I bought my first tractor in 1934, traded four horses and some horse-drawn plows for a used Farmall tractor on iron rims with lugs. This was a great step toward progress and in 1937 had rubber tires put on it and this was really a big improvement.

In 1947 the most wonderful thing and a blessing for the dry land farmer came into existence with the beginning of irrigation in Parmer County. The 160 acres we rented from Sue Stephens had one of the first irrigation wells drilled in the county. This was a sight to behold and what a crop we had that year. We had our irrigation well drilled on our farm in 1954.

In 1945 another dream came true with the coming of the electricity lines. (The R.E.A.) Then the kerosene lamps, the sad irons, the old iceboxes and windchargers went out of use and on the shelves.

About 1946 the dirt road from our place to Friona was paved. There were five houses from our place into town when we moved here. Two at Hub, the Wright house just south of town, the Clyde Goodwine house and the Walker house, known now as the Crow place.

In 1958 we sold the farm and moved to our present home in Friona at 804 W. 9th Street.

Next year (1975) will mark our 50th year here on the Great Plains of Texas. In recent years it has been called the Golden Spread. In our fifty years here we have seen good times and bad times, happy times, and sad times but most of all God has granted us the most blessed time of all and that is the time spent in serving and worshipping him on this earth.

Our children are: Mrs. Leo Bails, Route 1, Friona; Mrs. C.B. Hanson, Athens, Texas; Mrs. Butch Freeman, Tulia, Texas; Ray Lee Hadley, Friona, Texas; Mrs. Alfred Beavers, Friona, Texas; Mrs. Windle Sikes, Bovina, Texas; and Mrs. Thomas Shoemaker, Friona, Texas.

HARTWELL

Mrs. Jeannette Hartwell, a widow, bought the XIT Ranch headquarters north of Bovina in 1918 from Col. A.J. Bestor, a man of Dutch heritage who came from South Africa with the intention of raising eucalyptus trees for their oil. This venture proved unsuccessful so he sold the ranch and returned to South Africa.

Mrs. Hartwell and her sister from Plainview, Texas, Donna Gardner, farmed and

HARTWELL HOME, formally XIT headquarters.

MRS. MABELLE SCHLENKER HARTWELL and children, Tommy, John, and Jeanette.

DONNA GARDNER, Alice Held, Mrs. Jeanette Hartwell, on the Bovina Ranch, 1921.

FIRST COMBINE in Parmer Co., Bovina, 1921.

HOLT CATERPILLAR TRACTOR—Bovina Ranch, 1921.

MRS. JEANETTE HARTWELL and niece, Jeanette Held.

MISS DONNA GARDNER and her pet bear, Bovina, 1921.

MR. JOHN HARTWELL, Doughboy.

MR. AND MRS. FRANK HASTINGS, May 20, 1915.

raised sheep. Later, John Hartwell, Mrs. Hartwell's only child, joined them after he was discharged from the army. They had the first combine in Parmer County which they pulled with a Holt Caterpillar tractor.

In 1927 Mrs. Hartwell had a farm sale, then moved to Amarillo to be with her sister, who had married George Williams. She died in 1929 in Amarillo.

John Hartwell married Mabelle Schlenker. They lived in Kansas City, Missouri several years where their three children were born. Later they returned to the ranch where the children graduated from Bovina High School. The oldest, Jeanette, now lives in Philadelphia, Pennsylvania, and John lives in Pratt, Kansas, and Tom in Dalhart, Texas. Mr. Hartwell died in 1952. Mrs. Hartwell lives in Friona.

FRANK HASTINGS—1902

Frank Hastings came to Bovina in 1902 when there were only a few buildings. Most had a small business in front and the family lived in the back. He came looking for work. He located a job as a carpenter, painter and sometimes cook, at the Star Ranch near Lazbuddie. When the buildings were completed, he worked as a cowboy, caring for windmills, building tanks and fencing.

In the winter, he was moved to Bovina to check out cake and other supplies for the ranch.

Finally Laird-Herring opened a general mercantile store in Bovina about 1905. With Luther Barnes (a Star Ranch employee also), as manager and Hastings as assistant.

In 1906 Mr. Tom Houghland bought a store from Bill Mersfielder across the street, and later on bought the Laird-Herring Mercantile. At that time, Barnes and Hastings bought stock in the company. It was enlarged and incorporated as the Bovina Mercantile Company at Houghland's original site. In 1915 Barnes & Hastings bought the Houghlands' stock. Also Houghland Grocery at Memphis, Texas operated by Barnes.

Frank Hastings was born in Parker County,

MR. AND MRS. TOM HASTINGS (Pearl Dean)

LATIN STUDENTS—Eulalie Sprawls, H.H. Smith, Sara Eastland, Hallie Hoghland, Ina Davis, Roy Heco and Mrs. Pearl Hastings, teacher.

Texas in 1881, one of 13 children of W.W. Hastings and Margaret Ann Hastings.

The parents, Frank and the family still at home, moved to Swisher County near Tulia in 1892.

Frank Hastings served as Deputy Sheriff from about 1904 to 1906 when Parmer County was attached to Deaf Smith County. He served under Sheriff Inmon of Hereford.

Frank Hastings and Leora Tidenberg were married in Amarillo, Texas on May 20, 1915. They went to the San Francisco Exposition on their honeymoon and returned by way of Salt Lake City, Denver and Colorado Springs and sightseeing there.

Mr. and Mrs. Frank Hastings have been around Bovina a long time and are among those who were instrumental in the development of this area of West Texas.

They came to what is now Parmer County in the early 1900's and have seen the changes that have occurred since that time, from the breaking up and selling of the famed XIT Ranch to the flourishing irrigated farm land that it now is.

Frank Hastings was one of 13 children born to W.W. and Margaret Hastings in Parker County between Weatherford and Decatur in 1881. At the age of 10, in 1892, he and the brothers and sisters still living at home

moved to the Plains northwest of Tulia with their parents.

The father, a farmer and rancher, had been to the area and filed claim on a section of land in Swisher County and built one of the first two-room houses in the county. Most dwellings at that time were dug-outs. And later filed on three more sections.

The Hastings' chartered an immigrant car on the railroad, loaded all their household goods, livestock, farm implements, tools, etc. and headed northwest. Frank, his brother and father, rode out in the immigrant car to look after the livestock on the long trip, while the remainder of the family rode the passenger train.

They arrived in Amarillo by rail, unloaded the wagons and teams, piled on their household items and started the 50 miles through open country to their new home.

The Hastings brood moved into the little two-room house, but before long they needed more room so the "kids" dug out a cellar under the house, which became the new kitchen.

During those years there was an abundance of antelope on the plains, Mr. Hastings said, but the country was being settled all around and only a few mustangs were left.

Star Ranch Hand

When he was about 20 years old, Hastings began to go out on his own, wandered over the Plains, into New Mexico, and when money began to run out, came to this area, spent the night in Bovina and went to the Star Ranch headquarters, located about two miles north of Lazbuddie and was given a job as a carpenter and painter.

Kelly Bros. and A. Laird had just bought

269

90,000 acres of the XIT Ranch and started improvements. At that time the XIT Ranch would only sell large blocks of land, the minimum 50,000 acres, Hastings said.

The area began to settle up and the next year, Hastings was moved to Bovina during the winters by the Star Ranch to keep track of supplies coming in to the ranch by rail, see that they were loaded and sent to headquarters.

Bovina was the largest cattle shipping point in the nation in those years, stock pens lined the railroad tracks and herds covered the open land waiting to be loaded. Loading cattle continued all the time, Hastings said, but there were never enough cars to take care of the herds arriving all the way from Midland and Big Spring area and in between. Even though cattlemen on the South Plains could ship their cattle nearby, they brought them to Bovina because in between was open land for free grazing and Bovina was a direct line to market in Kansas City, which could get the cattle there at least 24 hours earlier.

Contrary to what many people think, Hastings said most of the cow hands over the area were young boys under 20, some of them runaways. However, when they came to town or arrived here at the end of a drive, the cowboys behaved well and the impression that they "shot up the towns and lived it up" is highly exaggerated.

Hastings said the cowboys would "rig up" a dance sometimes and that he had loaned shoes to cowboys who had only boots with them. One never saw a cow hand dancing in boots and spurs as depicted on television.

Little trouble was had with the cowboys, he said. Occasionally some of them would go to Texico and have a little too much to drink, but raised little ruckus either there or in Bovina.

Railroad Made Towns

Hastings pointed out that the towns in this area were made by the railroad, which was laid in 1898 from Amarillo to Roswell, N.M. with old material discarded from other roads. J.J. Haggerman of Roswell built the railroad, which extended on out to Pecos, thus first being called the Pecos Valley Railroad.

When Hastings came to Bovina in the early 1900's the railroad had been taken over by the Santa Fe.

In 1905 the Belen cut-off was laid straight west from Texico. The railroad company put up company shops and started the city of Clovis. Then a spur was built south from Clovis to intersect the railroad about 10 miles northeast of Portales. At that time the track from that intersection into Texico was removed.

When the railroad was first built, back in 1898, the engineer was given a log showing the average yearly rainfall all along the route from Amarillo to Roswell. The log showed that the average rainfall in the Kenna and Elida area between Portales and Roswell was seven inches.

The engineer built the tracks, culverts, etc. accordingly, not expecting any weather threats. That year Hastings said that a "gully washer" came—one of those this country gets about every 20 years. The culverts were washed out as well as several miles of track.

The engineer was taking quite a beating. Railroad people were calling him a "bum" engineer. The engineer retaliated that it was really the railroad's fault, because when he was given the weather log, "You didn't tell me it fell all at once."

Mr. and Mrs. Hastings recall that a Mrs. Nichols hired a tutor for the Nichols children and the first kind of "schooling" was offered here in a room over one of the stores in town. Three or four other children living here also attended the classes. They say that Mrs. Kate McLain Queen, deceased, claimed she was one of those first students.

The first Bovina school building was the old Catholic Church.

Tidenberg Family, Dec. 9, 1909

In the meantime, Miss Leora Tidenberg was born in Pennsylvania to Mr. and Mrs. J.A. Tidenberg. Her father had come to the Plains and bought 80 acres four miles north of town. A brother-in-law had also purchased 80 acres.

At this time, the syndicate had surveyed the XIT land, was sending out land agents and selling it at prices that were outrageous at that time—$28 per acre. The country was being flooded with people from the north who had bought 80, 160 or sometimes a half section of land.

They all came to settle their land and

270

among them were Mr. and Mrs. Tidenberg and their eight children. They travelled by railroad and brought few of their belongings. The family arrived in Bovina in a snowstorm. Mr. Tidenberg and three other men, who planned to live with the family, had intended to immediately build a dwelling, but the snowstorm curtailed their plans, the group lived in a hotel for two weeks. By that time they were really poor, Mrs Hastings laughingly said, "but we didn't know it." When weather would permit, the men secured materials and built a little temporary house, actually a shack she said, that had a division which made a small upstairs.

The family survived two winters in the house, and when many of the people from the north "gave up" and went back to their northern homes, the Tidenbergs were able to secure a four room house.

The only reason the Tidenbergs could hold on to their farming operations on the Plains was because the brother-in-law went back to Pennsylvania and worked as a carpenter to help make the payment, while Mrs. Hastings' father raised maize, cane and maybe a little wheat. He also herded sheep for ranchers the first year, then later bought his own sheep.

The first year they lived on the Plains, it did not rain until July, but the fall was late so Tidenberg managed to raise a little maize and sold it for seed.

Mr. and Mrs. Tidenberg lived here for the remainder of their lives.

Couple Marry

The Hastings first met in about 1909 when the Tidenbergs bought groceries in the general store. However, it wasn't until about 1912 that they paid much attention to each other. They married on May 20, 1915 in Amarillo.

The young couple had wanted to keep their plans a secret, so decided to go to Amarillo for the ceremony. The news leaked out and some of their friends, thinking they were already married, opened the train window and showered them with rice. They came back through Bovina on their honeymoon enroute by train to the San Francisco Exposition.

The couple continued operating their store here until selling it about 1921. A year later the building burned, as had a rooming house

LAIRD HERRING MERCANTILE CO. in 1905. First Bovina Post Office Building, left background.

and grocery store back in 1910 or 1911. Since there was no fire department, saving a burning structure was impossible.

Hastings had invested in cattle and land during the years and decided to sell his business to look after his other interests. He still owns land near Bovina that he bought at $10 per acre. His land is rented now, but he still enjoys watching his crops grow and discussing farming problems with his renter and friends.

Active Citizens

The Hastings joined the Methodist Church in Bovina in 1917 and have been active members since that time. Mr. Hastings served on the school board back about 1919 and for years afterwards. A few Mexicans began migrating to this area about that time and education for the children became an issue. During his tenure on the board, he was instrumental in building an adobe school for these children and the Methodist preacher, Rev. B.Y. Dickenson, was the teacher.

The Bovina pioneers have two children, Miss Anna Hastings of Plainview and Mrs. Robert E. (Alethea) Wilson of Bovina and four grandchildren, Ann Lynn, Kregg, Candy and April Wilson. Both the couple's children finished high school in Bovina, as did Mrs. Hastings and the three older grandchildren. In fact, after attending college in Canyon, Mrs. Hastings returned to Bovina and taught the first, second and third grades for a year, 1914-1915.

In 1961 the Masonic Lodge presented Hastings with a 50-year pin, having been a member that long, and now in 1966, he has been a Mason for 55 years. Mrs. Hastings was a charter member of the Order of Eastern

EDD ROSS on wagon, left to right—Sheep Hill, Luther Barnes, Fent Stallings, (in sweater), Mr. Tom Hoghland, other unknown.

INTERIOR OF Bovina Mercantile Co. Grocery and Hardware Side of Business. The men are left to right, Luther Barnes, Frank Hastings, Fent Stallings, Sheep Hill (man with Beard), Edd Ross. Boy unidentified.

Star here, although she claims she was never active.

Mrs. Hastings remains busy trying to find information on her family back in Pennsylvania. She has the old family Bible, published in 1856, which is printed in German with each page ornately surrounded by flowers and scroll work.

Hastings continued operating the store until selling it in about 1921.

He had invested in land and cattle and decided to devote full time to ranching and farming.

They endeavored to be faithful members of the Methodist Church through the years, and be of help in community projects when possible. They hope they have accomplished some good.

In 1961 the Masonic Lodge presented Frank with a 50 year pin and certificate.

In 1965, they celebrated their 50th wedding anniversary and are grateful to relatives and friends that came to help make it a happy occasion.

Their two children are: Miss Anna Hastings of Plainview, Texas and Alethea (Mrs. Robert Wilson) of Bovina, Texas and four grandchildren—Anna Lynn, Kregg, Candy and April Wilson; and one great grandson, Robby Dyer, son of Ronny and Candy Wilson Dyer.

Recently, Mrs. Ann Corn, German teacher in Bovina, translated some notes in the Bible written in German by Mrs. Hastings' Grandmother Tidenberg, which revealed a few facts Mrs. Hastings had not previously known.

The West Texas pioneers now live in a large white brick home in Bovina and stay busy keeping one of the neater and lovelier yards in the town.

In 1965, they celebrated their 50th wedding anniversary.

HILLS FAMILY

In 1908, my father and mother, Mr. and Mrs. Fred L. Hills, decided to sell their Missouri farm in Fulton, Callaway County, Missouri and move to Texas. My father had been a farmer all his life and attended the Aurora Academy in Illinois. My mother was a teacher in Kansas and attended Manhattan College in that State in the early 1880's. I am their daughter, Grace, now Grace H. Whitener. I was then 13 years old. In October, 1908, after selling the farm at Fulton, my father chartered a railroad car with all our household furnishings plus horses, two cows, three turkeys, two dozen chickens, two or three hogs, my beautiful blue maltese cat and our collie aboard. The farm was in West Texas, nine miles north of Farwell, one mile east of the New Mexico line and seven miles west of Bovina. The land in this country was all owned at that time by the Farwells of Chicago and it was a part of the million acres which they had received for building the capitol of Texas at Austin. It had been known as the X.I.T. Ranch and we came at a time to see the last big cattle herds disappear. I remember when a bad blizzard would come in the winter, these herds would drift with the wind and snow and I've seen dead cattle after a storm frozen and still standing—others lying frozen.

Our land was as bare as your hand except

for the native Buffalo and Gamma grass. In the fall of the year the Gamma seed was very nourishing and made the coats of the animals shine.

The first thing my father did was drill a well. It was 200 feet deep. Then he built shelter for the animals and also pens. Later he started the house. It was a comfortable five-room house with pantry and closets and one small room upstairs.

How happy my mother and I were when my father wrote and said, "Come." However, when we arrived at Texico on December 28, 1908, the house was not quite complete due to unforeseen happenings. So we boarded at a neighbor's house, Niles George, for a few days and when we moved in the partitions were not all in between the rooms. However, we were happy to be together and it didn't take long for it to all be finished. My beautiful cat was killed by coyotes before we ever got settled.

Of course, there were no fences and I helped my father survey our land. Then my father broke the land, using a sod plow and four horses and walking behind the plow.

We ordered our trees and my father planted peach, plum and apple trees and a wind break planted around it and the house of black mulberries. This made a wonderful wind break and bore many berries which were enjoyed by ourselves and our neighbors in that fruit-scarce country. Fruit was so scarce we resorted to various things to take its place; such as garden lemons, which grew on a vine; and ground cherries, which grew on a bush. My mother canned these things for winter. They had to be carefully seasoned with lemon juice and sugar to give them a sort of zip; but they were delicious when done properly. The garden lemons looked and tasted like pears when canned.

In 1914 we had our first peach crop—great big, delicious Elbertas. There were bushels and bushels and people came from all over to buy. It was the first bearing orchard in that country—but my father had worked hard. During long, dry spells, he would dig deep around each tree and pour a barrel of water to each one and let it soak in and cover with dry dirt to hold the moisture in.

Our closest school was the Billingsley School four miles northeast from our home,

and for several months I walked back and forth each day. About two miles from us I had to go across a draw or sort of ravine and down in this draw one morning were seven coyotes. They did not run when they saw me—just stood looking at me and I became quite frightened. After that my father bought me a regular cow pony and I spent much of my time riding. It was my job to round up the stock and to ride the nine miles into Farwell at least once a week to get the mail. When we came from Missouri, I had my side saddle as it was thought very unladylike to ride astride in that staid old state; but it was not long until my father decided I would be much safer riding astride and bought me a beautiful cowboy saddle and how proud I was of it. In the art of riding I became quite proficient.

It soon became evident to my father that four miles was too far to be from school, so he and other neighbors got together and voted at the Billingsley School to divide the District. There had to be a certain number of children in the District before it could be divided and we had enough, so we got our school called the Daniel School. I can't think of the names of all the pupils; but there were Blanche and Lonnie Daniels, Annie, Willie and Ernest Scherkenbach, two Wilson children, three Hill children and myself. Mrs. Carl Wirth was our teacher. Later in 1914, after I returned from school in Illinois, I taught this same school one term.

My mother and father were both good nurses and good in caring for the sick and in that new country so far from doctors they were in much demand, my mother especially was called on for everything from childbirth to cases of pneumonia and croupe and Mother even helped a doctor in an operation performed in a neighbor's home one time.

Many covered wagons passed our place with families in them bound for New Mexico and Arizona, where there was still homesteading. Sometimes they camped for the night near us and bought milk and eggs from us, other times we gave them milk and eggs and other things. Sometimes there was a sick baby in the wagon and Mother would help the young wife. It seemed she always had some remedy on hand.

At the time we came there was no Church or Sunday School in our community. My father helped organize the first Sunday School in the Billingsley Schoolhouse and he was the first Sunday School Superintendent. There was a Congregational preacher, Rev. Hurbert, who came out from Farwell once a month and preached for us. We had great times in the neighborhood and had picnics there with dinner on the ground. Only there were no shade trees and we put up tables in the schoolhouse.

We also organized a Literary Society both for the young and older and we had many good times. Music was not forgotten and we had songs everyone could sing and organized a male quartet. I played the organ for these affairs and when we went to practice, my father and I would go horseback in the evenings, sometimes as far as 20 miles after chores were done in the evening. I shall never forget those wonderful rides across the prairie at night with my father. This was in the winter time as summers were too busy.

August 19, 1916, I married Noah L. Whitener. Three children were born to us—Fred, Dorothy and Noah L. Jr. They are all married now and I have nine grandchildren and four great-grandchildren. I am very fortunate in this day when families are so scattered that they all live close to me. Noah L., Sr. passed away in 1945.

The Whitener's lived in the Community of Pleasant Hill in New Mexico, only a couple of miles from my father's farm in Texas. They were also pioneers of that new country, coming to New Mexico in 1906—six years before that Territory became a state. Everyone did dry land farming and Mr. Whitener and his boys, Noah and Caruthers were very successful farmers. That was in the days before irrigation; but they did well in raising wheat and other crops.

One time while my children and I were living in Espanola, New Mexico, my daughter, Dorothy, was telephone operator of the little town in the northwestern part of the State. A man came in to have her make a long distance call to New York. Meanwhile, he asked her name and he said, "Are you any relation to the D.P. Whitener, who is "Wheat King" of New Mexico?" Of course, she said, "He is my Grandfather."

The other sons, Caruthers and his wife, are retired and live in Farwell, Texas. Their son,

Howard and his family still live on the old Whitener place in New Mexico. Their daughter, Marjorie Jean and her family, The Donald Watkins, live on a farm near Farwell.

Written by Grace Hills Whitener

BILL HINKLE DIES; WAS RODEO STAR

Amarillo Daily News
March 2, 1972

Bill Hinkle, born in 1881 in "Bull Town"—which changed its name to Bovina when the post office was established in 1899—died Tuesday in Kissimmee, Fla.

Hinkle, a rodeo star, storyteller and cowboy who spent his childhood with the likes of Bat Masterson and Wyatt Earp, had been ill for several weeks.

He promoted rodeos around the country as well as appearing in shows with Buffalo Bill Cody and Annie Oakley. He wrote short stories and told long stories about the days when his father, George Hinkle, defeated Masterson in an election for sheriff of Dodge City, Kansas.

Hinkle grew up in Dodge City and Fort Smith, Ark., after his folks moved from Bull Town, one of the divisional headquarters of the XIT Ranch.

Throughout a long life he exchanged letters with some of the men who were the living legends of the West.

His letters led to a correspondence and friendship with the late Will Rogers and Tom Mix. In recent years he had counted Arthur Godfrey and Tennessee Ernie Ford among his pen pals.

Hinkle once served as a body guard for President Theodore Roosevelt on an expedition to uncharted portions of South America. At the time, Hinkle was an agent of the U.S. Border Patrol.

October 19, 1907 J.M. Neely and F.L. Spring to buy bldg. presently occ. as C.H.—if could not contract to Henry Sloan & C.M. Clark $1380.00.

Commissioners Court Notes

RICHARD COKE HOPPING, 1905
State Line Tribune, Farwell, 1908

It was the year of 1905 that young Richard Coke Hopping and his beautiful little wife, Lelia, with their four children moved from Portales to Texico, New Mexico, where Mr. Hopping and Mr. Mart Robertson became partners in a mercantile store. Texico was a thriving little frontier town; both men were well liked; and their investment was a good one. They had a very prosperous business for several years. There was no town of Farwell at that time.

A barb wire fence at Texico marked the boundary line of New Mexico on the East. One Sunday afternoon Mr. Hopping said to his wife, "Let's go into Texas and select a site for our new home." The children, thinking that a trip to another State would be a long, interesting journey, asked to accompany them. Indeed, their disappointment was great to learn that on the other side of the barb wire fence lay the great State of Texas. After that experience they had the mistaken idea that all the States of our glorious Nation were separated by barb wire fences—just as fences separated the pastures of the big ranches in the West.

In 1907 the little town of Farwell was founded across the fence from Texico. Mr. Hopping and Mr. Robertson moved their mercantile business to the new town. It was the only "Mercantile" in the area, and they were well pleased with the business which came to them from the new "settlers." "As long as nature favored West Texas with rains, it blossomed like a flower garden, but there came three years of drouth. Since there were no crops, there was no money. Coke and Mr. Robertson sold merchandise on the books. Three fourths of the newcomers went back East to pick cotton, hoe on farms, do anything to get something to eat," said Mr. Hopping in his book, "A Texas Ranger in Chuck Wagon Days."

The Mercantile Business had to be closed in the fall of 1909. Mr. Hopping had invested all of his savings in the store. Now, all was gone—lost. He was deeply in debt. What should he do? He and Mrs. Hopping talked about their problem and solved it together.

There was a certain freedom in this new undeveloped land of West Texas which they loved and which stirred their imagination. They didn't want to leave. They were still young and vibrant, eager to find their place and their mission in God's beautiful world. They began again with grim determination to build a brighter future for themselves and for their children.

They sold their pretty home in Farwell which they had built next door to the Robertson Family. They cleared their indebtedness, and Mr. Hopping bought on credit an eighty acre tract of land two and one half miles east of Farwell from Mr. J.D. Hamlin, the Syndicate Manager. Soon Mr. Hopping had a half dug-out on his land ready for his family to move into.

Mrs. Hopping, with her understanding heart and wisdom, knowing that home is where the heart is and where love abounds, made this humble dwelling comfortable for her beloved husband and their little children. Often she was reminded of her Grandmother's admonition, telling her that the thirty-first chapter of Proverbs was written by the wise King Solomon to depict the virtuous woman and the ideal home-maker, and as her birthday is August the twenty-seventh, then the twenty-seventh verse of the thirty-first Chapter of Proverbs applied directly to her, and that she must seek to emulate in her life the words given there.

"She looketh well to the ways of her household, and eateth not the bread of idleness." Truly, her duties were many. There was the washing of clothes and linens to be done on the old fashioned rub board. There was no such thing as an electric washing machine and dryer. Water was heated in a big iron pot in the yard unless it was too cold outside for her labors. Then, she heated the water on the kitchen stove in a large tin wash boiler. Of course, the ironing came next, which was done with heavy flat irons heated on the kitchen stove. Another chore which had to be done each day was the care of the milk and butter. Since there was no refrigeration, a milk trough was set up near the windmill and so arranged that fresh water ran through a large container in which the crock jars of milk were set. The container was a big zinc pan about five feet long, three feet wide and about six or eight inches deep. This was placed on a homemade table. As the milk was brought in fresh and warm, it was strained, poured into jars, and they were set in the cool, running water with clean wet rags wrapped around the jars. Mrs. Hopping never seemed to tire of the churning. She would get a good magazine or book after the cream had been placed in the old fashioned churn with the dasher in it. Then, as her right arm and hand brought the dasher up and down in the rich, sweet cream, she would indulge in the delight of reading from a favorite magazine, known as the "Delineator" or she would enjoy the delving into some great novel or any good book of fiction. Often these few minutes with the churning were her only moments of relaxation during the day, and at times this pleasure was denied her, for her baby, seeing her seated, would crawl to her and demand to be taken into her arms and lap, and instead of living in the dreams of a wonderful romance, she would be singing a lullaby to her little one. However, she always felt repaid for her labors, for the buttermilk and fresh, sweet butter were always enjoyed when placed on her table. Her sons helped her with the gardening for fresh vegetables when they were in season were a necessity for her table. Although today Mrs. Hopping will tell you that she was not a good cook, for she did not like to work in the kitchen, yet the verdict of her children is that there was never a better cook. It was a real treat, they always felt, to be greeted with the appetizing aroma of hot bread just from the oven as they came from an active, busy day at school. No one could bake the delicious rolls and hot cinnamons like their mother.

Mr. and Mrs. Hopping were both sincere and devout Christians. One of their first acts in moving to a new Community was to place their membership in the Baptist Church which they loved and taught their children to love. Of course, the children were always enrolled in the Public Schools of the Community also, and the older ones remember attending the first Public School in Farwell. It was conducted in the Congregational Church which was a stone building.

Mrs. Hopping still retains her sense of humor and enjoys looking back on the early days when she and "Coke" were young. She often says, "I wouldn't trade places with any

one. I married the best man in the world, and my people used to say of me, 'Now that Lelia has married Coke, she thinks that she has the whole world by the tail and a down hill pull on it'." Once a friend was asking her about the hardships which she endured as a pioneer. She replied, "They are all forgotten now. Those were very happy days When I had Coke and the little children around me. Why, if I had the gift of a poet, I would even write a tribute to the **Cowchips,** for they brought warmth and comfort to many of the little humble homes of the West when coal, wood, and gas were not available. I have enjoyed many meals with Coke at the cowboys' chuck wagon when the meat stew and the sour dough biscuits were prepared over a cowchip fire. Then sometimes, I wonder what has become of sunbonnets that we used to wear. I often told my girls not to go out in the wind and sun without their bonnets, for if they did go without them, their freckles would run together, and their faces would be black. Later, Jake saw a Negro for the first time. He was a porter on the train, and remembering my words, my little son asked me, 'Mama, did that man go without his bonnet?' "

Mrs. Hopping, although she had little time for social activities, loved her friends, and delighted in her association with them. Once she met with a little sewing circle. Various kinds of fancy work was being done by the members, such as needle point, knitting, crocheting, and embroidery. Mrs. Hopping's fingers were busy too. One friend, seeing that her work was not being displayed as a work of art said to her, "Mrs. Hopping, don't you do any fancy work?"

"Oh, yes," she answered, "Right now, I am putting embroidery on the seats of my boys' pants," and so it was true that every moment had to be used in keeping her children clothed and fed and in school. She was a wonderful seamstress, and in one day she could cut the pattern for a dress for one of their daughters. Then cut the material by the

August 17, 1907 Parmer No. 185 on alphabetical list of 254 counties.

Commissioners Court Notes

pattern, sew it up, and the next day the child could wear it.

In a recent publication of a Crosbyton newspaper, Billye Marye Stockton, the daughter of Mr. and Mrs. Sid Hopping, paid the following tribute to her Grandmother, Mrs. R.C. Hopping, and also expressed appreciation for the contributions made by the pioneers of Crosbyton. Mrs. Stockton's home is in Crosbyton.

"My Grandmother, Mrs. R.C. Hopping, marked her 92nd birthday last month, and I feel this calls for a tribute to her and also to a number of pioneer men and women in the Crosbyton area who are a rare breed of people.

They came to this country when it was only grassland, snakes, coyotes, and a few antelope. They helped it grow into thriving cities and irrigated farmland. They raised their children to be God-fearing, hard working people who expected to take their place in their communities as workers and leaders, not laggards. They didn't have Daylight Saving Time. Their day started by sun-up and lasted until all light was gone.

"They had to be strong to survive. Many lived in dug-outs, a far cry from the fine homes which dot the rural plains today.

"My thanks to 'Mama' Hopping and to those like her who have given us a fine heritage. May we preserve it and do our best to deserve it."

After the closing of the Mercantile Business, Mr. Hopping accepted a position with Mr. Wallace Good, owner of the Sixty-Nine Ranch near Bovina, and served as foreman for a year. In 1910, he was elected Sheriff of Parmer County and served eight years in this office. He also served as an Inspector for the Panhandle and Southwestern Cattlemen's Association. He was commissioned a Texas Ranger and was appointed to the Mounted Police Force of New Mexico. His days were busy ones, and he knew the fatigue brought about by too many duties and too long hours of labor, but each task was approached with quiet sincerity and with zeal, and a determination to fulfil each obligation. His experiences in these law enforcement offices are vividly described in his book "A Sheriff Ranger in Chuck Wagon Days." In writing about him, one person said, "Young Coke

Hopping was fully aware of the danger he would face as a sheriff in the days when the West laughed at law, when guns were cheap, and life was cheaper. He knew too, of the loneliness it would mean for his lovely wife, Lelia, and for their family. But love of country ran deep in Coke, and he was determined to build a law abiding West where his children could grow up in peace and security. That was why Coke began his long and exciting career as a western sheriff. That was why Lelia, courageous and unflinching, stood by her husband while he pursued horse thieves in the great mountains and canyons of the West, while he dodged the bullets of cattle rustlers, and fought gun battles with murderers." He was away from home much of the time, but the joys that he knew and loved best were the periods of rest and recreation that he spent with his wife and children.

After leaving Farwell in the fall of 1918, the family moved to Littlefield, and Mr. Hopping served as Judge of Lamb County eight years. He was a public spirited citizen. He enjoyed the development of the new town and manifested great interest in its school and churches. He loved the people and entered wholeheartedly into their activities. In later years, he was made President of the "Old Settlers Reunion" of Lamb County, an organization which has done much to bring the Pioneers together and to lighten the duties of every day life in times of social enjoyment. Mrs. "Gus" Shaw was the outstanding leader, and the first President of this Pioneer Organization.

In 1926 Mr. Hopping and his family moved to Lubbock. He accepted the position as sales manager for the colonization of the lands of the Spade Ranch which was owned by Mr. W.L. Ellwood.

The dugout which was two and one-half miles east of Farwell was boarded up on the inside, and was well ventilated with several windows where it was built above the level of the ground. At the southwest corner were the stairs from the outside entrance. A long din-

May 11 1908 J.C. Temple and V.L. Anderson build jail, cost $212.50.

Commissioners Court Notes

ing table extended from the stairway to the northwest corner of the room. A long bench was behind the table and against the wall on the west. There was always a mad rush on school mornings to prepare breakfast, and to get the children dressed and off to school. Mr. Hopping solved the problem. He always helped his wife prepare breakfast, which usually consisted of a cooked cereal, preferably oatmeal, bacon, eggs, hot biscuits and butter with King Comus Cane Syrup. Of course the parents drank coffee, but not the children, they had a glass of milk. Their father promised each child a nickel to dress in five minutes. There was no cheating. All were required to be dressed, to have face and hands washed, teeth brushed, and hair combed and to be seated at the table in time to hear their father ask the blessing, as he always did at each meal. The children sat on the bench behind the table, and the name of each one was written on the wall behind his or her place at the table. A tally was kept of the times each one dressed in five minutes by placing a pencil mark on the wall under the name. A careful record was kept. Knowing how eagerly his children rushed to their stockings on Christmas morning and that getting dressed became a real task on that day because of the interest in their gifts, their father promised a quarter to the one who could dress in five minutes on Christmas Day. Finally, the long looked-for morning arrived. Flora Besst awakened early, slipped out of bed, and found her precious doll, clad in a blue satin dress which her mother had made. The loveliest doll she had ever had. She took the doll to bed with her, and when the alarm sounded, she jumped out of bed and dressed in five minutes. She did not receive her quarter, for her father had heard her stealthy steps earlier and knew that she had already seen all of her Christmas gifts. At the end of the school year, although each one had a little spending money, Jake had earned the most cash. Flora Besst always argued that boys could dress faster than girls because they didn't have to put on as many clothes and they didn't have long hair to brush an braid.

The dugout was a home of short duration. A small three room house with a lean-to joining the house to the dugout was soon built, and later, Mr. Hopping bought a three room frame school house from the school, and moved it to the farm property. The school building was joined to the small house. The large school rooms were divided into several rooms, and at last the family enjoyed the luxury of having the ample space they needed for living quarters. Perhaps the greatest luxury of all was the bathroom which their home now afforded them. Oh! the joy which each one experienced in bathing in a real bath tub instead of a small wash tub near a stove heater where one side of the bather almost blistered and the other side chilled.

There was another member of the Hopping Family which we have not yet mentioned. His name was Jumbo, and he was the pet pony beloved by all. He was not a large pony as his name would indicate, but was the opposite. He was not a prancing beauty of noble stock. He was only a sweet little roan, petted, and spoiled, and seemingly indispensible to the members of the household. Mrs. Hopping often said that he helped to educate her children. LaVerna and Flora Besst were the first to ride him to school. They learned at an early age to throw their side saddle on his back and to mount him with the greatest of ease. They rode him double with LaVerna in the saddle and Flora Besst behind the saddle. They felt that they were really accomplished riders when they could put him through his various gaits without having to hold on. He was a wonderful pacer, and they enjoyed this smooth easy gait most of all, but of course, it was always fun to gallop. They had never heard of barrel races or they would have tried them.

As the younger children reached school age, Jumbo was hitched to the buggy and driven to school. Through the school hours he was unhitched or unsaddled, hobbled and permitted to graze near the school. Oh! The freedom and privileges given in a small town and in a small school will never be forgotten. There were no nice bus rides to school in those days. Often for short rides, as many children as could find a place to sit on Jumbo's back would climb up on him, and he never seemed to object. They could crawl all over him and under him, and he would exhibit great patience. However, he was not perfect, for sometimes he would indulge in willful, naughty habits. One day Mrs. Hopping heard an anguished cry and rushed out to rescue the injured. "Berna" as LaVerna was affectionaly called, was the victim. Jumbo had one of her long, beautiful braids of hair in his mouth, and with seeming great delight was swinging his head up and down, almost lifting poor Berna off the ground with each upward sling of his head. Her only offense was that she had drawn the girth tighter than Jumbo liked it.

Another incident which always brought forth gales of laughter when recounted was the time that LaVerna and Flora Besst were returning home from school on a warm sultry day, following a rain. They came to a puddle of mud and water in the middle of the road. Jumbo refused to go around it. LaVerna coaxed, kicked, and scolded him but to no avail. He walked very deliberately into the water and lay down. Perhaps Jumbo was more comfortable and cooler, after this episode, but the girls were not. They were terribly embarrassed, because a lady sitting on her front porch nearby laughed gleefully at the sight. When Jumbo was ready to resume his journey, he arose with the girls still on his back, shook himself, and trotted off home. Neither girl had lost her balance on her mount, but they arrived home spattered with mud and water, and tearfully tried to explain through their anger what had happened to them.

LaVerna, their first born, was ever the pride and joy of her parents, and when young Johnny Jones asked for her hand in marriage, it was hard for them to consent, for she was only fifteen years old; however, on February 3, 1909, with only the family present, they became man and wife in a quiet home wedding. The family was living at the Sixty-Nine Ranch at the time. Her life with Johnny was a very unhappy one, and like many teenage marriages, ended in divorce. They had one son, Vertner Wray, born December 7, 1910.

Later, LaVerna attended another year in

the Farwell High School, and then took a Commercial Course in Wayland College at Plainview. She secured a position in the city and remained there to work. While in Plainview she met and married Hollis T. Wingo. To their union were born three children: Lelia Eileen (Eileen), Truman Earl (Truman), and Richard Coke (Coke).

Mr. and Mrs. Hopping's creed could have been "cheaper by the dozen" for other children often came and made the Hopping home their home. Loved and cared for as their own was their Grandson, Wray Jones, LaVerna's son who spent many years of his childhood and even later years with them. There was also Mr. Hopping's nephew and niece, George Jake and Sara Sue Landers, whose mother passed away when they were very small children, and there was Toll Dycus who had suffered the loss of his mother—these three children were welcomed and spent long periods of time with the family and were loved by all.

Jacob Wray, always known as Jake, was a sturdy little fellow with brown hair and hazel eyes. He was ever alert and manly, industrious and thrifty. In looking back over his childhood in Farwell, everyone remembers how much he disliked being small and always fought the idea of anyone thinking he was effeminate in any way. He defied anyone to say or even to think that he was a "Sissy." Therefore, his embarrassment was great one morning when his mother gave him his sister's coat to wear to school because he had left his own at the school the day before. Then to add insult to injury, she put her garters on him to hold his stockings on him, because he had lost his own garters. The little boys those days wore short, straight-legged pants, and when not going barefoot, they wore long, black, ribbed cotton hose. Jake was determined not to enter the school room in that red coat, nor was he inclined to take the risk of those satin covered garters with large roseate bows dropping down and showing below his pants. Not one of the children ever said "no" to Mama, so he dressed as she told him to do, but before reching the school, he hung his coat and garters on a mesquite bush far away from the school where he could pick them up on his way home. Mama never knew until later years the trouble he had that day with his sagging stockings.

Then came the First World War. In 1918 Jake had just finished the Farwell High School. He graduated with honors, serving as Valedictorian of his class. He felt the call to go into the Service of his Country. He was still a little fellow but big of heart and with great patriotic zeal. He and one of his close friends, Coke Caraway, decided to enlist in the Army. Coke too was a small lad, so just before taking the Physical Examination they tried to build up their chances of being accepted by adding to their weight. They drank a great quantity of buttermilk and ate bananas. They did not pass the physical. Later, Jake was admitted to the Texas National Guard. Again, luck was against him or shall we say with him, for the Armistice was signed the day before he was to report for duty.

Earl, the second son, possessed a bright, sunshiney disposition. In childhood he never had a care or worry of any kind. Any trouble was lightly dismissed. One day when Earl was about three years old his father came home and found Earl playing in mud and water, really making mud pies. His once clean little Buster Brown suit was wet and muddy. His father, in a shocked voice, said, "Earl, don't you know your mother doesn't want you to do that?" "Yes, but my mother isn't here," Earl replied with a mischievous smile, and a twinkle in his blue eyes. Earl was very popular with his father's friends. He was given a beautiful buckskin pony by Mr. Barto Osborne of Farwell, and while the family was living in the Sixty-Nine Ranch, Mr. Wallace Good gave him a nice saddle. He was now fully equipped to be a real cowboy, which seems to be the dream of nearly every young West Texan.

One time, eight of the children had the German Measles. It was during the winter of the First World War. LaVerna was married and in her home at the time, so she escaped the quarantine which was placed on the Hopping family. Poor Mrs. Hopping! It seemed that one child at a time would awaken in the morning really speckled with the troublesome rash and fever. Each morning she had a new patient. Before the quarantine the three boys became very restless. They were the very last ones to be sick. After they were feeling better, but still not dismissed by the doctor, Earl thought of a way to get from under the tiresome yoke. He inveigled Jake and Sidney to help him. This was the plan: When Mama was busy in the kitchen, they would slip out to the pens and turn the milk calves out. Surely, they couldn't help it, if the calves ran down Main Street, and the boys had to chase them to get them back into pens. Everything went according to plans. The three brothers had a gay time running up and down and around town chasing the calves which they finally drove back into the pens where they belonged. The Doctor came to see them, found the boys none the worse for their unusual activities, lifted the quarantine, and dismissed all the cases of measles which had been in the household.

Earl, who married Lydia Crockett, has one daughter, Michael, who is now Mrs. Johnny Johnston. They all live in Kerrville, Texas. Earl and his son-in-law own and operate several filling stations.

Sidney was a sincere, quiet, and studious little fellow. He was always earnest in keeping up with all his duties, appointments, and assignments, but he too had his mischievous moments. When he was in his early teens he had a mount which afforded great fun for the boys. Sid traded a bicycle seat to a neighbor for an old donkey which was an excellent example of the old saying "Stubborn as a mule." There were times when no amount of coaxing could persuade the old animal to move. Sidney would often take him to town and bet with his friends, both men and boys, that they couldn't ride him. Such a challenge had to be met. Immediately, on being mounted before the rider was safely seated, the old donkey would lower his head and begin bucking. Every rider that was thrown off had to give Sidney a quarter.

After Sidney graduated from high school, he went to the Mashed O Ranch to work for the summer. It was his first job, and he began his life as a cowboy with all the zeal and enthusiasm of youth. How proud he was of his

May 8, 1916 Old jail at Friona sold to C.F. Kobe $6.30.

Commissioners Court Notes

first pay check of $20.00! After receiving his pay he was invited by a group of the cowboys to go with them to a rodeo at Arch, New Mexico. Oh! the fun he would have! He knew that it would be a great day for him. He was filled with excitement as he thought of the joy he would have in spending his own money. Money he had earned through his own labors. But Alas! when he arrived in Arch and needed to cash his check, he had lost it. He searched in his billfold, in every pocket, but no check. It was through the kindness of his companions that he was able to return to the Mashed O's that night.

Sidney married Loraine Pass of Ralls, Texas, and they have two children, Billy Marye Stockton, who lives in Crosbyton, Texas, and Clifford Coke who married Eva Jane Fields and lives in Springlake, Texas. Billye's husband, T.W. Stockton, Jr., is a farmer, and Clifford Coke is employed by the Byers Grain and Elevator Business in Springlake.

Lillian, a little girl with blue eyes and dark hair, added much happiness to the household. She is active, alert, and intensely interested in all about her. She possessed an affectionate, sensitive nature. When things went wrong, she always wanted to do her part to help make things right again, and in reminiscing she tells the following incident in her own words:

"Perhaps there are some adventures that should be called misadventures. Mama's prudent economy finally provided her with money to buy five pure strain barred rock hens and a setting of eggs for each. I'm sure she saw in her dreams luxuries and lovely things that this investment would eventually bring to her family. But as a little child, I could only remember her great pride in her chickens. One night, I heard Mama and Papa discussing the fact that mites and lice were eating her hens. How to get rid of those lice had both Mama and Papa pretty worried.

Since I slept on a trundle bed in their room, I heard the story, and I did **so** want to be helpful. The next day I went out to study those hens. Finally, I decided what to do. If I hung the chickens by the heels, the lice would drop off. 'Twas pretty hard to get those big, pecking, scolding chickens from their nest without breaking those precious eggs. Hanging them on the high roosts was a task too, but I managed.

The next morning, Mama discovered her poor wonderful chickens—cold, stiff, and quite dead. All five settings of eggs—cold, and the little chicks just ready to hatch—dead too. Mama! Oh, My! Mama was too sick to be articulate. I sensed that she might be dangerous if she discovered my misplanning. So believe me, I lied out of this one! Furthermore, I never ever, tried to find out if the lice dropped off!"

Lillian always followed her brothers in their play and always wanted to be included in their games. She watched them with great adoration, and her older sisters, LaVerna and Flora Besst were shining examples, in Lillian's eyes, of great wisdom. She felt that they knew most everything, and of course, they relished her admiration. She often tried to imitate them, especially in their manner of speaking, and this sometimes got her into trouble. She even adopted some of their vocabulary, which did not always advance her knowledge of the English language. Once when she was a Freshman in the Texas Technological College at Lubbock, she wrote a theme in which she used the descriptive word "solemncholy" instead of "melancholy." Another impressive word was "edrapation" meaning, of course, "a small amount." For example, one might put a small "edrapation" of sugar in his coffee. The English instructor indicated that coined words were interesting but not admissable. Thus the red ink on her papers marked not only the teacher's cortections, but also the end of the "Age of Innocence" for Lillian.

Lillian and her husband, Frank Hayne, are very successful teachers now. They have many years of teaching experience to their credit and are employed in the Eagle Mountain High School, Eagle Mountain, California.

The next baby to make her arrival into the family was a little blonde with fair complexion and blue eyes. She was just as cute and petite as her name which is "Patti." As a

Liquor Election—August 14, 1916—141 for, 18 against, prohibition that is!

Commissioners Court Notes

small child she was a quiet and demure little girl. Patti was one month younger than her nephew Wray, Berna's son. They were inseparable in the home. Wherever one went, the other went. What ever one did, the other also did. Now, Patti says that there is one incident of her childhood which she always remembers with nausea. Her mother's help was a woman who dipped snuff and always chewed gum. When ready for a dip of snuff, she always stuck her gum on the top of her snuff box, and then placed the snuff box with its wad of gum on the nearest table or on the window sill. The wad of gum grew in size for she never threw any away. She just added new gum to that in her mouth, so it seemed. The wad just got bigger and bigger. This habit of the woman's always fascinated Patti and Wray, so one day they watched for the opportune time and seeing the snuff box and gum on the window sill, they slipped over very quietly, secured the gum, divided it, and put it in their mouths to chew. Their mothers could never understand the splashing and spluttering which ensued in the bathroom.

Patti is now married to Mr. Earl B. Hobbs of Lubbock. They have two children, Earl Bryan Jr., who is in the military service and is now located in Kentucky, after having finished his time as a helicopter pilot in Viet Nam. Sylvia Ann (Sylvia), their daughter, is attending the Southwestern Baptist Theological Seminary in Fort Worth.

Another little girl made her appearance in the Hopping Family on one still, moonlight night in June. Mr. Hopping was away from home seeking cattle rustlers in Kansas. This night will never be forgotten by the three oldest children. There was anxiety and a tenseness of feeling exhibited by each one. The telephone was out of order. Berna began making the first preparations for Dorothy's arrival and providing as best she could for her mother's needs and comfort. There were no cars in Farwell at this time, and the horses were in the back of the pasture, quite a distance from the home. Jake and Flora Besst ran as fast as their legs could carry them to get the doctor. They stopped at their nearest neighbor's home which was about two miles from their home. Mrs. Colthorpe, a kind, gracious, and sweet neighbor telephoned the doctor, but she did not wait for him. She hur-

ried to Mrs. Hopping's bedside, and rendered well the duties of a mid-wife. The baby arrived before the doctor did.

Dorothy had a happy, carefree childhood, even though she had many painful, unhappy experiences. She was overly active, always doing something first and then thinking about it afterwards. When asked to tell some incident of her childhood, she said, "My goodness! tell about the time I fell off the porch when I was a baby and cut off the end of my nose on a tin can. Mama just stuck my nose together and held me in her arms until it quit hurting. I still have the scar although it isn't noticeable. Then, there was the time I wanted to plait Jumbo's tail and he kicked and broke my arm. I remember riding a bicycle once and falling on the pavement and broke my ankle. I was a big girl then, however, in my teens. Another time when I was small, I climbed on old Bob, a pet pony, out in the pasture. I had neither halter nor bridle, but he was gentle, and I thought it would be fun to take a ride, for I had nothing else to do. Papa came along with a load of hay. Bob took out after the truck at full speed, hoping to get a big bite of the appetizing alfalfa. He stepped in a hole, and I fell off head first. When I became conscious again, Bob was standing perfectly still with one foot on my face, but none of his weight was on that foot. My face was bruised but there were no scars left from this adventure!"

There were several grandsons who were in service during World War II. Wray Jones was in the Navy, Truman Wingo was in the Army Air Corps, Coke Wingo was in the Army, and Pat Boone Jr. was in the Army. All saw foreign service but Coke. Dorothy was the only one among the girls in the military service, and she was a member of the Women's Army Corps and served nearly four years.

During the Korean War, Clifford Hopping served in the United States Navy.

Doris is the youngest of the Hopping "Bunch." She was the one who sat on her father's knee the longest time, and together she and he sang many of the popular songs of the day which they learned from the Edison records. Also, because she was the youngest, she was the one that her mother cuddled and caressed the most. There was not another baby to push her away or to take her place.

She often listened to the conversations between her parents for they were her constant companions. Sometimes, to their embarrassment, she would repeat things that she heard them say. Once they had as neighbors a fine family whose religious belief was that man should not shave. There were several young men in the family whose hair was a beautiful shade of red, and their beards were long, red and wavy. Their eyes were a deep blue and their skin was very fair. Although their appearance was very unusual to the Hopping children, they were handsome men. Their occupation was farming. Mrs. Hopping, in fun and joking with her husband, called them "My pretty Dutchman." One day one of them was delivering a load of grain to Mr. Hopping. Doris followed her father to the barn and proceeded to ask questions. Mr. Hopping, with great patience, was trying to answer her and to make the necessary explanations. Finally, this question came out, "Papa, is this Mama's pretty Dutchman?" To this question, although Doris repeated it several times, her father had no answer.

Doris and her husband, John S. Pomeroy, have a very attractive ranch near Monett, Missouri, which they call the "Agua Fria Ranch." They operate and live on their ranch and enjoy their neighbors and friends in Missouri very much. John, from a former marriage, has three children, Donald, Beverly, and Jerry. Doris loves these three as her very own, and helped rear them. However, they are all married now and in their own homes.

Flora Besst, the second daughter, is living in Littlefield, Texas, where she moved with her parents in the fall of 1918. She was married in 1921 to a wonderful young man, named Pat H. Boone. He was just starting out in the cattle business, a vocation which he always enjoyed, and he later became the owner and operator of his grandfather's ranch near Elida, New Mexico. His grandfather was William P. Littlefield, who was a brother of the late Major George Littlefield, the founder of the town of Littlefield.

Pat H. Boone, Jr., Flora Besst's and Pat's son, is now serving as the District Judge of the 154th District of the State of Texas, presiding over the District Court in Parmer, Bailey, and Lamb Counties.

A Tribute to Our Parents
(With apologies to
Genevieve Brunson)

Beneath the roof of our home
Love and happiness did abound.
Laughter rang within its walls,
And all felt comradeship's close tie.
Little ones expressed their joys
In merry songs and romping play.
Hospitality was often shared
To cheer the hearts of many friends.
Love of God was taught and country too,
And in the quiet evening hours
Repose beside a warm stove fire
Where we sat to read or chat or dream—
Forgot were all the worldly cares,
We enjoyed the peace and love of home.

Now, the happy family circle has been broken, God in his infinite wisdom and great love has gathered five of the loveliest blossoms from this **Bunch of Prairie Wild Flowers.** He needed them for his beautiful Garden Above. One by one He has transplanted them beside the River of Living Water, but our Faith and Hope is that some day we shall join them there. Richard Coke Hopping, born August 20, 1875, died September 29, 1954.

LaVerna Hopping Wingo, born December 5, 1894, died September 18, 1966.

Jacob Wray Hopping, born September 23, 1900, died February 16, 1942.

Jane Wray Hopping (Jake's and Velma Jane's first baby died at birth).

Richard Coke Wingo, (LaVerna's and Hollis' son) born December 30, 1934, died June, 1963.

Pat H. Boone (Flora Besst's husband) born November 14, 1897, died July 22, 1963.

The following poem was written by Claude Miller of Wichita Falls, Texas, as a tribute to a lifelong friend, the late Judge Richard Coke Hopping.

Coke

Can you see that glorious twinkle in his eye?
Well, that's love for all the folks beneath the sky,
He was sheriff, judge, and ranger
And to fear, he's not a stranger,
And to know he's waiting for us
In that great, sweet by and by.

He was all that friends may cherish
And his soul may never perish,
In the saddle on the range—was at his best
Humble cowboys loved him better
And obeyed him to the letter
On the wide and tawny prairies of the West.

Then at home his joy was keener
There his pastures always greener
Mid his loved ones all about the old ranch
door.
Now that smile I see serene
At his little wife, a queen.
Welcome always were the rich as well as the
poor.

Let us always think of Coke
As a faithful, sturdy oak.
On the plains, I'm sure the people won't
forget,
How he loved to meet and mingle
With his merry eyes a jingle
And I am sure the sweetest man we ever met.

HISTORY OF ERNEST ARNOLD
AND SOPHIA HROMAS

We arrived in Texico, New Mexico, on snowy November 19,1919, from Wills Point, Texas. We traveled in a Model T Touring car. Everything was sold in Wills Point and all our worldly goods were put in the car—a little bedding, a feather bed, can goods and some cash. Our daughter Ernestine was 4 and Arnold was 2. (Our last child, Evelyn, was born in 1922.)

It took 3 days to make the trip. We arrived in Texico on Thanksgiving Day and stayed in the Texico Hotel owned by Mrs. Murphy.

Our reason for being here was that Ernest Hromas decided he wanted land of his own. He had heard about West Texas, so he boarded a train to "go west." He met Mr. Sam Lawrence, a land agent for the Capitol Reservation Lands in Sweetwater, Texas. They arrived in Farwell and stayed at the Farwell Inn Hotel, which burned down De-

ERNEST ARNOLD and Sophia Hromas in 1921.

MR. AND MRS. E.A. HROMAS, Ernestine, Evelyn, Anold with friends in 1925.

cember 17, 1919. It was located just south of the present park. Mr. Hromas was looking for 160 acres and was shown 2 probable sites. He chose the northeast quarter of a section 6 miles south of Bovina—10 miles east of Farwell. The price was $30.00 an acre purchased November 1st, 1919. (The E.A. Hromas Family Farm was the NE-4 Section 16, Twp. 10, South, Range 2 East and located about 6 miles South of Bovina.)

"We rented a 3 room house and bought a bed, mattress, 4 chairs, and a stove. We lived there until December 26th (a little over a month). We had finished building a barn on the new farm which was 14'x18' with a car shed on the north and a horseshed on the south. The barn had a loft, also. We lived in the barn until 1925 and then moved into a 2

284

E.A. HROMAS FARM HOME built in 1929. Picture made Sept. 23, 1945.

HROMAS MEN in 1926 left to right, John Hromas, Sr., father of Ernest, Frank, Bill and Joe each lived in Parmer County at one time (all deceased).

EVELYN, ARNOLD AND Ernestine Hromas with 1929 F-20 Farmall Tractor.

room washhouse. We lived in it until the new home was finished in 1929. This house had six rooms, including a bath. We had nearly 1,200 square feet for $1,200.00 cash money. The whole family pitched in and worked on this."

We started farming with one walking plow, a sod planter, and 4 horses. One team of horses cost $250.00 and another team cost $124.00—the cheaper pair turned out to be the better. The first year we were able to break and plant only 14 acres, but made a very good crop. Seven inches of rain fell that year. For the first several years, the first rain came exactly on May 14th.

We raised kaffir corn and crooked-head maize. We harvested it with a pocket knife or heading knife. We could hand head 5 wagons loads a day. The horses were trained to "giddy-up" and "whoa" to allow for this hand work. It took around 45 days to harvest our crop.

After the first year of sod planting, the land had to be listed twice—single bottom pulled by 4 horses. We always started listing in

March and could do about 6 or 7 acres a day. After the crops were up, they had to be cultivated with a go-devil. Our go-devil was an Avery brand. There were not many weeds to speak of until about 1925, then the careless or pig weeds started to make trouble in our crops.

We bought a F-20 International Farmall tractor from Mr. Hartwell in Bovina in 1929. It was equiped with a two row lister-planter and cost $850.00. The tractor and plow continued to be used until we quit farming in 1953.

Ernest did carpenter work full time, then plowed after he came home. Sophia raised chickens and sold eggs, using the money to buy groceries and managing to have some left over. She also raised a large garden, did all our canning, and sometimes sold extras or gave it away.

This essentially takes us up to 1930.

EARLY DAY HISTORY
OF PARMER COUNTY, TEXAS
By Mrs. O.M. Jennings

In December of 1922, Mr. and Mrs. J.E.W, Jennings, a daughter Vera, a son, Finis, of the home and three married sons: C.M., E.M., and Ohpel N., with their families set out from Cone (Crosby County) to what was to be their new home in the southeastern part of Parmer County, Texas. It consisted of one raw (un-broken) section, a half section improved and one section leased. It lay ten miles, following wagon trails northeast of Muleshoe in Bailey County.

285

O.N. AND VERA JENNINGS

JENNINGS THRESHING MACHINE

Most of the country was in grass with few fences and fewer graded roads. For other than staples, Clovis, New Mexico, Amarillo or Lubbock, Texas, was our shopping centers. Land could be bought very cheaply when compared to current prices and it was also plentiful. The unbroken section cost the amazing sum of $17.50 per acre. These facts prompted our move as land was higher and hard to find in our part of Crosby County.

Irrigation was almost unknown at this time but was soon discovered which caused the price to quickly zoom to unbelievable heights in price. Forty years later some was known to have sold from $400 to a few cases of going at $800 per acre. Economy flourished in this great underground water belt of West Texas known now the world over.

The move itself would be almost as interesting as a parade of today. A hugh Avery engine chugged along pulling first a "Hugher" threshing machine followed by a long string of wagons loaded to capacity with household furniture and odds and ends of farm equipment. The mule drawn wagons piled still higher with more of the same. Tractors pulling various other pieces of farm machinery were followed by truck loads of cattle. Two nights were spent on the road, one at Olton, Texas and one in Plainview, Texas. The women and children drove through in a Ford car in one day; considering the roads, etc., this was indeed good time.

Luckily the one house on the half section was a large two story with ample sized rooms to afford accommodation, though somewhat crowded for all. This too was soon overcome. Wells were quickly drilled on each quarter section, two room temporary shacks were quickly thrown up, fences strung and the land broken out and made ready for the

abundant crops to follow.

Becoming acclimated and overcoming our loneliness were our first hardships. The first few winters were especially rough. We thought we knew the west but were quite unprepared for our first encounter with the real thing. One occasion stands out clearly today. Late one afternoon the stillness was broken by a low rumbling noise. Rushing outside we witnessed our first stampede, sandstorm, and blizzard all in one. The wind had suddenly changed to the north pushing a cloud of sand. The temperature changed to freezing just as suddenly. There were quite a few cattle on the Charlie Hinkson ranch joining us on the west. It was these plus the roar of the wind that had created the thundering sound as they plunged headlong into, over, and under the fences to the south, trampling each other and anything that chanced to get in the way. It was weeks before they were found, rounded up, and herded back home. This all done on horseback. Snow drifted over the fences in many places.

The following July 4th was also memorable. A rodeo and barbeque with its various entertainments and contests was held on the Matthiesen ranch near the UL community. Everyone for miles around attended and took part even though it was cold enough for some of the ladies to come decked out in fur coats. A few snow-flakes did fall but it was agreed that it was too cold to turn into a regular snowstorm.

There were few roads and one could travel

March 11, 1917 New jail cost $3000—1st story.

Commissioners Court Notes

286

SCENES ON THE JENNINGS HOMESTEAD

SCENES ON THE JENNINGS HOMESTEAD.

in almost any direction following the crooked wagon and dow trails. Prairie dog mounds dotted the area with rattlesnakes their co-inhabitants. We got our mail at Muleshoe which boasted one general store which also housed the post office. Soon a hardware store, an implement building, theater, filling station, cafe and hotel went up. These were mostly of locally made adobe brick managed mostly by men of Mexican decent and on main street.

People began moving in and changes came quickly. Graded roads, following mostly section (square mile) lines were built. This was done by a Mr. Head using a team of twelve of the largest mules to be found and which he drove himself hitched to an enormous grader. Quite a feat for that day, or any day, as a matter of fact. Roads helped bring about the magic development of the country.

As soon as the family got settled a Presbyterian Church was organized at the little one room school building know as "Cracker Box" (jestingly named because of its size.) Sunday School was held each Sunday with preaching by the Rev. E.W.L. Jennings as his health permitted. Ministers of various denominations filled in. The church disbanded when the building was moved.

The first year, Vera rode horseback and attended a one room one teacher school located one and a half miles south of present Lazbuddie High School. It was made into a two room; two teacher school the following year, merely by hanging a curtain down the center of the room. This was the original Star Ranch school better known as "Roaming Charlie" because of its many moves from one

community to another. This being its fourth move with one more to follow; the present Lazbuddie school. The small Jennings children walked and attended "Cracker Box" taught by Mrs. Buck Lee. It was soon moved a few hundred yards onto the Hinkson Ranch and made into a two room two teacher to accommodate the increased enrollment. This one soon consolidated and moved west being named Plainview school. Later consolidating with the Jesko school to form Midway. Midway finally joined Lazbuddie to help form the elaborate system of today.

Singing in the homes and all day singings were the popular entertainment of the day. "Cracker Box" school boasted of one of the more proficient quartets around. It consisted of T.C. Hennington, Walter Hapke, E.M. Jennings, and Walter Noble. Rev. G.O.Dean (father of the now famous Jimmy Dean) assumed Mr. Hennington's position when he moved away. Mrs. E.M. Jennings was general pianist unless she sang with the group which she often did. Mrs. O.N. Jennings was substitute pianist. People traveled for miles around to the various communities which as a general rule had a quartet of its own. The Stamps Bros. type of songs were the most popular and they were sometimes present at the singings to enliven and lend glamour and interest. Frequently there were "dinners on the ground." This was basket dinners spread together not on the ground but one long table made up of small tables placed end to end. Food was indeed plentiful and elaborate at times as all the dishes were prepared by families of the community.

C.M. and Finis still live at their original home places. E.M. is now Reverend E.M.

SCENES ON THE JENNINGS HOMESTEAD.

SCENES ON THE JENNINGS HOMESTEAD.

Jennings of the Presbyterian Church and semi-retired in Lubbock, Texas. He has held pastorates in various towns and cities of our southern states. O.N. lives at Muleshoe while farming and cattle feeding at Lazbuddie and ranching and cattle raising at DeKalb.

Few families lived in this vicinity in the early 1920's. These were the Hinkson's, Joel and Buck Lee's; Walter Hapke's; Widmires; Holzerlands; Rowdens; Henningtons; Jack Lynns; Chad Greens; Peacocks; and Smiths. After 1925 came the Collins: Kimbroughs; Wenners; and Wagnons. Still later the Jarmans; Wilsons; and Eubanks.
By: Mrs. O.M. Jennings, P.O. Box 343, Muleshoe, Texas.

Mr. James Enoch Wright Jennings and wife Margaret Virginia Nunn Jennings came to Parmer County in 1922. They bought the Smith place with a two-story house on it. Finis and Vera were still at home.

Oris Jennings and wife Effie Jacobs and their three children, Elvis, Nerine and Helen, also came in the winter of '22. Ophel and wife Ruby Davis and son, Joe Bates, came in the early 1923. Ernest and wife Gladys Ragle and three sons, R.M., Cecil and Homer Eugene also came in the Spring of '23. All came from Crosby County, Texas.

The Jennings' all settled in the "Cracker Box" community and children went to school there. Church and Sunday School were also held in this small school house. Vera rode horseback to the school which is now Lazbuddie. She later went to the Muleshoe school and stayed with Mr. and Mrs. E.R. Hart. She then went to Bethel College in McKenzie, Tennessee. She became ill there and died in a Lubbock hospital in 1926.

Ernest and Ophel brought a tractor, threshing machine, and wagons from Crosby

County cross-country which took three days. They also broke out much of the sod around the community.

Mr. T.C. Hennington, Walter Noble, Walter Hapke and Ernest Jennings made up a quartet which sang at many conventions and different social functions in the schools around.

Finis later married Alwilda Noble, who taught school at the Cracker Box School.

Ernest and family later moved away and he attended school in McKenzie, Tenn., Texas Tech and has pastored Cumberland Presbyterian Church in Texas, Tennessee, Missouri, Alabama, Arkansas. The other families stayed on the farms.

JESKO FAMILY HISTORY

In the early 1880's a family of Polish immigrants, Michael and Hedwig Jesko, arrived in New York seeking freedom for themselves and two of their three children. (They had to leave the oldest daughter in the old country with relatives for lack of money to bring her with them. They sent for her in a couple of years.)

They kept pushing westward until, at last, they found a place and settled in a factory town, which was Michigan City, Indiana.

By all working and saving they had enough to buy some land, all in timber. As the land was cleared of the timber, the ground would be prepared for cultivation.

One of these two teenagers of the family was Steve Jesko. He worked for different farmers in the communities and there he met Martha Dreyer, a young girl that arrived with her parents from Germany about the same time as the Jesko's did. They lived around Michigan City a couple of years after they

288

JESKO FAMILY, 1911.

THE JESKO CLAN

married. Then Dad and Mother and small daughter Anna (now deceased, 1961) moved to Chicago, where Dad worked in a meat packing plant for several years. While living in Chicago there were three sons born, Matt, Joe, and Harry (deceased 1950).

When Harry was small, Dad and Mother decided a farm would be a much better place for the children to grow up on. They acquired about 100 acres of timber land not too far from his parents. They cleared a few acres and built a home and a barn. As years went on the family added two more boys, Alex (deceased, 1966) and Ed; three girls, Cecelia (deceased 1965), Gertrude and Elizabeth.

In 1907 Dad heard of inexpensive land in Texas. A land agent visited around in Indiana, and several men became interested in the new development. The land was described and advertised as good and level land, and what the agents showed the prospectors was that type of land.

Dad was the only one with nerve to make the move. He came out and looked at the land, and liked it very much. He dreamed of the future, with his growing sons, of having easier life than cutting, sawing, and hauling timber in all kinds of weather. But early life, even in Texas, was by no means easy. There were many hardships and disappointments. Cold weather, bad winters, when it was almost impossible to get to town for bare necessities and supplies, and years when crops were almost failures.

In March of 1908, Dad Jesko loaded a family car, the railroad furnished with what it would hold of the family's belongings. It was called an immigrant car. It contained four mules, two horses, one cow, one calf, one sow, one dog, a wagon, a surrey, and household furniture, besides feed for the livestock

MAT JESKO 3rd—Harry Jesko 5th

enroute. Some extra hay was stacked in one end of the car, where Matt, Joe, Alex, and Ed were stowed away. Mother, the girls and Harry came later, in May, by passenger train. It took four days then to make the trip by rail.

When Dad and the boys arrived in Friona, there were the agents to take them to their new home. A Mr. Saxcine was the overseer of several cars that took the land agents and prospectors out to look over the land. Dad had paid down on a half section of level land northwest of Friona. It was close to the old landmark, now known as Finley. When the agents showed this place to Dad and it sloped badly toward the draw, Dad refused it. So the agents put Dad on another place and there they put up a tent and staked their livestock. Soon they found out it had already been sold. They made another move about six miles south of Finley; there no water was to be found. Another move put them fourteen miles south of Friona. As there were no improvements on the place, the family lived in a house some five or six miles east, called the Four Mile. It was one of the ranch houses belonging to Star Ranch. They lived there for a

ED AND ALEX JESKO—Celia and Gertrude Jesko on their first "school bus."

MAT JESKO driving army mules.

JESKOS THRESHING, 1924.

few months until their home was finished enough to move in.

They built a two story house about 30 x 34 feet. Later porches, bath, and kitchen were added. The lumber was hauled from Friona, taking more than a day for round trip. (Traveling in these days were on open pasture trails.) Late one evening while coming through the Running Water Draw with a load of lumber, an animal much larger than a dog was walking down a cattle trail not too far from where they were. The noises of the wagon and lumber did not seem to affect the pace of this creature. Later, they heard several people at Friona and Bovina talking of a Lobo Wolf being seen around out in the Draw.

When living at Finley there were three herds of wild horses that would molest and bother the tame horses. They finally became so brave as to come close to the tent where our animals were staked. Some of the wild horses were shot at before they would leave the farm stock alone. There were many herds of antelope also. The farming was slow going as the sod was dry and hard. We would plow as long as there was enough moisture, then plant the seed. We managed enough feed to carry the livestock through the first winter. The sow that was brought along farrowed 13 of the prettiest pigs we ever had; the night the freight car was unloaded at Friona. The first job was to build her a pen which was made of some bales of alfalfa that were brought along for stock feed. All 13 of these pigs were raised, and they provided meat for the family. Other litters meant a little cash along too.

The first crops were maize, corn, and kaffir corn, wheat, and oats. Oats was a short season crop, and made wonderful feed for mules and horses.

Mother also planted a garden from seed she had brought from Indiana. She almost always managed to raise enough for the family to live through the year. Most fruits then were bought dried, as apples, peaches, prunes, raisins, and apricots. Mother had small fruits, known as ground cherries and wonder berries, in her garden. These and vegetables were canned during the summer months.

Two more children were born after moving to Texas. A girl, Helen; and a son, Steve (deceased 1966).

The first school was built about one mile north of what is now Clay's Corner. A family by the name of Presgrove lived on the present Robert Kimbrought place. The three Presgrove children and four Jesko children were the only ones in school at that time. In a year or two the Presgroves moved, leaving only the Jesko's. Miss Lucy Goodwine and Miss Ruth Essex taught school in one of the upstairs rooms of the Jesko home for several years. As more settlers began to move in, the

JOE JESKO on wagon, W. Nobles heading machine.

school was moved two miles north of its first location and made a permanent structure; naming it "The Jesko School." Some of the first families: Wiley Simmons; Mr. (Smitty) Smith, and his sisters, Misses Lula and Carrie; Revens; Bill Johnsons; W.J. Coffmans; John Crim; W.S. Memefee; and others.

In 1928 a four room brick building was built for Jesko School. Church and Sunday School services were held almost every Sunday; different denominations alternating services. On Valentine's Sunday, 1937, it burned. The fall of 1937 the two school districts of Jesko and Plainview were consolidated and formed Midway School. We had many pleasant meetings as church, Sunday School, PTA, and community meetings continues. In 1948, Midway consolidated with Lazbuddie which is now one of the four leading communities of Parmer County.

Dad Jesko passed away in 1925; Mother, 1945.

By Joe and Ida Jesko

History of Early Days
In Parmer County, Texas
By Susie Jesko

Born in Youkton, South Dakota, December 24, 1895—Moved to Texas December, 1908.

My father, Peter Kaiser, came down on an excursion trip with George G. Wright Company and bought land out near the old Star Ranch South of Friona, Texas. It is now called Lazbuddie Community.

We were one of many pioneers who settled on ranch land after the large cattle raisers sold their ranches and it was divided into acreage for farms.

There were very few neighbors when we moved one and one-half miles southeast of the Old Star Ranch. My father came down in the freight train with a few head of cows, two horses, some furniture, etc.; while Mother brought the family of kids down. We arrived ahead of Dad in Friona one night after dark. The wind was blowing at a high gait, and we were taken to possibly the only rooming house in town: The Wentworth's Room House. We were all tired from the trip and worst of all, we were all sick; every one of us. We had to stay there over a week before Dad arrived. The wind blew for two weeks—day and night—and never let up. We were so disgusted we were all ready to go back by the time Dad arrived.

He set up a small shack on the farm we were to make our home. There we spent our first Christmas. We had many dust storms in those days and our little shack was by no means built for winter weather. We slept on the bare floor all in a row. We learned to eat red beans and salt pork which were both filling and the cheapest thing we could buy. No one of the family would ever ask what we were having for dinner today, because it was always beans.

Dad hired two men—John Badey and Charlie Gibson—to drill our well. That took several days and we had to feed and bed those two men. They were two jolly men and had lots of fun with our set up and us kids. One night it snowed and the snow came in through the cracks of the walls and on top of the shack. The next morning they had to go on top of the roof and sweep the snow off or we probably would have drowned. One of the men kept saying: "Snow in Panhandle, but this morning it is Pan with out a handle." We really had tough going. Next we built a grainery. It was two rooms and had a wall through the middle; one side was the kitchen with a little cellar under the floor. It was about four feet square, just about big enough for a hundred pound sack of potatoes to set in.

We toughed it out till spring when we got fences built and a garden started and things

September 17, 1917 $25,000 borrowed til taxes come in.

Commissioners Court Notes

began to look brighter. Our only way of getting around was a covered wagon. We went to Friona or Bovina once every two weeks for groceries. It was about as far to one as it was the other—twenty-five to thirty miles—and it would take all day to go and get back by night. I remember one time I went to Bovina with Dad and coming back we got lost after dark. There were no roads and we cut across the country. We finally came to a fence and followed it for several miles till we came to our gate.

Our neighbors were few. Bill Reeds lived on the Star Ranch. The other neighbors were Joe Pauls; Steve Jeskos; Otto Trieders. After a few years a family by the name of Brooks moved a few miles north of the Star Ranch, the Presgroves settled west of the Ranch, and we could see people settling down here and there. We saw many covered wagons traveling across the country. More and more people moved in as years passed.

A trail we used to take going to Friona went by the "Four-Mile House" where the Jesko's lived. Usually some of the Jesko's went with us to town. I can well remember when I saw Harry Jesko for the first time. A little barefoot boy whom I married in 1919. At that time he was about ten years old . He was following one of his older brothers home from the field as we were coming back from Friona. Barefoot and walking behind, every few steps he took he would stop and pick the sandburrs out of first one foot and then the other; finally he stopped and sat down to pick them from both feet. You can guess he not only had them in his feet; he was also needing help elsewhere.

One Fourth of July there was a big celebration in Friona. I remember all of the neighbors met at the Star Ranch. There they all filled a wagon drawn by four horses and went to the celebration. Will Reed was our driver and everyone sang, joked, and were happy on the way having lots of fun. We stayed till a late hour that night, then departed for home. Everything went fine till we got out a few miles and it began to rain. It came down in buckets full. We all huddled close under several umbrellas. That worked fine for some while some of us had the rain coming down the umbrella in our laps. We were all soaked before we got home. During all this rain, Will

Reed was yodelling and singing away.

In the fall the neighbors would get together and go to the Sandhills to pick plums. We would take plenty of food and stay several days picking plums. Frank Reed was our cook for one day and when meal time came around, he served us a dish he called "Lick-ah-ma-goods." He had mixed tomatoes, corn, hominy and—all in one kettle. It was a very good name for it and it was good; at least we had to like it as it was all he had prepared for dinner.

Another pioneer discovery was: We found that dry cow chips made a good fire and from then on we burned cow chips instead of coal. For several years we would gather wagon loads of them to burn in our big range cook stove. There were no gas stoves, no electricity in those days. We used oil lamps and wood burning stoves.

My mother baked bread all the time, and once in a while she would make cookies, which was really a treat. My brother, Theodore, once said, "Why doesn't Mother bake us a tub full of them while she is at it?" Pioneering was tough, but I believe we were as happy in those days as we are now.

After a few years, the settlers decided to consolidate the districts and moved the school house where all the children could go to one school; they moved the school north across the draw to what was known as Red Tower. We attended school there several years, then it was moved again to about two miles west of the Star Ranch. Walking was the main transportation of getting to school.

After I got out of school I went to Wichita, Kansas, to work. I got a job in a tailor shop. My sisters, Thresa and Marie lived there. After several months, Harry Jesko came up and went to work in a broomcorn factory. After we married (1919), we moved to Laverne, Oklahoma and farmed for a few years. In 1925 we moved to Garden City, Kansas and farmed. Ruth Ann was born in July, 1926. In 1929, we moved back to Texas, returning to the home place. My folks moved to Corpus

Sept. 10, 1917 A.L. Ralls allowed $50.00 for Parmer exhibit at International Soil Show—Peoria, Illinois.

Commissioners Court Notes

Christi, Texas. We farmed and raised sheep. In 1931, Raymond was born.

Rain was scarce and it was dry and windy. There were lots of thistles and the winds blew them across the country; sometimes piling them high over the fences. The sand would blow day and night for weeks at a time.

I remember one dust storm that scared us all out of our wits: It came from the North, March, 1935. A crowd was gathered at Ed Jesko's place when we saw it come boiling in. We all took for our homes, driving like mad to beat the storm. We got to Lazbuddie and knowing where there was a dug-out, we headed for it. The storm was approaching fast. We just made it to the Nelson McCurdy refuge in time. The dugout was full of scared neighbors: some were praying, some were crying, and some were so scared they couldn't talk. We all thought the end had come. In a few minutes, the storm had hit, it got pitch dark. In less than an hour it was clear and was daylight again. We all came out to see what had happened. All was still as a mouse and much colder. The air was light, and full of electricity. It took us quite awhile to get our cars started. When we got home, we found all the tops blown off our feed stacks. Our herd of sheep had been fed with the bundles of feed that had been blown everywhere.

After a few years we traded the home place for some raw land north of Muleshoe, Texas, in the community of Midway. The trade was made with Pop Mansfield. There we built grainaries, brick home, and farmed and raised white face cattle. Wheat and maize were our main crops—funny thing, we didn't know cotton would grow that far north.

In 1947 we sold the farm to D.L. Morrison and moved to Farwell, Texas where we bought an old house on Second Street from a Mr. Nobles. We remodeled it and fixed it

Jan. 1, 1917 25c poll tax—21 to 60 years old, not included were Indians, insane, blind, deaf and dumb or those who have lost one foot or one hand.

Commissioners Court Notes

nicely. In the fall of 1950 we were involved in an auto accident on the Oklahoma Lane road. We both were seriously injured and Harry died of his injuries. A few years later, I sold my home on Second Street to Mim Sprowls and built a home on First Street. I now live in Clovis, New Mexico, and Mose Glasscock lives in the home on First Street in Farwell, Texas.

I spent most of my life in Texas and I think that even though we saw many hard times in pioneering this part of the country, Texas still can't be beat. You can't wish for anything that you can't find in Texas.
In Texas:
One can Seymour (see more) and
One can Seagraves (see graves)
Take a bath in Sweetwater and
Eat in Plainview.
Where else can you do this?

FRED ELDON KEPLEY
By Bonnie Jean Paine

Land fever has been a common malady of men since time began, but it hit my dad, Fred Eldon Kepley, in 1919. He first went to the Fort Sumner, New Mexico area that year, but a blue norther blew in the night he got there and cooled his fever. He decided to go on home to Byers, Texas, via Farwell, where his brother-in-law, Dr. Gerard A. Foote lived.

Dr. Foote showed Daddy around the Farwell area, and he made a good guide, since he had had his office above the Faville Drug Store in Texico, New Mexico since 1917 and knew the area well from his numerous house calls. Daddy didn't come to the Oklahoma Lane community without knowing the disadvantages of this country because Dr. Foote illustrated this point about the varying weather by telling him of the hot, blistering sun in summer and about the time he almost lost his life trying to reach a sick patient during the flu epidemic when his car stalled in a snow drift. Dr. Foote had to make a house call to Bovina to see Press Abbott, so Daddy accompanied him and they came back by the way of the Oklahoma Lane community. It was in this community that Daddy decided to settle.

Daddy went back to Byers, Texas, sold his home and moved by train with his wife and daughter, Ora. Mother (Flora Foote Kepley) had doubts about moving, because at that time this area was called "The Great American Desert" by historians. Two lines from a partly remembered song kept running through her mind as they traveled: ". . . Out on the desert, hot and dry . . ." Mother must have really had the pioneering spirit though because the land Daddy bought had just four things on it besides the native grass . . . the four iron pipes marking the boundries. They went to work though and put up a 12' x 14' tent and they lived in it until they could get a well drilled and a house built. They got a deep, pure, water well drilled, but the first building they constructed was a four foot square out-house. This building still stands along with a house built in 1920. I (Bonnie Jean Paine), was born in this house. Daddy built a new house in 1926 and converted the two room house into a dairy barn.

Hard work with little pay was still ahead. The land was virgin soil, so Rupert Paul, of the Texico-Farwell area, brought his Hartpar tractor and slowly turned the grassland into a farm. Daddy says the only way he could have stayed those first few years was by the "cow-sow-hen" route, meaning that he had his own meat, eggs, milk and a garden when money was short. Money was short many times because the depression hit just nine years after the big move. Sudan seed was $1.00 per cwt., milo was 22 cents per cwt., wheat, 25 cents per bushel and good corn went for $4.00 a ton. Hogs were 5 cents a pound and eggs were 10 cents a dozen. In the poor price years, Daddy used corn to heat with instead of coal, because coal was $8.00 per ton. My sister, Gloria (now Mrs. J.W. Herington of West Camp), was born during the later depression years.

Daddy planted thirty-five dry land crops and never failed to harvest one, but some were pretty short. One year the boll worms hit the cotton crop and something had to be done, so a spray rig was built on a wagon and the entire crop was sprayed by mixing the spray in a barrel and using man power to pump it into the nozzles. They had to get up about four o'clock before the wind came up and spray after night after the wind died down. The cotton was also pulled by hand and the boys that pulled the cotton stayed at our house. One year we had four boys staying in the house and a man and his wife in a little room out back and a large family in a house in the pasture. That year (about 1928) it rained seventeen days straight and Mother had to cook for her family and the four extra boys and part of the time for the man and his wife. The day it got pretty enough to pull cotton part of the boys left and didn't even pay board.

Hog killing time was always a time for several neighbors to get together. Daddy always killed one hog for each member of the family and one for the hired hand. He always seemed to choose the coldest day in the fall to do this. He cooled the meat out good, sugar cured it and hung it in the "meat room," as the little room over the cellar was called. The parts of the hog that would not keep were always eaten before we were allowed to cut into the cured meat.

Mother always planted a big garden and Daddy set out orchards on both sides of the house, so we always had plenty of fruits and vegetables to can. Mother put up a thousand quarts of various fruits and vegetables one year. During the depression years we had our own wheat and corn ground into flour and corn meal. Lots of food was needed though because it was ten miles to Farwell and ten miles to Bovina and trips to town weren't made too often. There were usually extra people to cook for. At threshing time there were fifteen to eighteen men to cook for.

Ora, now Mrs. Charles Smith, of Clovis, New Mexico, went to Sunnyside school which was a one room school before it was consolidated with two other schools. The late P.A. Lee and Nelson C. Smith, Willie May Vogarty and Erma White were teachers in this school.

I am now Mrs. Turner Paine and I graduated from Oklahoma Lane after the new gym was built. Oklahoma Lane then had eleven grades.

Feb. 9, 1915 Office of sheep inspector discontinued.

Commissioners Court Notes

My sister, Gloria, started to school at Oklahoma Lane but soon moved to Farwell when Farwell, West Camp and Oklahoma Lane consolidated.

Daddy served on the school board off and on through the years and was a charter member and director of the Federal Land Bank and was instrumental in organizing the Production Credit Association. He also helped get electricity to the Oklahoma Lane community.

Daddy says he is a Hoosier by birth, 67 years a Texan by choice and 54 years in Parmer County on the same farm, —Parmer County, the best county in the state of Texas.

MR. AND MRS. R.H. KINSLEY

R.H. Kinsley was an early day (1909) Friona merchant, who contributed much to development of the surrounding trade territory.

Kinsley operated the first water well drilling service in combination with a hardware store. He came to Friona as a young man from Upper Sandusky, Ohio.

A few years after his marriage to Miss Pearl Stuckey of the same city, Kinsley came to Friona on an excursion train with his father-in-law, G. Stuckey, who had a similar business in Ohio.

Both men were favorably impressed with the opportunities offered by this section of the country and decided to pioneer here. In February of 1909, Kinsley came to Friona and helped start the business here.

His wife came down in April of the same year and the couple rented a house located in the south part of town. Later they moved into the two story house located in the first block north of the First Baptist Church.

The first few years the Kinsleys were in business here their merchandise consisted mostly of windmill repairs, hardware items and furniture. Later after motor cars became more popular, they added gasoline pumps in front of the store and were in the filling station business.

They moved to a house on Woodland and this was their home until their death.

Mrs. Kinsley served as bookkeeper, clerk, and during times of help shortages, filling

OUT FOR A SPIN WITH THE KINSLEYS.

station attendant. She related that from the very first she was impressed with the friendliness of residents of the city and had a desire to be a part of a growing community.

Before Mr. Kinsley's death in 1939, he purchased three other tracts of land. A quarter section of land which was purchased by Mr. Stuckey in 1909 was later bought by Mr. and Mrs. Kinsley.

Mrs. Kinsley was a charter member of the Friona Woman's Club which was organized in October, 1909. She was also a long time member of the Union Congregational Church and the Eastern Star Lodge.

Mr. and Mrs. Kinsley have contributed much to the town they chose to help build. Land was donated to the Girl Scouts for a Girl Scout permanent home.

Copied from **The Friona Star.**

J.L. LANDRUM FAMILY
SOME OLDEN DAY HAPPENINGS

The family of J.L. Landrum of Floydada, Texas came to Parmer County and Friona in about June of 1925. My father first came to Bovina in the summer of 1924, where he bought grain and loaded it in boxcars to be shipped by rail to terminals.

Mr. F.S. Truitt, also of Floydada, Texas and my father who was a carpenter and contractor, decided to go into the lumber and building business in Friona. They did this in

September 21, 1917 Citizens clamor for Cannon Ball Stock.

Commissioners Court Notes

THE TALLEST girl in the picture is Ella Marie Scarbrough. Next to her is Joyce Braidfoot, Ray Landrum is holding Joel, George and Dorothy Chesnut.

the early part of 1925.

Our first home was about four miles east of town. The unpaved highway was on the south side of the railroad at this time.

We lived there for a few months before moving to town and into an adobe warehouse near the stockyards, where we lived for about two months, until my dad could build us a house. He was so busy building for others that our house had to wait.

Our first real home in Friona was a house on Main Street across from the park. Our next home was across the street north of the present post office.

There were six of us children. I am the eldest of the group, then my sister, Marie, now Mrs. Vernon Scarbrough, living in Monenci, Arizona; then my sister, Dorothy, now Mrs. Henry Chesnut living in Huron, California; my sister, Joyce, now Mrs. Joyce Braidfott, living in Clovis, New Mexico; also my brother, Joel, living in Albuquerque, New Mexico.

I took saxophone lessons and began playing in the school orchestra while still in grade school. One of the main entertainments in those days was the picture show in the old red school house auditorium on Saturday nights. They had one picture projector and the show was on ten minute reels, each show consisting of eight or ten reels. So a few minutes' time elapsed between each reel. The orchestra members got to see the show free for playing a number between each reel. Needless to say the orchestra was usually there on time and in full force.

After getting into high school, a few of us in the orchestra met in the "Dutch" Hanson home and played popular tunes of the times. We were good enough that we were asked to play for a few dances. "Dutch" Hanson was postmaster at this time. One time Mr. Hanson asked me to just play the notes and not the fly specks too.

Along about the time I was a senior in high school, I took a train trip to Hagerman, N.M. On the way home I saw some "English Oval" cigarettes for sale on the train. I bought a package and after I had been home a few days, I was at "Fat" Hughes' barber shop and decided I would be real big and impress my friends by smoking one of these fancy cigarettes. About the time I got it fired up, my dad walked past the barbershop. He turned around and came in not saying a word. Just took me by the arm and led me home, where he gave me considerable chastisement with a razor strap. That dulled my smoking pleasure for some time.

I worked for Mr. F.N. Welch for seven wheat harvests straight beginning in about 1926, I think. Wheat was the principal crop for most everyone then.

During the depression years when wheat dropped to as low as 15c per bushel, my dad and Mr. Truitt built a large grainary south of the school property. They bought wheat from people who owed them for lunches at a dollar per bushel against their debts. They filled the grainary and held the wheat until it was worth a dollar again.

My dad built most of the older buildings on main street now. Among the last buildings he built was the school building next to the highway, which is now the Junior High School.

My dad was the mayor when the city put in its first water system. Prior to that time, "Uncle Andy" Wentworth had piped water to a lot of the town from his home well and large water storage tank. This was about 1928. A lot of the residents had their own windmills pumping into a barrel. No running water in the house—you just ran to the barrel and carried a bucket of water to the house. Most houses then had outside toilets.

On Halloween nights, a number of the toilets were mysteriously overturned. Quite a number of strange things occurred on Halloween nights. One time I remember that the bank had repossessed a real large steel-wheeled tractor. Its rear wheels were at least six feet high. For several years it had been parked about two blocks north of the bank at that time. Anyhow a bunch of the boys decided that if the tractor belonged to the bank, it should be parked in front of the bank. About fifty boys got together and after much energy was expended, the tractor was left in front of the bank. The bank at that time in the building at 5th and Main. I heard also of someone's milk cow being left on the stage of the school auditorium one Halloween night. The auditorium was on the second floor, too.

I imagine Friona's population in 1925 was about four or five hundred. The highway was on the south side of the railroad and many of the businesses were located along the highway. Among them were the Friona Consumers, Sylvester's Blacksmith Shop, a tourist court, a service station or two and a grain elevator, probably Friona Wheat Growers. Hix Oil Co. had a nice building which had a cafe as well as a "roof Garden" where dances were held during summer months. Sometimes roller skaters used the floor.

The elevators did not handle grain as fast then as they do now. During harvest time, trucks were often lined up two abreast for several blocks both north and south of the elevators.

My dad and Frank Truitt's dad would put a grain bed on the lumber yard truck during harvest season and Frank and I would haul wheat. Our dads furnished the truck and expenses and gave Frank and I one-half of what we made. A day or two Frank and I made as much as $25.00 per day each. Hauling was a cent a mile per bushel. Each time that we got to town with a load we would stop at F.L. Spring's store or at J.J. Crawford's store and have a bottle of pop. The pop was two for 15c. One time we would charge the pop to my Dad. Next trip we would charge it to Frank's dad. Anyway at the end of harvest when my dad paid the bills at Spring's and Crawford's he noticed all this pop on the grocery bills. We added the pop only and it came to over $15.00. That was another time I was reprimanded severely. He said that besides the money it cost it would surely damage the insides of a person.

In those days the Frio draw would go on a rampage once or twice a year, flooding the businesses along the highway. Usually the water would get as much as a foot or two over the rail crossing and the ground was lower along the highway. A dike or levee was finally put up to keep the water in the draw as it traversed the area.

I think it was in 1937-38 at a time the draw was up, that a passenger train headed west, was stalled by empty floating oil drums from the Texaco Agency near the depot. Some of these drums were rolled into balls of metal by the train's wheels. The train had to wait until the water went down so the crushed barrels could be removed. Charlie Bainum took his motor boat and got the engineer from the engine and took him to the depot.

Sometimes the draw would be up when it was dry here, but had rained in New Mexico.

Mr. Floyd Reeve owned the school busses when we came here. He bought some International truck chassis and my dad built the bus bodies. The buses were heated by running the exhaust pipes along the floor and out the rear end. (Energy saving even then.) The busses were mostly driven by high school boys.

The first electricity for the city was provided by a power plant located where the present city offices are now. The power plant consisted of a huge three cylinder diesel engine and generator. The exhaust pipe was about a foot in diameter, and could be heard without difficulty over most of the town. The plant ran fairly well in the daytime but conked out frequently at night. Most people had lights only not many electrical appliances then. Just a bare bulb hanging in the center of the room. No wall plugs or wall switches. I think I was probably the first and

September 28, 1917 Cannon Ball Capitol— Ten Million $

Commissioners Court Notes

297

possibly only boat builder in Friona. One spring Sunday in 1932 we had eight inches of rain. All the lakes were full, no one had a boat. The drug store was a kind of social gathering place then and was owned by J.R. Roden. J.R. and Dr. R.R. Wills got to talking about how we should have a boat. I worked at the drug store. Since my dad was in the lumber business, I volunteered to build the boat. Five men agreed to furnish the finances. We decided to power the boat with a Model T Ford engine, which we bought from Mr. Claridge Fallwell. The motor cost us $5.00 and ran real well.

It took about a month to build the 16-foot boat. Daily I was instructed by everyone as to how to properly build a boat. Some of my advisors said that the weight of the motor alone would sink the boat. There was a fellow named Holbert Wells who was around the drug store a lot on weekends. His favorite expression was "Oh, Helen!" That was the name we chose for the boat. The name was painted on by our local sign man, a fellow by the name of Michel. The night before our official launching, someone painted out a part of our name, a part of the E and all of the N.

The launching was quite embarrassing. We loaded the boat on a truck and went out to the Reeve Lake at the Northwest corner of town. It took all the men who could get around the boat to lift it. When we got it in the water, half of the propellor was above the water. One of my principal advisors told me not to put the propellor shaft through the floor of the boat as it would be harder to make waterproof and that besides it would sink so low it would be under water anyway. Anyhow, the boat traveled fine with only half of the propellor under the boat this time and about a week later on another Sunday had our second launching of the boat. What was so embarrassing about our first launching was that practically everyone in town came to see. Most everyone had a good laugh at least.

The boat cost a total of $62.50 not counting my labor, which would have been real expensive, what with my being a boat building authority and all.

My mother and father celebrated their 50th anniversary in December of 1961. My father passed away in July of 1964 at their home in Tucumcari, N.M. Mother is living at Retirement Ranch in Clovis.

Written by Ray Landrum

O.F. LANGE

When O.F. Lange first saw Friona, he was just a little disheartened and didn't think he would stay, but it only took thirty days for him to decide that it was the "best city, and the best people" and he has made his home here ever since.

It was on June 7, 1919 that Lange hit town. He had only been out of the Army for two weeks. He had most recently been stationed in San Antonio. His original home was Llano, Texas. Since his father was a lumberman, he grew up in the lumber business. He knew the senior Mr. Rockwell, who owned Rockwell Bros. Lumber Co. in Friona. Mr. Rockwell asked Lange if he would like to have a lumber yard—Lange said "yes" and his career in Friona began.

The Friona lumber business was opened January 1, 1907 and is still under the same ownership. James M. Rockwell, the original owner is now deceased and the business is owned by two sons, James and Henry.

Lange says when he first came to Friona, the average house probably cost about $1000 and a person could build a "really nice" home for $3000. At that time, cattle raising was the principal industry and most of his business was in the form of materials for barns, fences, feed troughs and things needed around the farm. He feels that merchants have progressed with the times. People build nicer homes now, and there are so many more things to include in a home today. Back then, he recalls, a house was just so many rooms and most of them contained very few, if any, closets.

But he says, laughingly, people just didn't have as many clothes and other belongings then as they do now.

Almost a one-man Chamber of Commerce for Friona, Lange says about 380 people lived in Friona when he arrived here. But he notes that there has always been a gradual growth, and as far as he knows, no set-backs or decline in population.

After Lange accepted the job in Friona, he tried to find his home-to-be on the map. It wasn't there. But he bought his ticket on the train and was on his way. When the porter yelled "Friona," he looked and didn't see much. "Which side of the tracks is town on," he asked the porter. "Just don't make no difference," the man answered.

His first years, the young men in town found various ways to entertain themselves. They played baseball, pitched washers and played dominoes and cards.

He met his wife, Rose Conway, at Black and they were married in 1924 in Clovis. Since that time, they have made their home in Friona.

LAWRENCE LILLARDS

With a sense of humor, a remarkable memory for the past, and a love of living, Mr. and Mrs. Lawrence Lillard of Friona, who are truly pioneers of the area, watch with interest as "their town" thrives and grows. And they have seen the changes that have been wrought in most of the 50 years the town has been established.

Mr. Lillard arrived in Friona in 1907, and his wife came to the prairie town in 1909. Her original home was Ashland County, Ohio; and her husband was a native of Ray County, Mo. Both landed in Friona because their families purchased land in the highly advertised "land of opportunity."

Mr. Lillard was 19 years old when he first set eyes on the community that would be his home for the years to come. His family had sent all their belongings by rail, and they came through the country by passenger train. The family included the mother and father and Lawrence and his brother, Claud. Claud is now deceased. Another brother was born in Friona.

The Lillards lived in the place that is now known as the Elzie Jennings place, and they operated a mercantile store.

Mrs. Lillard's family, the Maurers, had a similar story. The father purchased land in Friona and came to Parmer County in 1908.

C.L. LILLARD, Carrie, Virginia, and Frank.

He built a house on the farm and his family joined him in 1909. Mrs. Lillard still owns the beautiful corner china closet that her mother brought along on the trip to their new home. She also has several chairs and a love seat that belonged to her mother.

Original plans for the Maurers were to stay five years and return to their first home. They went back for visits, but they never wanted to remain for long, she says. She was also 19 years old when she first saw Friona.

After her arrival, Mrs. Lillard made an important trip to Farwell, to take the examination to enable her to teach school in Texas. She had to study Texas school laws and Texas history before she was eligible. Then she began her teaching career with 14 students at Buckeye School, north of Friona. Of her pupils, two of the students still live in Friona—her brother, Carl Maurer and E.E. Taylor, a retired farmer.

Their ride to school each day was quite an event for Mrs. Lillard and Carl. They lived about 1½ miles from the school and transportation was a burro and two-wheel cart. They had what was known as a "persuader stick" which was a long stick with a tack on the end of it. When the burro stalled, one of the Maurers used the persuader on the animal, while the other held the reins.

After teaching at Buckeye two years, Mrs. Lillard taught school at Summerfield for two years, then was the teacher at Buckeye for another year. When she was at Summerfield, it took her about 2½ hours to get to town, so

October 26, 1917 Westward the Star of Empire—addv.

Commissioners Court Notes

EDITH AND LAWRENCE LILLARD, horseback.

LAWRENCE AND EDITH LILLARD on the Self Rouch Farm wheat crop of 1914.

EDITH MAURER between her parents, George and Belle Maurer.

she passed the time crocheting.

One day, she was so busy with her handwork, she noticed too late that her horse had walked into a mud bog. The animal stalled and she had to take off her shoes and wade out of the bog.

She says the little Buckeye school house was a comfortable little building and was heated by a coal stove. "I was also the janitor" she states, and Carl helped her get the fire going and the school room ready for classwork. Her salary at Buckeye was $40 a month. At that time, school was held only six months out of the year because of insufficient funds.

Asked how they became acquainted, the Lillards explained that the Maurer family stayed at the Lillard home after their arrival in Friona, for about a week. They were waiting for their train car of household goods to arrive.

In their courtin' days, young people around Friona found companionship to be wonderful. They got together for parties, met at various houses for Sunday meals together, and the most enjoyable entertainment of all, was a trip to the breaks. They recall one trip when they traveled in covered wagons and took enormous amounts of food, to last a week. A large group of young people made the trip, with chaperones going along with them.

After their marriage, the Lillards lived on a farm, where the Friona airport is now located. They were married at the home of the Congregational minister, then drove to Hereford via horse and buggy for a 23-hour honeymoon. On their way home, they stopped at a vegetable grower's place and bought enough plants to start their first garden. "We came back and went to work and have been working ever since" quips Lillard. They stayed on that particular farm for five years.

Mrs. Lillard recalls that her wedding dress was a blue basketweave suit, with a hobble skirt.

The newly-married couple purchased their furniture from E.B. Black for about $150 or $160 and set up housekeeping. They had a stove already and new purchases included a rocking chair, 4 dining chairs to go with their home-made table, a sewing machine, a rug and a fancy brass bed. They couldn't recall if other furniture was included.

Mrs. Lillard later owned one of the first washing machines with a motor, in the area.

Later the Lillards moved to her family's home place 7½ miles north of Friona. They lived there from 1918 to 1944, when they moved into their present home in town. Previous to settling down for their present routine, they took a three month tour of Mexico, which is a highlight of their lives.

HAROLD M. LILLARD on Iron Wheel Tricycle.

LAWRENCE LILLARD and friend at 5th and Summitt in 1908.

LAWRENCE AND EDITH LILLARD—1914.

They pretty well saw the country, from one end to the other. Then they "came home and went to work," he adds.

The Lillards are looking forward to the 50th anniversary celebration of Friona, and are hoping many of the old-timers and their friends of the early years can attend. It is nothing unusual for one of the early settlers to stop by and see the couple, when they pass through Friona.

The Lillards have a son, Harold, who is married and has three children—Jim Carl, Nan and Miles.

EDITH LILLARD'S STORY OF THEIR COMING TO TEXAS
Taken from tape recorder
Jan. 31, 1970.

We came to Texas in 1909. My father had contacted George G. Wright, Land Agent of Chicago a couple of years before that time. They had agents in all the North Central States and these agents kept coming and distributing their literature, telling it was the land of plenty, land of honey, where everything would grow. They thought that would be the place for them to come.

We read all the literature and decided my Father should make a trip to Texas and look the situation over and see if they should buy some land. I don't know if he bought the land

Nov. 16, 1917 The Cannon Ball is Gliding—addv.

Commissioners Court Notes

at that time. Of course he came down and was contacted by Agents down here, and the boys were there with their automobiles to take them out to see the land, when they arrived at the station at Friona. They were met by all the different Agents in their cars.

Mary Dorcas: Was it a train load of prospectors?

Yes, it was a whole train load of prospectors. These Agents would go out to their cars and each Agent would take a load of his prospectors out to look at the land. Well, they traveled pretty fast; didn't give them much of a chance to look at the foliage to see how dry it was or how far they went. Sometimes they went 20 miles and you would think it five or ten miles to the place where they stopped; they fooled them in this respect.

They would say "We are out in the region of Finley." Several people, Mr. Goodwine, Mr. Guyer and Mr. Jesko bought land around Finley, but they could not get water; so they had to move to other places on the Plains. Because they could not get water, the land company did move them.

MRS. EDITH LILLARD and Carl Maurer, her younger brother, enroute to Buckeye school.

Mary Dorcas: Where they had dry wells, were they out the cost of the wells?

Clyde: Yes, Dad was. He had dug three dry holes.

My Father bought a half section of land at that time; it was selling at $20.00 to $21.00 per acre, but closer in it was a little higher.

Clyde: Dad paid $18.00 per acre for land that was out farther, but he could have bought land cheaper.

In 1908 my Father came down and improved the land he had bought, which was seven and a half miles northwest of Friona.

Lucille: How was it you met Uncle Lawerence?

He put down a well, built a story and a half house, barn and sheds. Then in the spring of 1909 we came down with the idea that we would stay five years. When he returned to Ohio he loaded an emigrant car with three or four hogs to butcher, baby chicks, two fine Durham milk cows, farm machinery and some household goods. We came on the George C. Wright, Special. Then my father came with the emigrant car about a week later.

My father had made arrangements for us to stay with the John Lillard family until he arrived with the car.

Lucille: And they had a young man who took a fancy to Aunt Edith?

Well, I don't know how much of a fancy, but he was nice to me and took me around and introduced me to Miss Roxie Witherspoon, who later became Mrs. Fertch, also Floy Knode, who later became Mrs. T.J. Crawford, who were both teachers in the school. We moved to the farm April 1, 1909 and ground was covered with snow at the time. We made a good garden that year, and it was looking nice. Then one morning when we got up cows were all around the house, and the garden was trampled and eaten by the cows. We soon learned we should have fenced that plot as the cattle had the range of the country and very few fences to stop them. But in spite of bad luck with garden, we always had plenty to eat and never went hungry.

When my Father was down here, he had met Roxie Witherspoon and had told her that I had planned to be a teacher, and that it was my goal to be one of the younger teachers. They were organizing a new district out north called the Buckeye District. I had in mind to teach, and I did. I taught school that Fall in the Buckeye School. This school was about 5 miles north of town and east of our place. I had 14 pupils and all grades. I taught 6 months and then they ran out of funds.

Lucille: How much money did you get?

I got $40.00 per month.

Carl and I used to drive to school in a donkey cart. The next year I finished out the term in the Friona school as one of the teachers got sick. Some of my pupils were Earsel Taylor, Orville Stevick and Clyde Goodwine.

In the summer Elsie Goodwine and I went to summer school at Denton to keep our Teacher's Certificates valid. I later taught several years at Summerfield.

GEORGE W. MAGNESS

It was August 13, 1920 that the possessions of the George W. Magness family were loaded into a big boxcar and ready to leave Vernon, Texas for their new home in Parmer County. It was a great day in my life. I suppose it was the spirit of adventure, the idea of pioneering and the making of new friends that challenged me.

In our family at that time were Chester L. Magness, Morgan (Muggs) Magness and we three girls: Loucile, Eunice, and Estellene. Our car, an old Willis 6, Overland—seven passenger too—was loaded as full as the box car; for we were going to cover only as much territory each day as the box cars. Now that can be slow moving at times. And so it was not until August 20 (I remember this, as it was Mother's birthday) that we arrived at Farwell. The town was even smaller than I could imagine. Tripplett's store was the very first that I entered.

Waiting at the railroad station was my Grandfather Dan Magness and Clay Beavers, an old time friend, also from Vernon. They had their wagon team each and ready to help get us to the new farm.

It was a long way out to the place that was destined to become Oklahoma Lane Community. Every mile of raw cow trail was longer than I ever knew miles could be. The houses along the way were the Moore house that stood back from the road and is still there. Then the next one was the old Christian home, this had been built by Oscar Goddard a year or so before and sold it to Mr. C.E. Christian. Not too far away and a little further east was the old Massey home. Then, the Fowler home, and a vacant house and the small building that once had been an office building—my father had had this moved from Farwell previously as a corn bin. But into it we were moving to live until our new home was completed.

Across the road, the J.F. Foster family resided, they were helpful neighbors and it was from them that we obtained water until our well was dug. The windmill played an important part in our life, no, oh, no we never thought of the inconvenience of not having water piped into the house. Neither did we think anything about our bath being taken from a wash tub. Talk about the good old days! I like these new fandangles that make life so simple.

Friends and neighbors were wonderful, we learned to work together. In a raw country there was much to be done. Churches to be organized, schools to be built, roads to be improved—step by step we have seen that country become one of great prosperity, as far as agriculture is concerned. Little did we dream that there could be so much grown on that once grass land.

Social life was simple, very simple when it is looked back upon. A party now and then where swing games were played. They are now called folk games. And we made

whoopee to the tune of old Joe Clark or maybe it was Tideeeo. The girls were nice or not, according to the way they were swung in the dance—nice if she did not allow waist swings—horrible if a boy's arm fell any way near her waist line. Oh, well, that was forty years ago!

The Foster family who lived across the road from the Magness farm, became of great significance to me—Carrie was a good friend near my own age, and Tom was a little older. Through eight years of dating off and on, we enjoyed life, according to our feeling toward each other. Then, in January of 1929, we were married. But that is getting ahead of the story.

I must tell of the happenings that took place in my own life. We were poor, yes, of course we were, but we never felt it. And I actually do not think that any one else did very much. We had plenty to eat, most that we grew ourselves. Not much to wear, but we were not cold or hungry—we wore the same clothes both winter and summer, too—but then that was a day of not too much civilization. But I am modern enough to appreciate the fact that we have fewer petticoats and no long handled underwear, at all.

Outstanding events were the annual pie supper as a money raising project that paid for treats and a Christmas tree for everyone in the community. There was always a pretty girl contest, and an ugly man contest. The pies brought a lot of money, if the lovers were framed—for who wanted their best girl eating with someone else, and what lad didn't want to know just how good a cook his future wife was. I never let Tom know that I could not bake a pie fit to eat, then or now.

But the Christmas tree with its glitter and twinkle. Every child was thrilled, at the sight, and every fair miss wondered just what the surprise was to be to her. Old Santa Claus was played many times by my father—but I do believe that Frank Ayers played the first one. Then perhaps Ed McGuire did his fair amount of Santaing. It was fun, it was looked

January 11, 1918 C.A. Robertson starts C.B. in Arizona.

Commissioners Court Notes

303

forward to, it had a wonderful spirit, and not always a spirit of Christ, but there always seemed to be a few faithful ones to quiet down the more spirited ones. So things just went along year after year.

History was in its making also. The following years after World War I, meant a great many changes, prosperity was at a low ebb; the depression hit, it was truly a sad time. Some way things moved forward in spite of it all. Fortunate were those that could grow much of their food at home. It was during the time of this challenge that our daughters were born. They are Bonnie Marlene and Bettie Darlene.

This is a list of the immediate family of George Washington Magness and his wife, Cordelia Elizabeth Collier Magness at the time of moving to Parmer County: Chester Luther Magness; Morgan (called Muggs) Magness; Anna Loucille Magness (Foster); Eunice Salina Magness (Vinson, whom she divorced, later married Ketner); Estellene Martha Magness (Billington). The neighbors that I remember are: John Franklin Foster and his wife, Margaret Henderson Foster, and their immediate family: Charles Ernest Foster, Pearl Foster (Grissom), Willie Nelson Foster, Thomas Franklin Foster, Carrie Elizabeth Foster (Christian), Mrs. Fowler, a widow Gertrude Fowler, Carl Fowler, Vashti Fowler, Chester Fowler, The Frank W. Ayers Family, Bertha, his wife, Mable—Velva (daughters) and two sons deceased.

Written by Loucille Magness Foster

OTIS EDWARD MASSEY FAMILY

The History of the Otis Edward Massey Family as was re-created by Mr. Massey, assisted by two daughters, Elizabeth and Geneva, May 15, 1974.

Otis Edward Massey was the first child born to Mr. and Mrs. B.T. Massey on October 10, 1890, just in the edge of Dallas County, Texas. Soon after Otis was born, the B.T. Massey family moved over into Ellis County, Texas near Midlothian soon after this Midlothian was to be our home for the next several years. There were six children born to Mr. and Mrs. B.T. Massey, named Otis Edward, Beulah, Burton, twin boys Raymond and Ferman, and Norfleet. Ferman did not live very long and is buried at Midlothian, Texas.

In 1903, the Wright Brothers appeared at the State Fair in Dallas and flew their plane, the Kitty Hawk, 150 feet above the ground. Otis witnessed this first flight. He started to school at Newton Branch near Midlothian, Texas. This school was also known as Oger Hole. The famous outlaw, Clyde Barrow, was one of the pupils at that time. Otis went to another school known as Onward. These

August 17, 1917 First occupant escapes new jail.

Commissioners Court Notes

MR. AND MRS. OTIS MASSEY—wedding

OTIS MASSEY FAMILY just before coming to Parmer County.

were country schools. His first school teacher was Miss Georgia Poindexter and she is still living.

Otis Massey bought his first buggy in the fall of 1907 from Padget Brothers, in Dallas, Texas. He was musically inclined and learned to play the banjo and guitar and mandolin and played with some of the neighbor boys and this became a way of entertainment for the community. Otis continued to farm with his father. In October, 1910, a family from West Point, Tenn. moved to this community. This family was the G.W. Price family. This family consisted of three girls and one boy, namely Beulah, Flora and Mary and Marvin, who were twins.

Beulah Elizabeth Price was born April 27, 1894 at West Point, Tenn. Beulah Price and Otis Massey were properly introduced at a party at Mr. Dee Johnson's who was an uncle of Beulah Price. This romance blossomed into marriage of Beulah and Otis on December 22, 1912. They set up their first housekeeping January 13, 1913. He continued to farm with his father and soon got a farm of his own consisting of about 80 acres. He later rented more land which brought his farming acreage over 100 acres.

Otis Massey's father, B.T. Massey, purchased his first Model T. car on March 13, 1913 and this was his first experience at driving a car.

The first child was born to Otis and Beulah

Massey on September 30, 1913 and she was named Elizabeth Alphonsus Massey.

Otis and Beulah continued to farm in this same community for the next several years and during this time the following children were born: Edward Eugene Massey, September 19, 1914; Gordon William Massey, December 19, 1915; Geneva Ruth Massey, July 1, 1917; Russell Andrew Massey, August 22, 1919; Stanley Price Massey, April 18, 1921; and Frances Louise Massey, December 20, 1923. The family doctor was Dr. W.C. Brown and of course, all were born in the family home, assisted by neighbor women.

The first two children, Elizabeth and Edward, started to school the same year in September, 1921 and went to the little country school nearby named Walnut Grove. They walked to school with the neighbor children. The next two children started to this same school.

In 1924 the Massey family got the expansion fever. The family doctor, W.C. Brown, had possession of some land near Houston and he offered this layout to Otis Massey if it suited him. He loaded his family in the car and went to Houston to visit this layout. This was Mr. and Mrs. Otis Massey and seven children driving a Dodge touring car. This was a very nice trip but did not suit our liking because of so much water and rough country. They returned to Midlothian but were still searching for new land. Otis Massey bought his first tractor in 1919. This was a Fordson. He used this in his farming to a good advantage.

In July, 1925, Otis Massey made a trip to the Panhandle of Texas with some of the friends in and around Midlothian. He liked

THE MASSEY FAMILY BAND

BACK ROW: Otis Massey, G.W. Price. Front row: Gordon, Edward, Russell and Stanley Massey.

what he saw and came back so that he could bring his family out West to see what they would think of this part of the world. Otis came back to Midlothian and told his children that he had found the "perfect land." "People were so lazy out there," he said, "that the wind pumped the water and the cows cut the wood."

This sounded good to the children who did not like to chop cotton in the rocks and then have to pick the cotton in the fall. The boys had to help with the hay baler which was a hard, hot, dirty job too. In July, the Massey family made this same trip to see this "perfect land." Mr. Massey had told his children that they could not find a rock anywhere but if we did he would give us something. We visited with some friends of the family at Silverton, Texas. This family was the Dee Garvin family. While visiting here, Geneva thought she found a white rock on the banks of a earth tank and she thought she would kick this loose and show it to her father. Instead of this being a rock, it was a duck egg that had been mashed in the soft bank and it had spoiled. She was a mess—needless to say. It was Elizabeth's job to clean her up and this did not make for very good relations for some time. But pleasant memories now.

We continued our trip on toward Friona, Bovina, Farwell and back down to Sudan, Texas where we spent the night on a return trip to Midlothian, Texas. We visited in Bovina, Texas with Mr. J. Sam Gaines who operated a service station. We enjoyed ice water and fellowship with Mr. Gaines.

When we returned to Midlothian, Otis Massey contacted these friends that he made

the first trip out with and they decided to come back to Friona to buy some land. These men were Mr. Ed Smith and Nick Lindtop and Mr. E.T. West. We all bought some land from the Syndicate Capital Land Company. Mr. Massey bought 160 acres described as SE¼-T4S-R4E Sec. 26 and paid $30 per acre for this land. This was located three miles east and four miles south of Friona, Texas.

In the fall of 1925 the crops were harvested and returns from the crop settled for and plans were made to move to Friona, Texas. We made the necessary arrangements for a freight boxcar to ship a part or the most of the farm machinery, part of the household furniture, horses, cows, and farming tools including our Fordson tractor. The railroad required that a person ride the freight car with livestock so a friend of ours decided to "Go West" too. His name was Jennings Duke. He rode this freight car with the family collie dog as his companion. Otis Massey and family loaded the remainder of their possessions in the Dodge touring car and a Model T truck. Mrs. Massey drove the car with the seven children and Mr. Massey drove the truck. In this truck we had a registered Chester white brood sow. We had her cornered off in the back of the truck. On the trip out she got tired of this riding and decided to change locations. She climbed out over the high sideboards on this truck and fell to the ground. She broke herself up pretty badly but was not killed instantly. Mrs. Massey had a terrible time trying to outrun the Model T

FRANCIS IN THE Dodge touring car, left to right, Elizabeth, Russell, Stanley, Gordon, Mrs. Massey, Geneva.

ELIZABETH MASSEY and 5 row "go-devil."

truck to tell Mr. Massey that he had lost his hog. This happened somewhere near the caprock around Quitaque, Texas. We finally all got stopped and turned around and located the injured hog. We loaded her back in the truck and continued our way to Farwell, Texas where we were to make our headquarters until we could establish living quarters on our land. The old sow died soon after we got to Farwell. We spent two or three nights in a vacant part of the building that was being used by the Capital Syndicate Land Company. Our freight car was routed to Friona, Texas for unloading.

We arranged for some lumber to build a three-sided barn to house our family and livestock in until we could get our house built. We started to move on to our land November 11, 1925. This was a real experience. The family in one end of the barn and the milk cows and horses in the other end with tarpaulins used for doors. Shortly after we moved in it snowed but we made it fine and none the less for weather. Four of the children started to school the first of the week. The school bus route came right by our farm and this was a real experience for Elizabeth, Edward, Gordon and Geneva. Their first day in school "in town" was really something. Mr. Grant Music was our bus driver and Mr. F.W. Reeve owned and oper-

ated the buses that transported all students to Friona to school.

Our house that we were to build was a three room house—one bedroom, living room, and a long kitchen, dining room on the back. We had a water well dug with a wooden tower. This had a Lone Star mill that pumped the water. This was really living, because we had been used to drawing our water from the open wells. We still had to carry the water in buckets from the windmill to the house but this was an improvement. This was a new experience not only for the Massey family but also for the man who dug this well. He was new at the business. But this was a successful venture. We had a good well and good water. We have forgotten the name of the man who did this work.

In the early spring of 1926, we begun to break out the sod and prepare for farming in the West. We soon learned that the horses and plows and the Fordson tractor that we had brought with us were not powerful enough for this job. Otis started searching for more powerful machinery to break out the virgin sod. There was three families living near where we located—the Nathan Morton family to the north about ½ mile; the Carlton family about ½ mile to the south and another family farther east and south by the name of Kaltwasser. Mr. Morton had lived here for some time and he had been farming with tractors. He had a 15-30 International tractor and an Emerson 6 disc breaking plow that we worked out a trade with. Farming on the plains was quite differently from East Texas farming and we had a lot of experiences in store for us.

THE NEW TRACTOR

EDWARD MASSEY AND CECIL BOREN.

The country was sparsely settled and when we started to Friona for groceries and other supplies, we did not go the way the road went, we just headed in the northwesterly direction of Friona. If the conditions were just right, we would see Friona from our home. The only established homes between our farm and Friona were the Nathan Morton, Elmer Euler farm, the Widmier farm and the Goodwine farm.

The superintendent of schools was Mr. Buckner.

Our first crop consisted of Maize, corn, and red top cane. The first crop was a real treat for us. Otis Massey continued his search for better machinery in order to till the soil more efficiently. He went to Hereford, Texas and visited with an implement dealer who made a trade with him to go to Amarillo to bring a load of machinery back to Hereford. In this load was to be a sod planter which he would use on the farm. He was driving the Model T truck that we had moved from Midlothian, Texas. On his return trip from Amarillo from Hereford to his farm home, he got his truck stuck and had to leave it in the mud. He started walking home and lost his direction and walked and wandered all night. At day break he found himself and finally made it home and took the car back to get the truck out of the mud. Another experience in our new surroundings.

We soon learned the art of making dobies—dirt bricks—to build buildings for storage of our grain crops and machinery and livestock. This was a hard job but proved successful. With the family all working at the job, we soon had enough dobies to build our first chicken house. This made a warm building in the winter and a cool building in the summer. We built a large grainary that measured 14 x 28 ft. We stored our wheat and maize crop and cane in this grainary.

Other people begun to move into this country. Soon we had neighbors in all directions. Some of the names we can recall were the Sandifers, the R.G. Wiley, W.F. Cogdill, J.W. Hutton, the Hines family, the Crooks, the P.B. Griffiths, the Ed Boggess family, Enfields, and Taylors.

We all became acquainted and helped each other with the farming operations. And when harvest time came this was a community affair too. The neighbors traded work with each other and made the work lighter for all. Otis Massey bought his first combine from Mr. J.W. Parr. He agreed to harvest so much crop for Mr. Parr for this combine. Little by little we begun to accumulate the necessary farming tools to work our land. The community begun to settle with people from different parts of the country. The most of the people came from Oklahoma and it got to be a common question "What part of Oklahoma are you from?" It was most unusual to meet someone who did not come from Oklahoma. But we all soon became acquainted and this was a way of life and entertainment for us.

On January 7, 1927 Betty May Massey was born to our family. The doctor in attendance was Dr. McElroy assisted by neighbor women—Mrs. Wiley and Mrs. Cogdill.

When school was out in May, all hands and the cook worked in the fields to get our crop

MAKING ADOBE BLOCKS

I HELPED TOO!

started. We became self sufficient within ourselves. We raised a big garden, canned for the winter months, raised our own hogs for butcher and butchered our own beef. We would hang our beef on the windmill tower in the winter time and wrap it in cloth material to protect it from dirt and possible animals that might climb the tower to try to eat our meat. This was a treat to have good fresh beef all during the winter. We cured our pork and ate it during the summer months when we could not keep the beef. We had chickens enough to supply our eggs, and also have chickens to eat. We sold eggs and separated the milk and sold the cream for additional income for the family.

We made good crops and got a reasonable price for it. We financed with the Friona State Bank in Friona. The president of the bank was A.W. Henschel. We bought our groceries from Mr. T.J. Crawford. Mr. Ed White was a clerk in the store at this time. The town of Friona was rather small. It only consisted of Mr. Crawford's store, the post office, the depot, the school building and a few other stores and service stations. We only went to town when it was necessary. We got our mail at the post office in Friona.

The second year our children went to school, the school became overcrowded and to take care of this situation, the students who were in the first few grades of school were sent to school at Hub. This was the first 3 or 4 grades. This was held in the church house at the Hub. This school term was only the one year and all the students went to Friona from then on. Gordon and Geneva attended this school. Elizabeth and Edward went to the school in Friona. The bus would

come back by Hub and pick up the students and take them to their homes.

We had rented other land that people had bought for investment purposes and wanted someone to farm it for them. We soon were farming a lot more land than we ever could have farmed at Midlothian. We were renting land from Mr. E.T. West and Mr. Fred Lamb and the land that we had bought.

On March 20, 1929 Morris Wayne Massey was born into our family. This brought our family to nine children. Russell and Stanley had started to school and this made six children in school. This increased expenses and responsibilities. Frances started soon after this and there was times that we had 7 children in school. A large family has its advantages as well as its disadvantages. We learned to work together and to play together. In 1929 we had a good wheat crop and Otis surprised his wife by buying a new Maytag washing machine powered by a gasoline motor. Up to this time we washed on scrub board and open boiling pot which was real labor with a family the size of ours. The Maytag machine was delivered one day while Mrs. Massey was driving the wheat truck to haul the wheat from the combines to the elevators. When she came in that night the children had the washer sitting in the kitchen door running. She was sure surprised. It had a rubber hose on it that had to be placed outside to carry the gas vapors away from the machine. In playing with the machine, we flooded the motor and it nearly did not start; but soon with a little experimenting, we were well on our way to washing with a power machine. We thought we were "rich." The wheat crop was good and we bought a new

309

HEY THERE!

piano and Elizabeth was enrolled in the mail order music course of piano with the Conservatory of Music from Ft. Worth, Texas. This was to be the starting of the Massey String Band. Otis still played the guitar, mandolin and French harp, and this was a lot of family entertainment when "dad" played for the family. Dad was also the "family barber." This was an all day job when hair cutting time came around.

We had our own shoe repair implements too. Mrs. Massey repaired shoes while Mr. Massey had to be busy in the fields or when it became necessary. Mrs. Massey did the family sewing also. Many hours were required to keep the family clothed. Mrs. Massey made a hand in the fields along with the children. We would pack our lunch and go to the fields and stay all day. Some of the older children would stay with the babies in the wagon or car or truck whichever it was necessary for us to use. We learned many different ways to accomplish the work that had to be done.

We experienced lots of hardships but seemed to grow stronger through each trial. We attended church in Friona but not very regularly. There was the Methodist church, the Congregational church and the Baptist church. We prospered by our move to Friona and even though there were times that our faith may have faltered we knew that we had prospered by our move. We had not been back to our home town of Midlothian since we left in Nov. 1925 until 1929. After the harvest was over, Mr. Massey figured out a way he could use wagon bows to make a top over the truck bed to protect the children from the wind and sun to make the trip back to Midlothian. We packed our clothes in boxes made of wood and we used these boxes for seats in the truck and headed back to Midlothan. Our family enjoyed home made ice cream and since there was such a large group of us, we took our 2 gallon ice cream freezer along. This was a very enjoyable vacation but we were glad to get back to Friona and our Home in the West. We continued to increase our farming operation and continued to prosper but the years ahead of us were to be very disappointing and difficult.

The last child was born to our family on February 25, 1932. This was Marvin Ray Massey. The attending doctor was Dr. R.R. Wills.

The Massey family has set some kind of record in our life time. Mr. Massey's parents celebrated their 50th Wedding Anniversary on Nov. 3, 1939.

Mrs. Massey's parents celebrated their 50th Wedding Anniversary on July 20, 1942.

Mr. and Mrs. Otis Massey celebrated their 50th Wedding Anniversary in Dec. 1962.

Their 10 children all have senior rings and high school diplomas from Friona High School and three of the 10 graduated with honors—Geneva was Salutatorian of her Class in 1936; Stanley was Salutatorian in 1938; and Betty was Co-Valedictorian in 1945. Four of the children, Geneva, Stanley, Frances and Betty attended Draughon's Business College, Lubbock, two Elizabeth and Edward attended Texas Tech for part of a semester in 1933; two served in World War II—Russell and Stanley. Mr. and Mrs. Massey boasted 5 generations in their life time on both sides of the family. We think this is some kind of record.

Mrs. Massey died July 10, 1963 and was laid to rest in the Friona Cemetery.

Edward Eugene Massey died March 24, 1967.

Gordon Weldon Massey died September 10, 1968.

Edward Eugene Massey died March 24, 1967. Gordon Weldon Massey died September 10, 1968 and are both buried near Mrs. Massey in the Friona Cemetery.

WILLIAM AMBROS MASSIE, 1918, in Friona.

WILLIAM AMBROS MASSIE

William Ambros Massie married Mattie Bell Browning in Springfield, Kentucky in the year 1880. They had six children—Anna Julia (1881); Jesse Devan (1888); Edwin Kennedy (1891); and Laura Janet (1895). They lived in LaGrange, Kentucky until 1906 when the family moved to the Llano Community near Claude, Texas. There they tended and raised cattle and horses. Jesse Devan married Ora Bell Hamilton and lived around Claude until his death in 1959. They had four children—J.D., William Meryle, Floyd Boone and Cleo Bell.

In wagons drawn by horses, the rest of the Massie Family moved to Hollene, New Mexico in the year 1913; then in 1914 they made their last move to Friona, Texas. Will H. Massie was sent to France in 1917 where he served in World War I. While he was away, the family lost most of their cattle during the winter of 1918-1919. The story goes that snow covered the ground from October to April.

W.A. Massie died in 1925 with a cancerous stomach.

The family rented grass from the Capitol Freehold Syndicate then bought some land from Mr. Dutch Hanson. They lived there several years then they bought land from a Mr. Ballard. This is where the home place is now. They also bought a section from the Federal Land Bank in 1939.

Lula married D.M. Ballard and moved to Colorado; they had five children. Laura married Ross R. Pollard who was with the railroad in Friona. They moved to Oklahoma. They raised one daughter. Will, Ed and Anna never married and lived in Friona all their lives.

In 1943 William Meryle and Olive Smiley Massie came to Friona to attend the funeral of his grandmother, Mattie Bell. Meryle was stationed in Lubbock at the air base at this time. On December 31, 1945, Meryle, Olive and their daughter, Marcia Lynn, moved to Friona to go into farming and ranching with his two uncles, Will and Ed Massie.

Olive and Meryle had two other daughters, Betty Merylene and Jaynette Lea. Will died in 1967 and Ed in 1961.

HOWARD MAYFIELD

Howard Mayfield was living with the Frank Loflin family at Anadarko, Oklahoma when they decided to move to Parmer County near Friona. Some neighbors had been out here and went back telling what a good country it was. They brought their household goods and stock in a railroad car. Mr. Mayfield broke out sod land with a mule team. He acquired 80 acres just one mile west of the Syndicate Hotel. His first house was a 14 x 20 one-room house.

He remembers whirlwinds, dust storms, and floods. One whirlwind picked up a shed on a neighbor's place, whirled it around in the air and put it back down without damaging it. The same wind picked up a stack of bundles and laid them out in a row across a field just like a binder had left them.

Mr. Mayfield drove a school bus for the Friona School. He was a member of the Friona Baseball Team.

In 1921 he married Miss Mary Tackett of Oklahoma. Their three daughters are Mrs. Dorothy Lovelace and Mrs. Peggy Snyder of Farwell and Mrs. Betty Jean Blackburn of Albuquerque.

GLEN E. McCRATE FAMILY

Mr. and Mrs. Glen E. McCrate and their son, Woodrow, moved to Black, Texas, from Texico, N.M. in January, 1923. Glen E. McCrate was the Depot Agent for the Santa Fe Railroad at that time. There were three operators and one Depot Agent, the track crew and also three water well pumpers and the section foreman. These above mentioned made up the railway employees. There was not a store or Post Office at Black at that time, so the mail was sent into Friona.

In 1924, Glen E. McCrate built a little store building about 24 feet square. In 1925 he built a larger store and a Post Office was also established for Black early in 1926.

The Black School at that time had some 28 pupils. Families living in, around and near Black in 1923 were: the McKinneys, Makes, Coneways, Stanfords, Overtons, Robersons, Hines, Bennetts, McDonalds, Reese, Scheihagens, Hansons, Wilsons and Browders.

Our family had many wonderful times at the Black School house. It was the center of the Black Community. Speaking for myself, our happiest years were spent at Black, Texas, and three of my four children went to grade school at Black.

McFARLAND FAMILY

Mr. and Mrs. J.B. McFarland moved from Killeen, Bell County, Texas to Friona, Parmer County, Texas in September, 1925. They shipped their household goods and livestock which were horses, mules, and Jersey cows on an immigrant train.

Mr. and Mrs. McFarland and eight of their 10 children made the trip to Friona in two Model T cars. They rented a house on the Green Valley Farm and began improving a section of land five miles northwest of town. They drilled a well, built an adobe house, chicken house, and sheds for the stock and began farming.

One daughter, Kathy, went to Brownsville, Texas to teach school and one son, Lonnie, was married and lived in Bell County.

Lora Mae taught school in Amherst, Texas, and Ilene entered Texas Tech in 1922. Granville, Martha, Robert Hines, Geraldine, and Charline graduated from Friona High School. One son Maurice died in 1937.

Mr. and Mrs. McFarland were members of First Baptist Church and were active in church and civic affairs and the building of the Parmer County Community Hospital.

Mr. McFarland passed away in 1958 at the age of 80. Mrs. McFarland in 1972 at the age of 92.

The children are: Katy (Mrs. Claude Osborn), Friona, Texas; Lonnie McFarland, Pierre, South Dakota; Lora Mae McFarland, Clovis, New Mexico; Ilene (Mrs. Sloan Osborn), Friona, Texas; Granville McFarland, Friona, Texas; Martha (Mrs. Roy) Clements, Friona, Texas; Robert H. McFarland, Tucumcari, New Mexico; Geraldine (Mrs. George) Taylor, Friona, Texas; and Charline (Mrs. Roy Lee) Jones, Ruidoso, New Mexico.

E.W. McGUIRE
By Mrs. E.W. McGuire

In January, 1916, Edward W. McGuire, Tom Hooser, Jim Johnson, and a Mr. Stewart from Vera, Knox County, Texas, went west to eastern New Mexico looking for land on which to homestead. Finding nothing, they started back home and spent the night in the Nichols Hotel in Texico, New Mexico. Mr. Nichols' son-in-law, Judge J.D. Hamlin, had the agency for the Capitol Reservation Land, and this was the beginning of the big land sales to new settlers. Judge Hamlin came to the hotel and told them about the future possibilities. Soon after the men returned home, a Mr. Hartshorn, an agent for the Capital Reservation Land, made a trip to Knox County looking for prospective buyers. He told of the abundance of rainfall in 1915, of how one could plant grain on the sod and it would grow; also of the wonderful fruit grown south of Farwell. As a result of his sales talk, five men, Ed McGuire; his brother-in-law, John J. Scribner; and friends, Tom Hooser, Jim Johnson and Joe Johnson returned with Mr. Hartshorn, and after seeing the country, each bought 80 acres at $16 an acre with an option to buy the remaining 240 acres of the half section of their choice. This was seven miles east of Farwell and was the first land bought in what is now the Oklahoma Lane Community. Destined to become the first settlers of what was later to become the Oklahoma Lane Community, the men each bought land adjoining the other and in

May 21, 1919 C.A. Robertson—Cannon Ball booming in Utah & Wyoming.

Commissioners Court Notes

ED McGUIRE, Tom and Alice Hoosier, Lillie & John Scribner. Children are: Pauline and Elmo Hoosier, Clifford McGuire, Noami, Vivian and Kathrine Scribner.

ED McGUIRE and Henry Thomas harvesting milo maize with a push header. (Four mules and Ed McGuire on a White Horse.)

ED McGUIRE, Clifford McGuire and R.A. Hawkins with a two-headed calf born on the Ed McGuire Farm. The calf did not live.

this way were able to be of help to one another. Of these five, only one, Ed McGuire, survived the ordeal of pioneering. The other four men soon moved away.

On March 5, 1916, John and Lillie Scribner and their two children, Vivian, 5, and Catherine, 2½; Cora McGuire and son, Clifford, 5; and Ed's father, J.H. McGuire, who also bought 160 acres east of Ed's, arrived in Farwell via passenger train. They were greeted by an outstanding sandstorm and can still remember the sand stinging their legs as they walked across from the Santa Fe depot to the Nichols Hotel where they stayed overnight. The next day Ed McGuire arrived with the immigrant rail car containing the household goods, horses, mules, chickens, turkeys, a cow and farm implements. The Scribners and McGuires immediately moved into the old Franklin house in the southwest part of Texico, their temporary living quarters.

"The next day after arriving in Texico we fixed our lunch and started out to see our new homes. You can't imagine how we felt trying to locate an 80-acre plot in a 96,000-acre cow pasture! The grass was almost knee high, with a liberal sprinkling of loco. Each section corner was marked by an iron post with the section number on it. There was not a house between our place and Farwell or Bovina and only three toward Muleshoe. We have seen cattle trailing two and three miles long just east of our place on their way to Bovina, which was the shipping point."

McGuire, Scribner and Dr. J.M. McCuan ordered lumber from south Texas and built little two-room houses. The Scribners were

expecting a baby, so their house was completed in time for the new arrival. Naomi Scribner was the first baby born in the present Oklahoma Lane Community, May 11, 1916.

One well was dug that the Hooser, Scribner and McGuire families shared, and another that was shared by the Johnson brothers. Soon the five original families were settled in small homes and the work was begun preparing land for planting their first crop. Ed McGuire had about twenty acres planted in corn that did really well, but each time a land salesman would come along with prospective buyers they would stop and each take a sample along with them, thus cutting down the yield considerably. The grass was beautiful and supplied good grazing for the stock. However, the horses and mules seemed to have a good appetite for the heavy infestation of loco weed. As a result, for several years many of the settlers had to destroy their animals which became completely insane (locoed) from eating the weed.

ROBERT McGILL hauling feed from McGuires farm into Farwell for Mr. Jim Walling. Clifford McGuire rode to the Knox School on the sled.

(MULES, SLED, Two Men and Bundle Wagon in Background.) Ed McGuire and Robert McGill hauling feed on a sled when the snow was on the ground for so long in 1918.

MY FIRST SCHOOL ON THE PLAINS—The Knox School Building. Mrs. Bess White, teacher, Clifford McGuire on lower left front row (mother of Joel Preston White)

Soon after the first five families arrived, others began moving into the community. In April, 1916, Mrs. Fowler and her four children, Carl, Gertrude, Vashti and Chester, arrived from Oklahoma. They camped by a well on their property until their two-room house was completed. In December, 1916, the Ben Bates and John Bates families moved to the Tom Hooser place, as Tom and family had already moved to Floydada. Mr. and Mrs. A.L. Tandy and four of their children, Fay, Maurine, Frances and Guy, became part of the growing population after settling on land bought from both Joe Johnson and John Scribner. A real estate agent, Mr. Massey, who had come here from Oklahoma, sold land to a number of Oklahoma people. Some of the early settlers were the Ben Hendricksons, the Frank Ayres and his parents, the George Roberts, the Tiptons, the W.A. Doshers, the Godards, Mr. and Mrs. Jim Perkins and Clyde, John and Ina (Perkins) West

and Obereta. Their son, Loren West, was born the next year. In 1922, Clyde Perkins went back to Oklahoma to marry Thelma Foshee, and returned to the Oklahoma Lane community with his bride. Other early settlers included Mr. and Mrs. C.E. Christian, John, Clarence, Grace, Rose, Everette and Anna; Mr. and Mrs. R.G. (Dick) Hammonds, Hollis, Bob, Cassie Mae, Dollie—Fern, Frankie and Bobbie Jo were born here; Mr. and Mrs. Willis Magness and Clyde; Mr. and Mrs. George Magness and children; Mr. and Mrs. Fred Kepley and Ora—Jean and Gloria were born here; Mrs. Martha V. McGill (Cora McGuire's mother), Bob, Clarence and Homer. Alice (Grandma) Roberson, Cullen, Dave and maybe other children and the J.C. Robersons all came from Canada. J.C. Roberson opened a general store around 1922 in what is now Lariat. The J. Frank Foster family, the W.I. Rundells, the Robert Rundells, the Warnie Hursts, the P.A. Lees, the George Boltons, the D.W. Carpenters, the J.R. Caldwells, the Joe T. Hannas, the Ernest Hromases, the Frank Hromases, the J.I. Gobers, the Nortons, the E.A. Berrys, the Nelson C. Smiths, the Conda Jonses, the Sam and Earl Billingsleys, the Lee Thompsons, the Lee Sudderths, the Karl Zocks, the Swedes, the Kubes, the Kaltwassers, the Grafs, and the Sherman Woods also settled early.

In December, 1916, several families gathered together for Christmas. Cora McGuire and Lillie Scribner made the "tree" out of a box covered with bright colored material and

OKLAHOMA LANE COMMUNITY Easter Egg Hunt in 1917. (Large group of people with teams and wagons to the right and left backgrounds.)

THE FIRST CHRISTMAS TREE, 1916, Oklahoma Lane. Boards and strings across the corner of the room at the Ed McGuire Home. Families attending the Christmas Tree were the Ben Bates, John Bates, John Scribner and Ed McGuires.

a board tacked across the corner of the room to hang gifts on. John Scribner was Santa Claus, to the delight of all the children. This was actually the beginning of the annual Community Christmas Tree. The two Bates families and Scribners ate Christmas dinner with the McGuires. The men spent the day working on Ben Bates' house. The next year at Christmas time, someone gave a dead peach tree which the women wrapped in green crepe paper and trimmed with strings of cranberries and popcorn. In later years, the men would travel to the brakes in New Mexico to get real trees for the community tree. When everyone gathered for the Community Christmas Tree in 1919, Cora McGuire, Ina West, Mrs. Frank Ayres and Mattie Lee Richards had made little sacks of colored netting so each person would get a sack of fruits and candy. The tradition of an annual Community Christmas Tree with a big tree, Santa Claus, and sacks of goodies for everyone has continued to the present.

The community was growing rapidly and a school building became necessary. In 1917 the first school was built one mile west of McGuires and was called the Knox school since so many families had come from Knox County. Miss Matilda Tidenburg from north of Bovina was the first teacher, but she stayed only one month. Mrs. Gilliland F. Parker from Hereford finished the term. Miss Lula Sullivan taught the second term. Another teacher was Mrs. A.D. (Bess) White. In 1920 Miss Mattie Lee Richardson came from Knox County and taught one year. Two other schools were built in the district—the McElroy school in the south side of the district and the Sunnyside School one mile

south and three east of McGuires. Two early teachers in the Sunnyside School were Miss Anna Foster and P.A. Lee. In 1920 the Knox and Sunnyside schools consolidated. Mr. Jim Perkins sold five acres and gave five acres to the school system if they would call it Oklahoma.

So many people living on that road were from Oklahoma, so the new school was officially named Oklahoma Lane by Mr. George Temple, an employee of Judge Hamlin. The two little school buildings were moved to the new location. The little one-room Knox schoolhouse was moved with three Fordson tractors, belonging to Mr. Hammonds, Mr. Christian and Mr. Willis Magness. Mr. George Magness walked ahead and directed the drivers so they would not run into any prairie dog holes, and Mr. Fred Kepley followed to keep the building pulled straight so it would not get out of line. Some of the first teachers at the Oklahoma Lane School were Mr. P.A. Lee, Miss Anna Foster, Mr. Nelson C. Smith and Miss Jo DeOliveria. Bonds were voted for a new school building and work was begun on it in the fall of 1923. The building had three high school class rooms and an auditorium upstairs and grade school and

THE ED McGUIRE HOME from 1917 to 1925. Clifford McGuire on his horse, Nell. This is the home where Nova, Lois and Jimmy McGuire were born.

home economics rooms down stairs, along with a big furnace room and coal storage room.

After the new building was built, more teachers were added. A vocational agriculture teacher, Mr. Gourley, was instructor for Oklahoma Lane, Farwell and Bovina, and Miss Barnes was home economics instructor for the three schools. There was a music department and on many occasions Mr. Joe Head, who maintained the roads in the community using mules, would stop by the school and lead songs for the children. Mr. Clyde Perkins became the first custodian and bus foreman after his first crop got hailed out. Mr. R.S. Tucker took over the custodial duties and remained there until consolidation with Farwell when he joined the Farwell School and worked there until he became disabled. Lester Norton became bus foreman. A school supply and candy store was across the street. The two old schools were used for teacherages and later sold to individuals. Mr. J.H. McGuire bought one and moved it to his farm for a rent house. Several years later bonds were voted and E. McGuire and Clyde Perkins went to Dallas to make arrangements for the construction of the elementary classrooms and gymnasium-auditorium to replace the outdoor basketball courts. Miss Dorothy Harris, who became Mrs. Dee Brown and still resides in the community, was one of the first teachers in the new elementary school. The Oklahoma Lane School consolidated with Farwell Public School in 1949, with some on the east side of the school district going to Lazbuddie and on the north going to Bovina. The gymnasium was used for a community skating rink and basketball court for several years. The old high school was later torn down and the elementary-gymnasium sold to the Oklahoma Lane Methodist Church and was remodeled into a church.

The first Sunday School was organized in 1917 with Mr. R.A. Hawkins as superintendent. It met in the afternoons so preachers from other places could come and preach. Some of the first preachers were Rev. J.F. Nix, Sam Tipton and Bro. Savage. Mr. and Mrs. B.N. Graham were loyal supporters also. After the new school was built there was a Union Sunday School and preaching. Then Oklahoma Lane became known far and wide for their Sunday night singings with such singers as Virgil O. and Frank Stamps and their quartets, Otis Echols, Joe Head, Olin Birch, Otis Thompson and others coming from many areas, including Dallas, Nashville, Tennessee, etc. Many big singing conventions were held at Oklahoma Lane with all day singing and dinner on the ground. Singing schools were conducted by well-known personalities for a week or longer. Then the churches were built—the Methodist first and then the Baptist. Soon the Sunday evening singings began to be taken over by Sunday evening preaching. Parsonages were built for the preachers and their families. After Oklahoma Lane School consolidated with Farwell, the Methodist Church bought the Oklahoma Lane schoolhouse, using the classrooms for Sunday School rooms and converting the gymnasium into a sanctuary and fellowship hall. The Baptist Church built a parsonage, then later built a new sanctuary, converting the old one into additional classrooms.

The Ed McGuires had four children, Clifford, Nova, Lois and Jimmy—all but Clifford being born at the farm in Oklahoma Lane and completing high school there. Clifford finished at Farwell. "We have seen many hardships as well as happy times," relates Mrs. McGuire. "In November, 1918, the big snow began, and it was March, 1919, before we saw the ground. We had to grub feed out

CLIFFORD McGUIRE, Katherine and Vivian Scribner. (Standing in front of pond of water with a dog.)

of shocks in the field and haul it in on sleds to feed the stock. The flu epidemic in 1919 was bad, when Ed and I had to care for my mother, brother and many of the neighbors. We've been wiped out by hails a number of times. The depression hit hard with cotton dropping to 4c and 5c a pound and grain to 20c and 30c a hundred.·

"Many, many changes have come about with irrigation, machinery to replace the mules and walking plows, electricity, telephones and many other things too numerous to mention. A familiar sight on about the coldest day of the winter was the hog killing when the neighbors got together for hog butchering and preparing the meat, then rendering lard in the old iron pots and making lye soap out of the cracklings or left over old lard. The electric milking machines and cream separators replaced the old hand operations, and now it is a very rare thing to see a milk cow, with the convenient cartons of milk on the grocery shelves or even delivered to the door.

"The grain crops had to be hand headed. The sudan, cane and millet had to be bundled and shocked, then threshed by the old threshing machine manned by neighbors working together to thresh for one and then another for weeks and weeks. We, the women, had to prepare huge meals to feed the threshing crews. All this has been replaced by the modern four-, six- and eight-row combines. The back-aching job of hand picking cotton is now done two and four rows at a time with modern harvesters.

"Fuel and electricity for cooking and heat-ing has replaced the burning of corn cobs, cow chips and coal. Modern washing machines sure beat the sore knuckles on a rub board.

"Although Ed McGuire was taken in death in 1964, he lived to see many of these changes in the land he helped to settle. A large percentage of the original settlers are now dead, but many of their children and grandchildren still live in the area and farm the land that was once one big open cow pasture."

THE D.H. MEADE FAMILY

One family, consisting of my father and mother, myself and brother Harry arrived in Friona January 12th, 1909. My parents are originally from Virginia but moved to Texas from Camden, Indiana, seeking a milder climate.

Dad had made a trip there earlier and purchased a half section of land about a mile west of town on which was a small house, a well and a barn. Later he bought some adjoining land to add to his farm.

Coming out of the cold winter in Indiana we found the climate much warmer when we arrived. Always being used to trees, especially fruit trees, one of our first projects was to plant an orchard and build a fence around it. No one had warned Dad of the winds, tumbling weeds and sand and before the end of spring we found the fence and several rows of trees buried in sand caught by the tumbling weeds against the fence.

The town was just getting started. A land company was selling land around Friona and had built some business buildings. Also a show house near the depot which was the first house we saw when we got off the train. I remember a coal yard run by "Daddy Foster." The land company ran excursions there regularly of prospective settlers. Most everyone turned out to see the excursion train come in.

Cattle was being grazed all around Friona and for some time after. So, in order to farm, the first thing was fences which did not always keep the cattle out when they got near water.

There was one church and a one room school house. The second year we were there

BIRTHDAY PARTY AT THE MEADE HOME.

we had two rooms. Miss Floy Knowd, later Mrs. T.J. Crawford, taught the upper grades and a Miss Davis the lower grades in the Congregational Church. My father was on the school board when the first brick school building was erected. This building later burned.

Many families moved there that year and the following year. Some did not stay but those that did worked hard to build their homes and their farms and worked close together to build up the town and community. The nearest doctor was at Hereford and we had to shop in Hereford for many things those first years. As I look back, those old settlers were very close to each other and shared much together.

J.H. (JIM) MEARS

The year was 1919 when a lad of 18 arrived in Hale County, Texas and he had come all the way from Tennessee. After serving 82 days in the army then the war had ended and Uncle Sam had no further use for his service.

MR. MEARS, SAM AND J.C.

MRS. MEARS, SAM AND J.C.

He had heard of this far west country and wanted very much to get away from the mountains of Tennessee where everyone seemed to be dealing in moonshine.

He landed in Abernathy in Hale County in 1919. He went to work for the Overton family and then followed them to Parmer County when they moved further west to find grass for their expanding sheep flocks. Working for the Overtons and for himself for several years or until the Overtons, Elbert and Walter, bought a large ranch in New Mexico and moved there, he went into farming for himself. He lived in a dugout for three years, 1925, 1926 and 1927.

In the mean time he had met and courted a young lady in Parmer County. She was Opal Hand, the daughter of Mr. and Mrs. J.I. Hand. They were married in 1927. In 1934 he bought a place in the Lakeview district. This place was about 7 miles east of Friona.

They have two children. J.C. who graduated from Friona High School after attending grade school in Lakeview is working for Phillips Petroleum Co. He has two children whose mother died when they were very young.

Sam also graduated from Friona High School and the grade school at Lakeview. After working for some years he married Donna Miller, daughter of Roy and Eva Miller. He is now farming the home place. They have two children, Clint and Sarah.

Jim married during the big depression in the 1930's and had a hard struggle during the

JIM MEARS—HORSEMAN!

drought and depression. He sold eggs and cream for the very low price of 10 cents per dozen for eggs and cream not much better. He sold a 600 pound sow for six dollars. Also sold what little wheat he could raise for 16 cents per bushel. But with the coming of better times he has been able to improve the place and add irrigation wells.

Tragedy struck early in the family. Opal became ill and passed away in 1951. Jim stayed with the boys until they left to go out to work on their own and he still resides on the home place.

EARLY DAY HISTORY
OF PARMER COUNTY, TEXAS
By Mrs. W.S. Menefee

In January 1925 in a 1923 Chevrolet curtains buttoned on, Walter S. Menefee and his wife, Lena, moved from near Greenville, Tex., to West Texas bringing their four children. He had previously bought ¼ section of land 12 miles north and one mile east of Muleshoe, Texas. Bought more later.

The wife and children remained in Slaton a week while a shed was built for them to live in. Her brother and two of his children came along to help build and see what West Texas looked like. His brothers rode in the boxcar bringing furniture, chickens, turkeys, six head of horses, a cow, and boad arch posts (bois d'ark). He then fenced the land with barb wire, built a small corral around the shed with horses in it and furniture stacked around. At night horses would rub themselves on the piano that was covered in can-

vas. It misted some and they knew it was ruining the furniture. At night they would move bedsprings and bedding inside the shed to sleep on but outside at morning so they would have room enough to cook and eat.

Soon their grass carpet wore off until it was very dusty. My! what an appetite those men had. I never cooked so many red beans and cornbread. In two weeks they had a four room house built but no windows set in. They moved in and were so happy to be on a good floor and beds to sleep on. At night they boarded up windows but put glass in as soon as they could. During that time temperature dropped to below zero about 6 degrees.

The Menefee's had been taught by parents that there were good people everywhere you went and the Lord may be sending them to this (seemingly foreign) place. To be sure there were good neighbors.

The Jeskos, Treiders, Jennings, Nobles, proved to be good neighbors, also the Coffmans. Mother Jesko (deceased) gave them plants for the garden they had never known before and all proved to be real friends in sickness.

Mrs. Menefee's only brother (a bachelor) was very sick in 1926 and died in March in their home. Rattlesnakes were killed in their yard as turkeys were fussing over something which turned out to be a rattlesnake. Little 2 year old Ruth was playing around a car sitting near the door when a little rattler was found and killed.

How they longed for trees as they had been used to having them. When spring came they went a few miles and dug locus sprouts and set out which soon made trees they were so glad to have. They did not get but 60 acres of the sod land broken and planted but had rented about that much from a neighbor Mr. Coffman.

One morning they awoke to see a herd of cattle in the 60 acres. Of course there was discouragement for they had devoured and destroyed much of it. Cattle men from other counties had bought cattle and turned them loose on the free grass and it was detrimental to newcomers. There was no stock law. Had to cross nine cattle guards or open wire gaps to even get to Muleshoe for mail and groceries. Once a week neighbors would go get the mail and bring out for them or they would go themselves and bring for all.

The first year we went regular to First Baptist church in Muleshoe which met in the school house. In 1926 a Baptist church was organized as there was a school house and post office named Lazbuddie. Members included the Menefees, Heaths, Shaws, Mrs. Pyritz, and Mrs. Welch and Elizabeth and others; Menefee was Sunday School superintendent ten years, and was an ordained deacon as was Mr. T.C. Hennington.

The Menefee children were Rubymae, married Paul Syms of Hereford, Texas. She taught school at Jesko and Paul drove the bus; they later moved to Albuquerque, N. Mex. Paul died Nov. 2. Rubymae is very low at this writing. She has taught school in Albuquerque, N. M. for the past 20 years, her last day being October 14, 1966.

The second daughter, Frances, married Juel Treider of Lazbuddie, and they are now living on their farm.

Joe Scott, a son, married Mary Lou Barnes of Lazbuddie, and now are living in Friona.

Ruth married Sam Long in 1941 after graduating from High School at Muleshoe, Texas, and are now living in Hereford, Texas.

In coming to Parmer County, there were six in the family; now there are 59 living children, grandchildren, and in-laws, and 29 great-grandchildren.

W.S. served as commissioner at different times. He passed away Sept. 8, 1958, two days past their golden wedding anniversary, in a Friona hospital. Mrs. Menefee lived on the farm eleven miles north and one mile east of Muleshoe for six years alone. She then moved to Kings Manor retirement home in Hereford, Texas. It is a lovely home and she is not lonely among so many good people.

She still drives her car and has any privilege she had at her own home; and she has a private room with bathroom, maid service and good meals.

She belongs to and attends First Baptist Church when not providentially hindered.

THE MOSELEY FAMILY

David and Eva Moseley moved from Hammon, Oklahoma to a farm, five miles south of Friona, on October 1, 1926. They had heard of the plains area and Mr. Moseley came with other prospective buyers and stayed at the Syndicate Hotel, southeast of Friona. He bought land on Christmas Day, 1925.

In the winter of 1926 Mr. Moseley built a small shack on a wagon bed, to bring a sod plow and stove and bed, to his new farm. It took him and a neighbor eight days to drive a team of four mules and they arrived March 8, 1926. For the next several weeks they broke the grass, planted a crop, and built a corral. Neighbors took care of the mules when they returned to Oklahoma.

During the summer Mr. Moseley and brother-in-law, Mr. J.W. Hutton, returned and built a small house for the family. It was one long room with a dirt floor, one door and three small windows.

Mrs. Moseley, her mother, Louisa Collier and daughter Edith, age 6, arrived October 1, 1926 by Model T Ford car about 2 p.m. and were awed by the vastness of the treeless plains. Neighbors were a mile or more, but a bond was established between them that would last a life time. The household goods and stock were shipped by train, and when it began to rain the first night, the dirt floor seemed like a small creekbed, before dawn came. It had rained hard all night. The cooking was done on a bachelor (coal) stove with a round oven on the stove pipe. Mrs. Moseley enjoyed cooking and entertained many people at her table, with good food and fellowship.

Improvements were made when money and time were available. The house was divided into three rooms and a floor was laid. Later a screened porch was built on the south side of the house.

The family hauled water from a neighbor, Mr. Blankenship until the spring of 1927 when two gray mares were traded to Charlie Adams, to drill a hole. The windmill and pipe were purchased from Jerry Blackwell.

A small adobe well house was built and later a lean-to room was added to this. One rainy night, twenty-five people spent the night with the Moseleys.

On January 22, 1927 a son, Hugh Edward, was born at the home and delivered by Dr. A.P. McElroy. On October 24, 1928 a son, Jack, was delivered by the same doctor.

Mr. and Mrs. Moseley spent happy days and long hours working and paying for the land, and bringing up their family.

PRESTON ROBINSON NICHOLS

Mr. Preston Robinson Nichols, nicknamed Ted, died January 11, 1967. The following account of his childhood days is given by his wife, Ruth Nichols.

Ted was born in Bovina, Texas on April 6, 1900 on his mother's 44th birthday. His father was William Henry Nichols and his mother was Erie Rose Nichols. He had three older brothers, Horace A., C. Fowler, and W. Harry Nichols; three older sisters, Adelia, (Mrs. Webb), Kate, (Mrs. Judge J.D. Hamlin), who died September 1940 in Lima, Peru, South America and is buried there, Florence (Mrs. Gallady) 87 years old at the time of this writing in 1967. Mrs. Gallady has a son, John Robert Armstrong of Farwell, Texas. Her first husband was John Armstrong, a manager of the southern division of the XIT ranch before he was killed in line of duty.

"Ted" Nichols was the first white child born in Parmer County (after its organization) his wife relates. Mr. Joe Killough often told her how he, being a cowboy in 1900, rode all day to see the new baby after the word got out, as he had not seen one in a long time. Many cowboys did the same thing.

Ted's father worked for the railroad on coming to Bovina. The family had to live in a tent until a house could be built. Ted's mother was a very industrious woman, although the family came west from around Victoria, Texas due to severe asthma attacks she suffered. It was told that she served many cowboys their first Thanksgiving Dinner (in a long time) for 25c a piece. The family later moved to Texico where Mrs. Nichols opened a hotel when Texico was "booming."

B.E. NOBLES FAMILY

Mr. and Mrs. B.E. Nobles with their son, Mack, and daughter, Estelle, left Deport, Texas in Lamar County and moved to Farwell, Texas in September of 1907. They traveled by train. Their household goods were shipped from Detroit, Texas, the nearest shipping point, and the boxcar came on the newly extended Santa Fe Line into New Mexico. At that time a carload of household goods could be shipped across the state for fifty-two dollars. Mr. Nobles' decision to go to Farwell was influenced by his brothers, Millard and H.A. Nobles, who lived in Amarillo and operated a Wholesale Grocery Company there. They felt all this part of Texas had a future.

Mr. Nobles bought the Daniels' Grocery and employed Mr. Daniels' son, Wick, to assist him. Later, he moved the store next door to The Farwell State Bank and added a Dry Goods Department.

Their first home was just over the line in New Mexico, but later they built a home in southwest Farwell.

The two children attended school in The Congregational Church, the only school in town at the time. Later a high school was built and they attended it.

Two hardships were the frequent sandstorms and the extremely cold winters. Coming from an altitude of just above sea level to Farwell's 4100 feet was quite an adjustment to make.

The family was Presbyterian and when they first arrived, they attended services held in a business building. The preacher walked all the way from St. Vrain. This congregation soon disbanded however, and they joined what is now The Hamlin Memorial Methodist Church. Mr and Mrs. Nobles were both very active in church work. Mr. Nobles served for years as Superintendent of Sunday School and a member of the Church Board.

Mr. Nobles was always interested in civic affairs. He served at one time as a County Commissioner and many years later was Justice of the Peace. He was instrumental in organizing the first Masonic Lodge in Farwell.

In 1922 Mr. Nobles disposed of his business and retired. He and Mrs. Nobles lived in the home they built until they died in 1947. He died in January of that year and Mrs. Nobles died a month later. They are both buried in the Clovis Cemetery.

After serving in World War One in France, Mack Nobles moved to Amarillo. Several years later he married Frances Burgess of Amarillo. They have a son, Edward B.

Nobles, who is an attorney in Amarillo and three grandchildren.

Estelle Nobles married James H. Curry of Texico. They live in Alhambra, California. They have two sons and five grandchildren, all living in California.

T.A. O'BRIAN SR. FAMILY

With five children to support, Mr. T.A. O'Brian came to Texas to look at the country that so many people from Medford, Oklahoma were so interested in. He decided it offered more opportunities for them—so he went back to Medford, had a farm sale, and moved the family to Parmer County, Friona, Texas in August, 1928.

This was a desolate looking place to ones who had trees and creeks nearby. Mr. O'Brian used to say you could see farther and see less than any place he'd been. Another thing, he jokingly said that he thought the salesman said you could grow nuts in this country but after a few years he decided he meant "go nuts."

The family other than Mr. and Mrs. O'Brian were, Kenneth, Russel, Marion, Tom and Julia. We came to Texas in a 1927 Model T Ford truck with all our worldly possessions. The hill coming out on the plains this side of Miami, Texas was like a mountain and the old truck barely made it.

A 24 x 28 wooden structure house was built. This was a story and a half house. This was covered with black tar paper—intended for stucco but ran out of money. We had no more hardships than lots of people.

We used lots of home remedies such as skunk-grease, hog-lard and turpentine for colds, etc. Also onion syrup.

In the winters we took heated bricks to bed to warm up the beds. Many a sheet was scorched or burned. We hauled water a quarter of a mile as we had no running water, no electricity as most other people around us.

The neighbors got together during winter, usually the coldest day, and butchered hogs. That called for another day for rendering lard, frying down sausage. We always ended the rendering of lard day off by frying doughnuts in the grease before putting in three and five gallon containers. Sausage was fried, packed in crock jars, then fresh lard poured over them and they kept indefinitely.

Neighbors also had threshing days when the women cooked for all the crews. There were 10 or 12 families that came out here about the same time and settled on adjoining land. Arch Vincents, Mace Haws, Claude Beggersloff, Otho Derrick, K.R. Henry, John Ransom, Louise Wilson, Ray Walker, Walt Ayers and E.L. Fairchild. The rest had money to go back during dust bowl days and before but the O'Brians and E.L. Fairchilds didn't have the money to leave.

For entertainment we had parties in the homes. There were also lots of checkers, pitch, and dominoes played. Also some dances were had in the homes. It shined the floors up good.

In the summer there would be a man come along about once with a team and wagon who peddled laces, threads, dress material, few toys, and just about anything one could get in town. Also caravans of gypsies stopped in to sell their wares.

The mail came three times a week. I think a Mr. Harry was our first mail carrier.

Tom and Julia went to school at Lakeview School. They rode an old school bus, and sometimes cars. Mr. Charles Russell was the bus driver. Mrs. Carter, Miss Floy Bridges were the teachers in 1928-1929. Then Mr. and Mrs. Boston taught in the 1930's.

Kenneth and Russell helped their dad with the living and income by working out. Marian went to Canyon to college in 1930. In the 30's is when activity and wind and sand started picking up in this area. Another enjoyment we had was a donkey and cart that we had lots of enjoyment out of.

Roads to Friona were trails in places.

HAMLIN OVERSTREET

Lubbock, Texas Sunday Morning, Feb. 25, 1973

Hamlin Overstreet Recalls Roaring Days of Farwell, Texico

It was the last frontier—wide open gambling, 16 saloons, a big red light district, shootings, rustling and all the rest that went with westward expansion.

It was Texico in 1906 when Hamlin Overstreet, now of Farwell, arrived there as a boy of 10. His uncle had helped found the town, along with the sister settlement of Farwell on the Texas side, and his grandfather was dealing in real estate.

Land could be bought in New Mexico, but the Texas side was part of the famed XIT Ranch, three million acres of land traded by the State of Texas for the capital of Austin.

"They burned off Prairie grass nearly waist high to survey this town," said Overstreet, who spent 50 years of his life selling and managing land affairs following the breakup of the vast ranch.

Land he sold for $25 an acre in 1925 "couldn't be bought for $425 today. I sold the last 35 acres of the three million acres several years ago, a little tract between the railroad tracks right here in Farwell," he said. "My whole life has been with them."

There were the years—the "boom and bust" years—that came before Overstreet joined himself to the breakup of the XIT and the settlement of the western plains of Texas.

There were great plans in the beginning for the Texico-Farwell area. It was founded as a division point for the Santa Fe Railway Co. building southwest from Amarillo, past Bovina on the XIT which was the "largest shipping point in the world" at the time.

Overstreet's uncle—James D. Hamlin, who was legal representative for the XIT owners for years—helped lay out the town, casting his lot with the new frontier after leaving an imprint on early Amarillo.

Overstreet reminisced about Parmer County and XIT history following publication of a book about Hamlin who handled the family westward. Hamlin stopped over in Amarillo, en route to the Klondike, and stayed. His father followed with the Overstreets coming a bit later. When Clovis later became the division point, many Texico and Farwell residents moved their homes or businesses over there.

Excitement was an every day affair when young Overstreet arrived from Saint Louis—cattle drives, track builders, cowpunchers, rustlers, "and everything else." Cattle came "clear from the Pecos Valley" to XIT holding pens at Bovina.

The big cattle drives were gone, but Overstreet got to see some pretty big herds moving to the railroad and later going northwestward to company holdings for finishing before shipment to the Chicago Markets.

The fall Overstreet arrived "hundreds of cattle froze to death along the railroad tracks" just outside Farwell.

Overstreet recalls that the Texico saloons would be going wide open at 3 a.m. when he met his father, who traveled for a pharmaceutical company, at the train.

"There were a lot of killings," he said. "We'd hear them hollering and there'd be a cowpuncher riding his bronc right down main street over there."

Trouble came from the difference in life made by the state line. On one side there was wide open rangeland and the other swarmed with small settlers.

Texico was "wet" while Farwell was "dry." Excitement was born in Texico but took in Farwell when it got going.

Hard feelings resulted when unbranded XIT calves strayed across the line and never made it back. Straying was often times helped along, draining the XIT of calf crop.

"No XIT cowboy was allowed to carry a branding iron on his saddle," Overstreet explained, noting that because of this many calves were not branded and could be enticed to other pastures.

Loss of calf crop was one of the things leading to the breakup of the gigantic ranch, which was still operated in 1906.

Overstreet went to his first school in a rock church, then to a portable building before completing his schooling in a schoolhouse erected in 1910 when his grandfather was chairman of the school board.

"I would have graduated in 1913 but I was the only one in the class. So, I quit a year and worked for the Santa Fe in Amarillo," he explained.

After finishing "the junior college at Clarendon" Overstreet went into banking business in 1916 in Farwell.

"Every morning about 10, I would make the rounds of the saloons in Texico and pick up their deposits . . . stacks of checks, American Express checks. Then it was legal to ship whiskey and they shipped it all over this country. I have seen three or four express trucks loaded with case whiskey at the depot."

The company constructed buildings to the south of the bank and put in several stores to encourage New Mexico farmers to shop in Farwell. There were "no farmers or inhabitants" east of Farwell and customers had to be drawn across the state line.

They didn't come in encouraging numbers so the mercantile and hardware stores moved back across the railroad tracks to Texico.

Breakup of the XIT began when all ranch equipment was sold in 1912.

A bank opened in Texico in 1917 with saloons to the side and across the street. The day Overstreet was to go to work there, a man was killed in one of the saloons, but he showed up for work anyway.

He was in the bank the morning a federal marshal showed up with warrants for a "real wheeler-dealer" who was promoting many things in Texico, including a motor company.

The Cannonball Motor Co. had sample cars built to promoting many things in Texico, company never got off the ground.

After a stint with the Clovis bank, Overstreet returned to Farwell in 1925 to work for "the company" in the bank building the company had purchased after the bank moved.

Sales methods were much like those today in land development.

"We built a hotel out east of Bovina and various agents in Oklahoma and Kansas would bring their prospects down," Overstreet said.

"We wouldn't take them to town or the real estate people there would get hold of them. We would take them out to this hotel and entertain them, show them the land. Then they would come to me and I'd take their application."

Land sold in spurts—sales stopping and starting for no apparent reason—at "very reasonable rates" with a series of annual payments set up.

"They couldn't meet their notes and we would extend them and extend them. Finally, we had to take a lot of this land back."

"When we sold it, it was in sod. When we got it back, it was in cultivation. That put us in the landlord business with several hundred tenants."

Land in grass was leased for 25 cents an acre with farm land crop and one-fourth of the cotton.

A change came about in the early 1930's. The company had only 25,000 acres left and decided that was not enough "to justify keeping the trust open. It bought out the smaller shareholders for cash and gave Overstreet the job of dividing the land—"Some improved, some not improved, some grazing and some farming"—among the 10 largest shareholders. He made the division and continued to manage the land.

Water—"There are several thousand irrigation wells in Parmer County"—changed the whole complexion of farming on land that once knew XIT cattle.

Some land, Overstreet said should never have been turned by a plow. It should have remained grassland, but back then "They put a plow to everything and ruined good land.

Rolling ranch or flat farm, the scene has changed greatly since Overstreet rode XIT rangeland to reach Texico—a town that "boomed and Busted" in the grand tradition of a pioneer settlement reaching for tomorrow.

It was Farwell, that stayed in the shadow of Texico in the booming years, which gradually grew to a settled town, serving a farm community with new modern homes growing on its perimeter.

He keeps an office in the old bank building that now sports a historical medallion for its importance to the development of the county.

"I did millions of dollars worth of business in a bare office up front and now I have this fancy office and don't use it," he said.

He does use it for sitting and talking about yesterday, how every bit of history was—when it was happening.

Today is nice and prosperous around Farwell, but there is a far-away look coupled with a hint of humor to the eye when Overstreet thinks of yesterday and all it held.

"I'm very glad I got to see it in its natural state."

JOE PAUL
By: Grace Paul

My report of this community in Parmer County—Lazbuddie—must begin in the year

THE JOE PAUL HOME at Lazbuddie, one of the most unique buildings in Texas. The lumber came from the fence around the 1893 Columbian Exposition in Chicago, Ill. commemorating the 400th anniversary of the discovery of America. Rail freighted to Friona was hauled by wagon to Lazbuddie.

1905. In that year my father, Mr. Joe Paul, my mother and seven really tired and disagreeable children landed and the peaceful cattle country was never the same again. The historical old Star Ranch soon began to take on a slight appearance of a settlement. Wire fences enclosed plots of land and the turning plow began its work. Many people came with high hopes and settled down to business living in shacks or half finished houses. Some became disheartened by the high wind, sand, drought, and blue northers and left. About five families, namely Frank Reeds, Steve Jeskos, John Treiders, Joe Pauls and Pete Kaisers stayed on.

I can't remember how or why the other families were not in on the first school, but I do remember that there had to be seven school-age children at that time to get a state supported school; and that we furnished four and the Kaiser's had three. However, we had not been in school since February the year before; but our parents thought school was all important. The next year we had a school—three months in length and one teacher who was really careful and cautious about the horse she rode to school. She boarded at the Old Star Ranch house and had been told by one of the hands that the horse was really viscious at times when he saw something unusual—the horse was blind! This one-room school was located approximately halfway between our home and the Kaiser home. Both families of children walked to school. The Paul children, three or four miles; the Kaiser children, two miles, because they were closer to a windmill and we could carry water from it. This was the mill where Rudoulf Pyrtz later lived.

The next project was a place of worship—non-denominational. The meeting place, in the school building. This practice came the first year the school building was completed. We used old literature from the Friona Congregational Church and our Bibles, Circuit Preachers, or some sort of preaching was held once a month. All services were non-denominational. After church and Sunday school, we all went home with first one family, then another for dinner. After dinner, baseball, basketball, or horseshoe games were a community affair. Other amusements were paly parties, singings, dances, box suppers, and picnic camp-outs in the sand hills to gather wild plums.

The fourth of July was always a big celebration. Relay races, potato races, bronc riding, sack races, etc., with basket dinners and lemonade. I do not understand now how we had time for all this for these were the days before tractors, cars, or modern home conveniences.

The community's school age children had increased until now the school building was moved to a new location; a quarter mile east of Star Ranch. This same building now housed two teachers. Room division was made by a curtain down the center of the building the long way. We carried water from the Star Ranch windmill. Red Tower school consolidated with us; that is the reason we had the second teacher. The school house didn't stay long in this location. Two or three years, as Red Tower school withdrew it was back on its own. The next move was a mile north of the Paul home or where Andy Brown now lives. We still maintained two teachers even though Red Tower went back on their own. At this location, the school stayed for about five years. But once again, this school house moved. This time about two miles east and a little south of the store or where the Merriott's lived. We still had two teachers and I was one of them. Now the reason for following this old building around is that it was certainly the center of all community activities. The teachers ordered the school books at the end of the year and we ordered books for 27 children. This allowed for five extra children and all the books were were permitted to order by law. But Old Star Ranch sold out to Shirley-Green and by the following Thankstiving we had 54 children seated on kegs and bricks along the front of the stage everywhere, and using school books sufficient for 27 children. It was also in this year that I had to go to Friona to get my voucher signed as the new-comers had not been here long enough to qualify for trusteeship and the older settlers had moved away; except for the Treiders, Jeskos and Pauls.

I will never forget that year. I was teaching five children in the same family who ranged in age from 6 to 17 years of age; none had ever been in school before. That year was pandamonium, but Viola Treider and I somehow suffered through. However good came of this condition. Star Ranch, Jesko, Cracker Box, and Red Tower all consolidated and Lazbuddie came into being. The name Lazbuddie was coined from the names of the older Shirley and Green who had bought out Star Ranch. Laz from Laz Green and Buddie from Andrew Shirley's nickname.The school now had five teachers and all camped around in these moved-in school buildings. This lasted only a few years, then Old Red, the first brick building, was constructed.

After Star Ranch sold out, things changed rather rapidly. The Pioneer days were gone and a modern era began. The Lazbuddie store came into existance. My brother, Charley, bought the first bill of groceries. The storekeeper made out the bill on a piece of brown paper bag. Also our famous traveling school house came to a halt in the form of Lazbuddie's first teacherage. It is still in use. The next year a Post Office was granted and housed in a corner of the store. This store and Post Office were a welcomed addition for in the early days we went to town only about once every three months and the freighters for Star Ranch brought the community mail from Bovina only when they made trips for cake and supplies. Some people were beginning to own cars. This relieved my mother some of her task of delivering babies or doctoring in general. We were a rather close knit community—everyone helped in their own particular way.

In the early days we raised our own wheat and took it to the Great West Mills in Hereford, Texas to be ground into flour and breakfast food. We made our hominy, cheese, butter, soap, rugs, quilts, corn meal, raised our beans, dried our apples, and if our debts permitted, killed and cured our own meat. Otherwise we ate rabbit, wild ducks, and sand hill cranes. We heated our house and cooked our meals with cow chips. Today we would be considered poverty subjects. Then we were proud of our ability to make ends meet. Not that I want to know modern times, I am certainly vastly proud of it because I can look back and see how very far we have come. Rural routes, paved roads, cotton gins, rural electrification, radio, television, telephones, school busses carrying the children to an excellent modern school. Irrigation wells with the help of fertilizer produce crops in abundance, modern farm tools, modern home appliances, all make country life very, very desirable.

There are three modern churches and many, many beautiful homes in our community. It is awe inspiring when you look back at this land that at the turn of the century sold from $3 to $12 an acre and now in 1966 is selling from $400 to $700 per acre. Last year, Parmer County, of which Lazbuddie is a part, led not only the State but the Nation in the production of grain sorghums. When I ran a test on this water in college chemistry, it proved to be like Ivory Soap— 99.6 percent pure.

I am proud to be a part—a very small part—in the making of this great community. Now what makes a community great? I think it is the ability and drive that makes its people want to achieve by their own initiative and persistance to do for themselves, and independence that never accepts defeat if the effort has been for the good of its people. And Lazbuddie has a goodly portion of this breed of people—the fast vanishing breed from the American scene.

Jan. 12, 1917 Ozark Trail Convention—Oklahoma City.

Commissioners Court Notes

THE POPE FAMILY

Oscar Theodore Pope and Bertha Myrtle Eaton were married March 16, 1902 in Weatherford, Oklahoma. They moved with their five children to Parmer County on November 26, 1925 from Tipton, Oklahoma, leaving one little girl, Ardith Marie who was buried in Arapehoe, Oklahoma. They broke out land three miles east of Hub which at one time was called Homeland.

Their oldest son Lloyd was married to Lillian Hale when they moved to Parmer County. Their only child Billy Ray was born in 1926. He now lives with his wife in Alaska. Lloyd lived, farmed, was a school bus driver and mail carrier for many years. Living in Parmer County until his death October 19, 1941. Lillian lives in Portales, New Mexico.

Coy Orville Pope went back to Tipton, Oklahoma and married Jewel George. They farmed in Parmer County until 1934 moving then to Crane, Texas where he became associated with Gulf Oil Company. They had two children, Donald Lee, who is a major in the Air Force stationed at Phoenix, Arizona and Coyelene Ulrick who lives in Midland, Texas. Coy died August 27, 1958. Jewel died January 29, 1973.

Alva Leroy served in the armed services for several years and married Iris Dixson. They had one daughter, Patsy Wright, who now lives in New Jersey. Alva and Iris lived many years at Imperial, Texas. Alva died February 24, 1966. Iris now lives at St. Elmo, Illinois.

Vivian Irene Pope married Everet Walter Talbot. His family having moved to Parmer County in 1919. They had one daughter, Edd Url Luttrull, who lives in Elk City, Oklahoma. Vivian and Everet lived and farmed in Parmer County until his death June 6, 1963. Vivian now lives in Elk City, Oklahoma.

Velta (Jackie) Pope married Forrest State whose family moved to Parmer County in 1929. They had one daughter, Donna Richie, who now lives in Pryor, Oklahoma. They moved to Missouri in 1933. They now live at Gravois Mills, Missouri.

Oscar and Bertha Pope celebrated 56½ years of married life, 32½ years being in Parmer County. Bertha died at age 73, January 19, 1959, and Oscar died December 8, 1960 at age of 84. Both are buried in the Friona cemetery.

FRANK LESLIE REED
A Short Family History
As Written By His Son,
G.E. (Bud) Reed

Being one of the long time residents of Parmer County, Texas, my father and mother came to Parmer County, Texas, in 1907, moving here from Lenox, Iowa. I have many times reflected upon the things my mother, Martha Ann Reed, whose maiden name was Ethington, told me about the way she felt when she first arrived in Friona, Texas. At that time, she said there was only a few buildings, consisting of the depot, a livery stable, one store, a small rooming house and a small lumber and coal business. My parents shipped their entire household goods, horses, cows, and other belongings to Friona in one box car, in those days called an immigrant car, and Daddy came along with it on the freight train. My mother came on the passenger train about two weeks later, by herself. She said that it was the first time she had been away from home. She considered it as quite an adventure because she didn't realize that there was so much country in the world without houses, trees, or people. When she arrived in Friona, she was met at the depot by Daddy. They spent the night in a rooming house as it was too far to go to the ranch that night. They got out early the next morning to drive the 25 miles by buggy. At that time there were only two or three homes between Friona and the Star Ranch, and the only thing Mother remembered seeing was some cattle and a few barbed wire fences. The buggy trip took most of the day. If Mother could have had a choice that day, she would have gone right back to Iowa. However, there was not a choice as they had already invested their savings in the move and they had to go on from there.

When they arrived at the ranch, Mother was surprised to see a large two-story ranch

January 12, 1917 Com. plans to draw Ozark Trails to Farwell.

Commissioners Court Notes

327

FRANK LESLIE REED—1882-1947.

house containing eight rooms on the first floor, and six rooms on the second floor. Nearby stood two large barns. A family by the name of Curtis lived in a part of the ranch house. When my Daddy arrived with his cargo he set up housekeeping in another part of the house and still everyone had plenty of room. I believe my mother told me that the Curtis family lived there for about two years, which was good for mother in that she didn't get so lonesome. Daddy did not have so much time to be lonesome as Mother did, because the first year he was there he plowed 80 acres of sod and planted it to feed crops. At that time, 80 acres was a large farm for the equipment he had, which consisted of a walking sod plow and a two-section harrow, a one row lister and a one row knife sled and four draft horses. In addition to farming, my daddy worked on the ranch when he could to help meet expenses. The first crop year for Daddy was not very good as it did not rain very much. The second year crop was better because of more rain fall and Daddy had broken out more sod land.

During that same period of time from 1907 to 1910 there were other families moving into the community of the Star Ranch. They were as follows: Joe Paul, Ernest Earl Worm, Steven Jesko, Peter Kaiser, and my Uncle W.O. "Bill" Reed. About this same time there was another settlement started some eight miles east of the Star Ranch which was known as Big Square. These families were some of our closest neighbors, and some of

the family names that I remember were: Habers, Micks, Wires, Stiles, and the Burtons.

The old Star Ranch headquarters where Mother and Daddy lived was centrally located among the neighbors and due to this fact it was more or less the gathering place for the community, and it was the custom then for them to get together for a dance. The upstairs rooms were built in a long hall like affair for that purpose. The Fourth of July celebration generally brought all the neighbors to the Star Ranch for a rodeo. Also on Sundays when the weather was pretty the neighbors would gather here for baseball games or to ride broncs for amusement and pass time as there wasn't any place to go and the means of transportation, which was horse back, in wagons and buggies was too slow to travel any great distance for a Sunday outing.

Due to the fact that the Star Ranch headquarters was one of the earliest settled and established ranches in this part of the country, it was more or less a stopping place for people who were crossing the country. I remember as a child seeing someone coming toward our place either by horse back, wagon or buggy, I knew that we were going to have company for a day or two because there was no other stopping place for many, many miles. On several occasions people from back East were crossing this part of the country on their way to New Mexico to file on land, would stop at the ranch to get water and feed for their livestock and make camp and they sometimes stayed for three or four days.

I do not know what year the first school was built in our district nor how much territory the district covered. During the year of 1914 or 1915 the Bill Hall family moved into our district some three miles west of where we lived. There were three children of school age in the Bill Hall family and they went to school with my older sister, Mable Pearl Reed. The school house was about three miles South and East of our home, which was some distance for children to travel by foot, or by buggy or horseback. Due to this fact the school trustees and men of the community got together and decided that something should be done about the situation. They discussed the matter and figured out a location that would more evenly divide the distance the children would have to travel to school. A date was set and the school house was moved to a new location which was only one-half mile East of our house. This new location made it very convenient for my sister and I to walk to school, however, this did not last very long. Within a couple of years the Charley Benton family moved into the western part of our school district. Therefore the little school house had to be moved again to keep it in the center of the school population. This time the building was located three miles west of the Star Ranch headquarters. During the eight years (1915 to 1923) that I attended the Star Ranch school the school building was moved three times. Soon thereafter the Star School consolidated with other districts and the little school building was moved to the present location of Lazbuddie High School, which is some two miles West of the original school ground.

During the seventeen years that my parents lived on the Star Ranch they endured many hardships of hard winters, cheap cattle prices and dry summers. The first hard winter they endured here was in 1911, when the snows came early and every few days it would snow more until it was almost impossible for Daddy to get to town for supplies. Mother told me how she worried about being stranded so far out in the country with two babies and what they could do in case of sickness, however, we all stayed well and had no problems from the standpoint of health. The major concern was food for the family and livestock. Mother said we had plenty to eat such as it was, but a very small variety. Caring for the livestock was no easy task and at that time very little farming was being carried on and due to this fact many cattle died of starvation. The next spring and summer the grass was good and the livestock that survived the winter had plenty to eat and did well. During the next few years more land was put into cultivation and also the cattle population increased and most people soon overcame their loss and began to look forward to a brighter future for themselves and their families. The winter of 1915 or 1916 was a rather severe winter which caused more loss and hardship, but not as great as in 1911 because people were much better prepared

to feed and care for their livestock. Up to this time I was not old enough to realize much about any of the worry and hardships that the older people had to endure. I remember Mother and Daddy talking of the year of 1917 being a good year as they raised good feed crops and a real good calf crop and got good prices for both cattle and grain.

The year of 1918, I shall never forget and so far as I know the winter of 1918-1919 was the most severe we have ever had here on the plains of Texas. We had raised a good crop of feed and had harvested it with grain binders and had the feed in shocks in the field, but before it was hauled out to be threshed the weather turned bad and the first snow came in the early part of November. Just before Thanksgiving we had a real blizzard with the snow drifts almost covering the shocks of feed. Another snow came before the first snows had melted away and another big snow fell by Christmas time, and travel and communications were next to impossible. The snow drifts were so deep in some places that we could not get through them with a two horse wagon. A short time before Christmas, Daddy had gathered enough material and built a sled and with the help of four good mules he made the trip to Friona after groceries and other supplies for the family and also some of our near neighbors.

The Spanish Influenza epidemic was very severe in the year of 1918 and nearly everyone in the country had that dread disease. I remember on Christmas morning of 1918 as we were having breakfast Daddy told Mother that he was afraid he might be taking the flu as he didn't feel very well. He and his brother, Earl Worm, who was working for us at the time, decided that we should move the cattle into the barns and corrals to make it easier on us to care for them during the bad weather. Daddy and I caught our saddle horses and started out to gather the cattle and Daddy asked Earl to start feeding the cattle. The feeding of the cattle was a big job because the feed shocks had to be dug out of

Jan. 26, 1917 Ozark Trail meet at Hereford, Tex.—Far. attend.

Commissioners Court Notes

the snow drifts with a shovel. By this time it had begun to snow again and it took Daddy and I until afternoon to get the cattle into the corrals. When we went to the house for dinner, Daddy was feeling so badly he could not eat anything. Mother tried to get him to stay at the house that afternoon as it was still snowing and very cold. He told her that we had to get the cattle separated and penned like he wanted them so in case he did come down with the flu it would be much easier for Earl and I to care for them. We worked until dark getting the cattle fed and for a nine year old boy, I had what I thought was a pretty rough Christmas day. By this time, Daddy was completely exhausted and past going, and was so sick by the next morning he could not get out of bed. For the next few days, Earl and I did very well caring for the livestock, although we could not dig as much feed out of the snow banks as the cattle could have eaten, we did manage to keep them from suffering from hunger. About the time Daddy was able to be up from his bout with the flu, Earl took the flu and was not able to work for a few days. My mother took Earl's place with the feeding and with her determination and ability, plus what Daddy in his weakened condition could help, we managed to partially feed and take care of the cattle. Our cattle suffered some from cold and hunger but we did not have nearly as great a death loss as some people in the country due to the fact that we had gathered our cattle into the barns, sheds and windbreak protection.

After World War I the farmers and ranchers in our area suffered from low prices in cattle and grain, for some two or three years then conditions began to change for the better. We raised several good crops and prices got generally better. Along about this time the land in Parmer County began to sell and change hands and more people from other parts of the country began coming here and buying land to put to cultivation. In 1924 Daddy and Mother sold their land at Lazbuddie to W.M. "Bill" Sherley, and bought land three miles north of Friona. We moved from the ranch to the new location in January of 1925. This was quite a change for our family as our livelihood on the ranch had been a lot of cattle and a little farming, and now the

situation switched to a lot of farming and a little bit of livestock. I helped Mother and Daddy with the farming until I finished high school in 1928, which was the year that Daddy bought his first farm tractor. We expanded our farming operation and broke out more sod. Then came the thirties with the depression and dust bowl days which was another hard blow to the farmers, but somehow we stayed and lived through them.

At this writing I am 56 years of age and have made my home in Parmer County the entire time. I can remember this country from the time it was practically all in native grass and then the early dry land farming days and now nearly all the land is in cultivation and under irrigation.

During the years I have travelled over a large portion of the United States, but I like Texas as a whole and Parmer County best.
(s) G.E. "Bud" Reed
A long time resident of Parmer County, Texas

W.O. REED

EARLY DAY HISTORY
OF PARMER COUNTY, TEXAS
By W.O. Reed
Lenox, Ia. April, 1965

Mr. & Mrs. Joe (and Ida) Jesko
Dear Friends:

I sure was glad to hear from you. We all stood the winter pretty good. We have had lots of snow and rain. No big snow; 2 to 5 inches. The ground is full of water, we did not get any of the floods and tornados. I guess it was awful in the north, about 250 or more killed and lots wounded. About 31,000 had to flee their homes. I guess the Mississippi River down the east of Iowa is still rising. Frank and Mattie came down there in 1908 by the 1st of March. Ben Curtis never did own the ranch; he was the foreman of the Star Ranch. Kelly of Chicago was the owner. Kelly bought the 90,000 acre ranch from Farwell brothers in about 1900—Got 3,0000,000 acres from the Government for building the State House of Texas (at $1.00 per acre). That was the Syndicate Ranch; headquarter at Bovina. They sold the small ranch off—90,000 acres, Star Ranch, H.L. Ranch, Spring Lake, and Hassel Ranch. I think all about 90 to 115 thousand acres. Kelly gave $2.50 an acre for Star Ranch. Kelly was a Stockyards of Commission man in Chicago. Ben Curtis ran the Star Ranch for Kelly. They kept cattle there til May or June 1st. Frank lived in the big house with Curtis. About the size of the house; 40 ft. square with a 60 foot wing, 20 feet wide on the west porch on the east side, south side to west end of wing.

The George G. Wright Land Company began selling that land for Kelly, I think in 1907. I am getting a little ahead of my story.

A fellow by the name of Laird was running a lumber yard at Bovina. Kelly got him to put the buildings out there. Two large barns 108 feet long, 40 feet wide. The horse barn burned down about 8 or 10 years after Frank lived there. The other they called the cake house where they kept cotton seed cake. Frank said there was a man run a freight wagons; pulled them with 15 burros, four in a brest, the head team three head. Don't know where they hauled from, a long way, I guess.

Joe Paul and family came down there in 1908, I think the same time Frank did. Charley Brooks family; Milo Lassen family; Leak family; Smiley family; A.R. Gregory, a bachelor; Don Kentrel batched on the Taylor place. It belonged to a railroad contractor that built the road between Farwell and Plainview. Didn't know his name. Charley Mopes and Mr. and Mrs. Hamil all lived across the draw northeast of Star Ranch. Milo Lassen lived at Red Tower, 6 miles northeast of Ranch. They had a school house in the neighborhood. I think they all came there in 1908. Erma and I came in January, 1909. Pete Kaiser and family, George Sturt, Oaks Weaver and family; John and Jim Rogers families lived 3 or 4 miles south of Lazbuddie on farm owned by Ralph Flanigan from Omaha, Nebraska. Henry Bledsoe, I think lived on the Oakes place in 1923-24, went to Colorado . He was a big farmer and stockman. I think he was a partner with G.G. Wright Land Company, and land people went off and left. Lis Presgrove and family lived at Keffer Ranch, southwest of Star Ranch, southwest of Laura Treider 2 or 3 miles. Ira Stouton came down in 1910. We lived on the Jennings place, south of Laura Treider place 1910. Left there in January 1911, went back to Iowa.

Mr. Weaver's wife died in 1908 just before we came down there. They had 4 or 5 small children. There was a Mexican family came through and lost two little children and they buried them out there on the Prairie not very far from the Oakes and Weaver places, and they buried Mrs. Weaver with the children. Some of our boys built a fence around their graves. I never did see the place. Mr. Weaver then moved to Bovina with his children and in a little while they put Mr. Weaver in for Sheriff. I got pretty well acquainted with him. He was a friend of everyone. He came down there from Classring (?), Iowa, a town six miles from Lenox, Iowa, our town. I never did know him here.

About the schools, Kaiser's had a school down in that part of the country, but nobody had too many kids. Paul's, Kaiser's, and Jesko's, Lis Presgroves, Otto Treider's; was about all I knew at that time. But in 1923 when we moved back, there were lots of kids and they had moved the school house one mile south of where Lazbuddie is now, I guess had a full house. We boarded the teacher in 1909, Miss Effie Walden that term. Erma and Effie wrote back and forth for a long time. She married a rancher from the Amarillo area. Dollie Clark taught in 1923 or '24 and boarded at our place. She married ChattonFloyd Penson, after he died, she married another man in Colorado. She was back and visited us six or seven years ago. Her folks came to Friona from Gravity, Iowa, about 20 miles from Lenox. Viola Geisler taught down there too, I don't remember where she boarded.

Daddy Hogland ran a store at Bovina: Bovina Mercantile Co. in 1909 and 1910. Luther Barnes and Frank Hastings worked at the store. We traded there. Jack Anderson ran a barber shop in Bovina in 1910. He used to come to our places for dances. Later on our visits there, I always stopped by to see Jack as he had moved his shop to Friona, he always was the same.

In 1924 we took 52 bales of cotton to Friona Gin, which was run by Benn F. Ridge—first gin in Friona. The bales brought $53.00. Got 19c per pound. A man came out in spring of 1924, and said if farmers would put out cotton enough, he would put up a gin in Friona. He told me Henry Bledsoe was going to put out 600 acres and would bring him 600 bales of cotton. I told him I would put out 100 acres and if I raised any, I would come to Friona with it. Bledsoe put out his 600 acres and contracted Mexicans to hoe it for $3. an acre. It looked like a weed patch. He picked eleven bales and took to Farwell. Pickers all quit and that was it. Benn Ridge put a gin in Friona and I think only ginned 168 bales all together. We took in 52 of them. Frank put out 50 acres of cotton and didn't get a stand. Plowed it up and put it in cane.

Back in 1907 and for 4 or 5 years, George G. Wright Land Co. ran an Excursion train to Friona every two weeks. It came to Friona on Tuesday and left on Thursday. They kept about eight autos at Friona for use in showing land buyers around. They would take them to Star Ranch and go from there to show land, then come back to the Ranch and make the contracts. After Frank and Mattie; and Erma and I came down, the Land Company would bring their bunch to Star Ranch and we would board them. If man and wife they would stay at the Ranch, and single men would room down at the "Four Mile House" south east of the Ranch. A place the ranch owned called Carter Corner. They kept about 40 cots down there for their customers to sleep, and they would come back to the Ranch to eat. They would return to Friona on Thursday, then would load the suckers on waiting train and leave for Kansas City, never letting them talk to anybody at Friona.

Friona would not let the negro porter off the train the two days it set on the side track there. Fleas were pretty bad down there at that time. Lots of dissatisfied people would stay one or two years and leave forgetting they had land. The ones who stayed two years, stayed on. It was pretty hard to stay two years, but all had good times. We would have a dance once in a while at the Ranch. The dance hall was upstairs a 40 x 20 foot all one room. Everyone in neighborhood would bring food and all enjoyed it. Girls and boys would come from Amarillo on horseback, stay all night at Ranch. We would dance all night Saturday night, and on Sunday play baseball. Star Ranch had a team along with Dimmitt, Spring Lake, H L. Ranch; all had good ball teams. The Fourth of July, 1909, had a Barbeque at Friona and Rodeo. The cars the Land Company had at Friona had no tops and cowboys and auto drivers went out on Syndicate land where there were herds of wild horses and rope their rodeo horses. Roped one horse they ran for 100 miles, an out-law horse stallion, Syndicate Brand. That one had gotten out and was running with wild horses. They really celebrated Fourth of July at Friona. I took a big wagon from the Ranch and 4 horses and took a load of neighbors to Friona and stayed till after dark. On the road home came up a big rain and thunder storm; everyone got soaked. I was driving. It was so dark, we were facing the storm and when it lightened my lead team was turned around by side of other team. I swung them all around and got back on trail. Every body felt pretty good to get such a good rain. We were about halfway home, and waited a little bit til the rain was over, and the moon came out, we continued on home. When we got home, it hadn't rained a bit, dry as a bone. I think if you ask Ralph Paul, he will remember that. I don't remember who all was on the trip, about as big a load as we could take in a big wagon. Maybe Laura and Otto Treider, Raymond and Jewell were pretty small at that time. Probably Grace and Greta Paul was along. If so, they would remember.

Always your friend,
W.O. Reed
Lenox, Iowa

FLOYD W. REEVE

Parmer County was just a little over two years old and populated by approximately 1000 people when Mr. and Mrs. Floyd W. Reeve and seven weeks old daughter, Esther, arrived from Friendswood, Indiana. The date was September, 1909 and the young family had arrived in Friona via a semi-monthly "Home Seekers" excursion train of the George G. Wright Land Company of Kansas City.

On a train car they had also brought with them a load which consisted of a registered Percheron stallion, a blue bull, Topsy (a high bred racing trotter), eight other horses, a dog, white wyndotte chickens, household items including a leather davenport, both dried and canned fruits, a buggy and a com-

ETHEL INEZ HADLEY and Floyd White Reeve on their wedding day.

MR. REEVE building an adobe house.

MR. REEVE builds an adobe house.

plete "set of farm tools fit for Indiana farming, but unsuitable for Texas farming."

The town of Friona at this time consisted of a train depot, a hotel, a bank, a boarding house (which later became the present Floyd W. Reeve residence), the old Maurer house, a watering tub, (located about 200 feet east of the present main street crossing), a school (a 20 x 40 foot frame building), "Daddy" Foster's scale shed from which he supplied the newcomers with coal, a livery stable and the Wentworth house which was the highest spot of the townsite and was also used for privately owned water works and approximately 10 or 12 other residences.

After the Reeves arrived in Friona, they had a long nine mile wagon ride to the four-roomed house of a cousin, D.M. Ballard, with whom they lived until they had time to build their own home.

With the help of two carpenters who had arrived in the area on the same immigrant train, the two families managed to complete the four-roomed Reeve house in about a month. The location of their first home was seven miles west and three miles north of Friona on a "raw and wholly unimproved section of land."

For a week at a time, there were big cattle drives on the trails as the XIT Ranch several miles distant moved cattle. Five men and 1000 head of cattle could make three to seven miles a day on their way to shipping pens.

Wild mustangs and antelope were there.

There were prairie-dog towns and rattlesnake dens. Coyotes were so numerous they were sometimes a menace to family pets. The dog they had brought from Indiana soon learned this fact. He had taken out in pursuit of a coyote only to return shortly, yelping, with a pack of coyotes on his heels. Floyd shot his old army Springfield western rifle at the pack. He succeeded not only in frightening them away, but started a bunch of wild mustangs out of a lake bed a few hundred yards away.

And so it was about 18 months after their marriage in March, 1908, Floyd and Ethel found themselves fulfilling a dream that he had held even before their marriage—that of establishing a home in the wide expanses of lush prairie land that had been described to him as the "future heart of America."

While attending a business college in Indiana, Floyd had waited tables in a boarding house to help finance his way through college. One of the residents of this boarding house was a land agent for a company who was selling land in the Texas Panhandle and it was he who supplied young Reeve with the pictures of "wonderful feed crops in the shock, golden wheat waving in the breeze,

REEVE-BALLARD FAMILY

A GOOD DAY for drying clothes.

clear, blue sky, cattle, sheep and horses grazing in great herds and standing by lakes with their shadows cast in clear water."

These pictures were vividly stamped in the memory of the farm raised boy even though he was currently preparing himself for the business world. After finishing school, he went to work in a small town bank and this was before the day of the general use of the adding machine and typewriter. Is it any wonder that the long columns of figures that had to be added and the piles of statements that had to be hand written soon presented a "night marish" picture that encouraged Floyd to recall more and more frequently the ones of the Texas Panhandle? In the meantime, his father had "Panhandle fever," too, and had purchased land from the George G. Wright Land Company. With this financial backing, then, the young Reeves decided to go to Texas to look after the land interests of the elder Reeve.

The life they chose, therefore, was by no means the easiest or even the most secure. They started with nothing much but their youth, good health, a staunch Quaker background, and their dreams. Materially they had the land that belonged to Floyd's father and the house they had built. And they were soon to learn that too much had been paid for the land. What his father thought was a bargain at $20.00 an acre was actually an extravagance. Adjoining the land of the W.H. Fuqua farm was later offered at $5.00 an acre.

To stock the land required money—which was a scarce item. But Floyd was able to buy 1000 head of sheep with "no money down and plenty of time to pay" and went into debt also for feed and equipment. Within five

years the sheep had paid for themselves and the Reeves were out of debt.

Those had been five lean years, however, filled with hard work and a growing family. Esther now had a sister and two brothers: Mary, Hadley and Glenn. And still another son, Charles, was to be born to the family before Ethel was able to regain a prized possession she had given up with her marriage.

She had studied long hours at the piano and her teacher encouraged her to go on the concert stage with her piano. The concert stage she didn't really mind abandoning, but her piano was another thing. Some day she would get another one . . . . Four babies and eight years later, that dream was fulfilled when Floyd traded a horse for a piano and brought it home to her.

As Esther approached school age, the family moved into Friona, but before long they moved again into the country to the V Bar Ranch. Here the school age youngsters commuted to school by car and stayed over night with a teacher if adverse weather kept Floyd from driving in to pick them up—which it occasionally did.

The sheep business had been prosperous, but Floyd decided to go into the cattle business chiefly because as he said, "The boys I was running around with were cowboys and rode horses while I was a foot and couldn't stand it."

The cattle business proved to be a financial success, too, and brought about the fourth

June 15, 1917 Ozark Trails Convention in Amarillo.

Commissioners Court Notes

THE REEVE SEXTET

MISS ETHOL BALLARD and Miss Malinda Reeve. Cow not named, picture not dated.

MALINDA REEVE and Ethel Ballard, 1911.

move for the growing family. From the big profit he had made on his sheep and cattle, they purchased the "finest house in Friona" (what is now the Harold Lillard home) and once again moved into town. It was here their sixth child, Ruth, was born.

Then during the winter of 1918-1919 an exceptionally severe winter set in and all the cattlemen were in trouble. Blizzards and deep snow killed off much stock and a general slump in cattle prices sent many of them into bankruptcy. Floyd was no foreigner to trouble. He did manage to hold his cattle for two years on 30 sections of rented grass land. The local banker extended his loan for the rent and he was able to raise enough kafir corn and maize following that terrible winter to keep holding the cattle.

Again the family moved back into the country, this time to cut expenses, for a small four-roomed house was furnished free with the rent of the land. By holding on until 1923, Floyd was finally able to sell all but 123 head of calves at enough to pay off all his debts. There was nothing left, except his 123 calves, but he had not declared bankruptcy and he owed no man . . . . And he remembered that someone had once said, "There are just two sources of wealth: natural resources and human resourcefullness."

With the 123 calves and his "human resourcefullness," Floyd was back in the cattle business within three years. A short time after that, they were able to buy land again and build on it—a three bedroom adobe brick house with concrete floors and a bath (with a tin tub).

Floyd and his sons were still in the cattle business and farming on the side, but their

pasture land was disappearing as more and more of it was being plowed under by wheat farmers. So he decided to venture into dairy farming and purchased 30 head of short horned dairy cattle and a flock of turkeys. The turkey business didn't prosper, for as Floyd put it, "They drowned on level ground."

Then just the fall before Ruth was to start to school, the family made a seventh and final move into Friona. Floyd had traded some land for a fleet of 10 school buses and the huge house in town—the boarding house they had seen when they first set foot in Friona many years before.

When Parmer County had first been organized in 1906, it was out into school districts as near six miles square as possible with plans for a school house to be placed near the middle of each district. The county school board wanted to keep the districts as small as possible for they felt that three miles was enough distance for any child to have to walk

March 9, 1917 Parmer and D. Smith com. co-op on Ozark Trail.

Commissioners Court Notes

MALINDA REEVE, Ethel Ballard, and Melville Ballard (the victim).

to school! Within a short time, however, these small districts learned they could legally and economically have their children transported with tax money and the smaller districts began consolidating. In 1923 the Friona school district voted to consolidate with the adjacent district and became an independent district a year later. Transporting the children within the larger school district became a "business" which Floyd and his two older sons decided to buy into. During 1926 and 1927 Hadley and Glenn drove two of the school buses.

Farming had always been a side-line but by now Floyd and his sons were dry-land farming two sections of land in addition to running the fleet of school buses. These were the depression years. Floyd and Ethel managed to "keep their heads above water" during those trying years and somehow see to it that their six sons and daughters each received a high school diploma from Friona High School and a college degree from West Texas University.

Finally in 1937 Floyd sold the buses and traded some of his land for the Chevrolet agency. Together with Hadley and Glenn, they formed the Reeve Chevrolet Company, but still had farming as a side-line. Eventually irrigation came to the Panhandle, so much of the dryland farming became irrigated and the value of the land greatly increased.

Throughout the years, the influence of these two Parmer County pioneers has been felt in many areas. Ethel's community service was most often connected with something musical. She was church pianist for many years in the Congregational Church. Floyd served in various ways—as Friona's mayor, Sunday School teacher, life member of

Masonic Lodge (presented to him in 1962), president of the school board, election judge, county commissioner and columnist for the weekly "Friona Star" as "Farmer John," a staunch Republican, who gave his views on many subjects, but most often political.

In the saga of any family, there are always those moments of tragedy or near tragedy and the Reeve family saga is no exception.

There was the heavy suitcase that fell from overhead on the train rack that barely missed Esther at seven weeks . . . or the near panic at one and a half when she caught a thimble in her throat . . . and the shock of her accidental death in 1966.

There was the day the older children played on the banks of the Frio draw as they frequently did. Those who know of its reputation know of its sudden treachery, but the four Reeve children playing there were not aware of anything ominous, for it was a clear, bright day in Texas. In childish glee, they had run across the draw and into the house to tell their mother of the penny they had found. Moments after they entered the house, a wall of water, having gathered from a cloud burst in New Mexico, engulfed the very spot they had crossed.

There was the run-away horse with Glenn the rider. The horse jumped the fence and the rider was raked off . . . And yet another time Glenn escaped serious injury when the car he was driving was hit by a train switching at the Clovis crossing.

A small boy tumbled down some steps, and there was Hadley with a broken arm which mended slightly crooked. And it was only Hadley who had presence of mind enough to "do something" when a wooden croquet ball, which was being used in a game of "Annie-Annie over," came down on top of baby Ruth's head and knocked her unconscious. The other children scattered in fright, but Hadley stayed and blew in her face . . . It was Hadley who had a childhood illness that remained undiagnosed until he reached manhood. But the diagnosis came too late, for the rheumatic fever had already badly damaged his heart and his life was cut short in 1957 at the age of 45.

Ruth had been born in 1919 after the peak of the influenza epidemic that followed World War I. Influenza was no respector of

336

age, however, so Ruth did not escape it. She was a very sick baby and when she was still not walking at the age of 18 months, her parents feared her bout with the flu might have left her permanently crippled. Shortly after her second birthday, however, their concern was dissolved when she finally walked as any normal child should. It was Ruth and a little friend several years later who tied their jump ropes on the back of the school bus parked in front of the house. Not aware of this, Hadley got into the bus to drive it to the bus barn about a block away. Ruth's friend was able to get her rope untied before the bus pulled away. But Ruth was not so lucky. Instead she held on to the bus, trying to untie her rope as she ran. She had been warned never to hang on to a moving vehicle, but for the moment, she ignored the warning, for she wanted the rope and she knew it would be locked inside the barn over night if she didn't get it off. But the bus was going faster than she could run and she finally turned loose about half way to the barn. Just as she did, the dangling jump rope wrapped around her ankle and dragged her to the ground. Fortunately Hadley heard her screams, but not before she had some skinned and bruised spots to explain to her mother when she went crying into the house.

It was on the Saturday night before Easter Sunday when Mary was ten years old that she dreamed of swallowing pins. She awakened critically ill...diphtheria. She was out of school the rest of the year...and during her convalescence, she could not see, talk or walk. Even a year later she could not run and play as the other children did, and she was a senior in high school before the doctor felt she was physically strong enough to have what remained of her tonsils removed. It was Mary, many years later, who went boating on Lake Wichita when both she and her date fell in. Neither could swim but some how he managed to drag an unconscious Mary to safety and shortly thereafter, she learned to swim!

Charles only had a slight case of diptheria and the other four were given anti-toxen which spared them from the disease entirely. But it was Charles who brought a different crises to the family a few years later. The car was not running properly, so Charles, sus-pecting water in the gasoline, had drained it out on the ground. He had driven the car several feet away and set fire to the gasoline to see if it would burn with so much water in it. But he was not prepared for the liquid to run down a slight incline toward the car—nor was he prepared for it to burn so well! So when he saw the fire igniting the spare tire on the back of the car, he raced into the house but calmly announced, "Papa, I think the car is on fire." The car was saved but it did have to have new paint and a spare tire.

Floyd and Ethel had weathered blizzards, dust storms, prairie fires and their children's accidents and illnesses, but their most critical vigil was Floyd's own fight against double pneumonia. At the time, the nearest doctor and hospital were 30 miles distance. He was critically ill and it is a tribute to the doctors who saved him, for the miracle drugs of today were then unknown.

Parmer County and Friona had undergone much change by the time they celebrated their golden wedding anniversary in 1958...and they had been a part of that change. Floyd spoke for them both when he said with warmth and meaning, "It is a worthwhile feeling to have had a part in the development of a community."

Floyd W. Reeve passed away shortly after his 85th birthday in May 1963.

The family continues to grow and from Floyd and Ethel's six children there have been 10 grandsons, 5 granddaughters, 5 great grandsons and 4 great granddaughters. All of them, with the exception of Charles and Ruth and their families (who live in Connecticut and California respectively) have remained in Texas within a 150 mile radius of Friona.

RUDOLPH J. RENNER FAMILY

Rudolph Renner and Clara Baker first met in the summer of 1920 at Shattuck, Oklahoma. One year later, on October 24, 1921 they were united in marriage at Arnett, Oklahoma by Judge Clark.

In April of 1922 they leased a farm two miles south of Clara's parents place. They bought the owners livestock and farm equipment here they started their farming career by planting row crop and feed for their livestock. It was hard work but much enjoyment to raise their own livestock and garden. Rudolph helped his father-in-law with his farming that spring and summer. It was here on this farm that their first son, John William was born on November 1, 1922.

Clara's father became ill in 1923 and passed away in January 1924. Rudolph was left to farm his land along with his own that he had leased, so they moved into a small two room house on this place. Clara's mother and three younger sisters continued to live in the large family house. Rudolph did a lot of trading and by now had accumulated quite a few head of cattle and had enough horses to do his own farming.

On November 16, 1924 Aubrey Lee was born on his grandfather's homestead. They made good crops this year and Rudolph was still trading for most anything he could. He would say, "I'll trade anything except my wife and two little boys, I married my wife for keeps."

In the spring of 1924 they rented a farm eight miles east of the place they were living on. They moved to this farm and again raised a good crop of wheat and spring crop. Their garden was good and supplied the food for the family. They received notice in the early winter of 1925 that this land they were farming could not be rented another year. The decision to move to West Texas was made. Rudolph had worked in this part of the country, for three years before they married.

He knew what great opportunities there were for a young couple here. In January of 1926 he came to Friona and bought their present farm southeast of Friona. Selling their surplus farm equipment and some livestock at a public farm sale on February 15, 1926 they loaded an Immigrant Train car with the rest of their belongings and headed for Friona. They bought farming equipment including an old tractor, two cows, chickens, and household furniture. How well they remember this day. Rudolph, Clara, their two small sons, Johnnie and Lee and Clara's sister Rebecca Weis and two sons. Leslie and Johnnie came in the Model T. It rained on them all the way which was a long day's drive in a Model T without a top. They had a water well drilled and built a 12x24 shack to live in. The H.H. Weis family was moving to Texas at

this time and both families lived in this house. It became quite crowded with four little boys and both families belongings in this little house, but the weather was warm and the out of doors was big and lovely. There were no fences or roads, only cattle trails as far as the eye could see. It rained a lot that spring and on the night of March 29, 1926 it rained all night until 9:00 a.m. the next day, then turned to the worst blizzard this family had ever lived through. Their shack was not at all comfortable but with Rebecca's "Home Comfort Range" blazing all day they survived. The snow was blowing in everywhere. They kept the four little boys in bed all day to keep warm and before the day was over they had baby chickens, the old mother hens and their dog in this little shack. It was a blessing the storm lasted only until night, but to them there never was a storm like this one, and never be another the same, at least after this they were prepared for blizzards. Rudolph broke sod and planted row crops. Time came for him to go to Oklahoma to harvest his wheat crop there. With plenty of rain here for the crops to grow, he stayed in Oklahoma and worked with the threshing crew until they finished his wheat. He was in Oklahoma 40 days. When he came home he could hardly believe his eyes how the crops had grown. On October 24, 1927, another son was born to bless this family, Rudolph Jr.

There was a lot of hard hand work to be done on this new place, fences to be built and also shed and shelter for the livestock. Rudolph's love for baseball was always present. This was the only form of recreation that was of interest to him. On Sunday afternoons he would go play baseball with the local neighbor boys. In the spring of 1930 they built their present farm home. It was here their first daughter, Lillie Mae, was born on May 13, 1930.

Depression hit hard at this time as it did for everyone else. They raised their own chickens and had their fryers and eggs. They also had their own milk cows which supplied

June 29, 1917 Ozark Trail lost to Roswell short line.

Commissioners Court Notes

them with fresh butter, cream and all the milk a family could use and also had some to market to help supply other household needs. They traded wheat for flour. Homemade bread and noodles went a long way in those days. "Dust Bowl Days" were especially hard for those to imagine who didn't live at this time.

Mary Joyce, their second daughter, was born on December 17, 1934. Delmer Earl (Cotton) was born on February 23, 1938. This bringing this family total to four boys and two girls. Time went only too fast for this happy family. By this time the older ones were in school and there was much work and planning to be done for clothing and such.

ERIC VANCE RUSHING

Eric Vance Rushing was born on April 5, 1896 in New Burnside, Illinois. His folks came to Oklahoma Indian Territory when he was four years old.

Mattie Carrington was born on June 1, 1898 at Natural Dam, Arkansas. She attended the same teacher's college that Eric's sister, Mary, attended. She came home with Mary for a weekend and this is how she and Eric met.

Eric and Mattie were married on May 30, 1917 in Ada, Oklahoma. Their children are Eric M. born May 16, 1918 in Ada, Oklahoma, Roberta, born on September 2, 1920 in Ada, Oklahoma and Bonna Lee, born February 15, 1922 in Francis, Oklahoma.

In 1927 the family moved to Friona, Texas, for health reasons. In March of that year they opened a general store in Friona, in the building where Bill's T.V. and Appliance Store is located now. They lived in the back of the store until they sold it in 1931 and bought a variety store from Uncle Andy Wentworth.

GEORGE A. SACHS

George A. Sachs was born on December 27, 1875 in Hastings, Nebraska and moved to Marysville, Kansas in 1882. He grew up in Kansas and came to Texas in 1908 for health reasons. He lived on the Escarbada Ranch and kept cattle on his land just south of the ranch. While there he helped build the Lutheran Church in the Rhea Community.

Clara Bultemeier was born January 22, 1888 in Decatur, Indiana. In 1911 she came to Texas with her father to see the land he had bought in the Rhea Community, and to visit relatives there. She and George met on this visit.

George and Clara were married on June 23, 1913 in Decatur, Indiana. They returned to Texas and lived on the Escarbada Ranch until 1917. Two children were born while there, Melvin, on June 18, 1914 and Irene, on January 7, 1916.

RUSHING'S STORE, Mr. and Mrs. E.V. Rushing, Mrs. McElroy, Mr. Butch Routh—1927.

GEORGE AND CLARA SACHS on their wedding day.

MOVING DAY—1917.

GEORGE SACHS sent this card to Clara Bultemeier about two months before they were married.

MELVIN AND IRENE eating watermelon out of their wagon.

In 1917 they bought a house and barn from Mr. Seamond, father of Clyde Seamond, of Friona. The house was located just west of the present post office in Friona. They moved the house to their land in the northwest corner of Parmer County, using a steam engine, teams and skids. The barn was torn down and rebuilt south of their house. Two more children were born here, Evelyn, on

April 16, 1918 and Ruth, on May 16, 1920.

George Sachs died December 23, 1920 and was buried in the Rhea Cemetery. Mrs. Sachs continued to live on the place, renting the land out until the children were old enough to help with the farming and chores. Life was mingled with hardships and pleasures, mostly pleasant memories to a child growing up.

Each of the children attended Rhea School, which was located near the Floyd Schlenker home. These are also pleasant memories. Some of the teachers who come to mind are the Fowlers, Corinne Tipton, David and Gladys Sides, Greta Paul, and others just as dear to think of. Two of our bus drivers were Boye Taylor and Harold Schlenker who made riding a bus lots of fun.

THE S.J. SANDERS FAMILY

Mr. and Mrs. S.J. Sanders and five children came here to Friona from Como, Texas in 1925. They farmed south of town most of their lives until moving to Mineola, Texas in 1955. Mr. Sanders lived to be ninety years old and passed away five years ago. Mrs. Sanders is still living at age of 89.

MR. AND MRS. S.J. SANDERS.

July 6, 1917 Ozark Trail short liners to meet in Clovis.

Commissioners Court Notes

340

ROBERT ALLEN SISK FAMILY

Robert Allen (Bob) Sisk was born in Jackson County, Alabama, January 29, 1890. He married Katharen Elizabeth Pillow in 1910 in Montague County, Texas. They moved to Friona, Texas, October 31, 1927 as he was Section Foreman for the Santa Fe Railroad. Bob and Katharen had seven children: Florence, Flossie, Zelma, Ony, Lucille, Cecil, and Steve. Katharen passed away in Friona in 1928. She was buried in Hereford, Texas.

In 1927 the Draw came down. Bob had to carry the small children from the house to the railroad which was under water. Bob had to build up under the tracks so the trains could pass. In 1928 Bob traded sections with Mr. Woods who was at Bovina. He still lives there with a daughter, Mrs. Lester Rhineheart.

J.M. SPOHN

J.M. Spohn and his wife, Amelia, and their five children, Samuel Oscar, Mary, Clara, Henry and Robert, came to Texas from Kansas in 1908. They first settled in Deaf Smith County, about 19 miles northwest of Friona. They could not get water at that location so they moved to a place six miles west of Friona in Parmer County. When moving their house, the movers stopped for the night. The place where they stopped was in a buffalo wallow. It rained that night and it was two weeks before they could get the house moved again as it was surrounded by water. The members of the family still living at this time are Mrs. Clara Miller, Clovis, N.M., Mrs. Mary Ford of Mineola and Bob Spohn of Friona.

FLOYD SCHLENKER

The Friona Star
Thursday, September 16, 1971

Malinda Schlenker
Rhea Area Resident Is Typical Pioneer
By June Floyd

Soon after the turn of the century Evan Hadley Reeve, who lived in Indiana, became interested in "Going West." A few years later he purchased land in the north central part of Parmer County, Texas, and planned to develop it into a cattle ranch.

One of his daughters, Malinda, graduated from high school in Indiana in 1907. She, too, had a pioneering spirit. This combined with her ambition to teach school, brought the young woman to the Texas Panhandle in 1909.

Evan Hadley Reeve died before realizing his ambition to become a "West Texan," but his widow, Adeline Reeve, and their children moved to the ranch. Mrs. Reeve was interested in the affairs of the community she lived in and at one time served on the school board.

Miss Malinda first taught school at a one room school in the Rhea Community.

She said, "At first I just had children from two families, and one of them was the Schlenker family.

After teaching two years, Miss Malinda was married to Floyd Schlenker December 25, 1912 at the Reeve Ranch.

Mrs. Schlenker related, "Our first home was on a claim over on the state line. After we proved up on it, we sold it and bought this section, where I have lived ever since."

Their first home in Parmer County was a combination of the house they had lived in in Curry County, New Mexico and another one they bought from someone in the neighborhood. Later the couple built a new house in the same location.

"I've lived in this location nearly 60 years and have no intention of moving," said the soft spoken pioneer woman.

The Schlenkers had three children, Amelia, Sarah and Carl. Amelia, who is now Mrs. James Rankin, lives in California; Sarah, who is now Mrs. Elmo Dean, lives in the Rhea Community; and Carl lives in Friona.

Schlenker, who died in 1955, was a farmer and cattleman. They first did dry land farming, but later began to irrigate. For a number of years the family raised registered Hereford cattle, hogs and small grain crops.

Billy Sifford and his wife, the former Florence Dean, and their two sons, live near Mrs. Schlenker and he takes care of the farming and livestock operations.

In addition to her duties as a wife, mother

CHARLES SCHLENKER FAMILY, 1917—Back row—Esther, Oscar, Willard, Mabelle. Second row—Louisa, Harold, Florence, Vula. Third row—Mrs. Amelia Schlenker, Helen, Mr. Charles Schlenker, John, Floyd.

and homemaker, Mrs. Schlenker has always found time for community, church and club activities. She is a long time member of Friona Woman's Club and Union Congregational Church.

Grandchildren, in addition to Florence Dean Sifford are Gladys Dean Spring of Bovina, Lindy Dean Varner of Phoenix, Arizona, Mrs. Bob Johnson and Carleen Schlenker, both of Friona, Jim Schlenker, who is a student at West Texas State University, Canyon, and Floyd Schlenker, who attends South Plains Junior College, Levelland.

There are also six great-grandchildren.

Soon after her husband's death, Mrs. Schlenker shared her home with two girls from Hong Kong. Madeline and Catherine Chang stayed in the Schlenker home and attended high school here.

Following their graduation from Friona High School, the two went to California for further training and at the present are both married and both are registered nurses.

A hand carved chest imported from Hong Kong was a gift from the Chang sisters to Mrs. Schlenker and is cherished by her.

Mrs. Schlenker remembers that during her early years in this section of the country she usually went to Bovina to buy groceries and remarked, "The few miles difference in distance doesn't mean nearly so much now as it did then."

She is one of the few persons left living in the Rhea Community who has seen wide open prairies with wagon trails, wire gates and little else change into lush fields of irrigated crops criss crossed with paved roads.

On the 65th anniversary of Friona as a town, the Friona Star proudly salutes a pioneer woman who has lived nearby nearly that long.

CHARLES SCHLENKER

Charles Schlenker and Amelia Metz were married at Des Moines, Iowa, in 1890. Charles came to the Texas Panhandle on a "landseeker" train in 1906. He bought property, built a 35 x 20 foot shack, moved down two freight cars of equipment and sent for Amelia and their nine children.

Four years of drought and a winter of blizzards exhausted his finances and he worked for a neighbor for one dollar a day. In desperation he went to the new bank in Bovina and arranged to buy cattle. This proved to be the turning point in his career as a Panhandle pioneer. Industry, honesty, and common sense resulted in his becoming a wealthy cattleman and farmer.

He joined with F.L. Spring, J.W. Barnett and other hardy souls in organizing the county and establishing a school in their area. A young lady teacher who "boarded around" held classes for eight months of the year.

In all the records of Pioneer history there are none more worthy of mention than these hardworking Americans of German descent. Their interest lay in establishing homes and providing opportunities for coming generations. This is best demonstrated by a remark made by Charles when he and Amelia visited their old homesteads in Iowa.

"Do you want to be buried here?" Amelia asked.

"No, indeed," answered Charles, "Bury me in Friona. I don't feel that's coming soon but I want you to know that I would not give my ranch in the Panhandle for all of Polk County, Iowa!"

April 20, 1917 Nearing the goal of manufacturing tires.

Commissioners Court Notes

F.L. SPRING STORY

F.L. Spring, the genial owner of one of the Panhandle's few remaining true "country stores" doesn't like to be referred to as a pioneer. "I've been here only a little while," he says.

Perhaps he is referring to Friona itself when he makes this statement, because it would hardly stand up if all of Parmer County is considered. The Springs came here from Aldridge, Illinois, in 1905. They settled eight miles north of Bovina.

They moved to Friona in 1926, a fairly "recent" year, where he purchased a mercantile store that is still his present place of business. Business today is done in the Spring store in much the same fashion as in 1926.

The merchandise of the modestly furnished building on the southern end of Friona's Main Street has a homey arrangement. There are no fluorescent lights, gleaming stainless steel, or fancy display cases.

But there is an atmosphere, and the customers seem to appreciate it. Many of them do more than shop in the Spring store. They sit and pass the day for a few minutes while the grocery buying waits.

The slatted wooden benches on the front porch are worn slick with use, and it's a rare fall afternoon that several men with idle time can't be found sitting there.

The 40-hour workweek and the two-week vacation are household words nowadays, but Proprietor Spring hasn't been off work except twice in the 30 years he has been in business in Friona.

He used one of those times to go fishing for a few days.

It was raining on the day that F.L. Spring arrived in Parmer County. It must have continued to rain during his entire visit. Looking over the apparently limitless expanse of knee-high gramma grass so abundantly watered by Mother Nature, he concluded that this land must be superior to the fertile but more confined farmland of his native Illinois.

This was in the year 1905, when Frank Lewis Spring, age 34, made the decision to come west. Born in Cobden, Ill., he had spent both his childhood and youth in the Mississippi Valley, leaving the immediate area only for trips upstream to sell produce and livestock in St. Louis. On graduating from high school, he studied for a year at Lake Forest Academy near Chicago. He wanted to become a physician, but financial difficulties at home necessitated his withdrawal from college. Moving from Cobden with his mother and sister, Minnie, he established a farm and general store in Aldridge, Ill., on the river. He enjoyed farming and had "a good hog house, the place fixed real nice, a hired man, a clover pasture, and the nicest strawberries" according to someone he frequently visited in those days. This person was Ocie Adams, with whom he "used to come play cards, Flinch and Cinch" and to "go to the floating theater" on the Mississippi. In 1906 the local Baptist preacher officiated at the marriage of eighteen year old Ocie and thirty-five year old Frank in the Adams home. "Some people said I was a cradle robber," Mr. Spring laughed in later years.

At this time, the Texas Panhandle was in the process of rapid settlement. The old XIT had been divided by the Southwest Land Company of Chicago, which marketed the subdivided acreage through an army of land agents. One of them was George Hoyt, a brother-in-law of Frank Spring. On Hoyt's advice, Frank Spring took time off from his duties as farmer, grocer, postmaster and railroad agent of Aldridge, Illinois, and, at the invitation of the Southwest Land Company, rode the Sante Fe all the way to Bovina, Texas in September of 1905. After having seen the peanuts, corn, maize, and potatoes touted by land salesmen in Illinois as examples of Panhandle produce and then treating his eyes to daily rainfall and a Frio Draw full of water, there could be no doubting the value of Parmer County farmland. Thus, one of the next trains out of Pine Bluff, Arkansas carried Frank Spring, "Dad" Teeter, and a carload of grooved, finished lumber to Parmer County, Texas. Mr. Teeter, the carpenter, was commissioned for one hundred days at a price of one hundred dollars plus room and board to build a clapboard

June 22, 1917 Tire machinery on the way.
Commissioners Court Notes

343

house and barn according to Frank Spring's specifications. However, Mr. Teeter was given to tippling, a vice abetted by local cowboys who gave him whiskey. Since the good carpenter stuttered, he found it easier to sing rather than speak (especially after a visit from the cowboys), and would melodiously intone "you wanted the chimney here, but it went over there."

In 1906, Frank Spring returned to Illinois, married, chartered a railroad car for his furniture, and bought tickets for himself and his eighteen-year and eleven-month old bride. They enjoyed a 750 mile trip southwest on the Santa Fe, sometimes having radishes for breakfast. On reaching their final destination Mr. Spring presented the five feet, one hundred three pound Ocie Adams Spring with a brand new eight room, two story house, seven miles north of Bovina, surrounded by open pastures on each side, and sparsely populated by the Rhea Brothers' longhorn cattle and a few antelope and coyotes.

While the environment of Parmer County proved somewhat austere, it was by no means barren. In the years 1906-1913 when the family lived on the farm, there were some excellent crops consisting of Indian Corn, milo, kaffir corn, cane, peanuts, "the nicest watermelons you ever saw," and there was never a crop failure. The farm was composed of an original 320 acres, bought for $8.50 per acre, and another quarter purchased from the Schlenker family at $5.00 per acre which paid for itself the first year. There was livestock (for both beef and milk), hogs, and poultry. A team of mules "that didn't even match" consented to both farm work and transportation, but later a horse named A.V. was added, easing their burden. Farm machinery included a drill for wheat and a planter for corn which had a knife in front to break the sod. The first maize harvest was accomplished by hand, Mr. Spring and his brother-in-law, Hannibal Aldridge, using knives. The first farm help was provided by the two oldest Schlenker sons, fine boys about 14 and 15 years old. A Williams boy also helped and was once paid in nickels. The boy liked hard currency.

Mrs. Spring found the facilities around the house more than adequate. Her pantry was an entire room and included a flour barrel of 50-lb. capacity. While the dried-cow-chip fuel left considerable ashes in the stove, the only great inconvenience was the chore of carrying water from the windmill to the house. The well stock pantry was particularly handy during the first winter when the hardships of a three-day blizzard were countered by the making and eating of apples, peanut candy and fudge. Another potential catastrophe was a prairie fire which swept over the farm, blackening the entire surface, but failing to destroy the house owing to the lack of combustible vegetation in the yard and the fierce resistance of Mr. Spring with his wet gunny sack.

An avid hunter since his boyhood in Illinois, Mr. Spring enjoyed hunting the wild game such as antelope, rabbits, ducks and dove afforded by Parmer County. He hunted coyotes with greyhounds, and when the coyotes were eating his watermelons one year, he staked out a rooster and trapped one. He delighted in telling of how he had once killed an antelope with the butt of his gun, neglecting until the end of the story to explain that the animal had already been stunned by a bullet. Meanwhile, the Schlenker boys taught his sons to bag rabbits, chicken hawks and the like with flying fence staves.

The first boy, Frank Augustus, was born October 9, 1907, the first registered birth in Parmer County. Mr. Spring rode into Bovina on horseback, making it in time to fetch Dr. Oliver before the child was born. A second son, Edward Gardiner (Ese) was born on November 3, 1908. The first girl, Mary Olive, was born in 1911 and a third boy, Thomas Lewis, died shortly after birth in 1913.

While the town of Bovina was at that time on its way to becoming the world's greatest cattle shipping center, it was nonetheless a rather modest settlement consisting of two mercantile stores, one of which contained a bank in one corner, a hotel, a blacksmith shop, a wagon yard, lumber yard, railroad station, and Chancy Delano's barber shop. The town's first barber, Jack Anderson, also surveyed land. The mercantile store did a rather voluminous business, since the ranchers in that area bought cases of goods, such as bacon and dried apricots. Besides being a supply depot, Bovina was of course a cattle market. Mr. Spring's original herd of five milk cows and thirty-one steers soon grew to an estimated one hundred to two hundred head which he traded in Bovina. Buyers from Montana once purchased his calves for $30.00 per head. And at the railway depot in Bovina he received a $500.00 registered Hereford bull which was shipped from Kansas City, Mo. by Railway Express. He later purchased a $100.00 bull calf named Twyford.

The Bovina scene included many cowboys who rode into town wearing boots and chaps and hitched their horses at the mercantile stores where they traded. They were always polite, Mrs. Spring related, never failing to tip their hats to the ladies. Their numbers included some colorful characters like Tuey Bean, "Buttermilk Smith," Pres Abbott and Charley Butcher, "a real Dutchman from Holland." There was generally good decorum in Bovina; the cowhands pulled their shenanigans in Texico, where at that time, "every other door was a saloon." Mr. and Mrs. Spring did not realize that "Ole Tex," a dog brought on horseback as a gift to their son Frank, was not bought in Texico, but stolen there. The cowboys tried to buy it but failed to make a deal, so they stole it.

The only significant foul play occurring in Bovina during those times happened while Mr. Spring was in Bovina selling a load of corn. Mr. Spring recalled that two men on horseback, John Armstrong, the foreman of the XIT, and John Williams, a Bovina resident, were involved in an altercation which began with Armstrong accusing Williams of cattle theft and which climaxed with Williams shooting Armstrong with a 30-30 rifle. Mr. Armstrong's horse bolted and his foot hung in the stirrup, thus he was dragged for a distance before the horse could be halted. Mr. Spring was the fourth man to reach Armstrong who only uttered a sigh and expired. Mr. Spring later appeared as a character witness at the trial.

Aside from the aforementioned incident, life in Parmer County was for the most part decent and civilized. But there was little organized social life owing to the sparse population. The women would hitch up their mules and hold a "get together." Those who had "had elocution" gave speeches, and the Schlenkers could sing German songs. One winter around 1910, the Springs gave a party and since it had snowed, the three couples invited came by sled. "Old Man" Queen and his son Bud provided violin music after dinner and there was dancing until a midnight breakfast closed festivities. The temperature had dipped to a point such that a sled ride home was out of the question. So the women and children went to bed while the men tended the fire all night. Mrs. Spring reported that the morning's breakfast was without biscuits since the buttermilk had frozen.

The Spring family was often entertained by a graphophone which played cylindrical Edison phonograph records, such as "The Preacher and the Bear." A favorite family pastime (as was frequently the case in both Europe and America during those days) was the reading aloud of literature. Mr. Spring was particularly fond of Dickens and daughter Mary recalls readings from the Pickwick Papers, the Old Curiosity Shop, Oliver Twist and other classics of that day.

In 1913 the family moved into Bovina so that the children could attend school there. Mr. Spring enjoyed farming and raising livestock, but the move necessitated a gradual end to farming and a resumption of the merchant's trade. The farm was worked by hired help who lived in the farm house, which later was converted into a duplex and sold to two different families. Mr. Spring commuted to the farm to work and oversee his help, then took a job as a bookkeeper and clerk in Jack Carr's mercantile store.

Son Frank entered school at age five that year. Mary and Ese were soon to enter school, and the first grade teachers of the three oldest children (Mrs. Tom Hastings, Mrs. Frank Hastings, and Mrs. Reynolds) are still alive at this date. Both Frank and Ese won county declamation contests and, according to Mrs. Spring, both returned from Friona once "just covered with ribbons." Frank once bested the redoubtable Nelda Goodwine in a second grade reading contest. Mary was not a competitive scholar, but made consistently high grades. At Bovina, three more children were added, Paul Louis in 1916, Floyd Lee in 1919, and Lydia Marie in 1921. Paul "read constantly" during his first four years of school, but occupied some of his time with a dog and a shetland pony.

By this time the family had become motorized. In 1916 a Ford Model T was purchased for about $500.00, one of the first Model T's in Parmer County. Filled at the mercantile store's gas pump, it greatly expanded the family's mobility. For example, the buggy-ride to the photographer's in Farwell for two-year-old Frank's picture had involved a dawn-to-dusk round trip. By contrast the family could now take an afternoon fishing excursion at the Hereford stream or vacation in the White Mountains west of Roswell, New Mexico, in the summer of 1916, even though there were no paved roads in the area. One of the first cars in Bovina, owned by the Jersig family, had caused a chaos of runaway horses and gleeful children, but the Spring auto wreaked havoc only on family possessions. Mr. Spring was still shouting "Whoa" as the machine crashed through the rear planks of his first garage. He then repaired the garage. and the same thing happened again. The next time, he wanted to learn to drive properly before he repaired the garage.

Mr. Spring helped to organize Parmer County; he was the first county commissioner from Bovina, serving at this post for over ten years.

In 1925 Mr. Spring traded a quarter section of land for E. B. McLellan's general store in Friona. Mr. Spring operated the general store until shortly before his death in 1959.+ During the early years in Friona he served on the Friona School Board which built Friona's first separate high school building.

When he moved to Friona Mr. Spring built the family a house at 911 Cleveland Ave., with a windmill in back erected by R.H. Kinsley. Over the years Mr. Spring developed an extensive orchard of fruit and nut trees around his residence, fulfilling his prophecy that "anything will grow in this country if you can get water to it." Mrs. Spring continued to reside at the home until her death in 1970.

Included in Mr. and Mrs. Spring's legacy to the county are a number of children and grandchildren. They are: Frank A., of Friona, married to the former Ethel Ruth Collins. Their children: Mary Tom Isaac, of Colorado Springs, Colorado and Frank Lewis, of Urbana, Illinois.

Ese, of Friona, married to the former Opal

THE McSPADDEN BROTHERS helping Mr. F.L. Spring doctor a calf.

Venable. His children: Edward Gardner, of Hereford; David Lynn, of Amarillo, and Don Paul, of Bovina.

Mary Olive, of Amarillo.

Paul, of Friona, married to the former June Pleszewski. Their children: Susan Kay and John Louis.

Lee, of Friona, married to the former Anne Moore. Their children: Sylvia Anne and Sandra Lee.

Lydia, of Winkelman, Arizona. Married to Murl Sylvester, Jr. Their children: Sherry Lynn Chapman, of Winkelman, Arizona; Michael, of Globe, Arizona; and Gary, of Winkelman, Arizona.

+He called it "F.L. Spring's Old Fashioned General Store" and as long as he owned it, the store fit that description.

By Frank Lewis Spring II

STEINBOCK

Alexander Peter Steinbock married Lena Mehl on Feb. 18, 1925, just a week before coming to Texas. Before venturing out upon the prairie the young couple spent a night in Plainview, Texas. A cold wind blew in from the north and the natives treated the newcomers to all of the tall tales concerning the severity of Texas weather. Undaunted, the newlyweds joined the rest of the family in the bold venture and occupied one of the small new houses. Their furniture was meagre to say the least. Items of prime interest were a cookstove, bed, table and cream separator. The bride's mother had provided her with a dozen hens and a rooster; a thoughtful gift that paid huge dividends in the years to come.

Alex and Lena became the parents of two daughters, Fern Marie, who married Robert Broyles, and Wanda May, who married Bert Williams.

The elder Mr. John F. Steinbock passed away on June 2, 1932. His wife, Alma, on Dec. 28, 1951.

JOHN F. STEINBOCK

John F. Steinbock's family moved to the Lazbuddie community on February 23, 1925. They shipped their household goods to Friona by railroad and the families came from Frederick, Oklahoma by car.

There were thirty-seven people, of different families: Mr. and Mrs. John F. Steinbock and single children, Johnnie, Alfred, Carl, Frances, and Alma, and Walter and married sons Mr. and Mrs. William F. Steinbock, Mr. and Mrs. Alex Steinbock and Mr. and Mrs. Ed Steinbock and married daughter, Mr. and Mrs. Rudolph Pyritz and family, Gertrude, Clifford, Clarence, and Laverne. Their reason for coming here from their former homes was the price of land, $200 per acre, that was selling here for $27.50 per acre.

At first they all built two room houses of wood bought from Rockwell Bros. Lumber Company in Friona and hauled it 25 miles with mule teams and wagons. They had to break out the grasslands of native grass before they could plant crops.

These thirty-seven people lived in a four room square house until each family completed their two room houses. This house was on land worked by the rancher Henry Bledsoe who lived about two miles south. The Gordon Duncans from Frederick, Oklahoma bought this ranchhouse of the Bledsoes and land adjoining it. Elbert Nowell now owns this four-room old house. A nice home is on this place now, occupied by Raymond McGeehee who recently purchased the John F. Steinbock Estate in partnership with his brother, John McGeehee.

In the early days, entertainment consisted of barn dances, 42 and domino games, bridge and pinochle.

Hardships: No hospitals closer than Clovis, New Mexico, kerosene lamps, coal stoves, ice boxes (for which ice was far away), 18 miles to Muleshoe. Many farmers used homemade wooden boxes through which the windmills pumped water to keep milk, cheese, cream, and other things cool. After running through the box, the water ran on through pipes to water tanks which were used to water livestock.

Hail storms were one hardship to contend with, picking up the hailed out heads of grain was a terrific job.

The first school at Lazbuddie was a two room white wooden building about one mile south and one east of Lazbuddie store. Box supper and Union church meetings are remembered by oldtimers.

The J.E. Vaughan family of nine children: Eunice (married to J.L. Shuping and two sons, R.L. and Raymond); Myrtle (Mrs. William F. Steinbock); Edgar, Cecil, Charles, Theron (who lives on the Vaughn farm and farms for his mother, Anne Vaughn); Tommy, the youngest daughter, was born to the Vaughans a little over a year after settling near Lazbuddie. Nola Vaughn was later married to a pioneer family, the Otto Treiders' son Raymond.

J.L. Shuping started from Frederick, Okla. with a load of hay, two horses pulling the wagon, two mules being lead behind; when they arrived two weeks later, the hay was all fed to the mules.

The John Steinbock families bought 2½ sections from the Wright Land Company of Kansas City, Mo. A large three bedroom home of the widow, Alma, wife of John Steinbock, burned. Mrs. Steinbock built another three bedroom home on the same half section which the McGeehee's now own.

Most of the land is all now under irrigation, electricity, phones, and pavements are all part of the new scene.

Windmills which were so important in the early days are fast becoming a passing thing.

Another thing that is remembered: the great change in the road system. The road to Muleshoe, Friona, and Clovis, New Mexico, were winding dirt roads through prairie. Often times one would overtake a swift fox on the trip to town and a chase would ensue with the fox sometimes winning.

By Steinbock

MRS. S.C. STEVICK

Many changes have been made in the community since Mrs. Eva Stevick came here from Kalida, Ohio, in 1907. Her late husband, S.C. Stevick, had been in ill health for several years and the family came here seeking a change which they hoped would be helpful for him.

Eva Price was born December 2, 1874, and was married to S.C. Stevick November 19, 1890. When the Stevicks came to Friona, they had five children, Walter, Lottie, Goldie, Otha and Orville. Their children attended the first school in Friona. It was a one room school and started in 1908.

Two of Mrs. Stevick's most prized possessions are a Bible which has been in the Stevick family more than 100 years and an organ which was a gift to Mrs. Stevick from her grandmother more than 60 years ago.

Mrs. Stevick's children who are still living are Walter, Lottie, Otha and Orville. Grandchildren are Glen Stevick, Katie Stowers, Jimmie Kuykendall of Hereford, Betty Kuykendall of Fort Worth, and Larry Stevick.

Great-grandchildren are Janet, Ronnie and James Stevick, Helen, Jackie and Sharon Stowers, Billy, Susan, Lucretia, Bobby and Danny Kuykendall.

Mrs. Cora Frysinger of Lima, Ohio was a recent vsitor in the Stevick home. The two women are sisters and had not seen one another in 49 years. A brother, Ralph Price, also of Lima, visited Mrs. Stevick last year.

EVERT WALTER TALBOT

Evert Walter Talbot and Vivian Irene Pope were married April 5, 1929. On December 2, 1930 their only child was born, a daughter Edd Url. Evert farmed land his father bought in 1909 buying the land himself in 1949, the place being three miles west and four miles north of Friona. Edd Url graduated from Friona High School in 1949. In 1950 she married Dan Luttrell also of Friona. They had five children, Scott, an electrician, Dana Url, attending college at Oklahoma State University, Tamara, Darryl Talbot, and Kevin Lee of the home in Elk City, Oklahoma; Dan is a milk hauler. Evert farmed until

his death June 6, 1963, and Vivian now lives at the Heritage House Apartments in Elk City, Oklahoma. Evert is buried in the Friona Cemetery.

W.J. TALBOT

Walter John Talbot and Bessie Francis Donald married February 22, 1889. They moved to Parmer County in 1919, with their four girls and two boys. Elvira of Oregon, Lava deceased in 1965, Toad of California, Viola deceased in 1930, Victor of California, and Everet deceased in 1963. In 1909 Walter purchased land three miles west and four miles north of Friona which is still owned by Everet's widow, Vivian Talbot. Everet and Vivian were married on April 5, 1929. Bessie died in April, 1927 and Walter died in August, 1953, both being buried in the Friona Cemetery.

E.E. TAYLOR FAMILY

Grace Boatman Taylor, a pioneer settler of Parmer County, was born in Parke County, Indiana, June 2, 1892. She came to Texas with her parents, J.S and Eliza Boatman, and two brothers, Dan and Curtis Boatman, and located on a farm that her father had previously bought in 1910 which was 10 miles north of Friona, known as The Messenger Community. "As most everyone did, we had our furniture, horses, mules and one milk cow shipped by rail to Texas. Father was a carpenter so the boys did the farmwork. There may have been a dozen or more families that owned land out there that came from the northern or eastern states, Ohio, Iowa, Indiana, Illinois, and Missouri, were all represented."

This was in the horse and buggy days. There was nowhere to go or nothing to do especially on Sunday. It wasn't too long before a Sunday School was organized and people would meet in the homes for Sunday School. Sometimes a party would be held on Saturday night for the young folks and maybe a dinner for Christmas or Thanksgiving where everyone would bring food and eat together. It was at one of these gatherings that Grace

Boatman met Earsel Taylor and some three years later that they were married in 1913 by a Congregational preacher at his parsonage.

They lived in Friona for some time and worked for a well-drilling company. After working for the public for several years they settled on the farm again and noticed quite a few changes that had taken place. Lots of wheat was being grown instead of maize and some tractors were taking the place of horses. Wheat was a much better price and cattle grazing was a thing of the day. Then came the dust bowl days when large fields of young wheat would blow out in the spring during the windy season. "The Dirty-Thirties" as it was called will never be forgotten.

Several years later, irrigation was first brought to the Plains and to Parmer County which did more for the people there than any one thing. They knew they had the best land anywhere but they were short on water.

Earsel retired and they moved to Friona in 1955. Their home is 1304 W. 5th Street and they have six wonderful children, twins included. The twins have the honor of being the second set born in Parmer County. They had one son who lost his life in World War II. They are Baptist and members of the First Baptist Church in Friona. Earsel is an invalid and has been for the past three years.
Written by Grace Taylor

TIDENBERGS

The J.A. Tidenbergs (our parents) must have possessed an abundance of courage, when they moved their large family from Johnsburg, Pennsylvania to the plains of Texas, to pioneer in a new land.

We traveled by train, arriving in Bovina on December 9, 1909.

Dad had made a trip to Texas with a land excursion earlier that year. He returned to Pennsylvania with heads of maize and kaffir, "(the wonderful new grain) that was being raised on land level as a floor." He liked it very much and bought 80 acres of land, four miles north of Bovina. All 80 acres he broke with a walking sod plow and two mules.

An uncle came to build a house. In the meantime, we all stayed at the Major's boarding house. Everything was so new! The

MRS. MATILDA TIDENBURG and Mr. Porth wedding picture. Miss Matilda Tidenburg—the first teacher at Knox School. She taught about one month and resigned to marry Mr. Porth.

air, food and water were all so different! How we liked the good old southern biscuits Mrs. Majors made. Biscuits were seldom served in Pennsylvania and did not taste like these!

We could bring with us only our personal belongings. I remember a large wooden chest with some bedding. In it were packed dried fruit and jars of apple butter. Some of the jars were broken. There was apple butter all over everything. After that one of the quilts was always called "the apple butter quilt." Two of our treasures we had to leave behind were the old spinning wheel and the organ. But dad played in his own way. The children sang. Dad said, "Irene has the best voice." "But now the rest of you kids sing." Some of his favorite songs were "Bringing in the Sheaves," "Work for the Night is Coming," "What a Friend We Have in Jesus," and at Christmas time we sang "Away in the Manger," etc.

At last the house was ready. A long room with kitchen in one end and a bed in the other. The second story was the same length with beds for all the children. There was a ladder like steps that went upstairs. When the wind blew real hard, the house would rock us to sleep.

The school we attended was a one room building with six grades in all. All grades were taught by one teacher. It was two miles from home and we walked both ways each day. Later we went to Bovina School and we had an old mule we hitched to a cart. When we were late, Old Jack (our mule), would seem to go that much slower. Going home he did better, even though he had to face a "norther" (as the Texans called it). We turned our backs to the wind and let Old Jack take us home.

I can't remember that a doctor ever came to our house in those days. Nothing ever was too bad that Mother didn't know how to take care of it.

Our first income was from sheep herding and freighting. Dad bought some ewes for about 50c a head but lost part of them during the blizzards of the first year. Sometimes he worked day and night to keep them on top of the snow. I remember he came in all covered with snow. Mother met him at the door to brush away the snow and he would tell her how many we had lost since his last trip out. But after a few years we had a nice, large flock. We older children would take the covered wagon and herd them out two weeks at a time. We feared the coyotes and the rattlesnakes.

One of our disliked chores was gathering the winter fuel. We took the team and big wagon out and gathered "cow chips" for heating and cooking.

When many people from the north "gave up," and moved back, we were able to get a larger house with rented land. Our dad bought more cheaper land and some cows. We fared better and were able to build a house after a number of years.

Mr. and Mrs. J.A. Tidenberg lived north of Bovina the remainder of their lives and were the parents of: Leora (Mrs. C.F.) Hastings, Bovina, Texas; Matilda (Mrs. M.H.) Porth, Canon City, Colorado; Irene (Mrs. C.L.) Armstrong (deceased);Hillary Tidenberg (Gladys Stagner), Clovis, New Mexico; Naomi (Mrs. Carl) Porth, (deceased); Charles Tidenberg (Mary Lee Ellison), Santa Rosa, New Mexico; Ella Tidenberg, Colorado Springs, Colorado; Henry Tidenberg (Alice Brower), Montrose, Colorado. There are eight grandchildren and 18 great grandchildren and three great-great-grandchildren. Three of the Tidenberg girls had certificates to teach, and taught some. Irene taught last in Hereford.

We had no TV dinners and pizza pies. Only good wholesome, fresh food, garden vegetables, mutton, sorghum molasses, bacon, etc. One of the girls informed her teacher, "We use axle grease on our bread." She said, "Surely you don't mean axle grease?" One of the older kids explained, "She means bacon grease."

Our modern way of thinking I suppose would be: Those were the old days of hard work and hardships, but even then we had many good times as we all grew up together.

TIEFEL HISTORY

In July, 1910, the Tiefel Brothers and their families arrived in Friona, coming from Brazil, Indiana. They came by train bringing all of their possessions with them, Brother Ed riding in the car, containing their possessions to care for the livestock.

Those coming to Friona were Jake and Alvenia who had one son, Arthur. Arthur and his wife Bertha live in Hereford and have one son and one daughter. Born in Texas were Leona, now Mrs. Luther Webb of Marshall who has one daughter; Mary, now Mrs. Clyde Hussy of Federalway, Washington who has two sons and one daughter; George who lives in Hereford with his wife Caralee, they have two sons and two daughters.

Henry and Susie had two daughters. Helen, now Mrs. P.B. Sowell of Hereford (P.B. is deceased), has one son and one daughter. Eleanor, Mrs. A. Rogers, had two sons and one daughter. Both Eleanor and A. are deceased. Erma, born in Texas, was married to Thurmond Johnson. They had one son and one daughter. Thurmond is deceased. Erma is now married and lives in Hereford.

Ed Tiefel was never married.

The Tiefel's were contractors and builders and farmers. The home now owned by Mr. and Mrs. Raymond Adams, 302 E. 10th Street, was one of the first homes built in Friona by the Tiefels and occupied by them. They also helped construct the first brick school house and many other homes.

The object of coming to Parmer County was to purchase land and find a new and better way of life. Many hardships were endured and many pleasures were enjoyed. All survived the hardships and were stronger for having had the experience.

Henry and his family moved to a farm in the Messenger Community in 1911. More drought and sandstorms followed, and he was forced to go back into Friona and again do carpentering work but he was a farmer at heart.

The Tiefels were members of the Lutheran Church; there being no Lutheran Church in Friona, services were held in the home.

In late 1913 because of drought and a building slump the family moved to Hereford. Jake and Ed continued to contract and build. Henry moved on to Dawn to continue his beloved farming. Jake died in 1939, his wife, Alvenia in 1950. Ed died in 1960. Henry died in 1963. Susie, age 87, is still living at 336 E. 4th Street in Hereford, Texas.

Submitted by Helen Tiefel Sowell

WILLIAM LYLES TOWNSEN
FIRST JUDGE OF PARMER COUNTY

William Lyles Townsen was born in Tennessee on June 4th, 1853. He was the son of James Garrett Townsen who had married a Miss Mitchell several years earlier. The Townsens had eleven children, ten boys and one girl. The boys were Lafayett Jasper, Columbus Franklin, Julius Randolph, Josephus Rollings, John Washington, Henry Clay, James Madison, Alexander Perry, Thomas Jefferson and William Lyles. The only daughter was Maryan Elizabeth.

The father died in 1860 and Mrs. Townsen accompanied by young William and "brothers" (how many is not stated) came to the Lampassas River district of Texas in 1862.

In 1879 Jasper and William were among the group of cowboys that drove a herd of cattle to Fort Sumner, New Mexico. Others in the drive were Bob Mitchell, Pink Higgins, and Joe Straley.

William was elected sheriff of Lampassas county and served during 1887 and 1889. He later became a Texas Ranger.

In 1883 he was living in Coleman County

where he married Mildred, "Millie," V. Simmons, a native of Monroe, Louisiana. Her date of birth is given as 1864. They moved to Hale Center in 1901.

When Parmer County was organized in 1907 Townsen was named as Judge and began his new duties in the Parmerton Court House. He served as Parmer's first judge from June 8, 1907 until November 17, 1908.

After his active participation in poltics, W.L. and Millie Townsen operated the Townsen Hotel in Bovina during 1910 or 1911.

Later they worked on the Halsell Ranch in Hale County. Mrs. Townsen ran the kitchen and Mr. Townsen cared for the headquarters stock and buildings.

During 1916 and 1917 they were employed by the Warrens at the Muleshoe Ranch.

Two faded stone markers in the Hale Center Cemetery bear the final legend concerning these two early residents of Parmer County:
William Lyles Townsen died 1929
Mildred V. Townsen died 1951

CHARLIE ANDERSON TURNER

Charlie Anderson Turner was born in Center, Mississippi, June 20, 1896. He came to Miami, Texas July 13, 1917 at the age of 20 years. He returned to Leonard, Texas to marry Annis Daphne Elam on May 18, 1919, where he remained to farm at Lane, Texas for three years. It was here at Lane their first child, a daughter, Virginia, was born July 23, 1920. A son, Billy Wade, was born November 21, 1922. In December 1924 he moved to Bailey, Texas and farmed one year. In August, 1925 he bought a farm in Parmer County of 560 acres located four miles south and one west of Friona, Texas. There were no roads and no fences. He built a three-room house over a dugout basement, and a barn, and chicken house. They had to haul water for two years until their well was dug in 1927.

The crops raised were wheat, sudan, corn, and crook-neck maize. Crops were average and he was able to buy a header and began custom heading for other farmers. He went

MR. AND MRS. CHARLIE TURNER.

partners in 1929 on a combine and began custom combining also. He traded his work horses for his first Farmall tractor in 1929.

On December 24, 1929, a daughter, Betty Jean, was born. Depression came and the dust bowl days hit. Times were hard. In 1936 he rented more land, 1900 acres, located one mile east of Parmerton Switch, alongside the south side of the Santa Fe Railroad and Highway 60. It had two houses on it. While living there he raised wheat, maize, sheep, and cattle, and also custom combined and did thrashing of bundles for straw. In 1939 he bought 710 acres of land three miles west of Friona, located just north of Highway 60 and built a new house on the grassland in the fall of 1944, spring of '45. This was the family home until 1947 when the farm was sold, and Mr. and Mrs. Turner moved into Friona, where he owned and managed the White's Auto Store on Main Street. His son, Bill W. Turner, became his partner in 1949 for 19½ years. He retired at the age of 68 in 1964 when the store was sold. He now lives at 510 W. 14th with his wife Annis. They have three living children, eight grandchildren and seven great-grandchildren.

July 20, 1917 Western Tire Stock sales good.
Commissioners Court Notes

V.C. VENABLE
An Interview
14 July 1970

IN REFERENCE: PHOTOGRAPH made 28 May 1941 by Hamlin Y. Overstreet of the Frio Draw at Flood Stage in Friona, Texas, showing a stalled Santa Fe Passenger Train:

The stalled passenger train shown in this picture was the Santa Fe Railroad's Grand Canyon Special. This was before the Diesel Engine Era and this train was powered by a steam locomotive. In the highwater shown in the picture there was no way for the Engineer to get the engine to start the train as it just spun its drivers when the engine was engaged. There was not enough friction between the rails and the drive wheels for the engine to gain forward motion, and it was useless for the Engineer to drop sand out of his sandbox onto the rails because the swift moving waters of the Frio Draw would have carried the sand away before it hit the rails.

V.C. Venable and a co-worker by the name of Evelina Cervantez who were employed in the maintenance department of the Panhandle and Santa Fe Railroad Company, had the occasion to approach the stalled train from the west. They waded the water between the tracks until they reached the engine of the stalled train, where they inquired of the Engineer if they could help him get the train out of the high water. They suggested to the Engineer to cut the train in two-car parcels and maybe the locomotive could move. The Engineer remarked that he had already suggested this to the conductor, but the Conductor did not want the train cut. However, the Engineer gave Venable permission to cut the train. After Venable had un-coupled the first two cars (which were mail cars) and gave his signal, the Engineer engaged his engine with a lunge and the engine with the two cars began to move forward. The Engineer and Venable took the two cars on west to the next siding where they dropped the two cars and brought the engine back to the remaining train to repeat the process of hitching onto two more cars. Venable was in the process of coupling up the next two cars when the Train Conductor came through a door with an 18" emergency braking stick in his hand and swung at Venable who ducked just in time to miss the blow to the head by the stick. Venable's co-worker suggested that they drown the Conductor in the flooded draw right then, but Venable said no. The Engineer later said to Venable, "I told you that Conductor was stubborn about having his train cut." Mr. Venable believes that the conductor was so near scared to death for fear of losing his train and passengers that he probably thought he was protecting the train by said act.

The process of picking up two cars at a time was repeated until all the cars were pulled out of the Frio Draw and onto the railsiding after which the train was made up again in a mixed-up fashion as what had been rear cars on the passenger train were now up front behind the engine and the U.S. Mail cars were now at the rear of the train. Venable presumes that the train re-arranged in its proper car order when it arrived in Clovis before continuing its westward journey.

If the stalled train had not been rescued from the Frio Draw it would have surely toppled over during that night according to Venable, who said that on the following morning he and other workmen discovered that the backwash of the water going over the tracks had washed out the road bed beneath the south rail causing the south rail to be much lower than the north rail, which in all likelihood would have caused the passenger train to turn over into the high water and possibly drowning some of the passengers.

The Train Engineer, after the incident, related to the Railroad Officials that he did not know the man who had come to his rescue and helped him get the train out of the flooded draw, but that he presumed him to be a railroad man, since he knew how to uncouple the air lines with such precision. Venable of course knew how to do this from his experience working with section crews around "Work-Trains." Venable remarked that diligent search was made for the man who had helped the Engineer cut the passenger train into the two car parcels. He said a letter written by one of the Railroad Officials, was read to many of his co-workers but that the letter was never read to him or in his presence. He therefore would not go forward and volunteer that he was the man the letter writer was

in search of, because he did not know if the railroad company intended to fire such a man or to give him a raise in salary, so Venable remained mum about the whole matter as long as he remained in the employment of said railroad.

PART II

During this same rainy season in the summer of 1941, V.C. Venable was directed by his Foreman to the Railroad Bridge on Running Water Draw. Said bridge is about four miles up the draw from Bovina. His duty was to carefully observe the rushing water to see that they did not wash-out the bridge railings and if the bridge was damaged by the swift waters to flag down any approaching trains and to notify the dispatcher of trains to stop all trains coming that way. To perform his duties of observation and investigation at the bridge, Venable equipped himself with rubber boots, a rain gear slicker, a lantern and a long handled shovel. He made his way to the bridge late in the evening and waded through the water to a position under the bridge to see if any damage had occurred as a result of the swift running water. Venable was standing under the railroad bridge poking around with the shovel to see if any of the soil had been washed away from the bridge pilings, when all of a sudden the very ground upon which he was standing gave away and into the swirling water taking Venable and his gear with it. He lost his lantern and long handled shovel in the incident plus one of his rubber boots. As he was being swept down the current, Venable freed one of his arms from his rain gear slicker in case the slicker should become entangled in a barbed wire fence below the railroad bridge. Venable had a lot of experience, swimming in creeks in Erath County, Texas when said creeks were out of their banks and he knew how to "ride-it-down" which is to say to swim along with the current and not swim against it. Venable gradually swam his way toward the bank of

August 3, 1917 Western Tire plant at Pueblo, Colorado.

Commissioners Court Notes

the draw whereupon he was soon able to crawl out onto the bank and make his way back toward the railroad whereupon he noticed the head lamp of a freight train coming around the Bovina Curve and heading his way. Venable, having lost his lantern with which he could signal the trainmen, wondered what he could do to get the attention of the Engineer. He ran between the tracks toward the approaching train, and he happened to think that the rain gear slicker was white in color on its inside surface. He immediately began swinging the slicker from side to side between his out-stretched arms in a flagging motion and finally the train's head lamp caught a glimpse of his signal. The Engineer answered the signal with a blast on the whistle and began braking the train to a stop. Venable told the Engineer of the washed-out condition of the bridge on the Running Water Draw. The Engineer told Venable to notify the dispatcher that he would reverse his engine and began backing the train toward Bovina. Venable said the train had to be backed all the way to Canyon where it was re-routed to Clovis through Lubbock on the Galveston line. Venable then made his way to a telephone and informed the train dispatcher of the wash-out at the bridge and told him the freight train was being backed toward Canyon. Another West Bound train, according to the dispatcher, was between Canyon and Umbarger, but the dispatcher told Venable that he would stop the train, back it back to Canyon to clear the track for the first train.

Venable related during this interview that he did not become frightened during his brief swim in the swift waters of Running Water Draw because his previous experiences riding logs in the creeks of Erath County during his boyhood days.

Thus the interview ended.

CECIL L. VESTAL

Cecil L. Vestal and wife Lucy Merrill Vestal moved to Parmer County February 24, 1929 from Grayson County, Texas. They bought a 320 acre farm and lived on it, six miles south of Friona in the Hub Community. They had a daughter, Wana D. Vestal, and a son, C.L. Vestal, Jr. Wana married Loyde A. Brewer December 22, 1945 and lives at Friona, Texas. Their children were Byron Eugene, born Aug. 24, 1948, who lives at Arlington, Texas; Galen Ray, born June 26, 1950, and married Janet Scruggs of Olton Tex. on Jan. 1, 1972, and lives at Lubbock, Texas.

Loyde Brewer moved to Parmer County from Ellis County, Oklahoma in 1928, served in the U.S. Army four years during World War II in North Africa and Italy, and died Dec. 11, 1967.

C.L. Jr. married Nola Faye Smith April 20, 1947 and lives at Friona, Texas. Their children were Celia Faye, born Feb. 2, 1950, died Jan. 16, 1966; Susan Gaye, born March 23, 1952, and lives in Amarillo, Texas; and Burk Lee, born Nov. 20, 1961, and lives in Friona, Texas. C.L. Jr. served three and a half years in the U.S. Navy during World War II in the South Pacific and the Philippine Islands.

Cecil Vestal died April 15, 1953 and Lucy Vestal died Nov. 28, 1971 and they are buried in Friona Cemetery.

It was lovely weather when we came upon the plains by way of Turkey and Silverton that Sunday afternoon in late February 1929. Our model "T" Ford had given us some trouble and we stopped for repairs at Nazareth, but we reached our future home about 4 o'clock. Since a young couple was living in the two-room house, we had to wait till they moved out, and the arrival of our immigrant car hauling our livestock household things.

We looked around the place for awhile before we went into Friona, and one of those "almost instant dusters" blew in before we could get settled in for the night.

Our family spent their first night at The Friona Hotel. While our father was signing the register a Mrs. Martin who ran the place asked him questions like—where from, renting or did you buy, and from whom? When Dad replied that he had bought from the Capitol Syndicate, Mrs. Martin answered, "I don't know how much you paid, but you paid too damn much." She was right as the depression, drought, and "dust bowl" began that fall.

A young man from our home town had accompanied the immigrant car to feed and water the livestock during the trip which took them 3 or 4 days. It arrived on Tuesday so we moved out to the farm that day.

Dad just happened to meet up with Mr. G.L. Mingus who had a new '29 Chevrolet truck and he hauled our things out to the farm. Mr. David Moseley, a near neighbor, went to town and introduced himself to Dad and gave his assistance until we were settled in as comfortably as possible. This started a very close "life long" friendship with the Moseley family.

C.L. and I enrolled in the Friona school on Wednesday and found it to be larger and different from our previous school. It seemed that most of the students were fairly new themselves. Many people had moved here the fall of 1928 or three years before. Everyone was friendly and we soon felt established in our new school. The school buses were also quite a novelity.

The original owner of the land, a Mr. Bud Martin, had bought it as sod in the middle twenties. He broke out all but about 10 acres to leave for the house, barn, orchard, and other improvements. He secured proper help and made enough adobe blocks, by form, to build a six room house, barn and tank house. Mr. David Moseley had helped make the adobes and build the barn. He received $3.00 a day for his labor and considered that good pay for then.

A Finnell family from Fannin County lived on the place two years before we bought it.

The large two story barn with 4 granaries and the tank house were completed. The rest of the adobe lay out on the sod pasture in a stack and wasted away by rain and wind. Dad rescued enough of them to build a brooder house.

That six room house was badly needed. We moved from a six room house in Grayson County to a two room almost flat top shack on the farm. Most of our furniture was stored in the tank house and two of the granaries. What we absolutely needed was crowded into the shack.

We had moved from a rainy country and had tolerated wet land problems, but the ones we faced in that shack were quite a challenge. The average rainfall was more then than now. When it started raining we soon learned to get together all the big cook-

VESTAL FARM six miles south of Friona.

ing vessels and small tubs we owned to place under the leaks. If we lay still we could go ahead and sleep even with 3 or 4 pans on the bed to catch the dripping water.

With a good wheat harvest completed and fall crops looking promising our father and a carpenter, who was a friend of the family from Grayson County, built our five room bungalo house. We were delighted with it even if we did have to wait longer before we got it stuccoed.

An orchard with peaches, plums, cherries, and grapes was large enough to begin baring fruit. We had a large garden with plenty of water from the windmill to irrigate it.

Our parents had brought a half bushel of black walnuts with us. Looking forward to a large number of shade trees our mother and us "kids" planted about 50 nuts from the windmill to the road and north a short distance. Out of all that amount only one came up and it was the one nearest the well where it received enough water and care to become a tree. It lived over 35 years and had many crops of walnuts until it was injured by accident and died.

During our first summer here, our grandmother Mrs. Ida Merrill, began making her home with us several months during each year. She made Friona her home most of the time till her death in Sept. 1960.

Our family felt very much at home by the

September 7, 1917 Western Tire machinery installed.

Commissioners Court Notes

end of 1929. We had made close friends with the families of John and Art Benger, C.E. Allen, E.V. Rushing, and David Moseley. We attended the Methodist Church in Friona on Sunday mornings. Most Sunday afternoons there was either community singing or church at Hub. Rev. R.F. Jones, a farmer and Baptist minister who lived about 3 miles southwest of Hub, was the preacher.

The year ended with an abundance of new friends and experiences.

Wana Vestal Brewer
C.L. Vestal, Jr.

W.W. VINYARD RELATES EXPREIENCE AS SANTA FE AGENT

"I didn't want to come here," recalls W.W. Vinyard, former Sante Fe agent, "but at that time, the railroad could move you anywhere it wanted."

"At that time" it was 1914 and Vinyard was transferred to the position of Sante Fe agent at the Texico depot from the same position at Lockney, Texas.

Vinyard met his wife, Florence, in Lockney; however, they were not married until after he had been in Texico several months. According to Vinyard, she was teaching music in Lockney at the time, and he could not get leave from his duties long enough to return to Lockney to get married. Finally in desperation he wrote Florence, saying, "I'll meet you in Lubbock and we will get married if that is all right with you." She promptly agreed, and they were married in November, 1914.

Vinyard recalls that when he arrived in Texico on Jan. 30, 1914, it was cold with snow all over the ground. "I went over to the hotel in Texico for the night. It was a red tin building. The wind was blowing at 40 m.p.h. and the roof was loose. I didn't sleep much that night."

The first job that confronted him when he went to the depot the next day was to load some horses into a car. According to Vinyard, the section men who were supposed to cover the car with sand didn't come to work before 8 a.m. and it was 7:30.

Vinyard went to the coal house to get the sand, but it was frozen. After consulting the owner of the stock, who was anxious to get started, the two men loaded the car without sanding it.

When the traveling auditor checked Vinyard in that day, he told him "he could check me in today, but he had to check me out in 30 days." Vinyard ended up staying in his position for 45 years.

At the time he came to Texico, buying and selling liquor was legal. "It was not long until both Texas and Oklahoma permitted liquor shipments," he said. The Sante Fe Railroad paid Vinyard 10 per cent of the charges which were required for incoming and outgoing liquor shipments.

Vinyard said one time he loaded a whole baggage car with whiskey. He recalls that his salary increased rapidly during the time Texico was "wet" until the town went "dry" in 1917.

Working conditions for the railroad were not the best in the earlier days, according to Vinyard. "I worked seven days a week, sometimes 15 hours a day, with no overtime and no Sunday pay. He relates a time one Sunday morning when he was ordered to take one of his employees and ride the train to Muleshoe to load 32 cars of cattle. In those days, he says you just did what you were told.

When the eight-hour-day law was passed— Vinyard doesn't remember when, but he knows Woodrow Wilson was President— things started getting better. Even though he was still putting in 12 hours a day, he was paid a straight salary.

During World War II Vinyard had trouble finding anyone to work. "Up until that time you could pull guys off the street and they would come to work," he said.

Vinyard said when he came to Texico, there was not a regular agent. He didn't want the job because he knew there were two sets of books, and things would be difficult. At the time, he had no choice, because the railroad said either work in Texico or quit. Now, he says, the oldest employee may bid for the job.

His wife, Florence, taught piano in this area. They owned three pianos at one time— two in Texico and one in Clovis—recalls Vinyard.

The couple began their married life in the

rooms above the depot. Florence decided she wanted her piano sent up from Lockney, so Vinyard had it sent on the train. After six men struggled to get the piano up the winding staircase leading to their home, a drayman came up with an idea to hoist it through a window.

After that episode, when the Vinyards moved to a house and decided to sell the piano, they told the new owner he would have to figure a way to get the piano down. The new owner found the same drayman who got a horse and a rope and hoisted the piano down out of the window.

Vinyard still has a grand piano setting in his living room, which he says he will keep until his death. Mrs. Vinyard passed away several years ago.

The former Santa Fe agent retired in 1959. He is still living in Farwell where he spends his time in his yard or telling his friends and neighbors of those early days in Texico.

"SIS" GIVES THE Weir kids a ride.

HAZEL, DAD, MOM, MABEL, in the bean patch, 1912.

V.C. WEIR FAMILY

Mr. and Mrs. V.C. Weir and daughter, Carrie, and Mrs. Weir's mother, Mrs. Anderson, moved from Kentucky to Parmer County Texas in the spring of 1910. Mr. Weir's great aunt "Aunt Carrie" came in 1911 and made her home with the family. Their son, Glen, and a cousin, Cal Collins, came with Mr. Weir in 1909, and the boys stayed and built the house for the family. Another son, Scott, came with the family's household furniture, farming implements and livestock, in a railroad immigrant car called a "Zooloo". They located on a farm about 7 miles

northeast of Friona. They raised sheep for a few years and also farmed. One of the horses they brought with them was missing a few days after they arrived. They found him at the railroad stock yards where he had been unloaded from the immigrant car. They moved into Friona in 1919 or 1920.

Glen and his wife, Edna, started a grocery store on the corner of sixth and Main. Scott married Hazel Butcher of Farwell, in 1921. They had a cafe on the west side Main in the 600 block. Their son, "Sam" Weir is married and living at Seminole, Texas. Their daughter, Eunice Mae, "Sis" is Mrs. H. Jeffers and lives in Aurora, Colorado.

H.H. WEIS

H. Huldrich Weis, his wife the former Rebecca Baker, two sons, Leslie and John Lee, arrived in Parmer County from Shattuck, Oklahoma, on March 12th, 1926.

Their first stop was at the home of Rudolph J. Renner, a friend who had preceded them to Texas. Mr. Renner offered

THE ELDER WEIRS

357

them the use of a small frame building on his place and they occupied it until Mr. Weis could build a home. A large Home Comfort coal burning range served for cooking and heating. This temporary dwelling was not designed to withstand the onslaught of the norther that blew in two weeks after the Weises had "settled in." For thirty hours rain, sleet and snow, driven by a strong wind beat upon the house. Mrs. Weis remembers a pan of rising bread that became "frosted" with snow!

Mr. and Mrs. Weis, the boys and the four horses, four cows, and flock of chickens survived the blizzard in true pioneer fashion. A new house was built, a new son, Charles, was born and a new page of Parmer County history was written.

WENTWORTH FAMILY

Mr. and Mrs. A.N. Wentworth came to Friona from Crisco, Iowa about 1908 during the land opportunity deal. They farmed for a few years and sold the farm to Whaleys. He established the first blacksmith shop and later established the water works for the town; then owned and operated a cafe and variety store which he sold to Mr. and Mrs. E.V. Rushing when he retired about 1931. After his wife Laura passed away he moved back to Iowa to live with a daughter. He lived to be ninety years old.

WENTWORTH VARIETY STORE AND CAFE.

MRS. WENTWORTH and Marie Sander in store.

JOHN H. WEST

John H. West of Farwell began his travels in a Model T. His first car, purchased in 1915 was a Model T roadster. From that car, he has jumped to an airplane which will take him to Europe in September.

West is 79 years old. He has lived in Farwell since August 3, 1955. He moved to Oklahoma Lane in 1918. He bought a half section of land which he traded a short time later for some more land where he built his home.

His wife, who was the daughter of the late Jim Perkins and sister of Clyde Perkins of Oklahoma Lane, passed away May 3, 1963. She came with her husband and one child to the Oklahoma Lane community from Oklahoma. Their first child, a girl, Overeta Sudderth, now resides in Bovina. Their son, Loren, who lives in Abernathy, was born in Oklahoma Lane.

MR. A.N. WENTWORTH

After two years of farming, West decided to leave for the Burkburnett Oil Field north of Wichita Falls. In July, 1912, he came back to farm. He brought the team with which he used to haul rig material to carry his possessions back here.

West farmed dry land, raising milo and cane. He had a few cattle which he and his father-in-law ran together.

West says he remembers buying his first tractor from Nathan Tharp in 1935. "I traded all my horses for that tractor," he says. Farming was always in West's blood. "My aim in life was to be a farmer," he says.

"In 1910 I was in Dallas hauling gravel at 17 to help pave the streets. I found out then that I didn't like industrial jobs," he adds.

West delivered his crops to Farwell or Lariat. He also raised some cotton which he had to take to Sudan to get ginned. "There were no gins around here in the early days," he says.

He remembers that the family took off four or five days in the summer and went to the mountains near Ft. Sumner. "If we had longer, we went to Taos or Red River," he adds.

MARVIN WHALEY

Marvin Whaley and his wife, Beulah, and their two sons, Thomas and Watson, moved to Friona from their homestead just across the line in New Mexico so the boys could be near school. The move was made in 1920. Mrs. Whaley remembers that the school building had burned a short time before they came and that school was held in some temporary buildings. They still farmed their land in New Mexico and stayed there in the summer time. They came to Friona because the roads were better and there were no draws to cross.

Mrs. Whaley came with her parents from southeastern Iowa in 1906. Her father, Mr. Watson, came ahead and had a house ready for her and her mother when they arrived at Texico on Nov. 2, 1906. It was late at night when the train arrived and they got off some distance from the depot, and before they could get to the depot Mr. Watson had left, so they found a boarding house to stay at. It was several days before Mr. Watson found

them. She remembers the prairie fire that came up to the edge of town and a few days later a big blizzard which killed lots of cattle on the XIT Ranch.

The day after Christmas they moved to their homestead northwest of Texico. They had three wagons loaded with supplies and a surrey in which Mrs. Whaley and her mother rode. The team pulling the surrey was tied on behind one of the wagons. Her father broke the land with sod plow and mule team. Their entertainment consisted of community gatherings at the school and church. This is where she met her husband. They homesteaded on the "strip," a strip of land along the border, claimed by both states.

While at church one Sunday night it came a snow storm which lasted three days and nights. They all had to stay at the church. A Mrs. Charlie Foster cooked for them. Her husband owned the store at Hollene.

When the Whaleys first came to Friona they located on Woodland Street where Mrs. Whaley still lives. There was nothing west of them but a wire fence and nothing north to the highway except the Kinsley house. Mrs. Whaley, Watson and Tom still live at Friona. Watson married Alice Wiley and they have two girls, Connie, who is now Mrs. Ray Slagle and Louise, who is still in college.

JOHN WHITE

If it were possible for one to delve into the recorded minutes of the Friona Chamber of Commerce during the months of June and July, 1925, it is possible that one could get a true and recorded version of the events that led up to the founding of this newspaper, **The Friona Star.**

But, as those records are probably out of existence, or, at least, out of the reach of the ordinary individual, the contents of this narrative sketch must depend for its veracity and actuality upon the fickle memory of the writer.

At one of the meetings of the organization

January 25, 1918 Make tires within 40 days.
Commissioners Court Notes

MR. AND MRS. JOHN W. WHITE—1920.

HEADING CREW, 1921—George Messenger, Clyde Goodwine, Jim Goodwine, Fred White, Logan Sympson and John White.

MULE TEAM that hauled wheat from Bellview, N. Mexico.

SUNDAY SCHOOL, 1925.

above mentioned, and at about the time mentioned, the subject of securing a local newspaper for Friona was introduced and discussed with the result that the secretary was instructed to begin at once, efforts to locate an individual or group of individuals that would be willing and competent to undertake the establishment of such a newspaper.

Following advertising, which brought several propositions from a number of individuals, with correspondence and personal interviews with some of them, the secretary was able to report to the organization that a few of these applicants were willing to come to Friona, gather the news, solicit the advertising, and have the paper printed in some other town, provided the city would guarantee not less than $50 per week to the applicant, and the secretary was instructed by vote of the members present to make a deal with the one who had made the most promising offer.

The secretary, who had had some experience in the newspaper business, objected to such a move, on the grounds that such men were probably men who had made failure of the newspaper business in some other place, and would have nothing invested, and at any time he became dissatisfied with the job, he could put on his hat and walk out, leaving the organization with a newspaper on its hands with no one to care for it, and more in jest than otherwise, he stated that he could give them that kind of a paper.

Almost before it was realized, a motion was made and carried that the production of a local newspaper be assigned to the secretary as a part of his official duties, he to receive all revenues that might arise from such publication as recompense for his added labors. Selecting a name for the new publication was then taken up, and it finally decided to adopt the name suggested by A.W. Henschel, the then president of the Friona Bank, and the paper was christened, "The Friona Star," the name which it has borne during the 31 years of its existence and still bears. Credit for the name went to Mr. Henschel.

FRIONA LOOKING NORTH from what is now Hi-way 60—1919.

FRIONA, LOOKING NORTH, 1921

HEADING WHEAT—1920.

MAIN STREET LOOKING NORTH, 1921.

John W. White first came to Friona in 1908 when the Geo. G. Wright Land Co. was selling land for the owners of the famous XIT Ranch. The prospective buyers were taken in cars to the southwest part of Deaf Smith, about 15 to 18 miles northwest of Friona where there was a large hotel for them to stay in. This was at a proposed townsite called Findley. He, like others, bought land in this area, but did not move to Texas until several years later. The town of Findley never was developed.

John White was born May 23, 1868 in the southern part of Illinois. His mother died when he was one year old and he was taken care of by his "Aunt Mary" until he was old enough to go with his father and older brothers and help with the farming. He became a school teacher and taught for 12 years. In 1899 he married Florence B. Sympson. In 1906 he was appointed Deputy Sheriff and moved his family to the county seat town of Chester. Later he became associated with the local newspaper and engaged in job printing work.

On August 16, 1914 the family, John White

and his wife Florence and two children, Fred and Orma, arrived in Friona. A day or so later the immigrant car arrived bringing two horses, a Jersey cow and calf, some hogs and chickens along with the household furnishings. These were moved to a place two and a half miles northeast of town which is now the Massie place. This place was rented so the family could be closer to town and school. The children had bicycles which they rode to school, but when the weather was real bad "Old Dobbin" was hitched to the buckboard and brought them in. This was the family conveyance for a few years. Old Dobbin, as Orma remembers him, was a mild easy going critter until he was being saddled, then he would kick and bite at the same time, but if a calf got too close to his heels he would gently lift his hind foot and push it out of the way. Orma, eleven years old at the time, and Fred were riding Old Dobbin bareback one morning. She scooted back so Fred could get off, but got too far back and Old Dobbin's rear left the ground, sending her up in the air with nothing at all to hold on to. The first two times she came down she landed on the horse, but the third time she hit the ground. Her first thought was that her mother would not let her ride any more.

To ease the fuel shortage and save money, they picked up many cow chips for fuel.

In 1916 Mr. White purchased a farm adjoining the north side of Friona. The house stood on Main Street just north of what is now 14th Street. The west part of the farm extended farther south to the north side of what is now Highway 60, where the bank and hospital are now located.

Mr. White was on the school board when the first brick school building burned. When they started to rebuild he suggested that they consolidate with several adjoining districts and build a larger school and bring the children to school in buses. There was some doubt as to whether school money would be allowed to pay for the buses. He wrote to the state school superintendent and received the reply that it had never been done but to go ahead and try it, so Friona was the first district in the state to have bus transportation.

In 1925 he put his newspaper experience to work and started the **Friona Star.** In 1928 when Friona was incorporated he was elected the first Mayor with Jerry A. Blackwell and Jesse M. Osborn as commissioners.

The Whites joined the Congregational Church soon after coming to Friona and were active members, Mr. White having served as Sunday School Superintendent for many years. He also served as secretary for the first Chamber of Commerce.

After retiring from work with the newspaper he started a small job printing shop in his garage near his home and did small printing jobs as a hobby, which he continued until a year or two before his death in 1965 at the age of 97 years. His wife passed away in 1941. Fred and his wife, the former Glee Goodwine, live on the south side of Highway 60 in Friona where he had an automotive electrical business for many years. They have one son and three grandchildren. Orma, who married W.H. Flippin, Jr., now resides on the farm just north of town.

When Logan Sympson learned that his brother-in-law, John White, was moving to Texas, he asked to come with the immigrant car just to see the country. That was in August, 1914. He stayed all winter with the Whites and in March went back to Illinois and brought his mother, known as "Grandma Sympson," and his sister, Grace, to live in Friona. Grace later became the wife of Charlie M. Hart. They had three children, Roy, Wanda and Elda Hart.

Logan married Louise Cearley who was teaching school, and they moved to Amarillo.

E.B. AND DELIA WHITEFIELD

E.B. and Delia Whitefield came to Parmer County in 1925, after coming to Hale County in 1909 in a covered wagon with their three small children from Knox County. They settled first at Petersburg, then sold their place there and bought a section at Lakeview, also in Hale County, then sold that the following year and bought a place near Abernathy. Still trying to get away from the cotton county where the whole family was involved in raising this crop they looked still further west and finally traded their place at Abernathy for a place in the east part of Parmer County. The place was 11 miles southeast of Friona, in the Sullivan subdivision. At that time there was only one house between them and town—Friona. The rest was still grass land. A few roads had been freshly made with the mule-drawn graders but one could still take out across the trails through the pastures to get to town.

All farming was done by teams, with horses as far as the Whitefields were concerned as E.B. never bought many mules. Three fourths of the section was already being farmed so there was no problem in having to break fresh sod. Whitefield used a two row planter then and could take his six horse team, start on one side of the section making rows and end up on the far side with not a bobble in a row and every row straight as could be. Changing times caused more sod to be broken but by this time the tractor had made its appearance and was used for the heavy work of breaking sod or plowing wheat

September 13, 1918 Western to operate soon.
Commissioners Court Notes

DELIA AND E.B. WHITEFIELD—1920.

WHITEFIELD BOYS.

stubble while the teams were used for working row crops, harvesting and threshing. To supplement the income, sheep were added in 1928 and stayed a part of the farm scene from then on. And like so many then milk cows, which were brought from Hale County, played a big part in feeding the family as well as did hogs and chickens. The first combine was purchased in 1928 only to see a severe hail storm beat the wheat into the ground the night before the combine was to start rolling the next morning. Another one-half section just west of the place was added to the holding. It was all grass and came in very handy for the sheep.

Sudan for seed was one of the early cash crops and most of the other grain sorghums were for feed. Some wheat was also grown for a cash crop and that crop increased as the tractor came more into use. Sudan was cut with row binders, shocked and then hauled to the threshers with teams and wagons. Whitefield was lucky in having some of the neighbors, the O'Brians, with the know how and desire to buy and operate a thresher that was always available at harvest time. The straw was blown in huge stacks that was used to feed the stock during the winter months. The stocks were turned to the stacks and ate as they pleased. By spring the stack would all be gone. But fair times were not to last. During the late twenties, fair to good crops came to an end. 1931 was the last big wheat crop for years to come. But to top that prices were falling almost to nothing. The rains ceased, spring winds began to pick up the loose dust and whirl it skyward, to see it settling hun-

dreds of miles east and south. Months stretched into years with scant rain fall. Prices stayed so low that no one had any money and most could not pay debts, taxes and grocery bills. Livestock got thin and stayed that way all summer—no grass—no feed and no money to get feed. But the milk cows and chickens paid the Whitefield grocery bill. There was not even enough money to go to a picture show but everyone seemed to be in the same boat. People enjoyed the community gatherings and had great times together. The dust continued to pile high along fences, buildings and got into everything there was. During the severe storms, daylight turned into night within a few minutes. You couldn't even see a light if you were in the room where it was.

But then came 1941. Rain, more rain and still more rain. 45 inches here from spring through fall. So much rain the crops were as poor as when there was no rain. But prices began to rise and so did good crops and better times. But all this was marred by the war which lasted for several years. But the big depression was over and with the coming of irrigation everything was changing. Hardly any grass land left, new homes, businesses, modern machinery.

In 1925 the country out here was in the Black School District and as Black taught only through the seventh grade, high schoolers had to go to Friona. As there were four boys in the Whitefield family in school, two in high school and two in the grades, all were transferred to Friona, there was no bus to Black and they would have to furnish their

WHITEFIELD'S FIRST HOME IN FRIONA.

WHITEFIELD HOME—1929.

own way to Friona. And that was by Model T most of the time and by horseback or horse drawn wagon if there was coal or something heavy to bring from town.

Whitefield was elected to the School Board at Black in 1926. He served as trustee with W.R. Schiehagen and "Mac" McCrate. But as it was almost 15 miles to the south end of the district the people who were settling down there thought it was too far to send the children and petitioned to have the district split and form a new district. This was accomplished and in the summer of 1972 a new district, Lakeview, came into being. E.B. Whitefield, C.A. Quinn and J.M.W. Alexander were elected to serve as trustees. Whitefield served this district as trustee until it was annexed to the Friona Independent School District at the end of the 1944 school year. He was also Democrat chairman until his retirement from farming in 1947 and moved to Friona where he lived until he passed away in 1951.

There were five children of the home.

Opal graduated from Abernathy high School and Draughon's Business School of Plainview, Texas and married Bev Buchanan in February of 1927.

Heard graduated from Friona High in 1926, went to John Tarlton one year, then took up active farming until called to service during World War One. After the war he returned home to farm again, then moved to Severy, Kansas and then back to Clayton, N.M.

Otho (Hobe) graduated from Friona in 1928, spent two years at Texas Tech, then returned home to farm and raise sheep. He married Grace Eastep, in Lancaster, Texas in

E.B. AND MRS. WHITEFIELD'S daughter-in-law, Grace.

1947, bought a place near the old home place and resides there. Grace's 12 years at Friona totaled 30 years teaching in Texas in 1971.

Orville (Red) graduated in 1933, worked for several years or until called to service by Uncle Sam about the first month of the war. He served four year with the 13th Armored Division, mostly in North Africa and Italy, being one of the small group that landed on the Anzio Beach.

Weldon (Mike) graduated from Friona in 1934. He spent four years at Texas Tech, then entered the Air Force where he served until the war was over. He flew a number of missions from England and was there when the war was over. He was discharged as a Lieutenant Colonel and has made his home in Houston, Texas.

Mrs. E.B. Whitefield was active in the Lakeview Home Demonstration Club and a devoted mother to her family. One of the

DADDY OF THE HERD

"OLD SAL," mother of the horse herd.

highlights of the week for her was Saturday when they would go to town to shop and visit. Friona was then a Saturday town with the people coming from all around to shop and visit. She passed away in February of 1955.

Moving took lots of planning and doing. As all farming was done by teams there was lots of farm machinery as well as household goods. A model T truck was purchased to move the household goods. The wagons were loaded with machinery and other heavy goods and hauled the ninety odd miles by the horses. Whitefield and the older son, Heard, drove the horses. The trip was made in two days but the horses were very weary by that time. The truck came through the country to Pumpkin Center, a filling station-grocery store (now Spring Lake) north to Dimmitt to the Orzal Trail, Highway 86, thence west about 20 miles, and through a pasture by the old Mulheirn ranch and to the new White-field place. The rest of the family came in the Model T car. Hobe brought the truck through.

Horses, good horses, were long a part of the Whitefield operation. Big horses, that could drag the plow day after day and week after week. The first of a well known span of horses the Whitefield purchased and used so long was a pair of duns, Curt and Cord. Cord was as mean as the Devil and seldom ever saw his equal. Curt was docile and very dependable. And then there was Old Sal. Gentle, every ready to go. Buggy horse, work horse and the dam of the finest colts that ever grew. The offspring frequently topped a ton in weight. She produced or her offspring produced some of the best work horses that ever

pulled a plow. And thos offspring were still producing when they were eliminated by the coming of the tractors. Of course there were the saddle horses that were used by the children. Then they thought nothing of riding into town to play practice or other activities. Only once was there an injruy and that was when one reared and fell backward, breaking Heard's leg. Others of those horses long remembered was "Old Mexico," a giant of a horse topping 2100 pounds, Mares, Maude and Bess and many others. Among the saddle horses was "Little Red," Flexen, Speck, a retired cow horse when we got him and Black Beauty.

With livestock there was always the feed problem. And feed houses anxious to sell were thinking of ways to increase sales. And feed sacks, good cotton sacks, with beautiful prints. In fact the ladies would go pick out the print they wanted. Many a sack went into the making of a dress, apron, shorts fort the boys and many other things. Feed sacks clothed many a family and ours was one that used them.

During the late twenties and early thirties this part of the country was overrun with jackrabbits. Literally thousands of them. You could drive around your field every afternoon and shoot a dozen or more with the rifle. They were so bad that they were destroying the crops. Drives were organized to round them up and kill them. All the neighbors for miles around would gather then start out and surround fields, working towrd the center, until the rabbits were driven to the center then they were killed. Or perhaps they would ride on wagons with the rifles and

E.B. WHITEFIELD and sons, Orville and Mike, Heard hidden by old Dobbin's neck.

BEV AND DOYLE HARVESTING SUDAN.

drive through the fields, shooting all they could. Then a disease seemed to strike the rabbits and has kept them thinned out until they are no longer a menace to the crops.

Prices were pretty fair until after 1929 then the bottom seemed to drop out. With the last good wheat crop in 1931 most of that went as low as 25c per bushel. Eggs 10c or lower, we shipped lambs to Kansas City that sold for five and six cents per pound and an old ewe might bring one dollar each. Hogs were under 10c. Good cows and calves could be had from under $40.00 per pair. Old sows would bring about $1.00 per hundred. Everything else was priced accordingly. There just was not much money floating around.

As long as we were working horses, all row crops, which consisted of milo, corn planted in six foot rows, sudan, and some kind of sweet sorghums used to bundle and feed for the livestock. All milo was hand headed, in this we used two horses to the wagon, driving them down the row and cutting the heads by hand then transferring them to the wagon. Then when the wagons were full the heads were piled on the ground in ricks or maybe some put in the barn to feed the horses during the coming year. The ricks could then be threshed by pulling the thrasher to them which finally gave way to the combine. Our corn was gathered the same way and that generally lasted up into January of the following year. A corn sheller was used to get the grain from the ears. Trucks were coming into use so one was hired to get the grain to the elevator. Crops were worked with a one row sled or a two row sled and a two row go-devil, slightly different from the two sled. Most all land was listed with a one or two row lister. Also a big disc, three disc, plow was used for breaking. Then with the introduction of the tractor, one way plows became popular and could cover lots of ground. And then more and better plows and tractors began to appear that could work several times the acreage that the horse drawn plows would.

The Whitefields had been used to cheap fuel in the form of wood before they came to the plains. But out here there was no wood.

But there was coal freighted in by wagons or you had to drive miles to where the railroad came and haul it out yourself. Then there were times when finances did not allow the purchase of coal. But there were cow chips for the taking and they would burn. We did cook and heat with them at times. Many a time we would take cotton sacks and go out to the pastures where the cattle had run, gather a sack full, then dump it into the wagon to be hauled to the house. And then there was a time when corn was so cheap that it was used for fuel. That is corn on the ear, cob and all including the shuck and it did heat nicely.

All the early houses were without plumbing of any kind. The water was brought in from the wells in buckets and out at the well there was a barrel, usually a vinegar barrel—one made of staves—for the water to run into then from that piped out to water troughs—one a cooling milk trough for the water to pass through then into other troughs for the livestock to use. And we all had outside privies, usually out in one corner of the yard.

July 2, 1919 Dealers wanted—delivery by July 10th, 1919.

Commissioners Court Notes

The first house at Petersburg was rather small—a bedroom, living room combined and kitchen-dining room. Then another room was added for a dining place and another bedroom was attached to that. Then when this place was sold a brand new house was constructed on the new place at Lakeview. In the mean time we lived in a chicken house—the cooking was done outside, while the new house was completed. But in one year that place was sold and we bought a place near Abernathy and moved in to a three room house. There were seven of us now, the two younger boys, Orville and Weldon had been born while at Petersburg. Then another new house was built to accommodate the family but still no inside plumbing. Then this place was sold and the family moved to Parmer County into a four room house. Two bedrooms and a living-dining room and a kitchen. We got by with this for four years then in 1929 built a big new house with inside plumbing. One of the first rural houses to be so constructed. A Delco Plant was installed to furnish lights and an underground tank to hold casenhead gas was added to furnish fuel for cooking. And now good stoves to burn, kerosene was added for heating. That replaced the coal stove. Then there was the coming of the REA to bring electricity to all the county. Each day we would drive out to see how far or rather how much closer the working crews were to home in stringing the poles and lines and then there was that day the electricity was turned on and the Delco plant was run no more. Then with the coming of irrigation it was found that the motors could be run more cheaper on natural gas than they could any other kind of fuel. So soon natural gas lines were strung all throughout the country side. Electricity and natural gas—we were as modern as any place.

HARRY B. WHITLEY

In the spring of 1914, twenty year old Harry B. Whitley arrived at the one hundred section pasture south of Hub. He delivered the horse herd he had driven from his home ranch at Pilot Point, Denton County, Texas and remained to work as a cowboy on some of the area spreads. He was joined by three of his seven brothers, Virgil, Gene, and Tom. Harry and Virgil worked on the well-known Hay Hook Ranch while Gene and Tom found employment at Crawford's grocery in Friona.

After a few years of cowboying, Harry became a brand inspector for the Cattle Raisers Association. On June 3rd he married Miss Marye Harris at Denver, Colorado. Miss Harris had been born in Ponder, Texas, on October 13, 1897. She was a graduate of North Texas State College and Eastern New Mexico. University. Her career as a teacher spanned forty-three years and included schools in Ponder, Texas; Casper, Wyoming; Clovis, New Mexico; and Parmer County, Texas.

Mr. Whitley engaged in ranching for a number of years then became an inspector for the Texas Livestock Sanitary Board, which position he held until his retirement.

ESTELLE (WINN) DUNN COMBS INTERVIEW (PRAIRIE FIRE)

PRAIRIE FIRE ABOUT NOVEMBER, 1906

It started in New Mexico north of Fort Sumner and burned to near Amarillo. This fire went near the town of Bovina and Estelle Combs said that it was as light as day when the fire burned by Bovina one night. A snow storm came along and put out the fire.

A herd of 36 antelopes came to the Melugin place north of Farwell where about 40 acres of sod had been broken and the antelopes stayed there during the fire. The New Mexico settlers came over at night and butchered them.

The following notes were taken during an interview with Estelle Winn Dunn Combs by Hugh Moseley on June 29th, 1971.

Question: Mrs. Combs, for the record, I would like to ask you some personal information regarding your birthplace and birthdate.

Answer: I was born Estelle Winn, on October 5th, 1888 at Silver Valley in Coleman County, Texas.

My father was Gus Winn of Coleman County, Texas, who dealt in fine saddle horses. He sold horses in Monroe, Louisiana, and that is where he met and married my mother, Miss Jennie Simmons, who was a sister to Mildred (Millie) Simmons who married "Uncle Bill" Williams Lyles Townsen.

While I was growing up I lived with Aunt Millie and Uncle Bill Townsen as much or more than I did with my parents. I lived with them a part of the time that they lived at Parmerton when the County Seat was out there. I later lived with them at Bovina, when they were operating the Hotel there.

Question: Mrs. Combs, I have with me and want to show you two small models of the temporary courthouse buildings that were out at Parmerton and I want you to tell me how they were situated if you remember.

Answer: I do not remember the first model at all (the 28 x 30) but the other little building (28 x 40) I remember as being the courthouse there at Parmerton. It was a long building with small offices on either side of a hallway that I think was near the center of the building.

The courthouse building set off to itself in a plowed field and was quite some distance from the railroad. It was some 100 feet north or northwest from the windmill if you remember the windmill.

Question: Did the courthouse building face the railroad?

Answer: No, the building faced due east, I do not know why, but all the buildings at Parmerton faced the east as I remember it.

Question: Can you describe the house that your Uncle Bill and Aunt Millie Townsen lived in?

Answer: Yes, it was a three room house, two bedrooms and one front room. There was no kitchen in the Townsen house as we all ate at the cook shack.

Question: When you say we all ate at the cook shack, whom do you mean?

Answer: Uncle Bill, Aunt Minnie, myself (Estelle Winn), Norman Wilson, Sheriff E.T. Stevens, and also the comers and goers, that is to say the people who came to Parmerton to court or to tend to legal business. The McKay family (Jess McKay was the county clerk) did not eat at the cook shack as they had a kitchen in their house and they had two small children at that time so they cooked and ate at home. I can not recall the name of the woman that ran the cook shack. I can only remember two houses at Parmerton while we lived there, our house (Townsen House) and the McKay house. Norman Wilson ate at the cook shack and slept on a cot at the courthouse at night, I think.

Question: Can you remember if E.T. Stevens, Sheriff, lived at Parmerton while it was the county seat?

Answer: I remember Sheriff Stevens and his son, Pat Stevens. As a matter of Fact, Pat Stevens, when he was a boy, lived with Uncle Bill and Aunt Millie Townsen. It seems to me that he had lost his wife (Pat Stevens' mother) by death and he later married a widow by the name of Mollie Steele.

(Note: E.T. Stevens married Mollie Steele on October 7, 1907. Judge W.L. Townsen performed the marriage ceremony.)

I cannot remember for sure but I think Sheriff Stevens slept on a cot at the courthouse, at least a part of the time.

Question: Did you know John Armstrong, Postmaster at Bovina?

Answer: Yes, I knew him. Kate Nichols and I were on our way by foot from the post office which was located at the XIT Headquarter at that time, to downtown Bovina (North Street) on the date John Armstrong was shot from his horse by John Williams with a 30-30 rifle. We heard the shot fired.

JACK WOLTMON

INTERVIEW
with
JACK WOLTMON by Hugh Moseley on June 6th A.D. 1970 at The Security State Bank, Farwell, Texas.

Jack Woltmon, who was born in Floyd County, Texas, moved to Parmer County with his parents in ????.

Jack Woltmon attended the 5th grade in 1917 at the old Daniels School, which was situated on the North bank of the Running Water Draw, near the present site of the Freda Finley, deceased, home, which is on the Northeast quarter of Section 22, Block "A" Syndicate Subdivision.

Jack Woltmon says that there were 11 students at the Daniels School that year and that Miss Helen Ross, a sister of Mr. Charles Ross of Bovina, Texas, was the teacher.

Jack Woltmon attended the Texico Public School the following year.

Thus ended the interview.

ERNEST EARL WORM
By Earl Worm

Ernest Earl Worm was born May 17, 1888 in Lennox, Iowa, the son of Fredrick and Alta Rose Worm. There were eleven children of the home, nine boys and two girls. Mr. Worm is survived by a sister Nellie of Saint Joseph, Mo., and brothers, Clay of Long Beach, Calif., Bill of Lennox, Iowa, Harry of Waterloo, Iowa, Fred of Peru, Iowa, and Bennie of Manchester, Iowa.

Earl grew into manhood in Iowa, coming to Texas in 1907 where he made his home with a brother Frank Reed and his wife, Mattie, who both preceeded him in death. He was well known around Friona, Bovina, and Lazbuddie, working on the Star Ranch for many years. Counting also among his many friends the people of Muleshoe and Dimmitt area.

He was a veteran of World War I. Earl celebrated his 44th wedding anniversary this year, having been united in marriage on January 17, 1922, with Lulu Fern Burton. Making their home in the Big Square Community, they raised four sons: Ernest Edward, member of the armed forces, preceeded his father in death; James Edmond and Fredrick Otis, both of Sacramento, Calif.; Albert Keith of Clovis, N. Mex., and his wife Fern of the home mourn his passing. Also surviving are six grandchildren, nieces, nephews, and other close relatives.

Mr. Worm moved his family from Big Square back to Iowa in 1943. After the boys left for service in World War II, Mr. and Mrs. Worm moved to Sacramento, Calif., making their home there. He has been in falling health since his retirement seven years ago. He was visiting in the home of his son and other close relatives in and around Clovis when he was stricken with the last illness, entering Clovis Memorial Hospital, Sunday, February 27 and passing away Monday, March 7, 1966 at approximately 11:50 p.m.

Appendix

PARMER COUNTY, TEXAS

COUNTY JUDGES

	FROM:	TO:
William Lyles Townsen	June 8, 1907	Nov. 17, 1908
Rufus W. (Ward) McConnell	Nov. 18, 1908	Nov. 11, 1912
James D. Hamlin	Nov. 11, 1912	Dec. 31, 1924
Ernest F. Lokey	Jan. 1, 1925	Dec. 31, 1928
John H. Aldridge, Jr.	Jan. 1, 1929	Dec. 31, 1934
Walter Lander	Jan. 1, 1935	Dec. 31, 1938
Lee Thompson	Jan. 1, 1939	May 1st, 1945
A.D. Smith	May 1, 1945	Dec. 31, 1958
Loyde A. Brewer	Jan. 1, 1959	Dec. 12, 1967
Archie L. Tarter	Dec. 18, 1967	

Compiled by Hugh Moseley
Chairman, Parmer County
Historical Survey Committee

Dated: Feb. 8, 1971
Farwell, Texas 79325

PARMER COUNTY, TEXAS

SHERIFF and COLLECTOR OF TAXES

	FROM:	TO:
E.T. Stevens	June 8, 1907	Nov. 17, 1910
R.C. Hopping	Nov. 17, 1910	Dec. 31, 1918
James (John) H. Aldridge	Jan. 1, 1919	Dec. 31, 1922
James Henry Martin	Jan. 1, 1923	Dec. 31, 1930
W.W. "Bill" Hall	Jan. 1, 1931	Dec. 31, 1934
R. Earl Booth	Jan. 1, 1935	Dec. 31, 1948
Charles B. Lovelace	Jan. 1, 1949	Dec. 31, 1956

SHERIFF

Charles B. Lovelace	Jan. 1, 1957	

TAX ASSESSOR

J.B. McMinn	June 8, 1907	Nov. 17, 1908
C.G. Bratton	Nov. 17, 1908	Aug., 1921
Ben T. Little	Aug. 28, 1921	Dec. 31, 1922
John S. Potts	Jan. 1, 1923	Dec. 31, 1926
J. Willis Magness	Jan. 1, 1927	Dec. 31, 1932
R. Earl Booth	Jan. 1, 1933	Dec. 31, 1934

TAX ASSESSOR and COLLECTOR and SHERIFF

R. Earl Booth	Jan. 1, 1935	Dec. 31, 1948
Charles B. Lovelace	Jan. 1, 1949	Dec. 31, 1956

TAX ASSESSOR-COLLECTOR

Lee Thompson	Jan. 1, 1957	Aug. 31, 1963
Hugh E. Moseley	Sept. 1, 1963	

Compiled by Hugh Moseley,
Chairman, Parmer County
Historical Survey Committee

Dated: Feb. 8, 1971
Farwell, Texas 79325

PARMER COUNTY, TEXAS

COUNTY CLERK and DISTRICT CLERK

	FROM:	TO:
Jess F. McKay	June 8, 1907	Nov. 10, 1908

D.O. Stallings+		
James M. Hamlin	Nov. 11, 1908	Nov. 16, 1910
William McCandlish	Nov. 16, 1910	Nov. 11, 1912
Merton Dickson	Nov. 11, 1912	Dec. 31, 1916
B.N. Graham	Jan. 1, 1917	Dec. 31, 1926
Gordon McCuan	Jan. 1, 1927	Dec. 31, 1932
Eric Vance Rushing	Jan. 1, 1933	Dec. 31, 1940
D.K. Roberts	Jan. 1, 1941	Dec. 31, 1946
Loyde A. Brewer	Jan. 1, 1957	Dec. 31, 1954
Hugh E. Moseley	Jan. 1, 1955	Dec. 31, 1962

COUNTY CLERK
Mrs. Bonnie (Foster) Warren   Jan. 1, 1963

DISTRICT CLERK
Mrs. Dorothy (Thornton) Quickel   Jan. 1, 1963

Compiled by Hugh Moseley
Chairman, Parmer County
Historical Survey Committee
Dated: Feb. 8, 1971
Farwell, Texas, 79325

PARMER COUNTY, TEXAS

COUNTY TREASURERS

	FROM:	TO:
Norman Wilson	June 8, 1907	Nov. 16, 1910
Bob Kyker	Nov. 17, 1910	Dec. 31, 1916
T.J. Allen	Jan. 1, 1917	Nov. 11, 1917 (1)
M. Dickson (appointed)	Nov. 12, 1917	Dec. 31, 1920
W.M. Savage	Jan. 1, 1921	Nov. 13, 1922
Minnie Olivia Aldridge	Nov. 13, 1922	Dec. 31, 1928
Mrs. Lelah M. Robbins	Jan. 1, 1929	Dec. 17, 1929 (2)
John S. Potts (appointed)	Jan. 1, 1930	Dec. 31, 1930
Walter Lander	Jan. 1, 1931	Dec. 31, 1934
Roy B. Ezell	Jan. 1, 1935	March 4, 1950 (3)
Mrs. Mabel Reynolds	Jan. 1, 1951	

(1) Called into Military Service
(2) Death—December 17, 1929
(3) Death—March 4th, 1950

Compiled by Hugh Moseley
Chairman, Parmer County
Historical Survey Committee
Dated: Feb. 8, 1971
Farwell, Texas 79325

Evelyn (Kyker) Bradshaw, copy mailed 7-26-71

PARMER COUNTY, TEXAS

COUNTY ATTORNEYS

	FROM:	TO:
J.W. Sellars (appointed)	Aug. 12, 1907	Nov. 15, 1910
Sam G. Bratton	Nov. 16, 1910	Nov. 12, 1912
John D. Reese		
E.A. White		

+D.O. Stallings—Official Bond Dated June 10, 1907 and Recorded in Volume 1 Page 3, Parmer County Official Bond Records: D.O. Stallings was District Clerk—Pro Tempore for case pending before the District Court in Parmer County, in which E.L. Swenson was contestant and Jess F. McKay was contestee.

A.B. Crane
J.D. Thomas   Oct., 1925   Dec. 31, 1932
Perry T. Brown   Jan. 1, 1933
Ernest F. Lokey (appointed) Aug. 10, 1936 Dec. 31, 1936
Astynix Douglas Smith   Jan. 1, 1937   April 30, 1945
Sam Aldridge (appointed)   May 1, 1945   Dec. 31, 1954
William H. Sheehan   Jan. 1, 1955   Jan. 11, 1957
Hurshel R. Harding (appointed)   Jan. 12, 1957

Compiled by Hugh Moseley,
Chairman, Parmer County
Historical Survey Committee
Dated: Feb. 8, 1971
Farwell, Texas 79325

PARMER COUNTY, TEXAS

COUNTY COMMISSIONER, PRECINCT NUMBER 1

	FROM:	TO:
W.P. McMinn	June 8, 1907	May 27, 1908
C.S. Fergus (appointed)	June 5, 1908	Mar. 21, 1911
Dale W. McMillen (appointed)	Mar. 25, 1911	Aug. 14, 1911
W.E. Goodwine (appointed)	Aug. 24, 1911	Nov. 10, 1914
C.F. Kellner	Nov. 25, 1914	July 24, 1916?
Floyd White Reeve	Nov. 15, 1916	Dec. 31, 1922
D.H. Meade	Jan. 1, 1923	Dec. 31, 1924
Elbert Overton	Jan. 1, 1925	Dec. 31, 1926
Nat. Jones	Jan. 1, 1927	Dec. 31, 1928
D.H. Meade	Jan. 1, 1929	Dec. 31, 1930
J.M.W. Alexander	Jan. 1, 1931	Dec. 31, 1940
David Moseley	Jan. 1, 1941	Dec. 31, 1944
W.H. "Bill" Flippin, Jr.	Jan. 1, 1945	Dec. 31, 1948
Emmitt R. Day	Jan. 1, 1949	Dec. 31, 1952
Forrest W. Osborn	Jan. 1, 1953	Dec. 31, 1956
E.G. Phipps	Jan. 1, 1957	Dec. 31, 1960
Thomas Lewellen	Jan. 2, 1961	

Compiled by Hugh Moseley,
Chairman, Parmer County
Historical Committee
Dated: February 8, 1971
Farwell, Texas 79325

PARMER COUNTY, TEXAS

COUNTY COMMISSIONER, PRECINCT NUMBER 2

	FROM:	TO:
Frank L. Spring	June 8, 1907	Nov. 16, 1910
J.R. Champion	Nov. 16, 1910	Jan. 26, 1911
Frank L. Spring	Jan. 27, 1911	Dec. 31, 1914
D.O. Stallings	Jan. 1, 1915	Feb. 14, 1916
Geo. W. Lambert	Feb. 14, 1916	Nov. 15, 1916
James (John) H. Aldridge	Nov. 15, 1916	Dec. 31, 1918
Frank L. Spring	Jan. 1, 1919	Dec. 31, 1924
M.H. Martin	Jan. 1, 1925	Dec. 31, 1926
James A. Richards	Jan. 1, 1927	Dec. 31, 1930
Jack Carr	Jan. 1, 1931	Dec. 31, 1934
Floyd T. Schlenker	Jan. 1, 1935	Dec. 31, 1946
Charlie L. Callaway	Jan. 1, 1947	Dec. 31, 1950
Charley H. Jefferson	Jan. 1, 1951	

Compiled by Hugh Moseley,
Chairman, Parmer County
Historical Committee
Dated: Feb. 8, 1971
Farwell, Texas 79325

PARMER COUNTY, TEXAS

COUNTY COMMISSIONER, PRECINCT NUMBER 3

	FROM:	TO:
J.M. Neely	June 8, 1907	Dec. 22, 1908
J.F. Porter+		
R.C. Hopping (appointed)	Dec. 30, 1908	July 20, 1909
B.E. Nobles (appointed)	July 21, 1909	Nov. 15, 1912
F.W. McElroy	Dec. 9, 1912	Dec. 6, 1920
R.A. Hawkins	Dec. 6, 1920	Dec. 30, 1922
Charles E. Christian	Jan. 1, 1923	Feb. 2, 1929++
A.L. Tandy (appointed)	Feb. 11, 1929	Dec. 30, 1930
Lee Thompson (appointed)	Jan. 1, 1931	Dec. 31, 1936
Edd W. McGuire	Jan. 1, 1937	Dec. 31, 1938
Thomas E. Levy	Jan. 2, 1939	Dec. 31, 1940
Edd W. McGuire	Jan. 1, 1941	Dec. 31, 1942
Thomas E. Levy	Jan. 1, 1943	Dec. 31, 1948
A. Frank Phillips	Jan. 1, 1949	Oct. 27, 1949++
Earl F. Billingsley	Oct. 31, 1949	Dec. 31, 1954
Johnny H. McDonald	Jan. 1, 1955	Dec. 31, 1960
Guy Cox	Jan. 2, 1961	

+J.F. Porter was elected November 3, 1908 as County Commissioner, Precinct Number 3, however, he failed to qualify and R.C. Hopping was appointed to fill-out his term
++Death Date

Compiled by Hugh Moseley,
Chairman, Parmer County
Historical Committee
Dated: December 15, 1971
Farwell, Texas

PARMER COUNTY, TEXAS

COUNTY COMMISSIONERS, PRECINCT NUMBER 4

	FROM:	TO:
C.W. Arthur	August 17, 1907	Oct. 4, 1907
Robert E. Oakes (appointed)	April 28, 1908	Nov. 15, 1910
R.E. Flennikrn++	Nov. 15, 1910	Mar. 18, 1912
Peter Kaiser	March 18, 1912	Nov. 11, 1912
Stephen Jesko	Nov. 11, 1912	Nov. 10, 1914
Frank L. Reed	Nov. 10, 1914	Dec. 6, 1920
Henry Bledsoe	Dec. 6, 1920	Dec. 31, 1924
W.D. Knight	Jan. 1, 1925	Dec. 31, 1927
Robert L. Bledsoe (appointed)	Jan. 10, 1928	Dec. 31, 1928
Walter S. Menefee	January 1, 1929	Dec. 31, 1932
Joe Paul	Jan. 2, 1933	Dec. 31, 1936
Oris M. Jennings	Jan. 1, 1937	Dec. 31, 1944
Walter S. Menefee	Jan. 1, 1945	Dec. 31, 1950
Henry L. Ivy	Jan. 1, 1951	Dec. 31, 1958
George W. Crain	Jan. 1, 1959	Sept. 4, 1966+
Raymond Treider, Jr. (Appointed)	Sept. 28, 1966	

+Death Date
++Also known as Ralph E. Flennagan

Compiled by Hugh Moseley
Chairman, Parmer County
Historical Committee
Dated: December 15, 1971
Farwell, Texas

PARMER COUNTY CENSUS FIGURES

1880—0	1910—1,555
1890—70 (all on X.I.T. Ranch)	1920—1,699
1900—34	1930—5,868

POST OFFICES IN PARMER COUNTY, TEXAS
Postmasters and their date of appointment:
BOVINA Established January 31, 1899

William M. Guy	Jan. 31, 1899
George W. Winkler	March 9, 1899
John R. Armstrong	July 22, 1899
Ada W. Field	Dec. 16, 1903
Alba E. Poole	May 20, 1910
Eula McDonald	Sept. 7, 1912
Harriet P.Dean	May 22, 1916
Eula McDonald	Jan. 26, 1918
Lola L. Rumfield	June 13, 1919
Madge B. Martin	May 12, 1920
Sam N. Martin	June 6, 1921
Roy B. Ezell	Feb. 10, 1922
Della Ezell	March 10, 1922
Jeptha G. Flato	April 6, 1931
Johnny L. Stagner	Sept. 19, 1933
Edmund T. Caldwell	Apr. 29, 1935
Miss Alice B. Steelman	Oct. 1, 1945
(name changed by marriage to	
Mrs. Alice B. Moore, July 6, 1946)	
Marvin E. Ezell	June 1, 1947

FARWELL Established December 26, 1906

Minnie Burton	Dec. 26, 1906
Minne B. Francis	Jan. 3, 1908
Gustav A. Wulfman	July 16, 1923
Noma N. Lokey	Sept. 20, 1933
John D. Zahn	Apr. 11, 1958
Jesse F. Landrum	Mar. 10, 1961
Albert H. Smith	Aug. 19, 1961
James Robert Smart	June 29, 1963

FRIONA Established March 16, 1906

Sarah D. Olson	Mar. 16, 1907
Anna W. Dimond	April 2, 1908
Grace B. Little	Oct. 7, 1909
Grace B. McCandlish	May 2, 1910
David W. Sutton	Dec. 27, 1910
Lula E. Ernest	Oct. 26, 1916
Lula E. Ballard	Nov. 20, 1917
Mary A. Sutton	Dec. 4, 1918
William H. Musick	April 1, 1924
John A. Guyer	Nov. 19, 1924
Dayton W. Hanson	Apr. 26, 1932
Sloan H. Osborn	Sept. 22, 1933
Stelma Leo McLellan	Nov. 4, 1953
James Paul Fortenberry	June 4, 1956
(declined)	
Mrs. Martha Clements	June 24, 1961
Wright Williams	Dec. 16, 1963

PARMERTON Established September 14, 1907. Discontinued August 15, 1909. Mail sent thereafter to Friona.

William L. Townsen	Sept. 14, 1907

RHEA Established March 5, 1909. Discontinued March 31, 1924. Mail sent thereafter to Friona.

John W. Barnett	March 5, 1909
Hermann J. Reinking	Jan. 4, 1911
Charles F. Shroeder	Jan. 30, 1912
Ottomar E. Schmidt	Sept. 9, 1912
Pauline Gallmeier	Dec. 12, 1916
Emma Deffner	Apr. 28, 1919
Pauline Hoffman	July 8, 1921

BLACK Established April 26, 1912. Discontinued November 30, 1914, mail sent thereafter to Summerfield. Re-established March 6, 1915. Discontinued May 31, 1920, mail sent thereafter to Summerfield. Re-established February 16, 1926.

Joseph C. Baker	Apr. 26, 1912
Joseph J. Erdman	March 6, 1915
Albert S. Bell	April 5, 1916
Thomas E. Baker	Mar. 16, 1917
Bettie M. McCrate	Feb. 16, 1926
Woodrow McCrate	Apr. 9, 1936
Geneva L. Deaton	Dec. 8, 1936
William C. Neill	Nov. 1, 1939
Leslie L. Deaton	Apr. 1, 1945

LARIAT Established December 9, 1925

Mrs. Maggie L. Robertson	Dec. 9, 1925
Mrs. Lois Elizabeth Smith	Oct. 1, 1947

LAZBUDDIE: Established May 4, 1926

John H. Hennington	May 4, 1926
William M. Sherley +	Nov. 1, 1926
Otto L. Treider	Nov. 16, 1935
Mrs. Judith E. Taylor	April 1, 1942
Lorine V. Weems	Aug. 29, 1945
Elsie I. Clark	Feb. 29, 1948
Othale R. Mahan	July 24, 1948
Mrs. Mae Elizabeth Mahan	Mar. 31, 1951

The above information copied from U.S. Postal Records on file in the Panhandle-Plains Historical Museum, Canyon, Texas.

+W.M. (Bill) Sherley was the official Postmaster but never worked in the Post Office. He did take the Postal Examination because Mr. Otto T. Treider did not think he could pass the examination and he did not want to take the test anyway, but in later years (1935) he did take and pass the Postal Examination and was installed as Postmaster for Lazbuddie .

(The last paragraph of information was gained through personal interview with William M. Sherley on September 29, 1969 by Hugh Moseley.)

OFFICIAL LIST OF SCHOOL TRUSTEES, PARMER COUNTY, TEXAS.

Farwell Independent.
Farwell, Tex.

J.A. Oden, J.L. Walling, Bob Kyker, J.M. Hamlin, R.E. Maddux, A.R. Carter, D.W. Dunn.

Common School District No. 1.
P.O. Address Friona.

C.F. Kellner, W.W. Chivington, A.O. Drake.

Common School District No. 2.
P.O. Address Friona.

T.J. Drawford, D.H. Mead, F.E. Clennen.

Common School District No. 3.
P.O. Address Rhea.

Chas. Schlenker and H.B. Hunter.

Common School District No. 4.
P.O. Address Bovina.

H.E. Morey, E.P. Billingsley, S.M. Snodderly.

Common School District No. 5.
P.O. Address Bovina.

D.O. Stallings, F.W. Jersig and Alfred Berggren.

Common School District No. 6.
P.O. Address Friona.

S.O. Spohn, J.M. Spohn, R.P. Lee.

Common School District No. 7.
P.O. Address Friona.

A.J. James.

Common School District No. 8.
P.O. Address Bovina.

Joseph Paul, Peter Kaiser, F.L. Reed.

Common School District No. 9.
P.O. Address Bovina.

Stephen Jesko, Matt Jesko, Ira O. Stoughton.

Common School District No. 10.
P.O. Address Farwell.

Frank McElroy, W. Watkins, J.F. Hill.

Common School District No. 11.
P.O. Address Friona.

Geo. W. Maurier, Geo. F. Ballew, Henry Teifel.

COUNTY LINE DISTRICT No. 12. DEAF SMITH
GOVERNS.

Common School District No. 14.
P.O. Address Dimmitt.
Chas. Smiley.

Common School District No. 15.
P.O. Address Texico, N.M.

C.B. Daniel, F.L. Hills, J.T. Inmon.

Common School District No. 16
P.O. Address Bovina.

T.B. O'Neal, K. Killam.

Common School District No. 17.
P.O. Address Rhea.

Chas. Lovall, Ernest Schroeder, Chas. Schroeder.

VETERANS OF
WORLD WAR I

Honorable Discharges Filed
In Parmer County Courthouse

Page 1
Frank A. Wirth No. 1173740 U.S. Army
Sergent 1st Class, Repair Depot Detachment
Born: Cleveland, Ohio
Enlisted April 17, 1918 Waco, Texas
Discharged April 18, 1919 Montgomery, Alabama
Travel pay to Farwell, Texas
Recorded: May 6, 1919, B.N. Graham, Clerk
Page 2
Herman Schueler No. 4738737 U.S. Army
Pvt. 17th Co. 5th Bn. Depot Brigade United States
Army
Born: Decatur, Indiana
Enlisted: September 4th, 1918 Decatur, Indiana
Discharged: Camp Zachary Taylor, Kentucky on
December 5, 1918
Recorded: 16 June, 1919, B.N. Graham, Clerk

Page 3
William H. McDonald No. 1053862 U.S. Army
Pvt. 1st Class, Signal Corp. Co. G 4th Depot Bn.
Born: Collin County, Texas
Enlisted: June 1st, 1918, Amarillo, Texas
Discharged: Camp Bowie, Texas on 22nd May, 1919
Recorded: 16 June, 1919, B.N. Graham, Clerk
Page 4
Roland H. James No. 1056190 U.S. Army
Pvt. 1st Class M.D. Amb. Co. No. 10 Sec. "B" San Lo
No. 1
Born: Brunswick, Missouri
Enlisted: June 23, 1917 Fort Bliss, Texas
Discharged: Camp Baker, El Paso, Texas, Feb. 4th,
1919.
Recorded: 16 June, 1919 B.N. Graham, Clerk
Page 5
Raymond Davis No. 3069125 U.S. Army
Private Co. "E" 2nd Dev. Bn.
Born: Cuminp, Kansas
Enlisted: June 24, 1918, Farwell, Texas
Discharged: Camp Mac Arthur, Texas 18 Dec., 1918
Recorded: 16 June, 1919, B.N. Graham, Clerk

Page 6
Clarence Kenney No. 2242924 U.S. Army
Pvt. 1st Class Demobilization Detachment
Born: Fox, Oklahoma
Inducted: Oct. 9, 1917 at Bovina, Texas
Discharged: Camp Travis, Texas 22 May, 1919
Recorded: 19 June, 1919, B.N. Graham, Clerk
Page 7
James R. Dudley A.S. 2239822 U.S. Army
Crook Art. L.A. Co. B 315th A.M. Tn.
Born: Gainsville, Texas
Enlisted: Sept. 5th, 1917 Farwell, Texas
Discharged: Camp Bowie, Texas, 24 June, 1919
Recorded: 8th July, 1919, B.N. Graham, Co. Clerk
Page 8
Raymond A. McDonald No. 1054204 U.S. Army
Pvt. 1st Class 44th Service Co. S.C.
Cas. Det. Demob. Gro.
Born: Nocona, Texas
Enlisted: July 5, 1918, Fort Bliss, Texas
Discharged: Camp Pike, Arkansas, 6 August, 1919 .
Recorded: 9 August, 1919 B.N. Graham, Co. Clerk

Jack M. Baker No. 2225882 U.S. Army
Pvt. 1st Class Co. "B" 117th M.G. Bn. 31st Div.
Born: Waples, Texas
Enlisted: July 22, 1918 (Not Given)
Discharged: Camp Travis, Texas, 6 August 1919
Recorded: 29 August, 1919, B.N. Graham, Co. Clerk

Gottlieh Renner No. 3660 U.S. Army
Private Co. "C" 47th Inf. 4th Division
Born: Kupan, Russia
Inducted: August 10th, 1918,Farwell, Texas
Discharged: Camp Travis, Texas 7th August, 1919.
Recorded: 27 Sept., 1919, B.N. Graham, Co. Clerk

Byron William Standefer No. 3970072 U.S. Army
Waganer, Hqs. Troop, 18th Division
Born: Childress, Texas
Inducted: July 25, 1918, Santa Rosa, New Mexico
Discharged: Camp Travis, Texas, 13th February, 1919.
Recorded: 1st November, 1919, B.N. Graham, Co. Clerk

Everett L. Hecox No. 2231572 U.S. Army
Pvt. 1st Class 165th F.A. Brig. "Hg" Det.
Born: Manhatten, Kansas
Enlisted: Sept. 6th, 1917, Farwell, Texas
Discharged: Camp Bowie, Texas, 20 June, 1919
Recorded: 16 December, 1919, B.N. Graham, Co. Clerk, Mabelle Schlenker, Deputy

Isaac L. Clements No. 2249125 U.S. Army
Mech. 29 Co. T.C.
Born: Davilla, Texas
Enlisted: Feb. 22, 1918, Ralls, Texas
Discharged: Camp Bowie, Texas 14th July, 1919
Recorded: 15 April, 1920, B.N. Graham, Co. Clerk, Mabelle Schlenker, Deputy

John T. Miller No. 200396 U.S. Army
Sergent 1st Class, Co. "D" 52 & Tel Bn. S.C.
Born: Woodford, Texas
Enlisted: May 8, 1917, Amarillo, Texas
Discharged: Camp Travis, Texas, 13 August, 1919
Recorded: 16 April, 1920, B.N. Graham,Co. Clerk, Mabelle Schlenker, Deputy

William Henry Younger, Jr., (No I.D. number given)
U.S. Army
Captain Field Artillery
Born: Not Given
Enlisted: Not Given
Discharged: Camp Travis, Texas 18th August, 1919
Recorded: 24 April, 1920, B.N. Graham, Co. Clerk, Mabelle Schlenker, Deputy

Floyd L. Dotson No. 3522179 U.S. Army
Private Company "I" 86 Infantry
Born: Stephenville, Texas
Enlisted: July 22, 1918, Wills Point, Texas
Discharged: Camp Travis, Texas 3rd February, 1919
Recorded: 12 May, 1920, B.N. Graham, Co. Clerk, Mabelle Schlenker, Deputy

Clarence A. McGill No. 1494451 U.S. Army
Sgt. Co. K 144th Inf.
Born: Commerce, Texas
Enlisted: Nov. 29, 1913, Vernon, Texas
Discharged: Camp Bowie, Texas, 21 June, 1919

Recorded: 14 May, 1920, B.N. Graham, Co. Clerk, Mabelle Schlenker, Deputy

Mc D. Nobles No. 1481770 U.S. Army
Private D Company "F" 144 Infantry
Born: Depart, Texas
Enlisted: May 25, 1918, Farwell, Texas
Discharged: Camp Bowie, Texas 20 June, 1919
Recorded: 15 May, 1921, B.N. Graham, Co. Clerk

Nicholas J. Snodderly,
A Private of Company "A" of the 144th Mach. Gun Bn.
of United States National Guard
Born: Page County, Iowa
Enlisted: May 24, 1917, Portales, New Mexico
Discharged: Camp Kearney, 25 March, 1918
Recorded: 21 September, 1921, B.N. Graham, Co. Clerk

Ben Little No. 2230385 U.S. Army
Ord. Sgt. Ord. Office of Co. O A E F Pass.
Det. Demob Group
Born: Celena or Helena, Texas
Inducted: July 5, 1918, St. Johns, Arizona
Discharged: Camp Pike, Ark. 29 November, 1919
Recorded: 22 Sept., 1920, B.N. Graham, Co. Clerk

Raymond A. McDonald R 1054204
Private, Signal Corps, Dtcht., 8 Squadron S A R O
Born: Nocona, Texas
Enlisted: August 11th, 1920, Ft. Bliss, Texas
Discharged: Kelly Field, Texas 25 July, 1921
Recorded: 4 January, 1922, B.N. Graham, Co. Clerk

Fred F. Langer No. 1144755 U.S. Army
Pvt. 1st Class, J.R.S. No. 334
Born: Plainview, Minnesota
Inducted: June 15, 1918, Farwell, Texas
Discharged: Camp Pike, Arkansas, 21 July, 1919
Recorded: 11 October, 1922, B.N. Graham, Co. Clerk, Naomi Tidenberg, Deputy

Edward S. White No. 1996203 U.S. Army
Private Co. "A" 27th Bn . V G G
Born: Cora, Illinois (1894)
Inducted: Chester, Ill. Feb. 24, 1918
Discharged: Camp Grant, Illinois 29 December, 1918
Recorded: 4 January 1923, B.N. Graham, Co. Clerk

Giles Cross No. 2864844 U.S. Army
Pvt. 1st Class Co. "C" 549th Enquirers
Born: Nacona, Texas
Enlisted: May 9th, 1918, Carthage, Texas
Discharged: July 16, 1919, Camp Pike, Arkansas
Recorded: July 13, 1925, B.N. Graham, Clerk

William C. Woods No. 3522036 Pvt. unassigned
Co. "D" 168th Infantry
Born: Caddo, Oklahoma
Inducted: July 22, 1918, Sherman, Texas
Discharged: May 17, 1919 Camp Bowie, Texas
Recorded: April 29, 1929, Gordon McCuan, Clerk

Clifford H. Crume No. 3659210 U.S. Army
Pvt. Co. "B" 29th Div.
Born: Crone, Missouri
Enlisted: Aug. 5, 1918, Camp Cody, New Mexico
Discharged: June 11, 1919, Camp Dix, New Jersey
Recorded: March 13, 1931, Gordon McCuan, Clerk

Page 27
John D. Thomas No. 1126515 U.S. Army
Pvt. 1st Class, Co. "A" 3rd Infantry
Born: Springtown, Texas
Enlisted: May 29, 1918,Weatherford, Texas
Discharged: Jan. 31, 1919, Marfa, Texas
Recorded: March 17, 1931, Gordon McCuan, Clerk

Page 28
James Mears No. 4454967 U.S. Army
Pvt. S. A. T. C. Clemson College, S.C.
Born: Woodbury, Tennessee
Enlisted: Sept. 18, 1918,Woodbury, Tennessee
Discharged: Dec. 8, 1918, Clemson College, S.C.
Recorded: July 24, 1931, Gordon McCuan, Clerk

Page 29
Henry C. Ryals No. 1123693 U.S. Army
Pvt. (unassigned) last assigned Bat. "D" 3rd Tr.Art.
Born: Montague, Texas
Enlisted: May 29, 1918, Tucumcari, New Mexico
Discharged: Feb. 4, 1919, Camp Bowie, Texas
Recorded: April 5, 1922, Gordon McCuan, Clerk, Elma
Hood, Deputy

Page 30
Anguish O. Ford No. 3064993 U.S. Army
Pvt. Inf. C.C. 34th Infantry
Born: Madisonville, Texas
Inducted: May 25, 1918, Childress, Texas
Discharged: June 26, 1919, Camp Bowie, Texas
Recorded: Sept. 1, 1933, E.V. Rushing, Clerk

Page 31
William E. Anderson R 1586941 U.S. Army
Pvt. 1st Class Co. "A" 8th Machine Gun Battalion
Born: Myrtle, Missouri
Enlisted: July 25, 1919, Andernach, Germany
Discharged: Camp Pike, Arkansas, July 24, 1920
Prior Service: Sept. 19, 1917 to July 25, 1919
Entitled to travel pay to Andernach, Germany Application made for Victory Medal.
E.V. Rushing, Clerk, Mary Noble, Deputy

Page 32
William E. Anderson
Enlisted: Sept. 19, 1917 Pocahontas, Arkansas
Discharged: July 24, 1919, Nickenich, Germany
Recorded April 14, 1934, E.V. Rushing, Clerk, Mary
Noble, Deputy. He re-enlisted the day after he was discharged. (see page 31)

Page 33
John F. Williams No. 1254144 U.S. Army
Wagoner—Battery B 44th Artillery
Born: Austin, Texas
Enlisted: April 17, 1917, Ft. Sam Houston, Texas
Discharged: February 24, 1919, Camp Logan, Texas
Approved for Victory Medal with Champagne Marne,
St. Meuse—Argonne defensive
Recorded: July 13, 1934, E.V. Rushing, Clerk, Mary
Noble, Deputy

Page 34
Lonnie Smith No. 3655788 U.S. Army
Pvt. Co. "B" 168th Infantry
Born: Perryville, Arkansas
Enlisted: June 24, 1918, Seminole, Oklahoma
Discharged: May 16, 1919 , Camp Pike, Arkansas
Recorded: July 17, 1934, E.V. Rushing, Clerk, Mary
Noble, Deputy

Page 35
Sam F. Billingsley U.S. Army
Pvt. 25th Co. 7th Bn. 165th Depot Brigade
Born: Morgan's Mill, Texas

Inducted: July 24, 1918, Clarendon, Texas
Discharged: Jan. 22, 1919 Camp Travis, Texas
Recorded: Sept. 18, 1934, E.V. Rushing, Clerk

Page 36
Burlie Clay No. 1474043 U.S. Army
Pvt. 1st Cl. Quarter Master Corps No. 321
Born: Scullyville, Oklahoma
Enlisted: December 14, 1917, Oklahoma City, Oklahoma
Discharged: June 28, 1919, Ft. Sill, Oklahoma
Recorded: May 17, 1935, E.V. Rushing, Clerk, Mary
Jones, Deputy

Page 37
Wilbur D. Ross No. 530538 U.S. Army
Pvt. Co. "I" 63rd Infantry
Born: Hollidayburg, Pennsylvania
Inducted: May 25, 1918, Globe, Arizona
Discharged: June 20, 1919, Presidio of San Francisco
Recorded: May 27, 1935, E.V. Rushing, Clerk, Mary
Jones, Deputy

Page 38
Jim C. Holden No. 2217418 U.S. Army
Pvt. Co. "H" 357th Infantry
Certificate in lieu of lost or destroyed discharge certificate
Inducted: Oct. 3, 1917, Cordell, Oklahoma
Discharged: March 4, 1919
Given at the War Dept., Washington, D.C. April 20, 1931

Page 39
Seldon F. Warren No. 2245509 U.S. Army
1st Sgt. 5th Co. White Div. Bn. 165th D.B,
Born: Trenton, Missouri
Enlisted: Sept. 22, 1917, Farwell, Texas
Discharged: Jan. 29th, 1919 Camp Travis, Texas
Recorded: Oct. 31, 1935 E.V. Rushing

Page 40
Charles F. Dennis No. 1131558 U.S. Army
Pvt. Aero Squadron "G"
Born: Watts, Arkansas
Inducted: July 10, 1918, Mangum, Oklahoma
Discharged: June 27, 1919, Camp Bowie, Texas
Recorded: February 6, 1936, E.V. Rushing, Clerk,
Mary Jones, Deputy

Page 41
Devere K. Roberts No. 2224285 U.S. Army
Sgt. Co. "A" 359th Infantry
Born: Whitewright, Texas
Inducted: Sept. 8, 1917, Sherman, Texas (for period of
emergency)
Discharged: Nov. 27, 1918, Ft. Jay, New York
Recorded: Feb. 18, 1936, E.V. Rushing, Clerk, Mary
Jones, Deputy

Page 42
Homer A. Hyde No. 3655377 U.S. Army
Pvt. Hdg. 308th Infantry
Born: McKinney, Texas
Inducted: June 24, 1918, Walter, Oklahoma
Discharged: May 21, 1919, Camp Pike, Arkansas
Entitled to one (1) Gold Service Chevron
Recorded: Feb. 20, 1936, E.V. Rushing, Clerk, Mary
Jones, Deputy

Page 43
Francis O. Griffin No. 3027520 U.S. Army
Pvt. Med. Dept. Base Hosp. No. 216 Demol. Group
Born: Coal County, Ill.
Inducted: July 25, 1918, Shuttuck, Oklahoma
Discharged: July 28, 1919, Camp Pike, Arkansas
Recorded: Feb. 21, 1936. E.V. Rushing, Clerk, Mary
Jones, Deputy

Page 44
George Treider No. 1132899 U.S. Army
Cpl. Park Unit No. 479 Motor Transport Corps.
Born: Lawler, Iowa
Enlisted: Aug. 15, 1918, U of T Tr—Det. Camp Mabry, Austin, Texas
Discharged: April 2, 1919, Sheffield, Alabama
Recorded: March 4th, 1936. E.V. Rushing, Clerk, Mary Jones, Deputy

Page 45
Henry R. Lemons No. 978918 U.S. Army
Pvt. 1st Class, Demol Group
Born: Seymour, Missouri
Enlisted: May 27, 1918, Beaver, Oklahoma
Discharged: July 27, 1919, Camp Funston, Kansas
Recorded: July 27, 1936. E.V. Rushing, Clerk, DeAlva White, Dep.

Page 46
Coney A. Beckner, No. 2219104 U.S. Army
Pvt. 1st Class, Co. "D" 102 Ammunition Train
Born:
Inducted: March 29, 1918, Childress, Texas
Discharged: April 4, 1919
Recorded: August 10, 1939, E.V. Rushing, Clark, DeAlva White, Dep.
(Certificate in lieu of lost or destroyed Discharge Cert.)

Page 47
Willie N. Foster No. 505364 U.S. Army
Pvt. 23rd Company, Coast Artillery Corps.
Born: Elk City, Oklahoma
Enlisted: April 23, 1918, Fort Logan, Colo. (17 years of age)
Discharged: By reason of minority
Recorded: Jan. 9, 1937. E.V. Rushing, Clerk, DeAlva White, Dep.

Page 48
Samuel Stites No. 223365
Pvt. 1st, Int. Hq. Co. 343 F.A. Cos. Det. Demol. Group
Born: Dallas, Texas
Inducted: Oct. 3, 1917, Cordell, Oklahoma
Discharged: July 22, 1919, Camp Pike Arkansas
Recorded: July 2, 1938. E.V. Rushing, Clerk

Page 49
Leone A. Chronister No. R-3771751 U.S. Army
Pvt. 1st Class, Det. Quartermaster Corps.
Born:
Enlisted: April 15, 1919, Camp Dodge, Iowa
Discharged: April 14, 1920 (Certificate issued in lien of lost or destroyed Discharge Cert.)
Recorded: July 19, 1938. E.V. Rushing, Clerk, DeAlva White, Dep.

Page 50
Leone A. Chronister No. 3771751 U.S. Army
Pvt. Company E, 2nd Infantry
Enlisted: August 6, 1918, Jefferson Barracks, Missouri
Discharged: April 14, 1919 by reason of desire to re-enlist.
Re-enlisted: April 15, 1919
(Certificate issued in Lieu of Lost or Destroyed Discharge Cert.)
From the office of the Adjutant General 4-1-1936
Recorded: July 19, 1938 E.V. Rushing, Co. Clerk, DeAlva White, Dep.

Page 51
Charles R. Elliott No. 3656319 U.S. Army
Pvt. Prisoner of War Escort Co. No. 274, Casual Det. Demob. Group
Born: Naples, Texas

Inducted: June 27, 1918 Durrant, Oklahoma
Discharged: Sept. 24, 1919, Camp Pike, Ark.
Recorded: July 25, 1938, E.V. Rushing, Clerk, DeAlva White, Dep.

Page 52
Clyde Vivian Goodwine No. 1106136 U.S. Army
Pvt. S.A.T.C. West Texas State Norman College
Born: Kokoma, Indiana
Enlisted: Oct. 19, 1918, Canyon, Texas
Discharged: Nov. 26, 1918, (Per Telegram A.G.O.)
Recorded: Nov. 3rd, 1938. E.V. Rushing, Clerk, DeAlva White, Dep .

Page 53
Lee A. Clymore No. 2249283 U.S. Army
Pvt. 1st Class, Company "E", 359 Infantry
Born: Marshall County, Tennessee
Enlisted: Feb. 23, 1918, Bonham, Texas
Discharged: June 24, 1919, Camp Bowie, Texas
Recorded: Nov. 14, 1938. E.V. Rushing, Clerk, DeAlva White, Dep.

Page 54
Foister Rector No. 3911625 U.S. Army
Corporal 3rd Co. 2nd Bn. 164th Depot Brigade
Born: Buckeye, Tennessee
Enlisted: July 15, 1918, Springfield, Colo.
Discharged: Jan. 7, 1919, Camp Funston, Kansas
Recorded: Nov. 14, 1938. E.V. Rushing, Clerk, DeAlva White, Dep.

Page 55
David Moseley No. 2249527 U.S. Army
Corporal 358th Infantry
Born: Wood County, Texas
Enlisted: Feb. 22, 1918
Discharged: June 20, 1919 Camp Pike, Ark.
Recorded: Nov. 16, 1938. E.V. Rushing, Clerk. DeAlva White, Dep.

Page 56
John F. Stanford No. 2969352 U.S. Army
Pvt. 34th Co. 165th Depot Brigade
Born: Ben Wheeler, Texas
Enlisted: July 26, 1918, Vernon, Texas
Discharged: Feb. 24, 1919, Camp Francis, Texas
Recorded: Feb. 21, 1939, E.V. Rushing, Clerk, DeAlva White, Dep.

Page 57
Alva M. Seaton No. 1399864 U.S. Army
Corporal Co. "C," Med. Det. Co's. Det. Demob. Group
Born: Wakeeny, Kansas
Enlisted: Oct. 8, 1917, Shawnee, Oklahoma
Discharged: Sept. 12, 1919, Camp Pike, Arkansas
Recorded: Nov. 15, 1939, E.V. Rushing, Co. Clerk, DeAlva White, Dep.

Page 58
Edward J. Reiser U.S. Army
Pvt. Co. "A" 344 M.J. Infantry
Born: Monroe, Michigan
Enlisted: Sept. 20, 1917, Walters, Oklahoma
Discharged: June 23, 1919, Camp Pike, Ark.
Recorded: Jan. 16, 1940. E.V. Rushing, Clerk, DeAlva White, Dep.

Page 59
Arthur Appel No. 3817682 U.S. Army
Pvt. O.A.R.D. Camp Pike, Ark.
Born: Russia, State of
Enlisted: Aug. 26, 1918, Shattuck, Oklahoma
Discharged: May 13, 1919. Fort Sill, Okla.
Recorded: Feb. 26, 1940. E.V. Rushing, Clerk, DeAlva White, Dep.

Page 60
James C. Roach VC No. 777671 U.S. Army
Corporal, Det Veterinary Corps, Auxiliary Remount
Depot No. 333
Born: Celeste, Texas
Enlisted: Dec. 14, 1917, Ft. Sam Houston, Texas
Discharged: April 11, 1919 Camp Joseph, E. Johnston,
Fla.
Recorded: Jan. 7, 1941. D.K. Roberts, Co. Clerk

Page 61
Ralph Humble No. 4263701 U.S. Army
Pvt. QMC, Unassigned School for B & C
Born: Sedan, Kansas
Inducted: Aug. 26, 1918, Clayton, New Mexico
Discharged: June 29, 1919, Fort Riley, Kansas
Recorded: March 14, 1941, D.K. Roberts, Clerk,
DeAlva White, Dep.

Page 62
Virgil Bryan Whitley No. 3988179 U.S. Army
Pvt. 43rd Co., 165th Depot Brigade
Born:
Inducted: Sept. 2, 1918, Hereford, Texas
Discharged: Dec. 4th, 1918 by reason of demobilization
Recorded: May 15, 1941. D.K. Roberts, Co. Clerk,
DeAlva White, Dep.
(Certificate issued in Lieu of lost or destroyed Dis-
charge Cert.)

Page 64
Willie E. McCuan No. 1418653 U.S. Army
Pvt. Co. "F" 310th Inf. 78th Div.
Born: Granbury, Texas
Inducted: May 28, 1918, Granbury, Texas
Discharged: June 19th, 1919, Camp Travis, Texas
Recorded: May 6, 1942. D.K. Roberts, Clerk

Page 75
John W. McLean No. 3267084 U.S. Army
Pvt. Co. "A" 102nd Inf. attached 18th Recruit Co.
Born: Powersville, Missouri
Inducted: June 23, 1918, Milan, Missouri
Discharged: May 17, 1919, Jefferson Barracks, Mo.
Approved for Victory Medal
Recorded: Dec. 1, 1943. D.K. Roberts, Clerk, Dorothy
Lovelace, Dep.

Page 103
Talton W. Bewley No. 915518 U.S. Army
Wagoner Hdqrs. Det. 7th Demob.Group
Born: Iola, Missouri
Enlisted: Nov. 12, 1917, Ft. Logan, Calif.
Discharged: Aug. 7, 1919, Camp Pike, Ark.
Recorded: Apr. 4, 1946. D.K. Roberts, Clerk, Dorothy
Lovelace, Dep.

Page 104
George H. Brock No. 2229958 U.S. Army
Pvt. 1st Class M.G. Co. 328th Inf. 82nd Div.
Born: Bruceville, Texas
Inducted: Sept. 19, 1917 Marlin, Texas
Discharged: June 2, 1919, Camp Bowie, Texas
Recorded: Jan. 23, 1947. Loyde A. Brewer, Clerk

Page 107
Willie B. Norwood No. 1490867 U.S. Army
Corporal, Co. "I" 142nd Inf.
Born: Malven, Arkansas
Enlisted: June 30, 1917, Lubbock, Texas
Discharged: June 16, 1919, Camp Bowie, Texas
Recorded: Sept. 19, 1949. Loyde A. Brewer, Clerk

Page 108
Lee Hopingardner No. 2217051 U.S. Army
Pvt. Demobilization Det.
Born: Bethney, Missouri

Inducted: Sept. 19, 1917, Buffalo, Oklahoma
Discharged: April 16, 1919, Camp Travis, Texas
Recorded: Oct. 19, 1949. Loyde A. Brewer, Clerk

Page 109
Frank A. Phillips A.S.N. 3819269 U.S. Army
Pvt. Co. "E" 2nd Bn. Replacement Training Center
Born: Washita, Kansas
Enlisted: Aug. 27, 1918, Mt. Ida, Arkansas
Discharged: Dec. 16, 1918, Camp Pike, Ark.
Recorded: Nov. 21, 1949. Loyde A. Brewer, Clerk

Page 110
Harrison G. Beene No. 3028064 U.S. Army
Pvt. M.C. Casual Co. 747
Born: Leflore, Oklahoma
Inducted: July 25, 1918, Shawnee, Oklahoma
Discharged: April 5, 1919, Langleyfield, Virginia
Recorded: Feb. 14, 1950. Loyde A. Brewer, Clerk

Page 112
Matthew Jesko No. 1506117 U.S. Army
Wagoner Co. "G" 111th Arn. Fr.
Born: Chicago, Illinois
Inducted: Sept. 24, 1917, Farwell, Texas
Discharged: Mar. 31, 1919, Camp Bowie, Texas
Recorded: Mar. 24, 1950. Loyde A. Brewer

Page 113
August G. Kothe No. 3816213 U.S. Army
Pvt. Co. "I';' Hq. Bn. Army Service Corps
Born: Bryan, Nebraska
Inducted: August 25, 19?
Discharged: Aug. 13, 1919 Camp Pike, Arkansas
Recorded: Apr. 14, 1950 Loyde A. Brewer, Clerk

Page 114
Ephram Young No. 2230099 U.S. Army
Corporal Co. "F" 326th Infantry
Born: Shatta, Louisiana
Enlisted: 9-23-1917, Eastland, Texas
Discharged: June 23, 1919, Camp Bowie, Texas
Recorded: Apr. 27, 1950 Loyde A. Brewer

Page 115
Virgil Martin No. 1498685 U.S. Army
Pvt. 1st Class Co. "K" 144th Inf.
Born: Tom Bean, Texas
Enlisted: July 5, 1917, Ft. Sam Houston, Texas
Discharged: June 21, 1919, Camp Bowie, Texas
Recorded: May 4, 1950, Loyde A. Brewer, Clerk, Rosa
Lee Tabor, Dep.

Page 116
Earnest E. Hughes No. 1481667 U.S. Army
Pvt. Pol. 142nd Inf.
Born: Travis, Texas
Enlisted: May 25, 1918, Hollis, Oklahoma
Discharged: June 17, 1919, Camp Bowie, Texas
Recorded: Aug. 19. 1950. Loyde A. Brewer, Clerk, Rosa
Lee Tabor, Dep.

Page 117
Harry R. Jesko No. 1486180 U.S. Army
Cpl. M. g. Bn. Unassigned
(C.A. Co. D.) 132 Machine Gun Bn. 36 Div.
Born: Chicago, Illinois
Inducted: Sept. 23, 1917, Farwell, Texas
Discharged: Apr. 30, 1919. Camp Bowie, Texas
Recorded: Nov. 21, 1950, Loyde A. Brewer, Clerk

Page 118
Rochelle Christian 3026749 U.S. Army
Pvt. 1st Class Base Hospital No. 55
Born: Archer County, Texas
Inducted: July 25, 1918, Hobart, Oklahoma
Discharged: June 11, 1919, Camp Pike, Ark.
Recorded: Jan. 30, 1951 Loyde A. Brewer, Co. Clerk

Carl E. Hall
Inducted: June 24th, 1918, Kingfisher Co., Oklahoma
Discharged: July 1, 1918, Camp Cody, Deming, N.M.
Reason for discharge: Flat Feet
Recorded: Sept. 21, 1951, Loyd A. Brewer, Co. Clerk, Dorthy Quickel, Dep.

Page 120
William E. Payne No. 1097152 U.S. Army
Grade: Wagoner Battery F, 21st Field Artillery
Born: Kampner County, Mississippi
Enlisted: July 2, 1917, Ft. Sam Houston, Texas
Discharged: Aug. 9, 1919, Camp Travis, Texas
Recorded: May 26, 1952. Dorothy Quickel, Clerk
(Certificate in Lieu of lost or destroyed Discharge Papers)

Page 121
Harry Lee Scott No. 4280153 U.S. Army
Pvt. 1st Class, Prov. Tng. Reg. 1st Depot Brigade
Born: Topeka, Kansas
Inducted: Sept. 9, 1918, Maryville, Missouri
Discharged: Dec. 23, 1918
Recorded: Dec. 5, 1952. Loyde A. Brewer, Clerk

Page 122
Johnie Sidney Williams, U.S. Army
Pvt. Student Army Training Corps. Univ. of Oklahoma
Born: Louis, Oklahoma
Enlisted: Oct. 15, 1918, Hollis, Oklahoma
Discharged: April 15, 1919, Washington, D.C
Recorded: April 7, 1954. Loyde A. Brewer, Clerk

Page 123
Arthur D. McDonald No. 2250654 U.S. Army
Pvt. Supply Co. 47th Inf. Cas. Det. Demob. Group
Born: McCool, Mississippi
Inducted: Jan. 31, 1918, Durant, Okla.
Discharged: Aug. 7, 1919
Recorded: August 19, 1954. Loyde A. Brewer, Clerk

Page 124
Ottis Christopher Petree No. 4862329 U.S. Army
Private, Medical Det. 43rd Infantry
Born: Crawford, Texas
Enlisted: Sept. 4, 1918, Mangum, Oklahoma
Discharged: Feb. 24, 1919, Camp Logan, Texas
Recorded: Sept. 7, 1954, Loyde A. Brewer, Clerk, Bonnie Warren, Dep.

CIVIL WAR

Page 126, 127
Daniel Magness U.S. Army
Private, of Capt. M. Bimonton's Co. "B," 2nd Reg. of Light Artillery
Born: Marion County, Arkansas
Enrolled: May 28, 1864
Discharged: Dec. 20, 1865, Benton Barracks, Mo.
Recorded: Nov. 22, 1956 Hugh Moseley, Co.Clerk

Page 128
William H. Massie No. 1486184 U.S. Army
Pvt. 1st Class Co. "D" 132 M.G. Bn.
Born: Legrange, Kentucky
Enlisted: Sept. 24, 1917, Farwell, Texas
Discharged: June 18, 1919
Recorded: March 13, 1959 Hugh Moseley, Clerk, Dorothy Quickel, Dep.

Page 129
Marshall S. Wear (Weir) No. 1133584 U.S. Army
Private, Unassigned Univ. of Texas, Unit S.A.T.C. Vov., Sc. "B"
Born: Covinton, Kentucky
Enlisted: Aug. 1918, Farwell, Texas (Aug. 18, 1918)
Discharged: April 29, 1919
Recorded: Jan. 13, 1958. Hugh Moseley, Clerk, Dorothy Lovelace, Dep.

Page 130
Willie E. Smith No. 1484793 Inf.
Private, Machine Gun Co., 142 Inf.
Born: Uvalde, Texas
Enlisted: July 14, 1917, Cleburne, Texas
A.W.O.L. From March 31 to April 10, 1918. (No absence under G.O. 31-12 or 45-14)
Discharged: June 20, 1919, Camp Bowie, Texas
Recorded: July 29, 1958 Hugh Moseley, Co. Clerk

Page 131
Parker Mann No. 3060843 U.S. Army
Pvt. 1st Class, Pack Train No. 312
Born: In the State of Arkansas
Inducted: May 25th, 1918, Wichita Falls,Texas
Discharged: July 30, 1919, Camp Pike, Ark.
Recorded: March 10, 1960. Hugh Moseley, Co.Clerk

Page 132
Earnest G. Williams No. 4861866 U.S. Army
Private—Overseas Convalescent Center (Co. H., 80th Inf.)
Born: Cornish, Oklahoma
Inducted: Sept. 5, 1918, Duncan, Okla.
Discharged: April 22, 1919,Camp Logan, Texas
Recorded: Feb. 10, 1961. Hugh Moseley, Clerk, Dorothy Quickel, Dep.

Page 133
Asberry Broox Wilkinson, U.S. Navy
Hospital Apprentice, Second Class
Born: Harrold, Texas, Aug. 25, 1894
Enlisted: Dec. 14, 1917, Dallas, Texas
Discharged: June 27, 1919
Recorded: Apr. 25, 1961. Hugh Moseley, Co. Clerk

Page 134
Rolla E. Darling No. 156155 U.S. Army
Corporal, Co. "A," 2nd Engineers, U.S. Army
Born:
Enlisted: May 16, 1917, Ft. Logan, Colo.
Discharged: Aug. 14, 1919 (This certificate given in Lieu of lost or destroyed Discharge Certificate)
Recorded: Sept. 21, 1961. Hugh Moseley, Co. Clerk, Dorothy Quickel, Dep.

Page 161
Thomas I. Presley No. 1142425 U.S. Army
Private, Field Hosp. No. 24, Medical Dept.
Born:
Enlisted: Dec. 14, 1917, Ft. Bliss, Texas
Discharged: Apr. 29, 1918 by reason of disability
This certificate given in lieu of lost or destroyed Discharge Certificate.
Recorded: Oct. 18, 1921. B.N. Graham, Co. Clerk

Page 163
Dee Edison Farris No. 1147374, U.S. Naval Reserve
A Seaman, 2nd Class (Provisional)
Born: Chickasha, Okla.
Enrolled: Aug. 6, 1918, Oklahoma City for 4 years
Discharged: Sept. 30, 1921. Reason: Lack of Funds at 8th Naval Dist. New Orleans, La.
Recorded: Dec. 21, 1933. E.V. Rushing, Co. Clerk

Page 164
Clarence Knowles, U.S. Marine Corps
Private, U.S. Marine Corps
Born: Tyler, Texas, Oct. 21, 1901
Enrolled: May 4th, 1917, Norfolk, Virginia
Discharged: Feb. 12, 1918
Recorded: Feb. 8, 1936. E.V. Rushing, Co. Clerk.

The Farwell Times.

Pictorial Edition.

Vol. 2.   Farwell, Parmer County, Texas, Feb. 13, 1908.   No. 20.

Hon. J. D. Hamlin.

The above sketch is a snap shot likeness of one of our busiest citizens.

J. D. Hamlin was born near Louisville, Ky., about thirty-five years ago. About fifteen years back he located at Amarillo, Texas, where he conducted a large private school or college. During this period he was studying law, and was admitted to the Amarillo bar where he practised for several years, holding at one time the office of prosecuting attorney.

The construction of the Belen railroad Cut-off brought him to this section where he located the town of Texico, and later was employed by the Capitol Syndicate Company to handle their lands, and open up the town of Farwell. Practically he may be considered the founder of each of our twin cities.

During his residence here he has accumulated a large amount of choice property. Possessing a mind of wonderful resourcefulness and activity and a most impartial judgment, he is considered a safe adviser on most any subject his mind is directed to.

With an amiability almost angelic, he is regarded by all of our citizens as a personal friend. Generous to the extreme and accommodating to the last degree he has unconsciously made friends even among those who regard his interests as antagonistic to theirs.

He is a director in two of our National Banks and a member of several corporation Boards. In fact he is engaged in such a multiplicity of enterprises, it would be difficult to single out any one of them as his specialty, but we can safely say that there is no higher authority on real estate values and investments than J. D. Hamlin.

Capt. J. M. Kindred

The picture which we present above of Capt. J. M. Kindred is regarded as a good likeness. Mr Kindred was born in Kentucky. He began life as a school teacher, served in the army for three years during our Civil war. Entering as a raw private, he was promoted for repeated gallantry in action, and emerged at the close of the conflict as Brigade Quarter-master.

On returning to his native town, more or less turbulance existed in the district, and the citizens, realizing the need of a fearless, conscientious officer, selected him as high sheriff of the county, a position which he filled most acceptably until the close of his term. Declining re-election, he removed to Louisville, Ky. and engaged in busines there for several years. After this he visited Georgia and purchased hotel property, which he personally conducted for some time. Later on, hearing of the glories of the Texas Panhandle 20 years ago, he moved to Amarillo, Tex., at that time a mere hamlet on the line of the Fort Worth & Denver railroad. As the town developed into city proportions, the Amarillo citizens solicited him to become their postmaster, and following their petition the U. S. Government appointed him to the office, which he held for a period of about nine years.

His stock farm near Amarillo is now worth many times the price he originally sold it for, but he has recouped handsomely on his Amarillo town property which has greatly enhanced its original cost.

Sometime ago Mr. Kindred removed to this point and after a short sojourn, he was offered and accepted the presidency of the First National Bank of Texico, one of our three fiscal institutions here.

Possibly no one has done more in an active but unostentatious manner, to advance the interests of Texas and its Panhandle than Mr. Kindred. During the World's Fair at St. Louis, which he visited at his own expense, he was indefatigable in his efforts to advertise the state and induce immigrants to come to it.

In social life Mr. Kindred is considered as a most worthy accession to any circle. A man of strong force of character and consumate diplomacy of disposition he makes his presence felt in any community. In addition to his position as Bank President he is a member of the Farwell Board of School Trustees and is an active officer in his church. Mr. Kindred is nearing the limit of three score years and ten and honored by the confidence of our citizens with positions of trust usually relegated to younger men. He can also look back with pleasure over a life spent in doing good whenever the opportunity presented itself.

Long may he wave, and never waver.

C. H. Leftwich

C. H. Leftwich, one of the pioneers and promoters of Farwell-Texico represented by the below "cut" is a native of Virginia where he spent his boyhood days. When quite a young man he located in Knoxville, Tenn. He engaged as salesman for the wholesale queensware firm of Cullen & Newman. He remained with said firm, first in the house then on the road as traveling salesman, for several years. His business brought him to Texas about 20 years ago, where he bought land near Amarillo, and went into the cow business. In that line he was quite successful. When he sold out he owned one of the best improved small ranches in his section of the country.

He was afterward assistant post master at Amarillo, then city marshal, and tax collector for the years 1904 and 1905.

He is now farming and owns one of the most choice and best improved farms in Parmer county, Tex., two and one half miles east of Farwell. He is also engaged in buying and selling real estate. He is a stock holder and director in the First National Bank of Texico, N. M., and has been vice president for more than a year past. He has great confidence in the future of the Texico-Farwell country

G. A. Campbell.

G. A. Campbell, the pioneer confectionery man, is a native of Rogers, Ark., and after completing his education there he was engaged by the Rogers Wholesale Grocery Company as a traveling representative. After working as traveling salesman for four years he came to Texico and opened a first-class confectionery, and like all our energetic young business men, has prospered bountifully

Mr. Campbell numbers his friends by all he comes in contact with.

J. M. Hamlin.

The cut above is a likeness of Hon. J. M. Hamlin, one of Parmer county's well known business men.

He was born in Pittsburg, Pa., in the year 1843. His long line of ancestry is Maryland and Virginia stock.

During the early business career of his life he was engaged in the manufacturing of glass, then removed west, married in Louisville, Ky., where he spent a number of years in active business pursuits. Some twenty years or more ago he moved with his family to St. Louis, Mo., and became manager of the St. Louis Religious Press Association, having in addition the exclusive control of the advertising of several other journals of large circulation. The several duties of this line of work that he handled successfully for many years kept him prominently before the public so much that at one time he was nominated for congress in his district. While he secured the full strength of his party vote, he was defeated. At another election he was made one of Missouri's Presidential state electors. Notwithstanding these political honors he was never in any sense a politician.

Two years ago his attention was called to the southern Panhandle of Texas. Upon visiting it he found it so much to his liking that he engaged in business here, and also purchased a farm two miles from the twin cities, Farwell, Tex., and Texico, N. M.

He has beautified his home until he has one of the most attractive places on the plains of Texas.

Since his two years' residence here he is recognized as a strong factor in every needed enterprise. He was made one of the railroad delegates to look after a new railway enterprise. Was chairman of a committee sent to Austin to appear before the R. R. commission asking for Texas freight rates for his own town. His well prepared and impassioned appeal, together with the merit of the plea, secured a successful verdict.

As chairman of Farwell's first school board, he is actively enlisted in the cause of education.

He is a safe counselor and an honorable christian gentleman, whose life work is an open book.

E. T. Stevens.

Whose likeness we herewith produce is a native Texan, was born at Gonzales, Texas in 1852, where he remained until 1877. Came to Wichita Falls, Texas, where he engaged in the cattle business with the Fall Land and Cattle Co., and remained in the cattle business for fifteen years. In 1905, and in 1907 was elected to the office of Sheriff of Parmer county, which office he still ho'ds to the satisfaction of the entire County.

Mr. Stevens is a man that is well liked by all his many aquaintances and is today one of the foremost men in the County having won for himself by close attention and courteous treatment not only the respect of the law abiding citizens, but with the criminal element with which he has to contend. The Times feels that it has not words at its command to show its appreciation and regard for the citizenship of Mr. Stevens, as he is a man worthy of the citizenship of any country and one that we all feel justly proud of, and we hope to claim the citizenship of Mr Stevens during the remainder of his useful career.

E. R. Read.

Whose likeness we herewith present, was born at Richpond, Ky., 1876, beginning railroad work with the Texas Pacific R. R. Co., at Big Springs, Texas, at the age of 16. Mr Read has since that time been identified with railroad work. In 1894 he became identified with the Santa Fe R. R. on the Pecos Valley Lines as agent at Roswell, N. M., which position he held to the entire satisfaction of the company, until he was transferred to this place on December 8th, 1906. Since that time he has been local agent at this place and has filled that position to the satisfaction of an exacting public, and to the Railroad company.

Mr. Read is a man well liked by all who know him and enjoys the highest of esteem both at home and in railraid circles.

Dr Augustus Davis.

Augustus Davis was born near Shady Grove, Ky., in 1877, where he lived until entering the Hospital College of Medicine at Louisville, Ky., where he graduated with high honors in 1904.

After graduating, he, like many of our noble young men, turned his eye westward, and came to Texico in the fall of 1906, where he immediately engaged in the practice of medicine and has enjoyed a very lucrative practice since that date.

In social circles he holds an enviable position.

He was elected Noble Grand of the Independent Order of Odd Fellows at Texico, on January 1st, 1908, which position he holds to the entire satisfaction of his brother Odd Fellows.

Surely the western country is to be congratulated upon securing such a man as Augustus Davis to reside therein.

F. E. Kepple.

Prominent among our young men is Mr. Frank Kepple.

Mr. Kepple was born at Emporia, Kans., 1891 and graduated at the Emporia Business College in 1906, came to Texico in 1907, where he accepted a position as stenographer with the W. E. Schooler Land Company, which position he held to the entire satisfaction of the emyloyers. Mr. Kepple is now Public Stenographer, and is enjoying a liberal patronage, being courteous, accurate and prompt. Mr. Kepple enjoys the very best respect of the men he has served. Like many others of our stalwart young men who have accepted their lot in the west, he is prospering, well pleased and has the confidence of all his many acquaintances. We very respectfully call your attention to his card elsewhere in this issue.

Dr. A. D. Miller.

The author of the likeness below needs no introduction through the columns of the Times for Dr Miller is familiarly known to all our residents and numbers his friends by all who know him. He was born at Cedas Hill, Texas, in 1872. Studied Dentistry in the Curly Dental Parlors of Dallas, where he gained distinction as a dentist. He came to Texico in April, 1903, settling upon a claim three miles west of town at the time wnen it took courage and grit to prompt a man to settle upon and hold a claim. Today the Doctor prides himself upon having one of the best pieces of land in the county and it is a pleasure to point the finger of pride to the same to prospectors who come to this country.

He was elected Consul Commander of the Woodmen of the World January 1, 1908, and meets with the hearty approval of all the members of this praise worthy organization.

Cut Price Sale

In Order to Make Room for my Spring Stock of Goods which will arrive soon, I am giving a CUT PRICE SALE to last THIRTY DAYS. You will save money by taking advantage of this sale. Note the following Bargains:

$6.00 Hats now _____ $5.00
$3.50 Hats now _____ $3.00
$2.50 Hats now _____ $2.00

25 per cent Reduction on UNDERWEAR.

25 per cent Off on Gloves.

Sunflower Shoes.

MADE FOR US BY

Noyes-Norman
Shoe Co.

St. Joseph, Mo.

$3.50 Pants now _____ $3.00
$2.00 Pants now _____ $1.50
$1.50 Pants now _____ $1.00

$2.50 Wool Shirts now ___ $2.00
$1.25 Monarch Shirts now $1.00

$3.00 Corduroy Pants now $2.50

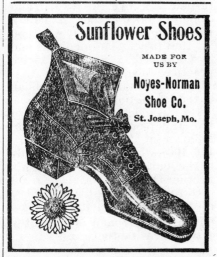

Sunflower Shoes

MADE FOR
US BY

Noyes-Norman
Shoe Co.

St. Joseph, Mo.

$6.00 Stetson Shoes now ___ $5.50
$6.00 Courtney Shoes now _ $5.00
$5.00 Courtney Shoes now _ $4.50
$3.50 Courtney Shoes now _ $3.25
$3.00 Courtney Shoes now _ $2.75

All Work Shoes at Cost.

NOT HERE FOR A WEEK, BUT HERE TO STAY.

J. M. Simmons
Gents Furnishing Store

First Door North of Texico Saloon

TEXICO, = = NEW MEXICO

L. C. Roberson.

Mr. Roberson, whose likeness we herewith produce needs no introduction on the part of the Times as he is favorably known to all of our citizens.

Mr. Roberson was born at Henrietta, Tex., August 28 1887. When but a lad he moved with his parents to Wichita Falls, Texas, entering the school there and graduated with high honors in the Wichita Falls Business College on May 12, 1905. He immediately came to Texico, and engaged in business under the firm name of Hopping & Roberson, Dec. 4, 1905. He remained with the firm of Hopping-Roberson Mercantile Co. last year when he was elected to the responsible position of Secretary and Treasurer of the company, which position he holds at present.

Mr. Roberson is a striking example of what a young man of energy and adaptation to business can attain, having risen rapidly to the responsible position he now holds.

Socially Mr. Roberson is a young man well liked by all his many friends and acquaintances, and especially esteemed by men in business, who by business relations come in contact with him. Truthfully we can say that should all of our young men de-vote themselves to business with the energy as has Mr Roberson. the age of young men would be an age to be looked upon with pride and praise.

Certainly we are to be congratulated upon having young men like Mr Roberson to live and mingle with us in the daily walk of life.

Ed. T. Massey.

Ed. T. Massey was born in Illinois 1873. At the age of five he moved with his parents to Kansas where he remained until 1891 when he settled at Gage, Okla., where he was engaged in the general mercantile business

for a number of years, and was elected and served the town of Gage as its first mayor. Mr. Massey remained at Gage until December 1905 when he came to Texico and associated himself with the Coker Triplett Mercantile Co. At present Mr. Massey is secretary of the Coker Triplett Co., president of the Texico Ice Light and Cold Storage Co.. secretary of the Texico Water Co., and one of the directors of the Roosevelt County Telephone Co. and President of the Trumpet Publishing Company.

Mr. Massey aside from being popular socially is one of our most prominent citizens finan cially and has done and is doing much for the up-building of the twin cities.

Post Cards.

You can get views of Farwell on post cards at

Farwell Drug Co.

R. C. Hopping.

Mr. R. C. Hopping was born in Granbury Texas, 1875 and remained there until the year 1901 when he came to New Mexico and engaged in the cattle business until December 1904, when he associated himself with Blankenship & Roberson in the general merchandise business in Texico; in March 1905 becoming a member of the Hopping & Roberson Mercantile Co., and in March 1907 he was made president of the Hopping & Roberson Mercantile Co.

Mr. Hopping is General Manager of the Farwell Wholesale Grocery Co Mr. Hopping is a highly educated gentleman having obtained his schooling in the best colleges in Texas, and has gradually by close attention and good business principles made for himself and family a living and fortune to be envied by anyone. Truly we can say we are glad to have Mr. Hopping live in our midst.

A Street Scene in Texico, N. M.

A. A. Maxwell.

A. A. Maxwell, cashier of the First National Bank of Texico, was born in Boston, Mass., and lived there continuously until his tenth birthday when he was sent to boarding school for the benefit that is commonly supposed to accrue to a boy upon leaving home.

He is the son of James Andley Maxwell, a civil engineer of repute in Southern Railroad circles and a lawyer of prominence in Boston, Mass.

Mr Maxwell went to Savannah, Georgia, on attaining his majority finding the business routine of Northeastern cities not too promising to a struggling young man.

The chances in the South were good and Mr. Maxwell says that the country is rapidly forging to the front commercial'y, but when it comes to the place for a young man the west is the arena.

Mr. Maxwell left Georgia over a year ago and came to Oklahoma and from there here. He is entirely satisfied with the country and believes in this particular spot in it. Texico and Farwell will be one of the cities of the Plains and he is convinced that the time is not far off.

C L. Main.

One of our most prominent and influential young men is C L. Main whose likeness we herewith produce. Mr. Main was born at Dover, Kan.,October 21st 1884. He graduated in 1902 in the commercial college at Tecumseh, Okla. After graduation he like other young men began looking for a location where he could be promoted by application to business and faithful work and rise into prominence. He came to Texico on the 29th day of October 1906. Before coming to Texico he was identified as assistant cashier of the First National Bank of Maud, Okla., and on November 1st 1906 he accepted the position with the First National Bank of Texico, which position he now holds to the credit of himgelf and to the entire satisfaction of all parties concerned. We are glad to know that Mr. Main i a permanent fixture with us and may his rapid progress never cease until he has reached the height of his ambition.

I am selling choice steaks and roasts from fed cattle. A word to the wise is sufficient. S. F. Wooding.   9tf

Hotel under construction in Farwell.

The Texico National Bank.

No financial institution in this section can point to a more satisfactory record of usefulness and conservative growth than the Texico National Bank. This Bank was organized as a State Bank March 20, 1906, but its business has grown to such an extent that the capital stock has been doubled, making the capital stock $30,000 fully paid up. The Texico Savings Bank and Trust Co., met with public favor from its inception, and the growth of the institution has been rapid, yet business is transacted on a conservative basis. The confidence of the people they have; integrity is evidently their watch word, and reliability their standard. With such methods as pursued by this Bank, would be hard to fail, and their strong financial business can be accounted for only by the conservative banking methods pursued by this management, always fair, cautious and liberal.

The Bank's career throughout has attracted widespread attention, possibly receives more write ups than any other bank in the territory. The manner in which they appeal to the people, then their advertisements are a credit to any banking institution. The following is an extract from a publication of the Santa Fe New Mexican: "Concrete examples are often more convincing than general statements. Up at Texico, a point on the boundary between New Mexico and the Panhandle of Texas, there is a bank which started business last spring with first day's deposit of $4,487.11; the 11 cents were not to be despised in those days either. But in one month the deposits had risen to $44,791 just 10 times the first days deposit. Fifty per cent increase brought the total to $61,000 at the end of the second month. The third month showed $70,000. The fourth $75,-000. In the dead of summer, the fifth month $89,000. Then a jump to $114,000, and now after eight months the total is over $150,000 or thirty-three times the total at the beginning."

The El Paso Herald says: "The Texico National Bank of Texico, N. M., advertises 'We do strictly banking, that's all'. It is as good a motto as a bank wants. The trouble with so many rail roads, insurance companies and banks nowadays is that they go into many lines outside their legitimate trade. Railroad executives go into stock jugling, insurance companies go into banking and bankers go into doubtful industrial venture for the benefit of the officers and directors. They would all be more serviceable to the public if they would follow their own trade."

The Texico National Bank is a money-making institution which is indicative of its prosperity, handing out to its stockholders every six months a handsome dividend besides setting aside a nice surplus which is added to its capital of $30,000, surplus $1,500. Total capital and surplus $31,500 for the year 1907 a dividend of 20 per cent was declared. With the exception of one bank between Roswell, N.M. and Hereford, Tex., they have the largest deposits. The First National Bank of Portales, N.M., which is a kindred bank, shows the largest deposits of any bank between the above mentioned places.

The Texico National Bank is connected with a line of the best organized Banks, their policies throughout have been watched with a degree of satisfaction attained by no other line of banks.

Their statements as made to the Comptroller of Currency, Dec. 3rd, 1907, proved their financial standing with their method of doing banking, their integrity of handling your business was supreme for the occasion. This Bank is a popular Bank, you are made to feel at home.

No deposit is too small for their attention, nor too large for their ability. By this policy they are all appreciated.

The officers of this bank are practical bankers. No change has been made in the management since its inception. W. O. Oldham, its president, is one of the best known bankers in the Territory. His broad ideas, safe and sound methods have achieved success when others have failed. He is cashier of the First National Bank of Portales Roosevelt county's largest bank. A. L. Breding, vice-president, is a man we all know; a prominent physician, also Texico's post master. B. D Oldham, cashier in whose hands the management is entrusted and whose likeness we herewith present

B. D. Oldham.

B. D. Oldham was born at Duffan, Tex.. March 11, 1876 where he spent his boynood days and after graduating in one of the best schools of Texas he came west in 1900, and was elected cashier of the Texico Savings Bank and Trust Company, now the Texico National Bank, at its organization in 1906 which position he now holds with great credit to that organization. Mr. Oldham, by his safe and conservative methods of banking has won for his bank an enviable reputation, as it is now one of the strongest banking institutions in Eastern New Mexico.

In social circles, Mr Oldham enjoys a very prominent position. Being courteous and obliging at all times to the public whether a customer of his bank or not, and too much cannot be said of his endeavors to build up that, for which he is most interested, the Texico National Bank.

E. H. Robinson.

The above we regard as a good likeness of E. H. Robinson. Mr. Robinson was born in Gallia County, Ohio, in 1864 where he spent the days of his boyhood. After completing his education at the Lebanon Normal School of Lebanon, Ohio, he taught school for about eight years in Ohio, then in Missouri for some time. After this time he was engaged in the general merchandise business in Eno, Ohio.

Like many others Mr. Robinson was attracted by the many advantages of our great and glorious west, and moved to Texico in July, 1905 where he immediately gained the respect and confidence of everyone who

he came in contact with. After sojourning in Texico for about one year Mr. Robinson accepted a position as teacher in our city school, where he taught for some time. Retiring from teaching school he entered in the real estate and insurance business under the name of the well known firm of Schooler & Robinson in which business he has prospered and is still engaged in the same line.

Mr. Robinson is a man that is easy to make friends with and is looked upon with the highest of esteem by all business men of the twin cities. He is a man so well liked by the people in general that we think it would be almost an impossibility for such a man not to come to the front. At the solicitation of his many friends Mr. Robinson has consented to become a candidate for County Superintendent of Public Instruction of Roosevelt County. We most cordially solicit the votes of Roosevelt county for Mr. Robinson in the election that will take place in the near future. Our hearty congratulations are extended to the public in having such a man in our midst.

Hobert R. Miller.

Below we represent a very prominent young man of the twin cities Mr. Miller was born near Howard, Elk County, Kansas, in 1881 where he spent the greater part of his life on his fathers ranch until he was twenty four years of age, when he was induced by the many advantages of the golden west to come westward. Selecting the country around Texico and Farwell as a desirable location, he decided to cast his lot with the people here and located at this place in January, 1906.

After Mr. Miller arrived at Texico he at once realized the wonderful productiveness of this country and accepted a position as traveling Immigration Agent for the W. E. Schooler Land and

Immigration Co., of Texico, New Mexico, and the S. M. Cotton Land and Immigration Co., of Amarillo, Texas. At this very beneficial work as well as profitable, Mr. Miller was engaged for one year, during which time he traveled some twenty thousand miles and induced many people to locate here. At the expiration of the time Mr. Miller decided to engage in the Real Estate business for himself, and was thereafter and up to a short time ago associated with The Wheat Land Company, of which he was President and General Manager during which time he was very successful.

Mr. Miller has studied Law extensively and was a short time ago admitted to practice before the Department of the Interior.

Recently Mr. Miller purchased W. E. Schooler's one half interest in the firm of Schooler & Robinson, a firm well known throughout the entire country.

In social circles Mr. Miller holds a very enviable position, being courteous to all, and obliging, he has won for himself the friendship of everyone he meets. He is a gentleman in every respect, bound to make friends in any community in which he may desire to locate. It is our earnest desire to have a man of Mr. Miller's ability with us permanently.

The
First National Bank

Farwell, Texas.

Officers:

Walter Farwell
President

D. A. Linthicum
Vice Pres.

Saunders Gregg
Cashier

With adequate equipment & exceptional facilities f o r handling all branches of the banking business, we are able to give customers the best service ❧ ❧ ❧ ❧ ❧ ❧

Let us show you how welll we can care for your business. . . . .

LLOYD,
THE PHOTOGRAPHER

Texico,   New Mex.

J. C. Nelson.

J. C. Nelson, Assistant Cashier of the Texico National Bank, was born in Little Rock Ark., in 1886 and remained there until at the age of twelve years he moved with his parents to Texas. Mr. Nelson is a graduate of Hill College at Waco, receiving his graduating diploma in 1902. Coming to New Mexico in 1907 he accepted a position with the First National Bank of Portales where h remained until about nine months ago when he accepted his present positio .

Mr. Nelson, is well liked by both his social and business associates and justly deserves the popularity he has attained.

Call on the Times when you need Job Work.

If you like the Times tell your neighbors, if not tell us. When you read your paper hand it to your neighbor if he is not a subscriber. We want the Times to reach every home in this part of the country and ask the readers to help us.

Residence of S. W. Pease, Texico.

DIRECTORY
FIRST CHRISTIAN CHURCH

......FARWELL, TEXAS......

Preaching the Second and Fourth Sunday in the Month.

Services at 10:30 A. M. and 6:30 P. M.

(Mountain Time)

J. T. WEBB, Pastor.

Bible School Every Sunday 9:30 A. M.

(Mountain Time)

PROF. McDONALD Superintendent.

Ladies Aid Every Thursday 2:30 P. M.

MRS. ANNA WARE, President.

"I was glad when they said unto me, Let us go into the House of the Lord."

P. E. Jordan.

The above is a likeness of P. E. Jordan, Assistant Cashier of the Texico National Bank. Mr. Jordan is a native Texan, was born at Farmersville, Texas, where he remained until October 1906. At that time coming to Texico and accepting the position he now holds with the Texico National Bank. Mr. Jordan is a typical southerner possessing the rare qualities of true southern blood, enjoying the friendship and esteem of all his many acquaintances and to the bank he has helped to make popular.

Residence of Ed T. Massey, Texico, N. M.

C. C. Marshall

C. C. Marshall, Vice President of the First National Bank of Texico was born at Girard, Illinois, December 6th 1860, graduated at Illinois College, at Jacksonville in 1879 and came South that year, located at Sherman, Texas, where he was engaged in business for eleven years. In 1893 he engaged in the Banking business at Cleburne, Texas, being assistant cashier of the National Bank of Cleburne for several years. He and his associates sold that Bank and Mr. Marshall organized The First National Bank of Venus, Texas, and was its first Cashier, remaining there four years, when he disposed of his banking interest and moved to Dallas, Texas, where he went into the wholesale manufacture of Buggies, being Vice President of the W. O. Brown company for two years, at the end of which time some of his former Banking associates induced him to come west and again go into the Banking business. Mr. Marshall assisted in organizing The First National Bank of Texico and was its Cashier from date of its organization until last month, when he was elected Vice President of that Institution, which position he still occupies. Mr. Marshall is a Banker of experience and ability. He is a firm believer in Farwell and its surrounding country, as evidenced by the fact that he has freely invested his money in Farwell property and farm lands near town. He has been a factor in the up-building of the town and community and is a public spirited citizen.

Residence of Alex Shipley, Farwell.

The First National Bank

Of Texico

BANKING BENEFITS

We keep books. ❧
A basis of credit.
Small deposits.
Grow with a growing Bank.

Your valuable papers.
We want the small account
Pay by check.
Absolute Security.

WEIGH THE ADVANTAGES

...First National Bank Of Texico...

The First National Bank of Texico.

The First National Bank of Texico opened in the spring of 1906. Its chief incorporators were L. T. Lester of Canyon City, Texas, J. P. Stone of Portales, New Mexico and C. C. Marshall of Dallas, Texas.

Business boomed as only business can boom in a new town and a new country. The Bank stayed open for business from nine o'clock in the morning until nine o'clock at night. New arrivals on every train brought money with them which they were unwilling to carry on their persons and they were glad to find a place to put it where it would be secure. There was almost as much banking done at night as in the day time and the appearance of the town was the same with the exception of darkness overhead and illumination on the streets. Music tinkled everywhere with the counters of the gambling tables and business was good.

Think of it. over two hundred thousand dollars on deposit at one time and a large portion of this money was left in this country on investment. Two hundred thousand dollars does not begin to be the figure that was invested but was the figure on one particular day and on many more days than one particular day that was held ready to be invested.

Take this to heart, think what one bank has done for this country. Then double it and treble it and think what this one bank together with other banks have done for this country. Hug this thought to your breast, you unbeliever in banks, see what has been done for you. It may never have come home to you, but everything done for everybody, has also done something for you.

At a recent meeting of the stockholders of The First National Bank of Texico, there was a radical change in its officers. It was thought that the officers of the bank should be of the people of the town and country and with this object in view Mr. J M. Kindred was elected President. Mr. Kindred has lived long here, having spent the last eighteen years on the Plains, and is known as a man of unimpeachable character and has many many friends.

Mr. R. L. Stringfellow, President of the Amarillo National Bank is a vice president, whose association with this bank as its vice president was sought because of the prestige such an association carried with it and also material advantages accruing to its standing as a first class business institution.

Mr. C. C. Marshall, also vice president, has been associated with the bank from its inception and has had wide experience in banking circles.

Mr. A. A. Maxwell, Cashier, has the detail work to look after.

This bank is especially well e quipped to handle any business. Its correspondents list is a large one and it has an advantage in having correspondents whose lists are also large thus eliminating much of the cost of collecting, which has been in vogue recently

The management is conservative you want to do business with people who watch their business closely. You want to deposit your money where it will be safe. Not only do you want your money safeguarded by strong safes and bolts and bonded employees, but you also want to know that it is being loaned to people who will pay it back, to people who will be a benefit to the community. With this feature of the business before them, the stockholders and directors brought into being a discount board which meets at the banking house every week and talks over the general features of the business and passes on any requested loans.

Primarily this was done to safeguard the business, but its effect is far-reaching. To the man who has money laid away and does not deposit it, this feature must do away with much of his prejudice. He can feel sure that his money is guarded from loss by robbery and from injudicious loans.

Residence of O M Conoley, Farwell.

Dr. A. L. Breeding.

Dr A. L. Breeding is a graduate of the St. Louis University,
and came to Texico from that city
in May of 1905. He was the first
practicing physician to locate in
the town, and has been actively
engaged in his profession since
that time. He has been in Texico
longer probably than anyone else
in business here.

Dr Breeding has won the confidence and esteem of those who
have made their home in Texico
and made for himself a position
of prominence and distinction in
both the business and social life
of the town.

January 1st., 1907, he was appointed Postmaster of Texico, is
vice president of the Texico National Bank, and also holds several other offices of responsibility. He is a member of the New
Mexico Medical Society and of the
American Medical Association.
He is a member of the Masonic
and Woodman lodges and of the
Methodist church. He is earnest and active in every move-
ment toward the improvement
and upbuilding of his home town
and has liberally assisted, both
financially and otherwise, every
measure toward building up the
town.

J. I. Phillips.

J. I. Phillips. the photographer, who made most of the photos
from which the cuts were made
for this edition. He is a fine
photographer and the work he
turns out is his best advertisement.

Interior of Coker-Triplett Store, Farwell.

Our Banks.

The recent financial panic found our Banks in excellent condition and able to successfully weather the storm. While a comparison of their statements of condition, as published in the local papers, for August 22nd, before the panic set in, and December 3rd, after it was practically over, shows a heavy decrease in deposits, it shows a corresponding decrease in loans. It argues well for the ability of our Bankers that they were able to call in their loans rapidly enough to meet the sudden and unexpected demand of their depositors, and shows the sound basis of the credits of the community. Their loans must necessarily have been good, else they would not have been able to collect them so promptly. Owing to the fact that the Banks in all important financial centers restricted currency payments, our Bankers deemed it wise to do the same here, not as a protection to themselves, because they did not need that protection but as a protection to the people. Currency for legitimate purposes was paid out in any amount, but for the purpose of placing it between the mattresses or in the

hosiery, it was wisely restricted, which again demonstrates the wisdom and ability of our Bankers, because it kept sufficient currency in circulation for all needs of the business community without the aid of the Bank's Kansas City or New York correspondents. Really, there was no panic here, it was only the fear that it might reach us that caused the uneasiness. The community, as well as the Bankers are to be congratulated on the manner in which the situation was handled. A happy after-thought comes to us in the knowledge of the fact that, although the Banks wanted their money, as their Depositors wanted theirs, not a single suit was instituted to enforce collection of the large amount which was paid into the Banks by their borrowers and cheerfully paid to their depositors.

Oliver's Livery Barn, Farwell.

The Farwell Times.

W. E. SCHOOLER, Proprietor

Published Every Thursday by Farwell Publishing Company.

One Dollar Per Year In Advance

Entered in the post office at Farwell, Texas as second-class mail matter.

Yours truly,
W. E. SCHOOLER.

This Edition.

In presenting to you this Special Edition of the Farwell Times it is our desire to fill a vacancy that we believe has been felt among our people for several years. In this Edition we have endeavored to bring our readers, and the public, face to face with those of our prominent men, and with the views of our county and town, that they may see the foundation upon which our great country is based. The policy of the Farwell Times has always been friendly to all and prejudiced against none. We have endeavored at all times to give to our readers a newspaper worthy of the name, not being based or prejudiced against any local individual or person.

We believe that our country has needed a scenic edition of some paper for some time and in producing this Edition we have endeavored to fill this want.

We cordially thank our friends for any and all assistance shown us in this matter, and hope you will justly appreciate our endeavors to give a paper second to none in any country.

Owing to the fact that we have been unable to get photos of all the business men and views of all the business houses in town this edition is hardly what we intended it should be, but we hope the readers will appreciate our efforts in doing what we have done at a great expense.

Mart Roberson.

Possibly the best and most favorably known man in this part of the plains country is Mart Roberson, whose likness we herewith produce. Mr. Roberson was born in Young county. Texas, August 24th 1859 and just prior to the Civil War he moved with his parents to Freestone county, Texas. Afterwards moving to the Choctaw Nation, I. T. At the age of 19 years Mr. Roberson returned to Young county and engaged in the cattle business. First associated himself with Hardisty & Neal, exclusive cattle raisers of Young County. Several years later Mr. Roberson came to the plains of the Panhandle and afterwards came to Roosevelt county, New Mexico, where he has been the leading cow man of this country for several years. During the time Mr. Roberson has been in the Cattle Business he has the distinction of having the praise and confidence of all the Cow boys that have been in his employ, as he has always been courteous and obliging to them. At present Mr. Roberson is a director of the Hopping & Roberson Mercantile Co., President of the Farwell Wholesale Grocery Company.

Mr, Roberson being a pioneer in this country is considered authority on all questions pertaining to the Plains Country and is looked upon as being one of the best posted cattle men on the plains. He is favorably known all over the plains by all the leading cattle men and if he has an enemy we have failed to hear him speak or spoken of. Mr. Roberson is a great believer in the possibilities of our new coutry and takes every opportunity of praising it to the many newcomers and prospecters here.

He has a suburban home in east Farwell that will compare favorably with the residences in cities much larger than Farwell and one that Farwell feels justly proud of.

We hope that "Uncle Mart" as he is familiarly known to his friends, may live to see many more summers, that we may enjoy his company and association.

S. H. Withers.

One of our most prominent and prospeorus business men was born on a farm in Mason county, West Virginia, July 4, 1872.

Both parents were of widely known and respected families of the two Virginias. Both of an ambitious nature and a desire to follow Greely's advice, at the age of 17, with the consent of his parents, he left hom with a little more than enough means to land him at Henrietta, Texas, where he worked on a cow ranch for the first year. The next year he entered the Baylor university, at Waco, Tex. After completing his education at this institution, he entered the employment of one of the first merchants at Henrietta, Texas, and later engaged in business for himself at Hennessey, Okla., where he was married to Miss Nellie Rhodes, daughter of a prominent citizen of that place.

When the Cherokee strip opened, he sold out his business at Hennessey and invested all his resources in Enid real estate. However, prices of real esta e were so depreciated by the panic of 1893 and having invested some borrowed capital, and in liquidating found himself in debt a few hundred dollars, for which he gave his note. Not discouraged he again set to work, and by patient industry he soon acquired sufficient means to pay this obligation and set himself up in business again.

Soon after the war with Spain he spent a year in traveling and prospecting in Cuba and other countries, after which he returned to the States and engaged in the general mercantile business at Addington, Okla., continued same until the first of January, 1907, at which time he closed out his business and came to New Mexico.

Mr. Withers has traveled over the greater part of the United States and has been at the opening up of the new countries in Oklahoma, but thinks this part of New Mexico and the Panhandle of Texas is the best of them all. To show his faith in the twin cities and surrounding country he has invested considerable means in both land and town property. He is actively engaged in the real estate and loan business and has an enviable reputation for straight-forward and careful dealings.

L. W. Avery.

L. W. Avery, whose likeness is herewith shown, is one of the most familiarly known men in the twin cities. Mr. Avery is a native of Detroit, Michigan, and previous to his coming to Farwell he was connected with some of the strongest railroad companies as Civil Engineer and Contractor, resigning the same to accept an offer made him by the Capitol Freehold Land and Investment Company to look after their interest at Farwell.

Since coming to Farwell Mr. Avery has made many warm friends and admirers He is

courteous and generous in all his dealings and wins the respect and friendship of all who come in contact with him.

He has complete charge of the Capitol Freehold Land and Investment Company's interests here, and he is managing the same very successfully.

Dr. J. T. Webb.

Dr. T. J. Webb whose likeness we herewith produce was born in Lockhart, Texas, 1883. After reaching manhood he attended the University of Nashville three years, graduated at the Memphis Hospital Medical College with high honors in

1904 and immediately began the practice of medicine at Thrifty, Texas, moving from there to Hale county where he practiced for one year. He then came to Texico where he settled and has

received an enviable practice since he has been with us.

Dr. Webb is very popular socially, and well liked by the people he comes in contact with and is regarded as one of our best physicians and authority on medicine. He being a young man we predict great things for him during his career as a practicing physician.

J. W. Sellars.

Mr. Sellars, the popular County Attorney of Parmer Co., was born at Warsaw, Mo., and while very young came to John-

son county, Texas, where he spent the rest of his time until a few months ago when he came to Farwell.

He graduated in 1890 from the Granbury College, and in 1898 he graduated from the Law Department of the State University of Texas.

He was Assistant County Attorney of Johnson County before coming to this place.

He is County Attorney of Parmer county and is holding his office in an able manner.

Being a young man with superior legal talent we predict for him a brilliant future.

Milton Brown, Jr.

Milton Brown, Jr., was born in Comanche, Texas, April 16th, 1882. When he was twelve years old he moved with his parents to Galveston. Was in the great storm there September 8, 1900. When he grew older he felt that he could have better opportunities in the west, so he came to New Mexico in 1901, and began working for the Kemp Lumber Company at Roswell, where he remained about four years.

In August, 1905, he came to Texico to work for the same company and has been here ever since.

He is local manager of the

Kemp Lumber Co. here and a stockholder in the same.

He holds the respect and esteem of the whole citizenship of the country, being a man of good business qualities and pleasant to deal with.

Socially Mr. Brown stands at the head. His opinions are regarded very highly in both business and social affairs. He is found always up-holding his home town and its institutions.

T. C. Taylor.

Is a native born of the state of Mississippi. Was reared in Northeast Texas, at and near Jefferson, once the metropolis of that great state. Was admitted to the practice of law in the year 1883, and for a short time practiced his profession at Linden, Texas.

After his marriage he removed to Gatesville, Texas, in the year 1887, where he resided until a short time before locating at Texico. He was elected by the people of Coryell county to the office of County Judge and served two terms from 1894-1898 Under his administration he built for his people a beautiful court house and jail, which stand as a monument to his memory.

He served his senatorial dis

trict as a member of the State Democratic Executive Committee during the period that the democratic party was split over the race between Governor Hogg and Judge George Clark for Governor of Texas.

He has recently been admitted to practice law before the Supreme and Interior Courts of New Mexico and is now engaged in the practice of law at Texico. He also practices his profession in Texas.

Judge Taylor is one of our most prominent lawyers, and is a man true to his convictions and to any trust placed in him.

S. F. Wooding.

S. F. Wooding was born May 29th, 1852, in Atlanta Georgia.

He was connected with the Georgia and Central railroads for a number of years. Entered the butcher business in 1875 in Atlanta. Moved to Chattanooga, Tenn., in 1882 and was in the

butcher and packing business there until 1887. Moved to Texas and again entered the butcher and packing business. Was superintendant of the Hays Packing Company at Gainsville, Texas and was also manager of the Fulton Market at the same place for a number of years. Moved to

Portales, New Mexico in 1902 and again entered the butcher business. Came to Texico in June 1905 and opened up a meat market which is one of the best in the great southwest.

Mr. Wooding is one of Texico's best and most substantial citizens and is always working for the advancement of the interests of the town. He is a large stockholder in some good banks and has many business interests. He stands at the head as a butcher and citizen.

O. R. Oliver.

O. R. Oliver was born at Texarkana, Tex., May 29, 1883.

After reaching manhood he came to Clarendon, Tex., where he was engaged as a cow puncher for several years. Coming to Texico in 1902, he engaged in the livery business and today has one of the most up-to-date barns in the southwest.

His motto is, "If you don't ride in the best turn outs, it's your own fault.

There is a KNOW-HOW to everything, and Wooding knows-how to sell dressed hogs at 7 cts per pound.

Shows Coming.

From Feb. 19 to 22 our show going people will have an opportunity to see several good shows.

On Feb. 19th Uncle Zeke's Musical Comedy, in 4 acts, will show at the opera house. They have a company of 20 people.

February 20 the celebrated Mahara Minstrels will entertain us with a good performance.

February 21 and 22 G. Whillen's moving picture show will be here. One feature of this show is the Thaw-White tragedy.

All the above named shows come well recommended.

F. C. KEPPLE
Public Stenogragher

Phone 12

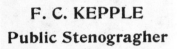

Mrs. W. W. Edwards left for Kansas City, Mo., Monday where she has gone to purchase an up-to-date stock of Spring Millinery. She will open business in the old stand formally occupied by Simmons the Gents Furnisher.

Guy Gamble.

Brick Block in Farwell.

Interior of First National Bank, Farwell.

Brief Description of This Country.

The land adjacent to the towns of Texico, N. M. and Farwell, Texas, is strictly agricultural. What once was thought to only be a plains grazing country has been developed within the last five years from that stage by the sturdy farmer to one of the richest farming belts to be found anywhere. Within the last five years thousands of acres of this land has been placed under a high state of cultivation and has proven a bountiful succucess in every instance.

The farmers who are coming to our part of the country are men who are willing to work and use their best abilities for the up-building of this great new country and it is our opinion alone goes a long way in development of any new country.

The soil is a loamy chocolate fat soil, ranging in depth from two to five feet, underlaid with a fine clay subsoil which makes the land inexhaustible.

The farmers who have had extensive experience in raising corn, wheat oats, cane, etc., elsewhere say that this country in their opinion cannot be surpassed for bountiful yield, or for quality of the product. Many thousand acres have been sown in wheat this year and from present indications a bountiful harvest will be reaped. Our climate is all that the most demanding could ask for. We are on an elevation of 4100 feet above sea level which makes the air pure and healthful, and there is no stagnant water or any cesspools and our towns as a general thing are kept clean and free from filth. The air is pure and taking all together we believe we have the most healthful country to be found anywhere, and if our friends in the north and east could realize some of the inducements offered by this country in the way of cheap homes they would leave the crowded countries in which they live and immigrate here.

Our schools are our pride. The plains country in and around the two towns that has so recently developed into the fine agricultural country has not been lacking in the interest on the part of the men who are helping to develop the same as they have been looking forward to the education of their children and have erected nice school buildings all over the country and in reach of every child of school age.

Practically all religious denominations are represented here and most of them have nice modern houses of worship. Taking everything into consideration we believe that we have the best country on earth in which to live and that we can offer every inducement to the most demanding request for good citizenship. We believe that we have everything that is necessary in laying the preliminary foundation for a great and glorious country and that there is no power that can check our advancement.

To our friends in the east and north and everywhere we bid you come and look into this matter for yourselves, for "Seeing is believing."

Familiar Farm Scenes.

The Farwell Real Estate Exchange.

Interior of Farwell Drug Store.

The Farwell Ice Plant.

In Conclusion.

We are taught that there is a time to begin and a time to end. We began some few weeks ago to accumulate data for the Special Edition of the Farwell Times, we have been doing so continuously since, but find that now as we progress the work is only just begining to develop but at the same time we find that time forbids that now as we go in to further detail with reference to our people and business enterprises, and that we must bring our efforts to a close. We find that there are other subjects of interest on which we would like to write and that we believe would be of interest to our readers, but time will not permit. We would have been glad to have said more concerning the great country in which we live but we would rather that those interested most would come and look the situation over for themselves.

During the last week we noticed that a terrible blizzard has been raging in the north and east and reaching as far south as our sister town on the north, Amarillo, while we have been enjoying the most delightful weather that it has ever been our pleasure to see anywhere. We fully sympathize with our northern friends, and bid you come live with us in the Land of Sunshine.

In concluding this Pictorial Edition of the Farwell Times we wish to thank those who have helped us in this matter, and shall at some other time take up the work where we have left it off and deal more extensively with the matter that so vitally concerns us.

J. C. Wells.

The above is a likeness of J. C. Wells who for some time past has been connected with the Times.

Mr. Wells is a native of Mississippi and came west with his parents and settled in the Panhandle country several years ago.

Mr. Wells has been true to his duties with the Times and we can truthfully say we feel proud to have him connected with us.

W. E. S.

FARWELL, TEXAS

County Seat of Parmer County.

The Ideal City to locate in as it is bound to be the Most Important City in this great country as Farwell is the Gateway to the Southwest, being on the State Line between Texas and New Mexico

The junction of four lines of the Santa Fe R. R. System from the North, East, South and West, and therefore the best Distributing Point, as is proven by the large wholesale houses that have come to Farwell.

Good Schools, Good Churches, Best Retail Stores, $40,000 Hotel under construction, Wholesale Houses, Material ordered for 1st. class Water system, Prettiest Residence District, Cheap Residence Lots, Cheap Business Lots.

And surrounded by the BEST FARMING COUNTRY in the Great Pan-Handle of Texas.   Farm land adjoining the town can be bought with a small payment down and the balance payable in Nine equal yearly installments with interest at six per cent.

If you are thinking of coming to the West, write us or stop off and you will not regret it.

We are Owners ——— Not Promoters.

Capitol Freehold Land & Investment Co.

Farwell Drug Company....

Prescriptions a specialty
We handle the most complete line of toilet articles
and druggist's sundries
to be found in the country

Try a Drink From Our Sanitary Fountain.

...Farwell Ice Co..

We manufacture ice by the latest improved methods, thus making our product absolutely pure. There is no danger of germs in ice made from distilled water. Leave orders at the office and the wagon will call every morning.

Wholesale Distributers the famous Lemp's and Schlitz Beers.

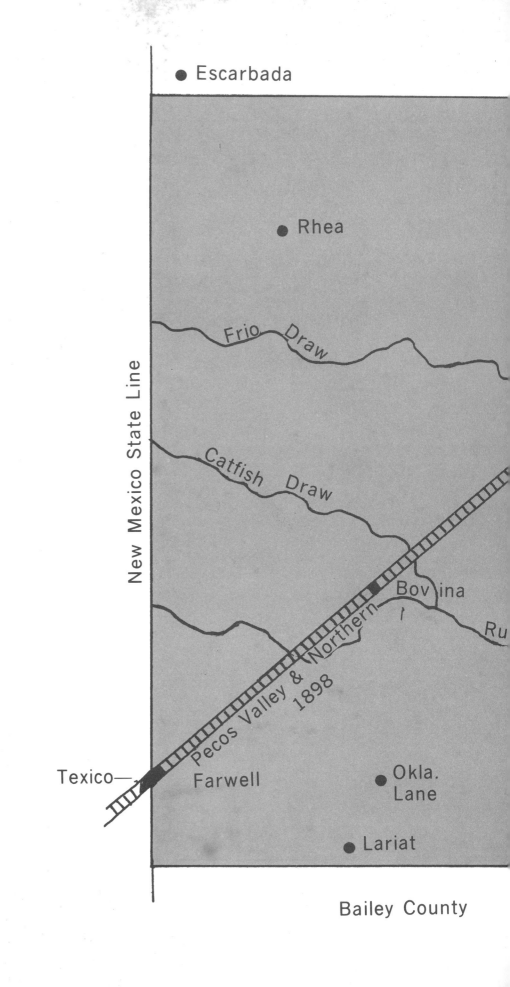